WORKS OF

SAHL

&

MĀSHĀ'ALLĀH

TRANSLATED BY

BENJAMIN N. DYKES, PHD

The Cazimi Press
Minneapolis, Minnesota
2008

Published and printed in the United States of America
by the Cazimi Press
621 5th Avenue SE, Minneapolis, MN 55414

Second printing 2010

© 2008 by Benjamin N. Dykes, Ph.D.

All rights reserved. No part of this publication may be reproduced, stored in or introduced into a retrieval system, or transmitted, in any form or by any means (electronic, mechanical, photocopying, recording or otherwise), without the prior written permission of both the copyright owner and the above publisher of this book.

The scanning, uploading, and distribution of this book via the Internet or via any other means without the permission of the publisher is illegal and punishable by law. Please purchase only authorized electronic editions and do not participate in or encourage electronic piracy of copyrighted materials. Your support of the author's rights is appreciated.

Library of Congress Control Number: 2008928418

ISBN-13: 978-1-934586-02-0

PUBLISHER'S NOTE:

This paperback reprint of *Works of Sahl & Māshā'allāh* represents the original hardcover edition with minor corrections to the Introduction, a few word corrections, and an updated Index. For other translations and lectures on traditional astrology and thought, see my site at www.bendykes.com.

Dr. Benjamin N. Dykes
October, 2010

Also available at www.bendykes.com:

Learn the principles of traditional astrology from two famous medieval astrologers, Abu Ma'shar and al-Qabisi! With over 120 figures and extensive commentary by Benjamin Dykes, this book is essential for students.

The three volumes of *Persian Nativities* represents works on natal interpretation and numerous predictive techniques by Masha'allah, Abu 'Ali al-Khayyat, 'Umar al-Tabari, Abu Bakr, and Abu Ma'shar. These works represent the natal portion of the *Essential Medieval Astrology* series.

This classic medieval text by Guido Bonatti, the *Book of Astronomy* is now available in paperback reprints. This famous work is a complete guide to basic principles, horary, elections, mundane, and natal astrology.

Expand your knowledge of astrology and esoteric thought with the *Logos & Light* audio series: downloadable, college-level lectures on CD at a fraction of the university cost! Ideal for people with some knowledge of traditional thought but who want to enrich their understanding.

Acknowledgments:

I have had wonderful conversations with, and received important support from, several friends in translating this book. Warm thanks and appreciation go (in alphabetical order) to: Christopher Bouchard, Chris Brennan, and Robert Schmidt. Special thanks to Terry Linder for his Arabic skills and interest in recovering the concepts behind traditional astrology.

TABLE OF CONTENTS

INTRODUCTION	VII
SAHL: THE *INTRODUCTION*	1
SAHL: THE *FIFTY JUDGMENTS*	51
SAHL: *ON QUESTIONS*	67
SAHL: *ON ELECTIONS*	187
SAHL: *ON TIMES*	223
MĀSHĀ'ALLĀH: *ON THE KNOWLEDGE OF THE MOTION OF THE ORB*	243
MĀSHĀ'ALLĀH: *ON THE ROOTS OF REVOLUTIONS*	299
MĀSHĀ'ALLĀH: *CHAPTER OF THE RAINS IN THE YEAR*	309
MĀSHĀ'ALLĀH: *ON RAINS*	315
MĀSHĀ'ALLĀH: *ON THE REVOLUTION OF THE YEARS OF THE WORLD*	325
MĀSHĀ'ALLĀH: *ON THE SIGNIFICATIONS OF THE PLANETS IN A NATIVITY*	361
MĀSHĀ'ALLĀH: *ON NATIVITIES*	391
MĀSHĀ'ALLĀH: *ON THE INTERPRETATION OF COGNITION*	417
MĀSHĀ'ALLĀH: *ON HIDDEN THINGS*	425
MĀSHĀ'ALLĀH: *BOOK ON RECEPTION*	437
MĀSHĀ'ALLĀH: *WHAT THE PLANETS SIGNIFY IN THE TWELVE DOMICILES OF THE CIRCLE*	499
BIBLIOGRAPHY	515
INDEX	523

Book Abbreviations:

Abu 'Ali al-Khayyat:	*The Judgments of Nativities*	*JN*
Abū Ma'shar:	*Liber Introductorii Maioris ad Scientiam Iudiciorum Astrorum (Great Introduction to the Knowledge of the Judgments of the Stars)*	*Gr. Intr.*
	On Historical Astrology: the Book of Religions and Dynasties (On the Great Conjunctions)	*OGC*
	The Abbreviation of the Introduction to Astrology	*Abbr.*
	The Flowers of Abū Ma'shar	*Flowers*
Al-Bīrūnī:	*The Book of Instruction in the Elements of the Art of Astrology*	*Instr.*
Boll *et al.*, eds.	*Catalogus Codicum Astrologorum Graecorum*	*CCAG*
Bonatti, Guido	*Book of Astronomy*	*BOA*
Dorotheus of Sidon:	*Carmen Astrologicum*	*Carmen*
Māshā'allāh:	*Book of Nativities*	*Nativities*
	Chapter of the Rains in the Year	*Chap. Rains*
	On Reception	*OR*
	On the Knowledge of the Motion of the Orb	*Orb*
	On the Interpretation of Cognition	*Cognition*
	On the Revolutions of the Years of the World	*On Rev.*
	On the Roots of Revolutions	*On Roots*
	On the Significations of the Planets in a Nativity	*On Sig. Planet.*
Māshā'allāh/Jirjis:	*What the Planets Signify in the Twelve Domiciles of the Circle*	*Twelve Dom.*
Ptolemy	*Tetrabiblos*	*Tet.*
Sahl bin Bishr:	*The Introduction*	*Introduct.*
	The Fifty Judgments	*Judgments*
	On Questions	*On Quest.*
	On Elections	*On Elect.*
Vettius Valens:	*The Anthology*	*Anth.*

Arabic Transliteration:

ا ى	ā	ض	ḍ
ب	b	ط	ṭ
ت	t	ظ	ẓ
ث	th	ع	ʿ
ح	ḥ	غ	gh
ج	j	ف	f
خ	kh	ق	q
د	d	ك	k
ذ	dh	ل	l
ر	r	م	m
ز	z	ن	n
س	s	ه ة	h
ش	sh	و	w, ū
ص	ṣ	ي	y, ī
		ء	ʾ

Arabic Terms:

Transliteration:	Meaning:
mubtazz	The most powerful planet in signification
hīlāj	The planet granting life in a nativity
kadukhudhāh	The planet indicating the years of life
tasīr	Primary directions, from Ar. "march/move."

Table of Figures

Figure 1: Transfer of Light ... 19
Figure 2: Prohibition of Light (First Way) ... 21
Figure 3: Prohibition of Light (Second Way) ... 23
Figure 4: Prohibition of Light (Third Way) ... 25
Figure 5: Prohibition of Light (Another Example) ... 27
Figure 6: Not-Reception ... 33
Figure 7: Pushing of Strength/Virtue ... 37
Figure 8: Pushing of Arrangement (or Disposition and Nature) ... 38
Figure 9: Besieging ... 48
Figure 10: Acquiring a Kingdom ... 75
Figure 11: The Four Elements ... 246
Figure 12: The Four Pivots ... 248
Figure 13: If the Sun were Equal to the Earth ... 256
Figure 14: If the Sun were Smaller than the Earth ... 257
Figure 15: The Sun is Greater than the Earth ... 258
Figure 16: The Moon 12° from the Sun ... 261
Figure 17: The Moon on the 7th Day ... 261
Figure 18: The Moon on the 14th Day ... 262
Figure 19: The Moon on the 21st Day ... 263
Figure 20: The Moon Joined to the Sun ... 263
Figure 21: The Moon Arising in the Morning ... 264
Figure 22: The Moon over Cities ... 266
Figure 23: The Orbs of the Moon ... 268
Figure 24: The Orbs of the Sun ... 269
Figure 25: The Ten Orbs ... 271
Figure 26: The Four Orbs ... 276
Figure 27: The Great Orb ... 278
Figure 28: The Orb of the Signs ... 279
Figure 29: The Eccentric Orb ... 280
Figure 30: The Orbs of Saturn ... 282
Figure 31: The Circles, Chords, and Points ... 286
Figure 32: The Eclipse of the Moon ... 287
Figure 33: The Stars Receiving the Sun's Light ... 289
Figure 34: The Eclipse of the Sun ... 292
Figure 35: Example 1, A Nocturnal Figure ... 404
Figure 36: Example 2, A Diurnal Figure ... 405
Figure 37: Example 3, A Diurnal Figure ... 406
Figure 38: Example 4, A Nocturnal Nativity ... 407
Figure 39: Example 5, A Nocturnal Nativity ... 408
Figure 40: Example 6, A Diurnal Nativity ... 409
Figure 41: Example 7, A Nocturnal Nativity ... 410
Figure 42: Example 8, A Diurnal Nativity ... 411

Figure 43: Example 9, A Nocturnal Nativity 412
Figure 44: Example 10, A Nocturnal Nativity 413
Figure 45: Example 11, A Nocturnal Nativity 414
Figure 46: Example 12, A Diurnal Nativity...415
Figure 47: Discovering the Intention 420
Figure 48: Mars Receiving Saturn by Domicile...439
Figure 49: Mars Receiving the Sun by Domicile...440
Figure 50: Saturn and the Sun Receiving Each Other by Exaltation............441
Figure 51: An Infirm Person, Will he be Liberated or Die? 450
Figure 52: An Infirm Person..455
Figure 53: Will the Relative get the Decedent's Goods? 466
Figure 54: Will he Acquire the Kingdom? 475
Figure 55: Will he Acquire a Kingdom this Year?..477
Figure 56: The Condition of a New General and a Rebel 491

INTRODUCTION

§1: Sahl and Māshā'allāh

The sixteen works translated in this volume were written by two of the most important and famous astrologers in the Arabic period of traditional astrology, Sahl bin Bishr and Māshā'allāh bin Atharī (or simply Māshā'allāh). Little is known about their lives, but both were Jews of Persian descent working in the 8th and 9th Centuries AD, and many of the works here were fundamental for later astrologers, who quoted them often (and sometimes copied their work without attribution). Some of these works have never been translated into any modern language; for others, it is their first English translation; for yet others, these are updated English translations based on cross-referencing between all of the works and access to some critical editions in Arabic. Collected together for the first time, they represent a huge contribution to astrological theory and practice, and will prove to be of great benefit to modern astrologers interested in traditional thought and techniques.

Māshā'allāh's[1] work represents some of the most important work to be produced in the early Arabic period. He was born in ca. 740 AD in Basra, Iraq, and died ca. 815 AD. As a young man he participated in a team of astrologers who cast the electional chart for the foundation of Baghdad for Caliph Al-Mansūr (dated July 31, 762), along with Nawbakht the Persian and 'Umar al-Tabarī. His output was large, covering at least 28 works by Pingree's count, but since some of the larger Arabic works were divided up and copied in smaller chunks, it is hard to know their exact number. An additional problem is that most of his work survives only in Latin, and other works are lost altogether.

Māshā'allāh represents a period in which Indian and Persian astrological practices were consciously informed with Hellenistic ones (primarily from Ptolemy and Dorotheus). From the Indian and Persian side there are mainly works of mundane astrology, and from the Hellenistic side there are nativities and elections. But as I will point out below, Māshā'allāh's writings also include both what we would recognize as traditional horary astrology, and an earlier type which casts "consultation" charts to divine the client's intention.

---

[1] My biographical information is based primarily on Holden 1996 and Pingree 1974.

As we look from our perspective at long-term influences in astrology, it is perhaps not too much of an overstatement to say that true medieval astrology begins with Māshā'allāh, or at least with his circle. For reasons of Islamic imperial politics, the effort to translate other scientific materials into Arabic, and through the influence of his pupil Abu 'Ali (whose *Judgments of Nativities* was so important to the medieval Latins), Māshā'allāh stood at the end of an era and the beginning of a new one, and his name and work were well-known and respected. It is a shame that so little of his work has been translated into modern languages. Apart from the eleven works translated here, there are approximately 6-10 others in Latin which should be translated in the future. According to Pingree, some of the works attributed to Māshā'allāh also appear in the list for Abū Ma'shar, so there is some dispute about authorship.

Sahl bin Bishr, known better by the Latinized names *Zael* or *Zahel*, was a Persian Jew who flourished in the first half of the 9th Century. So he was a contemporary of Māshā'allāh's, and while he knows Māshā'allāh's work, we do not know if they ever met. From the sources I have consulted, we know next to nothing about him, but Stegemann says he was an attendant of al-Hasan, the vizier under the Caliph al-Ma'mun, in Khurasan.

If Māshā'allāh and his circle formed the true beginning of medieval astrology from a linguistic and cultural-contribution perspective, Sahl's work stands out as a kind of reader-friendly repackaging of traditional material which made his work extremely influential for many centuries. His *Introduction* is notable for its list of technical terms, which reappears again and again in various forms in later astrologers' works. His clear principles of horary and electional astrology, the topics covered and his delineations, are all drawn on by later astrologers. (Māshā'allāh's own horary methods were not as popular as Sahl's.) His *Fifty Judgments* is a collection of handy sayings and principles which are reflected in both style and content in works by ibn Ezra, Bonatti, and collections of centiloquys. Two works I have not included in this volume (for various reasons) are his work on the magical use of precious stones, and a work on mundane astrology and weather prediction, known in Latin as the *Fatidica* or "Prophetic Sayings."

INTRODUCTION ix

§2: Stegemann and Dorotheus

In 1939 and 1942, two books on ancient and medieval astrology were published by the German scholar and philologist Viktor Stegemann. The first was his attempt at reconstructing the transmission and authentic work of Dorotheus from whatever Latin, Arabic, and Greek quotations and summaries he could find.[2] Stegemann already believed that much medieval natal and electional astrology is based on only a few sources, chief among them Dorotheus. In 1942 he continued work on this thesis, by publishing a critical Arabic, Greek, and Latin edition (with German translations of the Arabic) of Sahl's *Introduct.* §5, the list of technical terms with explanations and some examples.[3] Through references to the *CCAG* and other sources, and drawing on his Dorotheus work, Stegemann felt justified in his earlier belief about the centrality of Dorotheus to the medieval tradition.

Stegemann was more right than perhaps he knew. As the reader will see in my footnotes, I have cited, wherever possible and obvious, the passages in Pingree's *Carmen* on which Sahl depends. It turns out that principles and passages from Dorotheus form part or even a large bulk of material from *Introduct.*, *On Quest.*, *On Elect.*, and the *Fifty Judgments*. But as I mentioned before, Sahl's ability to reorganize and repackage, and to isolate theoretical statements from exposition, allowed him to reshape much of this material in a form recognizable as medieval astrology today. In fact, based on Stegemann and the translations in this book, it seems to me that pretty much all medieval astrology can be boiled down to three or four central books or types of books. The first two are real and known: Ptolemy's *Tetrabiblos* and Dorotheus's *Carmen*.[4] We could add to this a hypothetical Persian-style work on mundane astrology (perhaps even Māshā'allāh's own work *On Conjunctions, Religions, and Peoples*), and possibly another work on horary. If we had all three or four of these books (even apart from other sources like Valens and Rheto-

---

[2] Some of the many authors used by Stegemann include Hephaestio, al-Qasrani, al-Rijāl, Rhetorius, Abu Bakr, Abraham ibn Ezra, Leopold of Austria, 'Umar al-Tabarī, and many other authors and compilations. Pingree's later edition of Dorotheus's *Carmen* (dedicated to Stegemann) was not a continuation of Stegemann's project, but rather a translation of 'Umar al-Tabarī's Arabic version, which differs in certain respects from other versions.

[3] As I explain below, I use Stegemann's edition in parallel with the Latin. I also draw on Crofts's Arabic edition of *On Elect.*, and have provided a translation of Māshā'allāh's Arabic *Chap. Rains*.

[4] I note here that Crofts argues Sahl uses a totally different edition of *Carmen*. See my notes to *On Elect.* in §12 below.

rius), we could possibly reconstruct all of the main points of medieval astrology retrospectively—though of course it took them centuries of practice, reading, experimenting, commentary, and so on.

I had originally planned to include as footnotes all of Stegemann's commentary on the individual sections, which offer extensive references to many Hellenistic astrologers; but the commentary itself runs to almost thirty pages, and it really deserves its own translation, especially due to the numerous Greek quotations and references to the *CCAG*. But as a point of interest, I have here translated portions of Stegemann's own Introduction, to give the reader a sense of his thought. First we begin with some comments on the transmission of materials:

"The Arabic terminology of the planetary positions, based on conjoining and flowing away,[5] is found in situational horoscopy[6] (which works with the Moon and its position relative to the planets and the zodiacal signs), systematically handled openly for the first time in the *Textbook* of the Jew Sahl ibn Bishr ibn Habīb (ca. 785—845? in Khurasan, an attendant of al-Hasan, the Vizier under the Caliph al-Ma'mun). Sahl wrote in Arabic. We definitely have his textbook in a copy in the original language, as it was translated and excerpted by the Byzantines as well as in the West, in Latin transmissions in the Middle Ages, [and] enjoyed great respect—Zahel, as the author is called here, is afterwards much cited in the emergent astrological works in the West—the corresponding chapter is a suitable departure point for a small study that should be instructive for the connection of the Arabic with the ancient astrology, and the adoption of these terms in the medieval astrology of the Byzantines and the occidental West."

After a brief description of the structure of his own book, Stegemann continues:

"The outcome of this investigation into sources should be presented here to a certain extent only as theses. Everything (or very much) of what this terminological chapter of Sahl contains, goes for the most part back to the Greek astrologer Dorotheus of Sidon. He lived around

---

[5] *Defluxion.* That is, "separation."
[6] *Augenblickshoroskopie*, lit. "moment-horoscopy."

Christ's birth, and reached to the time of Tiberius. His influence on the astrology of late antiquity (possibly through the mediation of Theophilus of Edessa, as he came to Baghdad) allowed the Arabs to be attentive to him. Dorotheus's significance for the beginnings of Arabic astrology appears even greater (according to the results of this work) than I hitherto was able to make plausible.[7]

"In a succession of works I have hitherto been able to explain that, in the astrological literature of the Arabs from the Greeks, next to Ptolemy's *Tetrabiblos*, for great stretches the poet Dorotheus is written out and often also presented there, [even] where he is not expressly cited.

"The little writing at hand produces another example for this question, which the results I obtained earlier confirm; and it puts me in the [right] situation to append some further fragments of the hitherto arranged material. In essence, the interpretation applies only to one chapter of the *Introduction*; but according to the results one must suspect that Sahl has written his entire *Introduction* as an extensive application of Dorotheus. I believe we are now permitted to argue that the beginnings of astrology in the Arabic language rest on very few ancient writers. Systematic researches into the still unedited mass of the Arabic astrologers' manuscripts can definitely expect further results along the lines of this inquiry.

"With the importance that one allots to Sahl's writings in the area of the Mediterranean and in middle Europe (between the 13th and 16th/17th Centuries), it again appears impressive how dependent one still was, in these times of the reorganization of the Western spirit in the direction of modern natural science, on antiquity, except that those times could visualize the connection more than in general outlines. The Middle Ages in the occidental West, like in Byzantium, stands here in an unmediated contact with Hellenism, above all that of Ptolemaic Egypt and the astrology published there in the *Hermetica* and in the work of Nechepso-Petosiris. From these writings Dorotheus took most of his material. It wandered over the late antique East (Syria) to-

---

[7] Stegemann is referring to his 1939 compilation of Dorothean fragments.

ward Baghdad and the Middle East and into Arabian Egypt, in order to reach from there over north Africa (Tunisia) to Spain (Toledo) and Sicily, from where it was brought further to middle Europe and eastern Europe; then also manuscripts with the Latin translation of the *Introduction* can be found in the libraries of St. Petersburg and Krakow. The printed edition in the late 15th and early 16th Centuries completed what the manufacturers of astrological manuscripts had begun. Since then, printings of Sahl's works can be found in many great and small libraries in all of Europe. A great part of what they convey belongs, without it being recognizable, to the ancient astrologer Dorotheus of Sidon."

For the Arabic basis of his text, Stegemann used Manuscript #V 799 (formerly D.C. 116), at the Universitätsbibliothek in Leipzig. For his Latin, he relied on three manuscripts[8] and the 1493 printed edition (the same one I am using for other parts of Sahl). Following are some comments he makes about the middle Latin transmission:

"Writings of Sahl ibn Bishr, among them the *Book of Judgments*, belong to the earliest ones that were made accessible to the West in middle Latin translations. Of these translations, we already have manuscripts from the 12th Century; they were copied up to the 15th Century in increasing numbers, which suggests [both] their widespread use and—in the understanding of that time—their practical reliability in the study of astrology in western Europe.

"The Western translator of Sahl's work is unknown. We must seek him in western Europe, in Spain or southern France. Of the translators of the time, possibilities are Hermann of Dalmatia[9] (who made a name for himself through his transmission of the *Great Introduction* of Abū Ma'shar (1120 AD?)), Plato of Tivoli, and John of Spain; above all the

---

[8] They are: (1) Clm. 130 21, from the 12th Century (Catalogue #9264), and (2) Clm. 189 27, from the 13th Century (Catalogue #9265), both at the Staatsbibliothek in Munich. (3) "Soest, the Stadtbibliothek 24 #12, from the 13th Century (Catalogue #9266)."
[9] Now often called Hermann of Carinthia.

INTRODUCTION   xiii

last-named had translated numerous astrological books into Latin, among them likewise the *Great Introduction* of Abū Ma'shar."[10]

Following this Stegemann discusses the transmission of manuscripts and the quality of various editions, and why he chose 1493 as his printed source (it is the earliest, for one thing). Further discussion need not detain us here.[11]

For now I turn to other topics of interest to astrologers in this volume (§§3—11). After discussion these other topics, I will provide information and interesting details on each of the works, including my source texts for each (§§12—13).

§3: Five Relations to Domiciles

In these texts we see several configurations and conditions which Sahl and Māshā'allāh consider important, but which lack either formal definitions or clear statements about their theoretical background or practical value. But if we pay close attention to what Sahl and Māshā'allāh say throughout their works, we can find valuable hints and comments. In this section I would like to lay out briefly five relationships that planets have to the twelve domiciles, explaining what Sahl and Māshā'allāh say about them, what I believe their underlying concept is, and how they may be used. The five relationships are: (a) being the Lord of a domicile; (b) being in a domicile of one's own or another's; (c) aspecting one's own domicile by whole-sign aspect; (d) aspecting one's own Lord by whole-sign aspect; and (e) reception. These relations may not be very tightly interconnected, but they share certain features in common. I believe that if we can harness these relationships properly, our understanding of traditional astrology will increase greatly, and our practice will improve.

(a) Being the Lord of a domicile. This is the simplest and most abstract relation. All planets rule at least one domicile. And it is telling that the typical Arabic word for what we call the domicile Lord (*dominus domus*) is ṣāḥib,

---

[10] If we are confined to these three choices, there is no doubt it must be John of Spain. The styles of Hermann and Plato of Tivoli are very different from John's and this edition of Sahl.

[11] Stegemann also does much to compare the Arabic, Latin, and Greek editions of the *Introduction*. Hopefully it will be possible in the future to have complete translations of all of Stegemann's works, especially his reconstructed edition of Dorotheus (1939).

"owner." The basic concept behind being a domicile Lord is *ownership*. A related notion is that of *management*. The domicile Lord *owns* the domicile, and is its chief *manager*, much as we think of someone who owns his own home and is the head of the household. The domicile Lord is in charge and sets the rules for the home (even though the exalted Lord is in some sense higher still), so it is the default planet we look to in deciding how to judge a matter.

(b) Being in a domicile. This relationship runs a spectrum between being in one's own domicile or exaltation, to intermediate states such as being in a domicile of one's own triplicity, or perhaps the domicile of a sect-mate, to the other extreme of being peregrine (lit. "foreigner, pilgrim"), in a domicile in which one has no rulership. For now I wish to minimize the intermediate states. The contrast between a planet being in its own domicile (or exaltation) and being peregrine is one between being (1) independent, self-reliant and in control, and (2) being dependent and in a relative state of helplessness—i.e., reliant on the Lord of the domicile one is in. This is a logical extension of the concept of ownership and management.

These first two relationships are basic in traditional astrology, and they are found in plenty of other texts. But these works of Sahl and Māshā'allāh also speak of three other relationships, to which I now turn.

(c) Aspecting one's own domicile by whole-sign aspects. There are no references in these works to aspecting intermediate cusps, and references to planets aspecting the angular degrees are still somewhat speculative. But it is very clear that Sahl and Māshā'allāh are interested in whether or not a Lord aspects its own domicile by a whole-sign aspect. One of the key texts is *On Elect.* §§23b-c, where Sahl says "a planet which does not aspect its own domicile is like a man absent from his own house, who cannot repel nor prohibit anything from it. Indeed if a planet aspected its own domicile, it is like the master of a house who guards it: for whoever is in the house, fears him, and he who is outside fears to come to it." For Sahl, when a planet aspects its own domicile, it is able to *protect* it,[12] and *provide* for it in the sense that the aspect allows a matter to be perfected, and quickly so.[13] In one case he says that a planet aspecting its own domicile will show someone with a good family stock.[14]

---

[12] *On Elect.* §§23b-c.
[13] *On Quest.* §§10.1, 10.2, 13.11.
[14] *On Quest.* §10.5.

But if the planet does *not* aspect its own domicile (that is, if it is in the 2nd, 6th, 8th, or 12th from it), it can show that the person signified will be in some other land not his own;[15] or it shows someone not staying at home;[16] the Lord will be "inimical" to its own domicile, leading to duress and complications for the matter (so that even if the Lord can perfect a matter, it will not be in the way expected or desired);[17] the Lord will be "in need," craving and desiring and weak;[18] it will be poor, not able to do much,[19] or not even be able to provide what it signifies,[20] its abilities slow;[21] if it represents a clime in a mundane chart, that clime will suffer detriment.[22] Moreover, it will show someone of low stock,[23] as though the person signified is cut off from his roots, having no recognizable lineage; and it can show someone mischievous and deluding,[24] as though he is unreliable, departs from established norms, and is unconnected to normal lines of support and responsibility.

In other words, the aspect to one's own domicile shows a two-way relation to one's home and roots. On the one hand, the aspect from the Lord shows his protection of it, providing for its signification, and perfecting it. But this connection also shows that he is supported by it, and not in need. When he is not aspecting, he is in need, with the danger of mischief, he is weakened and cut off from home. *Providing* and *protection* seem to be the key concepts here, and they, too, are related to the notions of home, ownership, belonging.

It seems to me that the contrast here can be shown more vividly if we imagine the difference between (1) a head of household who goes out into the world but keeps in close contact with his family and his responsibilities there, being supported and acting as a provider and protector. This benefits both him and the home. But (2) a head of household who disappears for long periods of time, who does not support the home and cannot or will not take care of crises there, is cut off from its support and appears aimless, irresponsible, his background and morality under suspicion.

---

[15] *On Quest.* §10.8.
[16] *On Elect.* §46.
[17] *On Quest.* §10.2.
[18] *On Rev.* Chs. 11-12.
[19] *On Quest.* §13.11.
[20] *On Quest.* §4.2.
[21] *On Quest.* §9.6.
[22] *On Rev.* Intro.
[23] *On Quest.* §10.5.
[24] *On Elect.* §35.

So if the Lord of the Ascendant in a nativity is in the 2nd, 6th, 8th or 12th domiciles, then it will not aspect its own domicile. By its location it will show a key area of life the native finds himself in. But since the Lord wants to produce the native's life and well-being, being cut off from the rising sign means that he will be slower to realize the native's happiness, will find difficulty in doing so, will feel a lack of support or rootedness, might perhaps find himself surrounded by mischief or subject to matters not in his direct control. Now, all of this must be taken in context, and it may not apply equally easily to all situations. For instance, if the Lord of the 11th were in the 10th, then the native's friends will be involved in his advancement, profession, and honor. Although the Lord of the 11th is not aspecting the 11th domicile, it would not necessarily mean that the friends are ineffective. After all, the Lord is still aspecting the rising sign, and so we would still expect the friends to affect the native productively. But perhaps the delineation could be refined on the basis of this lack of aspect to the 11th, along with other features in the chart.

(d) The fourth relation is that of aspecting one's own dispositor by whole signs. I emphasize whole signs, because if the texts meant an aspect by orbs or exact degree, then it would immediately be a case of reception proper—but in these cases the texts never speak of reception, only aspecting one's own Lord (and especially the Moon aspecting her own Lord). So I take this to be a whole-sign aspect, just as in aspecting one's own domicile above.

In the case of the Moon, the indications are relatively straightforward and general, probably because she is the universal significatrix for everything on earth. If she aspects her Lord (by whole signs), then matters will go well, quickly, and smoothly for what she signifies (Sahl emphasizes this in elections).[25] But for other planets, there are few passages in the texts, and there seems to be a distinction. In general, a planet aspecting its Lord (by whole signs) will have its strength doubled for its task;[26] have joy and security;[27] and the person signified will be bold and faithful to his master; but if it did not aspect, the person signified will not be faithful.[28] However, in issues of conflict, imprisonment, and so on, if a planet aspects its Lord, then that Lord will have *control* over that planet, and it will not be good for it.[29]

---

[25] *On Elect.* §§35, 46, 47b, 51, 53, 59c, 104b, 126a, 138c, 140a; *On Quest.* §13.11.
[26] *On Quest.* §7.25.
[27] *On Rev.* Ch. 19.
[28] *On Quest.* §7.25.
[29] *On Quest.* §§7.25, 13.10.

To my mind this situation differs from reception (see below) in that reception concerns specifically the relation between receiver and received; but aspecting one's own Lord by whole sign concern's the planet's ability to *act*. Aspecting one's own Lord lacks the moral categories that are evident in reception: it is as though you are acting under the formal permission of, and are in contact with, your master. It enables you to act (or in the case of enmity, forbids you to act effectively) but doesn't say much about whether you are good, honest, have real support and friends—all of which reception shows.

(e) Reception is the most complicated of our five relations, and as one might guess by the very title of Māshā'allāh's *On Reception*, our authors have a lot to say about it. Reception obtains when one planet is in an aspect by degree (including corporal conjunction) with its domicile or exalted Lord. Sahl also says[30] that Māshā'allāh allows a less desirable form of reception involving the Lords of *two* of the minor dignities, and there is some indirect support for this claim in OR, when Māshā'allāh says reception by domicile or exaltation is a kind of "strong" reception.[31] Let me first describe what reception is supposed to do, and what concrete ideas are used to describe received planets; then I will summarize what I think the basic concepts are.

The first and most important thing reception does is guarantee perfection of a matter.[32] This is so not only for the final dispositor of a matter (see OR's use of a final dispositor), but for any of the planets which must commit disposition over the matter from one to another: if they receive each other as they transfer the light, they help ensure the integrity and success of the matter. But if the disposition arrives at a bad final dispositor without reception, then the outcome will be unfavorable.[33]

Reception is said to provide these results in several ways. Generally speaking, received benefics produce a stronger good, while received malefics impede less.[34] Reception takes away the evil from a situation, so that a

---

[30] *Introduct.* §5.8.
[31] OR Ch. 3. But elsewhere Māshā'allāh makes it seem that what makes reception weak or strong is if it is by aspect (weaker) or corporal conjunction (stronger). To me it is also unclear (based on OR Ch. 1) whether reception exists only *when* the aspect is perfected (or in orbs), or whether it will exist *now* provided the aspect *will* perfect while they are in their same signs.
[32] OR Ch. 5.
[33] OR Ch. 4.
[34] *Judgments* 25; *On Rev.* Ch. 23.

planet's signification will not suffer, even if it is in a bad place.[35] A received planet (or rather the person signified by it) will be able to bear its own problems more easily.[36] And one reason this seems to be so, is that the received planet is allowed to produce *itself*, despite bad circumstances. So for instance, in a question about illness and death, if the Lord of the 1st is received by the Lord of the 8th, the querent will live.[37] Although this aspect would normally be a classic sign of perfection—i.e., death—in such cases the Lord of the 1st is allowed to produce life. Likewise, if the Lord of the 1st received the Lord of the 8th, then although the Lord of the 8th is allowed to produce something like death and harm, the friendliness and benefic qualities conferred by reception will not allow the native to be destroyed.[38]

There are several qualities, including moral qualities, which reception is said to involve. Perfection with reception adds *esteem* (though whether this means one planet is esteeming the other in particular or not, is unclear);[39] planets in mutual reception will *make peace*, even if there is (or despite) a difficult aspect between them—so they will have good intentions and amenability toward one another;[40] a received planet's significations will be accompanied by *joy and security*;[41] a received planet has *allies*;[42] and *truth* and *knowledge* are involved: complete reception by domicile or exaltation involves truthful intentions, but a lack of reception can show a lack of knowledge, familiarity, or understanding.[43] Reception can take away someone's disgrace in a bad situation, or confer honor in a neutral one.[44] And in cases where a leader is deposed, if his significator is received (even if peregrine, which again means being a pilgrim or foreigner), it shows him returning home.[45]

Before trying to summarize the concepts behind these, there is another situation involving reception which Māshā'allāh mentions twice: being "separated from out of reception." Unfortunately Māshā'allāh is unclear as to exactly what is bad about this situation, and his two examples are mirror op-

---

[35] *On Quest.* §10.3.
[36] *OR* Ch. 3.
[37] *OR* Ch. 3.
[38] *OR* Ch. 4.
[39] *OR* Ch. 8.
[40] *OR* Ch. 1.
[41] *On Rev.* Ch. 19.
[42] *On Rev.* Ch. 25.
[43] *Introduct.* §§5.8-9.
[44] *On Quest.* §§10.3, 10.7.
[45] *On Quest.* §10.8.

posites of each other. In the first example,[46] he says that if the Lord of the Ascendant were separated from a planet receiving him, and if that dispositor were committing disposition in turn to another malefic not receiving *him* (or to a benefic Lord of a bad house), then it will be bad for the querent. Here, the Lord is now separated (or perhaps still separating?), but we are supposed to track what his dispositor is still doing. This sounds as though the Lord of the Ascendant is leaving the joy and safety of the hospitality that reception conferred—but why would the action of his dispositor still matter once he has left reception?

In the other example,[47] the Lord of the Ascendant (Venus) was doing the receiving. She was receiving Jupiter from her domicile, but was separating from him, and Māshā'allāh says this is "horrible." In this situation it makes sense that it would be horrible for Jupiter, because his hostess Venus is as it were withdrawing her hospitality—and indeed Māshā'allāh treats this as an indication that the matter will not be perfected.

So in one case, the received planet is separating, and in the other the receiver is separating. Both are said to be bad, but I can only understand the underlying logic behind the latter case.

If we put all these details together, I think we can see that reception is essentially about having a surrogate home—a form of support that does not depend on one's own ownership and responsibilities. Unlike being in one's own domicile, where one can rely on oneself, received planets have others helping and esteeming them; and it is as though the received planet is vouched for. This notion of a surrogate home explains why received planets have joy and security, can perfect reliably (because they have support), show a connection to home and returning home, have honor instead of disgrace, have allies, involve truthful intentions (as though they are trusted), and have peaceful relations with their receivers.

Note the claim that received malefics impede less. One might question this—after all, why shouldn't they be able to harm more, since they are so supported in their efforts? I think we can understand this somewhat better if we think of medieval feudal relations.[48] In the medieval period, attachment to a lord or other institutional authority (with its own moral and legal standards

---

[46] OR Ch. 3. Māshā'allāh means to include the Moon, but for simplicity's sake I omit her here.
[47] OR Ch. 7.
[48] Or medieval warrior culture in general, which might very well apply to the Islamic milieu in which Sahl and Māshā'allāh lived.

of conduct) was an important way of establishing oneself as stable, loyal, and dependable. The modern idea of the unattached individual existing by himself would have struck traditional people as strange and suspicious. If we imagine the difference between a warrior who is unattached to any fixed purpose—and thereby is unpredictable and dangerous—and one who has become *domesticated* and *disciplined* through service to a Lord, I think we can see analogically why a received malefic would impede matters less than an unreceived one.

To summarize, Sahl and Māshā'allāh offer us implicit concepts to understand and delineate several relationships planets may have to domiciles: (a) as an owner and manager of affairs; (b) as independent *versus* dependent and helpless; (c) as protecting and providing for its matters, and receiving support; (d) as being more able to act and effect its matters through the formal permission and relation with its Lord; and (e) through having a surrogate network of support and integration into the wider economy of the chart, to help it achieve success. If I am right about these underlying concepts, they could prove very productive for practicing astrologers when analyzing planetary conditions and configurations. But they may also be extended to other areas as well, such as testimony and witnessing, to which we now turn.

§4: Testimony

The period of transition from Hellenistic to Persian-Arabic astrology saw a transformation in the way astrologers dealt with two important areas: the use of signs and houses for topical matters, and the understanding of testimony and rulership. In this section I want to describe the changes in the latter, and propose an explanation as to why they might have made sense to the Persian and Arab astrologers.

When the Hellenistic astrologers wrote about planetary interactions, in addition to using vocabulary pertaining to status and estate-management (as we speak of the domicile Lord, the exalted Lord, *etc.*) and language of looking and seeing (whence we speak of "aspects"), they also used a legal vocabulary of "witnessing" and "giving testimony." These concepts are obviously linked, because in court one gives testimony about something one has witnessed or has personal knowledge of. So for instance, a Hellenistic astrologer may speak of some planet testifying to another planet. This conception of testimony and witnessing concerns what the planets are doing to the signs and each other.

Suppose someone is on trial for a crime, and a witness appears before the judge. The witness says, "I swear to *you* (judge) about *this thing* (crime) that I witnessed." Here, the witness has no intrinsic connection to the crime—it is simply something he witnessed. He is reporting to a third party about a separate event he witnessed, in which he has no personal stake. If Robert Schmidt is right, then this makes sense in an astrological context (which I will put in very broad strokes). For example, suppose we are asking about matters of the 7th house. According to Schmidt, the Lord of the 7th is like the judge. If there is a planet in a whole-sign aspect to the seventh sign, then this planet can act as a *witness* for 7th house matters because it "aspects" or "looks at" the seventh sign. If furthermore this planet is in aspect to the Lord of the 7th, then it can provide *testimony* to the Lord of the 7th about what it has witnessed. The testimony may be good or bad, helpful or not helpful; but it involves separate planets and signs, with the witnessing and testimony taking place by aspectual relationships, and the Lord of the 7th acts as the judge.

But by the 17th Century, this legal model had been discarded. In the astrology of masters like Lilly, there were two broad ways in which the concept of testimony was used. The first was a more subjective attitude, in which the planets' conditions provide testimony *to the astrologer*. So for instance, one might read that "If planet X is in a trine to planet Y, this is a testimony that the querent will get his money." The testimony derives from the planets' actual condition, but it counts as testimony *for the astrologer*. The second attitude was more objective, and tended to be blended with the concept of planetary strength by dignity. If we follow the practice of assigning point-values to dignities, where the domicile Lord of a place receives five points, the exalted Lord four points, and so on, then we might say that the planet with the most "testimonies" or "strengths" is the most relevant or powerful for the matter at hand.

Clearly the concept of testimony underwent a significant change, and these later attitudes bear only a passing resemblance to the legal concepts of antiquity. For when we speak of witnessing and testimony in a court, we are implying that there is a judge or jury who will decide the matter on the basis of the testimony. If the planets are testifying *to each other*, as in the Hellenistic model, then we would expect some one (or more) of the planets to be acting as the judge, giving the final decision as to how some astrological matter will play out. In fact this is the basis of Robert Schmidt's recent effort to establish the rules on how to differentiate between mere aspects, witnessing, and testimony, using (ideally) the Lord of a house as the judge. As I do not know the Hellenistic material or the Greek as well as he does, I cannot know whether the Hellenistic astrologers would have used his reconstructed method. But it makes sense to me that if the planets testify to each other, then the judge must also be one or more of the planets.

But the 17th Century attitudes do not reflect this approach. According to the first attitude, the stars are really testifying to the *astrologer*, and the astrologer is the judge. Of course, since astrology is a human science, a human does need to judge the chart for the client. But it makes a difference whether the astrologer is reporting what a planetary judge has already determined, or what he or she gathers from the planetary testimony. With respect to the second attitude, testimony is no longer given to anyone, but is an objective calculation pertaining only to the stars themselves—the astrologer merely counts up the testimonies.

So what happened in the 1,200-or-so years between late antique astrologers like Firmicus Maternus, and early modern astrologers like Lilly? I think the answer boils down to two changes. The first probably came about as a natural change within the profession of astrology itself, the second from another model of witnessing and testimony I will discuss below.

Of the 44 passages in this volume dealing with witnessing and testimony,[49] there are between 2 and 6 references to the older Hellenistic view.[50] In one,[51] which I believe derives from Theophilus of Edessa, the author states outright that "the witnesses are the planets when they are aspecting." Since "to aspect" means "to look at," this is equivalent to saying that planets witness when they are looking at something (in this case, the Ascendant). The text then delineates what it means when such witnessing planets "provide testimony" to the Moon and to the Ascendant. This short text matches Schmidt's idea about testimony and witnessing rather well, and goes along with the other passages suggesting a testimony-aspect link.

---

[49] I am uncertain about six of these passages. Four are wholly ambiguous to me (*On Times* §§4, 10; *On Rev.* Chs. 37, 41); two others connect testimony and strength in a way I do not understand, saying that we should look at a planet's "testimony and strength" (*On Rev.* Ch. 39) and at "the testimony of the planets and their strength in their own places" (*On Rev.* Ch. 21).

[50] The following seem certain: *On Quest.* §7.25, *On Elect.* §123b. Less certain ones include *On Quest.* §§9.5, 13.10; *On Elect.* §14b; OR Ch. 9.

[51] *On Quest.* §7.25.

To me it seems reasonable that this model might naturally have led astrologers to use shorthand formulations, gradually beginning to think of planetary conditions as being testimonies for the astrologer. If a chart has several planets giving testimony (with aspects) in the Hellenistic manner, then it is reasonable to say the chart has "many testimonies." And if a planet has many others testifying to it, then it is not too far a stretch to say that such-and-such planet has "many testimonies" and will play a central role in the chart. Now, since the astrologer is evaluating and ranking the planets in order to find the most important information, it is not a great leap to transfer this judging responsibility to the astrologer, and say that planetary conditions offer many testimonies *to the astrologer*. If so, then it would help to explain why medieval texts like the ones in this volume often speak in this way. Of the passages on testimony, between 13 and 19 treat testimony as something present for the astrologer—a trend which continues right into the 17th Century, as we have seen.[52]

If I am right, then the older use of testimony in connection with aspects naturally changed into the attitude that any aspect or planetary condition in the chart presents testimony to the astrologer for this or that topic; and thus between 15 and 25 of our 44 passages are accounted for.

I believe the second change came about due to another model of testimony which was present in antiquity and which we draw on even today. I argue that the religious model of bearing witness and testifying to religious conviction (which might have arisen out of the legal tradition) forms the basis of this change, and it linked the concept of testimony with having dignities in a particular sign. First let me present what I take to be a defining, explanatory passage in *Introduct.* §5.9, given both from the Arabic and the Latin. This section concerns what Sahl calls "not-reception":

(Arabic) Concerning those in which there will exist neither reception nor knowing.[53] So then the Moon or the owner of the rising,[54] when connected with a planet with no testimony in the place of the Moon or

---

[52] The thirteen that seem certain are: *Introduct.* §5.14, *On Quest.* §§1.7, 1.8, 7.19; *On Elect.* §57b; *On Times* §12; *Nativities* §6, Example 9; *On Rev.* Chs. 5, 12; OR Chs. 2, 4, 11, 12. Less certain are: *On Quest.* §§7.25, 13.9, 13.12; *Nativities* §1; *On Elect.* §14b; OR Ch. 9.
[53] This word can also mean "understanding" or "recognition."
[54] That is, the Lord of the rising sign.

the owner of the rising,⁵⁵ it does not understand it and does not receive it.

(Latin) But these are places in which neither reception nor knowledge⁵⁶ comes to be: namely if the Moon (or the Lord of the Ascendant) were joined to a planet which did not have testimony (that is, some dignity) in the place of the Moon (or the Lord of the Ascendant): it does not get to know him nor receive him.

Imagine that you are staying in someone's house, much as the Moon is imagined as being in another planet's domicile. The doorbell rings, and you see someone at the door. You do not recognize this person as being a member of the household, but he wants to speak to you and demands to be let in. The idea of this passage is that you do not let him in, because he has no membership there, and whatever he tells you might not be trustworthy. This would especially be true in a traditional culture wherein family and tribal membership is crucial: strangers outside the tribe are not to be trusted.

But how can we understand the notion that testimony has something to do with trustworthiness, familiarity, and membership? The answer lies in the religious tradition. In Judaism, Christianity, and later Islam, the defining act of religious commitment is the recitation or personal acceptance of the creed. For example, a defining creed of Judaism is the *Shema*:⁵⁷ "Hear, O Israel: the Lord is our God, the Lord is one." In Christianity, it is the acceptance and reciting of one or another of the standard creeds, such as the Apostle's Creed or the Nicene Creed ("I believe in the Father Almighty, Creator of Heaven and Earth..."). Likewise in Islam, the crucial step to becoming a Muslim is the recitation of the *Shahādah*, "There is no god but Allah, and Muhammad is his prophet." It is significant that in Greek, Hebrew, and Arabic, words for "witness" and "testify" and "swear an oath" are closely related. Our English word "martyr" derives from the Greek for "witness," showing the close relationship between legal and religious notions of bearing witness and offering testimony.

But unlike legal testimony, where the witness is not intrinsically involved in the actions witnessed, two things are created simultaneously when the reli-

---

⁵⁵ I.e., in their current positions.
⁵⁶ Reading *cognitio* for *coniunctio*. Like the Arabic, this word means learning, acquiring knowledge, and recognition.
⁵⁷ *Deut.* 6:4.

gious adherent bears witness to the truth of his or her creed: (1) a *personal identification* with the content, with the sense of a personal stake in it, and (2) *community membership*. When religious people "witness" to non-believers, the primary purpose is not to relate information as when giving testimony to a judge, but to *express their identification* with the spiritual content, especially in the hopes that the non-believer will come to have this identification, too. And bearing witness to this content makes one a member of the community, such as what was once called "Christendom" and what Muslims call the ʾ*umma*, the community of believers.

Now in fact there is more to this in the Arabic (and perhaps Pahlavi), which may help explain why the changes in the notion of testimony became especially evident with the Arabic and Persian writers. The ʾ*umma*, which is undoubtedly related to ʾ*umm*, "mother," is also related to the following words: ʾ*amuna*, "to be faithful, honest, trustworthy"; ʾ*amina*, "to be secure, safe"; ʾ*ammana*, "to secure, guarantee"; ʾ*amn* and ʾ*amān*, "security, safety"; *āmana*, "to believe in, have faith in." In other words, when someone recites the credal statement of the *Shahādah* (which itself means "testimony" or "witnessing"), one automatically becomes a member of a group whose members are considered honest and trustworthy, and who are offered protection and safety. The creed and community membership go hand-in-hand. By the very nature of these tribal notions embedded into Arabic, non-believers are not considered honest and worthy of protection.

If we keep in mind that the dignities traditionally had household management and membership concepts tied to them, and are sociologically related to relatives, the master of a household, and so on,[58] then we need only go back to Sahl's statement above, armed with these Arabic verbs and concepts, and the passage practically writes itself. If a planet in some sign is aspected by another planet, and this second planet has no membership or identification with that sign, then it is viewed as a stranger, untrustworthy, not having control over the matters of the sign, and so on. In a practical context this might mean that the planet's influence will be weaker, or (if a malefic) probably more destructive, and (if a benefic) less cooperative or constructive. Of the 44 passages dealing with testimony and witnessing, between 12 and 15 treat testimony as a matter of having a dignity in a sign.

Still, there is one other problem: granted that this new conception of dignity was in use for separate reasons, why did so little of the older legal model

---

[58] See §2 above.

survive? I would like to offer a conjecture, which probably cannot be proven. Sahl and Māshā'allāh were Persian Jews, living at a time when much of the region had only recently been conquered by the Muslims, who, while relying on unbelievers for financial and intellectual capital, formally mistrusted them and subjected them to various social and financial disadvantages under Sharia law. If someone like Māshā'allāh was observant, and especially if he knew Hebrew or another language in which the Jewish scriptures were written, he would have noted several things. First, he would have remembered that God forbids star worship,[59] but that in several places the Israelites are described as breaking this rule and worshipping stars as gods, pouring libations and so on.[60] He would also have known that the periodic downfall of the Jews was sometimes blamed on these star-worshipping practices. Second, he would have known that in Hebrew, words for the number seven (*sheva/siv'ah*) and for swearing an oath (*nisba'*) are related; and that a famous scene in *Gen.* 21:30-31 shows Abraham giving seven lambs to Abimelech, so that Abimelech may "be a witness" for Abraham; and that the traditional number of planets was seven. These facts, combined with their formally tentative position in Islamic society, may have given people like Māshā'allāh pause when reading passages in Hellenistic texts that speak of the planets doing things like swearing oaths, giving testimony, witnessing, and so on. Māshā'allāh would probably have recognized that only God should receive such oaths. After all, "the heavens declare the glory of God, and the firmament proclaims His handiwork."[61] The planets should not be witnessing and testifying to each other, but if anything, they should be testifying *to us about God.*

Then Māshā'allāh would have noted two other things. On the one hand, he would have seen that the legal model of testimony had largely been abandoned, having been reduced to a testimony for the astrologer. On the other, the concept of testimony had shifted to the notion of having a dignity in a sign. And these changes would have made sense because of the reasons already described. Now, in works such as *OR*, Māshā'allāh describes situations in which the Lord of the Ascendant does not aspect the rising sign. In order for the Lord of the Ascendant to have proper protecting and providing power over the rising sign (so as to be the significator of the querent), the Lord needs another planet which *does* aspect the rising sign, in order to ren-

---

[59] *Deut.* 4:19.
[60] *Amos* 5:26; *II Kings* 17:16, 21:5, 23:4-5, 23:11-12; *Zeph.* 1:5, *Jer.* 8:2, 19:13.
[61] *Ps.* 19:1.

der the Lord's light to it. According to Schmidt's reconstruction, this situation might normally have been described in terms of legal testimony and witnessing. But since Māshā'allāh saw that testimony was no longer used in such a fashion, and he might have had second thoughts about introducing it (given the religious and political reasons given above), he could have concluded that testimony language was no longer necessary. Instead, he could speak of the planets "rendering light" or "pushing disposition" to each other and to the rising signs. Therefore, the language of testimony does not appear in works like *OR* in the legal context, but rather in the form of testimony to the astrologer, or in terms of dignities, or in a third form as committing or pushing disposition.

To summarize, the Hellenistic legal model of witnessing and testimony was not so clear-cut and independent of other influences that it would necessarily avoid being changed. One natural change was the shifting of judgment responsibility onto the astrologer, so that planetary conditions acted as testimonies *for the astrologer* about this or that matter in the chart. But alongside this legal paradigm was a related, religious model. Like the legal model, the religious model relied on notions of trustworthiness; and due to some felicitous Arabic connections between faithfulness and trustworthiness, it was possible to say that the various Lords of signs, already being known as the owners and masters of signs, were also members of the signs, and their relationship to those signs was one of control, allegiance, and trustworthiness. Thus it was possible to say that a planet ruling a sign has a "testimony" in that sign, with further consequences for planetary relationships. Finally, it is possible (but not proven) that the ultimate disappearance of the legal model could have been motivated by two factors: the shifts already described, which made it seem less important, and possible hesitation about using the language of witnessing and testimony in a culture that abhorred idolatry.

§5: Detriment, Being, Corruption, and Descension

In the Latin edition of Sahl's *Introduct.* §5.0, Sahl introduces a number of planetary conditions and relationships that we recognize as the familiar transfers of light, prohibition, angular strength, and so on. The title of this Latin section is "On the effecting [*effectu*] and detriment [*detrimento*] of the planets." The noun *effectus* means "bringing about," "accomplishing." The noun *detrimentum* means "detriment, loss, harm." In themselves these seem like innocuous and ordinary terms, and indeed "detriment" is a common enough term in the Latin texts, as for example when a planet is said to suffer detriment or harm by having bad aspects to the malefics. But the title reads as though they ought to be opposites—yet "bringing about" and "harm" are not opposites.

The significance of the title only becomes clear when we look at the original Arabic title, which is "The chapter of explanation on being [*kawn*] and decay [*fasād*]." In this section I will argue that this presents an important metaphysical point that must inform our understanding of planetary interaction.

The Arabic *kawn* has as its root *kawwana*, "to form, fashion, create, bring into being, produce." The Arabic *fasād* has as its root *fasada*, "to become bad, corrupt, distorted, destroyed." Clearly creation and destruction are opposites, and Sahl means to say that his 16 conditions of the planets describe what they produce and destroy, or how their natures themselves are brought into being or corrupted by the conditions of a particular chart. This pairing of words has its origin in Greek philosophy, especially in the notion of "generation and corruption" as described by Aristotle, who used them as technical terms to account for the process of change. Even more significantly, where the Latin uses *detrimentum* elsewhere in *Introduct.* and *On Elect.*, the Arabic (for the texts I have) employs *fasād*.[62] Consequently, Sahl uses *fasād* as a *general* term referring to any kind of corruption or decay, whether in planetary interactions or in the general sense of harm: a planet being harmed by the malefics, example, will have increased *fasād*.[63]

If we take this knowledge of the Arabic and investigate the Latin further, we find that the Latin is not so far off, after all. The root of *effectus* is *efficio*, which like the Arabic means to "bring about, bring to pass, cause to be, produce." But the root of *detrimentum* is where things get interesting. The root of this noun is *detero*, which does not really mean "to harm," but rather "to wear away (especially by rubbing)," "to wear out," "pound, grind," and in a military context it describes when a fleeing army breaks apart and disintegrates. The theme here is disintegration, which is opposed to bringing something into being.

---

[62] The one exception is at *Introduct.* §5.16, where the Latin inserts it without any corresponding term in the Arabic.
[63] *On Elect.* §122e.

There are two things we may conclude from this: first, the Latin translators did not arbitrarily choose words like "detriment," but they thoughtfully considered what the Arabic meant (even if this thoughtfulness was forgotten and taken for granted by later astrologers). Second, and more importantly, it means that when we do traditional astrology *we must employ the jargon and attitude of traditional physics and metaphysics.* Many modern astrologers try to adopt modern scientific concepts, either in order to make astrology more palatable to scientists, or as an honest attempt to update astrological thinking. But even if these modern concepts have value, they are still very removed from the world we experience: speaking about waves and forces does not translate directly into practical delineation. Traditional astrology, on the other hand, puts us directly into the concrete world in which we see events, things, and relationships come to be, exist for a while, and pass away. It points ultimately to a cosmological model in which our very lives, as described in the natal figure, are phases in the universal process of change, in which we cannot assume the Enlightenment model of the sacredness and sovereignty of the individual, however we think our personal soul or intellect might survive death. This notion of planetary configurations as expressions of creation and destruction, of coming to be and passing away, is very profound for the practice of traditional astrology and its modern resurrection.

However, we ought to notice that this word *detrimentum*, "detriment" or "wearing away," is used in another special context in later astrology. It is true that it is often used to describe adverse planetary conditions in general—that is fine, and this could be described as a further sense in which adverse conditions destroy planetary effects or make them decay. If we took this usage seriously at every turn, it could have a revolutionary effect on astrological delineation. But all astrologers nowadays are familiar with the word "detriment" as a very specific debility: that is, the seventh sign from a planet's domicile. So Mars, who has Aries as his domicile, has Libra as his detriment. And when Mars is in Libra, we say he is "in his detriment."

It might come as a surprise to learn that most medieval texts (including those in this volume) do not refer to the seventh sign as the sign of "detriment." It seems to be a later development. The medieval texts are very much concerned with the descension or fall (the opposite of exaltation), but they do not give a formal name to the opposite of one's domicile, and rarely mention it.[64] However, given what they *do* say about this sign, and what the original meaning of *detrimentum* was, I think we can reconstruct what the real meaning of the sign of detriment is, assuming that we should give it greater prominence than the medieval astrologers generally do.

Let us review some of the ways in which the opposite of the domicile is described in these texts. For instance, a planet in such a place will "impede [hinder] itself";[65] if a planet in such a position signifies the querent, he will "dread the purpose concerning which he asked: for it will be severe for him";[66] it is a "bad place," belonging to a planet's bad fortune, and it is weakened there;[67] it is a place of "enmity";[68] it signifies "contrariety."[69] We might add to this ibn Ezra's aphorisms that a planet in its own detriment is like someone who does not completely desire the quaesited matter, and is like a person fighting himself.[70] And it is standard in horary charts for wars and conflicts that the Lord of the Ascendant in the seventh (or vice versa) shows that the querent (or the enemy) is conquered or captured.[71]

At first glance it might seem as though this is just a list of generally bad things. But the deeper connection between these characteristics is that they involve threats to the being of the planet itself. Self-hindering, the contradiction or self-defeating attitude of both wanting and dreading something, contrariety, fighting oneself, being overcome and conquered—these ideas boil down to a planet encountering what is contrary to its defining activity and being. In a practical sense this means the planet's (1) disintegration and dispersal, and (2) loss of control. Typically in ancient physics, beings in the proper sense (like humans, for instance) have a kind of integrity and organization and internal control. But when enough changes and oppositions are introduced, the being's activity is less controlled, less reliable, more disorganized—until something like total change (i.e., death and destruction) takes place.

---

[64] Māshā'allāh even omits the sign of detriment when he has an explicit opportunity to do so (*OR Intro.*). In *OR* Ch. 12, Māshā'allāh does not seem to care that Jupiter is in the sign of his detriment. How he would have delineated this Jupiter when taking it into account is another matter; but my sense is that he would definitely have noted it if Jupiter were in the sign of his descension.
[65] *Introduct.* §5.10, #10.
[66] *Judgments* 50.
[67] *On Rev.* Ch. 26.
[68] *On Quest.* §7.25.
[69] *On Quest.* §10.2.
[70] Ibn Ezra pp. 133 (#49), 136 (#86).
[71] See, e.g., *On Quest.* §7.25.

One way to explain this enmity, disintegration, and so on, would be in terms of ancient theories of change, such that the elemental qualities of hot, cold, wet, and dry suffer change into their opposites. Jean-Baptiste Morin seems to have something like this in mind when he says that a planet in the sign of its detriment is corrupted because it has no "affinity" with it, and has an "incompatibility" with it.[72] So for instance, Venus in Aries would experience the contrariety between her moistening quality and Aries's drying quality, which would hinder or threaten her normal activity and being. But I am not sure this is the right way to look at it. Medieval astrologers do pay attention to the elemental qualities, but it is not clear to me that this model provides the right basis for this topic. For example, Venus rules Taurus, which is cold and dry, while the sign of her detriment, Scorpio, is cold and wet. But if elemental qualities were the underlying cause of the detriment, one would expect her to fare better in Scorpio than in Taurus, and Taurus would cause her to suffer changes in her qualities.

If indeed the sign of detriment is meant to express this notion of decay, disintegration, and contrariety in the way that *detrimentum* or *fasād* is used by Sahl to describe planetary interactions and any kind of harm generally, then perhaps it gets this meaning simply by being an opposite to the domicile, and it has nothing to do with systems of elemental qualities or relationships of planetary dispositors. We should take the sign of detriment simply as a special case of *detrimentum/fasād*, because a planet's domicile illustrates the place of a planet's safety, integrity, control, and resources—its opposite domicile, then, would signify the opposite of all that. Thus when we see a planet in the sign of its detriment, we should not simply think "bad," but think "disintegration, loss of control, lack of definition and solidity."

We can compare this attempt of the Persian-Arab-Latin astrologers to define detriment more broadly, with Rhetorius's explanation of the detriments.[73] In the *Thesaurus*, Rhetorius explains why the domicile of a given planet is the opposite of another, and he uses the notion of contraries: so the domiciles of the Sun and Moon are contrary to those of Saturn because *light* (which the luminaries signify) is the contrary to *darkness* (which Saturn signifies). Likewise Mercury signifies the intellect while Jupiter signifies material gain, and these two impulses are contrary (by which he must mean *intellect*

---

[72] Morin pp. 26-27.
[73] Rhetorius Ch. 8.

and *matter*, though this is something of a stretch in my mind, since wealth is not the same as matter itself).

Now, for Rhetorius the question is, "why are the domiciles of planet X contrary to those of planet Y?" This has more to do with how planets are inimical to each other or represent contraries, so it is not quite the same as asking what the sign of detriment itself is. Nor does Rhetorius state that it is bad for a planet to be in the sign of its detriment. According to Rhetorius's approach, the reason why it might be bad for Venus to be in Mars's domicile is not because *the domicile* is opposite her own, but because *Mars* signifies things contrary to her. And this is tantamount to saying that when Venus is in the domicile of Mars, she becomes Martial or is conditioned by Martial things. But by the same token, Venus would become Jovial in Jupiter's signs, and Saturnian in Saturn's signs, which leads us away from the question of the sign of detriment as a special illustration of a more basic principle. True, according to this account it would be worse to be in a domicile whose Lord signified opposite things. But this sort of explanation (a) pushes the burden of explanation to the planets, not the signs and their relations, and (b) offers different explanations for each planet, since each pair of contraries is different. For instance, if the Moon is in Capricorn and Venus in Aries, they are each in the sign of their detriment—they share the same condition. Normally we would want an explanation of this condition which would equally apply to both planets. But on Rhetorius's explanation, the Moon and Venus find difficulties for *different* reasons: the Moon finds difficulties because of Saturn, and Venus because of Mars. However useful this is (and it is useful), it does not act as a general explanation for *what* detriment is and *why* it is bad, in terms of the relations of the signs themselves. I suggest the Persian-Arab-Latin astrologers were trying to do just this with their use of *detrimentum/fasād*, because it dealt with the principles of being and decay. Since coming-into-being and decay or destruction are opposites, they can thematize at a more fundamental level both planetary conditions generally, and the difference between being in one's domicile and being in its opposite.

From here we can move to a discussion of descension or fall (Ar. *hubūṭah*, "downfall"), which is the domicile opposite the sign of exaltation. In the medieval texts, the descension is not only of greater concern for the astrologers, but it is described differently than the sign of detriment is. The signs of exaltation and descension have more of an evaluative and comparative sense to their meaning, unlike the starker opposition of being-decay or domicile-detriment. A planet in its descension is like one in sorrow, prison, and distress;[74] it is a place of "worthlessness" relative to a planet's interests;[75] someone represented by a planet in its descension will have hatred for its own situation, and be restricted there;[76] sociologically it signifies someone low-class or brought low. These meanings convey the themes of esteem and contempt, prominence and obscurity, noble and base. If a planet (or a person signified by a planet) naturally seeks dominance and prominence, then the sign of the descension will represent a threat different from that of the detriment. The sign of detriment represents a threat to one's whole being or operative ability, whereas the sign of the descension represents operational irrelevance, distance from what matters, and ineffectiveness. This does not mean that both planets and detriment and in descension might not signify bad or even powerful events (as for example if Mars is in Cancer or Saturn in Leo), but the underlying concept that informs the events differs in the two cases.

In *Introduct.* §5.9, Sahl offers a second example of what he calls "not-reception," when planets with certain dignity-relations do not take kindly to each other when in aspect. Sahl envisions a planet like the Moon applying to another planet, while the Moon is in the sign of the other planet's descension (for example, the Moon applying to Saturn while she is in Aries). In such a case, the Moon would be like someone approaching Saturn from the house of his enemies, and he will neither receive[77] nor esteem her. The threat here is not so much to Saturn's integrity or being (which is more like the detriment), but to his status and relevance. The "enemies" represented by Aries do not seek to destroy him, but to bring him down low and make him insignificant.

Sahl suggests what this means in delineations, and it generally signifies that the person represented by the applying planet (here the Moon) will not achieve any or much success in a matter, if the slower planet is the one we hope to achieve perfection with. In *On Quest.* §1.6, Sahl says that if the applying planet is in the descension of the heavier planet, it will show the detriment and destruction of the matter. And if the heavier planet were in the descension of the lighter, applying planet (without reception), then the per-

---

[74] *Judgments* 4.
[75] *OR* Ch. 10.
[76] *OR* Ch. 10.
[77] In the more general sense of accepting her influence, being well-inclined to her influence.

son signified by the lighter planet will be in a bad situation, and be unable to perfect the matter—as though the matter is being handed to someone who represents its downfall. There are other valuable passages along these lines in *On Quest.* §10.7.

If I am right, then the Persian-Arab-Latin astrologers were interested in applying metaphysical concepts of being and change to relationships between planets; and they did so because they took seriously a cosmological model in which the planets signified, or were the agents of, change. The astrologers applied the themes of being and decay to the effects of planetary configurations, and then the notion of decay more broadly to any adverse planetary conditions. At some point the groundwork for referring to a "sign of detriment" was laid, perhaps through an analogy between the domicile and being (and integrity, control, *etc.*), so that the opposite sign meant the decay and loss of all of this. They had some hints about this from the Hellenistic period, but understood and sought to solve the issue in a different way. On the other hand, oppositional themes continued to be used with respect to the exaltations and descensions, but using more comparative and socially-derived distinctions like high-low, esteemed-debased, and so on. The descension does not threaten the being and integrity of the planet in itself, but it threatens the prominence and influence a planet would normally have.

§6: The Consultation Chart

One striking feature in Sahl and especially Māshā'allāh is the use of the "consultation chart," a phrase I will use following Chris Brennan and his work on this concept.[78] Texts in this volume that definitely or probably employ the consultation model include *On Quest.* §13.18, perhaps §1.1, and probably §9.7; *Cognition* (all); *On Hidden Things* §§2, 6; *Twelve Dom.* (material in the section on Jupiter and dream interpretation).

It used to be thought that horary astrology's history reached as far back as the early Hellenistic period, though it seems now that it had its origin in Persia or India, somewhere around the 6th Century (see Brennan). Originally, what we now call horary was only electional astrology, choosing the auspicious times to begin an action. But over time a new practice arose, that in which the astrologer casts a time for the client's interview, and interprets the

---

[78] Brennan, 2007.

chart so as to divine the client's *thoughts*. According to Brennan, this probably did not even include an analysis of what the outcome of the thoughts would be, though this developed later on and can be seen clearly in Māshā'allāh's *Cognition*. Only in the Persian-Indian period mentioned did something like our familiar horary practice mature.

The use of consultation charts did indeed continue alongside horary proper (again, as we see in Māshā'allāh). It is preserved wholesale in late texts such as Leopold of Austria's *Compilatio*,[79] and is sometimes disguised as horary topics, much in the way that later editions of Dorotheus seemed to disguise electional material as horary questions. For instance, I strongly suspect that Sahl's whole treatment of dream interpretation in *On Quest.* (which Bonatti happily adopts) derives from the consultation tradition, and probably portions of al-Rijāl's treatment of the same topic.

The primary purpose of the consultation chart was to divine the client's thoughts or intentions. On the one hand this seems like a superfluous exercise, since presumably the client need only open his mouth and the astrologer will discover it then.[80] Or was this a way for an astrologer to show off? Or was it a kind of consideration before judgment, as when one compares the client's physiognomy with that indicated by the chart, to see if it is valid?

Māshā'allāh does say[81] that the client's intention will be more *accessible* if the client has reflected on the issue for 24 hours; otherwise the astrologer will not be able to find (or might find only with difficulty) the significator of the intention; and he suggests that a client who does not think about the question this long will not know how to ask properly—therefore, if the astrologer cannot find the significator of the question, it reflects confusion in the client's own mind. In *Cognition*, he says the intention will be more "truthful" after 24 hours of reflection—which I take to mean that the truth will be more accessible.

Still, there is more to the issue, since Māshā'allāh's statements do not explain why we should try to divine the client's intention in the first place. As I said, once the client speaks the astrologer would know rather quickly whether he or she is confused, without ever looking at a chart. I think we find a clue in *Cognition*, where Māshā'allāh speaks of three things to look at in a consulta-

---

[79] Leopold, Treatise 10, "On Intentions." Interestingly, Leopold gives the very same chart Māshā'allāh does in *Cognition*, but attributes it to Hermes.
[80] Though sometimes it might help clarify the issue by focusing on the crux of a matter, the details and causes of a scary but hazily-remembered dream, and so on.
[81] *On Hidden Things*, §2.

tion chart. The first is "for what reason" the questioner has come—this seems identical to the intention. The second is that one should know the *cause* of the interrogation. If we compare this statement to Bonatti's 1st *Consideration*,[82] we see Bonatti also speaking about what moves a man to pose a question—among which are the causal motions of the superior bodies. If we read Māshā'allāh's delineation of the chart in *Cognition*, a clearer picture emerges.

Perhaps going to a consultation astrologer, or casting a consultation-type chart, is like going to a gypsy fortune teller to see what she has to say. You may have lots of things you'd be curious to know about your affairs, but none of them in particular is on your mind for the consultation. The point of the reading is for the gypsy fortune teller to inform you as to what "the spirits" want you to know at this time. Just so, the consultation chart would say what God or the Universe is doing and informing you of now. So for instance, suppose the astrologer casts a consultation chart, and the Lord of the Ascendant is in the 3rd. On the horary model, the astrologer would have to wait until client speaks, in order to find out what the issue was. But on the consultation model, the astrologer begins to speak about 3rd house matters, assuming that—whatever else the client may be interested in—the Universe is moving the client because of 3rd house matters. The consultation model assumes that the chart or Universe knows what the consultation should be about; the horary model assumes that the client knows what it should be about.

But there is a tension between my image of the gypsy fortune teller and Māshā'allāh's own instruction that the client think about his intention for 24 hours. If the consultation were only meant to divine whatever the Universe were telling the client at that moment, why would one need to meditate on an intention at all? At the moment I see two possibilities.

The first possibility is that meditating on the question somehow aligns the client with the stars (in some unknown way), so that he is eventually led to the astrologer at the right time. Then the consultation chart will divine that intention and the astrologer can say something about it. The problem with this possibility is that it is very close to the full-blown horary model we find in astrologers like Bonatti, where God is introduced as the agent responsible for the client arriving at the right time and ensuring the truth of the chart. So as an interpretation of the consultation model it does not seem to fit well.

---

[82] *BOA* p. 264.

A second possibility is that *Cognition* is *already* a hybrid work, displaying attitudes from both the consultation and the horary model. On the one hand, Māshā'allāh does not say "I was asked," but rather proceeds directly to find the significator of the intention, what is causing the mother's illness, and what will come of it (consultation model). On the other hand, he indicates that the client should already have an intention in mind for 24 hours (horary model). To me this hybrid model seems more plausible, though it does not get us closer to solving the issue of consultation charts versus horary questions.

Someone might point out that one can do both horary and consultation charts at the same time—in fact, some astrologers do cast charts at the beginning of a horary session in order to discern their client's state of mind, if not this "intention" in Māshā'allāh's sense. That is true. But according to the evidence, consultation charts and horary did not *arise historically* at the same time, and they make different assumptions about the universe. Therefore we have to try to understand on *what* points they differ, and make conjectures as to *why* one might have come before the other.

The consultation model works well under the assumption of universal determinism. This view of the world was to a great extent accepted by the ancients and medievals—and many moderns.[83] The idea was that our lives are part of the physical cosmos, with its own rules and structure which are guided by, or reflected in, the planets. We cannot escape this situation. So when the client goes to the consultation astrologer, the astrologer can do no more than describe the situation the client is in or which concerns him, its cause, and predict its outcome. Moreover, only certain kinds of advice would likely apply: if the chart showed that the client's mother will die, then the astrologer could only advise various forms of emotional, legal, and financial preparation—he could not advise anything that would make the mother live.

Horary astrology, which seems to have emerged from the consultation model, works better under the assumption that humans have some power of free will allowing them to change the normal course of events. Some horary questions do not suggest their own advice, and some horary advice is close to the consultation model. Horary questions like "Is my wife pregnant" do not suggest advice, while other questions suggest the need for preparation just as in the consultation model. Horary advice that differs from this includes in-

---

[83] I should point out, however, that probably most modern scientific materialist atheists also still believe in the untrammeled free will invented by theologians.

structions by people like Sahl and Māshā'allāh. In response to the question "Will I get this position," Sahl and Māshā'allāh say that under one configuration of the chart, the client will get it *if* he strives for it. Presumably then it is up to the client to decide whether he will strive or not. Even here the issue is not clear-cut: if the world is pretty universally determined, then the client will have such-and-such a character either determining him to strive or not to strive—no free will is needed. Still, it is clear in later Christian authors like Bonatti that horary proper demands a conception of undetermined free will. Since we know that the determinism model predates the freedom model, it seems reasonable to say that a consultation model would predate the horary model, and perhaps that the horary model was introduced in order to remedy certain theological, psychological, or cosmological problems with the consultation model. More work needs to be done on this.

In sum, it seems that sometime in late antiquity the Persian and Indian astrologers developed a new model of astrological practice, the consultation model. At first this was used to find a significator of the client's intention, which was then delineated to divine the client's thoughts or concerns. Perhaps this was even an extension of mundane practice, in which one wants to know what is on the king's mind—what does he intend? Later, the delineation was extended to predict what the outcome of those concerns would be. It may have been during this predictive stage that astrologers adapted electional material from people like Dorotheus, to the consultation model. Thus questions about the best time to perform an act, became a delineation about what act a client intended, and then whether it would be successful. As a final step, a horary model emerged, which did two things: first, it put the responsibility of posing the question onto the client, rather than the chart suggesting it on its own; second, some older consultation material was still transmitted in the form of horary questions. The horary model was likely introduced to remedy some problems in the consultation model, but more work has to be done in order to understand the relationship between these types of charts, historical evidence for them, and conceptions of determinism and freedom.

§7: Angles and Stakes

Latin astrological texts typically speak of the four *anguli* (sing. *angulus*), which we translate as "angle." And "angle" is indeed one of the meanings of *angulus*. But the standard meaning of *angulus* is "corner," as in the corner of a room. In this section I will describe what the original Greek and Arabic words for the four *anguli* are, and how the Latins changed its meaning. I will also alert the reader to how I will render this word in different texts.

Originally, the Greeks called the four angles *kentra* (sing. *kentron*). This word is derived from the verb *kenteō*, which means to "prick, stab." A *kentron* is a sharp point, a goad for driving animals, it is used to describe one's sovereignty, the peg of a spinning top, and even the stationary point of a compass. This word is particularly valuable for speaking of the actual degrees of the angles, since they are points on the ecliptic; but they also suggest a point of goading or stimulation for planets near them, which is one reason why planets are said to be more active or powerful in them. But it is sometimes also used to describe the four angular signs (the first sign, fourth, seventh, and tenth), which means there is a fundamental ambiguity in the Greeks' use of this word. In his own recent translation work Robert Schmidt distinguishes a "goad" (the degrees of the angular axes) from a "pivot" (the angular whole signs), but the underlying word is still *kentron*. This ambiguity, as we will see, is passed on to the Persians, Arabs, and Latins. We have inherited this ambiguity and must try to figure out in each instance what they meant.

When the Persian and Arabic astrologers read this word *kentron*, they must have gone through some decision-making process to decide what Pahlavi or Arabic word to use. We are not privy to their deliberations. But it seems they went primarily with the notions of sticking or stabbing[84] (instead of rotating or pivoting), and used the Arabic *watad*, which means a stake or a peg, especially the stakes used in holding down a tent. Like the Greek, this word comes from a similar Arabic verb *wattada* or *watada*, which means "to drive in firmly, fix, secure." It is also part of a phrase which means to "stay at

---

[84] I also note that the notion of the stakes as "goads" still survives in Māshā'allāh, though *watad* itself does not suggest it (unless we assume the idea of goading an animal with a stick or pole). In *On Quest*. §6.1 and OR Ch. 8, the Latin Sahl and Māshā'allāh each say that the stakes "excite" or "stimulate" matters (*excitant*). Sahl's passage refers to horary charts about illness, and says that a malefic in the Midheaven shows that the patient will "stimulate" the infirmity upon himself due to his own willful disobedience of the doctor's orders.

home."[85] When they decided on this word, they must have been noticed their great luck in that the Greek meaning of a *kentron*, as a symbol of sovereignty, was also like their own metaphors in Arabic. For in classical Arabic, *watad* is used as a metaphor for mighty and firm power: a mighty Bedouin chieftain was called "he of many tent poles," because his power allowed him to have a bigger tent, which in turn required more stakes or poles.[86] They must also have remembered that in many ancient cultures the sky is likened to a tent, so it is as if these "stakes" hold the sky in place like a tent.[87] But they also kept to the normal meaning of the word, as when Māshā'allāh says that the stakes (or angles) "fix" matters—i.e., establish them.[88]

So the writers in Arabic judiciously considered what word to use when translating *kentron*. But a certain change was introduced during the Latin period, which is repeated in a certain way in English translations of Arabic works. Some translators, like Hugo of Santalla, chose the word *cardo* as a translation of *watad*. In Latin, a *cardo* is a pivot or hinge. True, the original Greek *kentron* did connote pivoting (as in the point of a compass or the peg on a spinning top). But *watad* does not have this connotation, and Hugo could not have justified his choice based on *watad* alone. Others, like John of Spain, chose *angulus*, which has no relation to either *watad* or *kentron*, but as everyone knows modern English-speaking astrologers regularly use the word "angle."

Why did translators like John of Spain choose *angulus* instead of some other term meaning a stake (*palus*), peg (*paxillus*), or even pole (*asser*), any of which would have accurately translated *watad*? I believe the answer is literally staring us in the face when we look at a square, medieval-style chart. In these square charts, the four angles are literally the four "corners" formed by the triangular houses facing the cardinal directions, and the point of this triangular corner is formed by the degrees of the axes of the Ascendant and Midheaven. So, seeing how astrological charts were drawn, he decided to call these places "corners."

Once John of Spain's translations were popularized, this word *angulus* simply became a standard technical term, and since then astrologers have not only been ignorant of its original Arabic meaning as "stake," but even of the

---

[85] Note that in horary questions about the location of someone/something missing, planets in angular houses signify it is close by or in the home.
[86] See Mannan p. 600.
[87] *Cf.* also *Introduct.* §4.
[88] *OR* Ch. 10.

fact that "angle" originally meant a "corner." We have been divorced from the original meaning of this term and its connotations for centuries.

This change has even affected modern translators of Arabic itself. For instance, when translating *watad* for his edition of Dorotheus, Pingree calls it a "cardine." Crofts likewise uses "cardinal point," and Burnett *et al.* use "angle" for their edition of al-Qabīsī, but "cardine" in Abū Ma'shar's *Abbr.* But *watad* does not have pivoting connotations (like *cardo*) and does not mean "angle" or "corner" (*angulus*). So even modern translators of Arabic have been affected by the Latin tradition's preferences.

I see my job in this book as primarily that of a translator and expositor of Latin material, even though I take advantage of the Arabic when I can. Partly this is because of my own interest in the Latin material; partly it is because most of Māshā'allāh's works exist only in Latin translation anyway, so I could not access much of his Arabic even if I wished to. In this book I will continue to use the word "angle," with the exception of (a) Sahl's *Introduct.* §5, (b) Sahl's *On Elect.*, and (c) Māshā'allāh's *Chap. Rains*, because we have the critical editions of the Arabic for them, and they clearly use *watad*. My reason for this is two-fold. First, the common word "angle" does not really mean anything conceptually related to *kentron* or *watad*, so it can continue to be used as a technical term, *provided that* we remember the original meanings. If I tried to be a purist and translated *angulus* as "corner" in every instance, then I would be reproducing John of Spain's diagram-based reasoning, which was partly responsible for the mix-up in the first place. So I will continue to use "angle" except in those instances above. The reason I will use "stake" for those other passages is to alert the modern reader of the original meanings, so as to encourage us to think more in line with the traditional astrologers.

Unfortunately, there is enough ambiguity in the original uses of *kentron* and *watad* that it is sometimes unclear whether we are speaking of angular degrees or whole-sign houses. Using "stake" or "angle" will not necessarily get us the answers we seek on this topic. But if the only issue here were between a *watad* as a whole sign and a *watad* as an ecliptical point, it would not always be that difficult to sort out. If for example a planet is said to aspect another "from out of a *watad*," this would probably mean "from the angular whole sign." In other cases it would not be so clear: if a planet is said to "aspect the Midheaven," this might be thought of either as by a whole-sign aspect or as a degree-based aspect to the degree of the Midheaven.

But the issue is more complicated due to two matters. First, in later medieval Latin astrology especially,[89] an angle is considered to be a *region following the degree of the axis*, and not simply a whole sign or the degree itself. And of course the notion of a region then borders on the topic of quadrant houses for topical matters. Secondly, we have the ongoing issue that the degrees of the Midheaven-IC axis do not always fall on the "correct" whole sign. So for instance, let the rising sign be Aries, and let the degree of the Midheaven fall in Sagittarius, the ninth whole sign. The "angle" could refer to (a) the tenth whole sign Capricorn, or (b) the degree of the Midheaven in Sagittarius itself, or (c) a region following the cusp, encompassing part of Sagittarius and part of Capricorn, or possibly even (d) Sagittarius itself, which might count as an angle simply because the cusp is on it. We are dealing with signs, cusps, regions of power, and, later on, quadrant houses for topics.

I propose we look at the use of angles and stakes in this volume in three groups. First, there are all of the passages from *Introduct.* §5, *On Elect.*, and *Chap. Rains* which mention stakes in general. The reason for isolating these passages is that we will have no worries about mistranslations or interpolations by Latin translators and editors. Second, there are the passages in *On Elect.* especially, but also others, which speak of the "angle of the earth" or "stake of the earth," i.e., the 4th. Since the rising sign and the seventh sign will always coincide with the degrees of the Ascendant and Descendant, we must look to Midheaven and the 4th to see what Sahl and Māshā'allāh do with the fact that the Midheaven-IC axis may not fall on the fourth and tenth signs. Third, we should look at Latin passages which might shed light on how they viewed these axes and whole signs.

§7a: Stakes in General in the Arabic Works

In the works for which we have the critical editions of Arabic, there are several standard phrases used to describe the stakes, with other passages mentioning multiple uses. In addition there are several passages whose meanings are suggestive but unclear.

(1) "The stakes of *x*" and "aspect from a stake." In the three passages mentioning "the stakes of *x*,"[90] Sahl speaks of planets being in each other's

---

[89] But also in *Carmen*—see below.
[90] *On Elect.* §§ 61a, 64a, 131a.

stakes: planets in the stakes of the Moon or in the stakes of the malefics. All of these passages have a whole-sign meaning, since traditional authorities specifically warn us that it is bad for a planet to have malefics in the same sign, or the fourth or seventh or tenth from itself. In the two passages mentioning an "aspect from a stake,"[91] it is recommended that Jupiter aspect Saturn from a stake or a trine aspect, and that we should beware a conjoining of the Moon with Saturn from a stake, or that the Moon be joined also with a benefic from a trine, sextile, or from a stake. In these cases, I believe we are dealing solely with whole signs, where planets are joined with each other in the same sign, the fourth, seventh, and tenth from their own location (as with "in the stakes of x"). I also note that the section from *Carmen*[92] whence the latter passage derives does not suggest anything but whole signs, except for an ambiguous statement about the "stake, the house of fathers."

(2) "In the stakes." In these four passages,[93] we are told not to put the Lord of the Ascendant or the Moon in a stake, or in the stakes of the Ascendant; to beware putting the malefics in the stakes, or to make the significators be joined in the stakes; or to look for a connection in the stakes. Read in context, especially given the two references to the Ascendant in these passages, they are most likely all references to whole-sign houses from the Ascendant.

(3) "Cadent from the stakes." In these four passages,[94] it is said to be bad if the Moon or other planet is cadent (lit. "falling") from the stakes, or connected to a planet cadent/falling from the stakes, or falling from the stakes and not aspecting the rising sign (which is described as being in the sixth or twelfth). In these cases the evidence is ambiguous. On the one hand this could be taken as planets moving by primary motion away from the cusps of the axes, since the axes define the points at which planets rise, culminate and decline (or fall), set, and reach their lowest point—after which they fall away from them.[95] On the other hand, Sahl's insistence that a planet cadent from the stakes and not aspecting the Ascendant means that it is in the sixth or twelfth, is definitely a whole-sign reference—since the sixth and twelfth signs do not aspect the rising sign, but the third and ninth signs do; and a planet that merely falls away from the degree of the Ascendant would still be in the

---

[91] *On Elect.* §§48, 114a.
[92] *Carmen* V.21-25.
[93] *On Elect.* §§24, 34, 86b; *Chap. Rains* §1.
[94] *On Elect.* §22d; *Introduct.* §5.2, 5.15 #1, 5.16 #7.
[95] See for instance *Judgments* 44.

rising sign itself. So this group of statements is still somewhat ambiguous, and perhaps both types are represented in them.

(4) "In the succeedents of the stakes." This passage,[96] in the context of hunting, warns us to put the Lord of the seventh in the succeedents of the stakes, because "if he were cadent, it signifies that the prey will escape after he caught it." This statement is ambiguous. On the one hand, to "succeed" means to "follow after," but since the houses to not move but only the signs do, then really only the succeedent whole signs can follow the angular whole signs. On the other hand, one of the senses of being "cadent from the stakes" was to be moving away from the cusp of an axis, which suggests that perhaps being succeedent is a matter of quadrant regions, as well. In this case my best guess is that both of these references (being succeedent, being cadent) are meant in a whole-sign manner.

(5) Quadrants defined by stakes. In these two passages,[97] Sahl describes the ascending and descending of the planets in each hemisphere of the chart, which seems to refer unequivocally to the cusps of the axes. In the latter passage, he even refers to the cusp of the IC as the "stake of the earth," which I will address below.

(6) "Reaching/entering the stakes." In these two passages,[98] the Moon is said to reach the stakes or enter one of the stakes, and to then be joined to Mercury or Venus. This puts the weight on the side of whole signs, but it is possible that Māshā'allāh is referring to regions defined by the axes (see next paragraph).

(7) "Erecting/recording the stakes." In these two passages,[99] Māshā'allāh merely means that when predicting the weather, we need to cast a special chart and determine the degrees of the axes. It is possible that these are the stakes which the Moon is supposed to reach or enter by transit in (6); but they could also be the angular whole signs from the rising sign at the time the chart was cast.

(8) Finally, there are eight "multiple use" or other passages,[100] where different uses are meant, or the uses are ambiguous or do not conform to the stock phrases above. In the first passage,[101] we are told to put the benefics in

---

[96] *On Elect.* §138a.
[97] *On Elect.* §§66a, 70b.
[98] *Chap. Rains*, §§3, 4.
[99] *Chap. Rains*, §§1, 2.
[100] *On Elect.* §§5b, 101, 104a-b, 108b, 109-111, 123b; *Introduct.* §5.1, 5.14 #1.
[101] *On Elect.* §5b.

stakes and make the malefics be cadent from them. Looking at both Crofts and the Latin, I take this to refer to the angular whole signs from the rising sign, and the signs cadent (not aspecting) them (or at least, not aspecting the rising sign).

In the second,[102] we are told there should be a conjunction of the Moon with Jupiter from the stakes or a good place from the Ascendant (which must be a whole-sign reference), but we are to beware the conjunction of the Moon with Mars "and the stakes" (which I take to be whole-sign squares and the opposition to the Moon's sign); and that Mars and Saturn should be "following" or in the "succeedents" of the stakes (which repeats the ambiguity in [4] above).

In the third,[103] we are told that Jupiter should be in the Ascendant or the seventh, with the Moon testifying to him from one of the stakes, and that Saturn and Mars should not be in one of the stakes. The context here suggests angular whole signs from the rising sign.

In the fourth,[104] the Moon is to be in the stakes or in the succeedents of the stakes, aspecting the Ascendant (otherwise, if she is impeded, she should be cadent from the Ascendant); and the Lord of the Ascendant and her Lord should be in stakes. The bit about aspecting the Ascendant or being cadent from it, is a whole-sign reference. It is likely that the rest of the references denote whole signs as well, which further suggests a whole-sign interpretation of (2)—(4) above.

In the fifth,[105] the concept of "approach" or "advancement" refers to a planet being in a stake or in what follows the stake (i.e., a succeedent). This is somewhat ambiguous due to the unclarity of "approach/advancement." For "approach/advancement" could refer to primary motion, or it could be a metaphor for what the planet signifies—e.g., that a querent's *matter* will advance. If this were solely a whole-sign reference to primary motion, then while it makes sense to say a planet in a succeedent sign is advancing toward its future placement as an angular sign, a planet in the angular sign does not have to approach anything—the angular whole sign would already *be* angular. On the other hand, if this approach or advancement referred to approaching the cusp by primary motion, then we are dealing with a regional concept: a planet in the region defined by the cusp or stake, or one in the region follow-

---

[102] *On Elect.* §§109-111.
[103] *On Elect.* §123b.
[104] *On Elect.* §§104a-b.
[105] *Introduct.* §5.1.

ing that one, would each be approaching and advancing toward the cusp. But if we take this advancement to be metaphorical, then this passage could refer equally to either whole signs or regional divisions.

In the sixth passage,[106] it is good for planets to be in a good place from the rising—that is, the stakes and what is following that, from the places which aspect the rising sign. The phrase "aspect the rising sign" here suggests whole signs, but it would equally well refer to regions from the cusp that are *also* in a whole-sign position to aspect the rising sign.

In the seventh passage,[107] we are told in the context of elections that we should adapt the traveler's nativity, namely its Ascendant and its stakes. This seems to be a whole-sign reference, but it could also refer to adapting the degrees of the axes.

In the eighth passage,[108] we are told that if the Sun is cadent (or falling), there will be no good for him; but in the ninth, third, and fifth, there will be some success; and in the western stake and the fourth, there will be a scarcity of good with slowness. All of the places which show success aspect the rising sign, which suggests that by "cadent" here (and by extension, being in the stakes) Sahl is referring to whole signs.

§7b: The Stake of the Earth

Since the degrees of the Ascendant and Descendant will always fall on the first and seventh signs, but the degrees of the Midheaven and IC will not, perhaps we should see how Sahl and Māshā'allāh treat the MC-IC axis, to help us understand how they deal with the stakes in that context. It might seem clear that only the fourth and tenth signs are stakes, since three Latin passages say explicitly that the "angle of the earth" (the 4th) is the same as the fourth sign.[109] But matters are not so simple. In the first place, although both *Introduct.* §5 and *On Elect.* use the phrase "stake of the earth," neither the Arabic nor the Latin in those works ever clarifies that it is the fourth sign. So it is possible that these clarifications in the rest of the works are only interpolations by Latin translators. Second, one of these references[110] derives

---

[106] *Introduct.* §5.14 #1.
[107] *On Elect.* §101.
[108] *On Elect.* §108b.
[109] *Introduct.* §4 par. 5, 9; *On Quest.* §9.5.
[110] *Introduct.* §9.

from Ptolemy's use of the axes to define quadrants, so we cannot assume that the entire fourth sign is meant. These apparently clear statements present a mixed bag.

Sahl is absolutely aware of the fact that the MC-IC axis will not always fall onto the fourth sign, and he makes some statements to the effect that his exposition is only idealized. In the first of these three statements,[111] Sahl says the Ascendant should be a fixed sign, "and likewise the sign of the result." Now, if the stakes were only whole signs, then the fourth sign would always be the same quadruplicity as the rising sign—so he is asking the astrologer to frame elections so that the axes fall on the correct signs. In the second statement,[112] Sahl points out that sometimes "it will not be fitting that the Lord of the Ascendant should aspect the Lord of the tenth (like if the Ascendant were Leo, and the angles correct)." If the rising sign were Leo, then Taurus (ruled by Venus) would be the tenth sign, and indeed Venus and the Sun cannot be in aspect. But there would be no reason to speak of the angles being correct (*recti*) unless the "tenth" were sometimes not the tenth whole sign, but another one. But it also seems that the Lord of the tenth is equivalent to the Lord of the degree of the Midheaven.

Finally, the most important statement showing Sahl's awareness of the problem comes in *On Quest.* §1.7. There, Sahl describes what features of the chart will show a lasting and stable result. He says it is best if the rising sign is a fixed or common one, "and the angles stable (that is, that the Midheaven is the tenth sign, and the angle of the earth the fourth sign—and the Midheaven is not the ninth sign, nor does the angle of the earth fall on the third sign). This exposition of the angles is of the stable ones." This is a very important statement, for (1) it not only suggests that while the angle of the earth (and of the Midheaven) is a whole sign, it is not necessarily the fourth and tenth signs but only those that the MC-IC axis *happens* to fall on; and (2) it suggests that perhaps *whenever* Sahl (and perhaps Māshā'allāh) speak about the angle of the earth and suggest it is the fourth, they are only speaking about *idealized conditions*. This potentially throws a monkey wrench into the whole matter.

What we should do, then, is collect all of the instances of "angle of the earth" besides these, and also (in §6c below) other instances of "stakes" and "angles," and see if grouping them together might draw out some themes.

---

[111] *On Elect.* §125a.
[112] *On Quest.* §10.2.

(1) Our texts present four passages that clearly relate the stake of the earth to the degrees of the axes.[113] Two of them refer to the ascending and descending hemispheres of the chart as defined by the axes. A third refers to the quadrants as defined by axes. The fourth defines the angles as the "points" of the axes, though it does refer to the point of the Midheaven as the "point of the tenth." None of these statements tries to treat the stakes in a topical sense (profession, marriage, *etc*.), but only in terms of how we may divide the chart according to primary motion. To these we may add a fifth[114] which treats the stakes again in terms of quadrants and the ascending and descending hemispheres.

(2) Eight passages[115] treat the stake of the earth in what is *probably* a whole-sign sense (i.e., as the fourth sign). They are too varied in detail to summarize them here, but four deserve comment. One[116] says that the 4th domicile (or "house") is the angle of the earth, and the 5th domicile (or "house") succeeds it. I have already suggested that this is probably a whole-sign reference, since the signs move toward the axes. Two others[117] are derived from a passage in Dorotheus, who largely uses whole signs for everything except for some special rules I will address below in §6d. A fourth one[118] suggests whole signs to me because each one of the domiciles listed aspects the rising sign.

(3) Finally, five passages[119] are ambiguous to me. The first comes from a chart in which the Moon is both in the fourth sign and the fourth quadrant house, and Sahl says she is in the "angle of the earth." Nothing definite can be deduced from this example. The second seems to refer to whole signs, but I can see it reading as quadrant houses as well. The third is so brief ("wherefore if they came together with the angle of the earth") I cannot make much of it. It seems to me the fourth could be read as whole signs or quadrant houses. The fifth refers to directions in space, which sounds like the quadrant divisions by axes, but could also be whole signs.

These, then, are all of the instances of "stake/angle of the earth" in our texts. In the previous section we saw that whole signs overwhelmingly (but

---

[113] *On Quest.* §7.16; *On Elect.* §§66a-b, 70b; *On Times* §1.
[114] *On Times* §3.
[115] *Introduct.* §3; *On Quest.* §§7.13, 7.17, 9.2, 9.5 (two passages), 9.6; *On Rev.* Ch. 6.
[116] *Introduct.* §3.
[117] *On Quest.* §7.13.
[118] *On Rev.* Ch. 6.
[119] *On Quest.* §1.8, 7.17, 7.23; *On Rev.* Chs. 2, 6, 14.

not definitively) covered the instances in which planets were in a stake, aspecting from it, being in it, and being cadent or succeedent from one. But the 5° rule in *Judgments* 44, and Sahl's awareness of the problem of the MC-IC axis means we cannot assume it always means this. If there is a solution to all or most of these passages, we might have to segregate them by function, so that cusps are meant in one instance because they perform some function, while whole signs are meant in others because they perform another function.

In this section we saw that the passages which explicitly refer to the fourth sign are undercut by Sahl's admission that it is not always so, and his suggestion that he will idealize the charts; some others appear to refer to the fourth sign; others clearly come from dividing the chart by the axes in order to derive quadrants and hemispheres; and a few others are ambiguous. By themselves we still cannot say definitively what Sahl and Māshā'allāh take the stakes (or the stake of earth in particular) to be.

§7c: *Other Statements about Stakes/Angles*

Finally, let us look at some other statements of interest from the Latin texts which pertain to the stakes or angles in general.

(1) Four statements[120] clearly equate the stakes with the angular whole signs from the Ascendant. The statement by Sahl specifically says that the zodical circle is divided into twelve signs, and he specifically names the first, fourth, seventh, and tenth signs as the angles. Another statement by Māshā'allāh[121] says that the Midheaven is the tenth sign. But the other two by Māshā'allāh are of special interest. In the chart for Ch. 7, Māshā'allāh treats the entire rising sign as the angle or stake, so that Mars, who is in the second sign and only about 8° from the degree of the Ascendant, is specifically said *not* to be in the angle. In the chart for Ch. 12, Venus is placed about 5° 30' earlier than the rising degree but in the rising sign, and is said to be in the "ascending angle [stake]." She is not even said to be cadent. These statements speak strongly in support of a whole-sign interpretation of the angles.

---

[120] *Introduct.* §4 par. 2; *OR* Chs. 7, 10, 12.
[121] *OR* Ch. 10.

(2) There is a lone statement[122] by Māshā'allāh instructing us to set up the Ascendant and the Midheaven when casting a chart. If the Midheaven is a stake, then he is treating the stake as an axial degree.

(3) Finally, there is one other statement by Sahl.[123] Sahl says that a planet is not cadent (i.e., "falling") from the angles except after 5°, and follows it with an example: if the angle were the tenth degree of Aries, every planet in less than 5° of Aries will be cadent and not considered to be in the angle.[124] Sahl and Māshā'allāh may have disagreed on this very point—for Sahl recomments this 5° rule in a general way (not just in the context of longevity procedures, as Māshā'allāh does). But Māshā'allāh's example in OR Ch. 12 does *not* appear to follow this rule. It could be that the source for the 5° rule for cadence generally was invented by Sahl himself! But I do note that in OR Ch. 12 Māshā'allāh does say that the more cadent a planet is from the angles, the worse for what a planet signifies. If cadency were purely a matter of whole signs, then it should not make a difference how far away a cadent planet is.

After surveying all of these passages, it would seem we have a bewildering confusion. We have found stakes to refer to whole signs, quadrants/hemispheres, axial points; we have found a possible disagreement between Sahl and Māshā'allāh on the 5° rule; Sahl's possible idealization of charts; and regions of power. But I would remind the reader that the ambiguity in the word "stake" or "angle" derives ultimately from the Hellenistic authors' own ambiguous use of *kentron* to mean an angular whole sign house, and the degrees of the axes.

So far, very little has been said about the use of quadrant houses or powerful regions around the axes. But we do know that the use of quadrant houses for topics appeared within the next few centuries (if it was not already underway), and we do know that both angular signs and regions about the axes are both said to give "strength," and that the regions about the axes are later used as topical houses. Since later astrologers drew on works such as those in this volume, we ought to see if there is any reason suppose Sahl and Māshā'allāh used these concepts, or could have acted as sources for them.

Now in point of fact, there are only two references[125] in all of these works to something which sounds like quadrant house cusps, and several

---

[122] OR Ch. 8.
[123] *Judgments* 44.
[124] See §7d below for more on this passage.
[125] *On Elect.* §§36-38b; *On Times* §7.

others[126] which implicitly recognize them. The two explicit references refer to the "Lord of the degree of the house of trust [Ar. "hope"]" and the "degree of the house of death." Sahl says nothing more about whether this "degree" is the cusp of a house, or the first degree of a *domicile*. Of the implicit references, one uses Ptolemy's 5° rule for the determination of the *hīlāj* (which uses intermediate house cusps). Another is a somewhat confused passage by Sahl in which he combines a version of a rule of Dorotheus's with like statements by Ptolemy. It is this latter statement which acts as the springboard for the introduction of powerful regions around the angles, and the possibility of quadrant houses for topics. Several others in *On Nativities* speak of candidate *hīlājes* being within 5° of the "house" or "domicile" (*domus*) they are in. The third statement instructs us to set up the angles and "the rest of the places in the celestial figure by degrees and minutes."

When Sahl and Māshā'allāh read Dorotheus, they would have noticed that, most of the time, Dorotheus seems to treat the stakes or angles as the angular whole signs from the Ascendant. But they would also have read passages like *Carmen* IV.1.165, which says that a planet can be in the tenth but not in a stake—so they knew that a stake was not simply a sign. And they would have noticed the ambiguity in the word for "stake," since it sometimes stood for a sign, sometimes for the degree of an axis, and sometimes for regions of power about the axis.

In terms of the latter, they did in fact notice three places in *Carmen* in which Dorotheus introduces certain "15° rules" regarding planets in and about the axes. These three passages inspired three corresponding ones found in this volume. Let us look at all three passages by Sahl and Māshā'allāh, with their source texts in Dorotheus. Here is the first passage (emphasis mine):

> *On Nativities* §3: And if you found the *kadukhudhāh*, look at it: if it were *in an angle by degrees* or in its own domicile or in the exaltation or triplicity, safe from impediment (namely from retrogradation or from the combustion of the Sun), you will give it the greater years of the planet; which if it were in a succeedent of the angle and safe from malefics, you will give it the middle years; and if it were in the cadent of an angle, and did not have any dignity there, you will give it the lesser years.

---

[126] *OR* Ch. 11; *Judgments* 45; *On Rev.* Intro.

Carmen III.1.23-24: But if together with this a benefic is *in the ascendant in what is between it and fifteen degrees*, then mix this planet with the haylaj.

Both of these passages occur in the context of length of life treatments. In Māshā'allāh's version, we are to find the *kadukhudhāh*, and see if it is in "an angle by degrees." He does not say how many degrees, but this is a strength consideration, and he treats the angle both as an axial point *and* a region counted by degrees from it. In theory this could put a planet in the next sign, so long as it fell with in the prescribed region. What is puzzling is what he considers to be succeedent or cadent. If they are whole signs, then what is the rationale for the degree-based region? Note that he also applies the years of the planets, which Dorotheus does not do.

In Dorotheus's version, he seems to want the *kadukhudhāh* to be in the ascending sign, but in a 15° region from the rising degree: so he is treating the Ascendant both as a sign and an axial point, but adds to it a relevant degree-based region. As we look further in the text, Dorotheus also uses this region to decide which planets to which he will direct the degree of the Ascendant: namely, if they or their rays are in the 15° region. He does not say whether this region can extend to the next sign.

It is worthwhile to note that Dorotheus's use of this region does not simply seem to be a matter of strength or planetary relevance: it also seems topical, because the topic is life, Dorotheus speaks only of the Ascendant (and not the other angles), and the region is used to direct the Ascendant for crises in life. Although Māshā'allāh elaborates his own version of this rule and is somewhat unclear, we can imagine him seeing the possibility that a region from an angular degree, even possibly if it is in the next sign, might pertain to topics and not merely to strength. But he and Sahl would also have noticed another version of the rule:[127]

On Nativities §6: And if the first triplicity Lord were in the Ascendant, from the first degree up to the fifteenth, he will ascend to great riches; and if it were in an angle, closer[128] in degrees, it will be more useful for

---

[127] I use the stylized brackets to abbreviate the passage; the square brackets are Pingree's. In accordance with my standards I use "stake" instead of his "cardine."

[128] Reading *proprior* for *prior*, also following Abu 'Ali (*JN* p. 11): "And the closer it is to the degree of any angle…".

him. Which if it were in the second sign, from the first degree up the fifteenth, [it will be likewise].

Carmen I.26.3-8: Look at the lord of the triplicity of the sign in which is the shining luminary. If you find it in one of these four stakes in [such a way] that there are fifteen degrees [or less] between it and the stake, then predict about him that he will be most perfect in fortune and property. If it is in the second fifteen degrees, then predict {something less}...as the nearer it is to the degree of the stake, the higher it is for his rank in eminence and fortune. If that planet...is in the third fifteen degrees, then the owner of this nativity {will have something less still}...If you find the lord of the triplicity after these degrees until it reaches the next stake, then {it will be worse still}. But you should have these degrees in [the rising-times of] the ascendants...

The context in both passages is overall wealth and eminence in life. It will be easier to begin with Dorotheus. This is a strength consideration, measuring 15° increments from the degree of the stake, using ascensional degrees (*not* along the ecliptic), *regardless of sign boundaries*, to determine how strong the triplicity ruler is. The 15° are not topical, and "stake" is used solely in terms of axial points, with no reference to whole signs. But note that these instructions would hold just as good if the degree of the Midheaven were in the ninth sign, since planets after it in the ninth would be just as strong as planets following the degree of the Ascendant, even if the planet's ecliptical degrees were in the following signs. This encourages regional thinking instead of whole-sign thinking.

Māshā'allāh's version as it has come down to us has the appearance of referring to whole signs, especially given the reference to the second sign. But why should the last 15° of one sign be weaker than the first 15° of the following sign? I think this reference to the second sign is a mistake, probably by the Latin translator. Dorotheus says eminence will be reduced in the "second fifteen degrees." But, reading from the Arabic, a Latin translator might have read this as "in the second [sign], [in] fifteen degrees," giving the appearance of whole signs where there is none.[129] But the stake is still conceived of as defining regions of strength, and it is notable that these regions are at fixed points. In fact, a somewhat creative reader might see this as

---

[129] Then again, Māshā'allāh might also be borrowing from *Carmen* I.7, see below.

a kind of reference to intermediate cusps, since cusps in systems like Alchabitius semi-arcs are calculated using ascensions rather than ecliptical degrees—just as Dorotheus recommends using ascensions.

Finally and most importantly, we have two related Judgments from Sahl, which derive from *Carmen* I.5 and I.7. The context in Dorotheus is the prediction of upbringing—namely, whether the native will live, and what kind of life he will have; but Sahl universalizes this to apply to all stakes or angles:

> *Judgment* 44: If a planet were in the beginning of a sign, it will be weak until it is made firm in it, and walks through it by 6°. And a planet does not fall from the angles except after 5°. For example: if the angle were the tenth degree of Aries, every planet which is in less than 5° [of Aries] is cadent and is not thought to be in the angle.

> *Judgment* 45: And every planet which is after the angle by 15° will be just like one who is in the angle; and if the degree were to increase, he will have no strength. For example: If the angle were the tenth degree of the sign of Aries, then every planet which is from that same tenth degree up to 25° of the same Aries, is thought to be in that same angle. Which if one added 15° on top [of that], it will not be in the angle. But Ptolemy says a planet will be in the angle up into 25° after the angle.

> *Carmen* I.7.7-9: If you find a planet [such that there are] fifteen degrees between it and the ascendant, then, even if it is in the second sign from the ascendant, reckon its power as if it were in the ascendant. But if it goes beyond this, it has no strength in the ascendant and it is an indication of those who will have no upbringing.

The first point to make is that I believe Judgment 44 covers two topics. The first topic is covered in the first sentence. The rest of Judgment 44 introduces the topic of Judgment 45. So we can ignore the interesting but (for our purposes) irrelevant first sentence of Judgment 44. The last part of Judgment 44 and all of Judgment 45 pertain to regions of power around the axes, with the 5° rule and the accompanying 25° being taken from Ptolemy. We will ignore these borrowings from Ptolemy. Overall, we can say that the stake is treated here as an axial point and as a region that can overlap the next sign.

Here are some initial questions about Judgment 45:

a. What does it mean to be "just like" a planet in the stake? Is this purely a matter of strength, or could there be some topical significance here?

b. What does it mean to be "in" the stake—is this purely a matter of the 15° rule, or would a planet anywhere else in the rising sign also count?

c. Are the examples Sahl's own, or added by an interpolator? I think it does not matter much, since the source text in Dorotheus is clear about what is meant, and it pretty much matches what the examples say.

d. Why does Sahl say first that such a planet will be "just like" a planet in the stake, and then say that the same planet would be "in" the stake?

e. Sahl says that a planet outside the 15° region will have *no* strength. How does this square with Dorotheus? Here I think Sahl is abbreviating—he means to say it will not have power in the angle (as Dorotheus affirms), not that it will have no power at all.

f. Why does Sahl universalize this region to all stakes, when Dorotheus is speaking here about the Ascendant only, in the context of this technique?

In order to answer these questions and reconstruct what I think could be one basis for allowing quadrant-style houses for topics, we have to reconstruct what a Persian or Arab astrologer might have thought when reading *Carmen* I.5 and I.7.

In *Carmen* I.5, Dorotheus discusses which places (whole signs) are preferable in power to others in the chart. Preferable are the four angular whole signs, then the eleventh and fifth, then the seventh, then the fourth, then the ninth. The second sign is classified among those which are "not good." The basis for this classification could be that these good places aspect the rising sign (the third is usually considered ambiguous in Hellenistic astrology). So we could expect planets not in such signs to act badly vis-à-vis the rising sign and its matters.

But when our hypothetical astrologer reached I.7, he found something odd. Here Dorotheus discusses the matter of upbringing, and one thing he wants to see is benefics or planets in sect in the seven "good places." So far, so good. But then Dorotheus does something strange. Although the second sign was specifically listed as a bad place, the 15° rule in I.7 says that a planet in that sign—so long as it is within 15° of the rising degree—may have its power reckoned *as if it were in the Ascendant*, and if it is beyond this region it has *no strength in the Ascendant* and indicates *no* upbringing. At first it might seem as though this is simply a matter of strength, namely being in the powerful region about the rising degree. But Dorotheus does not say it will have power pure and simple, but that it will have power *as if* it were *in* the Ascendant. Our astrologer would also have noticed that these statements are not made about all of the stakes or angles, but only about the Ascendant, and the topic is the native's own survival and life—which is signified by the Ascendant. But normally a planet in the second sign would mean nothing for life, because in a whole-sign system, sign boundaries are house boundaries, and one sign cannot signify what another does.[130] Moreover, it had seemed that the good places were chosen precisely because they aspected the rising sign—but here we have a case where a planet not aspecting the rising sign can be treated *as if* it is *in* the Ascendant, simply by being in a particular region: and not just any region of mere strength, but in the region that signifies life: so a properly-placed, second-sign planet can signify life.

Then our hypothetical Persian astrologer might have gone a step further. As a faithful reader of Dorotheus, he would have noticed the other 15° rules discussed above. The first rule mentioned above speaks of the 15° region, and uses it topically to direct the Ascendant, if a malefic is in or casts its rays to the region. The second rule mentioned above describes graded regions of 15°, which have progressively less strength. This third rule uses a region to cover a sign not normally allowed, apparently saying that a planet in such a position can be reckoned as being in the Ascendant for topical purposes and not just purposes of strength. Our astrologer would not have thought that these were three distinct rules, because there is too much overlap between them. He would have applied the principle of charity and tried to see how all of the rules could be harmonized. He might have reasoned in the following way:

1. The rules apply to all stakes or angles, not just the Ascendant.

2. The 15° regions are graded and sequential, and do not just end after one region (as *Carmen* I.7 says).

3. Another important authority (Ptolemy) gives different values for what counts as being in the appropriate region (25° instead of 15°), so perhaps these values are rough conveniences.

4. One version of the rules says to use ascensional degrees, which would make a region of greater or lesser than 15° ecliptical degrees anyway, so perhaps there is some flexibility in what counts as the region. And the use of

---

[130] In fact, Valens says (*Anth.* II.5) that benefics in the second place are of no avail, and malefics there produce sluggish and diseased people who die early.

ascensional degrees makes sign boundaries (and thus whole-sign houses) irrelevant for this purpose.

5. Dorotheus's rule in I.26 and statement in IV.1 suggests that because the MC-IC axis can deviate from the tenth sign, these regions may be shorter and longer depending upon the latitude for which the chart is cast.

6. Since quadrant house systems were known, perhaps the quadrant house cusps could act as the divisions between the regions (which would have the added benefit of making them roughly equal in size, depending on the house system used).

7. Dorotheus's rules in I.7 and III.1 seem to have a topical character which breaks the normal rules about sign boundaries: planets or their rays in one sign can signify or be relevant to what those in another sign normally do.

Reasoning in this way, our astrologer might have come to the conclusion that quadrant house divisions simultaneously show strength *and* topical matters.

It is possible that some other way of looking at things could set all or most of the passages I have listed in a proper arrangement, and at this point I would like to make a suggestion along those lines. Please note that I am not trying to state The Truth about astrology, but I am interpreting and trying to reconcile what Sahl and Māshā'allāh say, based on the tradition they inherited and where it finally ended up.

First, there are uncontroversial uses of the stakes as axial degrees defining quadrants or hemispheres. These have their own particular meanings, such as the eastern quadrant signifying youth, the east, *etc.*, or the rising or setting half of the chart signifying parts of the body. These need not detain us here.

Second, there are the stakes as the whole-sign angles from the Ascendant or the Moon (or some other planet or Lot): so for instance, the rising sign, the fourth, the seventh, and the tenth. These angular signs signify more *notable* and *intense* actions upon the native (i.e., the rising sign), as do the angular signs from the Moon when the malefics are in them. The principle here is related to the fact that Sahl and Māshā'allāh want aspects to be kept within sign borders, so aspects in general (and the whole-sign angular aspects) pertain to planets' *effects on something else*. Planets in the angular whole signs from the Ascendant will have a notable effect for the native, but they might not be notable in themselves for matters they signify (see below). So, this is a functional and influenced-based notion of the angles, not a topical notion.

Likewise, the cadent and succeedent signs are the signs on either side of the angular ones. These triads show what has been, is passing away and is unstable or susceptible to change (cadents), what is present and notable (angular signs), and what is coming to be (succeedents). The cadent signs are not so much "weaker" than succeedents or angles, but their effect is less direct and notable—and their effects will be even less notable and more indirect on the native if they are cadent from the rising sign itself (the twelfth and sixth).

Third, the degrees of the axes and other quadrant houses can be used for topics, using the normal spans of the houses and the 5° rule for being cadent from these cusps. Planets in these houses can be delineated according to their natures and conditions, but their effects will be more or less notable and more or less direct (on the native) depending on whether they are in angular, cadent, or succeedent *signs*.

Fourth, planets closer to the axial degrees are indeed "stronger," according to the quadrant house region they are in, including the 5° rule as a way of determining when a planet ceases to have this strength by region.

Let me illustrate these proposals with a few examples:

1. Let the degree of the Descendant be at 14° Taurus extending to 12° Gemini, and let Mercury be in 20° Taurus and the Moon in 1° Gemini. According to this example, both Mercury and the Moon are in the 7th, and signify relationships. But Mercury is in the angular sign, and so will have a more notable and dramatic effect on the native than the Moon will. He is also quantitatively stronger than she is. The Moon is in a succeedent sign, and one which does not aspect the rising sign—so her effect will be less notable and more indirect, and less susceptible to control.

2. Let the rising sign be Sagittarius. But let the degree of the MC be in the ninth sign, Leo, at 14° extending to 20° Virgo (the tenth sign). Let there be a planet in late Leo and another in early Virgo. According to this example, both planets signify the profession. The planet in Leo will have a greater quantitative strength (and will likely produce some kind of profession according to its nature); but it will not have the kind of direct and intense effect that the planet in Virgo will have by being in the tenth sign. My sense is that while the planet close to the MC in

Leo will produce a profession quickly and early, the planet in Virgo will present ongoing, intense concerns in the profession and life generally, according to its nature and condition.

3. The same as (2), but now let there be a planet in the 11th house (but the tenth sign), at 25° Virgo. Such a planet will signify friends, and while it will not be as quantitatively strong as a planet in the 10th closer to the MC, by being in the tenth sign it will show notable, lasting, and intense matters pertaining to friends.

4. The same as (2), but now let there be a planet earlier than the MC, at 2° Leo. This planet is in a cadent sign and cadent from the cusp (since it is more than 5° away). Such a planet will be in the 9th house, signifying religion and travel. But its effect on the native will be less intense and notable, all other things being equal.

This is not a perfect arrangement, and these concepts need to be clarified. Also, context matters: if the planet in the 9th house in example (4) were the Lord of the Ascendant itself, then of course it would play a more central role in the nativity. But I think this arrangement, if developed further, could make good sense of the texts we have in this volume.

§8: Twelfth-Parts

Several passages in Sahl's *Introduct.*, *On Elect*, and *On Times* refer to adverse conditions of the Moon that relate to the so-called "twelfths" or "twelfth-parts" (and might also refer to Gemini as the twelfth sign from Cancer). There is some unclarity as to exactly what Sahl is describing, but later compilers like al-Rijāl and earlier sources like Dorotheus and Paul of Alexandria shed light on the matter. In order to propose good translations of these passages, we must understand what the twelfth-parts are, and that the difficulties in Sahl's passages are compounded by the fact that they were already understood in several ways in the Hellenistic period.

Olympiodorus[131] mentions three ways in which "twelfths" or "twelfth-parts" are understood, and Manilius[132] adds one more.

---

[131] Paulus p. 100.

1. According to Olympiodorus, a twelfth-part is first of all simply a zodiacal sign (or any 30° division of the zodiacal circle), since there are twelve zodiacal signs. One may see this in Hephaestio[133] and Ptolemy.[134] This possibility will feature in our discussion below.[135]

2. Secondly, a twelfth-part refers to the 2.5° sections of a zodiacal sign that result when we divide its 30° by 12. According to this method, each of these 2.5° sections is ruled by or refers to one of the zodiacal signs, beginning with itself. So for instance, the first 2.5° (or twelfth-part) of Virgo is ruled by Virgo. The next twelfth-part (2°30'—5°00') is ruled by Libra. The third twelfth-part (5°00—7°30') is ruled by Scorpio, and so on. When we run out of signs in our counting, we start over with Aries. Thus each sign has twelve twelfth-parts, each one of which is allotted to a zodiacal sign. Planets in a given twelfth-part will be affected in some way by the sign indicated. So for instance, if the Moon is in Virgo, she is modified by her presence in Virgo. But if she is in the Sagittarius twelfth-part of Virgo (7°30'—10°00'), then her signification will also be modified by, say, a planet actually in Sagittarius. This type of twelfth-part is described by writers such as Manilius,[136] Ptolemy,[137] Olympiodorus,[138] Rhetorius,[139] Abū Ma'shar,[140] al-Qabīsī,[141] al-Bīrūnī,[142] and Bonatti.[143] This is a rulership-based concept.

3. The third version is discussed by Olympiodorus and Paulus,[144] and for clarity's sake I will call this "Paulus's twelfth-part." The method seems akin to Lot calculations rather than the rulership version above, and it seems to pertain to *outcomes* and *where* a position's influence will wind up, not the qualitative modification of a planet itself as in the version above. According to these authors, Paulus's twelfth-part is to be used in nativities, when judging the overall quality of a native's life. First, identify which position's twelfth-

---

[132] Manilius pp. *liv*, II.738-48.
[133] Hephaestio, *Apotelesmatics* I.1.
[134] *Tet.* I.14.
[135] I tentatively add to this *Carmen* I.8.1-2, but this passage could also refer to the 2° 30' divisions. Likewise, Pingree tentatively adds *Carmen* IV.1.113.
[136] Manilius pp. II.693-721.
[137] *Tet.* I.22.
[138] Paulus p. 100.
[139] Rhetorius Ch. 18.
[140] *Gr. Intr.* V.18.
[141] Al-Qabīsī IV.15.
[142] Al-Bīrūnī §456.
[143] *BOA* pp. 1404-05.
[144] Paulus pp. 40-41, 99-103, 111.

part you wish to calculate (this may include any planet, angular cusp, or Lot), and multiply the ordinal number of its degree[145] by 13. Then, project this amount in degrees from the beginning of the sign in which the position is, and where the number ends will be the sign (and indeed a specific degree) which is called the "twelfth-part." For example, let the Moon be in the ninth degree (8°00'—8°59') of Aries. Multiply 9 by 13, which yields 117. Project 117° from the beginning of Aries (counting off in 30° increments for convenience), and the counting leaves off in 27° Cancer. So the Moon's projected twelfth-part is in Cancer.

The Hellenistic astrologers using this method looked to see where in the chart this resulting sign fell. For instance, it shows a good outcome if the sign is angular, or has benefic planets in it, or has the Lots of Fortune, Spirit, or Necessity (Mercury's Lot) in it, and so on. Ideally we do not want the twelfth-parts of malefic planets to fall on angles or on signs containing benefics, *etc.*

This method of Paulus is explicitly stated to be a modification of a more traditional version of multiplying and projecting. In the older method,[146] we multiply by 12 instead of 13. Obviously the older method will sometimes give a different result than Paulus's twelfth-part.

4. Finally, Manilius[147] offers a fourth version. Here, the 2.5° twelfth-part is divided into five sub-parts of 30' apiece, each one allotted to one of the five non-luminaries. Manilius does not explain how to allot the planets, but he says each planet will assume "power and authority" in its 30' division, and a planet's influence will be modified according to the twelfth-part it is in.

In sum, from the Hellenistic period we have four meanings for "twelfth-part": (1) a zodiacal sign itself, or any 30° division of the ecliptic; (2) a 2.5° division of any sign, which is itself allotted to a sign; (3) a Lot-like projection of a degree that shows its outcome or where its influence is effected; and (4) a 30' division of a 2.5° division, each of which is allotted to a non-luminary. Because of this diversity of meanings, we must be careful when we read the word "twelfth-part."[148]

---

[145] That is, if the planet is in the first degree (0° 00'—0° 59'), the ordinal number is 1; if in the second degree, 2; if in the thirtieth degree (29° 00'—29° 59'), 30.
[146] See also Rhetorius, *ibid.*; *Tet. ibid.*, Manilius II.722-737.
[147] Manilius II.738-748.
[148] Lat. *duodecima, duodenaria;* Ar. *āthaniya ʿashra* and var.

The difficulty in the Sahl texts was raised by Crofts,[149] though she did not know about another instance of this word in Sahl's *On Times*. In all, the problem stems from four passages, which we may put into two groups.

The first group pertains to elections for going out to war, and probably derives from Theophilus of Edessa, a contemporary of Māshā'allāh's, who wrote an entire book on war questions. The section from *On Times* whence we get one of our four passages, explicitly credits Theophilus for at least some of the techniques. So we can be reasonably certain that these passages come from a common tradition. They are as follows:

1. *On Elect.* [Latin] (§88c): "And you should not make the Ascendant and the Lord of its domicile impeded, if you were to begin a matter; likewise the **dignity[150] of the twelfth-part of the Moon**.

2. *On Times* (1493, 7th house matters): "And if the **dignity of the twelfth-part of the Moon** were in the Ascendant or in the tenth, or with the Sun at the same time with the Lord of his own domicile,[151] or with a planet which was then arising,[152] this will signify the quickness of the war."

The parallel phrasing of "dignity [allotment] of the twelfth-part of the Moon" further convinces me these come from the same source, probably Theophilus. In each case, we want the twelfth-part of the Moon to be in a good condition, and in the latter case it should be rising or in the tenth, *etc*. But the text does not tell us which method to use. Should we use the 2.5° version, or Paulus's version? Unless and until Theophilus is translated, we cannot say.

So much for the first group of passages, which do not present much of a textual problem. The real difficulties come from the second group of passages, both of which pertain to conditions of the Moon, and seem to derive from Dorotheus, *Carmen* V.5.5-8. In this passage, Dorotheus lists several bad conditions of the Moon in elections, which became the basis of later stan-

---

[149] Crofts, p. 154-55.
[150] The Arabic is *ḥazza*, which can mean a "share, allotment" (which is how Crofts reads it), or "luck, fortune," which is how the Latin translator reads it when he uses "dignity." Crofts is probably right here, since we are speaking of what twelfth-part has been allotted to the Moon.
[151] Following 1493. BN reads, "or [with?] the Sun, or with the Lord of the domicile."
[152] *Oritur*. This seems to mean pertaining-to-arising, since it is one of the phases that shows a change of times.

dardized lists in Sahl, , and others. Here are the key portions from Pingree's edition of Dorotheus:

> "If the Moon is in the dodecatemoria of Mars or Saturn…and if the Moon is in the last degrees of a sign, then it is according to this in the term of Saturn or Mars…"

The first thing we have to understand about this text is that Pingree's edition is taken from 'Umar al-Tabarī's translation. But this translation was already based on earlier Pahlavi translations, which were in turn based on the Greek. As Crofts points out, there is much evidence in Sahl's appropriation of Dorotheus to show that he did *not* use 'Umar's version, nor are there serious traces of Pahlavi. She argues that Sahl may have used another Arabic version, or perhaps had access to Greek sources.[153] For this reason, we cannot be absolutely sure that the quotation above is the true source for the problematic passages in Sahl below.

Second, note that the first part of the Dorotheus quote speaks of the Moon being "in" the twelfth-part of Mars or Saturn. But the Hellenistic accounts by Paulus, Olympiodorus, and others never use this sort of phrasing, since the twelfth-parts are always referred to signs, not planets. Only Manilius's brief version of his 30' divisions pertain to planets, and I have never heard of these actually being used by later astrologers. So there are several possibilities here, based on the versions of twelfth-parts we have seen. Dorotheus could be saying that the Moon is in the *sign* of Mars or Saturn (i.e., Capricorn, Aquarius, Aries, Scorpio); or that her 2.5° division or Pauline twelfth-part falls on Capricorn, Aquarius, *etc.*; or that he is speaking of the Manilian 30' division. None of these seem especially likely to me, but that the twelfth-part could mean "sign" is the most plausible.

Third, this is not the only place where Dorotheus speaks of twelfth-parts. In *Carmen* I.10.6, he uses the twelfth-part in a manner like Paulus and Olympiodorus—in the context of nativities, judging the life as a whole: "If you find the dodecatemorion of the Moon with malefics or they aspect it, then this is an indication of misfortune for the native." This sounds a lot like saying that we should find the twelfth-part of the Moon (by the 2.5° division or Paulus's method), and see if the malefics are in that sign or aspect it (proba-

---

[153] Crofts pp. *vi, x-xiii.*

bly by a square or opposition). The phrasing here is not like the Dorotheus passage above.

In Dorotheus then, we have one standard, nativity-based use of the twelfth-parts that is Hellenistic and presents no conceptual or linguistic problems; two ambiguous uses;[154] and we have a fourth use, in the context of elections, which is very ambiguous in its meaning and does not really match Hellenistic phrasing. It is this ambiguous passage in V.5.5-8 that was the source for Sahl and later writers. Now we can turn to the passages in Sahl, recreate Crofts's argument, and assess it.

3. *Introduct.* §5.16, *On the defects of the Moon*:

[Arabic:] [Sixth,] <...> and it is in Gemini, or it is in the last degrees of the sign, which is an unfortunate bound.	[Latin:] The sixth, that she is in the twelfth sign from her own domicile (the which sign is that of Gemini), or she is in the end of the degrees of signs (which are the bounds of the malefics).

4. *On Elect.* §22e (Ten impediments of the Moon):

[Arabic:] The eighth is when it is in a twelfth with a malefic or in opposition to its house or absent[155] from it.	[Latin:] The eighth, that she is in the twelfth sign from her own domicile (that is, in Gemini), with a malefic, or were she in the opposition of her own domicile, or absent from it.

Note that in passage (3), there is a lacuna in the Arabic, which Stegemann filled using the Latin. And he felt justified in doing so, because of the presence of the word "Gemini," which matched what the Latin said. On the face

---

[154] *Carmen* I.8.1-2, IV.1.113.
[155] Crofts explains this as when the Moon is not in a whole-sign aspect to Cancer—i.e., when she is cadent from her own domicile.

of it then, passage (3) refers to a *sign*, namely the twelfth sign from Cancer, and passage (4) to being in a *sign* with a malefic.

But according to Crofts, it was *Sahl* who committed the true error. Working from a different edition of Dorotheus, in basing passage (3) on *Carmen* V.5.5 Sahl mistook the statement about twelfth-parts to mean the *twelfth sign*, and so he clarified that that sign was Gemini. The Latin translator followed suit, accurately translating Sahl's mistake. According to this argument, when the Latin translator read in passage (4), he remembered what he had done before, and so inserted his own clarification about the twelfth sign from Cancer. Therefore (according to Crofts's argument), passages (3) and (4) should each read either "in a twelfth-part with a malefic," or, following *Carmen* V.5.5, "In the twelfth-part *of* a malefic," with no reference to Gemini at all.

There is some indirect support for Crofts's argument in al-Rijāl, who was drawing either on Sahl or on his own edition of Dorotheus. In a passage corresponding exactly to passage (4), al-Rijāl says (in the Latin):[156]

> "Eighth, when the twelfth-part of the Moon is with the malefics, or when she is contrary to her own domicile, or that she does not aspect her domicile by any aspect."

If Crofts is right, then none of these passages pertains to the twelfth sign from Cancer (i.e., Gemini), and they all pertain to twelfth-parts. However, there are certain problems with this solution:

a. If passages (3) and (4), along with al-Rijāl, have a common source in Dorotheus then why do they contain different information? Passage (3) mixes the twelfth sign or twelfth-part with the bounds of the malefics. But passage (4) and al-Rijāl mention a twelfth or twelfth-part and the Moon's other aspects to her own domicile. Bounds, signs and twelfth-parts, and aspects to one's domicile are different categories.

b. If passage (3) really has nothing to do with the twelfth sign from Cancer, but rather with the twelfth-parts and the malefics, then even if Sahl misread the word for "twelfth-part" in *Carmen* V.5.5, how could he have overlooked the explicit reference to Mars and Saturn there? That seems like a lot to overlook.

---

[156] Al-Rijāl (1485), VII.3.112' col. b.

c. Although al-Rijāl in the Latin version uses the word *duodenaria* ("twelfth" or "twelfth-part"), there is no reason to believe that it meant a twelfth-part any more than a twelfth (namely, a sign). It reads equally well if we assume it means that the Moon should not be in a *sign* with a malefic.

I propose the following solutions for the four passages we have discussed. As indicated above, passage (1) does refer to the sign indicated by the twelfth-part of the Moon (whether the 2.5° division or Paulus's). Likewise, passage (2) refers to her twelfth-part, and following Hellenistic practice we want to see it fall on certain auspicious places. For passage (3), Sahl probably misunderstood the term for "twelfth" and treated it wrongly as the twelfth sign from Cancer—perhaps encouraged in this reading because Gemini is one of the signs which does not aspect the Moon's domicile (which passage [4] warns against). But that does not mean it should be read as "twelfth-part." I suggest that passages (3) and (4) should read: "in a twelfth [i.e., a sign] with a malefic." If I am right, then 's passage should also read this way, and *duodenaria* in his work should mean simply a twelfth of the zodiac, that is, a sign.

§9: Committing Strength, Nature and Disposition

In my Introduction to *BOA* (pp. lxxiv-lxxvii) I described what I took to be Bonatti's position on committing disposition. Here I would like to update my comments and say something about how I see it appearing in Sahl and Māshā'allāh. Of course, if other texts in the future have more to say, I reserve the right to adapt my comments further.

Sahl's definitions of committing or pushing strength/virtue, nature, and arrangement/disposition[157] parallel quite nicely Abū Ma'shar's definitions in *Gr. Intr.* VII. There is an apparent discrepancy in their treatment of pushing disposition and nature, but that seems to be because Sahl combines the two and Abū Ma'shar distinguishes them. Based on the passages I have examined, I think Abū Ma'shar was right to do so. According to Sahl and Abū Ma'shar:

---

[157] *Introduct.* §§5.12-13.

INTRODUCTION

Pushing *strength/virtue* occurs when a planet is in its own dignity,[158] and is joining to another planet: for example, if Mars is in Aries and is joining to Jupiter. To my mind, this is like a powerful planet entrusting its matter to someone else, granting his own authority and resources to the other.

Pushing *nature* is when a planet is in a dignity of *another* planet, and joins to it: for example, if Mars is in Pisces and is joining to Jupiter. To my mind, this is like a planet committing what it is responsible for (in the chart) into the hands of a more powerful person, namely his immediate authority, the one hosting him.

Pushing *disposition/arrangement* is when a planet joins to another planet, pure and simple. Abū Ma'shar does not require any kind of dignity be involved.

To put it another way, pushing or committing of disposition occurs with every applying aspect;[159] but this will involve *strength/virtue* when the applying planet is in its own dignity; and *nature* when it is applying to its Lord (of whatever dignity).

However, there is a wrinkle. Apart from one place in which Māshā'allāh suggests that disposition can be committed without an aspect (and he does not explain how),[160] the texts seem consistent both in their statements and examples that the Moon does *not* require any dignity-relation in order to commit disposition; but the other planets *do*.[161] If this is so, then disposition is really a generic term that can apply to any planet's applying aspect; but for planets other than the Moon some dignity-relation is required. Any aspect still does something, but for any planet other than the Moon the entrusting of the responsibility and character of a matter requires *nature* and *strength/virtue*. The difference between this view and Bonatti's is that Bonatti did not believe Sahl really meant it when Sahl said the Moon can commit disposition by any aspect whatsoever without a dignity being involved. But Sahl and Māshā'allāh *do* seem to mean it.

---

[158] Sahl includes only the domicile, exaltation, and triplicity; Abū Ma'shar adds the bound and face.
[159] See e.g. OR Ch. 2; *On Quest*. §5.3.
[160] *On Rev.* Ch. 19.
[161] OR Chs. 3, 4; *cf. On Rev.* Chs. 8, 12.

§10: Timing Techniques in Sahl and Māshā'allāh

Sahl and Māshā'allāh employ the usual repertoire of profections, primary directions, and solar revolutions in their predictive techniques. In addition they employ "changing figure": when a key planet will change from northern to southern latitude, enters or leaves combustion, reaches a station, and so on (see *On Times* §1).

More varied are their use of transits and symbolic times based on distance. In the case of transits, the times they use include that at which: the Sun reaches the Ascendant or some other place; a planet enters its own domicile; a planet reaches any of the angles; a planet is joined to malefics or benefics (the context determining which matters); a pushing planet reaches the receiving planet by exact degree; the Moon or Lord of the Ascendant reaches a key planet (or vice versa); the Moon leaves a place.

For symbolic times based on distance, they include the distance between: a pushing planet and the planet receiving the disposition; a significator of time and a heavy planet; between two bodies generally; the Ascendant and a significator; the Lord of a particular domicile (or a significator) and any angle; the Moon and a planet; a planet and malefics or a particular Lord of a bad house; the receiver of disposition and its combustion. In these cases the units of time are generally a day for a degree, a month for a sign. They also occasionally use the minor planetary periods expressed in years or months. Most of these symbolic times can also be modified based on the angularity of the planets or their quadruplicity—for instance, a time might be expressed as days if the planets are in a quick place, but months in slow places.

There are other refinements and particular circumstances to consider, including perhaps a few here and there I have overlooked; but the above is a rather exhaustive list. Unfortunately, Sahl and Māshā'allāh do not tell us why they might pick one over the other. This is something perhaps which, as Bonatti would put it, they left "for the industry of the wise" to figure out.

§11: Optimal Places

Just as in *BOA*, the texts in this volume occasionally speak of *loci optimi*, literally the "best places." I continue to translate this as "optimal places" since, though they are supposed to be better than the other houses or domiciles, no criterion is given as to what would make them the "best." Now that we have the critical edition of Sahl's *On Elect.*, we know that at least Sahl's Arabic uses the adjective *jayyad*, "good" in this context. We do not yet know why the Latin translators turned a "good" place into an "optimal" or the "best" place, nor is it exactly clear which houses or domiciles count. They are almost always called optimal "from the Ascendant," which suggests that perhaps there are other derived-house possibilities with respect to other places. The Ascendant itself and the Midheaven are definitely optimal places,[162] but places "removed" from the angles (which must mean "cadent," as the 9th is)[163] or not aspecting the Ascendant (as the 12th, 2nd, 6th, and 8th) are not. Possibly the 7th is excluded, because it is a place of enmity relative to the Ascendant. This leaves only the Ascendant, the 4th, 5th, 10th, and 11th, though whether all of these count is unclear to me.

It is worth pointing out two things here, one etymological and one textual. Etymologically, *optimus* is the superlative form of *bonus* (good), which in Latin (and English) has merchant and wealth overtones (think of "consumer goods"), and *optimus* itself derives from *ops* or *opes*, which means "wealth, resources." Now, in Hellenistic astrology, places that are well-positioned or in a good place for the planets to "do business" are those which are in a whole-sign aspect to the rising sign (except for the third): so, the rising sign itself, the eleventh, tenth, ninth, seventh, fifth, and fourth. If we had a way of connecting the Latin translators directly with the Greek materials, then an "optimal place" could be a way of reflecting the connection between success, goodness, and benefit which is established in Hellenistic astrology. But we have an Arabic tradition standing between Greek and Latin. Still, it so happens that we can make the connection. For the Arabic *jayyad* can also mean "outstanding, excellent, first rate," which would definitely motivate a Latin translator to use the superlative *optimus*. Moreover, the root of *jayyad*, *jūd* or *jāda*, means "to improve, bestow liberally upon, grant, give lavishly," and so on. Therefore, it seems to me that the link between wealth, abundance, and the optimal places is established in all three languages. Based on these considerations, I conjecture that the "optimal" places from the Ascendant are the Ascendant itself, the 11th, the 10th, probably the 5th, and perhaps the 4th.

Māshā'allāh also offers an interesting list of criteria for the "goodness" of a place in *Cognition*. Here Māshā'allāh is trying to identify the best significator for the purpose at hand, and rather than identify a good place with a particu-

---

[162] *On Quest.* §10.6.
[163] *On Rev.* Ch. 41.

lar sign, he says that the goodness of a place has to do with a planet's (a) relationship to the Sun, (b) zodiacal sign or dignities, and (c) angularity. Of course these are central analytical criteria for the judgment of any planet. It is not clear to me that the "goodness" of place in this sense is the same as the "optimal" place spoken of above, but it is something to keep in mind. Definitely the best thing for any planet would be for it to be in an optimal place and also have a good relationship to the Sun and in a sign in which it had dignity.

§12: "Quantity"

Although the texts typically speak of the quantity or size of an orb, or the amount of concern a querent has, or a certain number of degrees, the word "quantity" is also used in other, astrologically more relevant ways. Many of these uses can be grasped easily; in others it is more difficult to say what is being communicated. Here I will summarize these other uses of "quantity," both those that are clear and those that are more conjectural:

1. Aspects are ranked in quantity, according to their severity. So for example, in the matter of how many people will suffer or be killed, a conjunction shows all; an opposition, half; a square, one-fourth.[164]

2. The quantity of impediment, referring to how bad a planet's condition is. For example, being cadent from the angles is worse for what a planet signifies, the farther away it is (the "more" cadent it is).[165] Or the matter of a question will be harmed, the worse the condition of the relevant rulers.[166] Or, when comparing the Lord of the Ascendant and the Moon with regard to their rulership over the querent, the one that is more impeded will be less able to manage the affairs effectively.[167]

3. The houses are ranked according to the severity of what they signify, so those with milder significations are quantitatively less bad. For instance, in conflicts a planet in the 2nd domicile might show

---

[164] *On Rev.* Ch. 28.
[165] *OR* Ch. 10.
[166] *OR* Ch. 2.
[167] *OR* Ch. 4.

taking someone's money; in the sixth or seventh, it shows making someone suffer under one's control; in the eighth, killing. The texts contain three such descriptions.[168]

4. The quantity of "quickness or slowness," referring to timing techniques. For example, if the distance between two planets were 25°, a "quick" place or a planet in a "quick" condition could turn this from 25 months into 25 days. All three of these references come from *On Times*.[169]

5. Different dignities can show the "greatness" of a person according to social status. For instance, if a malefic aspected the significator of the king in a mundane ingress chart, and the significator of the king had some dignity in that place, the dignity shows the kind of person signified by the malefic: if it were his domicile, the enemy is from among the king's household members; if it were his exaltation, the enemy is from among the nobles, and so on. All three of these uses come from *On Rev*.[170]

6. The "quantity of strength" of a planet seems to refer to its overall efficacy, as judged by its being in a place of its own dignity, or being angular or succeedent, or aspecting benefics, and so on. There are three references that link quantity and strength.[171]

7. (Conjectural) The "quantity of the nature" of a planet seems to refer to its benefic or malefic character. Here, "quantity" could refer to a planet's "greatness," where greatness is understood in terms of beneficence. There are three references to this kind of quantity.[172]

8. (Conjectural) The "quantity of the planet" refers to how inferior or superior it is in the celestial hierarchy. In charts of conflicts where the enemy will win, he will conquer the querent according to the "quantity of the planet" to which the Lord of the 7th is joined (and superior planets are considered better in conflicts).[173]

9. (Conjectural) Houses, especially the angles, can be ranked according to their suitability for a topic: so the Ascendant and the 10th

---

[168] *On Quest.* §§7.25, 9.1; *On Rev.* Intro.
[169] *On Times* §§ 3, 5, 7.
[170] *On Rev.* Chs. 14, 25, 29.
[171] *On Quest.* §13.14; *On Rev.* Chs. 6, 30.
[172] *Judgments* 7-8; OR Ch. 3.
[173] *On Quest.* §7.25.

have greater quantity with respect to matters of kingship, than do the 7th and 4th.[174]

10. (Uncertain) Māshā'allāh says that the greatest matters in mundane affairs, which come about due to the conjunctions of the three superior planets, will happen "according to the quantity of the stronger of them."[175] This could be a matter of inferiority and superiority (see above), since Saturn and Jupiter, the most superior planets, have the most important conjunctions. Or, it could mean that in any such conjunction, the one that is somehow "quantitatively" stronger, will determine the majority of the effects.

§13: Texts and Sources

In this section I will list my sources and make some brief comments on the works in this volume.

1. *Introduction.* My sources for this work include Stegemann 1942, BN (*Bibliothèque Nationale*) lat. 16204 pp. 422-41, and Locatellus 1493. For §5, I have put the translations of the Arabic (left) and Latin (right) in parallel columns, so the reader may see differences between them. I have also included all eight chart descriptions/examples from 1493 (these examples are also in BN, but often contain garbling or errors). Their presence in BN suggests that they appeared very early in the Latin tradition; and if John of Spain was Sahl's translator (and he probably was), and the BN manuscript was closely associated with his school,[176] then these might be examples of his own devising.

Also, in the Arabic column I have italicized the technical terms wherever they appear, so the reader can track them throughout §5. But this will not necessarily mean they are used in the same way or with the same words throughout the rest of the works, since one cannot be sure about the consistency of the various Latin translators.

2. *Fifty Judgments.* Sources: BN lat. 16204 pp. 441-45, and Locatellus 1493.

3. *On Questions.* Sources: BN lat. 16204 pp. 445-82, and Locatellus 1493.

4. *On Elections.* Sources: BN lat. 16204 pp. 488-500, Locatellus 1493, Crofts 1985. I have translated primarily from Crofts's Latin, but have also

---

[174] *On Quest.* §10.8.
[175] *On Roots* Ch. 9.
[176] See Lemay's comments in vol. IV of the *Gr. Intr.*, pp. 19*ff.*

consulted her critical edition and translation of the Arabic. As mentioned before, I will use the word "stake" instead of "angle" (Latin) or "cardinal point" (Crofts) throughout this work, so the reader may see some of the issues involved in Sahl's use of angles.

5. *On Times*. Sources: BN lat. 16204 pp. 482-88, and Locatellus 1493. Although some of this work seems a mess, it is a good example of how Sahl tries to organize material from his predecessors. Although the rest of Sahl's works have a style consistent with John of Spain and with each other, this work is somewhat different, with readings that differ much more between editions, and they have cramped and awkward and difficult phrasings. Perhaps someone else translated it, or the Arabic was so awkward or bare-bones that John of Spain (or whoever) just did the best he could.

6. *On the Knowledge of the Motion of the Orb*. Source: Weyssenburger 1504. Pingree (1975) has described the main points of this work and its sources, and should be read alongside it.

The introductory sections are instructive, as they derive from and engage with Platonic philosophy and some beliefs of unnamed Indians. In §1 Māshā'allāh says that the world is commanded, which implies law and a law-giver (namely, God). In modern science we take the notion of natural law wholly for granted, without realizing its root meaning as something received by a law-*giver*. Māshā'allāh is aware of this notion of law and command, because he immediately says the universe must comply with its command—it cannot choose, it does not merely follow the law sometimes, *etc*. The law is given and the world obeys, like a perfect slave. The world is also understood by the intellect—it is a rational world. So, in line with Greek, Jewish, and Christian themes, the world is rational and ordered, and (in some sense, with legal and religious concepts) ordained to be that way (and probably also "good," which is a Platonic conception).

Māshā'allāh then then opposes his view to some others, saying that some thinkers believed both God and the stars were makers or creators in an automatic and unintentional way, as when the Sun naturally gives off heat—but with the difference that at least God knows He is a creator. But then God would be unrelated to things created by the planets, and not having any rational intention in his own creation. Then God would be producing but with no particular concern for the world's intelligibility or consistency. In order to explain its consistency and intelligibility, the Indians must be wrong, and God is the sole or primary creator, and it is with intellect and rationality.

Later in §1 Māshā'allāh returns to a Platonic conception of the world, where things in the "womb" (the world, matter) are images of what is in the mind of God. There is an ambiguous reference to someone (God or maybe someone else) not knowing what is going to be or what he will will until he actually creates or wills it—but I'm not sure to whom this refers (probably to God). On the Platonic view, God does know what He is going to do, because He builds according to a plan. So perhaps the material about not knowing what will be willed until it is willed, pertains to the kind of creator that an un-self-aware star would be—perhaps it continues his objection to the Indians.

Māshā'allāh's elemental theory is adapted from Aristotelian views, and it may have some practical delineation value. The elemental qualities of hot and cold are strong/active and weak/passive respectively, and indicate lightness and heaviness respectively. But the dry and wet qualities are quick and slow, respectively. This means that while the hot elements (fire and air) are active and light, so they move away from the center of the earth, and the cold ones (earth, water) toward the center, the dry elements of earth and fire move more quickly—which is why fire is the uppermost element and the earth the lowermost one. Perhaps there is a way of understanding these in a practical way pertaining to the elements, signs and planets.

The material on winds and rains and plants is the most difficult because it involves theories of ancient physics and meteorology, so sometimes it is difficult to tell what kind of mechanisms and phenomena are being described.

7. *On the Roots of Revolutions*. Sources: BN lat. 16204, pp. 387-91, Hervagius 1533, Heller 1549. According to Carmody (p. 31), Heller's edition is a stylistically "improved" version, so I have favored BN and 1533.

8. *Chapter of the Rains in the Year*. Source: della Vida 1934. This was translated by Terry Linder, whose help has been invaluable. The editors of the *CCAG*, and also Burnett, think that this work is the Arabic version of *On Rains*. Probably Burnett simply read the *CCAG* editors' footnote and assumed they were right. In fact the reader will see the works are very different in style and content. Looking at them side by side, there are only a few clear points of contact between them. Perhaps they derive from a common source.

9. *On Rains*. Sources: BN lat. 7316a, *CCAG* XII, pp. 210-16. BN sometimes reads much better than *CCAG*, which is a reminder that a critical edition (*CCAG*) is only as good as its editor and his interest in the work.

10. *On Revolutions of the Years of the World.* Source: Heller 1549.

11. *On the Significations of the Planets in a Nativity.* Source: Heller 1549. Chapters 1-7 and 20-26 ought to be studied in conjunction with *Carmen* II.28-33, whence they derive. Based on some of the style and the Latin translator's use of the word *in* for "involved in, concerned with," I doubt it was translated by John of Spain.

At present I cannot see a clear delineation difference in this work between Māshā'allāh's use of the planets in bounds and those in the domiciles. But he does use planetary periods, transits, and perhaps primary directions when looking at the bounds. For instance, when he speaks of planetary periods, there seems to be one delineation for the period covered by the years, and then a different one after those years have expired. My impression of the transits is that they are only to be used when a planet transits into a such a bound as it was in, in the nativity. For instance, if Jupiter were in a bound of Saturn, he will have effects in his later transits to Saturn's other bounds—but not to the bounds of Mars, Venus, *etc.* Finally, we should remember that not all of these delineations can be true simultaneously. Probably Māshā'allāh only intended that we look up the delineation of an important planet like the Lord of the Ascendant or the *hīlāj*.

12. *On Nativities.* Sources: Kennedy and Pingree 1971, BN lat. 7324 15c pp. 73r-75v. Holden (*JN* pp. 86-90) made a partial translation of this through §4. I have translated the entirety and pointed out a few places in which I believe my reading is better. I treat Pingree's use of brackets (where he inserts a word into the text) as though it is part of the text itself, *unless* I disagree with him. The rest of the material in brackets is my own.

The length of life treatment in this work is indebted to Dorotheus, Paulus, and others. It begins with a different directive method, not the *hīlāj* method. It is largely based on *Carmen* III.1.14-18 and III.2, allowing the 4th, 5th, and 8th to be hylegiacal places. §§2-4 seem to be a mixture of elements from *Carmen* I.24 and III, possibly with some of *Tet.* III.11. The reader should also note that Māshā'allāh gives three different versions of the planets to examine, and the lists do not entirely match.

One strange feature of this text is the section in which Māshā'allāh reproduces a number of charts from Dorotheus, and some from other sources. In some of these charts intermediate cusp values are given, something which Māshā'allāh does not do elsewhere. I compared all of the possible latitude values and times for the charts with the degrees of the axes or intermediate cusps, and found that all charts could only have been cast for a very narrow band of latitude stretching from northern Spain, through Marseilles, northern Italy, and beyond: between 43° 12' — 43° 41 N. From this I surmise that a later Latin translator decided to cast the charts for his own latitude. But if the charts he found in his Arabic source had no cusp values, why did he assign the particular values he did? If we can find the sources of some of these charts, we might be closer to an answer. See also below for another possibility, that Māshā'allāh himself added these values for a location near the Black Sea.

13. *On the Interpretation of Cognition.* Sources: BN lat. 16204 pp. 422-24, Heller 1549. This work is an absolutely clear case of the medieval "consultation chart" mentioned above. As long as the client has been thinking about his issue for at least 24 hours, Māshā'allāh says we must find the significator of the intention and discover several things: *what* the topic is (which we discover from the significator); *whence* it has arisen (the planet the significator has most recently separated from); and its *end* (the planet to which the significator applies). Māshā'allāh gives us two different lists of criteria and comments on how to choose the significator.

The chart Māshā'allāh uses (and his exposition of it) is interesting for two reasons. First, he seems to violate his own rules. After deciding that Venus is the significator (using the rules), he then treats the Moon as the significator, because she is the Lady of Venus's domicile. Māshā'allāh may have had a reason to do this, but he nowhere states it. Second, I note that this chart is also found many centuries later in Leopold's *Compilatio* Tr. 10—attributed to Hermes! Unfortunately, since only a few positions are given on the chart, we cannot say whether it comes from Māshā'allāh's own lifetime or whether he—as in *On Nativities*—is cribbing from some other source and treating it as his own chart.

14. *On Hidden Things.* Sources: BN lat. 16204 pp. 424-28, Heller 1549. The "hidden" things in this work include the client's intention (i.e., through a consultation chart) and lost or hidden objects. The methods are very interesting, and there is a use of the twelfth-parts to divine a client's intention that is worth investigating. But even when Māshā'allāh names some of his Greek sources, it is unclear where he is getting his information from. The last section is unattributed in the manuscript and may simply be the Latin translator's own contribution, but I have included it.

INTRODUCTION

In §§3 and 5, Māshā'allāh (or whoever the author is, as Pingree thinks not all of it is by Māshā'allāh) describes two related but differently-stated rules for finding lost objects. The language of these passages is exceedingly tricky at first, but in comparing them I believe I have figured them out. They are worth trying out.

Method 1 (§3): Divide the client's home into four cardinal directions. Then find the Lord of the Ascendant. The triplicity of the sign the Lord is in, will show the part of the home the object is in (e.g., if the Lord of the Ascendant is in a fiery sign, the object is in the eastern part of the home). Disregard the other parts of the home. Then, divide the identified portion of the home into four sub-directions, and look at the Lord of the Lord of the Ascendant: the triplicity of his sign will show what sub-direction the object is in. (Presumably we could look at this Lord's Lord and repeat the process.) So, let us suppose the Lord of the Ascendant is in Sagittarius: the object is in the eastern part of the home. Divide the eastern part of the home into four cardinal directions, and look at the Lord of the Lord of the Ascendant. Let him be in Taurus (a southern sign). So the object is in the southern part of the eastern part of the home.

Method 2 (§5): Divide the home into four cardinal directions. Take the degree of the Lord of the hour (in the sign in which it is), and multiply that by 12. Starting with the beginning of the rising sign, project these degrees until the number is ended. The triplicity of the sign in which the counting ends, shows the direction inside the home. Divide this part of the home into four cardinal sub-parts. Find the Lord of the sign in which the number is ended, and note his degrees in the sign in which he is. Starting from the beginning of his sign, distribute these degrees through the signs, giving only 7° 30' to each sign.[177] The triplicity of the sign in which it is ended, will show the direction of the sub-part. One may then divide this sub-part as before, and do with the Lord of this latest sign, just as one did before, and so on until one finds the object.

For example, let Scorpio be rising, and let the Lord of the hour be Mercury, in 16° Capricorn. 16° x 12 = 192°. Starting with 0° Scorpio, project these degrees until you reach their end, at 12° Taurus. Taurus is an earthy sign, so the object is in the south. Now divide the southern part of the home into four directions. Look at the Lord of Taurus (Venus), and see how many

---

[177] One sign (30°) divided by 4 = 7° 30', allowing for the possibility that the counting may stop in any one of the four triplicities.

degrees of her sign she is in: let her be at 12° Aquarius. Starting at the beginning of Aquarius, project these 12° through the signs, allowing only 7° 30' per sign. Aquarius gets the first 7° 30', leaving 4° 30 left. The next sign, Pisces, gets those degrees. The counting is finished in Pisces, a watery sign, signifying the north. So the object is in the northern part of the southern part of the house. We could then look at the Lord of Pisces (Jupiter), and see where he is in his sign, and perform the same procedure again. According to the instructions, one can get within one cubit of the object!

15. *On Reception.* Source: Heller 1549. This is a wonderful and clear work on horary, which is made all the more valuable by the numerous charts and detailed delineations. Obviously I cannot summarize the whole work here, but I will list key features of Māshā'allāh's methods: (a) the heavy emphasis on reception when transferring light or committing disposition; (b) the use of transferring light and committing disposition until one reaches (c) the final dispositor, also called the "author" and the *mubtazz*.[178] Māshā'allāh also makes much use of the "changing" of signs, seeing what aspect a planet in a late degree will make once it has changed signs.

A short but interesting passage in Ch. 2 may have a connection with *Orb*. There, Māshā'allāh says: "And if there were a conjunction from a planet to the seven planets, the work in these will be by means of a system [*ratione*], namely where one renders and lifts up the light of one to another, until it arrives at the last of them." Although this is put in Latin, and we do not know Māshā'allāh's own Arabic word, the use of ratio may contribute a significant theoretical point, because *ratio* (Gr. *logos*) can also mean an argument—like a traditional syllogism.[179] Māshā'allāh or his translator could be implying that these transfers of light between planets are like the relationships between terms in a syllogism, whereby the major and minor terms are united through a third. On the standard view of syllogisms in modern languages, the analogy works this way. Take the so-called *Barbara* syllogism: "All A are B, All B are C, therefore All A are C." This is like saying: "Planet A transfers to B, Planet B transfers to C, therefore A transfers to C." Planet B is like the "middle term" through which equivalency is produced between the other two planets.

---

[178] The role of this planet seems very close to Sahl's final "receiver of the disposition" in *On Quest.* §10.2, which he may even have taken from Māshā'allāh.
[179] And it may relate to *Introduct.* §5.5, where a planet transferring light is said to make an "equivalency" between the other two planets.

But in fact, the analogy is even deeper. Māshā'allāh ideally wants the planets to be related to each other through reception, which means being in each other's dignities (this is true even though the discussion happens in the context of determining the primary significator). And in the original Greek, the Aristotelian logicians did not say "All A are B." Rather, they said "B belongs to all A." This notion of "belonging" easily fits into the astrological situation, since if one planet is in the domicile of the other, in some sense it could be said to belong to or be in the power of, its dispositor. And this matches especially well the notion I proposed earlier, that reception provides a surrogate home and a form of belonging for the received planet.

So this brief allusion by Māshā'allāh may be another way in which he believes that the world is a rational system (however it is commanded, as *Orb* states) which can be understood through the intellect: the objective structure of the world and logical structural principles merge, are ordained in this rational way by God, and can be understood through the human intellect.

There are two other observations I would make about *OR*. First, the chart in Ch. 4 has been dated by Hand to 791 AD, and it presents something of a puzzle. Its cusps, like all of those in *On Nativities*, also indicate a latitude similar to Marseilles. It is possible that this chart, and those in *On Nativities*, are indeed authentic to Māshā'allāh, but they were cast for a location around the Black Sea, where the 'Abbasid Caliphate was in power at the time.

Chapter 11 of this work is also odd. It has nothing to do with horary, but presents a set of length of life instructions. In his edition of *OR*, Hand doubts that Ch. 11 really is by Māshā'allāh. His argument comes down to saying that *On Nativities* is based on Dorotheus, and Ch. 11 on something else, which he says involves a more "static" approach to aspects. Now, it is true that *On Nativities* is heavily indebted to Dorotheus. But that in itself does not prove anything, since *OR* Ch. 11 derives largely from *Tet.* III.11, even down to its (garbled version of) adding and subtracting years based on aspectual degrees. There is no reason why Māshā'allāh could not have written one summary based on Dorotheus, and another based on Ptolemy. The puzzling question is why this chapter appears at all in *OR*.

There is a certain rare phrase that does seem to link Ch. 11 to Ch. 10. In the last paragraph of Ch. 10, Māshā'allāh speaks of a planet in its descension as being in a "well"; and the author of Ch. 11 speaks about a planet that is in its descension or "in a well." It is very rare for the Latin texts to use this word for "well" (*puteum*), and off-hand I cannot think of any other instance except when speaking about the so-called "welled" or "pitted" degrees. It would be very strange for this rare phrase, used in the same context in two consecutive chapters, to come about by accident—unless this was a phrase inserted by a Latin editor.

So we seem to have several options: (1) Māshā'allāh wrote both chapters and is responsible for both phrases about a "well," and had his own private reason for inserting this Ptolemaic chapter into the text. (2) Māshā'allāh wrote both chapters and phrases but did not intend them to be part of the same book: the arrangement in *OR* is the responsibility of some later compiler (though again, why Ch. 11 would knowingly be inserted into the middle of a book on another topic is a mystery); (3) Māshā'allāh did not write this chapter, and the phrase about a "well" appearing in Chapter 10 was then inserted into Chapter 11 as a helpful guide for the reader—but this does not explain why someone would knowingly insert a chapter not by Māshā'allāh. Or (4) Māshā'allāh did not write Ch. 11 at all. My bet is on (1) or (2).

Perhaps if Arabic versions of these two works were compared, we might get some answers. But Dorotheus and Ptolemy also have very different styles, so someone drawing from each and being faithful to the originals might indeed appear to yield different styles.

16. *What the Planets Signify in the Twelve Domiciles.* Sources: BN lat. 16204 pp. 428-32, BN lat. 7316 pp. 80v-82v. According to Carmody, only the first section of this work and the section on Saturn are attributed to or are actually the work of Jirjis, and only sometimes is the entire work attributed to Jirjis. In BN 16204 it is attributed to Jirjis. But since (according to Carmody) there is good reason to believe that at least most of it is by Māshā'allāh, I have included it here. I note incidentally that Bonatti (*BOA* Tr. 8 *passim*) uses all of this material to interpret the planets in the domiciles in *mundane* charts—and attributes it all to Abū Ma'shar!

This work seems to have been excerpted from a larger one, as the section on Venus alludes to some previous portion of it which contains timing methods. Whatever this larger work was, it seems to have been part of early horary or consultation chart practices: the section on Jupiter contains a reference to the divination of intentions.

INTRODUCTION   lxxxi

§14: Editorial Principles

- As in *BOA*, I will use different spellings depending on whether the Latin texts speak of houses, domiciles, or signs. When speaking of the "9th," this always means either house or domicile. The reader must keep in mind that "house" and "domicile" are the same word in Latin, and while I will write "house" or "domicile" depending on whether I think quadrant houses or whole-sign houses are being used, the reader should note that it is sometimes uncertain which is meant. When speaking of the "ninth," this always means either a sign (which I will indicate in brackets) or another masculine or neuter word like "place" or "angle." *However*, in the texts for the Arabic *Introduct.* §5 and *Chap. Rains,* I will always spell out the words ("ninth"), since Arabic does not have the same issues with gender and word endings in this matter.
- In this volume I now use "Lot" for the so-called Arabic "Parts." The word "Lot" is more faithful to the Arabic and Greek, and while the use of the word "Part" (*pars*) is supported in early Latin works like that of Firmicus Maternus (who treats degrees as "parts"), and also in *Orb*, it also causes some confusion when speaking about them.
- The reader will occasionally find statements about the planets "dismounting" in a sign or place. This translates the Latin *descendo*, which is usually used to mean "descend" and is the basis for the condition of being in one's own fall or descension. But it also can mean "to dismount," and accurately translates the Ar. *ḥalla*, "make a stop at, dismount at, encamp at." It simply means the planet is "in" that place. See Burnett 2006, p. 337.
- The Latin texts use *malus* and *infortuna* indifferently to designate malefic planets, and I have followed my practice from *BOA* by rendering both of these as "malefic." But there is a common phrase that one should pay attention to, namely when planets are encouraged to be "free from the malefics" (*liber a malis*). In Latin, while *malus* can mean "malefic [planet]," the neuter form *malum* also means "evil, bad." So for a planet to be *liber a malis* might always mean "free from the malefics," but it could just as equally mean "free from evils." Context must be our guide here. One way to deal with this ambiguity is to keep in mind that when we delineate we

should always take a comprehensive account of the good and bad influences affecting a planet's condition.

- In this volume I depart from my *BOA* practice of using "pilgrimage" to translate *peregrinor/peregrinatio*. I will use "foreign travel/journey" (unless pilgrimage makes the most sense) since that is what Crofts and Dorotheus prefer; but the reader must keep in the mind that for the medieval mind, pilgrimage and travel would have been understood in similar ways, and on a foreign journey one might also perform pilgrimages to local shrines.

- In my diagrams and descriptions of planetary positions, I stay as faithful as possible to the written Latin. In *OR*, the Heller diagrams and Hand's own translation are not faithful to the literal Latin. Typically the Latin uses ordinal numbers, but Heller and Hand tend to treat them as cardinal numbers. So if the text says that Mars is in the "fifth degree," that means anywhere between 4°—4° 59', and not at 5°. In some cases the Latin is ambiguous and I will point out those instances.

- I have already explained above that I will use "stake" instead of "angle" in the works for which I have the Arabic.

- The Latin texts make much use of the verb *recedo*, which means "withdraw, retire, move back, recede, pass away/vanish"—in other words, moving back from something. In *Introduct.* §5 it is used as a synonym for "withdrawal" or planetary separations. But in other cases it seems to refer to people moving away or withdrawing, or planets falling away from cusps by primary motion, and other meanings. I have decided to use the word "recede" as much as possible, in order to alert the reader that this verb is being used. But in *On Quest.* §§10.7-8, I will use "withdraw" when the text speaks of the king leaving the kingdom. Context can often be used to determine its precise meaning, but not always. Perhaps in the future (with more Arabic works) we will have a better sense of how to use this term consistently.

THE *INTRODUCTION*

The *Introduction* of Sahl the Israelite concerning the principles of judgments, begins:

§1: The first chapter, on the division of the signs and on the triplicities

In the name of the God of piety and compassion. Sahl bin Bishr the Israelite[1] said:

Know that the signs are twelve; and of them, six are masculine and six feminine. Therefore Aries is a masculine sign, of the signs of the day; and Taurus is a feminine one, of the signs of the night; and likewise a feminine one yields to a masculine one, and a masculine one a feminine one, up to the end of the signs.

And[2] of them, six are signs ascending in a straight fashion: that is, having straight ascension. And of them, six are [signs] ascending crookedly: that is, having crooked ascension. And those ascending in a straight fashion are from the beginning of Cancer up to the end of Sagittarius, because the breadth of each one of them is greater than its length, and it ascends in more than two equal hours: because of this they are named "those ascending in a straight fashion." And those ascending crookedly are from the beginning of Capricorn up to the end of Gemini, because the breadth of each one of them is less than its length, and [each] ascends in less than two equal hours: from this they are named "those ascending crookedly."

And of these, four are named "movable": that is, Aries, Cancer, Libra, Capricorn. And they are named "movable" for the reason that when the Sun enters into the beginnings of those signs, the weather changes to the substance of the following season.

And four of them are "fixed": that is, Taurus, Leo, Scorpio, and Aquarius. And they are called "fixed" for the reason that when the Sun enters their minutes, the weather is fixed in its own being, and is not changed. That is, if it were hot, it will be hot; and if it were cold, it will be cold; and if it were spring, it will be spring; and if it were autumn, it will be autumn.

---

[1] Reading with the Arabic for *Zahel bembiz ysmaelita*.
[2] See *Carmen* V.1.7-9.

And of them there are four common ones, which in Arabic are called two-bodied:³ which are Gemini, Virgo, Sagittarius, Pisces. And they are named "common" for the reason that if the Sun arrived to the middle of them, the weather is commingled: and its first half becomes hot, and the next cold; or the first half cold, and the next one hot.

And certain ones of them are called "four-footed": that is, Aries, Taurus, Leo, Capricorn, and the end of Sagittarius.

Certain ones of these signs are even fiery: that is, Aries, Leo, Sagittarius; and it is the first triplicity. And the second triplicity is the earthy one, and signifies whatever is in the earth and is born from out of the earth: that is, Taurus, Virgo, and Capricorn. And the third triplicity is the airy one, and signifies men and winds and whatever would be in the air: that is, Gemini, Libra, and Aquarius. The fourth is the watery one, and signifies waters and whatever is in the waters: that is, Cancer, Scorpio, and Pisces.

And certain ones of the signs are said to be dark: that is, Libra and Capricorn.

And there is a certain place in the signs which is called "burned up":⁴ and it is the end of Libra and the beginning of Scorpio.

And certain ones of these signs have half a voice: that is, Virgo, Capricorn, and Aquarius. And certain ones of them have voices: that is, Taurus, Aries, Gemini, Leo, Libra, Sagittarius. And of them, there are certain ones not having voices: that is, Cancer, Scorpio, Pisces.

And certain ones are half-way or common in the generation of children (that is, they are neither totally generating, nor totally sterile): that is, Taurus, Gemini, and Aquarius. And certain ones having more children: that is, Cancer, Scorpio, and Pisces. Indeed certain ones are sterile: Aries, Leo, Virgo, Libra, Sagittarius, and Capricorn.

And certain ones of them signify mountains and more difficult places: that is, Aries, Leo, Sagittarius. And certain ones signify inhabitable and flat places (that is, the countrysides and what is cultivated): namely Taurus, Virgo, and Capricorn. Indeed certain ones signify sandy places: that is, Gemini, Libra, and Aquarius. Certain ones even signify moist and watery places, or those which are next to water: that is, Cancer, Scorpio, and Pisces.

Therefore the fiery signs signify fire and every substance which pertains to it or which comes to be through it; and they signify noble things. And the

---

³ Following Holden's reading of Arabic, for the Latin *devet...deyn*.
⁴ I.e., "combust," the burnt path or *via combusta*.

signs of seed signify the earth and everything which is raised up from out of the earth. Also, the watery signs signify moist places, and every work which comes to be from out of moisture. And the signs generating more children signify the assembling of men.

Therefore the triplicity of Aries is hot, dry; of the natures it has red choler; and of the parts of the world, the east; the Lords of which triplicity are the Sun in the day, and Jupiter in the night, and their partner in the day and night is Saturn.

Also, the triplicity of Taurus is cold and dry; of the natures it has black choler; and of the parts of the world, the south; its Lords are Venus in the day and the Moon in the night; the partner of these in the day and night is Mars.

The triplicity of Gemini is hot and moist; and of the natures it has the sanguine; and of the parts of the world, the west; and the Lords of this triplicity are: in the day, Saturn, and in the night Mercury, and their partner in the day and night is Jupiter.

Indeed the triplicity of Cancer is cold and moist; of the natures, it has phlegm; of the parts of the world, the north; and the Lords of this triplicity are: Venus in the day and Mars in the night, whose partner in the day and night is the Moon.

§2: A chapter on the substances of the twelve signs, and what every sign signifies

Know that we have found, for every question or quaesited matter, a signification by which is signified whatever of the good and evil there would be in that same question—of the ways which the sages have expounded in the signification of questions and of matters, in terms of the substances of the twelve signs and the natures of the seven planets, and the places from which matters are taken up (just as the planets have, in terms of natures and significations)—just as we will arrange to describe, God willing.

§3

The first domicile, of the Ascendant and everything which is in it regarding questions (and the rest of the twelve signs)

The 1st domicile, whose beginning rises or ascends in the east at the hour of a question or nativity (or of some inception of a work): and this signifies life and death, because it is the Ascendant of the life of him with which his life arrives into the world, until he then goes out of the womb of his mother. For this sign ascends from the lower part of the earth to its upper one: and as though from darkness to light, so likewise did the native go out from the darkness of the womb to the light of this world, and from the narrowness of the uterus to the breadth of the air. And the one asking discloses his own question from the secrets of his own heart, and what was formerly hidden has begun to shine and is made plain. Therefore it signifies bodies and life and every beginning, and the motions of the body, and whatever were to come from something happening, and the establishment[5] or coming about of every matter; and every movable or rational thing, and the beginnings of all matters.

On the 2nd domicile

The 2nd domicile from the Ascendant does not aspect the ascending sign. It signifies the bringing together of substance; and the appurtenances[6] of life; and the condition of those serving; and taking [money] and donations.

On the 3rd domicile

The 3rd domicile is not wholly cadent from the Ascendant.[7] It signifies brothers and sisters [of the same mother and father], relatives and kin, and their condition; also patience and counsels, faith and religion, and conten-

---

[5] *Inchoationem.* In the sense of it starting to form.
[6] *Continentiam.* Following Niermeyer.
[7] Technically, it is cadent from the *angles*. But perhaps Sahl is drawing on Hellenistic tradition, which states that the 3rd is the least favorable of the domiciles that aspect the Ascendant. In that case, Sahl would be saying that the 3rd is only marginally more favorable than one actually cadent from the Ascendant.

tions in sects; letters, legations also, and legates; and foreign travels and dreams.

On the 4th domicile

The 4th domicile is said to be the angle of the earth. It signifies fathers and their being (that is, the origin and root); family relationships[8] and prisons; lands and the countryside; and villas and cities and every building; and every covered and concealed thing (or hidden treasures), and death and what is going to be after death (that is, what will happen to the dead person, namely from the grave, and whether the dead person would be dug up or cremated, or put on a gibbet, or thrown out in some place, and all the rest of the things which happen to the dead). And it signifies their end, and houses and lands (that is, real estate), and everything which is buried under the ground.

On the 5th domicile

The 5th domicile succeeds the angle of the earth. And it is a place of love, because it is of the triplicity and joy of the Ascendant; and it signifies children and everything in which there is trust; legates also, and donations; honor and seeking the friendships of women and friends; cities and the being of their citizens;[9] and the fruits of real estate.

On the 6th domicile

The 6th domicile is cadent from the Ascendant, nor does it aspect it. And it is a malign place, and signifies infirmities (both separable and inseparable), and the causes of infirmities; male slaves too, and female slaves; injustices; and changes from place to place.

On the 7th domicile

The 7th domicile is the western angle. And it signifies marriages and their matters; battles and contentions and contrarieties; and the comings-together

---

[8] *Parentelas.*
[9] See *On Quest.*, §7.25.

which come to be between two people; also, him who seeks and him who is sought (like a fugitive and robber), and something lost, and the rest of such like things; foreign travels and the losses of things, and their causes. And this sign is an enemy of the Ascendant, and every planet which is in it is opposed to the Ascendant.

On the 8th domicile

The 8th domicile succeeds the western angle. And it signifies death and killing and lethal poisons; and dread; and whatever is inherited from the dead; and everything which perishes; and labor and sorrow; also wars and contentions, and the footmen or allies of adversaries (or of those contending), and things consigned (that is, what are handed over to be preserved);[10] and farm-overseers, sluggishness,[11] and [bad] mental characteristics.[12]

On the 9th domicile

The 9th domicile is cadent from the Ascendant.[13] And it signifies foreign travels and journeys and the culture of deity, and all houses of religion; philosophy and the foresight of all matters; the wisdom of the stars, and divinations; letters and legates and legations, or rumors; dreams; faith; divine wisdom; and sanctity and religion; and all past and receding things; and a man put down from his honor or work;[14] and matters of the future world, and the foreknowledge of things that will be.

On the 10th domicile

The 10th domicile is said to be the angle of heaven. And it signifies the king or the kingdom; exaltation and empire; glory; and memory or the voice

---

[10] This pertains to the goods of a deceased person, as handled in a will. See *On Elect.*, §§97a-100.
[11] Reading *segnitias* for *segnities*. In Hellenistic astrology, the 8th domicile was known as the "idle" place.
[12] *Ingenia*. This word can also refer to trickery and traps.
[13] Really it is cadent from the angles, not the Ascendant.
[14] Because the 9th recedes and declines from the 10th.

of praise; also mothers[15] and substance [that is] stolen or taken away; judges, princes, and the authorities[16] of works; and every profession [or mastery].

On the 11th domicile

The 11th domicile succeeds the angle of heaven. And it signifies friends, trust and fortune; the substance of the king and his renderings or tributes,[17] and his soldiers and footmen; and the man who succeeds the king or first prince. And it signifies orations[18] and children.[19]

On the 12th domicile

The 12th domicile is cadent from the Ascendant, nor does it aspect it. It signifies enemies and labors; lamentations and sorrows; whisperings; distresses; jealousies and craftiness;[20] evil wills; and foreign travels;[21] malice, labor, prisons, and beasts.

§4: On the division of the circle, and the dignities or strengths of the domiciles

But the following things [are] more worthy than all the places of the circle, and the more praiseworthy among them in strength. They are distinguished thusly:[22]

The circle is divided into twelve signs, out of which four are named "angles": that is, the ascending sign, the fourth [sign], the seventh [sign], and the tenth [sign]. These signs are, as it were, the corners[23] of heaven, which sig-

---

[15] This shows that Sahl has adopted the mistaken interpretation of Ptolemy as attributing the 10th to mothers.
[16] *Praelatos.* I take this to refer to actual people, but the word comes from *praefero*, which has connotation of being held out, being displayed, presented. It is possible that the Latin translator picked this word to signify works that have fame and public reputation attached to them.
[17] I.e., taxes.
[18] Lat. *laudationes.* Specifically, eulogies, commendations, and good character testimony.
[19] Lat. *filios.* Perhaps in the particular sense of children fulfilling hopes?
[20] *Calliditates.*
[21] Bonatti says the 12th signifies the "longest" journeys (*BOA* p. 536).
[22] *Digniora autem omnibus circuli locis, ac laudabiliora seque invicem in fortitudine, succedentia sic distinguntur.*
[23] *Anguli*, i.e., "angles."

nify everything of matters which is present: that is, the presence of matters and strength in every matter.

And out of [the signs], four are called the "succeedents" (or the "followers") of the angles (that is, the ones ascending after them): that is, the second [sign], the fifth [sign], the eighth [sign], and the eleventh [sign]. These signify everything which is going to be, and whatever comes to be. And they follow from matters.

And the remaining four are said to be "cadent"[24] from the angles, which have receded and have fallen from the angles: which are the third [sign], the sixth [sign], the ninth [sign], and the twelfth [sign]. And these signify whatever of matters has receded and has gone away, by the command of God.

Stronger than all places of the circle, is the Ascendant: and this sign is more worthy than all the signs; and a planet which is in it is stronger than all the planets (and especially if that same planet were in its own domicile or in its own exaltation or triplicity or in the bound or in the face). Then the angle of heaven follows after in strength; then the western angle (that is, the seventh [sign] from the Ascendant) follows after; then the angle of the earth (that is, the fourth [sign] from the Ascendant) follows after. After these, the 11th domicile from the Ascendant follows this domicile in strength; and the 5th one this domicile;[25] and then the 9th. These seven places[26] are more praiseworthy and stronger: the first place[27] is better than the second; the second one better than the third, and so on.

And of the signs, after these ones, are chosen those recognized as good: the third sign from the Ascendant, because it is the place of the Moon's joy; then the second place from the Ascendant, because it ascends after the Ascendant.

But in the eighth sign from the Ascendant there is impediment and great misfortune, because it is the house of death and does not aspect the Ascendant. Also, the rest of the signs of the circle (that is, the sixth [sign] and the twelfth [sign]) are worse than all places, and less favorable;[28] and every planet which is in these places is of no profit: because the sixth sign from the Ascendant is the place of infirmities and defects and of all diseases (separable

---

[24] Lit., "falling."
[25] That is, the 4th.
[26] See *Carmen* I.5.
[27] That is, the first one listed (the 1st), then the second one listed (the 10th), *et cetera*.
[28] *Deteriora*. But see note to §5.0 below, on *deterioratio*. This might have connotations of being more contemptible or wicked.

and inseparable), and it is cadent from the Ascendant (nor does it aspect it), and it is the place of the joy of Mars; and the twelfth [sign] from the Ascendant is the place of enemies and of labor and sorrow; and it is cadent from the Ascendant (nor does it aspect it), and it is the place of the joy of Saturn (for Saturn rejoices in lamentation and wailing and tribulation).

And know that every sign aspects the third one in front of it, and the third one behind it (which is the eleventh sign): and this aspect is called the sextile, because it holds one-sixth of the circle (that is, 60° of the 360° of the whole circle). For example, a planet which was in the beginning of Aries, aspects him who is in Gemini in front of him,[29] and him who is in Aquarius behind him. And he aspects the fourth [sign] in front of him, and the fourth one behind him (that is, the tenth [sign]): and this aspect is called the square, because it holds one-fourth of the circle (that is, 90°). And he also aspects the fifth one in front of himself, and the fifth one behind himself (that is, the ninth): and this aspect is called the trine, because it has one-third of the circle (that is, 120°). It even aspects the seventh by opposition: and this aspect is of enmity. And if planets were in these signs, they are said to aspect one another.

On the aspects of the planets

These are the aspects of the planets: that is, the conjunction, sextile, and the square, trine, and the opposite. For the conjunction is when two planets are joined in one sign, and there are 12° and less between them:[30] this is the boundary of the conjunction. But the sextile aspect is from the third sign and from the eleventh.[31] The square aspect is from the fourth sign and the tenth. The trine aspect is from the fifth sign and the ninth. Indeed the opposite is from the seventh sign. Therefore the conjunction and opposition are stronger than these [other] aspects, and these are of stronger work and enmity; and these aspects signify enemies openly harming; and they signify contrarieties and participations. The square aspect is a middle: that is, it does not wholly expose enmities. And the second sextile aspect (that is, which comes to be from the eleventh) is stronger than the first sextile aspect. And

---

[29] Here and below Sahl does not even say the planet only aspects a particular *degree* in the relevant sign—he simply says it aspects the sign itself.
[30] I am not sure what the rationale behind the 12° is. Abū Ma'shar gives 15° as a relevant distance in *Gr. Intr.* VII.5.754.
[31] Note that Sahl does not specify degree-based distances as with the conjunction here.

the second square aspect (that is, which comes to be from the tenth) is stronger than the first square aspect. And of the trine aspects, the 9th domicile (that is, the second aspect) is stronger than the first trine aspect: and this aspect[32] is called "elevation," that is, "the higher."[33] But the signs which do not aspect each other, nor does a planet which is in them aspect another, are these: the second sign, the sixth, the eighth, and the twelfth. Indeed the rest besides these do aspect each other.

§5.0

The chapter of explanation on being and decay	*On the effecting and detriment of the planets*[34]
Know that everything indicated by the stars from what is created or is corrupted will be regarding 16 aspects. They are:[35]	Know that everything which the stars signify must be done or not, comes to be in 16 ways:
[1] *the approach*[36]	[1] This is *al-ʾiqbāl*[37] in Arabic, which in Latin is sounded "advancement."[38]

---

[32] I.e., the "second" aspect. See next footnote.
[33] In traditional astrology, the "first" or "leading" aspect is the sinister aspect cast forward in the order of signs (e.g., from a planet in Aries forward to Leo). The "second" or "following" aspect is the dexter aspect cast backwards against the order of signs (e.g., from a planet in Aries backwards to Sagittarius). Sahl or the Latin translator rephrases the description of the "second aspect" by making it seem as though it is coming *from* the earlier signs. But stated that way it would be a first or leading aspect from the earlier sign.
[34] See my Introduction for the use of "detriment" here for the Arabic "decay."
[35] Stegemann's critical edition shows that the Greek list is incomplete, has terms corresponding to the wrong Arabic term, and adds at least one term not actually in the Arabic list. I will match the Greek terms as best as I can to the correct terms here.
[36] Another possibility would be "arrival."
[37] Lat. *alicbel*. Gr. *to chrēmatistikon*, "the busy [place]," "able to conduct business." Stegemann translates this as *das Glück* ("good luck, happiness"), which is indeed another valid translation—except that it has nothing to do with planetary motion, and is not paired easily with the second term. We should follow the translations above rather than Stegemann in this case.

[2] *the falling-back*[39]	[2] *al-ʾidbār*,[40] that is, "making lower."[41]
[3] *the connection*	[3] *al-ʾittiṣāl*,[42] that is, "conjunction."
[4] *the departure,*	[4] *al-ʾinṣarāf*,[43] that is, "separation" or the disjoining of the planets from their conjunction;
[5] *the transmission,*	[5] *an-naql*,[44] that is, "transfer."
[6] *the collection,*	[6] *al-jamʿ*,[45] that is, "assembling" or "collection" (which sounds better).

---

[38] *Profectus*, which also has connotations of profit and of setting forth (as on a journey), as this word is the fourth principal part of both *proficio* (to profit, be successful) and *profiscor* (to set out, advance).
[39] This word has been difficult to translate. It comes from a root meaning to flee, turn one's back, or to veer toward the west. Literally it means "declining, setting," but given its root it means something like "being in a state of retreat or showing your back," and has a connotation of being low and bad. So there are three ideas here: declining or moving down, showing one's back, and being low or bad. Sociologically they must be related through the idea that only contemptible and worthless people flee from a fight or go into retreat. Stegemann favors *Sich-abwenden*, "turning away," and relates it to the Greek *apoklima*, "decline" (referring to cadent places). On the Latin side, *deterioratio* is a neologism that seems to mean "making something worse, lower, more wicked" (from the comparative *deterior*). But the astrological meaning of all of this is to be cadent or "falling" from an angle—that is, for a planet to have passed the angle by primary motion, and now to be declining from it and "showing its back" to the angle, so to speak. Finally, we note that this term is meant to be contrasted with "approach" above. With all of these meanings and relationships in mind, we feel that translating *al-ʾidbār* as "falling-back" is best, as is translating *deterioratio* as "making lower."
[40] Lat. *alidber*. Gr. *to achrēmatiston*, "the unbusy [place]," "unable to conduct business."
[41] *Deterioratio*. See footnote above.
[42] Lat. *alictisal*. Gr. *sunaphē*, "conjunction."
[43] Lat. *alinciraf*. Gr. *aporroia*, "separation" (lit. "flowing away").
[44] Lat. *annacl*. Gr. *metakomidē*, "transporting, conveying."
[45] Lat. *algemmee*. Gr. *theriōdēs*, "reaping, harvesting." But the Gr. *sunagōgē*, "gathering together," might also be appropriate here.

[7] *the prohibition,*	[7] *al-man͑*,[46] that is, "forbidding" or "prohibition."
[8] *the reception,*	[8] *al-qubūl*,[47] that is, "reception."
[9] *not-reception,*	[9] *ghayr al-qubūl*,[48] that is, "[not]-reception."[49]
[10] *void of movement,*	[10] *khalā as-sayr*,[50] that is, the "voiding of course."
[11] *the return,*	[11] *ar-radd*,[51] that is, "returning."
[12] *the pushing of strength,*	[12] *daf͑u-l-quwwah*,[52] that is, "pushing of virtue."
[13] *the pushing of arrangement [and] the nature,*	[13] *daf͑ at-tadbīr wa-at-tabī͑ah*,[53] that is "pushing of disposition and nature."
[14] *the strength,*	[14] *al-quwwah*,[54] that is, "virtue and strength."
[15] *the weakness,* and	[15] *ad-da͑f*,[55] that is, "weakness."

---

[46] Lat. *almane*. Gr. *empodismos*, "impediment, hindrance."
[47] Lat. *alcobol*.
[48] Lat. *gairalcobol*.
[49] Lat. *inreceptio*. This term is missing from the Arabic, but Stegemann has followed the Latin's lead and supplied it.
[50] Lat. *galaacen*. Gr. *kenodromia*, "void of course."
[51] Lat. *airchad*. Gr. *apostrophē*, "turning back/away."
[52] Lat. *dapha alchia*. Gr. *paradosis tēs dunameōs*, "bequeathing/transmission of the power/strength."
[53] Lat. *dapha aredir*. Gr. *paradosis tēs kubernēseōs*, "bequeathing/transmission of the steering."
[54] Lat. *alcdetih*. Gr. *dunamis*, "power/strength."
[55] Lat. *adof*. Gr. *astheneia*, "weakness."

[16] *the condition of the Moon.*

[16] *aḥwālu-l-qamar*,[56] that is, "the condition of the Moon."

§5.1

Concerning *the approach*. It is if the planet is in a stake[57] or in what follows the stake.

The exposition of *al-ʾiqbāl*. *Al-ʾiqbāl* is if a planet were in an angle or in one following an angle.

§5.2

Falling-back is if the planet is falling from the stakes.

Al-ʾidbār is like if a planet is cadent from the angles.

§5.3

The connection is if the light and quick star is pursuing the heavy star, the light one will be lesser in degree than the heavy one, and so the [light] planet continues to go towards the [heavy] planet, and closes in on it, and it will become [joined] with it in the degree, minute to minute: then it is called *connected*.

Al-ʾittiṣāl is when a light and quick planet would seek the conjunction of another, slower and heavier planet, and the lighter planet would be in fewer degrees than the slower one as long as he went to him, until he is joined to him and was in such a minute through an aspect: [and this is called] *al-ʾittiṣāl*,[58] that is, conjoined or stuck[59] together.

---

[56] Lat. *uvanuelhalcamar*. (No Greek given).
[57] Ar. *watad*. See Introduction.
[58] Lat. *Mutatil*, a misspelling.
[59] *Conglutinatus*.

And concerning when it has become [joined] with it, minute to minute, then it is *connected* with it, and at that time [it will be as if] in position[60] two men are under one covering.

The *connection* in position is a thread extending from the middle of the body of the light planet to the middle of the body of the heavy planet. The planet will not cease [to be thus] until it *departs* from the [other] planet by a complete degree. And so if the planets were coupled in one zodiacal sign, then the planet is not considered *departed* from the [other] planet until the lighter one *departs* the heavier one by half of its body. It is its light, because each of the planets has a body, a light, and individual parts, so half of the parts are from the front of the planet and half are from behind it. So when it is exceeding that distance, it is said to be separated.[61]

It is so called until he is separated from him by the space of one degree (and then it is called *al-ʾinṣarāf*, that is, separated from him).

But if the planets are conjoined in one sign, the planet is not said to be separated from the other until he would cross over him by a space of half of his orb (that is, of his light): because every planet has an orb of light, and individual parts:[62] and one-half of those parts is in front of the planet itself, and the other half is behind him. Provided that the planet has crossed over the other by that space, he is said to be separated from him.

---

[60] Ar. *bimanzilah*, "grade, rank, position," here evidently used as a synonym for the corporal conjunction, as both planets are in the same place. Stegemann ignores this word.
[61] The distinctions Sahl means to be drawing are between (a) applying or connecting but not yet connect*ed* (this is the 12° rule above); (b) actually connected (i.e., in the same degree); (a) separating but not wholly separat*ed* (i.e., no longer in the same degree); (d) wholly separated (by orbs).
[62] That is, degrees.

The chapter on the knowledge of the lights of the seven planets

Know that the body of the Sun is 30°, half in front of it and half behind it. If any of the planets were between the Sun from 1° to 15°, [the Sun] radiates[63] its light [over the planet], and it is *connected* with it. The light of the Moon is 12° in front of it and behind it. Saturn and Jupiter each have 9° in front of it and likewise[64] behind it. Mars has 8° in front of it and likewise behind it. Venus and Mercury each have 7° in front of them and similarly behind them. And by the amount of these lights, they *connect* one with another.[65]

The knowledge of the lights or orbs of the planets

Know that the orb of the Sun's light is one of 30°, half of which is in front of him (that is, 15° in front of the Sun itself, and 15° behind). And were there degrees between the Sun and one of the planets, from one up to fifteen, then he projects his own light over [the planet], and is conjoined to it. And the light of the Moon: 12° in front and 12° behind. And the light of Venus and Mercury (of each of them): 7° in front and 7° behind. By means of the quantity of this light, one is joined to another planet. The light of Saturn and Jupiter (of each of them): 9° in front and 9° behind. But the light of Mars is 8° in front and 8° behind.

---

[63] The Arabic is actually in the past tense here. For clarity we have used the present tense.
[64] Stegemann says *ebensoviel*, i.e., the same amount.
[65] Note these orbs are twice as big as those reported by later authorities such as Lilly (*Christian Astrology* I, p. 107).

So then if a planet observed [another] planet and it was struck by its light on its degree, then it is *connected* with it; and if it was not struck by its light, then it is "traveling towards the *connection*" until it is *connected*; and if the planet were in the last of the sign, [and] it is not *connected* with anything, and if the next sign was struck by its light, then whichever planet was first in that light is *connected* with it, even if the planet [which] was in the sign it will not see it.[66]

And if a planet looked at another, and were to hit its degree with its own light, it is said to be conjoined to him; and unless he would hit him with his own light, he is not called "conjoined" to him, but "going toward conjunction," until he begins to be joined to him. And if there were a planet at the end of some sign, joined to no one, and he were to hit the next sign with his own light, whichever one of the planets were more worthy in that light, he will be conjoined to it, even should the planet which was in the first sign not see it.

---

[66] Here Sahl allows out-of-sign conjunctions. But he does not allow out-of-sign *aspects*.

§5.4

Concerning the explanation of the departure

So if the degree of the lighter planet is going away from the degree of the heavier planet, and the lighter planet will be of a greater degree than the heavier one, then the observing is from the sign to the sign; and the *connection* is from the degree to the degree; and it is a saying of Māshā'allāh.[67]

The exposition of the receding or separation of the planets

The exposition of the receding or separation of the planets is if a lighter planet would go past another, heavier one, and it would begin to have more degrees, both in an aspect and in a conjunction. For an aspect is from a sign into a sign; but a conjunction is said to be from a degree into a degree. And this is the opinion of Māshā'allāh (that is, whom God willed to be a master).

§5.5

Concerning the explanation of the transfer

The transfer of light is if the lighter planet is departing from the heavier planet and connecting with another, then there is equivalency[68] between them, and there is a transfer of the nature of the first to the second with which it was connected.

On the transfer of light

The transfer of light from a planet to a planet is if a lighter planet is being separated from another, heavier one, and it would be joined to another: then it practically conjoins them and bears the nature of the first to the other (to whom he is being joined).

---

[67] Māshā'allāh repeats many times throughout OR that "true" corporal conjunctions and aspects are only by exact degree.
[68] Ar. *wāzā*.

An[69] example of that is if the rising[70] is Virgo and the question is about marriage, and the Moon is in the tenth degree of Gemini, and Mercury is in the eighth degree of Leo, and Jupiter is in the thirteenth degree of Pisces.

Mercury was the owner[71] of the rising and indicator of the question. It is not observing Jupiter (which is the owner of the sign of the marriage), because it is in the eighth sign from it. Rather, I looked to the Moon and found it departing from Mercury, and it is *connected* with Jupiter and *transferring the light* between them. Victory is indicated in the matter through the activity of envoys and those who go back and forth.

Of which matter [this] is an example: if the Ascendant were Virgo, and a question came to be about marriage; and the Moon was in the tenth degree of the sign of Gemini; and Mercury in the eighth degree of Leo; and Jupiter in the thirteenth degree of Pisces.

Mercury was the Lord of the Ascendant, [and] he was the significator of the question. He was not aspecting Jupiter (who is the Lord of the house of marriage), because he was in the eighth sign from him. Therefore I looked at the Moon, whom namely I found in the tenth degree of Gemini, separated from Mercury and joined to Jupiter: for she was bearing the light between each. And this signified the effecting of the matter—that is, the taking of a woman through the hands of legates and [the hands] of those running back and forth between each of them.

---

[69] I have depicted the chart according to Sahl's verbal description, though the Arabic manuscript (see Stegemann, p. 43) is given in a square form and uses the cardinal numbers rather than the ordinal ones.

[70] Ar. *aṭ-ṭālaʾ*. Sahl always means the rising *sign* in this text.

[71] Ar. *ṣāḥib*, that is, the Lord of the domicile. Sahl sticks nicely to the household management metaphor coming from Hellenistic astrology.

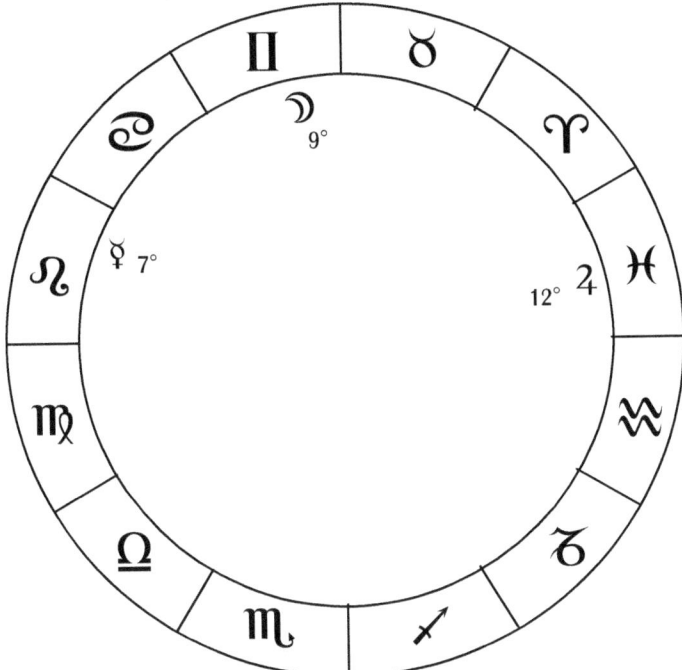

Figure 1: Transfer of Light

§5.6

On the collection[72] of the light of the planets

The collecting of the light is if the Lord of the rising and the Lord of the need[73] are *connecting* with a planet heavier than they; then it *collects* their strength and takes their light and their nature.	The collection of light is when the Lord of the Ascendant and the Lord of the quaesited matter are joined to a planet heavier than they, who would conjoin their strength and light, and would take up [or accept] their natures.

---

[72] Reading *collectione* for *coniunctione*.
[73] Ar. *al-hājah*. That is, the quaesited. Stegemann here uses *Sache*, "thing, matter," which is also a valid translation; but below he uses *Anliegen* ("cause, concern") for the same word. So, we have retained "need."

§5.7

*On the prohibition of light:
and it comes to be in three ways*

The prohibition is of three types.

Al-man^c, that is, prohibition, comes to be in three ways:

Of them, [the first] is the cutting-off of the light: and it is if a planet is between the Lord of the rising and the Lord of the need, less in degrees than one of them: then the *connection* with it is before the *connection* with the owner of the need.

[1] Of which one is called the cutting-off of light. And this comes to be when there is—between the Lord of the Ascendant and the Lord of the quaesited matter—some planet in fewer than the degrees of one of them, and there were a conjunction with that same one before the conjunction with the Lord of the matter would come to be.

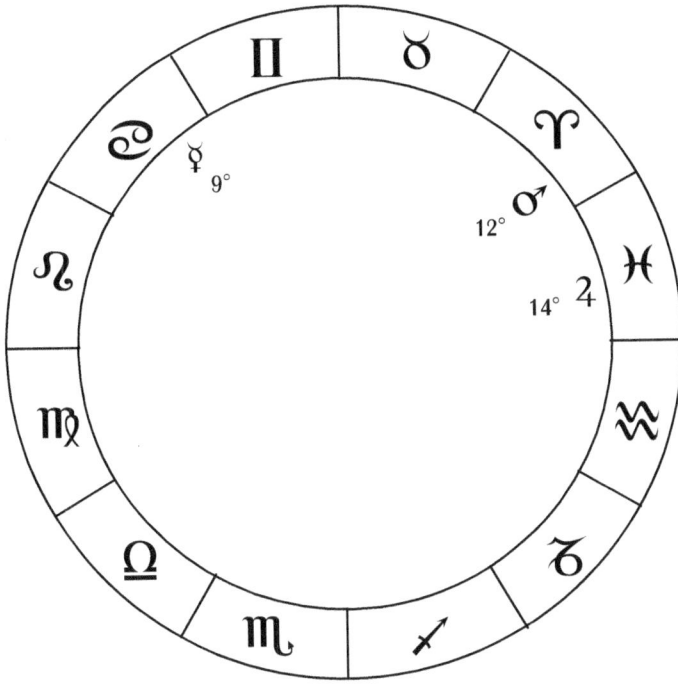

Figure 2: Prohibition of Light (First Way)

[1493:[74] Of which this is an example: like if the Ascendant was Virgo, and the question came to be about marriage.

---

[74] BN reads: "Of which [this] is an example: if the Ascendant had been Virgo, and a question came to be about marriage, and Mercury, the Lord of the Ascendant (who is the significator of the fiancée) in the fifteenth degree of the sign of Pisces; and Mars was in the thirteenth degree of Aries. Therefore Mars was cutting off the light of Mercury from Jupiter. And Mars was in the eighth sign from the Ascendant, in the sign of the Sun [?] of the substance of the woman. Therefore it signified that the destruction of this matter would come to be from the drawing-up of the dowry."

And Mercury the Lord of the Ascendant (who is the significator of the one asking) in the tenth degree of the sign of Cancer; and Jupiter, the Lord of the 7th domicile (who is the significator of the fiancée)[75] in the fifteenth degree of the sign of Pisces; and Mars was in the thirteenth degree of Aries. Therefore Mars was cutting off the light of Mercury from Jupiter; and Mars was in the eighth sign, that is, of the substance of the woman: it signified that the destruction of this matter would arise from the drawing-up[76] of the dowry.]

The second type is if there is a lighter planet and another heavy one and they are in one sign, and the lighter one *connects* with the heavy one. Then if another planet in the same sign *connects* to the assembly with the heavier planet and it is less than the lighter one, then the first one has really inserted itself between it and the connection (that is, it hinders them).[77]

The second way is if a light planet and another heavier one are both in one sign, and there would be a third one between them in the same sign, seeking the conjunction of the heavier one: this one takes away the conjunction of the first one.

---

[75] *Sponsae*, showing that the example assumes a male client.
[76] *Descriptione.* The querent pulls out of the arrangement due to disputes about the size or quality of the dowry.
[77] For this last clause (from "then the first one...") I am following Stegemann's German, which is more filled-out than the terse Arabic.

[1493: Of which [this] is an example: like if the Ascendant was Cancer, and a question came to be about marriage; and the Moon in the eighth degree of Gemini, and Mars in the tenth degree of the aforesaid sign; indeed Saturn in its twelfth degree, in front of Mars. Therefore, Mars separates the Moon and Saturn, and he takes away their conjunction and destroys their purpose.[78]]

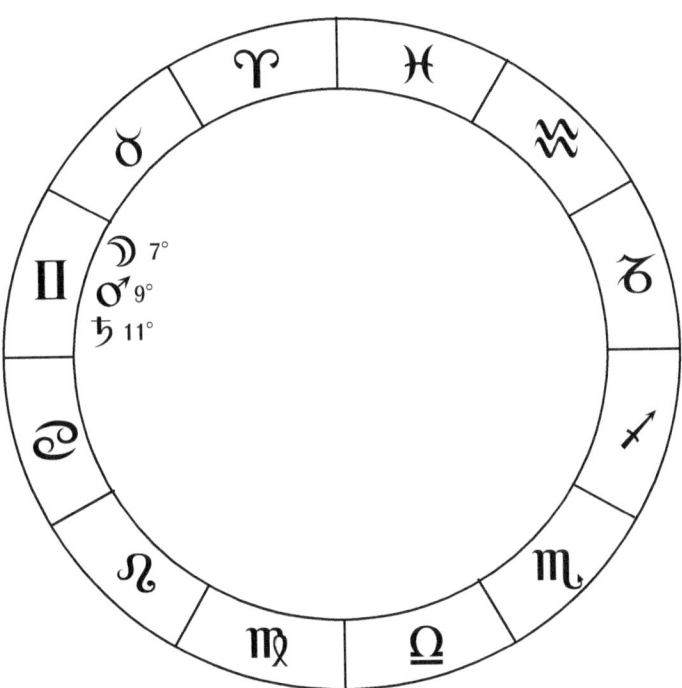

Figure 3: Prohibition of Light (Second Way)

---

[78] *Causam*, i.e., what they are trying to do *with each other*, not what they signify in themselves.

The third type is if the planet is *connected* with a planet that is heavier than it, and another is *connecting* with the heavy one by observation, and it is below the lighter one [in degrees]. Then the joined planet *prohibits* the planet that is observing from the *connection*.

The third way is if a light planet is joined to another heavier planet in one sign, and there would be another who would be joined to that same heavier one by aspect—who is below the lighter one in degrees, that is, in fewer degrees. Therefore the light planet who is with the heavy one in one sign, prohibits the conjunction of the other one who aspects.

And when it passes over, it is a true *connection*. And this type prohibits the *needs*, and its return is like the last two types.

And when he would cross over,[79] his conjunction would be true; and this way likewise prohibits the purposes, and returns[80] them just like the preceding ones did.

---

[79] *Transierit*, i.e., "transit."
[80] *Reddit*. The sense of the purpose being turned back is like when we say in English, "back to the drawing board."

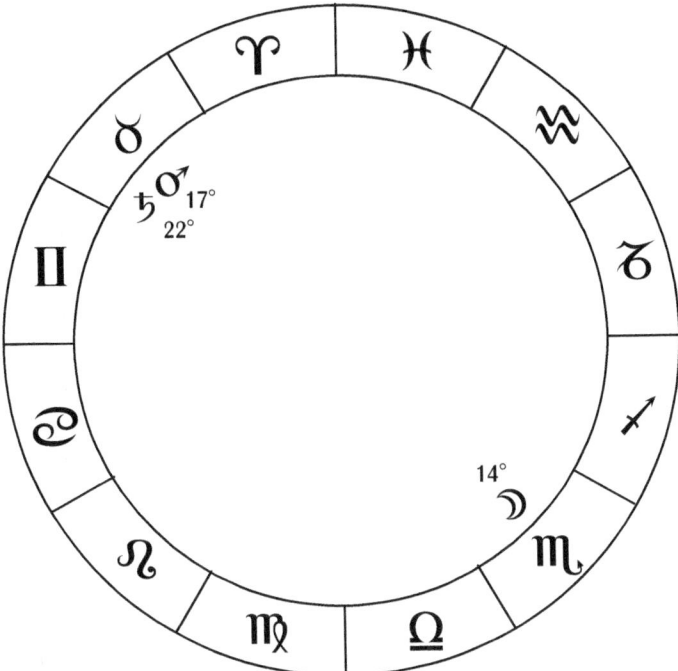

Figure 4: Prohibition of Light (Third Way)

[1493: Of which [this] is an example: like if the Ascendant was Cancer, and a question came to be about marriage; and the Moon, the Lady of the Ascendant (who is the significatrix of the one asking) was in the fifteenth degree of Scorpio; and Mars in the eighteenth[81] degree of Taurus; and Saturn in the twenty-third degree of the same Taurus.

---

[81] BN mistakenly says, "And Mars was in the tenth degree of Taurus…and Mars was below the degrees of the Moon, that is, by four degrees…" This cannot be right, else Mars would not be cutting off the light.

And Mars was above the degrees of the Moon (that is, in more degrees), and therefore he was cutting off the aspect between the Moon and Saturn, and he was prohibiting their conjunction. Because Mars was being joined to Saturn in one sign, and the conjunction of this is stronger than the conjunction of an aspect. For an aspect does not destroy a conjunction, but the conjunction destroys an aspect. And an aspect does not cut off an aspect, but it prohibits the purpose.[82] Indeed a conjunction cuts off an aspect.

And sometimes one planet is joined to another, but before he comes to him he is joined to another, and when he is joined to him, the conjunction itself is destroyed.]

---

[82] But what is the practical difference between cutting off light, and prohibiting a purpose?

If it were that a planet will be joined to a planet in a sign and was *pushing its arrangement* to another planet—that is, it enters into *connection* with it—then after that it arrives at the planet with which it was joined. And then the judgment[83] is carried out on the planet that was [previously][84] in conjunction.

Likewise, if a planet would be joined to another planet in one sign, and it would send its own disposition to an other—that is, it would be joined to another—who would be in another sign, and after the conjunction of this one by aspect he would arrive to the one with whom he is in one sign, and he is joined to him, the judgment will be according to the planet who is with him in the same sign.

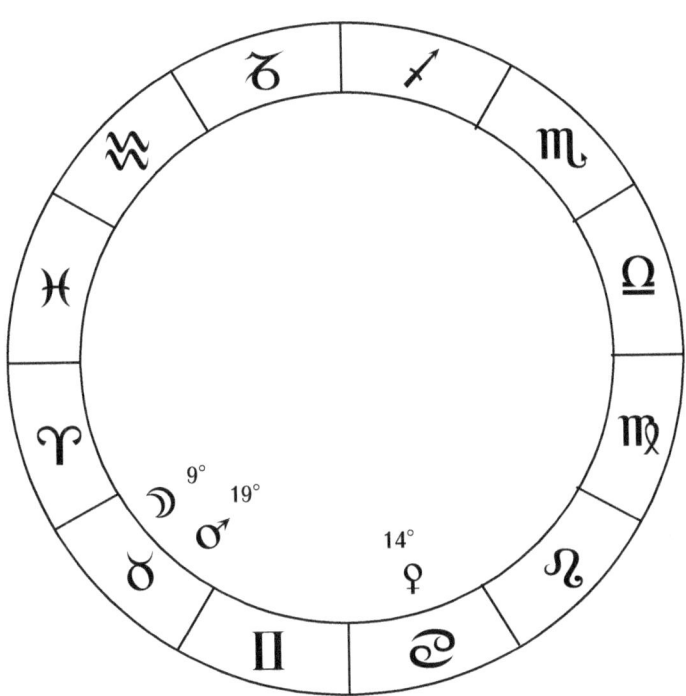

Figure 5: Prohibition of Light (Another Example)

---

[83] In the sense of finality, closing, a verdict.
[84] This is Stegemann's clarification, presumably referring to the planet in corporal conjunction, as in the Latin.

[1493: Of which [this] is an example: like if the Moon was in the tenth degree of Taurus, and Mars in the twentieth degree of the same Taurus; and the Moon would be joined to Venus by aspect before she would be joined to Mars; and Venus was in the fifteenth degree of Cancer. Even though Venus was in fewer degrees, still the judgment would be referred to Mars, because he was with the Moon in one sign.

And a conjunction of this kind is stronger than an aspect, as we have said. This is the exposition of those things which we said, because an aspect does not annul a conjunction, and a conjunction annuls an aspect.]

§5.8

Concerning the reception

The reception of the planets is when the planet is *connected* with [another planet] from its nobility or its house, and then it has complete *reception* with truthful intentions.

On the reception of the planets

But the reception[85] of the planets comes to be when a planet is joined to a planet from its domicile or exaltation: then it receives it with a good spirit and perfect reception.

---

[85] In the Arabic, "reception, approval, admission, acceptance."

Inferior to this *reception* is if it is *connecting* with a planet from a *triplicity* of that *connected* planet [...]⁸⁶

And there is another reception below this (that is, less than it), namely when a planet is joined to the planetary Lord of the triplicity and bound, or to the Lord of the bound and face (that is, when it is joined to a planet who has two or more of these lesser dignities in its own place): and then there will be a true reception. Indeed if it had only one, there will not be reception there.

...and so what contradicts this, the astrologer refuses it, and it does not recognize it, and it does not *receive* it, and does not see in it anything familiar.⁸⁷

And therefore say this:⁸⁸ because that which would be different from these, is at variance from the experienced astrologer, and is said to be as nothing.

---

⁸⁶ There is a gap in the Arabic. Note that what we have of the Arabic differs somewhat from the Latin, as Sahl seems to be suggesting that reception by just one lesser dignity will still be a reception, even if not the best. But the Latin disallows reception by just one dignity. Still, the Latin translator generally sticks very closely with the Arabic, and this would be a major and lengthy point to mistranslate.

⁸⁷ Ar. *'ahlā*, from the Arabic "family," but having the derivative meaning of "welcome." In this paragraph there is some ambiguity over who is refusing, knowing, and so on. It does at least seem that the astrologer should "refuse" or "disapprove" of these situations, but when read along with §5.9 below, it also seems that Sahl is speaking of the *planets* recognizing and greeting each other, and seeing family connections or memberships between themselves.

⁸⁸ Reading *hoc* for *hic*.

[1493: Of which this is an example: like if the Moon were in Aries, and she was being joined to Mars (who is the Lord of Aries): and then Mars would receive her, because she is in his domicile. Or, were she being joined to the Sun, the Sun would receive her, because it is the domicile of his exaltation. Or, were she in Taurus and she were being joined to Venus, or in Gemini and she were being joined to Mercury: this is perfect reception.

But the reception of triplicity is like if the Moon would be in Virgo, in the bound of Venus, and she would be joined to the same Venus. And Venus is the Lady of the triplicity of the Moon, and the Lady of her bound.

Or, if the Moon were in Gemini, in the bound of Saturn, and she would be joined to Saturn: Saturn would receive her, because he is the Lord of the triplicity and the bound. And were the Moon (or a planet) in such a likeness, she will be received. This is the opinion of Māshā'allāh on the reception of triplicity and bound.[89]

---

[89] Māshā'allāh alludes to the possibility of these other receptions in OR Ch. 3, where he speaks of a "strong" reception as involving the Lords of the domicile or exaltation (suggesting that reception by other Lords would be "weak").

And if the Moon were in this likeness, joined to some planet, and that planet were joined to the Lord of the domicile in which the Moon is (or to the Lord of the exaltation), the Moon will be received.[90]

And if the Moon were void in course, [and] after this were she to cross over to the next sign and were joined to the Lord of the first sign (or to the Lord of its exaltation), the Moon will be received. And if she were joined to a planet which was not the Lord of the first sign, nor[91] the Lord of its exaltation, it impedes her.][92]

---

[90] This appears to be something new.
[91] Reading *nec* for *aut*.
[92] This is the doctrine of changing signs, used here to aid the Moon in reception.

§5.9

Concerning those in which there will exist neither *reception* nor knowing.[93] So then the Moon or the owner of the rising, when *connected* with a planet with no testimony in the place of the Moon or the owner of the rising,[94] it does not understand it and does not *receive* it.

And likewise if the Moon or the owner of the rising is *connected* with a planet from its downfall,[96] it was as if it came to it from the house of its greatest enemy, and it does not *receive* it and it does not come near it.

But these are places in which neither reception nor knowledge[95] comes to be: namely if the Moon (or the Lord of the Ascendant) were joined to a planet which did not have testimony (that is, some dignity) in the place of the Moon (or the Lord of the Ascendant): it does not get to know him nor receive him.

Likewise if the Moon (or the Lord of the Ascendant) were joined to a planet, in its descension:[97] she will be like one who goes to him from the house of his own enemies: and he does not receive nor esteem her.[98]

---

[93] Again, this word can also mean "understanding" or "recognition."

[94] I.e., in their current positions.

[95] Reading *cognitio* for *coniunctio*. Like the Arabic, this word means learning, acquiring knowledge, and recognition (see the synonymous use of *cognoscit*, "get to know," below).

[96] I.e., its descension or fall (not detriment). Both Stegemann and the original Latin translator read this as though the slower planet is *in its own* descension. But that does not match the logic of the rest of the paragraph, nor the Arabic (*min hubūṭah*, "*from* its downfall"). Only the later interpolator (see example below from 1493) clearly sees what is happening. The diagram below only illustrates the first example.

[97] That is, if the Moon were in the descension of the other planet. See the facing Arabic version.

[98] Reading *eam* for *eum*. The idea is that the planet being joined to will not take kindly to the Moon (since she is in his descension).

[1493:[99] Of which an example is: like if the Moon is in Aries, and she would be joined to Saturn—or in Capricorn and joined to Jupiter, or in Cancer and joined to Mars, or in Libra and joined to the Sun, or in Virgo and joined to Venus; or in Pisces and joined to Mercury.

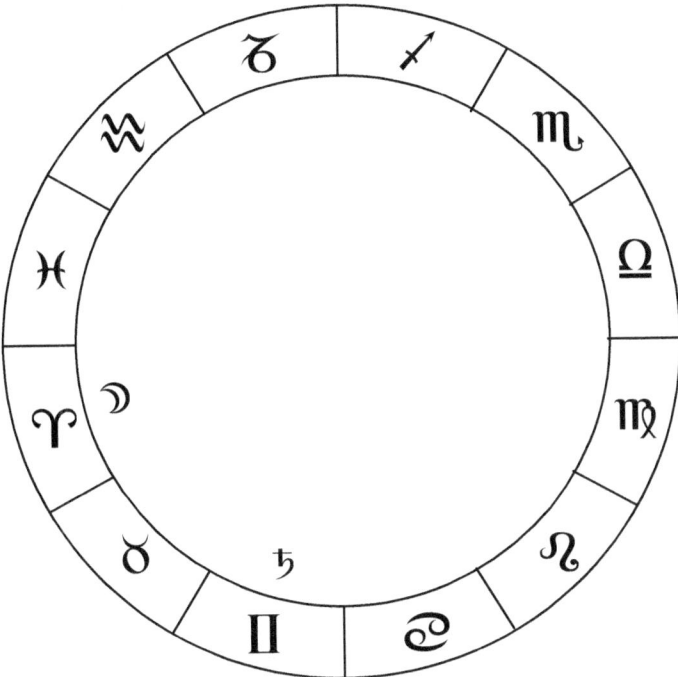

Figure 6: Not-Reception

---

[99] BN uses a shortened example and mistakenly uses the detriment instead of the descension in the first part: "Of which an example is if the Moon is in Aries, and would be joined to Venus, or in Libra and she would be joined to the Sun."

And if some significator were in its own descension, and were joined to a planet who did not have a power[100] (namely the domicile or exaltation) in the place of that significator, you will view him[101] as nothing, as if a strange vestment[102] was given to some querent.

And if a planet were joined to another planet in its own descension,[103] or that pushing planet were to descend,[104] it will make him go down, and it subtracts what would come to him from this.]

---

[100] BN reads *partem*, "portion, role."
[101] That is, the planet in its own descension. But BN reads, "*he* will view it." This is probably the more accurate reading.
[102] *Vestimentum ignotum*. Clearly the Latin translator sees a relation between strange or low-class clothing, and a planet in its own descension.
[103] That is, if the planet being joined to were in its own descension—provided that the applying planet were not the Lord of the domicile or the exaltation—which would help the planet in fall, as stated above.
[104] That is, if the applying planet were in its own descension, unreceived.

§5.10

Concerning the explanation of the void of movement

On the void course of a planet

So that is when the Moon is not *connecting* to any of the planets and none are joining to it. This is called the *void of movement* of the Moon and its body; there is futility in it and it is the planet of exile. It is the planet that is not *connecting* to any of the other planets.[105]

The exposition of a void course: if the Moon and her orb (and a planet) were void, and the planet were like one in exile, then it is said to be void in course: this is when it is joined to no planet, or none of the planets is joined to it.

§5.11

Concerning the explanation of the return

On the exposition of returning

It is if the planet or the Moon is *connecting* with a retrograding planet or [one that] is under the rays. It is then *returning* to what was before it and it is corrupt in its *arrangement* […][106]

The exposition of returning is when a planet or the Moon is joined to a retrograde planet (or one under the rays of the Sun), and it returns to him what it receives from him;[107] and it destroys the purpose.

---

[105] In the Arabic it is difficult to tell whether Sahl is only speaking about the Moon, or whether other planets may be called "void." Clearly the Latin translator means to include every planet. Stegemann reads: "And what the explanation of the "emptiness of the course" concerns, is this: when the Moon is not connecting itself with one of the planets, and is not accommodating itself to it, then this is called the emptiness of the course of the Moon, and [the emptiness of] its disc, which weakens it; and [the emptiness] of the planet that is pushed back, while it is not approaching one of the other planets."

[106] Stegemann says that both the Arabic and the Greek lack everything appearing in the Latin from 'Also, another way' to 'destroys his disposition.' He claims that this Latin passage proves Sahl was preserving statements by Dorotheus in *CCAG* V 3, 124, 14*ff.*

[107] That is, the retrograde or combust planet returns what the first planet or the Moon pushed onto it.

...and it signifies that the question does not have a beginning nor an end.

Also, another way concerns returning and judgment and destruction: like if there would be a planet (that is, a light one) who is cadent from the Ascendant, pushing to a cadent, heavy one: then it returns to him what it receives from him, and it destroys his disposition, and it signifies that the question does not have a beginning nor end.[108]

§5.12

Concerning the explanation of the pushing of strength

On the pushing of virtue

It is if the planet is *connecting* to the planet from its own house or its nobility or its triplicity.

The exposition of this matter is if a planet is joined to another from its own domicile or from the triplicity or from its own exaltation.

---

[108] Here cadence signifies the worthlessness or unusefulness or failure of what the planet signifies. 1493 has a more lengthy version with explanatory comments: "And there is another way of returning: like if a light planet which is joined in an angle, and it is joined to a planet cadent from the Ascendant. The beginning of the purpose belongs to [the light planet], because he who is joined, who signifies the beginning of the matter, was in an angle. And it will not have an end, because his receiver (who signifies the end of the matter) was cadent. And he who is joined, is light, and from him is the beginning of the matter. And the receiver [of what was pushed] is he who is heavy—and he is called the "receiver of the disposition." And the light one is called the "pusher of the disposition."

[1493: With such an example: like if namely the Moon were in Cancer or in Taurus, and she would be joined to Jupiter or to another of the planets, and she pushed her own virtue to him: wherefore she pushed, that is, "committed," her own disposition from her own domicile and exaltation. The remaining [planets] do likewise when they push the disposition from their own domiciles or exaltations.]

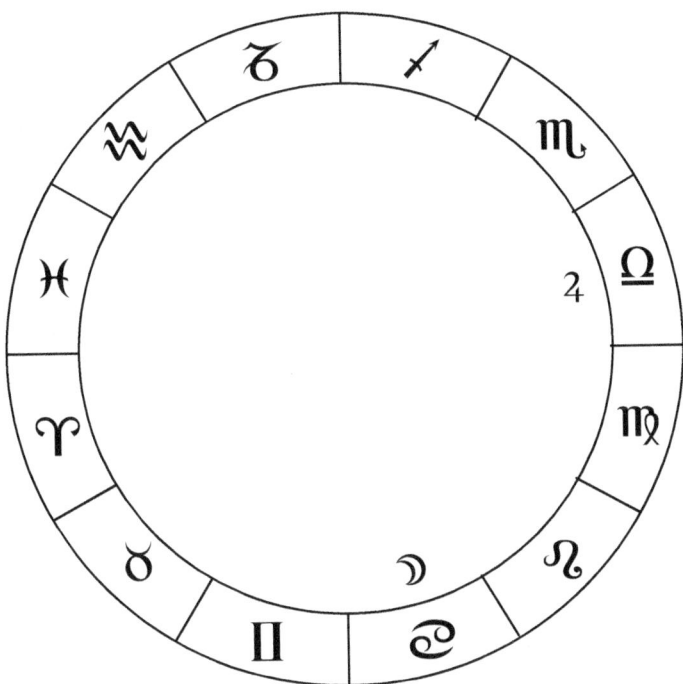

Figure 7: Pushing of Strength/Virtue

§5.13

Concerning the pushing of arrangement

It is if the planet is *connecting* from its house or its nobility, then it is *pushing* on it its *arrangement* and its nature.

On the pushing of disposition and nature

Also, the pushing of disposition and nature is if a planet would be joined with another planet from the domicile or exaltation [of the other], and it would push its own disposition or nature to it.

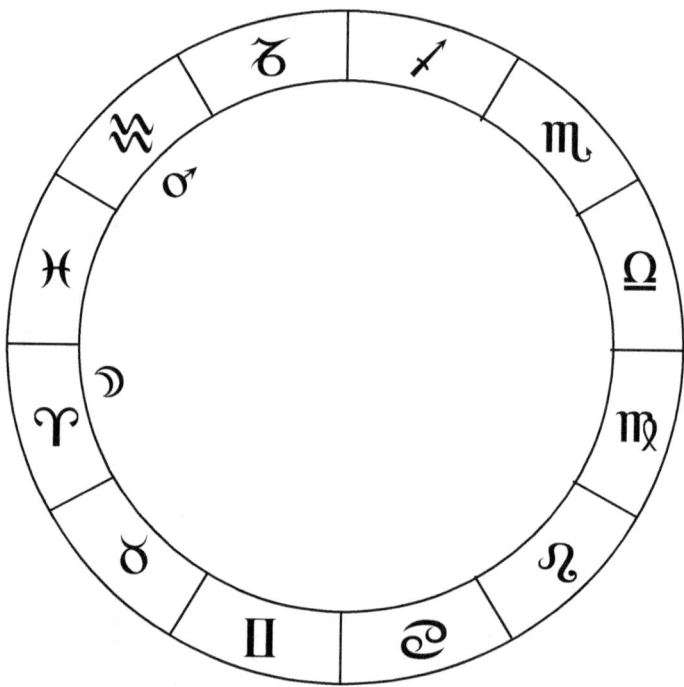

Figure 8: Pushing of Arrangement (or Disposition and Nature)

[1493: Of which an example is: if the Moon or one of the planets was in Aries, and was being joined to Mars (or she was in Gemini and was being joined to Mercury). And the Moon, if she were in Taurus or in Cancer, she pushes each (namely virtue and disposition); and if she were not in these two signs, she still pushes disposition.][109]

§5.14

On the strength of the planets

Concerning the explanation of the strength of the planets, that have no deficiency in the completion of the need, if they received or promised [such a thing].[110] Of them there are eleven types:

But the exposition of the strength of the planets (to which there is lacking a bad circumstance[111] or impediment to perfecting a purpose, if they received and promised [one])—this comes to be in eleven ways:

---

[109] See my Introduction for these different forms of pushing.
[110] Sahl repeats this idea of a planet "receiving and/or promising" something. At a minimum it sounds like a planet who simply signifies some matter and potentially promises an effect. Or perhaps it refers to planet like Māshā'allāh's final dispositor in *OR*, the last planet receiving disposition and responsible for effecting or destroying the matter.
[111] *Occasio*, here and at the end of the section.

If the planet will be in a good place from the rising: that is, in the stakes and what is following that, from the places which observe the rising.

Of which the first is that a planet is in a good place from the Ascendant: that is, it is in the angles and the succeedents of the angles (out of [such] places namely, those which[112] aspect the Ascendant).

The second is if the planet is in a thing from its share: that is, in its house or its nobility or a triplicity or its bound or its face or its joy.

The second is that a planet is in one of its own portions or dignities (that is, in its own domicile or exaltation or triplicity or bounds, or its own face or its own joy).

The third is if it is traveling the straight path.

The third is that it is direct.

The fourth is if an unfortunate is not with it in its sign, *connecting* with it, or observing it with a square or an opposition.

The fourth, that a malefic planet is not with it (that is, in the same sign in which it is), to which it is joined, or who aspects him from the opposition or from the square aspect.

The fifth is if it is not *connecting* with a star falling from the rising or with a star in its downfall.

The fifth, that it is not joined to a star cadent from the Ascendant, or to a planet which is in its own descension,[113] or [the planet] itself is in its own descension.

The sixth is if it is *received*.[114]

The sixth, that it is received.

---

[112] Reading *quae* or *qui* for *quia*, following the sense of the Arabic.
[113] That is, the planet being connected to—like if the Moon is joining to Venus in Virgo.
[114] The Arabic mistakenly adds a "not," which Stegemann says should be stricken, following the Latin.

The seventh is if it is one of the masculine planets: Saturn and Jupiter [and Mars], rising eastern in the dawn [...]¹¹⁵

The seventh, that the higher masculine planets (which are Saturn, Jupiter, and Mars) were oriental (that is, that they would appear in the morning, going out from under the rays of the Sun); and the feminine planets (that is, Venus, Mercury, the Moon) occidental (that is, appearing in the evening).

The eighth is if the planets are in their own light: that is, the masculine planets by day and the feminine planets by night.

The eighth, that the planets are in their own light: that is, the masculine planets in the day, and feminine ones in the night.¹¹⁶

The ninth is if the planets are in a firm sign.

The ninth, that planets are in fixed signs.

The tenth is if the planets are in the heart of the Sun, meaning when it was within one degree of it. The [planets of] fortune have an increase of fortune and the unfortunates are decreased in their evil.

The tenth, that the planets are in the heart of the Sun (that is, with the Sun in one degree): because then the benefics increase fortune and good, and it decreases¹¹⁷ the evil of the malefics.

---

115 Stegemann says the rest of the Arabic is missing, as well as the "and Mars."
116 This consideration is a hybrid of sect and gender.
117 Reading *minuitur* (with Arabic) for *confortatur* ("strengthens").

The eleventh is if the masculine planets are in a masculine quarter of the sides of the rising: and it is from the Midheaven to the rising and from the fourth to the seventh. And the feminine planets are in the feminine quarter: and it is from the seventh to the Midheaven and from the rising to the fourth. And the masculine planets are in a masculine sign and the feminine planets are in a feminine sign.	The eleventh is that masculine planets are in masculine quarters (of the parts of the circle of the Ascendant): that is, from the Midheaven to the Ascendant [and] from the fourth to the seventh, direct.[118] And feminine planets in feminine quarters: that is, from the seventh to the Midheaven and from the Ascendant to the fourth, direct. And masculine planets are in masculine signs and feminine planets in feminine signs.
These are the testimonies[119] which strengthen the planets, and there won't be deficiency in completing the need when they received or promised [one].	These are the testimonies by which the planets are strengthened, and they do not have a bad circumstance which would harm them in perfecting a purpose which they received and promised.

§5.15

Concerning the weakness of the planets	*On the weakness of the planets*
Their injuries are in the birth and the questions, and they are of ten types:	Indeed the weakness of the planets (and their impediment in nativities and questions) comes to be in ten ways:

---

[118] Sahl's Arabic does not have this "direct." It is unclear to me whether the Latin translator simply means they should be in direct motion, or whether there is some other feature of the quadrants or primary motion that is meant.

[119] Here "testimony" is meant in the sense of giving a testimony to the *astrologer*. See my Introduction for the topic of testimony.

If the planet is falling from the stakes and not looking to the rising, and that is in sixth and in the twelfth.

Secondly if the planet is in its retrogradation.

Thirdly, if the planet is under the rays.

Fourthly, if it is *connecting* to the unfortunate [planet] by conjunction or opposition or squaring.

Fifthly, if it is confined between two unfortunates: and [that is,] it is *departing* from an unfortunate and *connecting* to [another] unfortunate.

Sixthly is if the planet is in its downfall.

Seventhly, if it is *connecting* to a planet falling from the rising, or is *departing* from a planet in its *reception*.

Of which ways, one is that a planet is cadent from the angles and does not aspect the Ascendant (that is, in the sixth or twelfth).

The second is that a planet is retrograde.

The third, that it is under the rays of the Sun.

The fourth, that it would be joined to malefic planets from the conjunction or the opposition (that is, that it is with him in one sign or is in his seventh) or in his square aspect (which is the fourth sign).

The fifth, that it is besieged between two malefics: that is, if it would be separated from one malefic and joined to another.

The sixth, that a planet is in its own descension, or is being joined to a planet who is in its own descension.

The seventh, that it is being joined to a planet cadent from the Ascendant, or it is separated from a planet who was receiving it.

Eighthly, if the planet is in a house in which it has no testimony: no house and no nobility and no triplicity; and if the planet is a stranger, and the Sun is overtaking it: meaning that it is in front of the Sun.	The eighth, that a planet would be in a domicile in which it did not have testimony (that is, some dignity): that is, that it is not in its own domicile or own exaltation or triplicity, and so on, and that it is peregrine and already overtaken by the Sun (that is, in front of the Sun).
Ninthly, if the planet is with the Head or the Tail, then it will not have latitude.	The ninth, that a planet is with the Head or Tail: that is, if it had no latitude.[120]
Tenthly is when it was opposed: and it is when it was opposed to its house, meaning when it was in the seventh from its house, which is called the "unhealthy."[121]	The tenth, if the planets impeded themselves: that is, if they were in the opposition of their own domiciles (which is a certain impediment to them).
These are the gates that the corruption of the planets will be in for the births and the questions and works along those lines, and so I warn of these accounts [pertaining to] the capable, promising stars in [regards to] the need.	Therefore, these are the headings in which there is an impediment or detriment of the planets: that is, which come to be in nativities, in questions and in the rest of works. Therefore attend to these ways which we have stated, concerning a planet who receives disposition and who promises a purpose.

---

[120] This could mean that the planet is with *its own* Head or Tail (also known as the *jawzahirr*), not the Nodes of the Moon—otherwise this condition would be exceedingly rare. Or it could mean the Moon's Nodes, and Sahl is just being astronomically imprecise (since a planet could conjoin the Nodes but still have latitude).

[121] *Al-wabāl*. Stegemann reads this as "injury, disadvantage" (*Schaden*).

§5.16

On the defects of the Moon and her bad condition

Concerning the faults of the Moon, specifically the ill condition of the Moon in every affair and every beginning; and it is in ten types:

If the Moon is ignited under the Sun by 12°, and it is not passing the Sun, and after it.

Second, if the Moon is in the degrees of its downfall (which is Scorpio), or *connecting* with a star in its downfall.

Third, if the Moon is in the opposition of the Sun, under 12°, not reaching the opposition.

Fourth, if it is in conjunction to an unfortunate or looking to it from a square, or an opposition, or confined between two unfortunates, *departing* to an unfortunate.

Therefore the defects of the Moon and her bad condition, by which it makes the detriments of matters in every question and in every beginning, come to be in ten ways:

And the first is that the Moon is namely combust within the rays of the Sun, not yet transiting 12°, and likewise after him (but this is easier).

The second, that she is in the degrees of her own descension, or is joined to a planet in its own descension.[122]

The third, that she is in the opposition of the Sun, within 12°, not yet coming to the degree of the opposition.

The fourth, that she is joined to malefics, or they aspect her from the square aspect or from the opposition; or she is besieged between two malefics, namely separated from one and joined to the other.

---

[122] Or perhaps, to a planet in *her* descension.

Fifth, if it is with the Head or Tail in a sign, [with] less than 12° between them.	The fifth, that she is in the Head or Tail, and in one sign, and there is less than 12° between them.
[Sixth,] <…> and it is in Gemini, or it is in the last degrees of the sign, which is an unfortunate bound.[123]	The sixth, that she is in the twelfth sign from her own domicile (the which sign is that of Gemini), or she is in the end of the degrees of signs (which are the bounds of the malefics).
Seventh is if it is falling from the stakes or is *connecting* to a planet who is falling from the stakes.	The seventh, that she is cadent from the angles or joined to a planet cadent from the angles.
Eighth, it is in the ignited path: and it is the last of Libra and the first of Scorpio.	The eighth, that she is in the burnt path[124] (this is in the end of Libra and in the beginning of Scorpio).
Ninth, if it is savage and is *void of movement*, not *connecting* with any of the other planets.	The ninth, that she is wild[125] or void in course.
Tenth, if it is slow of movement: and it is when the adjustment is decreased from it, or it is in a decrease of light—and [that is] in the last of the month.[126]	The tenth, that she is slower in course (that is when her equation is taken away from her), or when her light is reduced (which is in the end of a lunar month).

---

[123] See my Introduction §7 for a discussion of this passage.
[124] I.e., the *via combusta*.
[125] Lat. *feralis*, or "feral."
[126] Stegemann reads: "10. That she is slow in her course, and that is if her average (speed) is detracted from her, or her light is diminished, that is, at the end of the month."

These are the faults of the Moon and its defects, in which no work should be begun, and they are not to be praised in a birth nor in a journey.	These are the aforesaid[127] defects of the Moon and her impediments, under which no work should be undertaken (that is, while the Moon is so, any work should not be begun nor praised in a nativity nor in foreign travel).

Know even the condition of the Moon in the increase of this light and its decrease: that is, while she waxes and while she is reduced: because the Moon, while she is being increased (that is, while she waxes), if Mars aspected her from the fourth sign or from the seventh,[128] or he were with her in one sign, Mars impedes her (because then she will be hot). But on the contrary, if Saturn were with her, and she is being decreased, or he aspected her from the square aspect or the opposition, it impedes her. Because if the Moon were greater in light (this is in the beginning of the month), and she were hot, Saturn does not impede her (because he is cold). And Mars impedes her because he is hot. And if she were less in light (this is in the end of the month), she will be cold: then Mars does not impede her, because he is hot; and Saturn does impede her, because he is cold.

And know that Saturn in diurnal nativities (and questions which are asked in the day), and in the beginning of the month, and in masculine signs, impedes less; and in the end of the months and in feminine signs, he impedes more; and Mars in the night and in feminine signs, and in the end of the month, impedes less; and in the day and in the beginning of the month and in masculine signs, he impedes more.

And a planet (nor the Moon, nor a sign) is not called "impeded" until the malefics are with it or they aspect it from the fourth sign or from the seventh, or from the tenth; nor is a planet (nor the Ascendant) called "fortunate" until the benefics are in the angles of that same planet (or in the angles of the Ascendant).

---

[127] Reading *praedicta* with 1493, for Stegemann's *praedicat*.
[128] This should probably also read, "or from the tenth," referring to the whole-sign angles of her position. See the end of the section below.

§6: On besieged planets

The exposition of a besieged planet is like if a planet is between two malefics, separated from one of them and joined to the other one, without the projection of the rays of another planet between them (that is, that no other planet projects its own rays between them): and more strongly so, and worse, if the separation and conjunction were from 7° and less. Of which an example is this: like if Mars is in the tenth degree of Cancer, and Saturn in the eighteenth degree of Aries, and the Moon in the thirteenth of Libra; and the Moon, separated from Mars from [her] second square aspect,[129] and joined to Saturn from the opposition: then the Moon will be besieged, because [she is] separated from the light of Mars and joined to the light of Saturn.

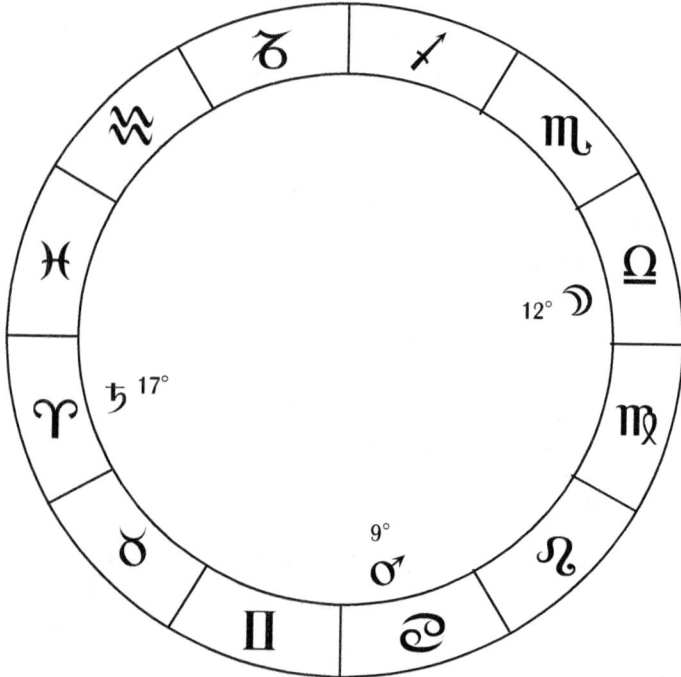

Figure 9: Besieging

---

[129] That is, from the dexter aspect she cast backwards from Libra to Cancer.

§7: On a planet in its own light

A planet is said to be in its own light: like Mars (who is nocturnal), if he were a significator in the night; and Saturn (who is diurnal) is said to be in his own light in the day.

§8: On the testimonies of the planets

Also, the exposition of those things which are said about the planets (that they have testimonies or parts or dignities): if a planet were in its own domicile, or in its own exaltation, or in the triplicity or in its own bound, or in its own face, it is profitable[130] if it is in a sign in which it would have testimonies.

§9: On the joys of the planets

But the exposition of the joys of the planets comes to be in four ways:

But first, their joy is from the circle: because Mercury rejoices in the Ascendant; and the Moon in the third; and Venus rejoices in the fifth; and Mars in the sixth; and the Sun in the ninth; and Jupiter in the eleventh; and Saturn rejoices in the twelfth.[131]

Second, the joy which they have[132] from their strength in their own domiciles. For Saturn rejoices in Aquarius, because it is [his] masculine sign. And Jupiter rejoices in Sagittarius; and Mars in Scorpio; the Sun in Leo; and Venus in Taurus; and Mercury in Virgo; and the Moon rejoices in Cancer.[133]

Third, because the diurnal planets rejoice if they were in the east: this is when they are rising in the morning; and the nocturnal planets rejoice when they appear in the evening in the western hemisphere.

---

[130] *Proficiens*, meaning "advancing, growing, profiting, being advantageous."
[131] Here they are arranged around the chart according to sect: the diurnal planets above the horizon, the nocturnal ones below, and Mercury in the rising sign, which is partly above and partly below the horizon. Also, the benefics and luminaries aspect the rising sign, while the malefics do not.
[132] Reading *habeant* with BN for *habet*.
[133] The planets ruling more than one sign (excluding Mercury) have their joy in the sign of their sect.

Then they have a fourth manner of joy: because Saturn and Jupiter and Mars rejoice if they were in the masculine part of the circle (which is from the Midheaven up to the Ascendant, and from the fourth sign to the seventh); indeed the Moon and Venus rejoice if they were in the feminine part (namely from the seventh up to the Midheaven, and from the Ascendant to the angle of the earth, which is the fourth sign). But Mercury rejoices in both parts: that is, if he were with masculine planets he rejoices in the masculine part; and if he were with the feminine ones he rejoices in the feminine part (on account of the diversity of these planets and their domiciles).

THE *FIFTY JUDGMENTS*

The principal judgments begin: and there are fifty

The first, on the reception of disposition through the Moon

Know that the significatrix (that is, the Moon), whose circle is closer to the earth than the circles of all the planets, is similar to the things of the world more so than all the planets. Do you not see that a man begins being small, then he grows until he is finished? The Moon does likewise. Therefore, consider the Moon as the significatrix of all matters: because her soundness is the soundness of every matter; and her detriment is the detriment of every matter. And she pushes (that is, "commits") her own disposition likewise to him [to] whom she projects her own rays, and to whom, of the planets, she is joined; and she changes her own being [or condition] to that planet (and this planet[1] is called the "receiver of the disposition" because he receives what had been committed to him). Therefore the Moon herself is these planets' bearer of information,[2] and she reconciles them and bears off from certain ones of them, to others.

Judgment 2: What the malefic or benefic planets would signify

The malefic planets signify detriment and evil on account of the excessiveness or overflowing of the power of cold and heat conquering and impeding in them. But if a benefic planet were in the domicile of a malefic (or in its exaltation), [the malefic] receives [the benefic] and restrains its own malice from him; or if there were an aspect of the malefics by a trine or sextile aspect, it would even be restrained by that, because it would be an aspect of friendship without any enmity. Indeed the benefics, because they are of a temperate nature and equal complexion (that is, because they are temperated from heat and cold), always profit and perform, were they to receive or not—but reception with them is more useful and better.[3]

---

[1] Reading *ipse* for *ipsa*.
[2] Lat. *delatrix*.
[3] *Cf. Tet.* I.5.

Judgment 3: On the impediment of the planets—three judgments

[1] There are two kinds of stars, namely the benefic and the malefic: therefore, wherever you saw malefic planets, say evil; and wherever you saw a benefic, say good.

Judgment 4[4]

[2] And a planet is called "impeded" while a malefic is projecting rays over its light according to the quantity which I told you concerning their orbs. And if it transited a bound of the malefics it is called "looking at the malefic," and [the malefic] would not be able to impede. And if a malefic transited a planet[5] by a complete degree, it sends in fear without the impediment of the body, and the malefic planet would not be able to act because it is separated from it. Likewise if a benefic transited a planet and were separated from it by a full degree,[6] he has hope, but the matter is not perfected. And every impeding [planet], if it were cadent from the Ascendant, sends fear and does not impede. Likewise if benefics were cadent from the Ascendant: it is hoped for, but the matter is not perfected.

Judgment 5[7]

[3] If a planet were in the angles of the malefics (that is, if it were with one, or in the fourth from him, or in the seventh or in the tenth), it will be like one who fights on his own behalf[8] against the tribulation and evil which descends upon him. And if [the malefic] transited it, and it were separated from it by a full degree (as I said to you before), he has already escaped the impediment of that malefic, and the malefic would be able to do nothing besides sending in fear. Therefore, observe these chapters: because they are of the secrets of questions.

---

[4] Continuing the judgments of impediment from *Judgments* 3.
[5] Reading *planetam* for *planeta*, in parallel with the following sentence.
[6] *Per gradum integrum*. *Integer* suggests that the degree itself is counted as a whole: so if the malefic were transiting a planet at 25° 57', it would be separated by a full degree as soon as it enters 26°, only 3' away.
[7] Continuing the judgments of impediment from *Judgments* 3.
[8] *Pro semetipso*.

Judgment 6: On the void course of the Moon

If the Moon were void in course—that is, joined to none of the planets—it signifies futility and annulment, and turning back from that same purpose,[9] and the impediment of that same purpose.

Judgment 7: On the conjunction of the Moon with the planets

The[10] conjunction of the Moon signifies what is going to be, and what is hoped for concerning matters, according to the quantity of the nature of the planet who receives the Moon's disposition (that is, if it were a benefic, good; if it were a malefic, evil).

Judgment 8: On the separation of the Moon from the planets

The[11] separation of the Moon from a planet signifies what is past and what has already gone away, according to the quantity of the nature of that planet from whom the Moon is being separated.

Judgment 9: On a planet in its own descension

If a planet were in its own descension, it signifies sorrow and prison and distress.

Judgment 10: On a retrograde planet

A retrograde planet signifies disobedience, and contradiction, and turning back and taking back, and diversity or discord.

---

[9] *Causa*, here and in the next clause.
[10] See *Carmen* V.28.
[11] See *Carmen* V.28.

Judgment 11: On a stationary planet

A planet in its own station signifies evil and what has already gone inactive.

Judgment 12: On the malefic planets

The malefics signify difficulty, and pressure, and haste in work.

Judgment 13: On a planet slow in course

If a planet were slow (that is if it walks slowly), it puts aside[12] its own number[13] or its own promise. That is, it makes a delay in number or its own promise, both in the good and the bad. It does likewise if it were in the domiciles of Saturn or Jupiter. And in the domiciles of the light planets, it hastens.

Judgment 14: On the conjunction of the Moon with planets in one minute

If the Moon were conjoined to some planet and she perfected her own conjunction (that is, if she were with it in one minute), look to see what is going to be concerning that question from the planet with whom the Moon is joined after this.

Judgment 15: On a planet's being at the end of a sign

If a planet were in the last degree of a sign, its strength has already receded from that sign, and its strength will be in the next sign: like a man who put his foot upon the threshold of the gate, wanting to go out—which if the house then fell, it would not impede him. Indeed if a planet were in the

---

[12] *Postponit*, the origin of our "postpone."
[13] This seems to refer to timing techniques—such planets will manifest more slowly and take more time.

twenty-ninth degree,[14] the strength of the planet will be in the same sign. Because there are three degrees of every planet in which its virtue is spread out—namely, the degree in which it is, and the degree which is behind it, and the degree which is in front of it.[15]

Judgment 16: On a planet which seeks and does not bring about a conjunction

Sometimes a planet seeks a conjunction, but it does not bring it about in its own sign until a planet imitates it through its own hastening.[16] And if it[17] were to catch up with it[18] in the next sign and it was not joined to another, the purpose is perfected. And if it were joined to another when it is changed [into the next sign], were it joined to it afterwards, the purpose will not be perfected (because it has already been commingled to the light of another planet).[19]

Judgment 17

[Suppose] a planet [is] wishing to be joined to a planet in one sign, but it cannot catch up with it in that same sign until it goes out to the next sign. And if it catches up with it in the next sign, then the purpose is perfected (unless he would then be joined to another);[20] but if it were joined with another by aspect, this does not hinder it, on account of what I have told you: because a conjunction which comes to be through an aspect does not annul a conjunction which comes to be by body in one sign. And a conjunction of this kind[21] annuls the one which comes to be by aspect. And an aspect does

---

[14] That is, from 28°00'—28° 59'.
[15] This seems related to Sahl's allowing of out-of-sign conjunctions (*Introduct.*, end of §5.3).
[16] *Donec imitetur ipsum planeta per festinationem suam.*
[17] The applying planet.
[18] The planet being applied to.
[19] For example, let Mercury be applying to Venus near the end of a sign. Before Mercury can complete the joining, Venus moves into the following sign. If Mercury can cross to that sign and join with her *before* Venus joins with a third planet, the purpose is perfected. But if Venus had already been joined (or perhaps were in the process of being joined) to another before Mercury could join with her, then the purpose will not be perfected.
[20] See *Judgments* 16.
[21] I.e., a corporal conjunction.

not cut off an aspect, but it prohibits the purpose; but a corporal conjunction cuts off an aspect.[22]

Judgment 18: On a malefic planet well disposed

If a malefic planet were oriental (that is, if it were to appear in the east in the morning), in its own domicile or in its own exaltation, and it was not joined to a malefic who would impede him, it is better and more worthy than a retrograde and impeded benefic.

Judgment 19: On malefic planets appearing as the Lords of purposes

If malefics were the Lords of purposes,[23] and the Lord of the Ascendant or the Moon were joined to them from a square aspect or the opposition (that is, from the fourth sign or from the seventh one),[24] they make the purpose but destroy it in the end. And if the malefics were those who are joined to benefics (that is, if the malefics would push and be joined to them), it will be better than if they were the ones receiving the disposition.

Judgment 20: On malefic planets in the Ascendant

If a malefic were in the Ascendant, in its own domicile or in the exaltation, it is restrained from evil; if however it is retrograde in the Ascendant, its evil is strengthened and its diversity and variation is multiplied.

Judgment 21: On a planet appearing in a sign similar to its own nature

If a planet were in, of the signs, its own character[25] and likeness, it will be agreeable for it: that is, if Saturn were in his own domicile or in the exaltation, or in a cold sign, and Mars were (just as I have told you before) in a hot

---

[22] See *Introduct.* §5.7, "the third way."
[23] That is, they rule the houses of the quaesited or the topic of an election.
[24] Again, this also includes the tenth sign from it.
[25] *Habitu*, a difficult word meaning "condition, style, quality, manner," *etc.*

sign, it will be good. Indeed if it were in the contrariety of its nature, it will be bad for it: just like water and oil, which are not commingled nor complected. And if it were in a sign similar to itself, they are commingled and complected just like water and milk.[26]

Judgment 22: On the benefics aspecting the malefics

When the benefics aspect the malefics, they decrease [the malefics'] impediment.

Judgment 23: On the malefics aspecting the benefics

When the malefics aspect the benefics from a square aspect or from the opposition, they decrease [the benefics'] fortune.

Judgment 24: On benefics cadent from the Ascendant

If the benefics were cadent from the Ascendant,[27] or retrograde, they will be impeded [and be] like the malefics.

Judgment 25: On planets when they are received

When planets are received, and they are benefics, their good will be stronger; and if they were malefics, their impediment will be less.

Judgment 26: On malefics appearing in a peregrine (or not-peregrine) sign

If the malefic planets were in a peregrine sign, and if they were not in their own domiciles (nor in the exaltation, nor in triplicity), they increase evil

---

[26] *Cf.* Abū Ma'shar's different forms of mixtures and complexions in *Gr. Intr.* VII.4.670-694.
[27] I.e., not aspecting the rising sign.

and their impediment is made greater; and if they were in signs in which they have testimony, they are restrained from evil, and altogether there will not be an impediment.

Judgment 27: *On the malefics, if they were the Lords of matters and well-disposed*

If the malefics were in their own domiciles (or in the exaltations or in triplicities or in their own bounds), and in the angles or in the followers of the angles, and they were the Lords of matters, their strength will be like the strength of benefics. Understand what I have said.

Judgment 28: *On benefics appearing peregrine or not-peregrine*

If the benefics were in a sign in which they do not have testimony, their fortune and good is decreased; and if they were in a sign in which there is testimony for them (that is, in their own domiciles or exaltations or triplicities or bounds), their fortune is made greater, and the matter is perfected, and good is increased.

Judgment 29: *On planets appearing in a malign place or under the rays*

If the benefics and malefics were in a malign place (that is, in one of the domiciles which I have said before), or they were under the rays, combust, they signify small and despicable things,[28] and the planets would not be able to signify good or evil on account of the weakness which is in them. Because if a planet were under the rays, combust, or in the opposition of the Sun, it will be weak, since in this place there is no usefulness nor anything of the good for benefic planets, nor anything of evil for the malefic ones: because the benefics signify a modicum of the good if they were under the rays, and likewise if the malefics were under the rays their impediment will be less.

---

[28] This is an arresting phrase.

Judgment 30: On planets appearing in their own dignities

And every benefic planet (or malefic), if it were in its own domicile or in the exaltation or in its own triplicity, and so on—whatever is in them of evil is turned away into the good. Marvel therefore at what I have told you, and take your measure of judging from it.

Judgment 31: On malefics appearing in the angles

If the malefics were in the angles of the Ascendant, and they impeded from the square aspect or the opposition, the malefics will be strong at harming, and their affliction will be greater, and especially and most particularly if they were stronger than the planet whom they oppress or impede (that is, if they were in a stronger place, that is, if they were to have some dignity); but if they aspected from a trine or from a sextile aspect, they are restrained from evil and their impediment is decreased.[29]

Judgment 32: On a consideration which must be had concerning the places of the planets

Always, a benefic does not signify except for fortune, and a malefic always signifies nothing except for evil (on account of the overflowing of its nature and the malignity of its complexion). Therefore it is necessary to look at the places of the planets—that is, their places from the Ascendant, and the signs in which they are: because even though a planet may be malefic, if it were in its own likeness, or in its own light,[30] or in its own domicile or exaltation or triplicity, or in a good place from the Ascendant, it signifies good.

---

[29] Trines and sextiles are likened to Jupiter and Venus, so indicating friendship; squares and oppositions are likened to Mars and Saturn, and indicate enmity. This correspondence is based on the relation of the domiciles to one another.

[30] Here "likeness" is not being proposed as a synonym for being in its own light. Earlier, "likeness" referred to a sign a planet ruled, or one of the same nature.

Judgment 33: On a benefic if it were badly disposed

If a benefic were not in its own light[31] (that is, if it were of the planets of the night, and it were a significator in the day, or it were of the planets of the day and were a significator in the night), or were it peregrine[32] from its own sign, or cadent from the Ascendant or under the rays, it impedes and is not profitable.[33]

Judgment 34: On that which Jupiter and Venus can[34] change

If Jupiter aspected a malefic, he changes its nature into the good; and Venus cannot turn a great thing (that is, the evil of Saturn) unless they would aspect Jupiter. For Jupiter loosens what Saturn binds up: that is, if Jupiter is joined to Saturn, he breaks [Saturn's] malice and changes it. And Venus loosens what Mars binds up.

Judgment 35: On that which the pushing of the planets to each other, signifies

If a malefic pushes (that is, it is joined) to a malefic, it is turned—that is, an evil is changed into another evil. And if a malefic is joined to a benefic, the evil is converted into good. Indeed if a benefic is joined to a malefic, it will find evil after the good. And commingle matters in this way.

Judgment 36: On that which the benefics free from the evils of the malefics

If the Moon (and the Lord of the Ascendant) were impeded[35] by the conjunction or from the square aspect or the opposition of the malefics, if then

---

[31] *Lumine.* Although the medieval Latin texts invariably use *lumen* for "light" (rather than *lux*), *lumen* also has the particular meaning of a period of the day—so sect issues are involved here. Here, "being in its own light" means "being a member of the sect in favor." So "light" refers to belonging to the "light of the luminary in charge."

[32] *Peregrinus*, literally, "a foreigner, foreign."

[33] *Non proficit.*

[34] Reading *possunt.*

[35] Reading *impedita* (referring to the Moon) for *impeditus*, since the sentence begins with her. But the Latin translator clearly means it to refer to either one of them.

benefics are joined to her from a square aspect, whatever would find a man in terms of destruction will be loosened by the benefics, and he will be freed from them. Likewise, if they[36] were joined to malefics from the square aspect, and benefics aspected from a trine aspect, the man will escape what happens to him in terms of that destruction, and he will fall into another; or he will hardly escape what happens to him in terms of the destruction, and he will not fall into another.[37]

Judgment 37: On a planet outside its own dignities and cadent from the angles

If a planet were not in its own domicile or in the exaltation or triplicity, or in its own bound or joy, and it were cadent from the angles, this will be an evil signification without any usefulness: and there is nothing of the good in the planet's impediment.

Judgment 38: On a planet under the rays toward the west

If[38] a planet were under the rays, toward the west (that is, if it arises in the evening), its strength will be weak as was said concerning the superiors: for there will be no strength for it, nor for its light; and its impediment will be less if it were a malefic; and if it were retrograde, it will be slow in all matters.[39]

---

[36] That is, the Moon or the Lord of the Ascendant.
[37] The rationale here seems to be related to whole-sign aspects, since a square from the benefics would place them in a position to oppose the evil itself. For instance, if the Moon were in the first, and a malefic were in the tenth, then a benefic in the fourth would be able to oppose the malefic; but if the benefic were sextile or trine the Moon in the third or fifth, it would not be in any aspect to the malefic and therefore be unable to deal with the evil directly.
[38] In this judgment, the occidental planets would either be headed toward combustion (superiors) or retrograding toward it (inferiors), or going direct but about to come out of the rays (inferiors).
[39] This latter point would only be possible for the inferiors, if they were retrograde and moving toward the Sun.

Judgment 39: On a planet under the rays within 12°

If planets were under the rays, they will be weak in all matters: that is, if there were less than 12° between them and the Sun (unless a planet is in the degree of the Sun, because then it will be strong).

Judgment 40: On a planet with the Sun

If a planet were far from the Sun by 12° in the morning from the east,[40] it will be strong in every beginning and in every work. And if it were prolonged from him by 15°, then it will be stronger—that is, then it will be in the greatest strength that it could be in. And if a planet were in front of the Sun from the side of the west (that is, if it would arise in the evening in the west), and there were from 15° up to 7° between it and the Sun, then it begins to be weakened from 7° until it comes to be in the heart of the Sun: the planet comes to be weaker than it could [ever] become. And if it were in the heart of the Sun, it will be strong through the heart of the Sun (thus he wants to be understood, like when it is with the Sun in one degree).[41]

Judgment 41: On a peregrine planet

If a planet were on a foreign journey,[42] that is, if it were not in one of its own dignities (as is the exaltation, face, and so on), its mind and nature becomes cunning.[43] And if it were not in its own domicile or exaltation and it were direct, and in a good place from the Ascendant, or in the Midheaven or in the eleventh, it will be good.

If the Moon is joined to some planet, he to whom she is joined is said to be the receiver of the Moon's disposition, and thus reception proceeds up until Saturn (because above Saturn there is no other who would receive disposition).

---

[40] That is, oriental from the Sun (in an earlier degree), rising before the Sun in the morning, but just going out of the beams. This judgment applies particularly to the superiors.
[41] This comment I have made parenthetical seems to be added by the Latin translator, as an interpretation of Sahl.
[42] *In peregrinatione.*
[43] *Callidus.*

Judgment 42: On the receiver of disposition

The receiver of disposition, if it were pertaining-to-sinking[44] by 12° and less in front of the Sun, it will be weak and crushed, and what it judges is not perfected; and if it were pertaining-to-arising,[45] it will be strong and skillful [and] excellent[46] in the judgment. Because an impeded planet is like a building: and if it were to fall, it is rebuilt, improved, and comes to be good.[47]

Judgment 43: On a planet in the 8th domicile[48]

If a planet were in the eighth from the Ascendant, and it were a benefic, it does not perform good nor evil; and if the malefics were in the same place, their evil is made greater.

Judgment 44: On a planet in the beginning of a sign and in the beginning of the angles

If a planet were in the beginning of a sign, it will be weak until it is made firm in it, and walks through it by 6°.[49] And a planet does not fall from the angles except after 5°.[50] For example: if the angle were the tenth degree of Aries, every planet which is in less than 5° [of Aries] is cadent and is not thought to be in the angle.[51]

---

[44] *Occidentalis.* That is, in a later degree than the Sun and setting after him.
[45] *Orientalis.* That is, in an earlier degree than the Sun and rising before him.
[46] *Perfectus.*
[47] The falling down/rebuilding metaphor clearly relates to entering the Sun's beams and then re-emerging on the other side.
[48] Reading "domicile," because the text reads *octavo* below (suggesting a sign).
[49] This could be based on the average size of a bound: 30°/5 bounds = 6° each.
[50] Here Sahl or his translator uses *post* ("after") an angle to indicate being in an "earlier degree" than the angle, having passed it by primary motion.
[51] Here the angle is being associated with quadrant houses; this notion clearly derives from *Tet.* III.11, where Ptolemy applies the so-called "five-degree rule" in the context of longevity determinations. See also *Judgments* 45. See my Introduction, §7c.

Judgment 45: *When a planet after the angle is understood to be in the angle*

And every planet which is after the angle by 15° will be just like one who is in the angle; and if the degree were to increase, he will have no strength. For example: If the angle were the tenth degree of the sign of Aries, then every planet which is from that same tenth degree up to 25° of the same Aries,[52] is thought to be in that same angle. Which if one added 15° on top [of that], it will not be in the angle. But Ptolemy says a planet will be in the angle up into 25° after the angle.[53]

Judgment 46: *What the planets would signify in the signs, concerning the stability of a matter*

If planets were in fixed signs, they signify fixity—that is, firmness and the stability of matters concerning which the question comes to be. And if they were in common signs, they signify the loosenings of matters and repetitions, and other things[54] will be attached to that matter (or some such other thing). And if they were in movable signs, they signify the speed of the conversions or changes of matters into good or evil.

Judgment 47: *What the signs would signify in questions*

A fixed sign signifies the fixity (that is, the firmness) of questions and of the matters concerning which the question comes to be, and every fixed and very firm and stable matter; and it is a good ally of the question. And the common signs signify matters which cannot come to be, and which are repeated a second time. And a movable sign signifies the speed of a matter's changing into something else.

---

[52] Omitting *vir* with BN.
[53] See my Introduction for a discussion of this difficult passage.
[54] *Altera*. This word has to do with repetition or pairs. See *On Elect.* §§16a-17.

Judgment 48: On a stationary planet

If a planet were to stand toward retrogradation (that is, if it were in its first station), it signifies the dissolution of a purpose, and disobedience; and if it were to stand toward direction (that is, if it were in its second station), it signifies forward direction after the slowness or duress of the matter. And every planet which is a significator and wished to go direct (that is, if it were in its second station) signifies the renewal of the actions of matters, and their action and strength or forward movement. And if it were in the first station, wishing to go retrograde, it signifies their destruction and slowness and dissolution.

Judgment 49: On a question made when the Moon is impeded

Know that on a day in which the Moon is impeded, everything concerning which it is asked on that day, will be impeded—unless the malefic impeding her is cadent from the Ascendant and weak, and the Moon did not then have a role[55] in the Ascendant: because if a malefic impedes the Moon, and he were cadent from the Ascendant, he introduces fear and worry; and if he were in the angles or in the followers of the angles,[56] he lets loose[57] fear onto the body.[58]

Judgment 50: On the planet to whom the Moon is joined; and concerning the Moon herself (and the Lord of the Ascendant) in the opposite of her own domicile

Know that the planet to whom the Moon is joined, signifies what is going to be, and the producing[59] of the matter. Which if she is joined to benefics, it signifies a good producing; and if she is joined to a malefic, it signifies a bad producing.

---

[55] *Partem*. This tends to mean having a dignity in the degree of the Ascendant.
[56] That is, the succeedents.
[57] *Ingerit corpori timorem*. *Ingero* has the more specific meaning of heaping or thrusting something on someone.
[58] See *Judgments* 4.
[59] *Proventum*, which has the more specific meaning of "issuing forth," as plants issue forth from the earth (whence in English we speak of fruits and vegetables as "produce").

And know that the Lord of the Ascendant (or the Moon), if it were in the opposition of its own domicile (that is, in the seventh of its own domicile), the master of the question[60] will dread the purpose concerning which he asked: for it will be severe for him. Know all of this.

---

[60] That is, the querent.

ON QUESTIONS

[Now] it follows concerning questions: and first concerning questions of the Ascendant, that is, the 1st domicile

§1.1

If you were asked about some question, you will begin to look just as I have told you before. For I have already established for you the manner from which it is taken in every matter: therefore you should not seek to deviate to something else, nor should you insert a purpose concerning which you were not asked, lest, in the purpose about which you are asked, you would insert something commingled [with it] concerning yourself—as for instance he who asks about a marriage, and when you were looking at this, he asks you about another matter which then came to him. If however you have reflected[1] before the consideration of diverse matters, it is just and right that you should accept each matter from its own heading. Nor is it right that someone might ask in one question about two matters which are of one kind.[2] And you should not look except for him who comes to you hoping, or under necessity, or sad, and who comes to you concerned or with labor. For he who came to you knowingly (as though one crafty or a tester), you should not look for him. Because the matter goes out[3] according to the quantity of the concern of the questioner in the matter about which he asks. Therefore, beware in these chapters: for then the question will be more useful if a man asked about himself, or were to send such a one who would ask for him who is concerned about his matter.

Therefore, know the intentions of men, because the consideration[4] and work comes to be according to the concern and intention of the questioner.

---

[1] Or, "planned" (*meditatus fueris*).
[2] If for example one asked multiple questions concerning money, the planetary combinations would likely give the same answer for each question.
[3] *Exit*. The sense here is of the question arising, appearing, and coming out of the querent's mouth in a certain way.
[4] Below he clarifies that the "consideration" is the astrologer's actual examination of the chart after receiving the question.

For were someone to ask, and his intention in that question were concerning his whole time [of his life], the places of the planets at the hour of the question signify his being for the whole time [of his life]. Likewise, if his intention was to ask about some matter in his year or in a month or in a day (or in whatever such), it will be so. Therefore, understand their intentions before the consideration: because every questioner does not ask except about that which is prevailing in him from the nature of the circle, with his being, about which he asks: namely, from the complexion of the circle, with its being concerning fortune or evil.[5] For they are the branches and parts.[6] Therefore he for whom a benefic comes up to or meets with the Lord[7] of his Ascendant and the Moon, he will be made fortunate; and to whom their impediment corresponds, he will be impeded. Wherefore [no] man asks about the presence of a significator's impediment (that is, of the Moon and the Lord of the Ascendant in the hour of the question or the nativity), unless [he is] impeded and bad (that is, made unfortunate and troubled), or a man who ought to find evils. Likewise fortune: no one asks about it except for every one made fortunate and a man who ought to have fortune. Nor should you be afraid if you were asked about diverse questions under one Ascendant, because the matters come to be diverse: which if more of them agreed in one being (that is, in good or evil), this will be benefic or malefic for them. For we see certain people made fortunate, and others like them made fortunate.

§1.2: A question about the durability and improvement of a matter

If however you were asked about some matter which ought to be profitable and be improved and be stable, look at the conjunction of the Lord of the Ascendant with the Lord of the matter, and the reception of the receiving planet (namely, of the planet who receives the disposition), whether it were the Lord of the matter or the Lord of the Ascendant (namely of the

---

[5] This almost sounds like the "consultation chart" tradition (see Introduction). Note that he is speaking about understanding the querent's *intentions*, not answering his *question*.
[6] Note the similarity between this material and Bonatti's statement that horary practice is like a tree in which questions are the trunk and the considerations of the chart's configuration are the branches (*BOA* p. 371). Bonatti's whole discussion (pp. 371-372) seems to be a reinterpretation of this passage.
[7] Reading *domino* for *domini*.

one who was heavier);[8] and look at his freedom from those things which I have told you regarding the impediments of the planets.

§1.3: A question about the instability of a matter and its changeability

If however it were a question about the instability of a matter or about movement (like foreign travel or change or the going-out of someone imprisoned, or someone's escape from tribulation and sorrow), look in these matters from the place of instability and receding (that is, from the cadents from the angles).

§1.4: A question about some matter pertaining to the twelve signs: if it will come to be or not

And if you were asked about some matter (of the matters which are in the twelve signs),[9] give the Ascendant and its Lord and the Moon as significators of that man who asks you; the sign of the quaesited matter and its Lord[10] to the quaesited matter.

After this,[11] look at the Lord of the Ascendant and the Moon, and the stronger of them (namely the one who was in an angle, and who aspected the Ascendant),[12] and begin from that one. Which if one of them were joined to the Lord of the matter, the matter will be perfected by means of the striving[13] of the one asking. And if you found the Lord of the matter joined with the Lord of the Ascendant, the matter will be perfected with the ease and eagerness[14] of the one asking, without striving, and without any

---

[8] Note that this is not a matter of reception proper, but of receiving disposition; and it needs an applying aspect from the lighter planet to the heavier one.
[9] See §13 for some questions not directly related to houses.
[10] Reading *eius* for *unius* ("the Lord of one").
[11] I have divided up this passage into three paragraphs, since Sahl says that there are three ways in which matters are perfected. But the reader will see that the first paragraph (which ought only to concern perfection "by joining") there is at least one other method: what I call perfection "by location." This method is found throughout Sahl and Māshā'allāh's OR.
[12] Note the similarity to Māshā'allāh's method for picking significators in OR.
[13] *Petitione*, from *peto*, "to strive, search, attach, sue for." But there is no intrinsic suggestion of legal action in the paragraph, so I have opted for the more generic "striving."
[14] *Studium*. This is meant in the sense of actively applying oneself to accomplishing the goal.

unreasonableness. And[15] if you found the Lord of the Ascendant or the Moon in the place of the matter, or you found the Lord of the matter in the Ascendant, the matter will be perfected unless the Ascendant is impeded and its Lord in his own descension or combust in it:[16] then it will not be. And[17] if you found the Lord of the Ascendant or the Moon to be joined to some planet in the place of the purpose,[18] or you found the Lord of the purpose joined to some planet in the Ascendant, and the planet had testimony in it (of domicile or exaltation or triplicity, and the rest), it will be perfected.

And if there were not any of all those things which we have said, then look to see (in the transfer of light) to the Moon or to some one of the light planets: which if you found it separated from the Lord of the Ascendant, and joined to the Lord of the matter, or separated from the Lord of the matter and joined to the Lord of the Ascendant, the matter is perfected by means of the hands of legates of those who run back and forth between each of them.

And if you did not find a planet between them who brings away the light of one of them to its partner, then look in the collection of light: which if you found the Lord of the matter and the Lord of the Ascendant (each of them, namely) joined to one planet heavier than they, and that planet aspected the place of the matter (or were in the Ascendant or in the Midheaven),[19] the matter will be perfected by means of the hands of a judge or man to whom they are sent.

Therefore, from these three methods the effecting of all matters comes to be: first, from the conjunction of the Lord of the Ascendant and the Moon and the Lord of the matter. Second, that some planet brings away the light between them (that is, it is being separated from one of them and would be conjoined to the other): then the matter comes to be through the hands of legates. Third, from the collection of light: that is, that they are both joined to some planet heavier than they, who conjoins their light, taking up the strength of each; and its judgment will be able to be taken up between them,

---

[15] This is perfection "by location."
[16] This probably means "combust, in the Ascendant."
[17] The sort of perfection described in this last paragraph seems to be a combination of perfection "by location" and "by joining," whereby some other planet in the Ascendant or the place of the matter is joined to the key significator.
[18] *Causae*, used here as a synonym for "the quaesited matter."
[19] *Cf. Introduct.* §5.6, which does not specifically mention a whole-sign aspect to the Ascendant or location in the Ascendant or Midheaven.

or through a man who will aid in that same matter. Therefore from these three first headings, the effecting of matters comes to be.[20]

After this, look to see (just as I have told you) at the receiver of the disposition from the one of them who is the heavier planet, whether it was the Lord of the Ascendant or the Lord of the matter, and the planet who collects the light, to see if it were free from the malefics, in the angles or in the followers of the angles (and it were not retrograde nor combust, nor cadent from the angles): the matter will be perfected after its attainment. And if the receiver [of the disposition] were retrograde, it will be dissolved after he thought he had attained it.

§1.5: A question if a matter will come to be with ease or with duress

And if you were asked whether he would attain it with ease or with duress, look to see if there were a conjunction from the Lord of the Ascendant and the Lord of the matter from a trine or from a sextile aspect: the attainment will be with ease; and if it were a conjunction from the square aspect or from their opposition, the attainment will be after duress and inconvenience and prolonging.

§1.6: A question if he will attain the matter through striving,[21] or he will have it without striving

And if you were asked whether he will attain it by means of striving or it would come to him by means of the other[22] without any striving, look at the Lord of the Ascendant and the Moon: if they are joined to the Lord of the

---

[20] Note that the type of perfection describes *how* the perfection will take place: by joining, through the querent's agency or somehow directly; by a transfer of light, through some third party or legate; through collection, by some judge or arbitrator who takes up the matter.

[21] *Petitione.* See above.

[22] Here and below, *utro.* The contrast being drawn is between the querent's significator being the lighter planet, or that of the quaesited. If the querent's significator is the lighter, than the perfection comes from him; if not, then it comes from "the other" direction: some person or thing represented by the quaesited.

matter, this will be with striving.²³ And if the Lord of the matter is joined to the Lord of the Ascendant, it will come by means of the other.²⁴

Moreover,²⁵ if the Lord of the Ascendant or the Moon were in the place of the matter, it will be with the striving and applying²⁶ of the questioner (that is, with his distress, and so on). Indeed if the Lord of the purpose were in the Ascendant, they will be diligent²⁷ concerning him in the matter, and it will be given to him voluntarily. Which if the question were about the arrangement of some honor, it will come by means of the other, and he will not come to the gates of kings on account of this.²⁸

And if the effecting of the matter were from the transfer of light, it will be through legates and those who run back and forth between them. If however the Moon were separated from the Lord of the Ascendant and were joined to the Lord of the matter, the legation will begin from the one asking.²⁹ Indeed if the Moon were separated from the Lord of the matter and joined to the Lord of the Ascendant, a legate will come to him, and there will be diligence upon him in this.³⁰

And if the attainment of the matter were from the collection of light, the attaining of the matter will be through some judge who enters in between them, or through one who enters in the matter until the attaining of the matter comes to be.

And know that if the Lord of the Ascendant or the Moon is joined to a planet from the descension of that planet,³¹ it signifies the detriment of the matter; as for example if she was joined to Mars out of Cancer, or to Jupiter out of Capricorn: for these destroy matters. Likewise, if planets were joined which were in the descension of those who do not receive them: it signifies

---

[23] That is, the querent (as the lighter planet) must go to the quaesited.
[24] So if the Lord of the matter is applying to the querent's significator, the matter will come to the querent.
[25] I have set this passage apart so it is obvious we are speaking about perfection by location.
[26] *Studium*, "eagerness, applying oneself to something, diligence," *etc.*
[27] *Studium*.
[28] That is, since someone else is arranging the matter, he will not have to go begging to the authority who grants the honor.
[29] Since the Moon is standardly a significator of the querent—or of the situation itself in which the querent is engaged.
[30] That is, a legate will come from the other side, and will be diligent in bringing matters about.
[31] See *Introduct.* §5.9.

the bad disposition³² of the master of the question in those things which he wants to do, and that the matter would not be perfected: of which an example is if the Moon would be joined to some planet which was in the third degree of Scorpio (which is the descension of the same Moon), or the Lord of the Ascendant is Mars, and he would be joined to a planet who is in the end of Cancer (which is his descension).

And know that if a malefic were the Lord of the matter, and the Lord of the Ascendant (or the Moon) were joined to him from the square aspect or opposition, and he did not receive them, the questioner will desire that the matter would not come to be on account of the evils or tribulations, and labors which enter in upon him in that matter.³³ If however there were a conjunction from the trine or sextile aspect, it will be decreased from this.

And if the Lord of the Ascendant or the Lord of the matter were one planet (that is, if the Lord of the Ascendant and the Lord of the matter were the same),³⁴ and it were received (that is, joined to the Lord of its own domicile or exaltation) and it were free from malefics,³⁵ the matter will be perfected; and if it were otherwise, the matter will be destroyed. Likewise if the Moon were joined to him and she were safe from defects, it will be perfected.

§1.7: The testimonies of the signs in the effecting of the matter

And know, because the testimonies of the signs in the effecting of matters are: that the Ascendant is a fixed sign or a common one, and the angles stable (that is, that the Midheaven is the tenth sign, and the angle of the earth the fourth sign—and the Midheaven is not the ninth sign, nor does the angle of the earth fall on the third sign).³⁶ This exposition of the angles is of the stable ones.

---

³² "Disposition" here does not mean "mental state," as later horary astrologers often want to assume. It means that the querent is in an *objectively* bad situation, badly prepared, not well-suited, *etc.*, *one component* of which might be having a bad mental state.

³³ Following BN. That is, the matter will have so many problems attached to it, that the querent will regret having asked about or having pursued the matter.

³⁴ *Cf.* §10.2.

³⁵ Reading *et fuerit liber a malis* with BN, for *vel situ erit liber a malis*. Remember that *malum* can also simply mean an "evil," so it could be read "and it were free from evils."

³⁶ Here Sahl is clearly speaking about the fact that the MC-IC axis can fall on signs not corresponding to the tenth and fourth, he is *not* necessarily advocating quadrant houses

§1.8: The testimonies of the planets in the effecting of matters

And[37] the testimonies of the stars in the effecting [of matters] are three, from which the Lord of the Ascendant and the Moon and the Lord of the matter are sought. If two of them (that is, the Lord of the Ascendant and the Lord of the matter) were free from the aforesaid malefics, two-thirds of the matter will be perfected; and if one of them were safe, one-third of the matter which he demanded[38] will be perfected—this is, if it had one testimony, he will have one-third. And if there were two testimonies, he will attain two-thirds of those things which he sought; and if the three testimonies were joined (that is, if the Lord of the Ascendant and the Lord of the matter and the Moon were safe from retrogradation and combustion—also from the malefics and from descension or fall), he will attain everything which he sought. And if they were received with their own two testimonies, and even he who received them were received, his good will be increased above that which he sought. Know therefore these questions, because they are conjoined to, and are consistent with, all matters.

---

for topics: he is only interested in whether the angles are *stable*. However, he seems to be contradicting his (or the Latin translator's) earlier statements (*Introduct.* §§3, 4, 9) that define the "angle of the earth" *as* the fourth sign or domicile. Perhaps in the earlier passages he is simply *assuming* an idealized chart—which seems to be confirmed in the next sentence, since he seems to say he will not overcomplicate matters by assuming unstable angles. Still, this does not help us much, because we still want to know in a given case whether, say, we should look at the tenth sign or the sign with the degree of the Midheaven to look for matters pertaining to honors, kings, *etc.*

[37] This passage bears a strong resemblance to *BOA* pp. 367-68.

[38] *Postulaverit.* "Demanded" is perhaps a bit too strong. The sense is that the querent is pursuing a matter and is trying hard to bring it about: so the astrological consultation is part of his overall prosecution of the matter.

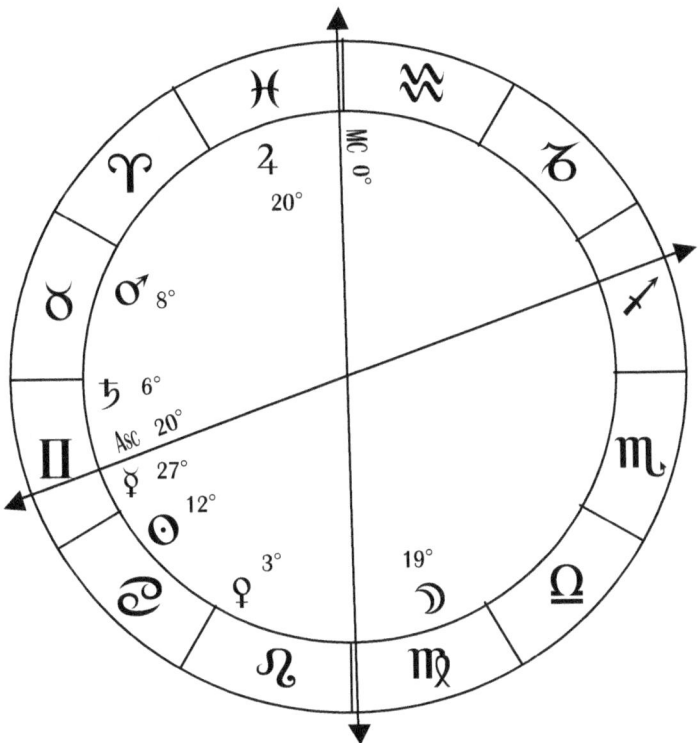

Figure 10: Acquiring a Kingdom

An example[39] of which matter is a certain question which was made for a kingdom—whether he would acquire it or not. And the Ascendant was the sign of Gemini, 20°; and the Midheaven, the first degree of the sign of Pisces; and the Sun in Cancer, 12°; and the Moon in Virgo, 19°; and Mercury in Gemini, 27°; and Mars in Taurus, 8°; and Venus in Leo, 3°; and Jupiter in Pisces, 20°, in the first station, wanting to go retrograde; and Saturn in Gemini, 6°.

Therefore I looked, in this question, to the ascending sign and its Lord, and the Moon (which are the significators of the one asking), and at the sign of the Midheaven and its Lord (which are the significators of the kingdom concerning which the question was). And the Ascendant was the sign of

---

[39] This chart was cast for a latitude of about 34°N. The date is approximately July 5, 824 AD GC, so it is likely a chart of Sahl's own. Bonatti's version of this chart (*BOA* p. 375) puts the Head and Tail of the Dragon at 22° of Pisces and Virgo respectively, though my dating puts them at 29°.

Gemini, and Mercury in it (namely the Ascendant), in the end of the sign. And Jupiter, who was the Lord of the matter, in the Midheaven in the twentieth degree.[40] And I found the Lord of the Ascendant separated from the Lord of the matter. Therefore I looked at the Moon, whom I found in the angle of the earth, joined to Jupiter from the opposition. And it signifies the attainment of the matter through winning and unreasonableness because they were joined from the opposition.[41] And if they had been joined from the sextile or trine aspect, the attaining would come to be with ease. And the Moon (who was joined to the Lord of the matter) was signifying that this would come to be through the striving and diligence of the one asking. And if the Lord of the matter had been the one who was being joined,[42] the attaining of the matter would be through the undertaking of him who would organize it, without the striving or inconvenience of the one asking.

Therefore, I looked even at Jupiter, who was the receiver of the disposition: and I found him in the Midheaven, in his first station, wanting to go retrograde, signifying the dissolution of the matter which I said;[43] and its detriment would be more quickly; and this will be from the direction of the king, on account of Jupiter (who was the Lord of the 10th domicile, which is the royal house, and who was signifying the king). And if the Lord of the Ascendant had been the receiver of the disposition, and he had been impeded, I would have said that the detriment would come to be from the one asking, and because of his own doing, because the Lord of the Ascendant was being changed from his own domicile into the domicile of substance, which signifies the quickness of the change of the one asking, and his journey for the sake of seeking substance to the place in which he was making a delay;[44] and he would not have received this, because when he went out from

---

[40] Perhaps there was some mix-up over the Arabic in the Latin translator's mind: above, Sahl said "20°" (*20. gradus*).
[41] That is, the aspect showed perfection by joining, and the opposition showed it would be with unreasonableness (or inconvenience), and a contention he would win.
[42] That is, if the Lord of the matter (Jupiter) had been the lighter, applying planet.
[43] See the rule for this above, §1.4.
[44] *Moram*, a delay, period of time, pause. BN reads: "which signifies the quickness of the change (of the one asking, and of his matters, through the seeking of substance), to the place in which he would make a delay." Meaning somewhat unclear. Bonatti's version (*BOA* p. 377) reads: "it signified that the querent changed his own purpose quickly [from one] to another, and because he was changed to the 2nd house, it seemed that the change would be the reason that he would acquire for himself substance which he did not have."

his own sign, he was joined to Mars; and he will not receive him. And[45] indeed this signified that he committed in his exit such a deed through which detriment and sorrow entered upon him. And because Mars was the Lord of the sixth from the Ascendant (which is the domicile of slaves and infirmities), he signified that that which I said would come to be from the direction of slaves and low-class persons, and from an infirmity.

And because Jupiter was the Lord of the matter, who wanted to go retrograde, and he was with the Tail, it signifies the dissolution which would enter in upon the man from whom the matter was sought, and a multitude of commingling;[46] and the separation of Mercury from the Lord of the matter signified that the questioner would be before that day,[47] that is, before the time itself in the hope of the matter: that is, he was hoping that it would be perfected for him; and since he was being separated from the Lord of the matter, he lost hope of it. Likewise in all matters generally.

§1.8: A chapter on the corruption[48] of the Ascendant[49]

And it is necessary that this should not be missing from it in nativities (and likewise questions). And indeed it corrupts questions, and corrupts the life of the native. Indeed Māshā'allāh, cutting off hidden things from this.[50] And it is that you should look at the star shining[51] or conquering in nativities and questions; and at the star with which the Lord of the Ascendant or the

---

[45] Here Sahl is shifting from saying what he *would* say if Mercury had been receiving the disposition, to stating that Mercury shows these problems *anyway*. As we will see below, Sahl does want to take Mercury into account, even though Jupiter by himself has already shown that the matter will be destroyed after it is thought to be attained.
[46] Perhaps the Latin translator means this in the sense of "confusion," or as we would say, "mixed messages" or a conflict in motives and decisions.
[47] Adding *ipsum* with BN.
[48] Reading *corruptione* for *coniunctione*.
[49] This section does not appear in BN. Moreover, its style changes somewhat. I believe this must be a later interpolation by a different author. Bonatti must have used the same source as 1493, as he gives his own version of this section (*BOA* pp. 378*ff*).
[50] This sentence fragment has no clear operative verb, and I am not sure of its function besides saying that Māshā'allāh has something to do with this doctrine.
[51] *Lucentem*. This is a verb not otherwise used by the Latin translator of Sahl, and a sign that something new is happening. *Luceo* means to shine or glow, and at first glance it seems to mean "aspect." But its pairing with *vinceo* ("conquer") also suggests some unexplained technical meaning.

Lord of the matter is joined,[52] or to whom the Moon is joined, when[53] the Moon is the partner of the Lord of the Ascendant—or [the star] is shining or conquering over the Ascendant and its Lord and the Lord of the matter in a question.

Therefore, consider the star conjoined to the one to which it is conjoined.[54] For if it is joined with a malefic who does not receive it, or with a retrograde star, or with a cadent one, or with a combust star, or with a star made unfortunate by the cutting-off[55] of light, the matter is corrupted. And if it is conjoined with a star, and that star is safe, and there is a conjunction to that star,[56] we look at the star with which that star is joined until the conjunctions are made less: then we look from the ones conjoined with it; and if it has one cutting off[57] according to what we have described in the first [statements above], the matter will be corrupted after it is made right.[58] And if it does not have one cutting off, then the question is complete. And if it is conjoined in the beginning of the matter with one made unfortunate, it is cut off with corruption; which if the unfortunate one is a reception without a square and without opposition, and without equality,[59] the matter will be completed when it is without opposition and without a square. And if it is conjoined in the beginning of the matter with a benefic, and it has no conjunction with one made unfortunate, the matter is completed. And if a star transfers light between each star, and the light and the star to which the light is transferred were cadent, upon the unfortunate one, not received, the matter is corrupted. And if the light of two stars is aggregated,[60] and the one aggregating between them were made unfortunate, the matter is corrupted. And if it is receiving one of them and not receiving the other one, it is corrupted.

---

[52] Reading *iunctus* for *iunctas*.
[53] *Quando*. One might expect *cum*, "since," since the Moon is generally one of the significators of the querent as well.
[54] This seems needlessly redundant—it seems we are simply to identify the special planet, and see to whom it is conjoined.
[55] *Abscisi*, which may be a misprint for *abscisione*.
[56] *Et stellae est coniunctio*, another seeming redundancy.
[57] *Et si est ei abscindens*. This paragraph has a number of dative possessives, which the Latin translator of Sahl does not normally use, another sign that this section has a strange origin.
[58] *Post rectificationem*.
[59] *Parilitas*. It is unclear what this means; perhaps a corporal conjunction?
[60] This might refer to the collection of light—again, the fact that the text uses *aggregatio* and not *collectio* is a further indication that some other translation has been interpolated here.

§2.1: The second sign or 2nd domicile, and whatever is in it concerning questions

If you were asked about some substance which is hoped for, whether he who asked you would find the substance or not: look at the Lord of the Ascendant and the Moon (who are the significators of the one asking), and the sign of substance and its Lord (which are the significators of substance). If the Lord of the Ascendant (and the Moon) is joined to the Lord of the domicile of substance, or the Lord of the domicile of substance were joined to the Lord of the Ascendant, or you found the Moon bearing away the light from the Lord of the domicile of substance to the Lord of the Ascendant, or from the Lord of the Ascendant to the Lord of the domicile of substance, he will attain the substance. Likewise, if Jupiter or Venus (which are benefics) were in the domicile of substance, he will find substance. And if there were nothing of those things which I have said, he will find nothing.[61] Indeed if the malefics were in the domicile of substance (which is the 2nd from the Ascendant), it signifies detriment in the substance of the house of the question. And if the Moon were void in course, then the questioner will not cease to be such until he dies.[62]

§2.2: A question about the kind of wealth

If however you were asked what kind of wealth it will be, look at the receiver of the disposition, whether it were the Lord of the Ascendant or the Lord of the matter (namely, the one which is heavier): which if he were in the Ascendant or in the second, he will find and acquire from the works of his own hands. And if he were in the third, from brothers and from friends. And if he were in the fourth, from the father or from parents[63] or from lands or from real estate. And if he were in the fifth, from children or from others in whom he has trust.[64] And if he were in the sixth, from infirmity and from slaves or from low-class persons. And if he were in the seventh, from women (if it were a feminine sign) or because of war or contention (if

---

[61] Sahl does not mention collection of light, but perhaps it is merely implied.
[62] But surely this must apply only to universal questions, such as "will I ever attain substance?" The question started out implying that there was a *particular* bit of wealth being sought.
[63] *Parentibus*, in the broader sense of older relatives.
[64] Perhaps because the fifth is opposite the eleventh?

it were masculine). And if he were in the eighth, from the things left over from the dead, and ancient things. And if he were in the ninth, from foreign travel and from sects or oratorical things. And if he were in the tenth, from kings and magistrates or from nobles. And if he were in the eleventh, from friends and business dealings or merchandizing. And if he were in the twelfth from the Ascendant, from enemies—and if it were a sign of quadrupeds, from beasts; and if it were of the signs of men, from prisons and their inhabitants. These are the natures of the twelve signs: the acquisition will be from wherever you found a benefic, from the substance and nature of that sign. And wherever you found malefics, thence will be detriment and confusion. Thus, look to see in all matters so that you know in what way there will be ease and what kind of disposition it will be.

§3: The third sign or 3rd domicile, with its questions

If you were asked about the being of the brother, look at the third sign (which is the sign of the brother) and its Lord, and the aspect of the benefic and malefic planets to it.[65] If you found the Lord of the third in the sixth from the Ascendant (which is the domicile of infirmity), or joined to the Lord of the sixth, say that his brother is taken infirm. Likewise if the Lord of the sixth were in the third. And if you found the Lord of the third in the fifth or in the second, his brother will be absent;[66] and if he were impeded in the twelfth, his brother will have an infirmity and sorrow; and if it is entering into combustion, he will not escape from this. You will announce likewise concerning the substance of the signs. And if he were to question you about his own father or mother, [take it] from the fourth; and concerning his own child, from the fifth from the Ascendant. And concerning his own slaves, from the sixth. And concerning his own wife, from the seventh, just as I told you before, if God wills.

---

[65] The "it" could be either the sign itself, or the Lord.
[66] The fifth is the third (short journeys) from the third, and the second is the twelfth (very long journeys, imprisonments) from the third.

§4.1: The fourth sign or 4th domicile, and concerning its questions

If you were asked about land (whether about a house or real estate) which someone sought—whether he would get it or not—look at the Lord of the Ascendant or the Moon (which are the significators of the one asking); the fourth sign and its Lord (which are the significators of the land). If the Lord of the Ascendant or the Moon were joined to the Lord of the fourth, or the Lord of the fourth were joined to the Lord of the Ascendant, or if the Lord of the Ascendant or the Moon were in the fourth, or the Lord of the fourth were in the Ascendant, he will get it. Which if the Moon would bear away the light from one of them to the other, he will get it through the hands of legates.

§4.2: On real estate which is obtained: what kind it is, and concerning a building and concerning everything which is in it

If[67] you were asked about some real estate which is obtained—what kind it is, its condition and its buildings, and whatever is in it, you will set up the Ascendant at the hour in which you were asked about it, and make it the significator of the farmers (namely, those of the farmers who work on it). And the fourth sign signifies the land and what kind it is. And the seventh sign signifies whatever is in it in terms of what follows [trees in size]—that which is less than trees.[68] And from the Midheaven, whatever is in it in terms of trees.

And if there were a malefic planet in the Ascendant, the farmers will be robbers and deceitful;[69] and if it were direct, they will remain on the land. Indeed if it were retrograde, they will flee from it. And if it were a benefic in the Ascendant, the farmers will be just and faithful. And if the benefic were direct, they will not go from the land. Indeed if it were retrograde, they will leave.

And if there were a benefic in the Midheaven, it signifies a multitude of trees; and if it were direct, its trees will be strong and abounding in fruit. Indeed if it were retrograde, they will suffer impediment and the buyer will

---

[67] For all of these 4th-house questions, see *Carmen* V.8-10.
[68] See *Carmen* V.10. This refers to grasses and herbs and plants.
[69] *Seductores*.

gather them up[70] and will sell all the fruits of the trees. Indeed if there were a malefic in the Midheaven, it signifies a scarcity of the fruit of the trees; and if it were retrograde, what remains in them will be sold. And if there were not a planet in the Midheaven, look at the Lord of the Midheaven: if it aspected the Midheaven, there will be trees in it; and if it were oriental, the trees will be newly planted; if indeed it were occidental, the trees will be from a planting of ancient people. And if it were direct, they will remain; indeed if it were retrograde, they will not remain but will be destroyed. And if the Lord of the Midheaven did not aspect his own place (that is, if he were in the second from it, or in the sixth, or in the eighth, or in the twelfth),[71] the land will be without trees.

After this, look at the seventh sign, just as I have told you before in the Midheaven for substance.

But for the land, look at the fourth sign from the Ascendant, to see if it were Aries, Leo or Sagittarius: the land will be mountainous[72] and hard to cultivate—that is, needing much cultivating. And if it were Taurus or Virgo or Capricorn, the land will be flat. And if it were[73] Gemini or Libra or Aquarius, it will be in two ways: that is, [both] mountainous and level. And if it were Cancer or Scorpio or Pisces, it will be watery or next to waters. And if the fourth sign were common (that is, Gemini or Virgo, Sagittarius or Pisces), the land will be in these two ways: this is, there will be mountains and level fields on the land.

And if you wished to rent out the land or its parts, or you wished to populate it, or to elect some such thing, look at the matter of the seller from the Ascendant; and that of the buyer from the seventh; and the end of his work and his purpose[74] from the Midheaven; and from the fourth sign, the end of the matter.

And if there were a benefic in the Ascendant, the seller will be fit, and he will be eager. And if there were a malefic in it, it will pain him to have sold, and he will be moved away from this,[75] or he wanted to sell it with craftiness and will not perfect it. And if there were a malefic in the seventh, the buyer

---

[70] Reading *comparebit* for *compariet*.
[71] That is, if he were in the eleventh, ninth, third, or fifth, since these places are cadent from the tenth.
[72] Reading *montosa* for *mortuosa*.
[73] Reading *fuerit* for *fuerint*.
[74] Reading as *causam*. That is, what his aim is, apart from how things will turn out (the fourth).
[75] That is, he will withdraw his offer. See *Carmen* V.8.2-3.

will turn back, that is, he will be pained and [the seller] will not hand it over to him; and if he did hand it over, he will enter into a quarrel and an abomination,[76] and it will not be perfected for him. And if there were a benefic in it, the buyer himself will be useful and fit. And if you found a malefic in the Midheaven, or it aspected it with an aspect of enmity, the business deal itself will not go forward. Indeed if there were a malefic in the fourth or it aspected it (that is, the fourth), the end will be in the greatest evil. And if it were a benefic, the end will be good and praiseworthy, if God wills.

§5.1: The fifth sign or 5th domicile, with its questions; and first, whether he would have a child from [a certain] woman or not

If someone were to ask you whether he would have a child from this woman or not, look at the Lord of the Ascendant and the Moon to see if they were joined to the Lord of the domicile of children, or [if] the Lord of the domicile of children were joined to the Lord of the Ascendant, or the Lord of the domicile of children were in the Ascendant, or the Lord of the Ascendant or the Moon were in the domicile of children, or you found a planet who renders the light between the Lord of the Ascendant and the Lord of the domicile of children: he will have a child. And if there were a rendering of light[77] in that same place, there will be a delay in this.[78]

After this, look to the receiver of the disposition (which is the heavier planet): which if he were free from the malefics (that is, if he was not joined to them, nor were they joined to him), and he was not cadent from the Ascendant nor combust, the child will live. And if the aforesaid planet were retrograde or combust, or were[79] cadent from the angles, after this [the child] will perish.

And if you found Jupiter in a good place from the Ascendant, and he were not impeded nor under the rays of the Sun, it signifies a pregnancy. And if a malefic planet were with Venus, it does not signify pregnancy. In-

---

[76] Dorotheus says there will be debauchery or prostitution or deception in it.
[77] I suspect this might be a "returning" of light, since earlier in the paragraph the rendering (*redditus*) signified pregnancy. Or perhaps Sahl means that if a planet *in* the fifth is transferring light between them, it is as though the light skips through the fifth—hence the delay, even with perfection.
[78] It is useful to keep track of all of the methods of perfection Sahl customarily uses: here he uses joining, location, and transfer of light. For some reason he omits collection.
[79] Reading *fuerit* for *erit*.

deed if the Moon were joined to malefics, know that she will not be impregnated. And if you found a benefic in the 5th (which is the domicile of children), the woman will be made pregnant; and if the malefics were in it, or they aspected it from the opposition or from the square aspect, it does not signify pregnancy.

§5.2: Whether a child will be born to him or not

And if a man or woman were to ask whether he [or she] would have a child or not,[80] look at the Ascendant. If benefics were in it, or[81] the Lord of the Ascendant were in the Ascendant or in the 10th or in the 11th[82] or in the 5th, and Jupiter were in an optimal place, a child will be born to him [or her]. And if the Lord of the Ascendant were in the 4th or in the 7th, and Jupiter in a good place, a child will be born to him after a delay from his question. But if you found a malefic in the Ascendant, or it aspected it from the opposition or from a square aspect, and the Lord of the Ascendant were in a bad place, and Jupiter were cadent or in the domicile of death or under the rays, it signifies a scarcity of children, and that they will endure [only] a middling amount [of time]—if there were [any children].

And you should not neglect to look at the fifth from the Ascendant, which is the sign of children: in which, if there were benefics, a child will be born to him quickly; and if malefics were in there, and you saw some good in the question, there will be a child but he will quickly see [the child's] death. And if you found Jupiter oriental in an angle, a child will be born to him quickly. Indeed if he were occidental in an angle (that is, if he appeared in the evening in the west),[83] and the Lord of the Ascendant were in a suitable place, one will be born to him slowly and after some delay.

---

[80] Sahl's description of this question focuses more on the Ascendant, which leads me to think this question is meant "absolutely": that is, "will I *ever* have children." This is to be distinguished from the previous question, in which there is a particular relationship already existing.

[81] Omitting *aspexerit* with BN. But perhaps the benefics aspecting the 5th would be good, too (though probably not definitive).

[82] Reading *undecimo* with BN for *secundo*.

[83] That is, setting after the Sun, out of the rays.

§5.3: Whether a woman is pregnant or not, and whether she will give birth or not

And if you were asked about some woman, whether she is pregnant or not, and whether she will give birth or not, or it would be perfected for her or not, look at the Lord of the Ascendant and the Moon (which are the significators of the children). If you found the Lord of the Ascendant and the Moon in the house of children, and the Lord of the house of children were in the Ascendant, free from the malefics, say that she is pregnant. And if the Lord of the Ascendant and the Moon pushed—that is, if they committed—their own disposition, there will be a pregnancy; and better than that if it were received. And if they were joined to a planet cadent from the Ascendant, it signifies detriment and that the pregnancy will be in vain—and more strongly than that if the Ascendant were a movable sign, or there were a malefic in an angle, or if the Moon were joined to a malefic: because all of these things signify detriment. But the receiver of the disposition (that is, the heavier planet who receives all the disposition from the Lord of the Ascendant or the Moon[84]), if it were free from the malefics (that is, if it was not joined to them nor were they joined to it), and it were in a good place, the pregnancy will be perfected.

§5.4: Whether the pregnancy is true or false

And if he were to ask about a pregnancy, whether it would be true or false (that is, whether it would come to effect or be in vain), look at the Lord of the Ascendant. Which if he were joined to a planet cadent from the Ascendant, nor to one receiving,[85] it signifies detriment. Likewise if he were joined to a retrograde planet—unless[86] the Moon were received, or the Lord of the Ascendant were in a good place from the Ascendant: because then it signifies pregnancy.

---

[84] Reading *luna* for *lunae*.
[85] *Recipienti*. I believe this means, "nor to one receiving *him*."
[86] Reading *nisi* with BN.

§5.5: Whether a pregnant woman will give birth to twins or not

And if you were asked about a pregnant woman, whether she would give birth to twins or not, look at the Ascendant in the hour in which you were asked, to see if it was a common sign, or if there were two benefic planets in the Ascendant or in the domicile of children: she will be pregnant with twins (that is, she carries twins). Likewise if you found the Sun and Moon in common signs. And if the Ascendant (nor the sign of children) was not common, nor were there what I said in them, nor were the luminaries in common signs, the pregnant woman carries only one [child].

§5.6: Whether she will give birth to a masculine or feminine [child]

And if you were asked whether she will give birth to a masculine or a feminine [child], look at the Lord of the Ascendant and the Lord of the domicile of children, to see if they were in masculine signs: it will be a masculine one in her belly; and if they were in feminine signs, it will be a feminine one in her belly. And if one of them were in a masculine sign and the other in a feminine sign, look at the sign in which the Moon is, and the planet to whom the Moon were joined. If the Moon were in a masculine sign and she were joined to a masculine planet, she will give birth to a masculine one. Indeed if the Moon were in a feminine sign or[87] she were joined to a feminine planet, she will give birth to a feminine one. And know that Mercury, if he were oriental (that is, when he rises before the Sun), will be masculine; and if he were occidental (that is, when he rises after the Sun), it will be feminine one, if God wills.

§6.1: The sixth sign or 6th domicile, with its questions: and first, if an infirm person will be healed or die

If[88] you were asked about an infirm person, whether he would be healed or die, look at the Ascendant. For the Ascendant signifies the doctor; and the

---

[87] The text reads *aut*, unlike the masculine situation, which said "and." It is difficult to say whether both of these situations (the gender of the sign and the gender of the planet) should read "or" or "and."
[88] See *Carmen* V.41.35-41, attributed to "Qitrinus the Sadwali."

Midheaven signifies the infirm person;[89] and the seventh sign signifies the infirmity;[90] indeed the fourth sign signifies the medicine.[91]

> If there were a malefic in the Ascendant, the medicine of the doctors will not profit him. But if there were a benefic in the Ascendant, the doctors' medicine and their cure will profit him.

> And if there were a malefic in the Midheaven, the infirm person will not be of aid to himself, but will stimulate[92] the infirmity upon himself—and[93] this because the infirm person will be disobedient to the instructions of the doctor. But if there were a benefic in the tenth, the infirm person will cure himself with those things which profit him.[94]

> And if there were a malefic in the seventh, he will be turned from infirmity to infirmity; and if there were a benefic in the same place,[95] health will come over him without any cure by which he could be cured.

> And if there were a malefic in the fourth sign, the medicine will increase the nature of [the illness's] strength [over] him—that is, the medicine will make him worse. And if there were a benefic in the same place, it will be profitable for him.

After this, look at the Lord of the Ascendant and the Moon, and begin[96] from that one which was in an angle and aspected the Ascendant, to see if it were free from the malefics and were not in the aspect of the Lord of the domicile of death (and especially in the fourth or seventh)[97]—which is the

---

[89] Reading *infirmum* for *infirmem*.
[90] Reading *infirmitatem* for *infirmitatum*.
[91] In this arrangement, the real subject of action is the doctor (Ascendant), who battles the infirmity (seventh); his goal (tenth) is the health of the patient, who is confronted by the medicine (fourth).
[92] *Excito*. Or, "stir up."
[93] Adding the rest of this sentence from BN.
[94] *Cum quibus sibi proficiunt.*
[95] Reading this clause from BN.
[96] Adding *incipe* from BN.
[97] If we follow this reading, then it means that, even if the Lord of the Ascendant or the Moon *were* in an angle and in aspect to the Lord of the eighth, it would be even worse if the angle were the seventh or the fourth. But BN reads, "and especially in the square or

eighth sign from the Ascendant—nor were it under the rays: it signifies health; and if it were joined to a benefic it even signifies health. If however the benefic were retrograde, it signifies the lengthiness[98] of the infirmity (but he will be healed).[99]

And if the Moon were not above the earth but she were joined to a planet which is above the earth, it signifies health. And if she were above the earth, it signifies health (unless the planetary receiver of the disposition would be entering combustion, because then it signifies death). And if the Moon were above the earth and were joined to a malefic below the earth, it signifies death. And if the Moon is joined to the Lord of the Ascendant, and [the Lord] were increased in light and number, it signifies the quickness of his healing and the improvement of his body.

And if the Lord of the Ascendant were below the earth, and the Moon were joined to a planet in the ninth from the Ascendant (wanting to be cadent),[100] it signifies death. And if the Lord of the Ascendant were joined to the Lord of the domicile of death, and with the Moon impeded, it signifies death. And if the Moon carried light from the Lord of the Ascendant to the Lord of the 8th, it will have to be feared, because it is evil.[101] And if he[102] were received, the infirmity will be prolonged. Indeed if the Lord of the Ascendant were joined to the Lord of the 8th from a trine aspect, and the Lord of the Ascendant were in an angle, [then] when the Lord of the domicile of death arrived at the degree of the ascending sign, it will signify death. And if some planet rendered[103] the light of the Lord of the Ascendant to the Lord of the eighth, and the Lord of the Ascendant were cadent, and the Lord of the eighth in an angle, it signifies death. And if the Lord of the domicile of death were in the Ascendant, and the Lord of the Ascendant or the Moon were impeded, it signifies death; and if the receiver

---

seventh aspect," i.e., simply clarifying that the square and opposition are the worse aspects to have with the Lord of the eighth.

[98] *Prolixitatem*.

[99] This parenthetical remark is from 1493.

[100] This is unusual, since both by whole-sign houses and quadrant houses, a planet in the ninth is cadent. Usually the phrase "wanting to _____" is filled by the phrase "go retrograde." I have not seen this construction with cadence before.

[101] I think this is because the Lord of the 8th would then be the "receiver of the disposition."

[102] I believe this is the Lord of the 8th.

[103] This example (and one above) shows that rendering is a broader concept, which can be synonymous with transfers of light. It does not simply mean the projection of light to an empty place in the zodiac (as the usage in some passages of Bonatti might suggest).

were impeded, it signifies death; and if the receiver of the disposition were impeded, it signifies a rupture[104]—that is, a relapse after healing.

Also, the presence of the Lord of the eighth in the angles [is] evil;[105] and if the Lord of the Ascendant were not above the earth, and he were joined to the Lord of the eighth in the fourth and in the domicile of death, it signifies death. And if the Lord of the eighth did not aspect the Lord of the Ascendant, but some planet rendered their light, and the Lord of the Ascendant were cadent, and the Lord of the eighth in an angle, it signifies death. And if the Lord of the Ascendant is entering combustion (that is, if there were less than 12° between him and the Sun), he will die. Likewise if he were combust and were not received.[106]

Which if a planet did not push disposition (that is, if it were a receiving planet),[107] and it were free from combustion, and the Moon were sound, it signifies escape. And if the domicile of infirmities[108] were a movable sign, the infirm person will be relieved at one time and made worse at another time. And if it were a common [sign], he will be changed from one infirmity to another. And if it were fixed, he will remain in one condition.

And if the Moon were separated from an oriental planet (that is, one rising in the east in the morning), the infirmity will be new and recent. And if the Moon were separated from an occidental planet (that is, one appearing in the late hour[109]) his infirmity is already prolonged. And if she were joined to an oriental planet, it signifies quickness. Indeed if the Moon were joined to an occidental planet, his infirmity will be prolonged—and better than this is if the benefics aspected the Lord of the Ascendant, and he himself were in a good place from the Ascendant. And worse will be the aspect of the malefics to him if it were from the square aspect or from the opposition, or [a malefic] were with him in one sign. And if the Moon were joined to a retrograde planet, it signifies the long-lastingness of the disease. And if she were joined to a slower planet, it signifies making worse, and it will render him afraid.

---

[104] *Fractionem.*
[105] Reading *mala* for *malum.*
[106] This must mean reception in the normal sense.
[107] Following 1493. BN says, "that is, if it were *not* a receiving planet."
[108] The 6th.
[109] *Sero.* This must mean "appearing in the west in the evening," to match the statement made above.

§6.2: On critical days by the place of the Moon

Know[110] even the place of the Moon on the seventh day from the beginning of his infirmity *and* of the question about it—and on the fourteenth and on the twenty-first and on the twenty-eighth day.[111] For the Moon, on the day she arrives to the malefics or to the Lord of the domicile of infirmity, the infirm person will be made worse on that same day; and when she arrives to the benefics or they aspected her, health and rest from the infirmity will happen to him.

And for knowing the condition of the infirm person on the seventh day, you will add 90° on top of the place of the Moon, and you will advance from the degree of the Moon: in which one the number arrived, there will be the place of the Moon on the seventh day. Indeed for the fourteenth day, add 180° on top of her place, and this is the opposition of her place in which was that day on which the infirmity or[112] the question began. And for the twenty-first day, add 270° on top of her place. Indeed on the twenty-seventh day the Moon returns to her place—that is, to the sign and to the degree in which she was at the beginning of the infirmity or question.[113] And as often as the Moon would be joined on these days to some benefic, so often will the infirm person find rest and improvement; and as often as she would be joined to a malefic, so often will his pain increase and be made burdensome.

§6.3: Whether someone is infirm or not

If you were asked about some man whether he is infirm or not, look at the Lord of the Ascendant (and the Moon): which if he were in the sixth from the Ascendant (which is the domicile of infirmities), or he were joined to the Lord of the sixth, or in his own descension, or combust under the rays, say he is taken ill; but lacking these, not.

---

[110] See *Carmen* V.41.10-18, attributed to "Qitrinus the Sadwali."
[111] Emphasis mine: we can look at the critical days from the decumbiture, but also from the time of the consultation. But we do not know if Sahl prefers one or the other.
[112] Note that now he says "or."
[113] This statement means we are not measuring the lunar month itself, but only the Moon's travel through the twelve signs—which would take less time than the average lunar month, since in a lunar month the Moon must travel even further to catch up with the Sun.

§6.4: Whether a slave will be freed from servitude or not

And if a slave were to ask whether he would be freed from servitude or not, look at the Lord of the Ascendant and the Moon. And if you found some one of them separated from the Lord of the Midheaven or from the Sun, or from the malefics, and it was not joined to any of those which I have said before,[114] say he is going to be free; but lacking this, not.

§6.5: A question if a slave, free from one [master], will serve another

And if a slave were to ask, asking "Should I go away from the hand of my master to another, or not," look in this at the Lord of the Ascendant to see if it is in an angle and is not joined to a planet cadent from the Ascendant: he will not go out from his hand. And if [the Lord of the Ascendant] were joined to some planet in the ninth or in the third, it signifies he is going out. Indeed if the Lord of the Ascendant were in an angle, impeded due to the opposition or due to the conjunction or from the square aspect [of the malefics], or he is entering combustion, he will die before he goes away from his master.

§6.6: A question whether the present master would be better for the slave, or a future one

And[115] if a slave were to ask you, saying "is my master (in whose house I am) better for me, or he whom I want, or to whose house I am setting out," look at the Lord of the Ascendant to see if he were received in the sign in which he is (that is, if he were joined to the Lord of his own domicile or exaltation): his master with whom he is, and the place in which he is, is better for him. Indeed if the Lord of the seventh were received, he to whom he wishes to go will be better for him.

Then, look at the planet from whom the Moon is being separated, and the planet to whom the Moon is being joined: and if the planet from whom the Moon is being separated were a benefic, his master with whom he is, is better

---

[114] I believe Sahl is referring to the previous chapter.
[115] For this question, see *Carmen* V.13.

for him; and if he to whom she is being joined received the Moon, [then] he whom he seeks will be better for him. And if she is not being joined to any, look at the Lord of the Ascendant and the Moon to see if one of them were received in the sign in which it is, or it was a sign in which it is its Lord, exaltation, or triplicity, and so on:[116] his master with whom he is, is better for him. Which if he were received in the second sign from that one in which he is, or it will be suitable for him,[117] then he to whom he goes will be better for him than his own master; and God knows best.

§6.7: A general question about the changing of matters from place to place: which one is better, either the one in which he is or the one to which it is changed

You will judge likewise for a man making a foreign journey, concerning his own condition in the land in which he is, or concerning his own condition in that one to which he is going to go (that is, if he were to ask which one of them will be better for him). Likewise, look in the revolution: that is, in the changing of any matter, when namely he[118] ought to be changed from mansion to mansion, and the condition of the man from house to house, and from land to land, and from one work to another. And however often you were asked about two matters, which of them would be better, look in this just as I have told you before.

---

[116] That is, if the Lord of the Ascendant is either received or is itself in a sign in which it has rulership by domicile, exaltation, triplicity, *etc.*

[117] I think what this means is the following: if the Lord of the Ascendant or the Moon is not currently received or in one of its own dignities, then change it to the next sign and see if it will then be received or in one of its own dignities—in that case, it indicates the former slave will be better after he "changes houses": that is, with the new master. The reader will see other cases in which Sahl changes planets to the next sign to see what will happen.

[118] It is hard to say based on the Latin whether this means the matter is changing from place to place (which must have some technical meaning) or the man himself is. This is connected to the difficulty earlier in the sentence: what is meant here by "revolution"—a solar revolution? Or does this refer to annual profections? Perhaps we are to apply these horary rules above to the solar revolution alone.

§6.8: On buying a slave: if the purchase would be perfected or not

And whenever you were asked about obtaining a slave, whether getting him would be perfected or not, look at the Lord of the Ascendant and the Moon to see if they were joined to the Lord of the sixth from the Ascendant,[119] or the Lord of the sixth from the Ascendant were joined to the Lord of the Ascendant: his purchase will be completed. And if the Lord of the Ascendant or the Moon were in the seventh from the Ascendant, or the Lord of the sixth were in the Ascendant, or you found a planet bearing away the light between the Lord of the Ascendant and the Lord of the sixth, he will attain this about which he asks. And if there were nothing of these things which I have told you, he will not attain this about which he asks.

§6.9: On one seeking a slave-girl: whether he will have her or not

And if you were asked by a man who seeks a slave-girl from someone, the Ascendant and its Lord and the Moon will belong to the one asking; and the seventh and its Lord belong to the one concerning whom he asks. Indeed the eleventh sign from the Ascendant will belong to the slave-girl.[120] Therefore, look at the conjunction of the Lord of the Ascendant and the Moon with him,[121] or with the transfer of [the light of] some planet between them, just as I have told you before in this chapter.[122]

---

[119] Omitting extra *domino ascendentis*, which seems to be a typesetter's mistake for its appearance later in the sentence.
[120] This question is interesting because of the way it construes what is at issue (and underscores the need to understand the question). The way Sahl conceives this, the real question is about a business deal with someone else (the seventh) over something that is hoped for (the eleventh). But why should this question differ from the previous one, in which one looked at the sixth for a male slave? Perhaps the male slave is wanted for heavy labor, while the female slave is wanted for another purpose understood in terms of the eleventh—perhaps for sexual pleasure, which could construe the 11th as the 5th (pleasure) from the 7th (seller).
[121] But with whom—the Lord of the eleventh, or the Lord of the seventh?
[122] This must refer to the previous question.

§6.10: If the master will have the substance of his dead [slave]

And if you were asked about what is left over from his dead [slave], whether the master would get it or not, look at the Lord of the Ascendant and the Moon to see if they were conjoined to the Lord of the seventh from the Ascendant (which is the second [sign] from the domicile of slaves): he will get it. Likewise, if the Lord of the seventh were joined to the Lord of the Ascendant, or the Lord of the seventh were in the Ascendant, or the Lord of the Ascendant or the Moon [were] in the seventh; or you found a planet bearing away the light from one of them to his partner: he will get it.

§6.11: If the one asking will have a possession (namely of a slave), or not

And if you were asked about possession, whether or not [the slave] would reach him who asked you,[123] look at the third sign from the Ascendant, which is the tenth domicile of the slaves. If you found the Lord of the Ascendant or the Moon conjoined to the Lord of the third from the Ascendant, or you found the Lord of the third joined to the Lord of the Ascendant, he will get it. Likewise, if the Lord of the Ascendant and the Moon were in the third, or the Lord of the third were in the Ascendant, or there were a planet transferring light between them (this is, from the Lord of the Ascendant to the Lord of the third, or from the Lord of the third to the Lord of the Ascendant), he will get the aforesaid possession through the hands of legates.

§7.1: The seventh sign or 7th domicile, with its questions: and first, if a marriage union will be perfected or not, and what kind of conjoining[124] there will be between them after it is perfected

If you were asked about a marriage union, whether it would be perfected or not, and if it were perfected, how the conjoining will be between them

---

[123] This question sounds like it has to do with slaves delivering some possessions; or perhaps it refers to a purchase of slaves?

[124] Reading *coniunctio* with BN for *conventio*.

([and] indeed if it were not perfected, from whom its separation or divorce will come to be),[125] put the Ascendant and its Lord and the Moon as belonging to the questioner; and the seventh sign and its Lord for the woman. If the Lord of the Ascendant or the Moon were joined to the Lord of the seventh, or were in the seventh, he will get the woman. Likewise if the Lord of the seventh were joined to the Lord of the Ascendant, or the Lord of the seventh were in the Ascendant, the matter comes to be with ease—and the desire[126] of the woman will be greater than the man's. And if the Moon were bearing away the light between them, legates will run back and forth between them, and the effecting of the matter will be through their hands.

After this, look at the receiver of the disposition (that is, the heavier planet), to see if it were impeded by the malefics from a square aspect or the opposition, or it was cadent: the matter will be destroyed after it has moved forward.

§7.2: A question about the impediment or detriment: what kind it will be

And if you were asked of what kind the detriment will be, look at the malefic itself which[127] impedes: if it were the Lord of the second from the Ascendant, or of the eighth, the detriment will be in connection with the drawing-up of the dowry. And if it were the Lord of the twelfth from the Ascendant, the detriment will be because of criticism of the woman's breeding.[128] And if it were the Lord of the sixth, it will be in connection with the man's breeding. And if it were the Lord of the fourth, it will be from the direction of the father. And if it were the Lord of the third, it will be from the direction of brothers. Understand thusly about the remaining signs, according to their natures.[129]

And if there were a planet cutting off the conjunction between them, there will be detriment because of the nature of its domicile: that is, if it

---

[125] The text's use of *coniugium* and *coniunctio* does not seem to be meant in a sexual sense, but only in the sense of the two people being joined together through legal marriage.
[126] *Voluntas*, in the general sense of wanting or wishing (not erotic desire).
[127] Reading *qui* with BN for *quod*.
[128] This must be due to the fact that the twelfth is the sixth from the seventh, indicating a low-class background for the woman.
[129] *Substantias*.

were the Lord of the 2nd domicile, or the 8th, there will be a complication in connection with the drawing-up of the dowry. And if it were the Lord of the third, it will be from the direction of the brothers; and the fourth, from the direction of the father and parents; and the fifth, because the woman is [already] married and has a child (this will be the occasion).[130] And if it were the Lord of the sixth, it will be because of infirmity, or because of a defect of his body, or in connection with slaves. And if it were a malefic planet who bears away the light between them, it will be from the direction of the legates.

§7.3: A question about the quality of their relationship[131]

Concerning the quality of their relationship, look at the conjunction which there was between the Lord of the Ascendant and the Lord of the quaesited matter: if they aspected each other from the seventh sign (which is the aspect of opposition),[132] it signifies the malice of the relationship and a multitude of contention; and if it were an aspect from the square, it signifies the goodness of the relationship, but sometimes there will be contention there; and if it were a trine or sextile aspect, it signifies esteem and the good quality of the relationship—and likewise if the Moon were received and if the Lord of the Ascendant were in an angle and it was the heavy planet (that is, the receiver):[133] the man will be raised up, ruling and conquering the woman. And whichever of them you found cadent or pushing, that one (namely the Lord of the Ascendant or the Lord of the matter) will be conquered and subject. Indeed if they were conjoined in one sign, it signifies contentions;[134] and if the Moon were aspecting the Ascendant and she were impeded, there will be insulting talk between them; and if there were a malefic in the Ascendant, this will be from the side of the man.[135] And understand thusly concerning the remaining signs, according to their natures.

---

[130] *Occasio*, which can simply mean a "reason," but also a "pretext" (which implies an inadequate reason).
[131] *Animi*, which can mean "mind, character, passions"; but here and below "relationship" makes more sense in terms of their mental attitude toward one another.
[132] This does not mean the seventh sign of the *chart*, but if they are in the seventh sign from *each other*.
[133] The receiver of the disposition.
[134] Reading *contentiones* with BN for *contemptiones*.
[135] The man is presumed to be the querent in this question.

And if you saw the Sun impeded, there will be an impediment upon the man; and if Venus were impeded, it will impede the woman. Indeed if the Moon were impeded, it will impede both.

§7.4: A question about a woman who runs away from her husband: if she will return or not

And[136] if you were asked about a woman (having gone out from her house due to her husband's anger), whether she would return to her house or not: look at Venus and the Sun, which are the significators of the man and woman. If Venus were above the earth in an optimal place from the Ascendant, and the Sun under the earth, announce the return of the woman to her house with a strong delay and duress.

And[137] if the Moon, at the hour in which [the woman] exited from her house (or at the hour of the question), were already transiting the prevention (that is, after one-half of the [lunar] month), her return to her house will be hastened. And if the Moon were increased in light (that is, in the beginning of the [lunar] month, her return will be with slowness.

And[138] if Venus, when [the woman] was exiting from her house, were retrograde and occidental, her return to her house will be of her own accord, voluntary, and penitent. And if [Venus] were oriental, going out from under the rays, and retrograde, she will return and her man will be penitent about her leaving—but it will not pain him concerning what he did, as it pains him in the first case; and it will pain her concerning her return, but it will not pain her concerning the thing which she did, just as she is pained in the first case.[139]

---

[136] In this paragraph, *cf. Carmen* V.17.1, 6.
[137] See *Carmen* V.17.7-8.
[138] *Cf. Carmen* V.17.9-10. Dorotheus seems to treat orientality and occidentality differently here.
[139] BN does not quite flesh out this last sentence as fully as it appears in 1493.

§7.5: A question about a woman: if she is a virgin or corrupted

And[140] if you were asked about a woman, whether she is a virgin or corrupted, look at the Ascendant at the hour in which you were asked, and at its Lord, and the Moon, to see if they were in fixed signs: she will be a virgin without all defect, and free from that about which she is defamed. And if they were in movable signs, or common ones, she will be corrupted. For she has already married—and if the woman believed herself to be a virgin, she is deluded and her virginity is taken.

And if the Moon were in a common or movable sign, and the Ascendant and its Lord in a fixed sign, she is already harassed by someone and her virginity is not well taken. And if the Moon were with Mars in a movable sign or a common one, the virginity is already taken in the friendship of men. And if Saturn were in the Ascendant with the Moon, in a common sign or a fixed one, he to whom she was conjoining used her contrary to nature,[141] and her virginity is not taken. And if Mars were in an angle of Venus[142] (that is, in the square aspect or the seventh),[143] and the Moon impeded by Mars, and Venus in Scorpio (or in its triplicity), she will not be a virgin. And if you found Mercury in front of Jupiter, in the triplicity of Venus or in her angle, and particularly [if] Mars were cadent from her, and he did not aspect [her], and Mars were in Aries or Leo or Sagittarius, she will be a virgin.

§7.6: Whether a woman has a child or not

And if you were asked, concerning a woman, whether she has a child or not, look at Venus to see if she were in Aquarius or Leo, and Mercury were with her: she has never given birth. Indeed if Venus and Mercury were in Scorpio or Taurus, she has a child; and if Mars and the Moon or Venus were in a common sign (besides Sagittarius), she has a child. (For Sagittarius signifies that the woman does not have a child, nor would she give birth, forever. But if she had given birth to a child, it will die.)

---

[140] See *Carmen* V.16. The material on the types of signs seems to be drawn from V.16.8-20, and that on the planetary aspects from V.16.1-7.
[141] Lit., "outside of nature" (*extra naturam*), evidently referring to oral or anal penetration.
[142] Reading *in angulo veneris* with BN for *in angulo vel secundo*.
[143] Remember that the "seventh" aspect is nothing more than a whole-sign opposition.

If however the malefics were in movable signs, her child will be due to injustice—that is, fornication and friendship—for she does not observe faith[fulness] with her husband. Indeed if the benefics were in common signs, her child will be due to justice; and if both [kinds], namely the benefics and malefics, were mixed in movable signs, she will be saddened because of her child.

A question about someone pregnant: if it is due to fornication or not

And if you were asked, concerning a pregnant woman, whether her child is due to justice, look at the sign of children, which is the fifth [sign] from the Ascendant: and if Mars or Saturn or Mercury aspected it,[144] her child will be due to fornication. And if the benefics aspected it, her child will be due to justice and will be legitimate.

§7.7: Whether a woman has a man whom she loves or who loves her

And if you were asked, concerning a woman, whether she has[145] a man who loves her or whom she herself loves ([that is,] whether or not there is some man who[146] loves her), look at the Lord of the Ascendant and the Moon, to see if one of them were with Mars in one degree: she has a friend with her in the house; and if they were in one sign and not in one degree, she has a neighbor near her; and if one of them were separated from Mars, she has a friend whom she used to love, but she has already dismissed him. And if some one of them is being joined to Mars, and it were in some one of his domiciles,[147] she has already loved a man who seeks her out, and she herself wants that he should have her. Indeed if some one of them were joined to Jupiter, at one time she has already loved a man higher and nobler than her, and she still loves him. And if [one of them] were joined to Mercury, she loves a young man more beautiful than her own first husband, and younger in age, and he is a writer and businessman. And if some one of them were

---

[144] Reading *eum* for *cum*.
[145] Reading *habeat* for *habeant*.
[146] Adding *qui*.
[147] The Latin is unclear as to which planet is supposed to be in whose domiciles: (a) Mars in his own, (b) Mars in the other's, (d) the other in its own, or (d) the other in Mars's. I have read it as (d).

joined to Venus, she loves a woman and is even occupied by women. If however Jupiter aspected Venus,[148] she has dismissed him because of religion which has happened to her. Indeed if the Sun aspected, a certain great man has already gazed upon her, and because of this she has dismissed him. And if Venus aspected, the woman has already taken him in.[149] Likewise all the planets according to their kind.

And know that Mercury (or Saturn), if they were in one sign and aspected[150] the Moon or the Lord of the Ascendant, [she has already taken this young man in betrothal, and likewise other young men];[151] and if the Moon is joined to them,[152] she loves an effeminate man with such a shape as I have said.

§7.8: On the contention of two people: which of them will win

And[153] if you were asked about a contention which was between two people—which of them will win and obtain victory—put the Ascendant and its Lord and the Moon for the questioner who is asking you, and the seventh and its Lord for the contender. After this, look to see if both planets were conjoined to each other from a sextile aspect or a trine: they will make an agreement before the contention. And if they were joined from a square aspect or from the opposition, they will not make an agreement except after a fight and contention. And if they each came together in one sign, there will be peace between them without the insertion of another, and without another who enters in between them for the reason of making peace. And if the Lord of the Midheaven aspected them, and there was a conjunction with

---

[148] Reading *Venerem* with BN for *illum*.
[149] *Percepit*, which also has connotations of taking in knowledge—the phrase seems to mean she has already had sexual relationships with the man in question.
[150] BN reads in the singular, but it does not make much sense by itself; moreover, later in the sentence it is clear we are dealing with both Mercury and Saturn together—probably in aspect to the other planets by whole sign.
[151] This is my best rendering of *iam percepit hoc iuvenis desponsatus, et similiter iuvenibus*. Bonatti's own text departs from this in certain respects, and is not close enough to tease out some other meaning. But he does say (*BOA* p. 445) that if multiple planets aspected the Lord of the 7th, she will have had sex with multiple people, especially if it is Saturn and Mercury. His treatment is much longer and may draw on multiple sources.
[152] Reading with 1493 for "light." This suggests an aspect by degree, so that the aspect earlier in the sentence was perhaps only by whole sign.
[153] See *Carmen* V.33.

him before one of them would be joined to the other, they will not make an agreement until they come into the presence of the king. And if the Moon transferred light between them, there will be a beginning of peace through the hands of legates.

After this, look at the place of each of the planets (namely that of the Lord of the Ascendant and the Lord of the matter, that is, of the Lord of the seventh), and their strength. Because through this you will understand the strength of those who are contending. For the stronger one is he whose significator is in an angle; and the one of them who is received will have more allies. And know that the beginning of peace will be from the pushing planet—that is, from that one who seeks the conjunction, he who is lighter, and from a cadent planet if it were lighter. And know that the Lord of the seventh, if he were in the Ascendant, signifies the strength of the one asking. And the Lord of the Ascendant in the seventh signifies the strength of him about whom it is asked: because he who is in the domicile of the adversary is[154] like someone conquered. And if one significator were retrograde, it signifies weakness and flight, also making deals and lies by him[155] whose significator it is: that is, if the Lord of the Ascendant were retrograde, it will be the weakness of the one asking; indeed if the Lord of the 7th were retrograde, it will be the weakness of the contender. If however the Lord of the Midheaven aspected them and he were retrograde, it signifies the injustice of judges, and the contention will be prolonged. Likewise if one of the significators were separated from the other (I say the significators are the Lord of the Ascendant and the Lord of the matter). And know that the luminaries, that is, the Sun and the Moon, if one of them were joined to one of the significators, or were in its domicile, he will be stronger and more worthy.

And if the Lord of the Ascendant were joined to the Lord of the Midheaven, the master of the question will seek aid from the king. Indeed if the Lord of the Midheaven were joined to the Lord of the Ascendant, the king will aid him without his [making a] request. And if the Lord of the seventh were joined to the Lord of the Midheaven, the contender will demand aid from the king. Indeed if the Lord of the Midheaven were joined to the Lord of the seventh, the king will aid the contender.

And if you knew the strength of each one of them [compared with] the other, and knew that they will not make an agreement, look at the king or

---

[154] Added from BN.
[155] Reading *illius* for *illi*.

judge who judges between them, from the Lord of the Midheaven. Then look to see which of their significators he aspects: that is, whether the aforesaid Lord of the Midheaven (who is the significator of the king or judge) is aspecting the Lord of the Ascendant or the Lord of the seventh. And know that the king or judge is with him whom he aspects. And if there were a peregrine planet in the Midheaven, not aspecting them, and the Lord of the Midheaven did not aspect them, they themselves set up amongst themselves [someone] who would justly judge between them.

If Saturn were in the Midheaven, and he himself were the Lord of the Midheaven, the judge will not judge justly nor truly. And if Mars impeded Saturn, the judge will be criticized on account of this, and he will be defamed from thence. And if Mars were in the Midheaven, the judge will be light, very quick, sharp, and speedy. Indeed if it were Jupiter, the judge will be just. And if it were Venus, he will be light and of a good mind, and take it up easily. And if it were Mercury, he will be sharp in sight.[156] And if the sign of the Midheaven were common, the first judge will not finish their judgment until they go to another judge.

§7.9: A question about buying and selling: what will be concerning it

And if you were asked about the purchase or sale of some thing, look in this to the Lord of the seventh and the Lord of the Ascendant, to see if they were joined: there will be an agreement between them, and there will be ease from the pushing planet (the one who is lighter). If however they were not joined, and you found a planet between them, rendering the light of one of them to the other, there will be an agreement through the hands of some man who enters between them. And if the Lord of the Ascendant were in the seventh, the buyer will be pursuing the seller; indeed if the Lord of the seventh were in the Ascendant, the seller will be pursuing the buyer.[157] And if there were a benefic in the Ascendant, it signifies the ease of the one selling, and his truth; indeed if there were a malefic in it, it signifies his duress and slowness and lying. If however there were a benefic in the 7th, it signifies the ease of the buyer and his truth; and a malefic, to the contrary.

---

[156] Perhaps this means he will easily perceive the issues and their correct resolution.
[157] This sentence assumes the querent (represented by the Lord of the Ascendant) is the buyer. See also §4.2.

And if the Moon were not separated from some planet, but she were joined [to one], the seller will sell the possession or thing, which [the buyer] does not buy [from him], but [the buyer] will possess it from someone [else]; but if he buys it, he has not given anything from its price. Indeed if she were separated and was not joined to some planet, there will be a delay in the purchase, and an agreement in principle. If however the planet from whom the Moon is being separated, enters combustion, the seller will die before his substance is rendered to [the buyer].

§7.10: A question about a fugitive, [and] about[158] substance or another lost thing: if it will be found

And if you were asked about a fugitive and about substance, or about some lost thing, put the Ascendant and its Lord for the one asking (namely for the master of the fugitive, whether the fugitive were a slave or someone else); indeed the seventh and its Lord and the Moon for the slave and the lost thing. Then, look to see if the Lord of the Ascendant is joined to the Lord of the seventh: the one asking will get the fugitive through an investigation and his own diligence. Likewise if the Lord of the Ascendant were in the seventh. And if the Lord of the seventh were joined to the Lord of the Ascendant, or the Lord of the seventh were in the Ascendant, he will come of his own will before he goes out of the land.

If however you found the Moon separated from the Lord of the Ascendant, and joined to the Lord of the seventh, someone will come to the master, who will show him where his slave is. And if she were separated from the Lord of the seventh and were joined to the Lord of the Ascendant, the slave will send to his master a legate who would seek safety for him. And if after this the Lord of the seventh were joined to the Lord of the Ascendant, the slave will return to his master of his own will.

If however the Lord of the seventh were joined to a malefic planet in an angle, the fugitive will be caught. But if the Lord of the Ascendant aspected the[159] malefic or the Lord of the seventh, his own master will catch him, but will render substance for him. And if one of the luminaries were joined to

---

[158] Reading *de* for *a*.
[159] I read "the," referring to the angular malefic just mentioned. This makes sense of the end of the sentence, indicating that while the querent will get the fugitive back only after undergoing the trouble of paying for him.

the Lord of the seventh, the place of the fugitive would not be able to be hidden. Also, if the Lord of the seventh were under the rays, it signifies the discovery of the fugitive. And if the Lord of the Ascendant aspected him,[160] he will be captured.

If the Lord of the seventh were joined to a malefic, the same fugitive will be captured; and if he were joined to a benefic, he will not be captured unless that benefic would be entering under the rays, or would be going retrograde, or would be impeded: because if it entered into combustion, it will signify his death; and if it were joined to a malefic and it[161] will enter under the rays in combustion, his corpse will be found. And if the Moon were joined to a malefic, he will get the fugitive. If however she were joined to a retrograde planet, he will return to [the master] of his own will. And if she[162] were joined to a standing planet (that is, one which was in its own station), in an angle or in what follows an angle, the fugitive or the one going astray will not be moved from his place until he is caught. But if the planet were in the first station, wishing to go retrograde, the fugitive will be caught and bound tight in fetters and will be rendered to his master. And if it were in the second station (when it wants to move forward), he will be caught in part, and will be tied up—after this, he will escape from captivity and he could be caught again. And if the planet to which the Moon is joined were direct, he will be rendered without fetters. Indeed if the Moon were under the rays and she were joined to Mars, the fugitive will be burnt to ashes by fire; and if she were joined to Saturn, he will die in the water. Indeed if the Moon aspected the Lord of her own domicile, the substance of the fugitive will be captured. And know that if there were a malefic in the ninth,[163] the fugitive will be captured and led back; and if it were a benefic in the same place, he would not be able to be caught. And if the Moon were increased in light and number, his capture will be slowed down; and in the decrease of light, he will be captured more quickly.

---

[160] I.e., the Lord of the seventh.
[161] I believe this refers to the Lord of the seventh.
[162] Reading *iuncta* with BN for *iunctus*.
[163] This could relate to the fact that the ninth is the tenth from the twelfth, and so it shows the government of prisoners. Note, too, that questions on prisoners can also be addressed via the ninth. See §9.5.

§7.11: A question about the place of the fugitive and the lost[164] thing, or the hiding-place

And[165] if you were asked about the place of the fugitive and the lost thing, or about the place of the stolen goods, look at the place of the Moon: if she were in the Ascendant, the fugitive will be in the direction of the east; and if she were in the Midheaven, the fugitive will be in the southern direction; and if she were in the seventh, he will be in the western direction; and if she were in the fourth, he will be in the northern one. And if she were not in any of the angles, look to the direction of the planet [and] her sign, namely in which she is; and judge upon the direction of the place of the Moon and of the sign in which she is.[166]

§7.12: A question if the fugitive's turning back to the place whence he has fled is better for him than going where he wants to

Which[167] if a fugitive (for whom you are looking) were to ask whether his turning back to the place whence he comes will be better for him than to go to where he wants, look at the Moon to see if she were separated from the malefics: his turning back to the place whence he had fled will be bad for him; and if she were separated from the benefics, his turning back will be better. If however she were joined to benefics, where he continues on to will be better for him; and if she were joined to malefics, where he continues on to will be bad for him.

---

164 Reading *perditae* for *proditae*.
165 See *Carmen* V.36.8-15.
166 Dorotheus means by quadrant direction, so that if she is in between the Ascendant and the 4th, he is in the northeast, *etc.*
167 This bears similarity to *Carmen* V.36.21-22, and V.13.1-4.

§7.13: A question about what was stolen:[168] whether the one asking would get it or not

If[169] you were asked about what was stolen, and whether the one asking would get it or not, put the Ascendant and its Lord and the Moon for the one asking (that is, the owner[170] of what was stolen); and the seventh and its Lord for the robber; and the Midheaven for what was stolen; indeed the angle of the earth for the place of what was stolen.

If the Lord of the Ascendant were joined to the Lord of the seventh, or the Lord of the Ascendant were in the seventh, the investigator will get the quaesited [matter], that is, the robber, with his investigation. And if, in addition to this conjunction, the Lord of the 2nd from the Ascendant (which is the domicile of substance) were under the rays, the questioner will get the robber with his investigation, but he will not get the stolen goods.

And if the Lord of the seventh were joined to the Lord of the Ascendant,[171] or the Lord of the seventh were in the Ascendant, the robber will return what he has stolen. And if, in addition to this conjunction, the Lord of the second from the Ascendant (who is the Lord of the domicile of substance) were under the rays, the robber will be found, but what was stolen will not be found. And if he had gone out from combustion, part of the stolen goods will be found.

And if the Lord of the Ascendant were joined to a planet in the angles (and better than this if it[172] were in the Midheaven), the questioner will get the robber. Indeed if he were joined to a cadent planet not aspecting the Ascendant,[173] it signifies the retreat of his fugitive. And if that planet were aspecting the Ascendant, it would be hoped for—that is, he would be able to have trust.

---

[168] *Latrocinium.* Technically this term refers either to the act of the robbery or to the robbers as a group. But here (and in *BOA*) it seems to refer either to what was stolen or to its location. I will translate it here in such terms.
[169] See *Carmen* V.35.20-24 for this paragraph.
[170] *Domino,* lit. "master."
[171] Following BN. 1493 switches the Ascendant and the seventh here, making the condition read as it had in the previous paragraph.
[172] That is, the other planet.
[173] Reading *aspicienti* for *aspiciens,* so as to refer to the cadent planet. *Aspiciens* would otherwise refer to the Lord of the Ascendant not aspecting the Ascendant, but that does not seem to be the sense here. This rule sounds like Māshā'allāh's in *OR*.

And if the Lord of the seventh were under the rays, it signifies the discovery of the robber—and better than that, if the Lord of the Ascendant aspected him: because this signifies that the master will have[174] the robber.[175]

And if the Lord of the seventh were joined,[176] in what I have said, with the Lord of the Midheaven, he will bring back the substance due to fear of the king. And if the Lord of the Ascendant were joined to the Lord of the Midheaven, the owner of the substance will threaten him through the king[177] or through another who is to be feared. And if they (namely the Lord of the Ascendant and the Lord of the seventh) did not aspect each other, the king (or someone other than him, who asked for him) will take the substance. And if the Lord of the seventh were joined with the Lord of the Midheaven, he will aid the robber, and so on.[178] And if the Lord of the Ascendant were joined with the Lord[179] of the Midheaven, the king will aid the owner of the substance.

And if the Moon transferred the light between each of the significators (that is, between the Lord of the Ascendant and the Lord of the seventh), it signifies the finding of the robber; and if the Lord of the seventh from the Ascendant were joined to the Lord of the third, the robber will go out from the region; if however it were in an angle from the Ascendant, he will not depart from his place.

And know what will happen to the robber through the aspects of the malefics to the seventh or to the Lord of the seventh.

And if the Moon were joined to the malefics, it signifies the taking away of the substance. And if she were joined to a benefic, and the benefic itself were under the rays and impeded, it signifies the taking away of substance. And if she were joined to a planet in the Ascendant or in the seventh, and that planet were free from the malefics, it signifies the finding of the substance.

---

[174] *Habebit*, in the stronger sense of the robber coming to be under the querent's control.
[175] This last phrase, "the master will have the robber," is missing in BN, which simply breaks off after "it signifies."
[176] Omitting "and the Lord of the Ascendant," who is dealt with in the next sentence.
[177] That is, he will threaten the thief with punishment by the king.
[178] This sentence is not in BN. Nor does it make much sense, since earlier in the paragraph it was said that the Lord of the seventh joined to the Lord of the Midheaven means the goods will be returned—which does not suggest a friendly relationship between the robber and the king.
[179] Reading *domino* for *domo*.

And[180] if the luminaries aspected each other from the trine or from the sextile aspect, it signifies the finding of what was stolen, and the lost thing, and so on. And if some one of the luminaries (that is, the Sun or the Moon) were in the Ascendant or in the Midheaven[181]…indeed if they aspected each other from the square aspect or the opposition, there will be an attaining [of what was stolen] after losing hope and complications. And if one of the luminaries aspected the Lot of Fortune, or it were with it in one sign, what was stolen will be found—and more quickly so if the Sun aspected. Indeed if the Moon aspected the Lot of Fortune, or she were joined to it in one sign, there will be some delay in the finding of it. If however one of the luminaries did not aspect the Lot of Fortune nor the Ascendant, and the luminaries did not aspect each other, what was stolen will not be found, forever.

§7.14: A question about that of the snatched substance which has disappeared or perished: will it be found or not

And if you wished to know whether what has disappeared would be found or not, look at the Lord of the Ascendant and the Moon to see if one of them were joined to the Lord of the second from the Ascendant, or some planet rendered its[182] light to him—that is, that he would bear away the light[183] between them: it signifies the attaining of the substance. Likewise if some planet joined their light—that is, both were joined to some planet heavier than they.[184] Which if the Lord of the second (who is the significator of substance) were in the Ascendant, it signifies the getting of the substance, even if after a little while. Likewise if the Lord of the second from the Ascendant were joined to a planet which was in the second sign from the Ascendant.[185] And if the Lord of the second from the Ascendant did not aspect, the substance will perish. Likewise if the Lord of the eighth from the Ascendant were joined to the Lord of the seventh (who is the significator of the robber). And if the Lord of the seventh were joined to the Lord of the

---

[180] See *Carmen* V.35.1-19.
[181] The sentence seems to break off here. Another possibility is that the two sentences go together: if one of the luminaries is angular *and* they are in a square or opposition.
[182] This must mean "the Lord of the Ascendant or the Moon," so that we have instances of perfection by joining and transfer here.
[183] Reading *lumen* for *limen*.
[184] I.e., by a collection of light.
[185] This would also be a case of reception.

second, it signifies the loss of the substance; which if the Lord of the eighth (who is the significator of the substance of the robber) were joined to the Lord of the second (who is the significator of the substance of the questioner, and of those things which he has lost), he will find the substance and take part of the substance of the robber—and better than that if the Lord of the Ascendant aspected them.[186]

For if the Lord of the Midheaven aspected, the king will take what I have said; and if the Lord of the eighth were joined to the Lord of the Midheaven (who is the significator of the king), the robber will appease the king with monies. If however the Lord of the second from the Ascendant did not aspect the Ascendant or its Lord, the substance will certainly be lost and there will be no hint of it. Indeed if the Lord of the second from the Ascendant were joined to the Lord of the third (and the ninth, or to some planet in them), or the Lord of the second was in them, it signifies the departure of the substance which was stolen from the region. And know that if the luminaries were each below the earth, the thief will be unknown forever. If however the Moon were in the Ascendant, and her Lord, and the Sun aspected them, what which disappeared or perished or was taken away by stealth,[187] will be found and returned quickly[188]—and more easily than that, if the aspect were a trine.

§7.15: A question about a robber: is he a foreigner[189] or not

And[190] if you wished to know whether the robber is a foreigner or not, look at the luminaries: if each of them aspected[191] the Ascendant, the robber will be from the household. And if one of them aspected the Ascendant and the other did not aspect, he will be commingled with them [socially], and he will not be of the household. Likewise if you found the Lord of the Ascendant in the Ascendant, or the Lord of the seventh were with the Lord of the Ascendant, the robber will be of the inhabitants of the house. And if the luminaries were in their own domiciles, aspecting the Ascendant and its Lord,

---

[186] Reading *aspexerit* for *asperit*.
[187] Reading *furtim* with BN, for *furto*.
[188] BN says, "on that very day."
[189] *Peregrinus*.
[190] The first part of this question is derived from *Carmen* V.35.75-78.
[191] Adding *aspexerit* from BN.

or in the domiciles of [the Lord] of the Ascendant, he will be of the inhabitants of the house.[192] And if they[193] were in their own triplicities, the robber will be of their relatives, but he does not stay with them in the house. And if they were in their own bounds or faces, he will be an intimate[194] of the inhabitants of the house, and it is thought that there is some relationship between them, and he visits them often. And[195] if the two luminaries were in some thing[196] of theirs which we have said, and one of them (and the Lord of the Ascendant) aspected the Ascendant,[197] he is an intimate of the people of that house, and he visits them often. Indeed if some one of the luminaries aspected the Ascendant and it did not aspect the seventh,[198] he did not enter the house before that time in which he stole, unless one of the luminaries is in a common sign: then he has already entered again, with the inhabitants knowing about it: because a common sign signifies repetition. If however one of the luminaries aspected the Lord of the Ascendant and did not aspect the Ascendant, he will be known to the inhabitants of the house, but he has not entered the house before.

But if the Lord[199] of the Ascendant has already fallen from the degree of the Ascendant, and there were with him another planet in that sign in which he is, closer to the degree of the Ascendant, the robber will be of certain people among the inhabitants of the house. Indeed if the Lord of the seventh were in the ninth from its own domicile, the robber will not be from that region. If however it were in the sixth or from the eighth from its own domicile, it will be a male slave or slave-girl. If however it were in its own exaltation, the robber will be noble. And if it were in its own domicile, it will be of the inhabitants of the house, known among them. And if it were in its own triplicity or in [its own] bound, or in its own face, he will not be known in the region. But, however, he will be known in his own neighborhood[200] and habitation.

---

[192] Reading this sentence as found in BN.
[193] Reading the plural here and below with BN.
[194] *Familiaris*.
[195] This sentence is missing in BN.
[196] This must mean "dignity." See *Introduct.* §5.14 #2.
[197] This phrase echoes the earlier sentence which I replaced with one from BN. I suspect that the sentence should read, "And one of them aspected the Ascendant *and its Lord*…"
[198] But any planet aspecting the Ascendant would be aspecting the seventh at the same time.
[199] Reading *dominus* for *domus*.
[200] Reading *vicino* for *vico*.

[§7.16: On the identity of the robber]

If indeed you came to know that the robber is of the household, and the Sun were the significator of the house,[201] it will be his father. Indeed if the Moon, it will be his mother. But if it were Venus, it will be his own wife. If however it were Saturn, it will be a slave or a foreigner. Indeed if it were Jupiter, he will be nobler than all who are in the house, and he will not come to be known in the theft: that is, someone about whom there will be no suspicion. Which if it were Mars, it will be his son or daughter or brother. And if it were Mercury, it will be of his intimate friends.

If however the significator of the robber[202] were peregrine, look at the Lot of Fortune: and if it were free from the malefics, the robber had never stolen before this time. Likewise if the Lord of the Ascendant were free from malefics. And[203] if Mars were separated from the Lord of the seventh, he was known by them in a theft before this.[204] And if Saturn aspected the Moon[205] or the Ascendant, the robber stole with cleverness and skill. If however Jupiter is the significator of the robber (that is, if he were the Lord of the seventh), he did not enter in order to steal, but he entered because of some other business: the robbery happened to him, and he stole. Indeed if Mars were the significator, he did not come to the theft until he had pierced[206] the house, or he dug under the wall of the house, or he broke the bolt, or he found a key. But if the significatrix were Venus, it signifies friendship and esteem, also partnership and boldness between them while he entered among them[207] for conversation, taking on the image and likeness of a visiting friend—and thus he robbed them. If however Mercury were the significator, the robber entered the house with cleverness and skill, or by some art.

---

[201] This must mean the Lord of the 7th domicile. See below.
[202] Below this is defined as the Lord of the seventh.
[203] The rest of this paragraph is based on *Carmen* V.35.131-38.
[204] Dorotheus says only that he has gotten into trouble before due to a theft, not that the current victims personally knew about it.
[205] Normally one would expect Sahl to say "if the Moon aspected Saturn," or "if the Moon would be joined to Saturn," since she is the lighter planet. Perhaps whole-sign aspects are meant, or else it is merely stylistic.
[206] *Perforavit*, which also has connotations of boring through something.
[207] Adding *inter eos* with BN.

For[208] the Sun and Moon, if they aspected the Ascendant, the robber will be of the inhabitants of the house.

If[209] however the significator of the robber were a benefic, he will be free.[210] Indeed if a malefic, he will be a slave. And if Venus or Mercury were the significator, the robber will be a young man or girl (and Mercury is of a younger age than Venus). And if Mars were the significator of the robber, he will be a complete[211] young man: that is, of perfected youth, [as well as Saturn—that is, Saturn will not be a youth.][212] Indeed Jupiter is older than Mars. And if it were Saturn, he will be a decrepit old man. If however [Saturn] were oriental, he will be of completed age.

But if the Moon were the significatrix, and it was in the beginning of the [lunar] month, he will be a young man; and if it were in the middle of the month, he will be of middle age, that is, a complete man; and if it were at the end of the month, he will be an old man. Indeed if the Sun were the significator and he were between the Ascendant and the Midheaven, the robber will be of the age of a young man: and thus you will not cease to increase it until you reach the angle of the earth: because this is the place of the end of life.

§7.17: A question about the place in which the stolen goods are

Indeed[213] if you were asked about the place of the stolen goods, look at the angle of the earth to see if it were Cancer or its triplicity: the stolen goods will be buried near water, and there will be its place. And if it were Aries or its triplicity, it will be in a place of beasts and in a place of fire. Indeed if it were Taurus or its triplicity, it will be in a place of oxen or cows—

---

[208] See *Carmen* V.35.75-77.
[209] This paragraph is a garbled mixture of *Carmen* V.35.108-115, and V.35.123-4. For one thing, in Dorotheus the initial statements about benefics and malefics refers to the planets *aspecting* the significator of the thief. Dorotheus's basic rules are that eastern planets are younger, western planets older; planets in stations are older, as are planets combust or under the rays.
[210] Free in the political sense, that is. See next sentence.
[211] *Collectus*, with the connotation that he is not middle aged but has finished his years of youth.
[212] I have rewritten this part a little, which in Dorotheus reads: "...and whenever [Saturn's] position is eastern, then according to this it indicates that the thief is mixed [middle-aged], is not one abounding in years nor a youth." The problem is that Sahl is trying to mix both of the passages cited above. The Latin here reads: *Et si fuerit Mars significator latronis, erit iuvenis collectus, id est, perfectae iuventutis plus Saturno, id est, plus iuvenis.*
[213] See *Carmen* V.35.27-37.

for Taurus signifies especially a place of cows. And Virgo signifies a place of harvests and the *annona*,[214] and Capricorn a place of sheep. And if it were Gemini or its triplicity, they will be in the residence or in a safe[215] or in a higher place from the ground. If however the stolen goods were in the house, and you wished to know their place in the house, look at the Lord of the fourth and the planet which was in that same place.[216] If however it were Saturn, they will be in the washroom of the house; and in a farther or filthier and deeper and darker place. And if it were Jupiter, it signifies a place of groves and of those praying.[217] And Mars signifies the kitchen or a place of fire. And the Sun signifies an enclosed part[218] of the house and a place of sitting[219] belonging the master of the house. Indeed Venus signifies the place of women's sitting. And Mercury signifies the place of a decorated building, and of books, or the place of the *annona* (and especially in Virgo). And if it were the Moon, it will be next to a well or cistern, or place of cleaning.

And know that the benefics, if they were in the fourth from the Ascendant, the stolen goods will be in a clean and beautiful place; and they have already been handed over to a certain noble. Indeed if there were a malefic in it, they will be in a horrid and stinking place, and have already been handed over to a certain ignoble person.

§7.18: A question whether the stolen object is one or more

And[220] if you were asked about the number of the stolen goods (if it were substance or something else which might be possessed), look at the signs which there are between the Moon and Mercury: and if they were equal, that about which you were asked will be combined, or more than one. Indeed if the signs between them were odd, it will be one thing.

---

214 This concept of *annona* goes back to antiquity. It is an annual grain rent paid by farmers, and can refer either to the value of the grain, or the grain itself. Throughout Sahl's and Māshā'allāh's works, it seems to mean the grain itself.
215 *Arca*. Or, a box or chest.
216 I.e., in the fourth.
217 *Oratorium*.
218 *Claustrum*. In medieval times this primarily referred to complexes in monasteries where the monks slept, or else walled-off areas like town walls. Perhaps this refers to where the master of the house (the Sun) spends time.
219 For example, where the master of the house has his den, office, or place to recline.
220 See *Carmen* V.35.72-74.

§7.19: A question whether he (concerning whom suspicion is had) is the robber or not

If however you were asked, about a captured man under suspicion, whether he was the robber or not, look for this just as you look for rumors to see whether or not they are true;[221] and even use the Moon in the testimony. Which if she were conjoined to a malefic, he will be a robber.

If you were asked, about some man, whether he has stolen something or not, look at the Lord of the Ascendant and the Moon—namely the stronger of them[222]—to see if it accepted something from the malefics (that is, if it were separated from them): he has stolen, and more truly so if it were separated from the Lord of the domicile of substance: that is, from the Lord of the second from the Ascendant. And if it did not accept something from the malefics, he has stolen nothing.

§7.20: A question about the stolen object: what it is

If[223] you were asked what is the thing itself which was stolen, look at the place of the Moon in the signs and the bounds:

> If she were in the bound of Saturn, it will be of those things which are necessary for the working of the earth. If however Saturn were in the Ascendant or in the tenth, in Taurus or in its triplicity (like Virgo and Capricorn)[224]...indeed if he were in the fourth from the Ascendant or in the seventh, it will be another substance. And if he were cadent from the Ascendant, and no one of the luminaries aspected him, or he were in Aries, it signifies the badness of the thing and its vileness, and

---

[221] Perhaps referring to §13.9.
[222] Probably referring to §1.4 above, but compare again to the rules laid out by Māshā'allāh in *Cognition* and *OR*.
[223] See *Carmen* V.35.44-56. Note that Dorotheus ignores the triplicities, and his account is briefer than Sahl's.
[224] This parenthetical remark is in 1493 but not in BN. But in both editions the sentence breaks off here. Dorotheus's account reads, "If...[the Moon] is in a term of Saturn while Saturn is in the midheaven or its exaltation, then it indicates that what was stolen is something costly and is one of the things which are necessary in farming the land or building or acquiring property. If Saturn is not in any of these places but is under the earth..." Dorotheus does not address every angle, as Sahl wants to here.

that it is a horrid or stinking thing. If however Saturn were in Gemini or in its triplicity, they will be two substances; and if Jupiter were in the Midheaven, aspecting Saturn, one of the substances will be gold; and if he were in the fourth or in the seventh from the Ascendant, it will be silver. Indeed if [Jupiter] were cadent from the angle, it will be lead or some such thing like this.

If however the Moon were in the bound of Jupiter, look at her[225] condition and her place, and [see] if some [planet] aspects her.[226] If it[227] were in Aries or in its triplicity (like Leo and Sagittarius), the thing will be gold or silver, and everything which comes to be through fire. But if Venus aspected Jupiter or Jupiter were in her[228] bound, it will be pearl; and if Jupiter were in Taurus or in its triplicity, the thing (that is, whatever it was) will be useful to the wealthy, or vestments, or it will be of vestments,[229] or it will pertain to vestments. Indeed if he were in Gemini or its triplicity (like Libra and Aquarius), the substance will be ensouled or something proceeding from animals. If indeed he were in Cancer and its triplicity (like Scorpio and Pisces), it will be taken out of the water, like pearl and so on.

But if the Moon were in the bound of Mars, the thing has already passed through fire, or fire has touched it in some way. Indeed if the Moon aspected Venus, dyeing has already been worked on it.

And if the Moon were in the bound of Venus, and in Aries or in its triplicity,[230] it will be gold or silver. And if she were in Taurus and its triplicity, or in Cancer and its triplicity, it will be an ornate vestment or a kind of precious silk vestment, woven in various colors and diverse pictures. And you will know the goodness of the substance, and its

---

[225] Throughout this paragraph it is a little unclear whether "he" (Jupiter) or "she" (the Moon) is meant, but I have tried to make this paragraph parallel the previous one.
[226] In this case both 1493 and BN clearly say "her."
[227] I believe this refers to the planet aspecting the Moon; but grammatically it could refer to her, as well.
[228] I believe this refers to Venus's bound.
[229] *Ex vestimento*, which suggests something made *out of* vestments; but what could be made out of vestments besides the vestments themselves?
[230] Here the logic seems to change: earlier, it seems we were to look at the triplicity of the Lord of the Moon's bound; now we are supposed to look at her own triplicity.

beauty, from the place of Venus in the signs: which if she were in Gemini and its triplicity, the matter will not be of the substances of animals. And if Venus has gone out from under the rays, it will be a new thing; indeed if she were retrograde, or in the end of her course or in diminished number, it will be an old thing, and wrapped.

[And[231] if the Moon were in the bound of Mercury, they will be books.] And if she were in Aries and its triplicity, it will be coins; and if she were in Gemini and its triplicity, the coins themselves will be taken from a little place or from some vessel which is covered in red leather.

After this, look at the place of the Moon:[232]

If she were in Aries, it will be an object which is put upon the head and face.

And if she were in Taurus, it will be an ornament or object which is suspended from the neck, or a precious substance.

And if she were in Gemini, it will be coins if Mercury aspected her; and if he did not aspect, it will be of leather.

And if she were in Cancer, it will be a thing taken out of the water, or something moist, or soaked.

And if she were in Leo and the Sun aspected her, it will be gold or silver; and if the Sun did not aspect her, it will be iron or yellow copper [or brass].[233]

Indeed if she were in Virgo and Mercury aspected her, it will be coins; and if he did not aspect, it will be vestments.

And if she were in Libra and Venus aspected her, it will be a thing which is sold on balance scales, and it has a good odor; it is also of the

---

[231] Adding material in brackets from Bonatti (*BOA* p. 474), in accordance with Dorotheus. The Sahl text does not formally introduce the bound of Mercury.
[232] See *Carmen* V.35.57-69.
[233] *Auricalcum* (var. *orichalcum*).

things by which women are ornamented. And[234] if [Venus] did not aspect her, it will be an animal, and it is traded in so that blood might be in it.[235]

And if she were in Scorpio and Mars aspected her, it will be gold or silver. And if he did not aspect, it will be crude ore,[236] or what is worked by fire, and it is gleaming.[237]

And if she were in Sagittarius, and Jupiter aspected her, it will not be one substance, or [it will be] a dyed thing; and if he did not aspect her, it will be a low-class thing below what I said, and it will not be precious.

And if she were in Capricorn, it will be an aged or shabby thing, and low-class; and if Saturn aspected her, it will be of the substance of the earth and seeds.

If however she were in Aquarius and its Lord aspected her, it will be an animal or something taken out of animals. And if Jupiter aspected her, it will be gold or silver. Indeed if the Sun and Mercury [aspected] the Moon, it will be coins, and they will be in leather.

And if she were in Pisces, and Jupiter aspected her, it will be pearls or amber or something brought forth from out of the water. If [Jupiter] did not aspect her, it will be silk and in various colors.[238]

---

[234] This sentence is not in BN, nor does Bonatti use it in *BOA*, nor does Dorotheus. It is worthwhile comparing this list of the Moon in the signs and of her position in the terms, with Dorotheus. In some cases the delineations seem to be swapped.
[235] *Mercetur ut in ea sanguis sit.*
[236] *Aes*, especially copper ore and alloys made with copper.
[237] *Splendidum.*
[238] Reading *coloris* with BN for *colores*.

§7.21: Concerning the taken or stolen thing: what it is, and on the manner of the thing[239]

§7.22: A question about a robber: whether he is masculine or feminine; or concerning *imbrione*[240]

And[241] if you were asked about a robber, whether he is masculine or feminine, or about *imbrione*, then consider what is ascending in the face of the Ascendant (in which the question comes to be), of the forms of men, and speak according to the substance of those forms:

And know that in the first face of Aries ascends the form of a black man wrapped up in white *kiswah*.[242] And in the second face ascends the form of a woman upon whom are red cloths. And in the third, the form of a man with a pale color, [and] red hair [on the head].

And in the first face of Taurus ascends a man—a spy—and a nude man.[243] And in the second face ascends a nude man in whose hand is a key. And in the third, a man in whose hand is a serpent and an arrow.

---

[239] This chapter is not found in BN, nor does it appear in *BOA*, and I cannot find a source text in Dorotheus. Moreover, the style changes suddenly, and it is a needless repetition of the previous topic. These facts make me doubt it comes from Sahl, so I omit it here.

[240] Word unknown, but because the chapter deals with outward appearance, it might be a Latinized form of the Ar. ʾ*abraza*, "to appear, manifest, expose." This chapter is not found in BN. I have remained faithful to the Latin, but have also consulted Bonatti (*BOA* pp. 477-480), who draws on this same material but sometimes elaborates helpfully.

[241] Dorotheus does have sign-based descriptions of the thief in *Carmen* V.35.94-97, but he does not use the decans as here, and he uses the sign in which the significator of the thief is. I also note that one would expect the decan of the *seventh* to indicate the thief (as in Bonatti), not that of the Ascendant.

[242] "Clothing" (Lat. *kise*).

[243] The word I have translated as "spy" (*speculator*) can also mean an "explorer" (and came to mean an estate manager in medieval times). The word has to do with watching and gathering information, as when a burglar cases out a house. But it is unclear from the text whether the spy is the same as the nude man, or not. Moreover, I would also point out that *nudus* ("nude") also has connotations of being lightly and poorly dressed in the way destitute people are. It may be that writers like Sahl are taking the more dramatic images of nudity and so on from traditional magical sources, but what they *mean* here and below is a shabby person with little clothing.

And in the first face of Gemini ascends [a man] in whose hand is a rod,[244] and another one serving. And in the second one, a man in whose hand is a tube,[245] and another bent.[246] And in the third, a man seeking arms.

[And if it were the first face of Cancer, it signifies that the thief is a well-dressed man with beautiful, fitted clothes, and with him is a young girl. And if it were the second face of Cancer, it signifies that it is a young girl, who readily carries a wreath of flowers, who is not a virgin, and has with her another girl who is a virgin. And if it were its third face, it signifies that it was one man and one woman who stole.][247]

And in the first face of Leo ascends the form of a lion, and a man upon whom there are diminished[248] cloths. And in the second one, the image [of a man] holding[249] his hands raised up, and a man on whose head is a crown. And in the third, a young man in whose hand is a whip and a man of intense sadness, and a foul face.

And in the first face of Virgo ascends the form of a good girl. And in the second, a black man upon whom are vestments of leather, and a man having[250] a crown. And in the third, a white woman, deaf.

And in the first face of Libra ascends the form of an angry man in whose hand there is a tube.[251] And in the second, two men serving,[252] and angry. And in the third, a man in whose hand is a bow, and a nude man.

---

[244] *Virga*, which can also be a switch for flogging—perhaps this means there is a team of robbers, one of whom dominates the other.
[245] *Fistula*. This can also mean a reed-pipe for playing, which is how Bonatti takes it.
[246] I take this to mean that the second person is stooped or curved in stature.
[247] I take this description from Bonatti, since it is missing in 1493.
[248] *Elevatus*. I use this rare meaning of *elevo* following Bonatti, who reads "short [or ripped]."
[249] Reading *habentis* for *habens*.
[250] Reading *habens*.
[251] *Fistulam*. Again, Bonatti connects this with reed-pipes and musical instruments.
[252] *Servientes*. This should be understood in the sense that they are slaves or menial, dependent people.

And in the first face of Scorpio ascends the form of a woman with a good face and body. And in the second, a nude man and a nude woman. And in the third, a man bent over his own knees.

And in the first face of Sagittarius ascends the form of a man, a shabby creature. And in the second, a woman on whom there are cloths.[253] And in the third, a man of a color like the color of gold.

And in the first face of Capricorn ascends the form of a woman, and a black man. And in the second, two women. And in the third, a black woman wise in works.

And in the first face of Aquarius ascends the form of a man. And in the second, the form of another man with a long beard. And in the third, an angry black man.

And in the first face of Pisces there ascends a man on whom there are good clothes. And in the second, a woman with a good face. And in the third, a nude man.

§7.23: A question about the association of two people, and what will be its end

And[254] if you were asked about the partnership and association of someone, look for the one asking from the Ascendant; and for his associate from the 7th; and for their being [or condition] from the Midheaven; and for their end, from the angle of the earth.

If the Lord of the Ascendant (and the Moon) were in movable signs, there will be confusion in their partnership—after this, it will endure. And if he were in fixed signs, their partnership will be durable. Indeed if he were in common signs, their partnership will be with wealth, and their association will be with security and the faithfulness of each of them toward the other.

---

[253] Bonatti says, "dressed well."
[254] See *Carmen* V.19.1-14.

And if there were malefics in the Ascendant, injury and lying and separation from the one asking. Likewise, if there were malefics in the 7th, the injury will come from his associate.

And if the Moon were conjoined to the Lord of her domicile, they will be separated with esteem and wealth. If indeed it did not aspect her, they will be separated through the suspicion they will have toward one another. Also, if the malefics were below the earth, they will be separated through[255] the bad evaluation which they will have toward each other. And if the benefics were in the Midheaven, their wealth will be multiplied. Indeed if the malefics were in the same place,[256] their wealth will be diminished. And if the Moon were joined to the Lord of her domicile in one [and the same] sign, and they were both joined to a malefic planet, they will not be separated except by death.

§7.24: A question of one wishing to go to a great man: if he will find him or not

And if a man wished to go to a great man, and he asked whether he would find him or not, look at the Lord of the seventh to see if he were in the angles: the [great] man will be in the place in which he is thought to be. And if he were in one following an angle, he will be near the place.[257] Indeed if he were cadent, the man will not be in the place.

§7.25: On a commander setting off to war, or another worried person when he asks about him

If[258] a commander setting off to war (or someone who is worried about him were to ask for him) were to ask (because even if[259] the king and his kingdom were stable, still, it could be that the commander will be conquered

---

255 Reading *per* with BN for *propter*.
256 I.e., the Midheaven.
257 The text reads "in his own place" (*in loco suo*), but this evidently refers to the place in which the querent believes him to be.
258 These questions bear a close resemblance to *Carmen* V.33, adapted from the topic of lawsuits to that of war; but it is also possible that Theophilus of Edessa, who was known for writing on military astrology, is the main source for this section. Of course, Theophilus himself might have adapted this same passage from Dorotheus.
259 Reading *etsi* with BN for *si*.

and killed, and another might come), put down the ascending degree and its Lord, and the planet from whom the Moon is being separated, for the one asking and the one undertaking it; and the seventh sign and its Lord, and the planet to which the Moon is being joined, for the enemy. If however there were no separation of the Moon, nor a conjunction, you should not admit her in this work. And know that the higher planets are stronger than the inferior planets in the cause[260] of war.

Look therefore at both significators (that is, the Lord of the Ascendant and the Lord of the seventh). If they were joined from a trine or a sextile aspect, and one of them received the other, there will be peace—and the beginning [of it] will be from the one pushing (that is, from the lighter planet). Indeed if they were conjoined from the square aspect or the opposition, and one of them received the other, there will be peace after a contention. If however one of them were retrograde, or in a place (namely in an unsuitable one, as the descension is, or the 6th or 8th or 12th)[261] from him who receives him, he will betray his partner and engage him according to the quantity of the substance of the house in which he is. If he were in the second from the Ascendant, it will give security to him: after this, he will accept his substance. And if he were in the sixth[262] or in the seventh, it will give security to him: after this, he will have him, and he will suffer difficulties[263] by him. And if he were in the eighth, he will kill and destroy him. And if the Lord of the seventh were retrograde in that which I have said, it signifies his flight after the safety. And if one of the significators were separated from the other, the war will endure between them. And if one of the significators were of the higher planets, and it were received in an angle, say that the Lord of that significator will win (unless he would be entering combustion). If however the Lord of the Ascendant were of the superiors, and he were cadent from the Ascendant, and the Lord of the seventh in an angle, and he were of the inferior ones, you will not judge that the questioner is supposed to win, until you see to whom the Lord of the seventh is joined: because if he is joined to a planet in an angle who receives him, the enemy will win, and

---

[260] *Causa*, primarily in the sense of the *pursuit* of war, but also generally in the sense of the *matter* of war.
[261] This reads as though Sahl is speaking of the 6th, etc., *from the enemy* by derived houses (i.e., being cadent from the enemy), but the next sentence makes it clear he means in those houses relative to the *Ascendant* (assuming the Lord of the Ascendant is the operative planet here, and not the Lord of the 7th).
[262] Reading *sexto* (and so on below) to follow the previous use of *secundo*.
[263] Or, "he will undergo/suffer punishment" (*patietur ab eo districtionem*).

he will get the questioner and will have strength and victory over him according to the quantity of that planet to whom the Lord of the seventh is joined. If however the Lord of the seventh were strong, and he were joined to a cadent planet who impedes him,[264] the Lord of the seventh (that is, the enemy) will not cease to have strength as long as he endured in his optimal place.[265] And when he is changed from that same place, he is weakened and will not cease to be weak until he (that is, the Lord of the seventh) would be impeded by the malefics or be burned up:[266] and then the enemy will perish. If indeed he is joined to no planet in the sign in which he is, change him[267] to the next sign; after this look at his conjunction with the planets.

And you should not judge by means of the strength of the inferior planets except by means of the goodness of its place from the Ascendant, and by means of his liberation from the impeding planets, and by means of the aid of the higher planets toward him.

And if the Lord of the Ascendant were in the seventh, it signifies the strength of the enemy, because [the Lord of the Ascendant] is being likened to one conquered—and more severely so if the Lord of the seventh aspected him: because it signifies that the enemy will get the one asking. And if the Lord of the seventh were in the Ascendant, it signifies the strength of the one asking; and if the Lord of the Ascendant aspected [the Lord of the seventh], the questioner will get the enemy.

And if the Lord of the Ascendant were in the eighth, or he were joined to the Lord of the eighth (or the Lord of the eighth were joined to him), it signifies the death of the master of the one asking. Likewise if the Lord of the seventh[268] were in the second from the Ascendant, or were joined to the Lord of the second (or the Lord of the second were joined to him): it signifies the death of the enemy—and more strongly so if the Lord of this domicile were impeded by malefics and did not receive the one pushing him (that is, the one who is joined).

And if the Lord of the Ascendant were joined to the Lord of the Midheaven, or the Lord of the Midheaven were joined to the Lord of the

---

[264] It is unclear to me whether the impeding takes place simply because the planet is cadent, or whether some other condition must be fulfilled in addition to being cadent.
[265] That is, so long as the planet is actually transiting that sign.
[266] I.e., enter combustion.
[267] Reading *muta* (imperative) for *mutabit*. Presumably this only means we should see what happens when he *actually* changes by transit.
[268] BN says, "eighth," but "seventh" makes more sense.

Ascendant, and the Lord of the Ascendant[269] were in the Midheaven, it signifies the strength of the one asking, in his own kingdom, and that he would get him who contends with him—and better than that if the receiver[270] were in an angle, because he will be unconquered:[271] for none would be able [to contend] with him, nor have trust in his[272] kingdom; and [the querent] will get him who contends with him. Likewise if the Lord of the seventh from the Ascendant were in the fourth or were joined to its Lord, or the Lord of the fourth were joined to him and the receiver were in an angle: the enemy will be unconquered; and none would be able [to contend] with him; and it will be feared concerning the kingdom of the one asking.

And if one of the significators were joined to some planet in an angle, or to the Lord of the angle—and better than that if he himself[273] were in an angle (because then it signifies the strength of the master[274] of that same significator)—and likewise if one of the two significators were in an angle, free from the malefics, received—and better than that if it were in a fixed sign, and if it were free from the malefics; and if it were in a mobile sign, it signifies his death quickly after his attainment.

And if the Lord of the Ascendant were in the twelfth from the Ascendant, it signifies the flight of the master of the question. Likewise, if the Lord of the seventh were in the sixth it signifies the flight of the enemy.

And if one significator were retrograde, it signifies the smashing and the weakness of the master of that same significator. And if the Lord of the tenth were in the Ascendant, it signifies that the king will extend aid to the one asking. Likewise if he were in the seventh from the Ascendant, it signifies that the king will aid the enemy.

Indeed if one of the luminaries pushed its own disposition to one of the significators (that is, if it were joined[275] to him), it signifies the strength of the master of that same significator, and that he will have aid from the king. And if the Moon were separated from the Lord of the Ascendant and she were joined to the Lord of the seventh, there will be victory for the enemy.

---

[269] Omitting redundant *caeli*.
[270] This is probably the receiver of the disposition.
[271] Reading *invictus* (as below) for *victus*.
[272] That is, of the Lord of the 7th, since he is the one being conquered in this scenario.
[273] That is, the significator.
[274] *Domini*. That is, of the querent or the enemy.
[275] Reading *iunctus* for *iunctum*.

And know that Saturn, if he were in an angle at the hour of the question, if he had no testimony, it signifies the long duration [or extent] of the war, until [Saturn] recedes from thence—and more strongly so if he were retrograde, because then the war will often be repeated.

And if the Moon were with Mars, and the benefics were cadent from her, then the questioner will be killed or captured.

And if the Sun were with the Head or the Tail when the war begins, there will be the greatest killing of each army, and there will not be peace between them. Which if the Lord of the Ascendant and the Lord of the seventh were with the Tail, there will not remain but few left in each army.

Also, look at the strength of the war and its terror from Mars and from his place from the Ascendant, and from him who aspects it. And look at a small amount of killing (and its multitude) from the Moon, and from her condition, and from her place. And look at the condition of the commanders and their age from the two significators. And look at the planet from whom Mars is being separated, and put this significator as belonging to the questioner and the inceptor; and [put] the one to whom Mars is being joined, as belonging to the enemy. After this, look at one of the two significators: because that one which was in a movable sign will be weaker, and flight is feared from him; and the one of them which was in a common sign signifies that the master of that significator will be persevering in the war, and a fixed sign will signify stability.[276]

Then look at their strength just as I will tell you. If one of the significators were in its own exaltation, it will be stronger than if it were in its own domicile; and the domicile is stronger than the triplicity; and the triplicity is stronger than the bound; and the bound is stronger than the face. Out of each of the planets, the more worthy one is the one who aspects the Lord of its own domicile, because then it doubles its own strength, and then it will be a planet more clever [than] if it were in its own descension or in the place of its enmity[277] and the Lord of its domicile did not aspect it.

And if one of the two significators were in its own exaltation, the master of that significator will be a king; if indeed it were in its own domicile, he will be of the relatives or the household members of the king; if it were in its own triplicity, he will be of the sons of nobles; if however it were in its

---

[276] Following BN at the end of this sentence.
[277] This probably means "in the sign of its detriment."

own bound, he will be below this; and if it were in its own face, he will be below that.

And if the Lord of the domicile of the significator were aspecting him, it signifies the boldness of the commander and his soldiers, and that he is faithful to the king. Indeed if the Lord of his domicile did not aspect him, he will not be well faithful.

And whichever one of the significators were retrograde and impeded, it will provoke [him] to falseness. And whichever one of them were direct and made fortunate, it will provoke [him] to truth and faith.

Also, look at Mars to see if he were in his own exaltation or in the exaltation of the Sun: war will be made manifest, and it will be renowned. Indeed if in addition he were in the Midheaven, the war will be made stronger until it is heard in the east and the west. And if he were in the Ascendant, it will be below what I have told you. And if he were in the angle of the west, there will be cunning and stability there, and the battle will be multiplied. If however Mars were in a fixed sign and he were not in an angle, the war will be below this. And if he were in a common sign the war will often be repeated and multiplied. Indeed if he were in a movable sign the war will be strong. And if he were in his own domicile or his own triplicity, it will be middling. And if he were in his own descension, the war will not be made bigger, but it will be separated in a short time. And announce according to what you see concerning the strength of Mars (and his weakness).

And know that if the Moon were in the Ascendant, and Mars in the seventh[278] (or, conversely, Mars in the Ascendant and the Moon in the seventh), he who goes to battle and who begins [it] will be killed.

And look at the multitude of the soldiers and the allies from the aspect of the planets to the significators and from their appearance in their own domiciles; and make the second sign and its Lord the significators of the soldiers of the one asking, and the eighth and its Lord as significators of the soldiers of the enemy;[279] and the eleventh sign and its Lord as significators of the allies and ministers of the king. Indeed the fifth [sign] and its Lord as significators of the being [or condition] of the city, and of those who are in it.[280]

---

[278] Reading *septimo* (indicating a place or sign) for 7.

[279] These questions assume that war pertains to the wills of the commanders and is between commanders—their soldier's wills and attitude, or the national attitude, is secondary.

[280] Perhaps, as the second from the fourth, it shows the goods and supplies of the city, and its civilian defenders (as though they are the allies of the city).

Indeed if there were benefics in the second sign from the Ascendant, or they aspected it, and the Lord of the second were in a good place, it signifies the strength of the soldiers of the one asking—and their faithfulness and their aid to him. Likewise, through the eighth from the Ascendant is signified the strength of the enemy's soldiers. And if the benefics which are in the second or the eighth from the Ascendant were in a common sign, or in a sign of many children, or in a movable one, announce the multitude of his soldiers. And if there were an oriental planet in the second domicile,[281] or the Lord of the second were oriental, the soldiers of the one asking seek truth. Indeed if he were retrograde, they will disobey him.[282] And if you found a malefic in the eleventh from the Ascendant, [and/or] the Lord of the eleventh retrograde,[283] the servants of the king and his allies are traitors—especially if there were a malefic planet or Mercury in the eighth from the Sun, and the Tail with the Sun: because even the king with his allies is an evildoer, very injurious or liable to cause injury.[284]

If however you came to find that the two commanders will come to an agreement, look at the planet which signifies this. If the one who enters in between them were in its own domicile, he will be one of their own; and if it were not in its own domicile, he will be a foreigner.[285] Indeed if it were Saturn, he will be an old man; and if it were Jupiter, he will be noble and great. If however it were Mars, he will be a commander from out of their commanders, and he wishes evil, and he consents to a lie.[286] And if it were the Sun, he will be the king or the head of an association.[287] And if it were Venus, he will be a man not having a discipline[288] nor good skills.[289] And if it

---

[281] BN reads, "And if [this planet] were in its own domicile, oriental…" But perhaps the reading above is correct because it matches the following clause.
[282] This contrast of "oriental" and retrograde suggests a Hellenistic understanding, where "oriental" simply means "outside of the beams and direct," no matter on which side of the Sun the planet falls.
[283] BN reads, "And if you found a malefic in the eleventh from the Ascendant, retrograde, the servants…"
[284] BN's reading is slightly different: "because even the king, with his associates, is an evildoer [though] very noble." 1493 is likely the correct reading.
[285] The distinction here is between someone who belongs to one of the two groups fighting, or someone from outside—"foreigner" here (*peregrinus*) should be considered loosely, since in the medieval period a foreigner could simply mean someone not from the city itself.
[286] Reading *consentiens* with BN for *sentiens*.
[287] *Congregationis*. This indicates a group of people with common social and political goals.
[288] Perhaps, a "trade" or "trained profession"?
[289] *Ingenium*.

were Mercury, he will be learned and wise, or a scribe. And if it were the Moon, he will be a man who will come between them with goodness and justice.

And look, for betrayal and cunning, to Mercury. If he were impeded under the rays from both planets,[290] there will be betrayal and cunning toward them (namely, from each one of them toward his associate).[291] And if Mars were with Mercury, the cunning and betrayal will appear, for it will be publicized and will not be able to be concealed.

But the witnesses are the planets when they are aspecting, and when they are in one sign. And if the Moon and Saturn were witnesses to the Ascendant, judge that the betrayal already was or will be. Likewise Jupiter, if he provided testimony to the Moon and to the Ascendant, it signifies good. Indeed if Venus were to provide testimony to the Moon and to the Ascendant, it does not signify betrayal. And if Mercury aspected the Ascendant or the Moon, it signifies cunning and betrayal: for the peacemaker which was between them is known from Mercury, which if he were under the rays, and the Moon with Mars or with the planet from whom Mars is being separated, the peacemaker himself will be captured. And if Mercury were oriental, difficulty will find him, and he will be freed from it. And if Mercury were in a common sign, the peacemaker who runs back and forth between them will not be [merely] one [person]. And if there were a malefic planet exalted[292] above Mercury, he will find a severe sentence and will be whipped. And if a benefic will be exalted above him, he will escape. And if he were impeded by Mars at the time, he who whips him will be of the warriors. And if it were the Sun, he will be the king or the head of armies.

Indeed, if you wished to have knowledge of the cause (from which the war was stirred up), look at Mars: because the planet from whom Mars is being separated signifies the one starting the war; and the one to whom Mars is being joined signifies the adversary.[293] If [Mars] were separated from benefics, the one starting [the war] and the questioner seeks truth; and if he were separated from the malefics, he does not seek truth. And if Mars were joined

---

[290] *Ex utrisque planetis.* Normally the phrase "under the rays" only refers to the Sun. This could refer to being besieged by the Lords of the Ascendant and the seventh.
[291] *Socium.* This statement seems to view war as a kind of partnership.
[292] This must refer to the Hellenistic "overcoming," in which there is a malefic in the tenth whole sign from the sign of Mercury.
[293] Unless Sahl is also allowing Mars to join to planets by retrogradation (either theirs or his), Mars would only be able to make these movements between Saturn and Jupiter: old men, ignoble men, and the clergy or the wealthy.

to benefics, the enemy seeks truth; indeed if a malefic were joined, he does not seek truth.

And if Mars were in the Ascendant, the war will be because of sustenance.[294]

And if he were in the second, it will be because of substance.

And if he were in the third, because of faith and religion.

And if he were in the fourth, it will be because of land.

Indeed if he were in the fifth, it signifies that the war comes to be because of substance, and that there is a kinship[295] between the commanders, and perhaps they will make an agreement; or the war will be because of a woman or a city; and especially if you found the Moon joined to Mercury from esteem, then the war will be because of the city toward which those wishing to take it are setting out.

And if he were in the sixth, the war will be because of a weak thing, and there will be much killing or wounding.

And if he were in the seventh, it will be because of an ancient enmity, and he does not seek substance.

And if he were in the eighth, it will be because of an ancient matter, with the seeking of blood—but if the Moon aspected the Lord of the Midheaven, this will be because of the substance of a kingdom, and the killing will be multiplied in each population.

And if he were in the ninth, because of faith.

And if the Moon were in the Midheaven and were joined to Mars from a square aspect or from the opposition, or she were with him in one

---

[294] *Victus.* Or, one's "way of life."
[295] *Propinquitas.*

sign, the war will be for the honor of the king or for making the king greater, and the seeking of a kingdom.

And if he were in the eleventh, it will be for friends and for those who are younger [or lesser] than the king.

And if he were in the twelfth, the war will be because of an ancient enmity, but there will not be a war: because Mars in the twelfth does not signify war, since he is cadent from the angle:[296] for[297] he will be heard, and those who set out for them will obey him, if God wills it.

§7.26: A question whether an army is big or small

And if you were asked about an army, whether it is big or middling, take from the Moon to Mercury the number of signs which are between them: which if they were even, the army will be big; indeed if they were odd, the army will be small.

After this, look to this chapter in the general matters of war, because it is universal in the general matters of war.

That is, that you ought to know that the Ascendant is the significator for the ones starting the war, and its reason; and that it is what has stirred up the war, and whether [the questioner] took it up in truth or with lies.

And the second [sign] from the Ascendant signifies whether a war will arise or not, and whether it will be for [his] profit or harm.

And the third [sign] from the Ascendant signifies arms, and what they are, and by what kinds of arms the victory and gain will be, and what kinds of arms are not necessary in that war.

---

[296] He is also cadent both from the Ascendant and the seventh. This may derive from the Hellenistic notion that planets cadent from the Ascendant are "turned away" from it, and so will not directly affect it—in this case, war will not touch the querent or the adversary.
[297] Taking the latter part of this sentence from BN.

And the fourth [sign] from the Ascendant signifies the place in which the war will be: namely, will it be flat or mountainous, and if it is on the shore of a great sea (that is, of a sea), or a small one, or next to a river, or if fruit-bearing trees are in that same place, or groves.[298]

And the fifth [sign] from the Ascendant signifies the honesty and readiness of the soldiers, and their advance, and [their] boldness or laziness.

And the sixth from the Ascendant signifies the animals of the soldiers, and what they are: that is, whether they are horses or asses or mules, or camels.

And the seventh signifies the enemy and the work of the *al-mijnaqah*[299] (that is, [the work] of the instruments with which stones are projected), and whether the war arises with cleverness and skill, [or] the contrary.

And the eighth signifies plagues[300] and captures and death; also the breaking up and flight of those conquered.

And the ninth [sign] signifies the work of scouts and the knowledge of the enemy's affairs, and his rumors and cunning actions.

And the tenth from the Ascendant signifies the customs or acts of the greater commander, and of the rest of the commanders which are under his authority.

And the eleventh signifies their organization, and what their battle array and gathering will be like, and how they advance, and their organization against the enemy.

---

[298] *Nemus*. This could also mean "plantations."
[299] "Catapult." 1493 reads *almagenie*, and BN either reads *almagenu* or *almagenii* (making a Latinized genitive). Another Arabic word for catapult is *al-minjanīq*, which is another possibility.
[300] *Plagas*, reading it in the medieval sense. In the classical sense, "afflictions, wounds, gashes."

And the twelfth signifies the city and those who are besieged and attacked in it.³⁰¹

Therefore, look at these twelve places and at the places of their Lords, and at their aspects to see which ones aspect whichever domicile of them (namely of the malefics and the benefics), and even which ones are in them—whether it is a benefic or malefic—and which one aspects the Lord of each domicile from out of those benefics and malefics.

After this, speak according to what you saw concerning the aspect of the benefics and the malefics, and concerning their strength and weakness: because if a benefic aspected a sign, it signifies fortune and good for that sign; and if a malefic aspected from a square aspect or the opposition, or it were in the same sign, it introduces impediment and evil into it (namely into what pertains to that sign according to its significations, about those things which I have expounded to you in this chapter).

§8: The eighth sign or 8ᵗʰ domicile, with its questions: and first, whether an absent person or some man is living or not

If³⁰² you were asked about an absent man, or about some other man, whether he is living or is dead, look at the Lord of the Ascendant and the Moon to see if they were in the fourth from the Ascendant or in the domicile of death (which is the 8ᵗʰ from the Ascendant), or they were combust or in their own descension or with the Lord of the domicile of death, or with the Lord of the fourth domicile: he will be dead. And if you found some one of them so, look at the aspect of the malefics and the benefics to them.³⁰³

If the Lord of the Ascendant were in the fourth, retrograde, or retrograde in his own descension, or retrograde in the domicile of death, or separated

---

³⁰¹ Note that this differs from his earlier statement about cities and the fifth. But perhaps the city's *besiegement* is what is operative here.
³⁰² In this chapter many conditions are stated, and it is not entirely clear whether they are all meant to hang together, or are distinct. After speaking of the Lord of the Ascendant and the Moon together, Sahl treats of the Lord of the Ascendant separately, then returns to the Moon—but I am unsure whether both the Lord's and the Moon's conditions are meant to be treated together, so that both must be met before death can be judged. I have broken the chapter up into thematic paragraphs, but the reader should remember that this is only for the sake of reading ease, and not necessarily reflective of Sahl's intent.
³⁰³ In the 1493 text the sentence does not end here, but the rest of the sentence is logically distinct, so I have broken this section into different sentences.

through retrogradation from the Lord of the domicile of death, look to see if he turns back to the degree of combustion: he will be dead.[304]

And if the Moon is joined to a planet below the earth, he will be dead. And if she is joined to a planet above the earth, he is living.

And if you found the Lord of the Ascendant in the 12th, with the malefics, or the malefics aspected him, and one of the luminaries were impeded, you will judge death for him. Also, if there were malefics in one sign with the luminaries (which are the Sun and the Moon) without the aspect of the benefics, it signifies death. And likewise if the Moon were with Mars in the fourth, and the benefics did not aspect her. Likewise if the Lot of Fortune were with the malefics in the fourth from the Ascendant, or in the sixth or the twelfth, and the benefics did not aspect her: they signify death.

And know therefore [that] what is above the earth signifies life; and what is below the earth signifies death. Therefore, if you found the Lord of the Ascendant combust under the rays and no benefic aspected him, and the Moon were under the earth, cadent from the Ascendant in the third or the sixth, know that he about whom the question is, is dead—especially if it came out that the Moon is in Scorpio in the third degree of it, impeded by Saturn: because it[305] naturally signifies death. Then you will establish the death of him about whom the question is.

§9.1: The ninth sign or 9th domicile, with its questions: and firstly whether there will be a foreign journey or not, and if it cannot be perfected, what prohibits it

If you were asked about a foreign journey, whether there would be one or not—and if it cannot be perfected, what it will be which impedes or prohibits it—look at the Lord of the Ascendant and the Moon (which are the significators of the one asking); and the ninth sign and its Lord (which are the significators of foreign travel).

If the Lord of the Ascendant (or the Moon) were in the ninth, or one of them were joined to the Lord of the ninth, the foreign travel will not be horrible for the querent [and he will go] of his own volition.[306] And if the Lord

---

[304] But the rest of the paragraph does not mention combustion, and combustion was only given as one possible condition in the previous one. Meaning uncertain.
[305] I believe Sahl means "Saturn."
[306] *A semetipso*, also relying on Bonatti's more detailed explanation (*BOA* p. 536).

of the ninth were in the Ascendant or were joined to the Lord of the Ascendant, the journey will happen to him such that it cannot be frustrated altogether. If however what I told you before about the condition of the Lord of the Ascendant and about the condition of the Lord of the ninth were not the case, and some planet rendered or brought away the light of one of them to the other (namely, a transfer of light), it signifies foreign travel. Which if this were not so, and you found the Lord of the Ascendant and the Lord of the ninth joined to a planet heavier than they, and that planet aspected the domicile of foreign travel,[307] it signifies the foreign travel; and if it did not aspect, he will not go on foreign travel.

Moreover, if the Lord of the Ascendant were in an angle and were joined to a planet which is on the left side of the Ascendant (that is, between the Ascendant and the third),[308] and it[309] were free from the malefics, it signifies foreign travel. If however the Lord of the Ascendant (and the Moon) were joined to a planet in an angle, he will not go on foreign travel. And if the significators were joined to each other (that is, the Lord of the Ascendant and the Lord of the ninth), and a peregrine malefic were in the Ascendant, impeding the Lord of the Ascendant or the Lord of the ninth, there will not be foreign travel—and this will happen from the side of the man (that is, from the side of the one asking): something will happen to him which will disturb and prohibit his foreign travel. And if that malefic were in the seventh,[310] it will come to him from that same land to which he wanted to set off, or from the matter which he was seeking, which would frustrate and prohibit his foreign travel. And if the malefic were in the Midheaven, a burden will come to him from the king or from him who is above him [in status] or who is in charge of him. And if the Lord of the Ascendant were joined to the Lord of the domicile of the journey after he was joined to a malefic from the opposition or from the conjunction or from the square aspect, or he was with it in one sign, announce a difficulty which will happen to him after the foreign travel, according to the quantity of the enmity of the planet (that is,

---

[307] Evidently by a whole-sign aspect. This is a new twist on the collection of light: perhaps it is not always required that the collecting planet should aspect the domicile of the quaesited, but it certainly would help.

[308] This must mean between the first degree of the rising sign and the last degree of the third sign.

[309] The Latin is unclear as to whether this refers to the Lord of the Ascendant or the other planet.

[310] Here and below we still seem to be dealing with the same sort of malefic as in the previous sentence, but in this case the malefic is in a different angle.

if it were the Lord of the sixth from the Ascendant, it will be an infirmity; and if it were the Lord of the fourth, it will be prison or some sorrow; and if it were the Lord of the eighth, it will be death; and if it were the Lord of the seventh or twelfth, it signifies difficulty from robbers and enemies); and if it aspected from the Ascendant, killing will be feared for him. Indeed if it aspected from the second from the Ascendant, it signifies the detriment of substance. Likewise, the [first] square aspect from the Ascendant signifies the impediment of the body, and the other, second square aspect (that is, from the tenth) signifies the detriment of substance.[311] And if you found the Lord of the Ascendant in the seventh or in the eighth, it signifies labor in foreign travel, and especially if he were a malefic.

Wherefore if the Lord of the Ascendant had already begun to arise from under the rays [of the Sun], or were already released from its impediment in which it had been, the foreign travel will be easy. And if you found the Lord of the Ascendant in the Ascendant or in his other domicile, nor [is he] already joined to the Lord of the ninth, he will not go on foreign travel,[312] especially if it were a fixed sign (because a fixed sign destroys a journey).

And if you found the Moon received, it signifies ease. Indeed if she were not received it signifies slowness and complications, and that he will attain nothing in that foreign travel, and it will be hateful and burdensome[313] at the home of him to whom he goes. The Lord of the Ascendant signifies likewise if he aspected her from the opposition.

And[314] know that the Ascendant signifies the one on foreign travel, and the Midheaven his quaesited matters or those he should seek. And the seventh [sign] from the Ascendant [signifies] the land to which he goes. Indeed the fourth [sign] from the Ascendant signifies the end of the matter. Therefore if there were benefics in the Ascendant, the condition of his mind and body will be useful; and if there were benefics in the Midheaven, his matters will be useful and successful; indeed if there were benefics in the seventh, he will see what he wanted and desired in the land into which he comes. And if you found some one of the malefics in the Ascendant or in the Midheaven, or in the sixth, infirmity and worthless labor and decrease will happen to

---

[311] I am not sure why Sahl is saying that the fourth pertains to the body and the tenth to substance.
[312] In other words, by the Lord of the Ascendant being in his own domicile, the querent will "stay in his own home."
[313] *Ponderosus*.
[314] See *Carmen* V.21.

him. If however you found benefics in the fourth from the Ascendant, the end of the matter will be according to what he wants and desires (if the malefics, to the contrary).

And[315] if you saw that[316] there would be foreign travel, and you wished to know to whom the foreigner is setting out, look at the Moon. If she were joined to the Sun, he travels to nobles or to the king. And if she were joined to Saturn, say that he is setting out for ignoble and low-class people. And if she were joined to Jupiter, say that he travels to nobles.[317] And if to Venus, to women. And if to Mercury, to writers and merchants and wise men. Indeed if the Moon were void in course, he leaves seeking [someone] familiar.[318] Which if she were separated from Saturn, he goes out on account of debt because he is threatened by his creditors. And if she were separated from Mars, he will be a fugitive (or like a fugitive) from the king.

Then look at the planet to which the Moon is joined: if it were in its own domicile, the man to whom he travels will be of the citizens of the region. And if it were in its own triplicity, he is not of its citizens, but comes to it and spends time in it. And if the Lord of the domicile of the planet to whom the Moon is joined, aspected [that planet], he will be well-known in the region; and if he did not aspect [that planet], he will be unknown in it. And if the aspect were from the square, he will be from out of that same region, between praiseworthy and blameworthy, nor is he wholly praised nor wholly blamed. And if the aspect were from the opposition, he will be hateful and contentious. If however the aspect were a sextile and a trine, he will be esteemed. And if he were conjoined to [the planet] in one sign, he will be of those who take away the substances of men by force.

After this, look at the malefic itself who impedes the Lord of the Ascendant or the Moon. If it is in the human signs (which are Gemini and its triplicity), warn him that he should beware of robbers and the cutters of roads. And if it were in the watery signs, he should beware of shipwreck. And if it were in the signs of animals, he should beware of the misfortune

---

[315] This paragraph is reminiscent of *Carmen* V.14.
[316] Reading *quod* for *quae*, following BN.
[317] Both BN and 1493 omit Mars. Bonatti (*BOA* p. 542) says, "And if she were joined to Mars, it signifies that he goes to warriors or to bellicose soldiers or pirates or to cutters of roads."
[318] *Notum*. *Notus* can also mean "well-known," but since we are talking about the Moon's voiding in course, which usually indicates nothing special or significant will happen, I take it to mean simply a routine person the querent already knows. Bonatti (*BOA* p. 542) says he will travel "to find an absent person who is known to him."

of beasts or from their strikes. Indeed if it were in the signs of seeds, he should beware of trees and thorns, and of a higher place, or from food in which there is poison. Indeed if the malefic were in Leo especially, the impediment will be because of a wolf; and in Scorpio especially, because of reptiles; and in Pisces especially [he should beware] of those things which spend time in water. And Mars is of greater impediment on land, and Saturn impedes more on the sea.[319]

§9.2: A question about the entrance of the foreigner into some city: what it will be like for him in it

Concerning the entrance of the one traveling, look, when the foreigner enters the city, to see what sign is ascending at the hour of his entrance. If the Lord of the 2nd domicile[320] from the Ascendant were retrograde, it signifies the quickness of his turning back, without the perfection of his business. Indeed if it were in its second station (when it wishes to be made direct), he will return [with a speed] between quickness and slowness, and he will perfect his business after losing hope. And if it were in its first station (when it wishes to go retrograde), he will slow down and turn back without the perfection of his business, and he will not find good. And if the Lord of the 2nd were in the Ascendant or in the Midheaven or in the 11th, the foreign journey will be sound and successful. And if it were in the 7th, difficulty and contention will happen to him on his foreign journey. Indeed if it were in the ninth or third, he will not rest in that land until he sets out to another one. If however it were in the fourth, and a malefic aspected him or were with him, this will be his last[321] foreign travel, and death in that region is feared for him, and he will not turn back by any means.

If however the Moon were joined to the Lord of the second in one sign, or he aspected her, or she were joined to Mercury in one sign, or Mars as-

---

[319] This sentence is clearly from *Carmen* V.35.42. But note that when hunting or fishing, it is the opposite: Mars is considered more helpful for hunting on land, and Saturn more helpful for fishing. See §§13.15-16, and *On Elect.* §140b. Perhaps the difference is that, when hunting and fishing, we want to harness the powers of bloodshed (Mars) on land, and the powers of the sea (Saturn), whereas when traveling we want to avoid these dangers.

[320] The reason we focus on the Lord of the 2nd must be because it is the sign immediately following the rising sign, and so it shows what comes next to the traveler.

[321] *Ultima*.

pected her, he will find plagues[322] and ruptures[323] and a horrible thing. Which if then the Moon were in the angle of the earth, he will die[324] from this. Indeed if she were in an angle outside of this one, the mark of the difficulty and rupture will remain in him. And if the Moon aspected Mars and no benefic aspected him, he will find plagues according to the content of the sign in which he is. Which if then the benefics aspected the Moon, there will be liberation concerning the difficulty which I stated, and healing for this infirmity, and a remedy for the rupturing and plagues will be found. Indeed if the benefics did not aspect, they will remain in this until he dies because of them.

§9.3: A question about the nature of the journey of princes or kings, and the nature of those who succeed them[325] or remain behind

And if you were asked about the nature of the journey of princes or kings, and the nature of those who succeed them or remain behind, look to the second from the Ascendant, to see if there were a malefic in it which did not have testimony: there will be some detriment after his departure in those who remain behind him (namely in his relatives and kingdom). If it were Mars, contention and war and the burning of fire; and if it were Saturn, robbers or infirmity or shipwreck. If however the malefic were received, it will not impede this, and it will be improved. Indeed if it were in its own descension, it[326] will be perfected and made greater;[327] and more strongly so if it were retrograde (because then it will signify dissolution and detriment).[328]

---

[322] *Plagas*, reading it in the medieval sense. In the classical sense, "afflictions, wounds, gashes."
[323] *Fractiones*. Earlier the Latin translator used this to denote an illness that returns or "breaks out" again. So it must refer to outbreaks of diseases of some sort. Bonatti (*BOA* p. 546) links this to wounds, including wounds from being tortured or maimed.
[324] Reading *morietur* with BN for *movetur*.
[325] I.e., of those who take the prince's place when he is gone.
[326] This probably refers to the disaster.
[327] Reading *magnificabitur* with BN for *monstrabitur*.
[328] This sentence is strange. Why would being in its own descension perfect the journey, but being retrograde indicate destruction "more strongly so"? Bonatti (*BOA* p. 548) interprets this passage somewhat differently: "If it were a malefic having dignity in the 2nd, and it were direct or were received, its malice is removed; nor will it impede by a very perceptible impediment. If indeed it were retrograde, its malice will not be wholly removed, however it will kill very little, because it is received. But if it were retrograde and were

Speak likewise about the benefics if they were in the second from the Ascendant, concerning success and good praise. And know that the Lord of the Ascendant or the Moon, if they were impeded, signifies sorrow and difficulty on the road.[329]

Which if there were a malefic above the earth between the Ascendant and the tenth, this will happen on his trip back; and if it were between the seventh and the tenth, on his departure; and if there were a malefic below the earth between the Ascendant and the fourth, in those things which he has acquired in his departure. Indeed if it were between the fourth and the seventh, in those things which he has acquired during his return.[330]

§9.4: A question whether the land in which the querent is, is better, or that one to which he is about to go

If[331] someone were to ask you, saying: "The land in which[332] I am—is it better for me, or that to which I want to go," look at the Moon to see if she were separated from a malefic: leaving will be better for him. Indeed if she were separated from benefics, staying is more useful for him. And if the condition [or nature][333] of the Lord of the Ascendant were good, staying is more useful for him; indeed if the condition [or nature] of the Lord of the seventh were better, going will be more useful for him.

And if he were to ask you: "See[334] for me [if] it is good if I should leave to this business matter, or I should do this or something else," look at the Lord of the Ascendant and the Moon. If they were separated from malefics and were joined to benefics, instruct him to do what he wants. Indeed if they

---

neither received nor in its dignity, its malice will be increased, and will kill more. You will say the same if it were in fall or in its descension."

[329] BN reads differently, omitting the Lord of the Ascendant: "Speak likewise concerning the benefics (or the Moon) if they were in the second from the Ascendant: if they were impeded, they signify sorrow and difficulty on the road."

[330] Bonatti thinks this passage is in error, and that the Latin translator has made the mistake. See his construal of this in *BOA* p. 548.

[331] This chapter is reminiscent of §6.6, and may simply be an adaption of it. See also §6.7 for another approach to this question.

[332] Reading *qua* for *aqua*.

[333] *Esse*. I believe this refers to whether the planet is angular, direct, *etc*. But it is possible that it refers to its intrinsic nature as benefic or malefic.

[334] Reading *vide* for *vides*.

were separated from benefics and joined to malefics, he should not approach the work.

§9.5: A question about someone conquered:[335] what will become of him

If[336] you were asked about some conquered person. Look in this just as you look in foreign travel: because you look for each in terms of their exit from their place—but under the heading of a conquered person, if the Lords of the angles (or certain ones of them) were in their own domiciles, in the angles, it signifies the holding back of certain ones of them in that year.[337]

After this,[338] you will look from the Lord of the Ascendant and his place: which if he were in an angle, it signifies the prolonging of the prison—and more strongly so if it were the angle of the earth (which if the Lord of the twelfth or one of the malefics aspected it,[339] he will find punishment[340] with prison). Indeed if the Lord of the Ascendant were cadent from the Ascendant, but he was joined to a planet in an angle, his prison will be prolonged after he was hoping to escape [it]. If however he were in an angle and were joined to a cadent planet, it signifies his liberation after losing hope.[341]

But if [the Lord of the Ascendant] were joined to a malefic planet which was in the angle of the earth (which is the fourth sign), or the Lord of the eighth (which is the sign of death) were in the Ascendant, he will not exit the prison until he dies. And if the Lord of the Ascendant (or the Moon) were

---

[335] 1493 reads this as "conquered" (*victo*), but BN reads it as "fettered" (*vincto*).

[336] *Cf. Carmen* V.27.

[337] This must mean that they are a first indication that the conquered person will not leave prison—along the same lines as the statement above (concerning foreign travel) that a planet in its own domicile will indicate someone who "stays at home" or will stay where he is.

[338] This must be a secondary consideration, if the Lords of the angles show continued detention.

[339] *Quem*, meaning "the angle," but Sahl or the Latin translator indicates in the next paragraph that this is the fourth sign.

[340] *Districtionem*. Or perhaps merely "difficulty."

[341] The statements so far show that the angles signify continued imprisonment; cadent houses or domiciles show escape. And the Lord's location is his starting condition—the planet receiving his light is his future condition. This is an example of how angles show stability, which normally is considered something good; but for an incarcerated person, it is not.

joined to some planet in the third or the ninth, it signifies liberation—and more easily so, if [the planet in the third or ninth] were not the Lord of any of the angles of the Ascendant,[342] and if one of them (that is the Lord of the Ascendant or the Moon) were joined to the Lord of the third or the ninth or to the receiver on the left [side] of the Ascendant: it signifies his liberation. And this will be from an action which he performs through himself, and no one will entreat on his behalf. Indeed if the Lord of the third or the ninth were joined to the Lord of the Ascendant, someone will work on his behalf, and he will be liberated without his own striving. Indeed if the Lord of the Ascendant were joined to the Lord of the 12th, and it[343] were on the left of the Ascendant, it signifies his flight from out of the prison. Likewise if the Lord of the third or the ninth were with the Lord of the twelfth. If however the Lord of the Ascendant were joined to the Lord of the third or the ninth, but the receiver (that is, the heavier one)[344] were in an angle, he will not go out until the receiver goes out of the sign and recedes from the angles.[345] And if the Lord of the domicile of the Moon were joined to the Lord of the Ascendant, it signifies a delay in leaving.

After this—after you have ceased to look with the Lord of the Ascendant and his conjunction with the stars, and in the conjunction of the stars with him—look at the place of the significator (that is the Moon) to see if she were in a mobile sign: it signifies the quickness of his liberation (except for Cancer, which is slow because it is her domicile):[346] and Aries and Libra are faster in freeing than Capricorn; and he will not delay in the prison, and he will find many allies in that same place. Indeed Capricorn signifies slowness, and solitude and sorrow, and because enemies labor so that he might be retained in fetters. And if she were in a fixed sign, it signifies the slowness of the exit (and slower than all is Aquarius). If however the Moon were in a common sign, and he was not liberated before the Moon goes out of that same sign, his imprisonment will be prolonged—and more strongly so if it

---

[342] Bonatti (*BOA* p. 556) reads all of this as though Sahl is speaking of the Lords of the third and ninth, not a planet in the third or ninth.
[343] It is unclear which Lord is meant here.
[344] I.e., the receiver of the disposition.
[345] I.e., until it leaves the angular sign, so that "receding" here must refer to going into the succeedent sign, not "being cadent."
[346] Remember that, just as above and in the case of journeys, a planet in its own domicile remains "in its own home"—here, the prison.

were a domicile of Jupiter and he himself did not aspect it.[347] Indeed, in the domiciles of Mercury, if he were in the prison itself he will find good and joy.[348]

Then look at [the Moon's] conjunction, to see if she were in an angle, and she were joined to a planet on the left of the Ascendant, and the Lord of the Ascendant testified: likewise it signifies liberation. And if the Moon were cadent and she were joined to some planet in an angle, it signifies the prolongation of the imprisonment unless the planet were the Lord of the third or ninth: then he will be liberated when that planet has changed.[349] And if she were cadent and were joined to a cadent planet who is the Lord of some angle, he will be in the hopes of going out until the planet enters some one of the angles of the Ascendant—and then he will lose hope. Which if the one to whom she is joined is the Lord of an angle, and he were in the third sign or the ninth, it will be better and easier to exit. And if she were joined with the Lord of some one of the angles (and especially to the Lord of the Ascendant), it signifies slowness.

And if the Lord of the Ascendant is entering under the rays, and there were a malefic in the fourth, he rarely lives. Which if the malefic were Mars, he will be killed after he exits from the prison. If however the Lord of the Ascendant has already crossed over combustion, he will become infirm with a strong infirmity. And if some one of the malefics were in some angle, by how much more you saw him farther from the degree of the Sun, by that much more will his infirmity be light—and he will be freed [from the infirmity] more quickly. And if he[350] were joined to the Lord of the eighth from the Ascendant, or to a malefic in the angle of the earth, he will die in prison. And if he were with Saturn, or aspected him from strength, it signifies the prolongation of the imprisonment, and sorrow and impediment in substance and the body. Indeed if he were with Mars, it signifies impediment and being bound. And if the Moon were then impeded, distress will find him and he

---

[347] *Eam*. This could refer to the Moon, but I take it to refer to the domicile itself by a whole-sign aspect.

[348] Reading as *si fuerit in ipso carcere*. But this does not quite make sense—presumably he is already in prison. In BN it is possible that the text reads as an abbreviated *nisi*, in which case it would read "*unless he is* in the prison itself, he will find good and joy." That is, he may be conquered but might have some freedom to pursue his own activities without being in a cell all day. But I am not sure which reading is the correct one.

[349] I.e., has changed into the next sign by secondary motion.

[350] I believe this refers to the Lord of the Ascendant.

will not be whipped. And if the Moon aspected the Lord of her own domicile, it will be easier; indeed if she did not aspect, it will be harder.

After this, look at the condition of the one asking from the Lord of the Ascendant, and the condition of the one who contends with him, from the Lord of the seventh. If they aspected each other from a trine or from a sextile aspect, he who provokes the other with ease, will seek him out, and with patience, desiring peace and being safe and sound. Indeed if they aspected each other from the opposition or from the square aspect, he will seek him out with severity and trouble, and he will be much persevering in the seeking of his justice.

§9.6: A question about the arrival of an absent person

If[351] you were asked about the arrival of an absent person, look at the Lord of the Ascendant and its place. If it were in the Ascendant or in the tenth, or it committed its own disposition to a planet which is in them, it signifies his arrival. And if the Lord of the Ascendant were in the ninth or in the Midheaven,[352] or it committed its own disposition to a planet in them, it signifies his arrival. Indeed if the Lord of the Ascendant were in the seventh from the Ascendant, or in the angle of the earth, there will be duress in his arrival, and delay; and it signifies that the absent person is in the land in which he is, not yet going out from thence. And if the Lord of the Ascendant were in the ninth or in the third from the Ascendant, and it were joined to a planet in the Ascendant, he is on his journey, wanting to return—likewise if the Lord of the Ascendant were in the eighth from the Ascendant, or in the second, and it were joined to a planet in the tenth (that is, in the Midheaven). If however the Lord of the Ascendant were cadent and was not joined to some planet in an angle, nor did it aspect the Ascendant, it will be bad because it signifies slowness. And if the Lord of the Ascendant or the Moon were joined to a retrograde planet, or were the Lord of the Ascendant retrograde and it aspected the Ascendant, it signifies his arrival.[353] And if the

---

[351] *Cf. Carmen* V.22.7-13.
[352] It is not clear to me whether Sahl is repeating himself, or whether he is implying a meaningful distinction between the "tenth" and the "Midheaven."
[353] This sentence could also be read thus: "If the Lord of the Ascendant or the Moon were joined to a retrograde planet (or were the Lord of the Ascendant retrograde), and it aspected the Ascendant..." On this reading a retrograde Lord of the Ascendant all by

Lord of the Ascendant were impeded, it signifies duress and the prolonging of the arrival.

If however what I said about the Lord of the Ascendant were not so,[354] look at the significatrix (which is the Moon): which if she committed her own disposition to the Lord of the Ascendant in the Ascendant, or near the Ascendant (namely by 2°),[355] it signifies the quickness of the return. And if the Lord of the Ascendant were in the seventh and in the one succeeding it, it will be prolonged.[356] If however the Moon were separated from the Lord of the fourth or the seventh (also the ninth or the third) and she were joined to the Lord of the Ascendant, it signifies the arrival. Again, if she were separated from a planet which was on the left of the Ascendant (that is, below the earth), and she were joined to a planet on the right of the Ascendant (that is, above the earth), it signifies the arrival. Indeed if the Moon were cadent and were joined to the right of the Ascendant to a planet in the tenth, it signifies arrival with delay, because if the Moon were on the right of the Ascendant she would be impeded: it signifies duress and the holding back of the arrival.[357]

§9.7: A question of a vision or dream[358]

The understanding of this is that you should always consider the ninth sign. Then, if you find a star in it, make [the star] the significator over the

---

itself indicates the arrival, as does it or the Moon being joined to a retrograde planet which *itself* aspects the Ascendant (as a rendering of light). BN has a slightly different reading: "If the Lord of the Ascendant or the Moon were joined to a retrograde planet, or were its Lord retrograde, and it aspected the Ascendant, it signifies his arrival." Here it is unclear who "its Lord" refers to.

[354] Presumably this means, "if none of the indicators of arrival are present, whether slow or fast."

[355] This parenthetical remark does not appear in BN. Is Sahl referring to the degree of the Ascendant, or that far from the borders of the whole sign?

[356] This means that the Lord of the Ascendant is in the seventh *or* the eighth (which is the sign succeeding the seventh).

[357] BN reads slightly differently (due to word order), and adds a little more: "Indeed if the Moon were cadent and were joined to a planet to the right of the Ascendant in the tenth, it signifies arrival with delay, because the Moon was on the right of the Ascendant; and if she had been on its left, it would be quicker; and if the Lord of the Ascendant had been impeded, it signifies duress and the holding back of the arrival."

[358] This chapter does not appear in BN, and contains numerous spelling and grammatical errors (unlike the rest of the work).

goodness or badness of the vision. If however you do not find a star in it, then consider the tenth: and if you found a star in it, then it is the significator over the goodness of the vision. Which if you did not find a star in it, then consider the Ascendant. And if you did not find a star in it, then consider the seventh. And if there were no star in it, then consider the fourth. Which if you did not find a star in it, then consider the third. Which if you did not find some one of the stars in this place, then the vision is not sound, and it is the deception of an unreal dream, and he did[359] not see it, or he has forgotten it.[360]

And if you *do* find some one of the stars in one of the aforesaid places, then you should know it: which if it is Saturn or the Tail, then he saw[361] a terrible thing of those things which bring fear. Then, look to see of which domicile that star is the Lord: then that which makes him fear, and terrifies him, is of the kind of the domicile of that planet. For if it is the Lord of the twelfth domicile, then that which terrifies him are enemies or their type—and say[362] likewise in the rest of the domiciles.

> And if the significator over the vision is Jupiter, then he saw kings and those placed high [in society] or made lofty, and those who are greater than all, and those likened to the nature of Jupiter.

> If however it is Mars, then he was seeing[363] a hunt or a duel, or [people] being joined [in conflict] by law,[364] or a dispute[365] or fight, or flesh, or blood or arms or an instrument [of war] or things which are like the nature of Mars.

> And if it is Venus, then he saw vestments and cloths and a good, estimable or aromatic or delightful thing, or pearls, or women, or girls or sodomitical boys, and the rest of the things which agree with the nature of Venus.

---

359 Reading *vidit* for *videt*.
360 Note that the rules for this question read largely like those of a consultation chart. Presumably the dreamer *knows* what he dreamt, but Sahl spends much time below trying to determine just that.
361 Reading *vidit* for *videt*.
362 Reading *dic* for *dicit*.
363 Reading *videbat* for *videbit*.
364 *Ex lege coniungi*. Perhaps this refers to lawsuits?
365 Reading *altercationem* for *alterationem*.

And if it is Mercury, then he saw something spiced [or aromatic] or *mischitas*³⁶⁶ or certain people giving speeches, or *denarii*³⁶⁷ or images or voices, or certain people buying and selling, and people altercating³⁶⁸ and things which are like the nature of Mercury.

And if it is the Sun, then he saw that³⁶⁹ he was flying between the heavens and the earth, or he saw light or fire, or a king, and things which are like the nature of the Sun.

And if it is the Moon, then he saw a woman, or the sea,³⁷⁰ or poor old ladies, or a stream.

And if it is the Tail, then he saw darkness, and dust, and whispering and murmuring. And if it is the Head, then he saw greenness and fragrance and gold, and the like.

And if the sign in which the significator is, is feminine, and the star signifies something of fear, then he saw a high, elevated place, or a high cliff, standing out on a crag,³⁷¹ or as though he fell from up high, or being raised up into a place, and a violent force, or a gusty wind. And if the star which signifies fear is in an earthy sign, then he is as it were stoned or surrounded [or besieged], or falling into a pit, or in a dark and narrow place; but he found his way out. And if it is in a fiery sign, then he saw a someone being hanged, or a burning up, or a flame, or fire, or fog [or gloom], or blackness. And if it is in a watery sign, then he saw drowning [or submersion] or a flood, or overflowing, or the sea, or danger.

Then look to see with what star the Lord of the Ascendant (and the significator of the vision) is joined: for if both (or one of them) are being joined with a benefic, then the harmful thing (of what he saw) will not pursue him. And if they are being joined with a malefic, then the harmful thing

---

³⁶⁶ Unknown word. It looks like it has connotations with mixtures (like foods with complex combinations of tastes?), but I cannot be sure.
³⁶⁷ A Roman coin.
³⁶⁸ Reading *altercantes* for *alterantes* ("changing"), but since Mercury also signifies interchanges between people, perhaps it should be "people changing."
³⁶⁹ Reading *quod* for *quare*.
³⁷⁰ Reading *mare* for *marem*.
³⁷¹ *Aut rupem altam supereminentem caute.*

of the vision will pursue him, according to the kind of the domicile of the one conjoined. For if it is the Lord of the *census*,[372] the harmful thing will pursue him in his *census*. And if it is the Lord of the seventh, the harmful thing will pursue him in women. And if it is the Lord of the fifth, then in children; and it happens likewise in the rest of the domiciles. And likewise, if the vision is agreeable, then look at the kind of the domicile of the one conjoined, with the significator,[373] and what is like it of the domiciles, and judge assistance from the kind of its domicile.

§10.1: The tenth sign or 10th domicile, with its questions: and firstly about a kingdom in which someone has confidence that he will attain it, or not

If you were asked about a kingdom in which someone had confidence, whether he would attain it or not, look at the Lord of the Ascendant and the Moon. If[374] the Lord of the Ascendant (or the Moon) were joined to the Lord of the tenth, and the receiver[375] aspected the Midheaven,[376] it signifies attaining it with success and eagerness, and with the seeking of the one questioning, and with his searching. Likewise if the Lord of the Ascendant (or the Moon) were in the tenth, not impeded. Indeed if the Lord of the Midheaven were in the Ascendant or were joined to the Lord of the Ascendant, he will attain the kingdom without seeking and inconvenience. It will be likewise if the Lord of the Midheaven were joined to a benefic in the Ascendant. Which if there were nothing of this which I have told you, and you saw a planet rendering their light (that is, transferring the light from one to another), then the questioner does not seek the matter through himself, but he seeks someone who will act on his behalf in this. If however the receiver of the disposition aspected toward the Midheaven, and it were free from

---

[372] The *census* was a system of assessing land and population for the purpose of levying taxes. Bonatti connects the *census* with the 2nd house (*BOA* p. 96). In this context I think the planet might be the Lord of the 11th, referring to the king's tribute or taxes; but it might be the Lord of the 2nd, the people's wealth. Then again it might also refer to the 4th, agricultural goods.
[373] Reading *significatore* for *significator*.
[374] Compare with OR Ch. 8.
[375] I take this to mean the Lord of the tenth, i.e., who is receiving their disposition.
[376] This seems to be a case of Abū Ma'shar's "rendering of light" (*Gr. Intr.* VII.5.985ff), discussed by Bonatti (*BOA* p. 217-18). But it is also a case of a planet aspecting its own domicile.

malefics, he will attain it. Indeed if it were impeded and did not aspect the Midheaven, this effort will be dissolved after going forward. And know that the malefics impede from the square or from the opposition (they destroy the question); but from the trine or from the sextile aspect, they impede less.[377] And if the light of the Lord of the Ascendant and the light of the Lord of the Midheaven were conjoined to some[378] planet (namely, if they were both joined with it and the planet itself were in the Ascendant or in the Midheaven), then[379] look at the Moon: which if she were joined to the Lord of the tenth, it will be.[380] If indeed she were joined to none of them, and she were free from the malefics, he will attain it, and he will have the aid[381] of many men. If however the Moon were not as I have said before, and there were a planet who conjoined her own light in the Midheaven, or she aspected him, and she were not cadent, nor did [she/it][382] go out from that same sign until the Lord of the Ascendant (and the Lord of the tenth) were joined to it, and [she/it] were free from the malefics, he will attain it wholly.

§10.2: A question about any matter: if he will attain it or not

If you saw the Lord of the Ascendant and the Lord of the tenth conjoined, look at the Moon to see if she committed her own disposition and strength to one of them, and she were received, and free from the malefics: expect its effecting.[383] Indeed if she committed her own disposition to none of them but she were received, it will be slower. If however she were not received, nor were she impeded, look at the receiver of the disposition from them: if it were free from the malefics, aspecting its own domicile, he will

---

[377] Reading with BN (but omitting a *non*). 1493 has two strange interpolations: "And know that *if* the malefics impeded from the square or from the opposition, *the master of the question will turn back from his associate, with a foul turning-back* (they destroy the question). But from the trine or from the sextile aspect, *he will return* (they impede less)."
[378] Reading *alicui* for *aliquis*.
[379] *Tunc.* It is unclear whether a sentence has broken off, or whether this complex condition is an antecedent for the following complex lunar consequent.
[380] Again, reading with BN. 1493 continues the interpolations: "...then look at the Moon: which if she were joined *with a good or beautiful turning-back*, and to the Lord of the Ascendant or the Lord of the tenth, there will be attainment."
[381] Reading *auxilium* with BN, for *auxilio*.
[382] It is unclear whether this refers to the Moon or the other planet. I suspect it refers to the other planet. See the third paragraph of the next chapter.
[383] Reading with BN for *annuntia ex toto et spera effectum*.

attain part of those things which he sought. And if [that planet] were impeded according to what I said about the impediment of the Moon, he will not attain it. And if the Lord of the tenth were joined to the Lord of the fourth, and the Lord of the fourth to the Lord of the Ascendant, he will attain it. Indeed if the Lord of the Ascendant were joined to the Lord of the fourth, and the Lord of the fourth were joined to the Lord of the Midheaven, he will attain it after losing hope. And if the Lord of the Ascendant received the disposition of the Moon, the seeking of the kingdom will be easier.

And know that if the Lord of the Ascendant were in its own domicile, he will be set up over the land in which he is; and if it were in its own exaltation, he will be set up over many lands, and especially a work of dignity. Indeed if it were in its own triplicity, it signifies a great work, but it will not be in his own land in which he is. If however it did not have testimony in its own place, he will be unknown in the land of which he is in charge.[384]

And know that perhaps the Lord of the Ascendant and of the tenth will be one planet (like if the Ascendant were Virgo and the tenth Gemini). Which if it were so, and that planet were received, and the Moon committed her own disposition and strength to him from an angle, he will attain it.[385] Indeed if the planet were received, and likewise the Moon were received and in a good place, and it aspected the place of the matter or its own domiciles, he will attain part of those things which he sought. If however it were not received, and the Moon were impeded, he will not attain what he sought. And perhaps it will not be fitting that the Lord of the Ascendant should aspect the Lord of the tenth (like if the Ascendant were Leo, and the angles correct):[386] then look at the place of the Sun and of Venus, each one by itself: which if they were received and aspected the Midheaven, it signifies their success. If indeed one of them were received, and the other not, look at the Moon to see if she committed her own disposition and strength to him who is not received: he will attain it. If however they were not received and the Moon were impeded and not received, nor did she aspect some one of them, and the one who receives the disposition aspected the Midheaven and

---

[384] Note that Sahl omits the bound; whether this is intentional or whether he is simply copying from another source, I do not know.
[385] *Cf.* end of §1.6.
[386] *Recti*, which also means "upright, straight," *etc.* If the angles were "correct," then Leo would be rising and the degree of the MC would be on Leo. But the Sun (ruling Leo) and Venus (ruling Taurus) cannot aspect each other, they can only be in corporal conjunction.

were not impeded, he will attain part of those things which he sought. And if a planet conjoined their light in an angle,[387] nor were it going out from its own place until it would be joined to it,[388] it signifies success and the attainment of those things which he sought.

After this, look at the Moon. If she were received and aspected the Midheaven, his strength and fortune is already perfected. And if the Moon were joined to the light of the Lord of the Midheaven or transited through him, and she were joined to his body and aspected the Midheaven, he will attain it. And if the Lord of the domicile in which the Moon is, aspected her, and they both aspected the tenth, he will attain it. And if the Moon did not run up to the light of some planet, in the sign in which it is, before it goes out of it, seeking the matter, he will not attain his matter unless the Lord of the Ascendant and the Lord of the matter would have strength and testimony in the places, and both aspected the place of the matter.

And know that the defect of the Moon and of the Lord of the Midheaven signifies the diminution of the matter in the working—and worse than that if the receiver of the Moon's disposition were impeded: because it signifies the detriment of the work. And if the Moon were joined to the Lord of the Ascendant or to the Lord of the Midheaven, it will help toward success. If[389] however the Lord of the Midheaven pushed strength and disposition to a planet who receives them, and who has strength in its own place and [that of] the matter, and it did not aspect the Midheaven, the matter will not be perfected in the same manner in which it is sought. And if the significator is inimical to its own domicile, it signifies duress and complications in the seeking of the matter: and enmity is like if it is in the twelfth of its own domicile, or in the second one, or in the sixth one, or in the eighth one. And if it aspected it from the seventh,[390] it signifies contrariety.

And know that the Lord of the Ascendant is the significator of those things which the lord of the kingdom runs into, in terms of praise and blame, and the rest of the things which are from that. And the Lord of the seventh is the significator of the work of his citizens, and the Midheaven and

---

[387] This sounds like the collection of light.
[388] I take this to mean, "if their light were applying to a planet in a whole-sign angle, and the angular planet did not leave the sign before the aspect was perfected."
[389] BN reads somewhat differently: "If however the significator pushed their strength to the disposition of the planet who is receiving them and who has strength in its own place and [that of] the matter..."
[390] That is, by opposition, which would place the planet in its own detriment.

its Lord are the significators of those things which come to be in his kingdom, in terms of the good or bad. And the eleventh [sign] and its Lord are the significators of those things which follow after him in his work (that is, in the kingdom).[391] And the ninth [sign] and its Lord are the significators of those things which were before him. And the fourth and its Lord are the significators of the end of his work.

Therefore, look for the significator of his acquisition and his substance from the second sign and its Lord, and from the Lot of Fortune and the goodness of its place and its Lord;[392] and from the eleventh and its Lord, his renderings[393] and his friends; and his brothers from the third sign and its Lord; and his slaves from the sixth and its Lord; indeed his enemies from the twelfth and its Lord. Therefore look at the aspect of the benefic and malefic planets to these places:[394] wherever there is a benefic, there will be good, joy, and wealth; and wherever he found a malefic, there will be impediment and fear and the taking away of [one's] hands from obedience,[395] and war.

§10.3: A question: on what will he spend the substance which the king has collected

And if you were asked on what he will spend the substance which he has collected, look at the Lord of the domicile of substance: if it were Mars, he will spend it and disperse it in every bad work (like a battle, and luxury, and drunkenness, and the rest of such things). And if it were Saturn, he will disturb his own mind and squander his own and another's substance. Indeed if it were Jupiter, he will spend it for the love of God, that is, in alms,[396] or on every good work. And if it were the Sun, he will sacrifice it on account of parents, and in the acquiring of a nobility. And if it were Venus, he will make up his own mind to engage in every delight. And if it were Mercury, on buying or selling, seeking wealth. If however it were the Moon, he will operate

---

[391] Or, "of those people who come after him in his work."
[392] Omitting "and writers from the second sign" with BN.
[393] *Redditus*. This must refer to taxes and tributes paid for him once he attains his new position.
[394] Obviously by whole signs.
[395] That is, desertion and betrayal. This phrase is also used in the *Flowers*.
[396] *Elemosinis*.

according to the nature of the planet to which she is joined. And if she were void in course, he will spend it until it is used up.

And the Lord of the Ascendant, too, signifies the nature of its end (because it is the fourth from the tenth) and his being deposed. Namely, if you found the Lord of the Ascendant either in the twelfth or the sixth or in the eighth, it signifies the disgracefulness of his deposing—and even more disgraceful if it were in the sixth or in the twelfth: then it signifies why one gets angry with him, and will have mistrust and get exercised, so that he who is set up after him rises up against him. If however the Lord of the Ascendant were received, the evil will be taken away (that is, he will not suffer any martyrdom, nor will he be conquered). Indeed if it were not received, and it were impeded in addition to what I said, what happens to him after his deposing will be worse than his deposing.

And if the Lord of the twelfth were joined to the Lord of the Ascendant, and he did not receive him,[397] the aforesaid commander[398] will be conquered—and even more strongly so if it were in one of the angles: which if it were in the tenth, he will be conquered in his own kingdom, in the eyes of all, and he will be placed publicly before them; and if it were in the Ascendant, it will be below what I [just] said; indeed if it were in the fourth, this will be in secret (but however, in his honor);[399] if however it were in the seventh, he will be handed over to citizens of his honor,[400] and he will find punishment from them. But if it were cadent from the angles, on the right of the Ascendant, and were commingled with the Lord of the twelfth, he will not be conquered in his own honor until he is dragged to the land in which he is to be detained. Indeed if it were on the left of the Ascendant, he will be conquered on the journey. And if he were joined to the Lord of the eighth after his separation from the Lord of the twelfth, it signifies his death in his being bound up. Indeed if he were joined to the Lord of the Midheaven after the Lord of the twelfth, he will find a kingdom after being bound up.

---

[397] Who is meant to receive whom?
[398] *Praefatus praepositus*, an unexpected expression in this translation. One would have expected *praedictus* combined with a more concrete noun like *rex, dux,* or *princeps*.
[399] I am not sure what this is supposed to mean (*in honore suo*). Perhaps he will be disposed while saving public face, as when disgraced politicians claim they are stepping down in order to "spend more time with their families."
[400] Reading *ipsius* with BN for *impervis*. Again, it is unclear to me what this phrase about honor means. But both the 4th and the 7th pertain to "honor," while apparently the 1st and 10th do not.

And know that Mars signifies being bound up just as the Lord of the seventh signifies it, if he is inimical to the Lord of the Ascendant: that is, if he were the Lord of the second or the eighth or the sixth or the seventh or the fourth (and the Lord of the eighth is more crafty, because it signifies death in his being bound up).

And look at the malefic who impedes the Lord of the Ascendant: if it were Saturn, [then it signifies] what I said about punishments, and he will be a martyr from out of prison, and by a beating of sticks. And if the one impeding were Mars, it will be because of chains and the pains of iron and the beating of whips.

§10.4: A question about the condition of the king from the one who set him up[401]

And if you wished to know the condition of him from the one who set him up, look from the Ascendant and its Lord for the one asking, and from the seventh and its Lord for him who set him up. If the Lord of the seventh received the Lord of the Ascendant or pushed his own strength[402] to him from the trine or sextile aspect, or the square, their matter will be conjoined in the best way. And if the Moon carried the light between them, she will be for him[403] who strives between them (namely who sends concord between them) *if* the Moon committed disposition to the receiver from a place of esteem. (And the malefics are wholly crafty from the square aspect or the opposition, and the benefics work from the square aspect and the opposition.) Which if the two significators were not joined to each other, and no star carried the light between them, what will be between them is not as they want it.

---

[401] *Constituerit.* I believe this refers to a succession between two people in an office: how they will get along after the succession.
[402] Remember that this is a technical term from *Introduct.* §5.12. Here the Lord of the 7th would be in its own dignity, and in an applying aspect to the Lord of the Ascendant.
[403] Reading *ei* for *eis*.

§10.5: A question concerning what land the master of the kingdom is from

If however you wished to know from what land the master of that kingdom is, look at the sign of the Midheaven to see if there were a planet there, and in its own domicile: he will be of the men of that land, and of the middle-class ones; and if in its own exaltation, he will be of the more noble of men. Indeed if it were in its own triplicity, he will be below this. And if it were not in its own domicile or exaltation or its own triplicity, he will be a foreigner.[404] And if the planet were eastern,[405] he will be of the citizens of the east; and if it were western, he will be of the citizens of the west. And if he were in the fourth from the Sun, he will be of the citizens of the north; indeed if he were in the tenth from the Sun, he will be of the citizens of the south. If however the planet were peregrine in the sign in which it is, and it did not aspect its own domicile nor exaltation, he will not be of good stock. And if there were not a planet in the Midheaven, talk about the Lord of the Midheaven just as I have told you before.

§10.6: A question about his entrance to the seat [of power]

And look at the hour of his entrance into the seat of his kingdom, provided that he did sit in the seat of his empire and undertook to rule and protect it. If his entrance was in the day, and the Sun were with Saturn, judge for him the speediness of his being deposed from that work (that is, from the kingdom). And if the benefics aspected the Sun, and you found the Lord of the Ascendant and the Sun in an optimal place from the Ascendant, and he[406] were in a fixed sign, his principate will be prolonged, and he will see what he wants in it. Indeed if the malefics aspected the Sun, and the malefic

---

[404] Again, Sahl omits the bound.
[405] The following classification seems to be a version of being "east/west relative to the Sun," described by Schmidt in his introduction to *Tet.* IV (pp. xiii-xiv). Being "oriental" here probably means being in the same sign as the Sun, and "occidental" means being opposite it. Note that being in the fourth sign from the Sun means being from the north, and being in the tenth, from the south. These are based on an analogy between the angular houses, which face the four cardinal directions.
[406] The Latin is in the singular, so I do not know which is meant. Surely it would be better if both the Lord of the Ascendant and the Sun were in fixed signs.

were Mars, and he were exalted[407] above [the Sun] from the Midheaven, and the Sun were in the Ascendant in a movable sign, some one of the citizens of that kingdom will be turned against him, who often terrifies him; or his end will be by means of death and killing. If however you found Jupiter in the Midheaven, and he were made fortunate, and the Sun were in an optimal place (and a strong one), his work will be in exaltation and increase, and in memory, and the collection of substances. And if you saw the Sun in the eighth or in the sixth, and the Lord of the Ascendant were in the Ascendant or in the Midheaven, and [the Lord of the Ascendant] were a benefic, the matter of this prince will be the best, but it signifies the death of him who set him up.

And if the entrance of his kingdom were in the night, look at the Moon just as I told you before about the Sun, and look at the Moon's being saved from the malefics: which if she were cleansed of the malefics and in a good place, it signifies the health of his body. Indeed if the Moon were with the malefics or joined to them, he will be deposed quickly from his honor, and he will have the greatest complaint, and a strong one.[408] And if the Moon were with the Head or the Tail, and there were 4° and less between them, he will not profit in that work. If however there were more than 4° between them, her impediment will be less until she transits 12° from the hour of her liberation from their evils.

Also, look at the Moon and the Ascendant and the Lords of their domiciles, and at the aspects of the benefics and the malefics toward [the domiciles]: if the benefics aspected them and their Lords, and their Lords were in good places, and the malefics were cadent and the benefics in the Midheaven, the prince will see what he loves. And if the Moon and the Lord of her domicile were in bad places, he will find evil in that region.

After this, look at the Ascendant at the hour of his entrance,[409] to see if its degree were of the bounds of the malefics, and the malefics aspected that same bound of the Ascendant: he will be weak in that work, and the worst accusation will be made [against him] in it. Indeed if the degree of the Ascendant were of the bounds of the benefics, and the benefics aspected them,

---

[407] This must originally have referred to the Hellenistic "overcoming," and simply means "if Mars is in the tenth sign from the Sun."
[408] I take this to mean that a complaint against him will not only be great, but also valid.
[409] I.e., as an event chart (or perhaps as an election proposed beforehand). Presumably such a chart would be cast with an eye to his natal chart or the horary showing success (the root).

the work will be perfected, and he will go out an honored man, and every good thing will be said about him, together with wealth which he will find because of his work.

And if there were a malefic in the Ascendant, his work will be bad, for he will find difficulty in it, and perhaps he will die in his work. If however there were a benefic in the Ascendant, and a malefic in the fourth, the beginning of the work will be praiseworthy and good, indeed its end bad. And if there were a malefic in the Ascendant and a benefic in the fourth, the beginning of the matter will be bad and its end will be good. And if you found the Tail in the Ascendant, and the Lord of the Ascendant were in a bad place, and there was a malefic in some one of the angles, also were the Moon impeded by the malefics, he will have low-class underofficials from the ignoble, who destroy his rule—and he will not cease to be sad and troubled and in fear so long as he endures in the work.

Wherefore if you found a benefic in the Ascendant at the hour of entrance, or you found the Lord of the Ascendant in the Midheaven—also, were the Lord of the Midheaven in a strong place, free from malefics—it signifies the goodness of the condition of that prince, and the prolonging of his principate. Indeed if there were a malefic in the Ascendant, and the Lord of the Ascendant a malefic, and the Lord of the Midheaven were in a bad place, judge that he will be deposed more quickly. And if you found the Lord of the Ascendant and the Lord of the Midheaven in the twelfth or in the sixth, judge his fall will be hastened unless Jupiter were oriental[410] in the Ascendant or in the Midheaven (because this will make his deposing slow down a little bit).

After this, look at the sign of the Midheaven and its Lord (to see where he is), and who aspects it and the Lord of the Midheaven. Which if [the Lord of the Midheaven] were in an angle and the benefics aspected him, it signifies the goodness of his condition; and if there were a benefic in the Midheaven, he will arrive in his work to better and more worthy things of his trust and will, and he will be considered worthy in that honor, and his rule will be strong, and his wealth will be multiplied. Indeed if the malefics were in the same place, he will find great difficulties in that work, and whatever he earned will be taken away from him through martyrdom and being bound up,[411] and by being deposed in the anger of his king, which [the king] will

---

[410] I am not sure in what sense this "oriental" is meant.
[411] Reading *vinctione* with BN for *convictione*.

have against him. And if a benefic aspected the Midheaven, and there were not a malefic in the same place, the work will be an advantage,[412] and good. But if a malefic aspected, it will destroy his work. If however a benefic *and* a malefic aspected [the Midheaven], see which one of them is in more degrees, and that one will conquer the other—but the other will take up a portion from him.

And if Mercury were with Jupiter in the Midheaven, his work will be overflowing by means of wisdom and counsel and reason and skill, and he will have a name and fame through it, it will increase (for the job in which he is in charge) the work and [its] delay, in the regions[413] (and especially if it[414] aspected the Moon). But if the Sun were in the Midheaven with them, without the aspect of the malefics, it signifies the prolonging of the sound of his name, and the attainment of his work in everything which he wishes, and the length of his life in that time. It will be likewise if Jupiter were with the Moon in the Midheaven, and Venus were in an optimal place. And whenever you find a benefic in the Midheaven, his difficulty will be decreased, and he will find good. Indeed if the malefics were in the same place, and the Lord of the Midheaven and the Lord of the Ascendant were cadent, he will endure [only] a middling amount in his work.

And whenever you find Mars[415] in the seventh from the Ascendant, and there were not a benefic in the Ascendant, he will die in the same work. Which if Saturn were in that same place, and a benefic in the Ascendant or in the seventh, he will not die, nor will be he killed in that work. Indeed if there were a benefic in the seventh, he will be deposed in a fine way, with honor and health.

And if there were a benefic in the fourth, he will be sound in body and his end will be according to what he wishes. Indeed if there were a malefic in the same place, he will find evil and impediment after he is deposed from the work, with prison and martyrdom and punishment, and in extended imprisonment. If however a benefic aspected the fourth, he will escape after the tribulation and punishment which he will find. Indeed if a benefic did not aspect the malefic which was in the fourth, he will be conquered and undergo punishments, and he will die in that same prison. But if the Lord of

---

[412] Reading *quaestum* for what looks like *quaetum* in both BN and 1493.
[413] *Et augebit operi suo cui praeest opus et dilationem in regionibus.* I am not sure what the astrological rationale for this is; but perhaps something is missing from the Latin.
[414] This must mean either Mercury or the Moon.
[415] Reading *martem* with BN for *mortem*.

the fourth were in the Ascendant or in the tenth, or in the rest of the optimal places, cleansed of the malefics, and likewise the Lord of the domicile of the Moon, it signifies the good end of the work.

§10.7: A question about the stability of the king, or about his withdrawal

And if you were asked about the stability of the king[416] or his withdrawal, look at the Lord of the Ascendant and the Lord of the tenth to see if they were conjoined. And were the receiver of the disposition (that is, the heavier of them) in an angle, the king will not be moved, nor will he depart from his kingdom. And if the receiver of the disposition were on the left of the Ascendant (that is, below the earth), he will depart from it, namely he will turn back. Which if the receiver of the disposition were received, it signifies the quickness of his turning back, with honor. If however the Lord of the Ascendant and the Lord of the tenth have already transited the light from one another, that is, if they were separated from each other, it signifies the moving away of the king.

Which if the Moon pushed her own disposition to a planet of a slower course, in an angle,[417] he will remain in his kingdom until that planet is burned up[418] or impeded in its own place or it withdraws:[419] then it signifies the taking away of his kingdom.

And if the Lord of the Ascendant were joined to the Lord of its descension, he will perform an action in which he will perish. Indeed if the Lord of his descension were joined to the Lord of the Ascendant, a lie will be said about him, and that [someone] would do this so long as he would live.[420]

And if the Lord of the Midheaven were joined to the Lord of its descension, the one in charge or the commander will destroy his own region. Indeed if the Lord of the descension of the Lord of the Midheaven were joined to the Lord of the Midheaven, his region will be destroyed.

---

[416] Reading *regis* with 1493 for *regni*.
[417] That is, the *other* planet is in an angle. See the parallel sentence below.
[418] I.e., enters combustion.
[419] I believe this means "until it changes into the next sign."
[420] *Et quod hoc fecit quousque vivat*. BN simply reads, "and that he did not do it" (*et quod hoc non fecit*). I am not sure which is the true Sahl, but 1493 is phrased in an odd, ungrammatical way.

And if the Lord of the Ascendant pushed its own disposition to a planet in an angle, the Lord of that kingdom will endure in his kingdom—and better than that if the receiver of the disposition were in some one of the angles except for the fourth (because it is the opposite of the 10th, and contrary to it).

Indeed if the Lord of the Ascendant were joined to some planet in the ninth from the Ascendant, or in the third, or with their Lords, there will be no doubt of his departure from his kingdom. Which if it were joined afterwards to some planet in an angle, he will return to his kingdom after moving away. And if the Lord of the Midheaven were in its own place, the king will not withdraw from his kingdom if the Moon were joined to him.

Also, if Jupiter were in an angle and had a portion[421] in it, or he received the Moon or the Lord of the Ascendant, he will remain in his kingdom until Jupiter encounters a malefic or is burned up[422] or recedes from his own place.

And know that the Lord of the Ascendant and the Lord of the Midheaven, if they were joined, and the receiver of the disposition were in a good place, not combust nor received, but it did not aspect the Midheaven, the prince will be set up over a kingdom that is not his but another's. Indeed if it did aspect the Midheaven, it signifies his stability in his own kingdom.

And if the Lord of the Ascendant and the Moon were in angles in movable signs, and the Moon were not received, the king will move away.

After this, look at the Moon to see if she pushed her own disposition to some planet in an angle: the master of the kingdom will not move away from his kingdom if the Lord of the Midheaven aspected his own place. Indeed if the Moon were joined to the Lord of the Ascendant and he were removed from the angles,[423] and evil would encounter the Lord of the Ascendant before the Moon is separated from him, he will be deposed from his kingdom. Moreover, if the Moon were joined to a peregrine planet in[424] the ninth or the third, or the Lord of them [were] in the place of foreign journeys, he will depart from his kingdom. If however it[425] were in the fourth sign, a movable

---

[421] I.e., a dignity, especially by domicile or exaltation.
[422] I.e., combust.
[423] I believe this means "cadent."
[424] BN says "from."
[425] Probably the peregrine planet.

one, the king will be removed—and more certainly[426] than that if the Moon is joined to the Lord of the end of the matter (that is, to the Lord of the fourth from the Ascendant), unless the Lord is in its own domicile: because then it will be better for him. And the Moon will be even more certain than that if she were joined to a planet in its own descension, or it were in the opposition of its own domicile. Indeed if the Moon were strong in her own place, and she were void in course, it signifies the cutting-off of that kingdom.

§10.8: A question about him who has withdrawn from his kingdom, or an absent king: whether he will return

And if you were asked about a man who has withdrawn from his kingdom, or about an absent king, whether he will return to his kingdom or not, look in this just as I have told you before in the first chapter, on the conjunction of the Lord of the Ascendant and the Lord of the Midheaven with each other. Which if they were joined, and the receiver of the disposition (from among [those two]) aspected the Midheaven, the king will return to his kingdom.[427] Indeed if it did not aspect the Midheaven, and the Moon were joined to a planet in the Midheaven, he will return.[428] And if the Lord of the Ascendant were retrograde, he will return again to his kingdom. And if the Moon, along with what I have told you, were in a movable sign, it will be faster for them. Indeed if the Lord of the Ascendant were not retrograde, and the Moon were joined to a planet in the Ascendant or in the Midheaven, he will return (likewise if the Moon were joined to the Lord of the Ascendant). And if he[429] were joined to the Lord of the domicile of foreign travel (that is, the ninth from the Ascendant), the Lord of the Ascendant will seek withdrawal of his own accord.[430] And if the Lord of the Midheaven were joined to the Lord of his own descension, it signifies the removal [or remoteness] of the king, even if it were in angles. And if the Lord of the

---

[426] *Callidius*, "more craftily." I do not see where the notion of cleverness or craftiness appears in these configurations, I am treating this as a misread for *certius*, "more certainly," here and in the next sentence.
[427] This sounds like a "rendering of light" *a la* Abū Ma'shar.
[428] This sounds like perfection "by location."
[429] The text reads "he" (*iunctus*), but it is worth mentioning that Bonatti reads this as referring to the Moon, which would also make sense given the previous sentence.
[430] *A semetipso.*

Ascendant were joined to the Lord of his descension, it even signifies removal [or remoteness]. If however the Lord of the Midheaven were in his own place, a removed [or remote] one will return to his own kingdom.

And if the Lord of the Midheaven were separated from the light of the Lord of the domicile of the end of matters (that is, the fourth from the Ascendant), he will return. If however he were joined to him, he will be removed. And if this same Lord of the fourth were joined to the Lord of the Midheaven, he will persevere in his own kingdom and another kingdom will be given to him. Indeed if the Lord of the fourth were joined to the Lord of the Ascendant, he will not be removed,[431] and a kingdom will come to him without his seeking it. And if the Lord of the Ascendant were separated from the Lord of the fourth, it signifies the firmness of the kingdom if the king were removed [or remote]—likewise if the Lord of the fourth were joined to him.[432] And if the Lord of the Ascendant and the Lord of the Midheaven were joined, and the Lord of the Midheaven did not aspect his own place, he will be set up over another land which he will be in charge of.

After this, look at the significatrix (that is, the Moon): which if she were joined to the Lord of the Midheaven, and the Lord of the Midheaven aspected his own place, he will return—and better than that if the Moon were in a movable sign. And if she pushed her own disposition to a peregrine planet in its own place, on the left of the Ascendant, he will be removed. If however the significator were received, he will return to his own kingdom. And if it were not received, he will be removed.

And if the Moon were joined to a planet in the ninth from the Ascendant, pronounce the withdrawal of the king. If however that planet were a benefic, and it were in a movable or fixed sign, he will return to his kingdom. Indeed if it were in a common sign, he will go to a kingdom outside the first kingdom, and he will rule for three years, because the receiver of the disposition of the Moon does not fall[433] until it comes to the twelfth place from the Ascendant; and in the second year, he will be in better work and in the great satisfaction of his will, unless first a malefic should come up to the Midheaven and go retrograde in it before the aforesaid hour. Because if a malefic were to come up to that same place, it will destroy his kingdom. And if the

---

[431] *Removebitur.* If the text had read *remotus erit*, this likely would mean "he will be remote [or far away]."
[432] I have ended this sentence here, although it is not clear in the 1493 text whether this completes the thought, or continues on with the next clause.
[433] Or, "is not cadent." This is clearly a kind of profection technique.

Moon were joined to benefics or were received, he will be praiseworthy in his kingdom. Indeed if she were joined to malefics, he will be blamed. And if she were joined to a planet in the tenth, he will not withdraw, and he will work for two years. And if she were joined to a planet in the eleventh, he will rule for one year. If however a malefic did not come up to the Midheaven and were retrograde there, and if she were joined to a planet in the fifth from the Ascendant, he will be in charge for two years and will withdraw in the third year. Indeed if she were joined to a planet in the fourth, he will be in charge for one year and be removed in the second.

And if you found the Moon and the Lord of the Midheaven both impeded by a corporal conjunction in an angle, he will not ever return to his position,[434] and he will be deposed and remain deposed according to the quantity of the place of the position. Indeed if you found the Moon and the Lord of the Midheaven made unfortunate, and if they were in common signs, his position will be made greater,[435] and he will be strong in his work; and if he went out from his position, he will return to it.

§10.9: A question if he will arrive to a kingdom or not[436]

And if someone were to ask you whether he would arrive to a kingdom or not, look at the Lord of the Ascendant and his significator (which is the Moon): if they were joined to the Lord of the Midheaven or to the Sun, or they were in the Midheaven, say yes; lacking this, not.

§11.1: The eleventh sign or 11th domicile, with its questions: and first, whether he would attain a matter which he hopes for

If you were asked about some matter which is hoped for and in which there is trust, like concerning dwellings from kings or an honor,[437] look at the Lord of the eleventh from the Ascendant: if it were joined to the Lord of the Ascendant, or the Lord of the Ascendant were joined to it, he will attain

---

[434] Reading *opus* as "position" (i.e., his "task") here and below.
[435] Reading *auge[bi]tur opus* with BN for *augebitur operi eius aliud*.
[436] Not in the sense of traveling to one, but in having a kingdom to rule.
[437] *Mansionibus*. That is, houses and/or tracts of land granted by a high official, or else as part of a promotion to some special duty.

the matter in which he had trust. If however it was a conjunction from the trine or from the sextile aspect, what I said will be with ease. Indeed if it were from the square aspect or the opposition, it will be on account of a difficulty. And if the Lord of the eleventh were in an angle, and the Moon [were] received, the trusted matter will be perfected according to how he wished it.

And if the receiver of the Moon's disposition were in a common sign, a middling amount of what he was hoping for will be attained. And if it were in a movable one, there will be difficulty in what I said. Indeed if it were in a fixed sign, he will attain what he hoped for perfectly. If however you found the receiver of the Moon's disposition impeded, the matter will be destroyed after its attainment. And if the receiver of [the Moon's] disposition were received, he will attain more than what he hoped for. And if the Lord of his Ascendant were received, he will have everything that he wished for.

§11.2: A question whether someone would be joined to his friend or not

And if he asked you about one person whom he said was a friend, and he said, "see whether I will be joined to him or not," look at the Lord of the Ascendant and the Moon, to see if they were joined to the Lord of the eleventh from the Ascendant: he will be joined (and likewise if the Lord of the eleventh would be joined with the Lord of the Ascendant). If however it were a conjunction from the trine aspect or the sextile, there will be joy, esteem, and happiness in their conjoining. If indeed it were from out of the square aspect or the opposition, there will be contrariety and contention in their conjoining, and each one of them will be contrary to his associate (also, in the opposition the contention will be stronger).

§11.3: A question about a hope not expressed: whether someone will attain according to his hope

And if you were asked about a matter which was not laid out to you, and he said to you, "I hope for a matter in which I have trust: see whether I may have it or not."[438] Look at the Lord of the Ascendant and the Moon to see if they were joined to benefics from out of the angles or from the followers of the angles: he will attain it. Indeed if they were not joined, say no. And if he were to name the matter [specifically], seek it from its own place in the circle according to what I expounded to you of the natures of the twelve significators.[439]

§12.1: The twelfth sign or 12th domicile, with its questions: and firstly, which beast will win the prize in a race

If you were asked about beasts, "which beast will win in the race," and the questioner had a beast in the contest, or he had a hunch about some one of the beasts, look at the Lord of the hour in which you were asked: which if it were in the Ascendant, the beast about which he has a hunch will beat all the [other] beasts. And if it were in the Midheaven, it will come in second (that is, it will come in after the first one); and likewise in the eleventh. And if it were in the seventh from the Ascendant, it will be the middle one of them. And if it were in the fourth, it will be last, and no beast will be after it. And if the Lord of the hour were in its own descension, the one riding that beast will be terrified,[440] and he will fall down from it. And if in addition to what I said the malefics aspected [the Lord of the hour], part of his body will be broken—the one the sign itself signified. Indeed if a malefic aspected it from the opposition, or were with [the Lord of the hour] in one sign, and the Lord of the Ascendant were in its own 8th domicile, he who races will die from the fall—and more certainly[441] than that, if the Lord of *that* domicile[442] or the Moon were impeded.

---

[438] Stated this way, it is a very generic universal question, and does not even pertain to the eleventh—which is why Sahl simply has one look at the general significators' relation to the benefics. Later in the paragraph he supposes the querent offers a particular question about a particular matter.

[439] Or, "of the twelve things signified," which suggests the houses more so than their Lords. This chapter seems like it belongs in §13, questions not obviously pertaining to a specific house.

[440] Reading *currens eandem bestiam terrebitur et cadet ex ea* with BN, for *currens eadem bestia terrebitur ex illo modo*.

[441] Reading *certius* for *callidius*. The translator's use of *callidus* is often unclear in its purpose, as I noted in §10.7.

[442] I.e., the Lord of the domicile which is the 8th from the Ascendant.

§12.2: A question: what is the color of the winning beast

If however someone who did not own a beast (among the other beasts) were to ask, namely saying, "which of them will win," look at the Lord of the hour.[443] Which if it were in the Ascendant or you found another planet in the Ascendant or in the Midheaven or in the eleventh, he who wins that day owns a beast according to the color of that planet.[444] Which if it were in some one of these places, and if the significator of the victor were in its own domicile or in its own exaltation or in its own triplicity, or in the bound or its own face, the beast who wins will be of good stock and well-known—and more worthily so if it were the domicile or exaltation. And what is outside of this will be bad. Indeed if it were not in one of these [places] which we have said, it will be unknown. And if in addition to what I said it were in its own descension, [the beast] has a malign style[445] and the worst spirit. And in its own exaltation and domicile, it will be of good stock; and in the triplicity, it is not known in its own land, and it will not be of good stock; indeed in the bound or the face, it will be known in the land but not of good stock—for it is not known from what land it is.

§12.3: A question about the age of the winning beast

And if you were asked about its age, look at the significator. If it were oriental, it will have two teeth; and if it were occidental, it will be filled up.[446] And if it were between both, it will be first—that is, having four teeth. And if you found nothing of those things which I have told you, look at the Ascendant. If it were the domicile of the Sun, the winning one will be from among the king's beasts. And if it were the domicile of Saturn, the beast will

---

[443] *Cf. On Hidden Things* §6, on the color of hidden object. There too, the Lord of the hour shows colors. Why? Could it be based on an analogy of the color of atmospheric light (which changes rapidly) and the hours (which change rapidly)?
[444] Obviously horses do not come in colors like red, blue, and so on. But since antiquity, animals representing teams or clans have been known by their colors: e.g., the Blues or Greens of the Romans, and the colored flags of the competing quarters of Siena in their annual horse race. So perhaps this is what Sahl means.
[445] *Consuetudinem,* "habit."
[446] The age of horses and camels can be tracked by the growth and distribution of teeth, but I am not sure whether the originator of this doctrine was referring to horses, camels, or some other beast.

be of great age, and perhaps it will not be of good stock (unless Saturn were in an angle or in an optimal place). And if it were in the domicile of Jupiter, the beast will belong[447] to someone honored who assists the king.[448] And if it were the domicile of Mars, the winning animal will belong to a certain duke [or commander] who puts on arms, and to a warrior. And if it were Venus's or Mercury's it will belong to some noble or the king or a woman or a writer. Indeed if it were the domicile of the Moon, it will belong to a certain businessman, and therefore the beast is being shown in order that it might be sold.

§12.4: A question about enemies in general: what there will be between them

And if you were asked about enemies in general, [look] from the twelfth domicile and its Lord; or, if one man were named to you, from the seventh and its Lord. Look to see what there is between them in their conjunctions, just as I have expounded to you.

For I have already expounded to you matters in questions in the twelve signs, and now I will lay it out for you those things which are not of the twelve signs, lest perhaps you should go astray: because the wise have already gone astray in this. And were it not in the twelve signs, take it from the substances of the planets, because [those] matters are more than can be comprehended [through the twelve signs].

§13.1: [Additional questions:] a question about a letter or a legate

If you were asked about a letter or a legate, look for him who has written the letter from the Ascendant, and from him from whom the Moon is being separated; and from the seventh and its Lord for him to whom it is written. Indeed [look for] whatever is hoped for or feared, or whatever was in the

---

[447] Following BN, omitting *bene vincens*.
[448] This is an interesting attribution, which echoes Vettius Valens's explanation as to why Jupiter is the secondary triplicity Lord of fire after the Sun: Jupiter is "the imitator and proxy of the king himself, the chooser of good things, the bestower of reputation and life: (*Anth.* II.1).

mind of each of the men, and their condition, from the Lord of the Ascendant and from the Lord of the seventh, and from their places according to the aspect of the benefics and the malefics toward them.

Whichever[449] one of them were in angles, or in a place in which it is received,[450] and aspected its own place, it will be greater and more worthy than the other. And if the planet from whom the Moon is separated were a benefic, or were it in its own exaltation, the letter will be from the master of the kingdom. Indeed if it were removed from the angles,[451] he has already had a kingdom (namely he was already removed from it). Indeed if it were in its own domicile, and it were in an angle, he will be of the known household friends[452]—he is also of the more worthy [people] of the household, and has some dignity. And the triplicity is below the domicile. Likewise the bound is below the triplicity, and the face below the bound. If however it were in a good place from the Ascendant, and were not received, he will have a dignity but he will not be praiseworthy—unwelcome among the men of his household. Indeed if it were in its own descension, and it were in an angle, he who wrote the letter will not be of good stock, but he will be with the king, and one who is honored. And if it were in its own descension and were cadent, he will not be of good stock, nor will he be known among men. If the master of the letter did not aspect the Ascendant nor the Lord of [its own] domicile,[453] he can do nothing: that is, he has nothing except for what he eats every day. And if then a benefic aspected him, he will be of those who work with their own hands, and they eat thusly. Indeed if the Moon were separated from malefics, and it were just as I have said, he will be in addition [someone who] suffers from a bad nature, hard in heart. And if the Moon were separated from a square aspect or the opposition, or from the conjunction, it signifies the strength of the master of the letter—and it will be more strongly so if the Moon were in an angle, in her own sign: because it signifies that he who wrote the letter is of good will in his matter; and that what is disturbing him is in the letter.

---

[449] This paragraph is good for looking at different dignities and receptions to figure out not only status, but how the factors work conceptually.
[450] Reading *recipitur* with BN for *recipit*.
[451] Based on the rest of this sentence, this probably means "is cadent," that is, in the third, sixth, ninth, or twelfth.
[452] Adding *amicis* with BN.
[453] Reading as *Si non aspexerit ascendens nec dominum domus dominus epistolae*, omitting *aut*. That is, if the Lord of the Ascendant does not aspect the rising sign, nor the Lord of the domicile it is currently in (though perhaps degree-based aspects are meant here).

After this, look for him to whom the letter goes, from the planet to which the Moon is being joined, and announce his condition according to what I told you concerning the planet from whom the Moon is separated.

And know that the Moon, if she were separated from Saturn, and Mercury were impeded, there will be labor in the letter, and a strong matter. And if she were separated from Jupiter, the letter will be from a noble man. And if it were from Mars, it will be a warrior who works by blood and who uses a sword.[454] And if it were from the Sun, it will be from the king. And if it were from Venus, it will be from a woman. Indeed if it were from Saturn, there will be some defect [or vice] in him.[455] If it were from Mercury, the letter will be from a writer or a businessman.

§13.2: A question about the nature of the man to whom the letter comes

And if you were asked about the nature of the man to whom the letter comes, look at the Moon and her conjunction in this: which if she is being joined to Saturn, the letter will be sent to an old man. Indeed if it were Jupiter, to a noble; and if it were Venus, to a woman; likewise for the rest of the planets according to their natures.[456]

§13.3: A question whether there is good or bad in the letter

And[457] if you were asked generally about the letter, whether there is good or bad in it, look at the separation of Mercury: because this will be in the letter. For all writing belongs to Mercury. Also, rumors belong to the Moon.[458] Also, the Lord of the ninth and the third have moderate participation in this. Therefore, if Mercury were separated from the benefics, there

---

[454] *Ferro*. Or, "iron." Sahl is speaking about warriors here, but remember that Mars signifies professions dealing with iron and fire generally.
[455] Reading *eo* with BN for *ea*.
[456] *Substantias*.
[457] See *Carmen* V.26.1-4.
[458] Due to her quick movement and the fact that rumors are spread among the common people.

will be good in the letter. And if he were separated from the malefics, there will be evil in it.

After this, look at the planet from whom Mercury is being separated, and Mercury himself—namely, at the stronger of them—and set this one up as the significator:

> Which if it were in the Ascendant, there will be health and profit in it, and repayment.

> And if it were in the second from the Ascendant, the letter will be through substance (namely, in donating and accepting it), and things like these which pertain to substance.

> And if it[459] were in the third, it will be because of a brother or a friend: in the letter he has narrated concerning a journey about which he is concerned, or he has inquired about its nature.

> And if it were in the fourth from the Ascendant, in the letter there will be some mention about some land, or perhaps the letter will be from a certain relative of his, who is older than him in age, or concerning an ancient thing.

> And if it were in the fifth, the letter will be about certain things which he hopes for, and it will be because of a child or friend.

> Indeed if it were in the sixth, the letter will be about a slave. If however, a malefic aspected that same place, the letter will be about an infirm person or for the sake of an infirm person.

> And if it were in the seventh, the letter will be concerning a woman, or about the condition of a woman.

> And if it were in the eighth, the letter will be about a dead person, or about what is left by the dead.

---

[459] Reading *fuerit* for *fuerint*.

And if it were in the ninth, there will be some admonition in the letter, or a preaching and reminder about God, and a mention of foreign travel, or about the removal of the king.

And if it were in the tenth, the letter will be because of[460] the king, and there is mention of the nobles and leaders in it.

And if it were in the eleventh, the letter will be because a friend, and there is something which pleases him in it, and it makes him return.[461]

And if it were in the twelfth, the letter will be about a contention or because of an enemy.

§13.4: A question: what is in the response letter, if you desire to know

And if a letter were written, and you wished to know what its response is, look at this from the second conjunction: because the first conjunction is [the first letter's] significator, of what arises from the letter; and the second conjunction is the significator of the response to that letter.[462]

§13.5: A question whether the letter is completed or not

And if you were asked about a letter, whether it is completed or not, look at the Moon to see if she were joined to Mercury: it is completed. And if she has already conjoined to him, and has transited through a quantity of 2°, or 3°, say it will be completed; but lacking this, not.

---

[460] *Ex.* Here and through the twelfth, it is possible that this should be read as "from," but in that case I would have expected the Latin translator to have used *de* or *a*.
[461] That is, the querent returns home because of what the friend (who apparently is from home) tells him.
[462] In other words, see to what planet Mercury joins after the planet already considered in the previous chapter.

§13.6: A question whether the letter is sealed or not

And if you were asked about a letter whether it is sealed or not, look at the Moon to see if she were joined to Mercury: say it will be sealed. And if she were separated from him, and transited him by a quantity of approximately 2°, and she has not transited him through the bound, say that it has already been sealed. And if you found Mercury with the Sun, and they both aspected the Ascendant, say it will be sealed; but lacking this, not.

§13.7: A question if a letter will go out from the king or not

And if you were asked (concerning a letter) whether it will go out from a prince or from the king, look at Mercury to see if he were separated from the Sun or from the [Lord of the] Midheaven by a modest separation:[463] say it will go out; but lacking this, not.

§13.8: A question if a letter would arrive to the king or not

And if you were asked (concerning a letter) whether it would arrive to the king or not, look at Mercury to see if he were joined to the Lord of the Midheaven or to the Sun: say it will arrive; but lacking this, not.

§13.9: A question about rumors: whether they are true or false

If you were asked about rumors, whether they are true or false, look at the Lord of the Ascendant or at the Moon (namely at the one of them which was in an angle), and begin from that one. Which if it were in an angle free from malefics, and was not joined to a cadent planet, the rumors will be true; if indeed it were in an angle and were joined to a cadent planet which did not receive it, there was mention of them, but they will not be perfected.[464] And

---

[463] Following the *Book of the Nine Judges*. Perhaps a "modest" separation is what he has mentioned before: around 2°.
[464] Reading *fuit de eis mentio sed non perficientur* with BN for *fuit de eis intentio sed non continuabuntur nec perficientur*.

if the Lord of the Ascendant[465] were not in an angle, and he were joined to a planet in an angle, the rumors will be true, and they will appear, if it were a benefic; if however it were a malefic and it did not receive the Lord of the Ascendant, the rumors will be false. And if the Lord of the Ascendant were joined to a cadent planet, the rumors will be false unless that planet receives the Lord of the Ascendant. Indeed if the Lord of the Ascendant were joined to a malefic who did not receive him, it signifies the destruction of the rumors, and this will be from the side of the master of the question.[466] And if a malefic were joined to the Lord of the Ascendant, the destruction of the rumors will come from another, and he will destroy the rumors.

After this, look at the Moon and her testimony with the Lord of the Ascendant. If the Lord of the Ascendant were of greater testimony, use his testimony. Indeed if the Moon were stronger, use her testimony with the Lord of the Ascendant.

> If the Lord of the Ascendant were in a movable sign or the Ascendant were movable, and certain ones of the malefics aspected him, the rumors will be lies.
>
> Likewise if the Moon were void in course.
>
> Likewise also if the Moon were joined to a retrograde planet, even if it may receive her.
>
> Likewise if the Moon were joined to a cadent planet—and more certainly than that[467] if it were a malefic, because it signifies lying even if [the malefic] were received.
>
> Indeed if she were in an angle, impeded, and the malefic did not receive her, the rumors will be false.
>
> And if she were joined to a planet in an angle who received her, it signifies the truth of the rumors (therefore you should not seek any other testimony with him). Indeed if she were joined to a benefic in an an-

---

[465] Here and below Sahl omits the Moon, but I take these conditions to also apply to the Moon if she is the stronger significator.
[466] I take this to mean that the querent will be able to deny or squash the rumors.
[467] Again, reading *certius* for *callidius*.

gle—and better than that if it were in the Midheaven or in the Ascendant—it signifies that the rumors are true. Which if the receiver[468] were then saved from the malefics and from retrogradation, the rumors will be perfected and they will be made better. Indeed if [the receiver] were impeded by a planet who did not receive *it*, or [it were impeded by] a retrograde planet, it signifies the destruction of the rumors after [the retrograde planet] goes direct.

Likewise if the Moon were joined to a planet in an angle (or outside it) which did not receive her, and the Moon were impeded (or she were joined to a retrograde planet): it signifies destruction after [the retrograde planet] goes direct.

And if the Moon were impeded in an angle, it signifies the destruction of the rumors.

And if she were joined to a cadent planet, it signifies lying if [the cadent planet] were not received.

And if she pushed her disposition to a planet in an angle, the rumors will be true. If however the planet were in the Midheaven, they will be rumors which men have already come to know, and they have appeared. And if it were in the Ascendant, it as already begin to appear. And if it were in the seventh, it already was and has appeared, and is appearing. Indeed if it were in the fourth, it will be secret.

§13.10: A question about a matter which is feared

And if a man were to ask about a matter which he fears, look at the Lord of the Ascendant to see if it were in some angle and it were free from the malefics: the rumors will be lies and nothing about that which he fears will reach him. And if the Lord of the Ascendant were in the bad places—that is, in the second and the sixth and the eighth and the twelfth—the rumor about the matter which he fears has already entered. If however the Lord of the Ascendant were in the bad places and the malefics have testified, he will fall

---

[468] Probably the receiver of the disposition.

into that which he fears; indeed if they did not testify,[469] it will be removed and will not increase concerning that of the fear which is in him. And if the malefics were in an angle and they aspected him from the angles, it will be worse for his condition.

Which if the malefic were itself the Lord of the eighth from the Ascendant, it signifies his death and destruction; and if it were otherwise, difficulties will find him.

And if the malefic were itself the Lord of the twelfth, he will fear punishments and being bound.[470]

Which if it were the Lord of the second, he will be captured in exchange for substance.[471]

If however the Lord of the Ascendant were in the twelfth and the Lord of the seventh or the twelfth did not aspect him,[472] he will escape and be freed, and [the enemy] will not have power over him. Likewise, if in addition the Moon were joined to a malefic, it will indicate[473] him unless the malefic is itself the Lord of her domicile; then it signifies that labor and difficulty will happen to him in his flight.[474] If however it were not the Lord of her domicile, it will point him out.

---

[469] In this sentence, "testify" seems to mean "aspect," but whether this is by whole-sign only or some degree-based aspect, is unclear.
[470] Reading *vinctionem* with BN for *iunctionem*.
[471] Both BN and 1493 omit the sixth.
[472] Following 1493. BN reads differently and seems to have something missing: "But if the Lord of the Ascendant were in the twelfth, and the Lord of the seventh or [*missing?*] did not aspect him (because it is the adversary), and it is in a cadent or the twelfth…".
[473] *Demonstrabit*. Both here and in the final sentence we have words for indicating and pointing out (*ostendo*). But I am not sure what they mean here—perhaps that he will become a visible target for enemies?
[474] Largely following BN in this sentence.

§13.11: A question if someone killed will be avenged or not, and if someone has suffered injury, will he be avenged or not, by making restitution for the injuries which he has undergone

If you were asked about someone killed, whether he would be avenged (or about someone who has suffered injuries, whether he could [be avenged] upon him who made the injuries to him, or if he would make restitution for the injuries which he made to him), look at the Ascendant and the angle of the end of the matter (which is the fourth [sign]) from the Ascendant. If they were movable signs, and the Moon were in a movable sign, he would not be able to do anything. If however the Lord of the Ascendant aspected the Ascendant, and the Lord of the domicile of the Moon the Moon, he will accomplish his matter quickly. Indeed if it were just as I said and the Lord of the fourth aspected the seventh, he will accomplish his matter and pour out the blood of the killer—unless the Moon is joined to the benefics, *if* after this the benefic was *not* joined to a malefic (because then he will be killed after the peace). And if the benefic were joined to malefics, he will be killed, unless it is a conjunction from a trine or from a sextile aspect: then it signifies that he will bear pains and be conquered by the sword. Which if the malefic were in a fixed sign, he will die in prison. Indeed if it were in a movable sign, and the Lord of its sign were quicker in course, and [the Lord] aspected [the malefic], he will release him[475] quickly.

And if he to whom the Moon is joined, were in a movable sign, and he aspected the Lord of his own domicile by an aspect of friendship, he will escape freely; and if the aspect were from the opposition or from the square aspect, he will escape by means of a battle, or through something like a battle. Indeed if the conjunction were in one sign, he will be released[476] quickly, or he will flee and be gone.

And if you found a benefic[477] in the Ascendant, his anger will be extinguished because of recruits.[478] And if the Moon in addition were joined to a strong malefic in his own place, the revenge will not be by recruits, for the king will avenge concerning it. And if a malefic were in the Ascendant, and

---

[475] *Dimittet.*
[476] *Dimittetur.*
[477] Reading *fortunam* with 1493 for *fortitudinem.*
[478] Reading *dilectorum* and *dilectis* below as the noun for recruits or hired guns, not as an adjectival noun for "delightful things."

the Moon were made fortunate, the[479] recruits (that is, belonging to the dead man), will put him and the killer under an obligation; and the king will aid him (the killer, that is), and will try to kill [the querent]. Which if the Lord of the Ascendant aspected the Ascendant, the recruits will get [the killer] after labor in the anger of the king. Indeed if the Lord of the Ascendant did not aspect the Ascendant, and the Lord of the domicile of the Moon aspected the Moon, the king will take him away without the willingness of his recruits. And know that every pain which Mars signified will have to do with iron and whips; and Saturn, through wood[480] and through the prolongation of prison and distress.

§13.12: A question about some thing, whether it is genuine or fake

And if you were asked about some thing[481] whether it is genuine or fake, look at the Lord of the Ascendant and the Moon: which if they were free from the malefics, the thing will be genuine in effect, and profitable. Indeed if they were impeded, the thing will be fake. And if it were gold, take the Sun as witness; for silver, the Moon.

§13.13: A question: which of two or three things is more worthy, and which will be acquired

And if you were asked about [1] two or three things, which of them is more worthy, and which of them is genuine or fake; or [2] for two rumors, which of them is true or false, [or] whether [3] about one matter or about two matters, which of them will be attained; or [4] about two or three beasts, which of them will win; or [5] about two men, which of them will attain his matter, look at the Lord of the Ascendant to see if it were in the angles, free from the malefics, and received: that which is named first, is more worthy and will be acquired. And if it were impeded in the angles, it will be that

---

[479] The rest of this sentence is from BN, which is at least clear and grammatical compared with 1493. I am assuming that the end of the sentence refers to the king trying to kill the querent—the Latin only says "him."
[480] *Angustiam.* This refers to planks and timbers, so I assume it could mean any punishment using wooden implements—flogging, the stocks, perhaps the rack?
[481] Following 1493, but BN actually says "alchemy" (*alkimia*), i.e., a purported precious metal gained by alchemical techniques.

which is named first—[but] it will be destroyed after this. And if the Lord of the Ascendant aspected the Ascendant, and it were in the succeedents of the angles, free from the malefics, received, the one named second will be acquired, and it is more worthy; if however it were impeded, it will be made fit, [and] will be destroyed afterwards. And if the Lord of the Ascendant were cadent, free from the malefics and received, the third one of the ones named will be more worthy and will be acquired; if it were impeded, there will be nothing of those which I said, and the question will be destroyed. And judge likewise concerning the Moon.[482]

§13.14: A question: if you were asked about many matters[483]

And if you were asked about many matters, you will set up the Moon as the significatrix of the one asking, and the stars (that is, the planets) will be his matters. Therefore, consider the conjunction of the Moon according to the number of the matters themselves: because the first conjunction will be the significator of the first question; and the second conjunction will be the significator of the second question; likewise [concerning] the matters according to the number which he named to you.

Therefore, look at the strength of each planet in the angles or in the succeedents of the angles; and in their being saved from retrogradation and from the malefics. Then commingle each planet in strength, and speak according to its quantity.

§13.15: A question about the acquisition[484] of a hunt, and of what sort its catch will be

And if you were asked about the acquisition of a hunt, and of what sort its catch would be, look at the Ascendant and the Lord of the hour (which is

---

[482] The unstated premise here seems to be that we favor the Lord of the Ascendant, *if* it aspects the rising sign; if not, we look at the Moon. This rule is also stated by Māshā'allāh throughout OR. Note that Sahl does not mention this for an angular Lord of the Ascendant, because all of the angles aspect the rising sign; but he mentions it for the succeedents.

[483] The previous question had to do with only one matter, in which there were several possible choices; this question has to do with unrelated matters asked at the same time.

[484] Reading *acquisitione* with BN for *inquisitione*.

strong in a hunt), and know the substance of the Ascendant (whether it is of the signs of quadrupeds, and so on); and after this look even at the substance of the seventh sign and that of the Ascendant while you proceed to the prey, or, were you asked about it, of which of the signs it is,[485] and where is the place of its Lord from the Lord of the Ascendant.[486] If they were joined from esteem,[487] it signifies the catching of what he sought (of the hunt) with ease. And if they were joined from a square aspect or the opposition, he will catch the prey with labor and fatigue. Indeed if they were not joined, he will have nothing, nor catch what he wanted. And if you found the seventh sign to be of quadrupeds, and its Lord or the Lord of the hour were in it, or in one of the angles, made fortunate, he will get the prey. And in the hour of Jupiter or in one of the angles, he will get roebucks.[488]

If however the Lord of the seventh were a malefic, and the benefics were cadent from him, he will torment himself in the search, and he will hunt moderately, and a defect or some impediment in this body will be feared for him if Saturn were the Lord of the seventh. Indeed if Mars[489] were the Lord of the seventh, and there were strength for him there, he will have his prey, and someone of those who are with him in the labor will create detriment for him, and [the prey] will be freed: because Mars has the substance of the hunt.

If however Jupiter aspected Mars, and he were the Lord of the hour or the Lord of the Ascendant, [the querent] will be saved from everything which he fears, and he will hunt easily; and he will have his thing without labor and fatigue. And if the seventh sign were of the airy signs, or of the earthy signs, and there were a benefic in it, and its Lord were a malefic, or the Lord of the hour were a malefic, he will be saved in his hunt and it will not extend to everything he wanted;[490] and the prey will be frightened and flee from him; and his searching will be strong, and he will torment himself in it (unless Jupiter or Mercury is with the malefic who is the Lord of the hour):

---

[485] I am unclear about the meaning of this phrase: *dum pergis venatum aut interrogatus fueris de eo, cuiuscumque signorum sit* (following BN).
[486] Following BN here and throughout.
[487] That is, from a sextile or trine.
[488] Here I am following 1493. BN reads: "And if you found the seventh sign to be of quadrupeds, and in the hours of Jupiter, or in one of the angles, roebucks." Perhaps the scribe of BN missed a line in his original.
[489] Adding *Mars* from 1493.
[490] *Non pertinget ad omne quod voluerit.* I take this to mean that he will catch much, but not all, of what he wanted to hunt.

for this signifies the badness of the malefic,[491] and it will not prohibit the hunt. Because Mercury has the greatest partnership with Mars on a hunt.

§13.16: A question whether the hunters would catch much or little

Moreover, if you were asked about the smallness of the catch, or about its multitude, look at the Midheaven when you go out to the hunt. If Mars were the Lord of the Midheaven, or you found him in that place, and he were in the aspect of Mercury or Jupiter, or in the aspect of one of them, and one of them (or the Lord of the Ascendant) were the Lord of the hour,[492] he will have much prey, and he will encounter it, and he would be able to hunt with his hands and he will not have labor—unless Saturn is aspecting Mars from an angle, or Saturn were in the Midheaven, or he is its Lord: for he sends a strong sorrow upon the master of the hunt in that for which [the hunter] hopes. If however Jupiter were cadent from him,[493] and Saturn were just as I have said, and Mars were in an angle, the master of the hunt will find impediment in his own body, and slowness in his journey; and in addition, he will not acquire the prey: because Saturn destroys a hunt, and he will heap slowness on its master, especially if the hunt were by land.

But in a hunt by sea, look at the Lord of the Ascendant, and the Moon, and the Lord of the seventh sign: indeed if the Ascendant were a watery sign, and the Moon were joined to Mars, or the Lord of the hour[494] were joined to Mars, and Venus were cadent from the aspect of the Moon, leave off this hunt according to your ability: because it has no strength nor usefulness (except with impediment). Indeed if the Moon were joined to Saturn, and Venus aspected the Moon, the catch will be multiplied. And Saturn does not impede the Moon in a hunt by water, unless Mars is aspecting the Moon. And in addition, Venus is even weakened, because Mars is the enemy of Venus. If Saturn aspected her, then shipwreck will be feared for its master, and the rest of the things like these: namely soaking and moisture.

---

[491] Or, "the badness of the evil" (*malitiam mali*). Still, I am not sure of this phrase's role.
[492] Omitting *vel*.
[493] I believe Sahl is referring to Mars.
[494] Reading *horae* with 1493 for *horum*.

§13.17: A question about a banquet and what the guests will eat

If you were invited to a banquet or to some party, or you were asked about the foods of some people (how many they will eat), look at the Ascendant to see if it were a movable sign: they will eat many appetizers.[495] And if it were fixed, they will eat one appetizer. Indeed if it were common, they will eat two.

And if the Moon were in the Ascendant, their food will be salted; and if Mars were in the Ascendant there will be some bitterness in it; and Jupiter signifies sweetness; indeed the Sun, sharpness (that is, the taste of celery or *eruca*[496] or mustard);[497] and Venus, a light taste,[498] and the rest of this kind, and what is rich [or greasy], that is, the flavor of grease[499] or dense meat[500] and what belongs to this.[501] And Mercury signifies a piercing[502] taste, and everything commingled; indeed Saturn signifies a violent and distasteful[503] taste.

After this, look at the separation of the Moon, and her conjunction. If she were separated from a malefic and were joined to a benefic from a square aspect or the opposition, it will not be able to come about but that the master of the food will give him a reason for the banquet (like it is for nuptials, or a circumcision, or all the rest such things in which men engage and which happen to them). And if it were from a trine aspect, or from the sextile, it will be because of a conference or retaliation,[504] and the rest. If however the

---

[495] *Pulmenta*. A *pulmentum* is a small meat dish served before a banquet or other large meal.
[496] *Erica* is an acrid herb used as an aphrodisiac (*eruca sativa*), but some of my dictionary sources also give white pepper and colewort. Whatever it was in the medieval mind, it seems to be a member of the cabbage family, and the word *eruca* is the source for our modern arugula.
[497] This parenthetical remark comes after Venus in the text, but it does not make sense that peppery and mustard-like tastes would be associated with her. Bonatti (*BOA* p. 627) associates this sentence with the Sun, so I have put it here.
[498] *Ventositatem*. My conjecture is that this refers to a taste lacking a clear or solid taste, as suggested by *ventosus*. Perhaps it means "having a light or delicate fragrance" (see below).
[499] Reading *sebi* for *sepi*.
[500] *Carnis crasse*. But a variant on *crassus* was also a medieval term for a whale or other large fish, so perhaps, in connection with the greasiness just mentioned, it refers to greasy or fatty fish?
[501] Reading as *huius*.
[502] *Acrem*, especially something acidic or sour, which affects the stomach.
[503] Reading *insapidum* (as a variant on *sapio*) for *insipidum*. It is possible that this means "unseasoned," but my sense is that it leans toward foul or unpleasant tastes.
[504] *Retributionis*. My sense of this is that the banquet is held in order that certain parties might get along and become allies, or to halt a conflict.

planet to whom the Moon is being joined were in an angle, their banquet will be one day; and if it were a common [sign], it will be more than one day.

And if the Lord of the domicile of the Moon aspected her, their banquet will be disturbed: for someone who will throw them into disarray [will be] at the banquet—then they will make peace, and afterwards they will return to the banquet.

And if the Moon were joined to Jupiter, it signifies the nobility of the banquet and the multitude of the appetizers.

And if she were joined to the Sun, it signifies the cleanliness or the beauty of the appetizers, or the multitude of sharp [foods].

And if she were joined to Venus, it signifies the beauty of the foods, and the multitude of their sweetness, with games and listening and laughter, and the sweetness of the odor.

And if she were joined to Mercury, it signifies the performances[505] of men in that same place, and that there will be someone who speaks wisdom, and tells it, and the appetizers will be multiplied, and the narrations of stories or fables, and they will use the meats of birds in the food.

And if the conjunction were with Saturn, it signifies the uncleanliness of their foods, and that the appetizers of fishes and whatever enters the water will be multiplied in that place.

Indeed, were the conjunction with Mars, it will signify that quarrels will fall between them, and that they will eat every hot thing;[506] and if he were in the Midheaven, it signifies that quarrels will fall between them.[507]

---

[505] *Pressuras.* I am reading this as though could be something like *praesturas*, from *praesto*, "to exhibit, perform." Otherwise, this means "pressure" or being pressed tight, and I am not sure what that could mean in this context, unless it means the guests will verbally "express" themselves. Given that speeches and stories are also mentioned, it amounts to the same thing.
[506] *Omne calidum.* I believe this means there will be only hot dishes and no cold ones.
[507] Ending the sentence here with BN. 1493 reads almost like a repeat of the previous clause.

Therefore, if you were invited to a banquet and the Moon were with Mars in one sign, or she were joined to him from one of the angles, you should not go to the banquet, because you will chastise yourself at its end. Likewise if she were with Saturn: because it signifies the uncleanliness of the foods, and their vileness[508]—and if you did go, you would not find sweetness in those foods which are there. Indeed if [the Moon] were with Venus or with Mercury, go: because you will see what pleases you; and likewise if it were Jupiter (and there will be multiplied in that same banquet, rice,[509] that is, a certain kind of grain[510] from which comes the best appetizers and grain).

After this, look at the Lord of the hour to see if it were in the Ascendant or in the Midheaven: the food will be brought in at the beginning of the session; and if it were removed from these two places, they will eat before it is served, and it will not be served until this star is removed from the Ascendant or from the Midheaven.[511] And if it were in the seventh or in the fourth, the food will not be served until the place is filled up. And however often the Moon were joined to Mars, their food will be hot.

And if you were asked [by a client] or you [yourself] were invited, and the Moon were in a watery sign, aspecting Saturn from a trine or a sextile aspect, they will eat trout. Indeed if the Moon were in Libra, they will eat grains or legumes; and if she were in Gemini or Aquarius, they will eat the meat of birds. And if Saturn aspected the Moon from a square aspect or the opposition, they will eat cold meat; and if the Sun were joined to Mars, the whole thing generally will be burnt; and if the Moon were in Libra or in its[512] square aspect, you should not eat cooked or raw vegetables;[513] and in Virgo or Libra, you should not approach grains; and if she were in Scorpio with the Tail, beware of lard;[514] and if she were in Leo, beware of consuming meat; and if she were in Sagittarius, you should not go near the meat of wild animals (that is, of wolves or bears); and in Pisces, you should not eat salted

---

[508] *Vilitatem.* Or, their low-class nature (as opposed to being fine, special foods).
[509] Lat. *alozor*. I take this to be from the Ar. *al-ʾarozz*. In a handwritten manuscript it would be easy for the translator to mistake whether the dot was over the *z* or the *r*, hence the transposed letters.
[510] *Annonae.*
[511] This use of "removed" suggests motion by primary motion, so that they will not eat until the planet becomes cadent, in up to 2 hours' time.
[512] It is unclear whether this means Mars's aspect, or the square aspect of Libra.
[513] Reading *holera* for *olera*.
[514] *Pinguedine.*

trout, nor fresh. Therefore, watch out for what I have told you about the places of the Moon with the malefics in these signs which I have named for you,[515] because they impede with a serious impediment.

And know that the Ascendant signifies the reason for the banquet: if it were the domicile of Venus, it will be because of nuptials; and if it were the domicile of Mercury, it will be on account of a child or because of children; indeed if it were in the domicile of Jupiter, a friend is preparing the party for him.

And the second [sign] from the Ascendant signifies the vessel in which they drink, and the furnishings of the house. If the second sign were common, their vessel will be colored; and if Mars were in the same sign, there will be copper in their vessel; and if it were Venus, there will be silver in it; and Jupiter, silver and gold; the Moon, glass; indeed Saturn, wood and earthenware.[516] And if the benefics were in the second sign, it signifies the beauty of the house's decoration. If however the benefic were peregrine, it will belong to someone else;[517] and if it had testimony in it, [the decoration] will be of the household.

And the third [sign] signifies those who are present at the banquet.

Indeed, the fourth [sign] from the Ascendant signifies the place where the banquet is held. Which if it were a common sign, their banquet will be on a porch [or portico]; and if the Sun or Jupiter were in it, their banquet will be in a closed part of the house, or in the south.[518]

And the fifth [sign] from the Ascendant signifies their beverages. If it were a common sign, their beverages will be diverse. And[519] if Jupiter

---

[515] This must mean that all of the signs listed above are only to be avoided when there is a square or opposition (by whole sign or by orbs, I am not sure) to one of the malefics while the Moon is there.
[516] *Testam*. Perhaps also, "shells."
[517] *Aliena*, undoubtedly meant to contrast with the following phrase.
[518] *Meridie*.
[519] For the rest of this paragraph, I largely follow BN. 1493 reads: "And if Jupiter or Mercury were in it, their drink will be of diverse wines; and if it were Saturn, it will be of sugar; and if Mars were [in] it, their drink will be most acidic, from dates. But if Mars were impeded by Saturn, their drink has already been made acidic. And if it were the Sun, there

were in it, or Mercury, their beverages will be made of dates. [And if Mars were in it, their drink will be acidic.]⁵²⁰ If however Mars were impeded by Saturn, their drinks will already be made pungent;⁵²¹ and if the Sun were in it, bitterness and acidity; and if it were Venus, they will drink a fermentation of dates. Indeed if were the Moon, their drinks will be water.

And the sixth [sign] from the Ascendant signifies the servers.

And the seventh [sign] from the Ascendant will belong to the butlers.

Indeed the eighth [sign] belongs to the bakers and cooks.

And the ninth [sign], those who serve its dishes.

Also, the tenth [sign] signifies the goodness of the foods, and whether he would rejoice with those invited, or not: because if the benefics were in the Midheaven, he will rejoice with them; and if the malefics were in it, they will be hateful to him and his friends.

And the eleventh [sign] signifies brothers and friends.

Indeed the twelfth [sign] signifies the master of the household, and whether he desires this or not.⁵²²

Therefore, look at the place of the benefics and the malefics in these twelve places. Were a benefic in any sign and its Lord made fortunate, judge good and joy for him who pertains to that domicile; and in whichever one there were a malefic, or its Lord were impeded, everything which pertains to that domicile, and all of its matters, will be destroyed.

---

will be bitterness and acidity in it. And if it were Venus, they will drink a fermentation of dates."
⁵²⁰ Adding from BN.
⁵²¹ This sounds like wine that has gone vinegary from exposure to the air.
⁵²² So, it signifies hidden anger or enmity behind the scenes!

§13.18: On the significations of the hours of the planets in questions[523]

These are the three partitions of the hours:

The first is divided into three parts: he who comes in the first part (belonging to the hour of the Sun) asks for the king or for [his] master or a man or a great evil whence he has great fear; in the middle [part], either on account of a great fear or an infirm person; in the end [part], about his livelihood or merchant business, and acquiring.

In the first part of the hour of Venus, he asks you about the taking of a wife or about the cares of women; in the middle [part], about the vestments of women or their decoration; in the end [or third part], for a reason which is being born or a friendship which cannot come to pass.

In the first part of the hour of Mercury, for a legal case[524] or personal fortune,[525] or a something engraved;[526] in the middle [part], for a fit vestment or for the soul of the one asking; in the end [or third part], because of loss.

In the first part of the hour of the Moon, for moving from place to place, or for an infirm person, or for something which has a blemish on it;[527] in the middle [part], for a reason which went out of his hand and is not returning, or for a man who comes from the road, or a beast, or for a man who is dying; in the end [or third part], for something going to be completed or because of something which is born of the earth.

In the first part of the hour of Saturn, because of a fleeing slave (if you are worried about him, [whether] he will return);[528] in the middle, for a strong man or an association which he wants to make, or he wants to walk from place to place, or some petition; at the end, for a bad cause whence he has already escaped.

In the first part of the hour of Jupiter, he comes to ask you with a particular name[529] or something public;[530] in the middle, for a vestment to be

---

[523] This section does not appear in BN, and the Latin style has changed. We should doubt that this really comes from Sahl. But it is interesting as an apparent example of "consultation chart" rules.
[524] *Causata.* My phrase "legal case" is somewhat speculative.
[525] Reading *avere* or *avero* for *avo*.
[526] *Causa sculpta.*
[527] Perhaps because the Moon's craters appear as blemishes or smears to the naked eye?
[528] *Si fatigas pro eo [utrum] revertitur.*
[529] *Proprio nomine.* This could also mean he comes on behalf of an important person.
[530] *Aliquod forum.* Perhaps, "market goods."

fitted, or for an infirm person to be healed;[531] at the end, for a man who made money and is now losing from his personal fortune.

In the first part of the hour of Mars,[532] stolen property [that is] red or gold or copper, or a vestment; in the middle, for an infirm person, especially one injured (perhaps by heat);[533] at the end, because of some deception or a purpose that is worked in fire.

The book of Sahl on questions has been completed.

---

[531] Reading *sanari* for *sanati*.
[532] Omitting a word that appears to be *primo*.
[533] *Afflicto vel calore.*

ON ELECTIONS

(§1) All are agreed that elections are weak, except [those] for kings. For these people (even should their elections be weakened) have a root—that is, their nativities—which strengthen every weak planet in the course.[1] (§2) Indeed you should not elect anything for the low-class and for merchants and for those who follow [in social status], unless [it is] more than [that]:[2] their nativities, and the revolutions of those years, and on the nativities of their children.

(§3a) However, [for] those of whom these things are not known, questions should be taken for them, and the effecting of their matter may be known from them—afterwards it should be elected for them according to this.[3] (§3b) Wherefore if[4] someone were to ask you about himself, it has already arrived at the good or evil from out of his own nativity, because it is he who has asked[5] you (that is, in the hour in which someone comes to you).[6]

(§3c) And if it is one whose quaesited matter will not come to be, or if the man who asks you (or who goes away to war) will die, beware therefore this kind of election.[7] (§4) For how would you elect for him whose root is

---

[1] Crofts does not explicitly say that the root *is* the nativity, but it is strongly implied: "kings have a root, which, if their choice is weak, strengthens their nativity and every weak planet in the course." This seems to mean that even a bad election will be able to take advantage of a good nativity, and even put weak natal planets to good use.

[2] The idea seems to be that if a king comes to us, we can assume he has a good nativity and that general success in life will be assured. But if a low-class person comes to us, we need to look at several possible charts, going beyond what we would look for in a king's election (i.e., looking at solar revolutions, *etc.*), and by looking at the low-class person's nativity.

[3] This passage suggests a hierarchy of desirable clients: powerful people with a known nativity; powerful people without a known nativity; lower-class people with a known nativity; lower-class people whose nativity is not known, but for whom we can cast a horary chart as a substitute for the nativity.

[4] *Dum*, which could also mean "while" or "provided that."

[5] Reading *quia ipse est qui te interrogavit*, omitting the extra *et est*.

[6] This sentence seems to describe a client who has *no* known charts (even a successful horary), so that the client is coming to the astrologer "cold." The implication, then, is that the nativity of such a person has already generally decided the outcome, and that his only possible hope is through a horary question; but lacking even that, Sahl is telling us to stay away.

[7] That is, if the querent has no known nativity, and the horary question shows bad results, consider the matter closed and do not proceed to an election.

destroyed, especially if in addition the first beginning and the old root on which one relies, is [also destroyed]?[8]

(§5a) Therefore, beware of electing for him whose root of the nativity or question signified something horrible. (§5b) [But] if it came to this, if you put all the benefics in stakes, and made the malefics be cadent from them, nothing will profit him; and every planet which did not agree with the Lord of his Ascendant would not profit the man anything,[9] (§5c) and especially for those who are low- and middle-class: because you do not know whether you might elect an Ascendant or star which is inimical to him in the root, or there were a malefic in that same ascending sign which you have elected for him.

(§6a) For this is to be warned against[10] for those who sail by sea, or for those who go on a foreign journey in one hour (whose intention is on [just] one foreign journey): but certain ones of them suffer shipwreck, indeed certain ones escape it, and certain ones of them discover substance (indeed certain ones discover nothing). For the condition[11] of certain ones cannot be likened to the conditions of others of them. (§6b) And I have already tested this many times in the bringing together of certain people who went out from a place in one hour, and they arrived at another region at one hour: but certain ones of them went back more quickly with the best substance, and certain ones took it slow in the same place; indeed certain ones of them perished before [they could] return to their own homes. For this happens to them because of their nativities and because of the division of them in those years themselves.[12]

(§7) We even see certain people rejoice and drink on a bad day and on a day to be feared (namely one of many impediments), and quarrels come to-

---

[8] The Latin text reads as though we are still speaking about a low-class client who has a bad nativity (the first or ancient root), and the substitute root (the horary question) is also bad or "destroyed." But in the more succinct Crofts version, it is unclear what chart is being referred to as the root: the nativity or the question. Either way, the point is taken.

[9] Crofts seems to read more correctly: "and make the malefics *and all the planets unsuitable to the lord of his ascendant* [be cadent]..."

[10] Reading *admoneatur* (following Crofts) for *admiratur*. The idea is that if you choose one election for a group of people, some of those people will inevitably have a better or worse relation between the election chart and their own nativities: therefore they will encounter different things on the journey.

[11] *Esse.*

[12] By "division of them" (Ar. *qismathum*), Sahl means primary directions (*qisma*). This could mean the direction of the Ascendant of the nativity, but that of the *hīlāj* is also possible. This underscores the need to match the election chart against the root and predictive techniques based on it.

gether and enter upon them on a good and praiseworthy day. (§8) And perhaps you will see the significator[13] joined to a malefic from a square aspect or the opposition (or it will be with it in one sign), but he will discover good in it: this does not happen unless[14] perhaps the malefics are more agreeable to it because they were the first Lords of the Ascendant[15] or the Lords of its division, or the Lords of the Ascendant of the revolution of the year.

(§9) If however you elected according to[16] the Ascendant of a question or nativity which you knew,[17] or on the Lord of the Ascendant (that is, the sign of the profection of the year), your election will be more worthy, because you would know what (of the stars) is in accord with it,[18] and what his Ascendant would be. Therefore be careful in this chapter, and let your work[19] be like your election.

(§10a) And know that the All-powerful and Highest has created every creature (namely the world and whatever there is in it) out of the four natures—that is, out of the four elements—and he put the earth in place and every thing which is above it (of what is rational and irrational, and of what is movable and immovable) in a circle; and between this and the circle he put subtle things which the wise know, (§10b) like that subtle circumstance[20] which he put between the stone of a magnet and iron, and the one that is between a father and a son, and between the one eating and food. Know this and understand it.

(§11a) Therefore from the concord which is between each of the two substances (namely the superior and the inferior), matters are combined properly; and they destroyed by adversity.[21] And the benefics are equal[22] (that

---

[13] Crofts reads "indicator" (*al-dalīl*).
[14] *Quare hoc nisi*.
[15] The Arabic reads, "the first Lord of the Ascendant." I am not sure what is meant by "first," as Sahl does not seem to use triplicity Lords in the way someone like Dorotheus does. Perhaps it simply means "one of the Lords."
[16] *Supra*, but following the Arabic.
[17] *Quam nosti*, following Arabic.
[18] Reading *ei* for *eis* (with Arabic).
[19] Crofts's Arabic reads this as "action," so it could mean that the inceptor's deed should be carefully undertaken just as the election is carefully chosen.
[20] *Occasio*. This word really means "occasion" or "pretext," i.e., the circumstance that allows something to happen. Crofts says "relation," which is easier to understand; but perhaps the Latin translator chose this word judiciously: instead of merely positing a relation, he wanted to emphasize that this relation is the *precondition* for there to be interaction between the parts of the cosmos.
[21] Crofts reads: "*when* there is harmony between the two essences, the higher and the lower, things are balanced, and when there is disharmony, they are upset" (emphasis

is, of a temperate nature), indeed the malefics of a harmful nature (and therefore they wish to impede); (§11b) but if they were received,[23] their [malefic] substance will not wholly be absent, [nor] their cunning of adversity;[24] and they are like thieves, and, of men, the citizens of evils, and from them comes adversity and discord, alteration also and the confusion of matters. Understand all of this.

(§12a) The Ascendant and whatever is in it concerning elections[25]

On the knowledge of the natures of the signs. The first of them are the movable signs. Know that the movable signs signify the mobility of matters, quickly [so], and there is nothing lasting in them, nor is their time prolonged. But it is good to sow seed in them, to buy, sell, and to be betrothed to[26] a woman (all of these are successful under them);[27] (§12b) and an infirm person will be freed quickly, also a contention will not be prolonged in them, and a fugitive will turn back quickly. Even foreign travel is useful in them; and if someone promised something in them, what is promised will not make progress.[28] Pronouncements, dreams and rumors will be false in them; a doctor should not cure under them, nor should any planting be planted under them, and a foundation should not be laid down under them—because it is bad. (§12c) And everything which you might begin in them (whose stability you want), will not be stable; but every unstable work (and hastenings) which you wanted to do, begin under them. (§13) And the faster [of] the movable ones are Aries and Cancer, for they have more crookedness and more mobility. Indeed Libra and Capricorn are the stronger and more temperate.

---

mine). In this paragraph, Crofts reads "imbalance" for every instance of "adversity" or "turning-against" (*adversitas*). The Latin translator seems to want to oppose "adversity" to the universal principle of "concord," but the operational pairing is really between temperance with imbalance *within* the general relation of concordance.

[22] *Aequales*. Or, "even, balanced."

[23] Following Crofts (for *reciperint*).

[24] *Adversitatis*. Crofts reads: "the malevolence of their imbalance."

[25] This heading must have been added by a later editor or translator. The section title in Crofts is actually the first sentence below (rendered in Crofts as: "The science of the natures of the signs").

[26] *Firmare*.

[27] This parenthetical comment belongs to the translator or a later editor.

[28] Or, "be successful." In Crofts, this says simply that he will not keep the promise.

(§14a) Next, the fixed ones are appropriate to every work whose stability and prolongation is sought, and what its author wants to be durable. (§14b) And it is good and useful to build in them, and to celebrate a wedding—after the engagement was in the movable ones.[29] And if a woman were divorced by her husband in them, she will not return to him. Indeed in judgments and inceptions in them, there will not be confidence[30] afterwards, unless the testimonies of the benefics would be multiplied in them.[31] (§14c) And he who was conquered[32] in them, his imprisonment will be prolonged; and he who grows angry in them, will not be able to be appeased quickly.[33] Indeed, agreements and claims[34] in them will be useful, and it will be good to build and lay foundations. (§15) But Scorpio is lighter than all the fixed [signs], and Leo more fixed; Aquarius is slower and worse, indeed Taurus is more level [or even].

(§16a) The[35] common signs are useful in partnerships and brotherhood, and whatever might be worked in them often will be repeated. Indeed to buy and to celebrate a wedding in them will not be useful nor advantageous, and there will be trickery[36] and deception in them; and he of whom something is charged in them, will escape and be relieved of that which is charged against him. (§16b) And he who is imprisoned in them will not be fixed in place (except in fear, in particular),[37] on account of the rarity of [the common signs'] appearance and emergence.[38] and he who goes out from prison, returns to that place; and he who is taken as a fugitive in them, returns a second time to his flight; and he who goes off to a judge in them, neither an opinion nor judgment is settled for him.[39] (§16c) Nor [if] someone goes away on a ship in them, for he who goes, will be changed from one [ship] to another. To whom something is promised in them, it will be dissolved and something of it will

---

[29] That is, we want the engagement to be quick (movable signs) but the celebration after the marriage to last a while (fixed signs).
[30] *Fiducia*.
[31] For this last point Crofts reads, "There is no satisfaction after making a judgement or starting an enterprise, unless the testimonies of the benefics are manifold."
[32] Reading *victus* for *vinctus*.
[33] Crofts says the reverse: that he *with whom* one is angry, cannot be *controlled*.
[34] *Condiciones et mercedes*, reading "claims" with Crofts.
[35] See *Carmen* V.4.1.
[36] *Ingenium*. This is a broad word that often refers to mental skills and character in general; but the Arabic Sahl means this in the sense of clever trickery.
[37] *In timore proprie*, which does not have a parallel in the Arabic.
[38] I follow Crofts here, but I do not understand why especially it is difficult for the common signs to appear.
[39] Crofts says he "will not receive a firm decision or judgment."

not be completed for him; and an infirm person will be healed in them, then will incur a relapse [of the infirmity]. (§17) Therefore, all of the good and evil which comes to a man in them is doubled upon him; and if someone dies in them, then after him another person near him[40] will die in that place. And alteration,[41] and the washing of the head and the beard, and the purification of gold and silver are appropriate in them, and sending boys [to learn their] letters.

(§18) If[42] however you wish to begin something of those things which I told you, then put the Moon and the Ascendant in those domiciles[43] agreeing with that which you want, and conjoin the Moon with benefics receiving [her] in that sign. And indeed the signs of the day are stronger in an operation of the day; and make the Ascendant diurnal [and put the Moon in diurnal signs].[44]

(§19a) The watery[45] signs are in conformity with hunting by land and sea; and the royal signs are in conformity with kings; and the signs which have voices are in conformity with him who plays the pipes and little songs;[46] and the fiery signs are in conformity with everything which is with fire; (§19b) and the signs of equality (in which day and night are made equal) are in conformity with truth and speaking truthfully and with him who works with scales; and the changeable signs[47] (and they are those in which night and day begin to be changed) are in conformity with change and with him who wants an alteration from thing to thing.

(§20a) And[48] consider, for every work which you want to begin, what is the nature of that sign from the orbs;[49] and conjoin the Moon and the Lord

---

[40] *In proximo*; following Crofts, signifying a neighbor or someone related, hence the evil is doubled in relation to the *first* dead person.

[41] According to Crofts, this is resettling one's home from one place to another.

[42] See *Carmen* V.4.5.

[43] Reading *et ascendens in illas domos* with Crofts, for *in ascendente illarum domorum*.

[44] This section in brackets is based on Crofts, as the Latin editions leave off. Dorotheus adds that we should put the Moon and the Ascendant in nocturnal signs for nocturnal elections.

[45] Following Crofts, instead of *aerae* (airy).

[46] Omitting *cum crudo et voci alhool*. This phrase has something to do with playing or singing crudely, but it does not match the Arabic (and seems incomplete), and the Arabized word *alhool* does not correspond to anything in the Arabic. Crofts says, "for those who play the nay and for lute-playing and singing."

[47] The tropical signs of Cancer and Capricorn.

[48] See *Carmen* V.30.

[49] The operative word here is *ex*, "from," but it is unclear to me whether *ex* has some technical reference here. Crofts's translation also says "from."

of the Ascendant with that substance; and the root[50] of that nature and its virtue is in the hour of the inception. (§21a) Which if you want that which is connected with[51] lords, and princes, and great men, and those put over cities, and visible people,[52] and the masters of fights and wealth,[53] then it is for you [to work] through the Sun; (§20b) and what is connected to lofty people, then it is for you [to work] through Jupiter; and that of farmers and the lowest people, then it is for you [to work] through Saturn; and that of generals and the lords of fights, then it is for you [to work] through Mars; and what is connected to women, then it is for you [to work] through Venus. (§20c) (And that of buying, and selling, and exchanges,[54] and the matters of writers and businessmen, then it is for you [to work] through Mercury. In the mixing with mistresses (of women) and an inquiry into what is connected to them, it is for you [to work] through the Moon.)[55] But purchases, and sales, and contentions, and matters of writing, and businessmen, are for Mercury; and, of women, in the commingling with queens and the inquiry into those things which are among them, through the Moon.

(§22a) Therefore if you wished to begin some work, adapt the Ascendant and its Lord, and the Moon and the Lord of the matter. And in the beginning of works, beware of the impediment of the Moon, just as Dorotheus[56] (and the rest of the sages) said—and there are ten ways:

(§22b) The first way is that she is combust under the Sun by 12°, and likewise after him (but it is easier after him).[57]

The second, that she is in the degree of her own descension.

---

[50] Crofts reads, "and *with* the root and strength of that nature…". Both the Latin and Arabic readings make the instructions repetitive.
[51] *Ex parte.* I have followed Crofts's translation. One should take this to mean elections *on behalf of* such people's actions, or matters merely *concerned with* them: e.g., one should strengthen the Sun both if a prince is the inceptor, and if the inceptor is a lowly person going to see the prince.
[52] *Spectabilium*, lit. "people who can be looked at." In other words, celebrities of every sort.
[53] *Pugnae et largorum.* Crofts reads "executioners and amnesty," and says the Latin is a mistranslation. Executions and amnesty pertain to public justice.
[54] *Altercationis.*
[55] This section is put into parentheses by Crofts, and is a repetition or slight elaboration of the next passage.
[56] See *Carmen* V.5.3-9, and compare to *Introduct.* §5.16.
[57] That is, after she has passed him and he is behind *her*.

The third, that she is in the opposition of the Sun.

(§22c) The fourth, that she is joined to malefics, or in the light of their square aspect or the opposition.

The fifth, that she is with the Head or the Tail from a degree to 12° (which is the boundary of an eclipse).

The sixth, that she is in the last degrees[58] of the signs (which are the bounds of the malefics).

(§22d) The seventh, that she is cadent from the stakes, or in the burnt path (which is the end of Libra and the beginning of Scorpio)—and this[59] is the worst that there is of the impediments of the Moon, and especially if it were the inception of a marriage or something concerning the matters of women, or buying, or selling, or foreign travel.

(§22e) The eighth, that she is in the twelfth sign[60] from her own domicile (that is, in Gemini), with a malefic, or were she in the opposition of her own domicile, or absent from it.[61]

(§22f) The ninth, that the Moon is slower in course: and this is what the sages call a likeness to the course of Saturn, so long as her course in a day is less than 12°, and [even] if it was one minute less (this is if her course in the day were less than her average course in one day), which is written in the *Canon*, that is, in the *Book of Courses*.[62]

---

[58] Reading *gradibus* for *gradus*.
[59] I do not know whether both of these count as the worst, or just one of them (and if so, which one).
[60] See my Introduction. Crofts reads this as though the Moon is in a twelfth-part with a malefic. But I propose that the original meaning is that "the twelfth-part of the Moon is with a malefic."
[61] Crofts explains this as when the Moon is not in a whole-sign aspect to Cancer—i.e., when she is cadent from her own domicile.
[62] The Arabic does not add this statement about a *Book of Courses* (which must be a book of tables and ephemerides like the *Zij*), but gives a description in terms of *kardajas*: the mathematical arc or sine of 1/96 of the circle: "when your calculation for the moon is in the first *kardaja* of its *kardajas*, so that the *kardaja* is from one to fifteen degrees" (Crofts, pp. 101, 157).

(§22g) The tenth, which Māshā'allāh and the sages of our time have said: this is if the Moon were void in course.

(§23a) And adapt the Moon according to your ability; and you should not put her waxing in any Ascendant, because this is to be feared on account of what happens to [the election's] master[63] because of infirmities in the body (unless the Lord of the Ascendant or a benefic[64] are aspecting the ascending [degree]):[65] (§23b) because a planet which does not aspect its own domicile is like a man absent from his own house, who cannot repel nor prohibit anything from it. (§23c) Indeed if a planet aspected its own domicile, it is like the master of a house who guards it: for whoever is in the house, fears him, and he who is outside fears to come to it.[66] (§24) And if the Lord of the Ascendant were a malefic, make him aspect[67] from a trine or sextile aspect. And beware lest you put the Lord[68] of the Ascendant or the Moon (if there were malefics aspecting the Moon) in a stake, and that you do not put them in the stakes of the Ascendant.[69]

(§25a) Nor should you make the Lot of Fortune, in all beginnings or questions, cadent from the aspect of the Moon or her conjunction; and you should not look at the Lord of the Lot of Fortune, nor should you care if the Lot is cadent from the Ascendant, *if* the Lot aspected the Ascendant and the Moon. (§25b) And strive to put the Lord of the Ascendant with the Lot, because this is more useful and of greater wealth. And you should never put

---

[63] I.e., the inceptor.
[64] Crofts reads, "and the lord of the house of the moon."
[65] Crofts herself has added *[gradum]* because the Latin reads *ascendentem* (implying a masculine subject) as opposed to its usual *ascendens*. But the Arabic itself does not specify the degree, implying only a whole-sign aspect. Crofts helpfully notes (p. 158) that if the Moon is in the Ascendant and the Lord of the Ascendant aspects the Ascendant, then both the Moon and the Ascendant will have their Lords/dispositors aspecting them which is often recommended by Sahl.
[66] In this context, it suggests that the Lord of the Ascendant can check the tendency of the Moon to create infirmities while she is in the Ascendant.
[67] Crofts states in a footnote and annotation (pp. 102, 158) that the malefic is supposed to aspect *the Moon or* the Ascendant, but I do not see where she gets the Moon from. To me it seems that only the Ascendant is pertinent here.
[68] I take this to mean *a malefic* Lord of the Ascendant. Crofts gives the following: "if there are two malefics in aspect with the moon from an angle, place it from the angles of the ascendant."
[69] The Arabic is vaguer and unclear what we are supposed to do or not do: "beware of placing the lord of the ascendant or the moon, if there are two malefics in aspect with the moon from the stake, place it from the stakes of the ascendant."

the Moon in the second, or the sixth, or the eighth, or the twelfth from the Lot, because this is horrible.[70]

(§26) And[71] always set up the Ascendant and the Moon, in all beginnings, in signs of straight ascension, because they signify ease and progress; and you should not put them in signs of crooked ascension, because they signify complication or hardship and slowness.

Also, the Ascendant and the fourth [sign] from it[72] signify what happens to that election.

(§27) Therefore, look at the benefics and the malefics from the places, both the strong and the weak,[73] and speak about the beginning of that matter and its end, from that strength and weakness.

(§28) And Dorotheus said, "If you saw the Moon impeded, and a matter is at hand which ought to come to be wholly and it cannot be put off, you should not give the Moon a role in the Ascendant: and make her cadent from the Ascendant, and put a benefic in the Ascendant, and strengthen the Ascendant and its Lord."[74]

(§29a) The second sign from the Ascendant, and whatever is in it of elections[75]

If you wished to elect the hour for the taking and lending[76] of money, let the Moon be in Leo or in Pisces, or in Scorpio or Sagittarius, or in Aquarius, and let her be defective in light, and let both benefics be deficient and aspecting the Moon or Ascendant.

(§29b) And let Mercury be cleansed of Mars, and [let] the Moon be with Jupiter or Mercury; and beware lest the Moon be impeded by any one of the malefics; nor let Mercury be joined to them [by corporal conjunction] or in their square aspect; nor let the benefics be cadent: (§29c) because if the

---

[70] See *Carmen* I.5.3-5.

[71] *Cf. Carmen* V.2.2-5. But Dorotheus says the opposite: signs of direct ascension show difficulty and slowness, those of crooked ascension will be faster.

[72] The Arabic adds the Lord of the fourth sign, as well.

[73] I take this to refer to the strong and weak places, not planets that are otherwise made strong or weak by other considerations.

[74] Crofts suggests that Sahl might be drawing on *Carmen* V.5.10-11. Even if it is true, Sahl understands the situation differently and makes some changes.

[75] *Cf. Carmen* V.20.

[76] Crofts only says "lending."

Moon were with Mars, he will fall in labor, and worry, and business dealings, and harshness or contention. And if she were impeded by Saturn, he will fall into something prolonged, and delay, and he will get out of it after distress and fatigue.

(§30a) If however you wished to conceal the lending, so that no one would be able to perceive it, let the Moon (while you take it or seek it) be under the rays, going toward the conjunction of the benefics after her separation from the Sun: for this is easier for the master [of the election], and more concealed, and it will not be made public. (§30b) For if the Moon were in her exit out of combustion, going out toward the conjunction of Mars, this will be made public and it will fall into the mouths of men, and in the mouths of those whom you do not want that they should know it. (§30c) And beware lest the Moon be in the circle of the signs (without latitude, that is, in the Head or Tail)[77] or in the burnt path, because this is horrible.

(§31) And Dorotheus said,[78] "You should not take what is loaned, nor should you loan something to someone, while the Moon is in the first degree of Leo or Gemini or Sagittarius, or [if] these signs[79] were ascending: because this is hateful for a loan especially." (Know this.)

(§32a) And[80] if you wished to partner with someone in substance or in a work, it is better for this that the Moon be cleansed of the malefics and joined to benefics, and that she be in common signs (so that it would be multiplied), or the Moon should be in Leo or in Taurus. (§32b) And it is to be abhorred for these things that the Moon should be in the lower signs[81] (and worse than the rest is Libra because the burnt path is in it; likewise abhorred is Aquarius). (§33) And let the Moon be received from a trine or sextile aspect, so that [the partners'] separation is good: because in the square aspect and the opposition there will be words between them (that is, a quarrel in the separation). Also, an aspect of esteem signifies the goodness or honesty of their separation, and their faithfulness and good will. (§34) And beware of the presence of the malefics in the stakes, because the Ascendant belongs to

---

[77] This parenthetical remark is by the Latin translator.
[78] See *Carmen* V.20.6.
[79] Dorotheus does not fault the entire sign, but only the degrees mentioned.
[80] *Cf. Carmen* V.19.1-14. Dorotheus lists each sign individually, but Sahl has tried to shorten things and makes a few changes. Sahl omits Aries, which Dorotheus says is bad; he makes Taurus good, which Dorotheus says is bad; he makes Capricorn bad, which Dorotheus says is good; and Sahl makes it ambiguous whether Pisces is good or bad—Dorotheus says it is good.
[81] That is, the signs of southern declination.

the one of them beginning the partnership, or him who is of lesser age; indeed the seventh [sign] belongs to the other partner;[82] and the tenth [sign] signifies what will be between them, and the multitude or scarcity of wealth; indeed from the fourth is known the going-out[83] of their matter. (§35) And beware lest the Lord of the Ascendant does not aspect the Ascendant, or that the Lord of the domicile of the Moon does not aspect the Moon: because if it were so, one of them[84] will delude his partner, and their matter will be made worse in the separation.

(§36) And if you wished to send forth [your] substance,[85] seeking its wealth, adapt the Moon and Mercury, and the Lord of the house of substance, not to mention the Lord of the degree of the house of trust.[86] (§37a) And let the Moon be joined to Mercury, and make Mars be cadent from each of them just as you are able; also adapt Mercury and purge him of defects. (§37b) If however Mercury were retrograde, adapt the Moon and the degree of the house of trust, and make Mercury be cadent from the light of Mars; and you should not make [Mercury] be cadent from the aspect of Venus and from the Lord of the eleventh. (§38) And let your trust (in the directing of substance and in the search for wealth) always be in Mercury, and the Moon, and the degree of the house of trust, and their Lords, and make Mars and his light be cadent from [Mercury and the Moon].[87]

(§39a) And[88] if you wished to elect the hour of a purchase, adapt the Lot of Fortune, and let it be in the domiciles of Jupiter, joined to benefics: because this will be better for the one buying than for the one selling. (§39b) And the Moon, if she were in signs of straight ascension, increased in light and number, and joined to benefics, whatever he would buy in that same hour, his master will lose in it:[89] for this is better for the one selling than for the one buying. (§39c) And let Mars be cadent from the Moon and Mercury, because in a sale and purchase Mars impedes, and he is the one who signifies

---

[82] As though the querent is a junior or inexperienced apprentice seeking to partner with a master.
[83] *Exitus*, that is, the end or final result.
[84] Crofts says "both."
[85] *Mittere*, a fair translation of the Arabic "channel." The text refers to investing your money in some activity in order to make a profit.
[86] I.e., the 11th.
[87] Following Crofts, who clarifies this.
[88] From here through §40, *cf. Carmen* V.9.1-7.
[89] By "it," Sahl means what is bought: the new owner will lose money on it, or lose the object itself.

labor and contention. (§39d) Likewise the Tail—therefore make it be cadent from the Moon especially (and it is below Mars).[90] (§40) And if you wished to sell, put the Moon in her own exaltation or triplicity, separated from the benefics and aspecting the malefics, but do not let her be joined to them.[91]

(§41) And if you wished to perform a work of alchemy, or a work which you wished to repeat, let this come to be [with] the Moon in common signs, cleansed of the malefics, and let the Ascendant be likewise—therefore adapt it. And if your work were in gold, strengthen the Sun and adapt him in its inception.[92]

(§42) [The third sign and whatever is in it concerning elections]

And whatever there is in the third sign concerning elections, were its portion to fall in the ninth and another portion in the domicile of friends, then we will state it, if God wills.[93]

(§43) The fourth sign and whatever is in it, in the manner of elections

If you wished to elect so that you might build a house, adapt the Moon and her Lord, the Ascendant and its Lord, also the Lot of Fortune and Mercury. (§44a) And make Mars be cadent from these significators which I have named for you, and you should never give him a role in anything concerning the building of houses. (§44b) And if it could not come about but that he did have a role, make Venus strong in her own place, and give her strength over Mars, and join her to him from a trine or sextile aspect: because Mars does not impede a matter of Venus, in view of the greatness of her friendship toward him. (§44c) And make Saturn be cadent from Venus according to your ability (on account of his enmity), with Mars and with the Moon, if

---

[90] Crofts says "when it is below Mars," but the sense of the Latin is that the Tail is below Mars *in destructiveness*—this is what the Latin *infra* means in comparative situations. It is not clear to me what it would mean for the Tail to be "below" Mars astronomically, especially since that would be a very rare situation, only taking place about once every two years.
[91] This seems to mean that she should be in a *whole sign* aspect to the malefics, but not *joined* to them by orbs.
[92] See *On Quest.* §13.12 for more on alchemy.
[93] The Latin speaks of this in the subjunctive, but Crofts simply says that some of the elections in the third sign "are in the ninth and some in the House of Friends," so that they will be discussed there.

they aspect each other from esteem.⁹⁴ (§45a) And⁹⁵ let the Moon be increased in light and number, and joined to Jupiter from a square aspect, because this is better than the opposition: and this signifies the beauty of the building and its perfection. (§45b) And beware lest Moon be with Saturn or the Tail, or Saturn be in the Ascendant or in the fourth: because this signifies slowness and duress in the work, and that it will not be erected; (§45c) or if it were erected or were inhabited, its inhabitants will not cease to suffer fears in it, and infirmities, and robbers, and tribulations from death, and the building will split open, and perhaps it will fall down. (§45d) And if Mars aspected [the Moon],⁹⁶ and it⁹⁷ was ascending (in the circle of the *awj* or the short one),⁹⁸ burning up and falling down will be feared for it; and let the Moon be then increased in light, because then it will be useful for its master.⁹⁹

(§46) And let the Lord of the domicile of the Moon be aspecting her, likewise let the Lord of the Ascendant be aspecting the Ascendant (and they should be cleansed of the malefics): because if they did not aspect, its master will not stay in it.

(§47a) And if you wished to destroy a house, let this be when the Moon descends in her own circle, and she were separated from the malefics and joined to benefics; and let the benefic itself be oriental or ascending direct, (§47b) or let the Moon be joined to the Lord of her own domicile out of esteem (that is, from the trine or sextile aspect), so that its destruction will be easier; indeed in the square aspect and the opposition, its destruction will be more difficult.

(§48) And if you wished to buy lands and to enter into them with someone,¹⁰⁰ or you wished to own land so that you might get from someone what it renders,¹⁰¹ let Saturn be in his own exaltation or in his own triplicity or

---

⁹⁴ Both the Arabic and the Latin seem to be missing the operative *and*, so that Saturn should be *both* (a) cadent from Venus *and* (b) in a good aspect with Mars and the Moon.
⁹⁵ From here to §47b, *cf. Carmen* V.6-7.
⁹⁶ Reading *eam* for *eum*, following Crofts.
⁹⁷ Crofts uses "it" for all planets, so it is unclear whether the Moon or Mars is meant. But it is probably Mars, due to the reference to burning and falling down later in the sentence.
⁹⁸ This parenthetical remark is by the Latin translator. Crofts understands this notion of "ascending" as simply meaning the left-hand side of the chart, i.e., from the IC to the Ascendant, to the MC.
⁹⁹ That is, the owner of the house.
¹⁰⁰ Crofts reads, "to occupy them with someone."
¹⁰¹ This is according to the Latin version, which suggests the rent, either as a portion of what is grown on it or as a portion of the proceeds after the crops are sold. Crofts reads, "you want to take a land or receive it from someone."

bound, and let Jupiter be in his aspect from a stake[102] or a trine aspect, and make Mars be cadent from them. (§49a) And let the Moon be in the beginning of [the lunar] month, aspecting Saturn from esteem, increased in number, also in the aspect of Jupiter. This signifies the populating of that land and its renderings. (§49b) Which if you were not able to have the aspect of Jupiter with Saturn, make it Venus instead of Jupiter, and you will make the watery signs fortunate: because if you made them fortunate with benefics, they will be better than the airy signs. (§49c) And let the Moon be in her own exaltation or in the Midheaven, and the Lord of the Ascendant aspecting her; also, let the Moon and the Ascendant be cleansed of the malefics and from defects.

(§50a) And if you wished to divert[103] a river or dig a well, let this be when Saturn is oriental, and the Moon under the earth in the third or fifth, free from malefics, made fortunate and received; (§50b) and beware lest there be one of the malefics in the Midheaven: because this is to be feared, lest the well tumble down or the river flow off.[104] (§50c) And let Saturn be in the eleventh from the Ascendant, and the Moon be joined to a benefic in a fixed sign, and the benefic itself ascending in the circle.[105] (§50d) And the better of the benefics is Jupiter. Which if you were unable to do this, put Jupiter[106] in the Midheaven, because this is more lasting for the river and more stable for the well.

(§51) And if you wished to plant palm trees, or fig trees and the rest of trees, let this be when the Moon is in a fixed sign, and the Lord of her domicile is aspecting her from the watery signs. (§52a) And let the Ascendant be a fixed or common sign, and the Lord of the Ascendant [be] ascending and oriental.[107] (§52b) Because if it were ascending and it were not oriental, they will sprout faster but they will make a delay in producing fruit; (§52c) and if it were oriental, descending, they will sprout slowly and produce fruit quickly (and if it were oriental, ascending, they will sprout quickly and produce fruit quickly); (§52d) and if it were occidental, descending, both [processes] will be slow: namely their arising and the fruit. (§53) And let the Lord of the Ascen-

---

102 My sense is that this refers to one of the whole-sign angles from Saturn, not from the Ascendant. *Cf.* §61a below, and my Introduction §6.
103 *Deducere.* Crofts reads, "make a river flow."
104 Or, "run dry" (Crofts).
105 Crofts reads, "let the benefic be joined to the moon in a fixed, ascending sign."
106 Omitting *(fortunas, id est)*. My reading matches Crofts.
107 It is hard to know which sense of oriental/occidental is meant here.

dant and the Lord of the domicile of the Moon be aspecting them,[108] and let them be free of the malefics and from combustion.

(§54) And if you wished to sow seed (or something beyond that you wished to work with),[109] let the Ascendant be a common sign, and its Lord in a movable sign, aspecting the Lord of its own domicile, and itself[110] free from the malefics: because if a malefic aspected him, the seed itself will encounter impediment. (§55a) Therefore, let the Moon be increased in light and number, because if the Moon were under the rays and defective in number, the seed itself vanish and nothing will sprout from it. (§55b) And if it were as I have told you before, with the Moon increased in number, the seed will sprout thinly, according to the quantity of that which is sown.

(§56) The fifth sign and whatever is in it in terms of elections

If you wished to elect the hour of conjoining [sexually], namely so that you would generate a male child, let the Ascendant and its Lord, and the Moon and the Lord of the domicile of children, be in masculine signs or in a masculine part of the circle at the hour of conjoining; and you should not put any but a masculine planet in the Ascendant of that same hour or in the sign of children. (§57a) And if you want that it be female, let these significators be in feminine signs and in a feminine part of the circle. (§57b) Which if you could not do this and these significators were diverse (that is, if certain ones of them were in masculine signs, indeed certain ones in feminine ones), let the Lord of the hour and the planet receiving the Moon's disposition be partners with those who had more testimony in the masculine signs and in a masculine part of the circle, and the child will be according to this.

(§58a) And[111] if there were a dead child in the uterus and you wished to take it out, let this be when the Moon is defective in light, descending from the circle of the signs to the seventh sign from the Ascendant (that is, from the Midheaven to the seventh),[112] aspecting the benefics from a trine or

---

[108] That is, the Lord of the domicile of the Moon the Moon, and the Lord of the Ascendant the Ascendant.
[109] Crofts says, "or everything which you never want to lose."
[110] That is, the Lord of the Ascendant.
[111] *Cf. Carmen*, V.18.
[112] Crofts says "descending from the belt," which seems to indicate that she should be in southern ecliptical latitude. In that case, she should both be in southern latitude *and* be in

square aspect with the aspect of Mars. (§58b) And better and more worthy than this is if the sign of the Moon and the Ascendant were of the feminine signs which are of straight ascension, and not in crooked signs.

(§59a) And if you wished to hand a child over for training, or to send him to a place in which he might be taught some profession or number, let your election be for this: and let the Moon be aspecting Mercury, and let them be free from the malefics. (§59b) And let the Ascendant be Gemini or Virgo, and let Mercury be oriental, ascending—and do not let him be descending, nor retrograde, (nor in his own first station),[113] nor in his own descension, nor let him be impeded—and let the Lord of the domicile of Mercury be likewise. (§59c) And you should not make the Moon be descending and deficient in light, because it makes the training slow down; and let the Lords of their domiciles be aspecting them.

(§60a) The sixth sign and whatever is in it in terms of elections

If some devil or an infestation of evil inhabitants were in some place or house, or some terrible thing which is to be feared had followed him (namely the inhabitant), or there were some phantasm appearing, and you wished to remove it from its place or from some man by means of a song[114] or some search[115] or trick, (§60b) beware lest the Moon or the Ascendant be in some one of these signs: namely in Leo and Cancer, in Scorpio and Aquarius. But let the Moon be in the rest outside of these, separated from the malefics and joined to benefics.

(§61a) And[116] if you wished to elect for taking medicine for those things which are bad,[117] that is, those who have spasms, or for taking medicine for a pain of the belly, or to make a plaster, let this be when the Moon [or] the Ascendant is in Libra or in Scorpio (and the Moon in it), joined to benefics, and you should not put one of the malefics in the stakes of the Moon.

---

the quadrant from the Midheaven to the seventh. But perhaps the phrase about the belt or zodiac is redundant, and it simply means that she should be in the named quadrant.
113 This phrase is in the critical Latin edition, but not in Crofts.
114 Or more likely, a spell or incantation, following Crofts. This must refer to some form of exorcism.
115 *Inquisitione.* Crofts reads "entreaty," which seems more to the point.
116 See *Carmen* V.38.2.
117 *Ad eos qui mali fuerint.* Meaning unclear. Crofts reads (for this whole introductory sentence) "for the bowels or for taking medicine for stomach-ache or for a pain in the belly."

(§61b) Which if it could not happen but that this does take place, let this be by a trine or sextile aspect, without the opposition and without the projection of the two rays,[118] or the entrance under the rays [of the Sun]: because if it were so, it will make pain and impediment.

(§62a) If however you wanted a cure for the head and whatever comes down from it (like gargling and vomiting), let the Ascendant[119] and the Moon be in Aries or Taurus, [and the Moon] defective in light and joined to benefics. And beware of the aspect of the Sun from the square aspect or the opposition in Aries especially, on account of the heat of the Sun. (§62b) But[120] for remedies which are projected into the nostrils (like suffumigations[121] and sneezing-powders and so on), let this be when Cancer or Leo or Virgo is ascending, and the Moon is joined to benefics; and do not let her be joined to the malefics, nor to a retrograde planet, nor to an impeded one.

(§63) And if you wanted a cure for the body (namely the hands and feet), let Capricorn or Aquarius or Pisces be ascending, and let the Moon be in them, joined to benefics.

(§64a) And if you wanted a cure for some old disease, let your election for doing this be when the Moon is in her triplicity (and the better one is Taurus, because it is of the diseases of the earth).[122] And let the Moon be cleansed of the malefics, and let there be benefics in the stakes of the Moon from Taurus, and it will be stronger and better. (§64b) [And look out] so that the old infirmity goes away and does not return to him who suffers it, and beware lest the Moon is joined to Saturn in particular, because it signifies the prolonging of the illness.

(§65a) And Māshā'allāh said,[123] "Look, in every cure which you wanted, at the place of the infirmity in the body: which if it were in the part of the head or throat or chest, cure it when the Moon is in Aries, and Taurus, and Gemini (which is the upper part); (§65b) and if it were in the part of the belly and lower in the pubic area and the navel, cure it when the Moon is in Cancer and Leo and Virgo: and this is the middle part. (§65c) Indeed if the

---

[118] Crofts believes this refers to the orbs of the planets, but that does not make sense to me. It probably refers to besieging.
[119] Omitting the redundant *Aries*.
[120] See *Carmen* V.38.1.
[121] That is, smoke or other odors inhaled through the nose (as when we inhale eucalyptus fumes to clear the sinuses).
[122] I am following Crofts's interpretation here, that this means either the watery or earthy triplicity; and that the earthy one (of which Taurus is a member) is better.
[123] Source unknown.

disease were in the lower part, namely in the anus and in the lower part of the body, cure it when the Moon is in Libra and Scorpio and Sagittarius. And let the Moon be joined to benefics, increased in light and number; (§65d) and if it were a disease from the knees below, up to the feet, cure it when the Moon is in Capricorn and Aquarius and Pisces."

(§66a) And it is even said that every pain which is from the head up to the navel ought to be cured when the Moon is between the stake of the earth, ascending up to the Midheaven, through this ascending part of the circle: and this is the place which is called the "upper part of the circle." (§66b) And if it were from the navel to the lower part of the feet, you will cure him when the Moon is between the tenth, descending to the stake of the earth, which is the lower part of the circle. (§66c) And let there be a benefic in the Ascendant: because if it were so, it signifies that he would be healed and progress.

(§67a) And[124] if there were some blister[125] in the eye, or some thing, and it were necessary that it be touched with iron or scarified, and there were a covering[126] over it, or it were in some place of the body for which it is necessary that it be touched by iron (like the cutting of a vein), let this be when the Moon is increased in light and number, (§67b) unless, however, [it is] in drawing away [fluids] by cupping: because then you will make the Moon defective in light and number, joined to benefics. And let Jupiter be above the earth in the Ascendant, or the eleventh, or the tenth or ninth;[127] and beware of [the Moon's][128] conjunction with Mars if the Moon were increased in light and number. (§67c) If however you were unable to put Jupiter in these places, let him be aspecting the Ascendant. And beware lest the Moon and the Ascendant be in the earthy signs, and lest the Nodes[129] be commingled with Mars (that is, having some communion with Mars); (§67d) and beware then, in the Moon's rising [out of the beams]—that is, when the Moon passes by the Sun through 12°; likewise in the prevention; or that Mars be in the Ascendant when [the doctor] cuts this off; and likewise Saturn, unless

---

[124] From here to §68b, and from §69a-d, cf. *Carmen* V.39-40.
[125] *Vesica*. Or, a pustule (Crofts) or cyst.
[126] *Coopertorium*. Crofts reads "film."
[127] The ninth does not appear in the Arabic.
[128] Crofts' text says "Beware of a joining with Mars, if the Moon is increasing in light and computation," and separates this from the previous statement about Jupiter. So I have replaced the Latin *eius*.
[129] Following Crofts; the Latin reads, "beware lest the Moon and the Ascendant be in earthy signs and *in Gemini*." But the Arabic reads *jawzahar*, referring to the Nodes.

Saturn is in the beginning of the [lunar] month and the Moon is increased in light and number. (§68a) Because if he were to cut something off from the body, or were to puncture it, it will putrefy, and the draining or puncturing will not profit the one suffering the infirmity. (§68b) And you should not cut a vein nor extract a tooth if the Moon were in a movable or common sign, clothed by the malefics (that is, commingled), unless the Moon is cleansed of the malefics or there were a strong benefic with the Moon, or she were joined to it[130] from a trine or sextile aspect.

(§69a) But pains which are in the eyes, like an inflammation and whiteness[131] and the rest of the infirmities which are cured by iron, let this be in the increase of the Moon's light and her number, according to what I told you [above], before this heading. (§69b) And let [the Moon] be cleansed of Mars in the curing of the eye in particular, because if he aspected, let him be held back[132] in this. Indeed if Saturn aspected then, if the Moon were increased in number and light in the beginning of [the lunar] month, it impedes less. (§69c) If however she were removed [or remote] from the prevention,[133] make the Moon aspect Mars from a trine aspect, and let her be joined to a benefic. And do not give strength to Mars in any curing of the eyes, because the sages agree concerning the impediment of Mars in the head. (§69d) And they even said everything which is cured with iron, look at the sovereignty of it from the body,[134] and you should not put the Moon nor the Ascendant in this sign, nor should you touch anything with iron if the Moon were in a common nor in a movable sign.

(§70a) If you wished to shave hairs with *an-nūrah*[135] (this is to remove hair with a certain kind of remedy), and so on, let this be when the Moon is in feminine signs, defective in light. (§70b) Which if you were unable to do this, you should not put her in hairy signs (as Aries is, and Leo, and the rest of the bestial signs), and let the Lord of the Ascendant be descending from the Midheaven to the stake of the earth.

(§71a) And[136] if you wished to make a purchase of slaves, beware lest the Moon be joined to malefics, or that there be a malefic below the earth, nor

---

[130] I believe this means "the malefic."
[131] *Phlegmon et albedo*. Crofts reads, "tumours and leucoma."
[132] *Abstineatur*. That is, do not let the doctor perform the procedure. Crofts reads, "...[Mars] will become more vehement in this."
[133] That is, after the Full Moon has passed.
[134] That is, see which sign rules the afflicted part of the body.
[135] A depilatory paste (Lat. *annora*).
[136] From here to §73, *cf. Carmen* V.11.

let the Moon be in a movable sign: (§71b) because it signifies that the slave will be unfaithful to [his] master, and he will not be stable in one condition; or he will be fleeing if the Moon were separated from malefics (except for Libra, which is more useful for this). (§72) But in fixed signs he will be enduring and supportive, and honoring his own master—except for Scorpio, because then he will be a whisperer,[137] and an accuser, and weak in words; and in Leo he will be desiring,[138] and on account of the gluttony of his belly a pain of the belly will happen to him; and he will be a robber. (§73) And let the Moon be in common signs, because this will be praiseworthy (except for Pisces, because he will consider betrayal in his own mind, and unfaithfulness toward his own masters, and he will be absent from them). And fear the conjunction of the Moon with the malefics, because if she were joined with malefics, it signifies that the slave will be sold. (§74) And if you wished to make a slave free, beware of the presence of the Moon in the twelve signs,[139] just as it is in the fifth book of Dorotheus.

(§75a) And if you wished to render a slave free (a freedman), let this be when the Moon is cleansed of defects, increased in light and number, and joined to benefics. (§75b) And let the benefic itself be oriental, increased: because if it were occidental [and] increased, he will find good but pains will happen to him, and he will not cease to be a failure[140] until he dies. (§75c) But in the increase of the Moon's light, he will be sound in body; and in the increase of number, it will signify the discovery of substance. (§76a) And let the Sun and the sign of the Midheaven[141] be cleansed of the malefics: because if they were impeded, the master will find impediment according to the nature of the sign. (§76b) And let the hour of liberation be when the luminaries aspect each other from a trine or sextile aspect, so that there will be concord and esteem between the slave and master, and he will find good from him: (§77a) for the square aspect is the middle, and the aspect of the opposition signifies that the slave will contend with his master. (§77b) And

---

[137] Reading *susurrator* for *susurro*.
[138] Or, ambitious. Crofts reads "greedy."
[139] From here to §77b, *cf. Carmen* V.13. Reading with Crofts for the Latin "twelfth sign." Crofts says "if you want to *gain anything* from slaves from the presence of the Moon in *the twelve signs*, it is in the fifth book of Dorotheus." This is a reference back to *Carmen* V.11, where Dorotheus speaks about the individual signs in purchasing a slave (see above).
[140] *Deficere*. This verb generally means to be lacking, to fail, to run short, to be weak.
[141] Crofts reads, "the sign *in* mid-heaven" (emphasis mine). This must mean the sign on which the degree of the Midheaven falls, since that sign will be crossing the meridian.

he who made a slave a freedman when the Moon was impeded, slavery will be better for him than freedom: therefore put the Moon in fixed signs.[142]

(§78a) The seventh sign and whatever is in it in terms of elections

If[143] you wanted the election of a marriage, beware lest the Moon be in the twelfth, and beware lest she be in signs which are not useful for this (which are Aries, Cancer, Capricorn, Aquarius). (§78b) And beware of the signs in which the malefics and the Tail were (if you wished to be engaged to a woman). And let this be when the Moon is joined to benefics and she is in a movable sign—and better than all of them together is the sign of Libra. (§79a) And[144] beware, in getting engaged, lest the Moon be in a fixed sign; (§79b) but in the [sexual] conjoining (that is, when someone goes in to his wife in order to use her), beware lest she be in a movable sign nor in a common one: but let this be when the Moon is in a fixed sign:[145] (§79c) and better than the rest are Leo and Taurus (indeed Scorpio and Aquarius are not useful for the woman). (§80a) And the middle of Taurus[146] is better [than] its beginning and end; indeed the first half of Gemini[147] is worse, and the end is good; also, Aries and Cancer are bad, indeed Leo is praiseworthy (except that each of them will not cease to destroy the substance of his partner). (§80b) And Virgo is useful for a woman who already had been married, but not for a virgin; Libra, too, is bad; indeed the beginning of Scorpio is useful, and its end bad, because it signifies that their partnership will not be prolonged. (§80c) Also, Sagittarius is bad, and likewise the beginning of Capricorn (its middle and end is good); Aquarius too is bad, and likewise Pisces.

(§81a) And there is no usefulness in marriage if Venus aspected the malefics. And let this be when Venus is in the domiciles of the benefics and their bounds, joined to the Lord of her own domicile. (§81b) If however [the Lord of her domicile] were a malefic, let her be separated from it, and let

---

[142] This "therefore"(*ergo*) is misplaced, since the Moon's being unimpeded does not entail that she be in fixed signs. In the Arabic these are two separate statements: slavery is better for someone if the Moon is impeded, *and* one should put the Moon in fixed signs.
[143] See *Carmen* V.16.8-20.
[144] From here to §84, see *Carmen* V.16.
[145] Undoubtedly so the sexual intercourse will last a long time.
[146] Perhaps because it is the decan of the Moon?
[147] Why? The first decan belongs to Jupiter and only the middle belongs to Mars.

Jupiter be overcoming[148] her, or Venus joined to him from a trine aspect; (§81c) and let the Moon and Jupiter and Venus be aspecting each other by a trine or sextile aspect, and the better of these is the trine aspect (and especially the triplicity of water). (§81d) And let the Moon be increased in light and number, free from the malefics, and let Venus always be in her own domicile or exaltation, or triplicity, or her own joy, or in the conjunction of Jupiter or Mercury, and Mercury made fortunate and strong. (§82a) Likewise adapt the Sun just as I have told you before, because from the Sun and the Ascendant is known the being [or condition] of the man;[149] and from Venus and the Moon and the seventh sign is known the being [or condition] of the woman. (§82b) Therefore beware of the aspect of the malefics to them from the conjunction or the square aspect or the opposition. (§83a) And if it were a woman [getting] married, let the Moon be in common signs and the work be according to what I have told you before. And let the Ascendant at the hour of the marriage[150] be of the signs which I told you before, so that the Moon would be in them. (§83b) And you should not put any of the malefics in the Ascendant, nor should one aspect it from enmity; and let one of the benefics be in the Midheaven. (§84) And Dorotheus said,[151] "Because then a child will be granted to them in that same year in which they are joined; which if [a watery sign][152] were in the degree of the Midheaven, the woman will become pregnant in the first conjoining."

(§85) The knowledge of the hours of going out to war. It is necessary that you should make the Ascendant one of the domiciles of the higher planets, of which the stronger is the domicile of Mars, if he were in a sextile or trine aspect of the Ascendant. (§86a) And let the Lord of the Ascendant be in the Ascendant or in the eleventh or the tenth;[153] and beware of the fourth or the

---

[148] Lat. *elevatus* ("lifted up, elevated"), but Dorotheus is clear he is referring to the Hellenistic "overcoming," whereby Jupiter is in the tenth whole sign from Venus (*Carmen* V.16.22).
[149] Crofts says "child," but this statement comes from *Carmen* V.16.1, which clearly says "man."
[150] Lat. *coniugii*. Crofts says "consummation," i.e., the first sexual intercourse after the marriage. *Coniugium* can have this connotation.
[151] This must refer to *Carmen* V.16.25-26. Here Dorotheus makes two statements, both in a synastry context: (a) if a benefic is in the Midheaven of each of the nativities of the man and woman, then they will conceive in the year of their first sexual intercourse; (b) if the tenth domicile of each is a fertile (watery) sign, they will conceive at their first sexual intercourse.
[152] Following Crofts.
[153] The Arabic omits "the tenth."

seventh and the eighth. And [the Lord of the Ascendant] should not be combust nor cadent, nor joined to a cadent planet who does not receive him.[154] (§86b) And make the Lord of the seventh be joined to the Lord of the Ascendant, or put him in the Ascendant or in the second, (§87a) with Mars.[155] If you wished that they be joined, [then] make them be conjoined in the stakes, so that they would encounter each other and war will fall between them. And join a benefic having a role in the Ascendant, to Mars, so that it might prohibit him from the Ascendant. (§87b) And you should not go to war unless Mars is in an aspect of friendship to the Lord of the Ascendant, like if he himself is the Lord of the Ascendant[156] and he is strong and in a good place, and not impeded, nor combust, and he is in signs of straight ascension. (§87c) And beware that you do not put him [anywhere] except in the *ḥayyiz*[157] of the Ascendant, so that his help will be toward him whom you are sending to war and him who sends the soldiers to war, because they will be freed,[158] by the command of God. (§88a) Even adapt the second and its Lord for the soldiers[159] of the one incepting, and the eighth and its Lord for the soldiers of the enemy; and you should not put the Lord of the eighth in the seventh, nor in the eighth, but put the Lord of the eighth in the second.

---

[154] Crofts makes it sound as though one should avoid the fourth, seventh, and eighth only *if* the Lord of the Ascendant is in one of these bad conditions.

[155] There has been some garbling in the Latin edition. According to Crofts, this section should read, "If you requested that they confront each other, place *Mars* in the stakes, so that there will be a confrontation and war will break out."

[156] Crofts reads, "Only go to war when Mars is in command in his course, that he can be the Lord of the Ascendant," with the rest of the conditions following. Still, it is a good idea for Mars to be in a good aspect to the Lord of the Ascendant.

[157] Lit., "domain, area." That is, Mars *should* be in the *ḥayyiz* of the Ascendant. This word is used in several ways in medieval astrology. Sometimes it is a synonym for "sect"; but in other cases it refers to a planet's location according to sect and gender: a diurnal planet above the earth by day or below it by night, and in a masculine sign (or a nocturnal planet below the earth by day or above it by night, and in a feminine sign). In Mars's case this changes somewhat, as he is a nocturnal planet (and should be below the earth by day or above it by night), but since he is masculine he should be in a masculine sign. Crofts follows al-Bīrūnī and takes this to be the meaning. However, I take this use of *ḥayyiz* simply to mean that Mars should be in the eastern area or hemisphere of the chart: note the following statements about Mars helping out the one going to war (which is represented by the Ascendant). I have seen it used this way in al-Rijāl.

[158] Or "saved," following Crofts.

[159] That is, the *allies* of the inceptor (and the eighth for the opponent's allies). See Crofts, "supporters."

(§88b) And put the Lot of Fortune and its Lord in the Ascendant or in the second, and you should not put them in the eighth nor in the seventh. (§88c) And you should not make the Ascendant and the Lord of its[160] domicile impeded, if you were to begin a matter; likewise the dignity of the twelfth-part of the Moon.[161] (§89a) Because it is necessary in the matter of war to adapt the stars of war: that is, Mars and Mercury, also the Moon and the Lord of her domicile. Therefore, look, in the adaptation of these things, and you should not be neglectful in this (nor should you hand it over to forgetfulness).

(§90a) And know that if you were to bring both armies forth[162] for war wisely, just as I have said above, he will gain the victory who, of them, was born at night and in whose nativity Mars had a role:[163] because Mars is the master of wars, and wars are committed to him. (§90b) And perhaps they will enter into an agreement or will give up the war (that is, if the place of their going out to war were good).[164]

(§91) And if you wished to buy arms and the instruments of war, let this be when Mars is in his own domicile or in the exaltation or his own triplicity, at the end of the [lunar] month: because the sages were careful lest the Moon be with Mars at the beginning of the [lunar] month (and at its end, it is more useful).

(§92) And if you wished to overwhelm fortresses,[165] let the inception of this work be when the Moon is impeded, without strength.

(§93) And if you wished to destroy some instrument of war,[166] begin this when Mercury is impeded and without strength.

(§94) And if you wished to destroy the opposition of the war,[167] let this be when Mars is impeded and without strength.

---

160 I believe this refers to the dispositor of the Lord of the Ascendant.
161 See my Introduction for a discussion of this passage, along with one from *On Times*.
162 *Produxeris*.
163 The Latin is more specific than the Arabic, which reads "who had Mars in his nativity." Obviously every nativity has Mars, but he might not have a *central* role in every one. A nocturnal nativity with a powerful Mars is obviously chosen because Mars belongs to the nocturnal sect and will therefore be of the sect in power. Sahl must be recommending we look to other favorable sect conditions and rulerships and placements: like Scorpio rising and Mars in the eleventh (which would also put him above the horizon).
164 Crofts reads, "if the position of the departure to battle of both of them works favorably." Perhaps this means they will not fight if each side seems to have an equal chance of winning.
165 Crofts reads, "demolish forts," but the idea is the same.
166 That is, instruments belonging to the enemy.
167 Crofts reads, "spoil the fighting." Evidently this means actions taken to halt the war.

(§95) And if you wished to destroy land, begin when the Moon is made unfortunate, not having strength.

(§96) And if you wished to destroy a place of idols and the place in which it is prayed to a devil and not to God, begin this when Venus is impeded and without strength.

(§97a) The eighth sign and whatever is in it in terms of elections

If[168] some man wished to make a will, he should not begin this when the Ascendant and the sign of the Moon are movable, because this signifies that the recommendation[169] of the will will be changed. (§97b) But let it be committed [to writing] when the Moon is defective in number and increased in light, and the Moon should not be joined to a planet under the rays (because this signifies the quickness of death). (§98) And more cunning[170] than this [is if] the Moon were with Mars or in his square, or in his opposite, or Mars were in the Ascendant or aspecting it from enmity: because this signifies that the recommendation will not be changed, and the infirm person will die from the same infirmity, and the recommendation will not be perfected after his death [or it will be stolen].[171] (§99) And if Saturn were [positioned] likewise from the Moon and the Ascendant [as Mars was], the life of the man will be prolonged, and the recommendation will be perfected after him, and it will not be changed in his life, nor after his death. (§100) And if Venus and Jupiter were in a like manner from the Moon and the Ascendant, the master of the recommendation will end his life and the recommendation will [not] follow.[172]

---

[168] From here to §100, cf. *Carmen* V.42.1-7.
[169] Lat. *commendatio*, referring to something entrusted to someone else to carry out—as when the will asks that something be carried out. This election is concerned with whether the wishes will be carried out.
[170] *Callidius*. But Crofts reads "worse," and based on other uses of *callidius* in these texts I think it might be a misread for *certius*, "more certainly."
[171] Adding missing phrase from Crofts.
[172] This sentence is garbled and incorrect in the Latin, and I have added "not" to give it a more correct sense. According to Crofts it should read, "the testator will live a little longer and change that testament."

(§101) The ninth sign and whatever is in it in terms of elections

You[173] should not neglect to direct the foreign travels of men based upon their nativities (namely, upon the Ascendant[174] of every nativity and its stakes). (§102a) And let the Moon be in its Ascendant or in its Midheaven; and adapt the Lord of the matter which you seek, and adapt the Lord of the Year, and the Lord of the Ascendant of the root and of the year.[175] (§102b) Which if you did not know what I said,[176] look (for him who came to you) from the Lord of the matter which is sought, to see where its place is from the Lord of the Ascendant.[177] (§103a) After this, indicate to him the hour suitable to his nativity or question (that is, you should not make the Ascendant of the question and its Lord cadent from the Ascendant of his departure). (§103b) And let the Ascendant of the departure be the tenth [sign] of the Ascendant of the question or nativity, if he sought a kingdom; and if he sought a business deal, the eleventh [sign] from the Ascendant of the question; and likewise in every matter which you sought, make that sign the Ascendant for him. (§104a) And let the Moon be in the stakes and in the succeedents of the stakes, if she were free from the malefics; and let her be aspecting the Ascendant. And indeed if she were impeded, make her be cadent from the Ascendant. (§104b) And let the Lord of the Ascendant and the Lord of the domicile of the Moon be in stakes, and let the Moon aspect the Lord of her own domicile. (§105a) And beware lest you put the Moon with malefics, or in their aspect from the square aspect or the opposition, because the aspect of the malefics to the Ascendant is easier than their aspect to the Moon[178]— (§105b) and this especially in foreign travel, because her conjunction with Mars in the beginning of the [lunar] month signifies robbers, or a king,[179] or fire. (§106a) And always beware lest you put the Moon in the fourth, but put her in the fifth (if she were made fortunate in this place, there will be less absence in the foreign travel, and more profit in

---

173 From here to §121, cf. *Carmen* V.21-24.
174 Reading with Crofts, for *ascensiones* ("ascensions").
175 So we must adapt: (a) the Lord of the matter in the election chart; (b) the profected Lord of the Year of the nativity; (c) the Lord of the natal Ascendant; (d) the Lord of the Ascendant in the solar revolution.
176 E.g., if the traveler did not know his own nativity, so that one could not adapt its features or that of the solar revolution.
177 That is, simply look at the Lord of the matter and the Lord of the Ascendant in the election chart itself.
178 This is an interesting claim I have not read elsewhere.
179 *Regem*, but this should read "tyrant" with Crofts, which makes more sense.

his matters, and more success in it, and also less loosening[180] of his body, and easier for his journey, and more for the safety of him who was with him). (§107) Even the presence of the Moon in the Ascendant in his entrance and departure is horrible, because infirmity will be feared for the one on foreign travel in his journey, or heavy labor in his body.

(§108a) If however it were a journey to the king, make the Moon be joined to the Sun or to the Lord of the Midheaven from a trine or sextile aspect, and let the Sun be in a good place in the Ascendant, or in the eleventh or in the tenth; (§108b) because if he were cadent, he will not find good from him;[181] and if he were in the ninth, or in the third and the fifth, it signifies labor and middling success. Likewise the western stake and the fourth [stake] signify a scarcity of good, with labor and slowness.

(§109) And if you sought nobles and judges, or the leaders of sects (that is, bishops and the rest such), let there be a conjunction of the Moon with Jupiter from the stakes, or in a good place from the Ascendant.

(§110) Indeed if your departure were to the leaders of battles, let there be a conjunction of the Moon with Mars from a trine or sextile aspect, and beware of his conjunction and the stakes;[182] and let Mars be in the ones following the stakes.[183]

(§111) And if your departure were to those who are of mature age, or to ignoble people, let her conjunction be with Saturn from friendship, and let Saturn be in the succeedents of the stakes.

(§112) Indeed if your departure were to women, join the Moon to Venus and let Venus be in a masculine sign; and if you could [make it] so that she is in the places which I told you before for a partnership, do so.

(§113a) And if your departure were to writers and merchants and the wise, let the conjunction be with Mercury. And beware lest Mercury be then under the rays, or retrograde, or the malefics aspect him, (§113b) because as often as there is a star to whom the Moon or a planet is joined, who is in the

---

[180] Crofts reads, "strain." The Latin idea seems to be that his body will not fall apart under the strain of travel.
[181] The Latin reads as though this means, "the traveler will not find good from the king." But Crofts reads as though the *astrologer* will find no good in the *Sun*. In practice it will not make a difference.
[182] This probably means Mars should not be in the whole-sign angles of the *Moon*.
[183] This suggests the angles of the *Ascendant*.

opposite of the Ascendant, or the Lord of the seventh [were] slow, or impeded,[184] it signifies complications and duress in those ways.

(§114a) If however it were a foreign journey by water, let the Moon be in signs of water, and beware of the conjunction of the Moon with Saturn from a stake in foreign journeys of water. And beware of [the malignity of] Saturn, so that he is not in a watery sign, and lest he be fixed in the Ascendant[185] of the departure, or with the Moon. (§114b) Which if it would not come about but that it were so, let the Moon be joined to him with a strong benefic (or in its[186] aspect) from a trine or sextile aspect, or from a stake, so that it would take away the malignity of Saturn due to shipwreck or impediment or a severe tempest.

(§115a) For in sailing the sea you should not make the luminaries impeded, because if they were adapted and safe from the malefics, and if they were not made fortunate by benefics, they signify safety and prosperity. (§115b) Indeed if they were impeded, the man will be dead or lost on his foreign journey. And you should not sail the sea when the Moon is between the old Moon and the new,[187] because this is horrible. (§115c) If however he sailed the sea on account of a business matter, adapt Mercury and the Moon especially, and let it[188] be aspecting Jupiter from Cancer or Pisces: (§115d) for Scorpio is horrible in sailing the sea on account of the place of Mars and his enmity against those sailing the sea. (§115e) And fear the bounds of the malefics in sailing the sea—wherefore in sailing the coast [or traveling over mountains][189] there is less impediment than in sailing the sea.

(§116) And if it were a foreign journey by land, the Moon should not be in watery signs, [but should be] cleansed of the malefics. And beware of the aspect of Mars in a foreign journey on the coast,[190] just as I have warned you

---

[184] This list is somewhat garbled in the Latin version. The three types of planets are: (a) a planet joined to the Moon; (b) a planet "in conjunction with" the Ascendant; (c) the Lord of the seventh. But surely one would also expect a planet opposing the Ascendant (as the Latin reads) to be significant.

[185] Crofts reads, "with command over the Ascendant of the departure or the Moon," which probably means being the Lord of the Ascendant or the Lord of the Moon's domicile.

[186] This probably means "the benefic's aspect."

[187] *In interlunio.* Crofts reads, "when the Moon is absent." I take this to mean the period when the Moon is under the rays of the Sun.

[188] Mercury or the Moon. This sentence in Crofts says we are to adapt Mercury *or* the Moon, not *and* the Moon.

[189] Filling in missing phrase from Crofts.

[190] Crofts reads, "land."

to beware of Saturn when sailing the sea. And beware lest the foreign journey be of any kind when the Moon is in Scorpio.

(§117a) And know that the healthiest [signs] are the earthy signs for him who wished to ride by land, and the watery ones for him who wished to sail in the water of the sea. And Saturn is of greater impediment in the sea, and more strongly so if he did not aspect Jupiter. (§117b) And beware, in a foreign journey on land and by sea, if the Moon is in the last image[191] of the sign of Libra. (Know all of this.)

(§118) And know that it is necessary (should you wish to) to adapt the region into which you are entering, so that you adapt the second from the Ascendant while you enter any kind of region which you wanted to: and if you did this, you have already adapted the region. (§119a) And you ought to adapt the Ascendant, and its Lord, and the Moon and the Lord of the second, if you can; therefore make it a benefic and let it be above the earth in the ninth or in the tenth or in the eleventh; (§119b) and never should you put it below the earth (namely in the fourth or fifth or sixth), because this is horrible in a foreign journey and in a work which you seek in that region; and let it be above the earth, whether it were a benefic or a malefic. (§120a) And strive so that the Lord of the domicile of the Moon is with the Lord of the second above the earth, and you should not put him under the earth, because this is not praiseworthy (unless that which you seek in that region is a matter which you wish to conceal, so that it does not appear until it is perfected). (§120b) And let the Moon then[192] be between 12° and 15° from the Sun—and better yet if the Moon, when she goes out from under the rays up to 3°, is made fortunate. For this is better and more praiseworthy than everything which you need in the concealment.[193] (§121) And if you sought a kingdom in that region, adapt the Midheaven and its Lord with the second from the Ascendant, and the Moon.

(§122a) After[194] this, look, in foreign travels (according to what Dorotheus said for foreign travels by water), at the place of the Moon in the signs. Which, if she were in the first face of Aries and the planets aspected (or they

---

[191] Normally I would take this to mean "face" or "decan," but Crofts provides an argument (based on Arabic usage, p. 184) that this means "paranatellonton," extra-zodiacal constellations rising at the same time. I am unsure about this. At any rate, the last portion of Libra is in the burnt path, so it would be bad no matter what the meaning of "image" is here.

[192] That is, if you *do* want the matter to be concealed.

[193] In other words, this is the best thing to do in matters of concealment.

[194] From here through §122e, cf. *Carmen* V.25.1-13.

did not aspect), it signifies the ease of his matter; (§122b) and if she were in Taurus, the impediment of Mars will be less for her[195]—if however Saturn aspected, it will impede [the inceptor] and will make a shipwreck for him; and in the second face of Gemini it signifies slowness, [but] after this safety; but in Cancer, safety from every impediment; (§122c) indeed in Leo, say impediment—and more strongly so if a malefic aspected; and in Virgo, say prosperity and slowness, and turning back;[196] and in Libra, if she had crossed ten degrees, you should not go on a foreign journey by land nor by sea; and in Scorpio, say sorrow; (§122d) and in Sagittarius, say before the journey is perfected he will turn back;[197] and in the beginning of Capricorn a little bit of good; and in Aquarius, say slowness and safety; and in Pisces say impediment and difficulty. (§122e) And if a malefic aspected, the detriment will increase; indeed if a benefic aspected, the impediment will be made better and the good will be strengthened. (Know this.)

(§123a) The tenth sign and whatever is in it in terms of elections

If you wished to set out with a king or prince to a region over which he already was in charge, let this be when Jupiter is in the Ascendant or in the seventh or in the ninth,[198] because this signifies that he who goes will find good and joy in that journey, and he will see what pleases him. (§123b) And beware lest you put Jupiter in the fourth, because this is horrible; and let the Moon (and Venus) testify to him from one of the stakes. And beware lest Saturn and Mars or Venus[199] be in the Ascendant or in one of the stakes. (§123c) And you should not put the Moon under the rays; and beware lest she be with the Tail or with the malefics, because there is no good in this: for if he were to go on a foreign journey, he will not return; and if he became infirm, he will die; and if he went off to war, he will be killed or overcome.

---

[195] This is an incorrect translation in the Latin edition: it should read (following Crofts), "tell him there will be losses." Nothing is stated about Mars in the Arabic.
[196] Crofts reads, "safety *but* a slow return" (emphasis mine).
[197] Crofts reads (with express puzzlement), "say that he will remove its colours." Dorotheus himself says, "calamities and misfortune from the waves will reach it" (*Carmen* V.25.9-10). Again, Dorotheus is speaking about journeys by sea.
[198] The Arabic omits the ninth.
[199] The Arabic omits Venus.

(§124) And if you wished to be raised up and moved to a kingdom,[200] let this be with the ascension of Leo,[201] and let the Sun be in Taurus in the Midheaven and the Moon in the Ascendant, joined to benefics or to the Lord of the Midheaven.

(§125a) And if you wished to introduce a king into the seat of his empire, let the Ascendant be a fixed sign, and likewise the fourth [sign], (§125b) and let the Lord of the Midheaven be free from the malefics, and the Lord of the Ascendant in a good place, received, and the Lord of the tenth should not aspect the eleventh from enmity. (§126a) And let the Moon be aspecting the Lord of her own domicile from friendship; also the Lord of the fourth sign should aspect the benefics. (§126b) If however you were unable to do it based on what I have told you before, let the Moon be received and the Lord of the fourth in a strong place, aspecting the benefics. (§126c) Which if you could not do this, make him be cadent from the Ascendant and its aspect, and put the benefics aspecting the fourth sign and the Midheaven.

(§127) And if you wished to elect the hour so that you would be set over the [tax] renderings,[202] let the Moon be joined to Saturn out of friendship in the beginning of the [lunar] month, and let her be in the domicile of Saturn, and the benefics aspecting her: because this signifies stability (and that the work will be stable); and let the Midheaven be a fixed sign, so that it will be one work.

(§128a) And if you wished to secure [military] standards,[203] let the Moon be in the domiciles of Mars, made fortunate, and let her be aspecting Mars from esteem, with the benefics, at the end of the [lunar] month, [with her] joined to them. (§128b) And the confirmation of those standards which are below the king[204] will be more worthy than this if the Moon is cleansed [of the malefics] and she is not in the domiciles of the malefics, nor in Cancer, (§128c) unless it is the standard of the master of the war: and let *this* be in the domiciles of Mars (and the better and more useful of them is Scorpio, on account of the strength of Mars, and his stability in it).

---

[200] Crofts reads, "enhance your reputation to the ruler." The Latin clearly assumes that the increased reputation has an official post as its goal.
[201] That is, Leo should be the ascending sign.
[202] Crofts reads, "to supervise levying taxes."
[203] These are the flags and standards used on the battlefield to make announcements and give commands.
[204] That is, of those who are not of royal status.

(§129a) And if you wished to make an enemy of the king, and you yourself were the one being inimical, let this be when the Moon is increased in light, and let the Moon and the Ascendant be cleansed of the malefics, (§129b) and let the Lord of the Ascendant be in an optimal place from the Ascendant, in one of his own dignities, direct and safe from the malefics (whether he was a benefic or a malefic). (§129c) And let the Lord of the seventh be in a bad place from the Ascendant, not aspecting a benefic nor the luminaries.

(§130) Indeed if he were angry with you, you should not appear to him unless the Moon is defective in light, and let [the Ascendant and its Lord, and the Moon, be impeded; and let][205] the Lord of the seventh be made fortunate in a good place from the Ascendant, so that it is stronger for your own matters.

(§131a) The eleventh sign and whatever is in it in terms of elections

If you wished to make a friendship with someone, let the Moon be cleansed of the stakes of the malefics, and let the Lord of the eleventh be aspecting the Ascendant from friendship. (§131b) And[206] make the Moon be joined to the substance of the planet which you seek: like Venus for women, and Mercury for writers, and all the circles according to what will come for this.[207]

(§132a) And if you wished to seek some thing from any man, let the Lord of the Ascendant be aspecting the Ascendant from friendship, and let the Ascendant be a fixed sign or a common one; and let the Moon be in [the Ascendant],[208] or in its triplicity[209] or square aspect; (§132b) and beware of the opposition, nor let [the Moon] be joined to malefics, or [beware] lest she is not aspecting the Lord of her own domicile. If however the Moon did not aspect the Lord of her own domicile, the matter will not be perfected.

---

[205] This phrase is missing in the Latin edition, but appears in Crofts.
[206] According to Crofts (p. 187), this section belongs to the following §§132a-134; cf. *Carmen* V.14 for all of this.
[207] The ending of this sentence is awkward. Crofts reads, "according to what that brings." It simply means we pick the natural significator of the type of person that pertains.
[208] Following Crofts, instead of having the Lord of the Ascendant be in the Ascendant—which would have contradicted the previous instruction.
[209] I.e., in a whole-sign trine.

(§132c) Therefore, seek matters[210] always when the Moon is increased in light and number, and the Lord of the Ascendant direct, and the Moon joined to benefics; if however the benefic were direct and the Moon joined to increased benefics, it will be increased. (§133) And beware lest Mercury be in a bad condition, because if he were impeded and he were received, it signifies inconvenience and duress, and a second turning-back in the seeking.[211]

(§134) And make the Moon be joined to the planet to which your matter pertains: like the Sun for a king and Mars for generals and those making war (likewise regarding the remaining Lords of the circles).

(§135) The twelfth sign and whatever is in it in terms of elections

If[212] you wished to buy a beast, let this be when the Moon is joined to benefics and they are direct and oriental, ascending; and beware the conjunction of the malefics, because then it is to be feared concerning the beast. (§136a) And if it were tamed and already ridden, buy it when the Ascendant is a common sign and the Moon in a fixed sign (except for Aquarius and Scorpio). (§136b) And let he to whom she is joined, be direct [and] ascending, so that the beast might increase in price and body: because if it were retrograde ascending, there will be diminishment in the body of the beast but the price will be increased; and if it were direct descending, it will be increased in body and the price will not be appropriate for it. (§137) Indeed if the beast were untamed, that is, not ridden, let the Ascendant be a common sign and the Moon in a movable sign, joined to a benefic; after this, do just as I told you before in the first heading.[213]

(§138a) And if you wished to go out to hunt, go out under a common sign, and let the Lord of the seventh be defective[214] and descending, and let him be in the succeedents of the stakes: because if he were cadent, it signifies that the prey will escape after he caught it. (§138b) And let the Moon, in every departure to hunt, be separated from Mars, made fortunate in an opti-

---

[210] Crofts makes this more specific: "ask for things." The instructions obviously do not pertain to every kind of seeking or undertaking.
[211] This last clause seems to be rendering the Arabic, "it indicates displeasure in the request and a mean refusal."
[212] From here to §137, cf. *Carmen*, V.12.
[213] This must mean in the first sentence of this chapter, i.e., §135, using the same criteria of ascending, descending, *etc.*
[214] Crofts reads, "decreasing."

mal place from the Ascendant. And you should not go out to hunt if the Moon were at the end of the signs, nor void in course, nor in a movable sign. (§138c) And beware lest the Lord of her own domicile does not aspect her, because if he did aspect her it will signify ease for him in the matter.

(§139a) And make Mercury be cleansed of the malefics in a hunt by water; if however you wanted a hunt in the mountains, let the Moon be in Aries and its triplicity; (§139b) if indeed it were a hunt for birds, let the Moon be in Gemini and its triplicity, joined to Mercury or separated from the same Mercury, [with] him descending: because this is better.

(§140a) And if you wanted a hunt by sea, let this be when the Ascendant is a common sign, and its Lord in a watery sign; and beware lest the Ascendant be a fiery sign. And let the Moon be aspecting the Lord of her own domicile. (§140b) And know that the impediment of the Moon with Mars in a hunt by sea will be worse and of more scarce profit: therefore beware of the impediment of Mars in a hunt by sea (and beware of the impediment of Saturn in a hunt by land). (§140c) Also, were you to adapt Venus and the Moon, and Mars did not impede them in a hunt by sea, the catch will be doubled (by its master) and multiplied, and its master will gain the greatest wealth, and the hunt will prosper by means of its master: (§140d) therefore let the Moon be joined to Venus, and let Mercury be with her; and if however Mercury were impeded by Saturn, it will not impede this. And beware lest Mars be in a watery sign and the Moon be joined to him, or Venus be joined to Mars.

(§141a) If[215] however you wanted to make flight or perform a concealed work, and [for] everyone who wished to flee or be hidden: let this be when the Moon is separated from the malefics and joined to benefics. And let the Moon be joined to Saturn under the rays, and let her be joined to benefics at the time of her going-out from under the rays.[216] (§141b) And the luminaries, if they were to arise[217] over some matter, they will uncover it and make it appear: therefore beware of their aspects in a like way.

---

[215] See *Carmen* V.5.3.
[216] Crofts makes this last clause apply to *Saturn*, not the Moon: "when he is joined to a benefic on emerging from the rays." But it seems to me that the statement applies better to the Moon. This was also mentioned before in §30a-b with specific reference to the Moon.
[217] *Orta fuerint*. I am not sure what this means; Crofts says "ascend over a thing." This could refer to the notion in *On Quest*. §7.13, that a luminary in the Ascendant or Midheaven (or aspecting the Lot of Fortune) indicates the discovery of a thief.

(§142) And if you sought someone fleeing, let this be when the Moon is joined to malefics or she is going out from under the rays: and in her going-out [from the rays] let her encounter a malefic from the square aspect or the opposition or conjunction;[218] and you should never put the Moon nor a planetary receiver of disposition in the fourth.

(§143) On that which is not in the twelve signs in terms of elections

And[219] if you wished to write a letter, let this be when the Moon is joined with Mercury, cleansed of the malefics; and let Mercury be strong and made fortunate, not retrograde, nor impeded, and let him and the Moon be cleansed of the malefics.

The *Book of Elections* of Sahl bin Bishr ends.

---

[218] The Arabic omits the conjunction.
[219] See *Carmen* V.15.

ON TIMES

§1

Know that times excite[1] motion. And[2] there is a beginning of motion which comes to be in the circle up to the end of time, a time in which the hour is adapted to each motion that begins, until it is ended with a complexion matching it or not matching—wherefore this signifies good or bad. And the general motions are according to what I will tell you, if God wills.

Know that the changing of figures, and the destruction or alteration[3] of motions in the general circle, signifies what (of the good or bad) is made stable in time. And the alteration or the changing of the figures is the changing of the planets from the east into the west,[4] and from the west into the east, also from the north into the south, and *vice versa*; and from it in latitude and longitude.

But the motion of the circle is that by which it is moved once from the east into the west in every day and night—that is, one circuit. Indeed the exposition of their motion in longitude is, because all the planets, after they are separated from the Sun (this is when they transit the body of the Sun) and made distant[5] from him through 180°, still they are oriental; from this, up to the completion of 360°, they are occidental.[6] And this motion which I have stated from the east to the west is accidental, not substantial.

And the "east"[7] of the planets is from the side of the motion of the circle: it signifies quickness. This[8] is like if it is between the Ascendant and the tenth, and between the seventh and the fourth. And the "west"[9] of them [is] namely like if a planet is between the fourth and the Ascendant, and what surpasses this (that is, what is between the tenth and the seventh). And this

---

[1] Reading *tempora excitant* with BN for *terra excitat*.
[2] This sentence seems garbled or incomplete in both BN and 1493.
[3] *Conversio.* This word can also mean "revolving," which could be relevant.
[4] *Ab oriente in occidentem.*
[5] Lit., "prolonged."
[6] This is significant because it is an early, clear statement of Renaissance-style doctrines or orientality. Note that it departs from traditional doctrine in that it does not distinguish between combustion and orientality.
[7] *Oriens.*
[8] This sentence does not appear in BN, but probably should have.
[9] *Occidens.*

place in the circle signifies slowness and delay, according to the sayings of the ancients.[10]

But Māshā'allāh[11] was different from them: that is, he disagrees with them in this. He makes the higher place of the circle [to be] namely whatever is elevated out of the circle and hastens to ascend and appear, and this is from the fourth backwards to the tenth: and this higher part is called "from the beginning of the motion of the circle in ascending"; after this, that which is between the fourth and the tenth backwards, to the slow and descending part, to the beginning of the descension of the circle and of its turning, and of the slowness of its appearing.[12] And this opinion is truer than the rest, according to proof. Moreover, the point of the east is the degree of the Ascendant, and the western point is the degree of the seventh; and the point of the tenth is the middle of heaven;[13] indeed the fourth point is the stake of the earth.

The motion of latitude is like if a planet is ascending in the north and descending in the north, or ascending in the south and descending in the south.

Also,[14] the changing of the figures of the planets is by means of [1] a conjunction of a planet with the Sun, up to the hour of its arising [out of the rays]; and [2] from this to its own first station, is a time; and [3] from its own first station up to the end of retrogradation and the beginning of its second station; and [4] the beginning of direct [motion] is a changing of time; and [5] from its direct [motion] up to the conjunction of the Sun is a time; and [6] from the motion of a planet from the superior circle, backwards to the Sun in his arrival to the degrees of the planets and the signs, is a time.[15] And [7] from the motion of the superior circle (which is from the east to the west); and [8] their changes to the places of the planets by body and light, is a time. And [9] from the direction of the degree of the Ascendant or some one of the planets, to any degree, one year and a month and a day or an hour, in front or behind, up to some one of the planets, to its rays and

---

[10] See e.g., *Tet.* III.14, end of chapter.
[11] Source unknown.
[12] In other words, the eastern hemisphere of the chart shows things hastening, and the western hemisphere shows things slowing down.
[13] *Caeli medium.*
[14] I have divided the following times according to what seemed right to me; but it would also be possible simply to divide them according to where the phrase "is a time" appears.
[15] I have translated this as one sentence, but it is possible that motion from the superior circle is meant to be distinct from the following clause, in which case *the Sun's* arrival to the degrees of the planets and times is a sign.

theirs,[16] and to the degrees of the signs and the Lots, is a time. And Māshā'allāh has already said before—and Abu 'Ali al-Khayyat[17] (that is, his successor)—they have said, "for, direct the degrees in longitude and latitude, in front and behind."[18] Therefore, the motions of the general circle, by which the times are known, come to be from these motions.

§2: The knowledge of the principal times

Know that the signs of the light planets and the signs of the heavy ones are: in the times of the light ones, days and months; and the signs of the heavy planets will be years. And generally speaking, if the significator were in fixed signs, it will signify years; and if it were in common ones, it will signify months; in movable signs, it will signify days.

Also, a fast place from the Ascendant (that is, the superior part) signifies the quickness of the time; and the slow part of the circle (which is the descending part) signifies slowness in time. The[19] Ascendant and the tenth [sign] signify quickness in time. And the seventh signifies months, and is slower; indeed the angle of the earth is slow, and signifies years. And if the planetary significator of the time were in common signs, it doubles the time.

§3: A chapter on finding the significator of the time

Know that it is not necessary for you to take the time from any planet, however strong it may be, unless it is the significator of the matter or has some role in the signification of the matter (apart from the luminaries, because they naturally signify times, which the others do not). For, you will take the time from the Lord of the Ascendant or from the Lord of the matter, or from the receiver of their disposition, or from a planet to which some one of them is joined (if they did not aspect each other), or from the luminaries, or from the receiver of the Moon's disposition—namely, from the one which

---

[16] Following 1493. BN reads, "behind, up to some one of the planets, and to their hour."
[17] *Abuabalgharat*. BN reads *Ahnahalgarat*. Abu 'Ali was a student of Māshā'allāh.
[18] Source unknown, but this is a pretty clear statement by a central authority that we are to practice both direct and converse directions, including planetary latitude into the calculations.
[19] This sentence is not in BN.

is stronger and more worthy in the question, and which conquers more in this. Set this one up as the significator of the time. Which if their similarity deceives you, that is, if you were not able to choose a significator because there are many similar things in signification, put one of the luminaries over the significator—namely, the one which aspects the Ascendant. If however you *did* find the significator of the time, this is the more worthy of times than the luminaries are. If however you took it from the luminaries, take it from the one which aspects the Ascendant.

And know that the general times in questions come to be in five[20] ways:

Of which the first is that you should look at the degrees which are between the pusher and receiver by light or by body, and you put down a year or a month or a day or an hour for every degree, according to the quantity of the quickness of the place, and its slowness.

The second way is that you should look to see when the informer[21] [of the time] arrives to him to whom the informer comes, by body, by degree and by minutes: namely when the light planet arrives at the heavy planet by body.

The third way is that you should look to see how many degrees there are between him who is being joined, and him to whom he is joined: and put those down as days.

The fourth[22] way is that you count from the Ascendant up to the place of the receiver of the disposition, or from the place of the receiver of the disposition to the Ascendant, a sign for every month.

The fifth way, that you should look to see how many are the lesser years of the significator of the time: and the time will be according to their quantity, of months or years. These are the five[23] ways.

---

[20] BN reads "six" (*vi*), clearly a mistake.
[21] *Delator.* I.e., the planet that reports or announces the time.
[22] Following 1493. BN reads, "And the fourth way is that you count from the *fourth* up to the place of the receiver of the disposition, up to the Ascendant, a sign for every month."
[23] BN reads "seven" (*vii*), clearly a mistake.

And[24] the time from the Moon is a month or two months, in number and the matter. And if she were in charge of the disposition, 25 months. And the time of Venus and Mercury in the matter and number: the matter in Venus [is] 10 months, and 8, and Mercury 5 months or even 3 months.[25] If however they were in charge of the disposition: in Mercury, if there were a cutting-off concerning him, he will signify 20 months, and Venus 8[26] years. And for the Sun, one year and 19 months. And for Mars, 18 months, or 15 years. And Jupiter, 12 months or 12 years. And Saturn, 30 months or 30 years.[27]

The science of the understanding of the nature of the times, of the five ways, in quickness and slowness (that is, which of them is faster or slower, slowness and quickness), is according to what I say.

Know that the pushing planet and the receiver is if each were in the eastern part from the Ascendant: it is necessary that the oriental planets from themselves[28] are faster in course. Therefore, put down an hour of the day for every degree which you found between them. And[29] if there were planets between the Midheaven up to the seventh,[30] it signifies months according to the quantity of degrees which there are between them. And if both planets were between the seventh and the fourth and the Ascendant, it signifies years and months, should the planets agree from themselves in their like agreement from the Ascendant. If however they were diverse, and there were an oriental and quick planet from it, and [an] occidental and slow [one] from the Ascendant, it signifies something in the middle—therefore, set up the time like that. If it were a time of the degrees which were between them, put down a

---

[24] There is a distinction here between timing (a) in "number and matter," and when the planet (b) is "in charge of" the disposition. I do not know where (a) comes from, conceptually or the actual numbers themselves; most of (b) are the minor years. Finally, some of the examples of (a) give two numbers, but I do not see what the difference is between them. But note below in §12, where some of these values for Venus and Mercury are explicitly used.
[25] "Or even three months" is not in BN.
[26] BN reads "7" (*vii*).
[27] BN omits Saturn.
[28] *A semetipsis*. The role of this phrase is unclear to me.
[29] What follows in the rest of the paragraph is from BN. 1493 reads: "And if there were two planets between the Midheaven up to the seventh, it signifies months according to the quantity of the degrees which there was between them. And if both planets were between the seventh and the fourth and the Ascendant, it signifies years and months, if the two planets agreed from themselves in their like agreement from the Ascendant. If however they were diverse, and there were an oriental quick planet from it and an occidental and slow one from the Ascendant, it signifies something in the middle—therefore, set up the time like that."
[30] Reading with 1493, for *ascendens*.

day for every degree; which if it passed by,[31] put down a month for every conjunction which was between them. Commingle therefore the times according to what I have laid out for you, from the role of the Ascendant and from the substance of the planet, and according to the sign in which it is, and by the figure of the planet. After this, test your measure in slowness and quickness, and you will not go astray, if God wills.

And know that these times are roots. And perhaps it will be an individual time without[32] these roots: because if the Moon were in the place of the matter, or she aspected the place of the matter, and if a planet[33] were joined to the Lord of the Ascendant or the Lord of the matter and it[34] aspected the place of the matter, it signifies the effecting of that matter in that same day. Which if the question were quick, and it signified days, and the days of slowness were against[35] the degrees of the parts of the planets, then you should not make the time a month until the orb of the Moon has passed by: because perhaps it[36] will be separated from one of the two planets,[37] and it enters between the Lord of the Ascendant and the Lord of the matter, or it enters the Ascendant or[38] the place of the matter, and the attaining of the matter will be in that same hour and that same day. And perhaps the hour will be from the degree of the significator to the degree of the Ascendant, a day for every degree. Or perhaps the time will be from the entrance of the Sun into the degree of the Ascendant or the place of the matter, or the place of the Lord of the matter. And the matter will be moved, and it will come with its perfection,[39] through its work in the times until[40] it enters the quarters of heaven; and therefore they compared it to the soul.[41] After this, look at the times of general matters in the twelve signs according to what I will describe to you [below], if God wills.

---

[31] This phrase is not in BN. It must mean that if the client waits so many days and the event has not come to pass, it must be counted in months (with more waiting to follow).
[32] BN reads, "from" (*ex*), a very different meaning.
[33] 1493 reads, "the Moon," which is probably what Sahl means.
[34] This probably refers to the planet the Moon is aspecting, as just mentioned (if we follow 1493).
[35] Reading as *contra*, though I am not sure what Sahl means.
[36] This probably refers to the Moon.
[37] "Of the two planets" is not in BN.
[38] Reading *aut* with 1493.
[39] BN reads: "And the matter will be moved before its perfection…" But it is possible that this is a misread for *profectionem*, "advancement," referring to the Sun's advancement through the signs (see following sentences).
[40] *Dum*. Perhaps, "while."
[41] I am not sure what this means.

§4: A chapter on the life of a man, in the Ascendant

If you were asked about the life of a man, from the sayings of the ancients, look at the Ascendant at the hour of the question, and at its Lord, and at the Lord of the conjunction or prevention which was before the question. And take the stronger of these significators, and the one which was greater by testimony: because he will be the *mubtazz*[42] (which is the significator of the hour). Therefore, direct this one just as you direct the *hīlāj* to the conjunction of the malefics and their aspects, giving a year to every degree, by the ascensions of that city. If however the benefics did not project their rays to that bound, the one asking will die in that same year. But the stronger of the rays, and the more killing one, is that which was from the square aspect or the opposition, whereby[43] perhaps it will kill, even if the benefics did project their rays to that bound. And if this *mubtazz*[44] were received, or the *hīlāj* were in charge, then if the one which was in charge were in an angle, oriental, it will give its own greater years; and if it were in the succeedents of the angles, it will give its middle years. Indeed if it were cadent from the angles, it will signify its own lesser years.

And Māshā'allāh said,[45] look at the Lord of the Ascendant and at the Moon, to see if they (or one of them) were joined to malefics, or were in combustion: take all the degrees which are between them and the malefics or combustion, and save[46] them. Because if the Lord of the Ascendant were in a fixed sign, take a year for every degree. And if it were in a common sign, take a month for every degree. Indeed if it were in a movable sign, you will take a day for every degree. And what comes out from the Lord of the Ascendant will be the number of life; indeed what comes out between the Moon and the malefics or combustion, will be the number of things suffered.

---

[42] *Alimbutar* (1493), *alumbtarum* (BN).
[43] Reading *qua* with BN, for *quare*.
[44] *Alimbutar* (1493), *almubta* (BN).
[45] This bears a resemblance to *On Nativities* §1, and Māshā'allāh does address the Lord of the Ascendant and Moon there. But in the paragraph that presents the above timing method, Māshā'allāh is speaking of the distance between a certain *mubtazz* and the planet to which it commits its disposition.
[46] That is, keep them in mind.

§5: A chapter: the domicile of substance

Indeed, the time of a question about substance, namely when he will find or attain it. If you wished to know [this], look at the number of degrees which there are between each of the significators, and know that the time of it will be according to the number of their degrees in days or months or years, according to the quantity of the quickness or slowness [of them]. Also, look to see when the Lord of the domicile of substance enters his own domicile or the Ascendant, or he will be joined to the benefics, and it will be then.

Indeed the third and fourth domicile is like[47] the rest of the chapters.

§6: A chapter: the domicile of children

If you were asked about a pregnant woman, when she will give birth, look to see how many degrees there are between the Lord of the domicile of children and the angle, in terms of signs and degrees, and put months for every sign, and a day for every degree: and in that same hour, she will give birth, if God wills.

§7: A chapter: the domicile of infirmity

But in the time of the healing of someone infirm, you should not make the Moon be cadent in her course, until she aspects her own place. Because if she were impeded, going[48] to the degree of the malefics or the degree of the house [domicile?] of death, direct her to the degree of the malefics; then, if the Moon is joined to the malefics before she arrives at the degree of the house [domicile?] of death, death will be feared for him before the Moon arrives at the house [domicile?] of death. Which if the malefic were Saturn, [it will be] according to the degrees which were between them (it will be months); and between her and Mars, a day or month according to the quan-

---

[47] Reading *iuxta* with BN.
[48] Following 1493. BN says *hīlāj* (Lat. *hiles*) where 1493 reads *iens* ("going") and skips over the issue of directing. I believe BN contains an error.

tity of strength and the quickness of the place, and its slowness. And you should not neglect the degree of combustion.

§8: The heading of the seventh sign for the times or hours of war, from the sayings of Theophilus

If you wished to know the time or hour in which a war ought to take place, look at the hour in which the Moon is joined to the Sun: if they were opposite, the war will hasten. Indeed if there were 20° between the Moon and the conjunction, the war will slow down. And if the Moon were with certain[49] planets in her own domicile, the war will come to be quickly (and especially if she aspected the Sun[50]).

And if the dignity of the twelfth-part of the Moon were in the Ascendant,[51] or with the Sun at the same time with the Lord of his own domicile,[52] or with a planet which was then arising,[53] this will signify the quickness of the war. And Theophilus said, if you wished to know the hour of the battle, and when it will be perfected, look at the luminaries to see if they aspect each other from a trine aspect, and they aspected the Ascendant: the war will be effected quickly. Indeed if they aspected each other from the square aspect, it will not be effected quickly, and the battle will last and be changed from its own place into the particular place of the one receiving.[54] And if they aspected each other from the opposition, the battle will not be perfected quickly.

And[55] if the Lot of Fortune were in the Midheaven, the war will be effected in those quadrants. And if the Sun, at the hour of the question, were

---

[49] What planets?
[50] Following 1493. BN omits "the Sun."
[51] Following 1493. BN reads, "And if the dignity of the Moon were in the twelfth-part[51] of the Ascendant or in the tenth …" See my Introduction for a discussion of this passage in concert with *On Elect.* §88c.
[52] Following 1493. BN reads, "or [with?] the Sun, or with the Lord of the domicile."
[53] *Oritur*. This seems to mean pertaining-to-arising, since it is one of the phases that shows a change of times.
[54] BN reads: "from its own place into a place, particularly those starting [the war]" (*in locum proprie incipientes*).
[55] Following 1493. BN reads: "And if the Lot of Fortune were in the Midheaven, the war will be effected in those opposites and triplicities, in the triplicities; and this comes to be if Jupiter and the Moon were aspecting the Ascendant by that number by which the Sun was aspecting at the hour of the question." 1493 seems to be more complete and coherent (though the paragraph is still not that clear).

in the square aspect of the Ascendant or he aspected from the opposition,[56] the effecting of the war will be in those oppositions and from the triplicities[57] and in the triplicities: and this comes to be if Jupiter (and the Moon) were aspecting the Ascendant in that manner in which the Sun was aspecting in the hour of the question.

And[58] look even at the Lot of Faith, and at the planet which was with Mars or in his square aspect, to see if they were made fortunate: it will be effected quickly. If they were bad, the war will be fixed,[59] and it will be burdensome and prolonged. But if the benefics were entangled with the Lord of the Lot, they will not[60] make delays when one of the armies wins, according to what you saw concerning the place of the benefic from the Lot.[61]

And Hermes said,[62] look, [concerning] the end of the cutting-off of war and of all things, at the luminaries and the Ascendant, and[63] at the benefics and malefics. Then you will know the times of matters and their cutting-off in terms of years and months and days. And he said, and look, in the slowness of victory (and its quickness) at the place of Saturn and Jupiter. If it were faster in course, victory will be quick for the one of them in whose clime Mars were—whether he were oriental or occidental. If however it were slower in course, the victory will be slow, and their matters will be prolonged, and will not easily be cut off. And if their significator (of Saturn and Jupiter) were direct after Mars,[64] it will hit hard in the land which was between both.[65]

---

[56] Omitting *quae dixi tibi*.

[57] Again, the whole-sign trine.

[58] Reading this paragraph with 1493. But I am not sure that this paragraph really even has to do with the Lot of Faith. My sense (reading BN) is that this paragraph continues the previous statement about the Sun, and the "Lot of Faith" is really the *domicile* of faith, which would be the 9th (or perhaps the 11th, as the domicile of trust). But that is a conjecture of mine. Perhaps it really refers to a Lot of Warfare, or perhaps even to the Lot of Fortune? BN reads: "And were he to aspect the Lot of Faith, and a planet which was with Mars in the square aspect, if they were made fortunate, it will be effected quickly. But if they were malefics [or bad], the war will be fixed and prolonged. If however the benefics were entangled [*indutae*], they do not make delays without one army being changed according to what you saw concerning the place of the benefic from the planet."

[59] Omitting *non* with BN.

[60] Omitting an apparent *nos* ("us") in BN.

[61] Reading *parte* with 1493 for *planeta*.

[62] Source unknown.

[63] Omitting *ultima graduum eorum*, which means something like "the end of their degrees" or "the extremities of their degrees," but *ultima* does not seem to be the right case and gender, and anyway I am not sure what this means. It is possible this refers to the degrees which they aspect by ray.

[64] *Directus post martem*. Meaning unclear.

[65] BN simply says, "it will be between each," saying nothing about hitting hard or striking.

Which if they were in a common sign, the war will be moderate and light; indeed in fixed[66] signs, the matter of the world will be severe and destroyed, and matters will be turned around just as they were after[wards].[67] And this opinion is out of the secrets of the sayings of Hermes.

The reminder about the domicile of death has already preceded, in the chapter on life

§9: The chapter of the ninth sign: on foreign travel, from the sayings of the ancients

If you wished to know the hour of the turning of one on a foreign journey back to his relatives and to his own home, look in the beginning of the foreign journey at the Lord of the Ascendant and the Moon. If you saw malefics in their square aspect or opposition, his foreign journey will be prolonged, and his turning-back will be slowed. And[68] if they were joined to benefics, it signifies the quickness of his turning-back. If they were joined to benefics after malefics, he will find evil in his foreign journey—[but] after this, he will escape and return to his relatives. And [the planet] with benefics [and then] malefics, [he will find good things and then delay].[69] And were you to find the Moon, at the beginning of the foreign journey, in the Ascendant, his staying on the foreign journey will be prolonged—and[70] especially if the Moon were in the domicile of foreign travel, not impeded—then, when she would come to her own square aspect or her own opposition, he will return well to his own place in which he was—it signifies his turning back. And if she were not impeded in that same sign, that is when you direct the Sun in his own place in the root, and in the trine or square aspect from his place. And if the Sun were impeded in the root, his stay will be according to the

---

[66] Reading *fixis* with BN for *inferioribus*. Moreover, BN ends the sentence here with *gravae*, reading "In fixed signs, burdened." This reading is more succinct and avoids the strange ending of the sentence according to 1493.
[67] *Fuerunt post*. Meaning unclear.
[68] This sentence does not appear in BN.
[69] Both BN and 1493 seem to be very garbled here. They read: *et ipse cum fortunis et malis Saturnus/sentitur per eum reversio et mora*, which could be read in several ways but only with the addition of other implied verbs and probably some changes of case.
[70] For the rest of the paragraph I follow BN, which has a logical series of sentences. 1493 is ambiguous and introduces the Sun without warning.

going-out of that malefic, and the applying[71] of some benefic to the place of that same malefic. Know likewise their strength to rule over enemies.[72] And speak according to this in his circle, in terms of years, months, and days: because Saturn, if he were the Lord of the Ascendant or were in the domicile of foreign travel, the foreign travel will be prolonged according to the orb of Saturn. Likewise if you found Jupiter and Saturn in an angle and they were retrograde: there will be a stay. But the rest are lighter than these planets in their motion.

§10: On the turning back of someone on a foreign journey

Māshā'allāh said:[73] for the hour of the arrival of one on a foreign journey, look at the Moon and the Lord of the hour, to see which of them is stronger: and if the stronger one of them were between the tenth and the fourth, take what there was between him and the Ascendant. If however the Lord of the hour were stronger, and a[74] malefic, what comes out in degrees will be hours. And if the Moon were stronger, take from what comes out: they will be days.[75]

And if you did not accept the signification from these, and the Lord[76] of the Ascendant were in the opposite of that which I said, and the Moon were the Lady of the hour, take what there was between her and the Ascendant, and what came out will be days: then it will happen. Moreover, if the Lord of the Ascendant were in the Midheaven, or turning back toward the Ascendant,[77] and if the Moon were greater in testimony and she were strong, and the Lord of the Ascendant was not aspecting the Ascendant nor the Lord of his own domicile, his turning-back will be according to this. And if the Lord of the domicile of the Moon were in a bad place, and the Moon in a good

---

[71] *Adiunctum*. Or, "attaching, joining to, directing to." It is unclear whether Sahl is speaking of primary directions or transits.
[72] *Scito similiter fortitudinem eorum praeesse inimicis*. This is not exactly grammatical, and I am not sure what Sahl is advising, but I see no other way to translate it.
[73] Source unknown.
[74] Reading with BN. 1493 says, "If however the Lord of the hour were a malefic...".
[75] Following BN. 1493 says, "take her thirteenth-part from that which comes out...". I am not sure if there even is such a thing as a "thirteenth-part" (*tertiadecima*), unless this refers somehow to her average daily course of about 13°.
[76] Adding from 1493.
[77] I am not sure what this means. Perhaps in the quadrant between the IC and the Ascendant, moving by primary motion to the Ascendant?

place from the Ascendant, and she did not aspect the Lord of her own domicile, the time of the turning-back will be according to what there was between her and her own domicile, in terms of degrees—if God wills.

§11: A chapter on a letter and rumors

If[78] you were asked about a letter or about rumors (when they will come), look at Mercury to see if he were in the Ascendant or in the twelfth (wanting to enter into the Ascendant), or [if] the Moon were joined to the Lord of the Ascendant, or [if] the Lord of the Ascendant[79] were joined to the Lord of the domicile of the Moon (or the Lord of the domicile of the Moon were joined to him), or [if] Mercury were the Lord of the Ascendant: the letter will come. And if he[80] were not in the Ascendant at the hour of its[81] entrance into the Ascendant, it will not[82] come. And if the Moon is being joined to Mercury at the hour of their conjunction,[83] or at the hour of the arrival of the Moon into the Ascendant, the letter will come. And if the Moon were bearing away [light] from Mercury into the degree of the Ascendant and to the Lord of the Ascendant, the time will be when the informer arrives to him to whom she is bearing away [the light]. And if you were asked about a letter, when it was written, look at the degrees which are between the Moon and the planet from whom she is being separated, and say that the letter was written according to the number of those degrees. Likewise, look at the degrees which you found between the Moon and the planet to whom she is being joined, and the time of the letter's arrival will be according to them.

---

[78] Compare with *On Quest*. §§13.5-8. In this passage it is sometimes unclear what planet is being discussed, but four central planets are involved: the Moon, Mercury, the Lord of the Moon's domicile, and the Lord of the Ascendant.
[79] Adding from 1493.
[80] I take this to mean Mercury, since he was mentioned as being in the Ascendant earlier.
[81] I am not sure what planet this means. If it meant Mercury, the rest of the clause would be redundant.
[82] Tentatively adding *non*.
[83] This phrase is redundant.

§12: The chapter of the tenth sign, on the king, from the sayings of Māshā'allāh[84]

Look at the hour of the withdrawing of that king whose entrance [into power] you came to know, or at the time in which the kingdom will receive [his] last will and testament, or at his question. And from these you will know the quantity of his period in the role, and whatever would be in it for him.[85] And from the hour of the confirmation of his election is known his honor and victory. But however often that planet (which signified the kingdom) were combust in one of the angles of the Ascendant, the king will be removed.

And if there were no planet in the Ascendant, look at the royal house. If you found in that place a planet having testimony in it, then when there was a malefic planet in that place, or the Lord of the descension of the Lord of the royal house, and it[86] then aspected the planet from which you had[87] the signification, the king will be removed.

But if you did not find a planet in one of these places, see to whom the Sun is being joined. If he were joined to Saturn and Mars, then when he arrives to the degree of the one to whom he is joined, in an angle, the king will be removed. And if he were joined to Jupiter, his withdrawal will be when Saturn arrives at the place of the Sun or to his opposition, or to his square aspect, or he was retrograde in that same place. Likewise if Venus were joined to [the Sun]. And if the Sun were removed as I said, and he were in the second or the ninth,[88] having testimony, then if Saturn or Mars were retrograde in that same place or in its opposition, the king will be removed.

And work in the night through the Moon just as you have worked in the day through the Sun—but you should not look for the time from the times of the planets,[89] but look to see whether the Moon is being joined to the Sun, whether she were joined to him or were separated from him, inasmuch

---

[84] The source for these comments might be one of the six sections of *The Book Known as the Twenty-Seventh*, entitled "On the Overthrow of the Government." See Pingree 1974, p. 161.
[85] Reading *quicquid ei fuerit in eo* with BN, for *et quid elucidatum ei fuerit in eo*.
[86] BN reads "they." We should probably take this to mean, "either, or both, whichever it is." Clearly having both such planets there making the aspect, would be an even stronger argument.
[87] Reading as *habuisti*.
[88] BN reads, "in the eleventh or in the eighth."
[89] BN reads, "but you should not look at the hours in the hours of the planets…"

as if she were being joined to a malefic, its time will be from the Sun, just as I have told you in [the Sun's] time.⁹⁰ And if she were not separated from the Sun, nor were she joined to him, see in this what I have told you: because his reign will not complete one year—therefore operate with this. And know that if the Lord of the Ascendant and the Lord of the tenth were combust in the angles, it signifies that his removal is already at hand. And if the Lord of the Sun's exaltation were impeded,⁹¹ one year will not be complete. Therefore, look in his hour before⁹² a year, for the combustion of the Lord of the Ascendant and of the Lord of the tenth, and the arrival of the malefics in their places.⁹³ And if the Moon were not the Lady of the exaltation, look at her conjunction with the planets: which if she were conjoined to Mercury, and he were in a fixed or common sign, it will signify 20 months; and if it were a movable sign, 10 months. Therefore, look at the planet to whom she is being joined: which if it were impeded by the malefics or by combustion, look to see how many degrees there are between it and the strength of the malefic or of the combustion, and the time will be how many there are.

But if, however, the Moon were received, and the Lord of her exaltation were received, a year will be perfected for him. Then look at the second year and revolve years for him. And know that if the Lord of its⁹⁴ place⁹⁵ were free from the malefics, he who enters [power] will remain in his kingdom one more year. Indeed if the Moon were received, look at the application of a malefic to the degree of the planet who is receiving the Moon, or at the lesser years of the Lord of the Ascendant, and commingle even between them the revolution of the year and its application. And if the Ascendant of the one entering [power] or his beginning, were of the domiciles of the higher planets,⁹⁶ [and the Lord of its domicile⁹⁷ signified the perfection of a year, revolve the years concerning him].⁹⁸ Which if a malefic were going retrograde in the Midheaven, or the Lord of the Midheaven [were going retrograde in the same], or the Lord of the Ascendant were in [the angles, it

---

⁹⁰ BN reads, "in his/its hours." See previous paragraph.
⁹¹ That is, the exalted Lord of the sign the Sun is in.
⁹² BN omits "before" (*ante*).
⁹³ That is, in the signs that the Lords of the Ascendant and of the tenth are in at the time of the chart.
⁹⁴ I am not sure which planet is meant.
⁹⁵ Reading *loci* with 1493 for *horum*.
⁹⁶ Following 1493.
⁹⁷ Reading *domus*. BN appears to read *dom* without the abbreviation for *us*.
⁹⁸ Material in brackets from BN.

signifies the destruction of the kingdom. And if there were a malefic in the Ascendant or the Lord of the Ascendant were combust in][99] the tenth, he will perish in his [reign]. And if it were retrograde in the second, it signifies the destruction of substance; and in the tenth it signifies the destruction of the position [or his work]; and in the eleventh, the destruction of the rents;[100] and in the Ascendant, the destruction of the soldiers.

Also, look at the planets which are in charge, to see if they were in angles and had strength: they give months or years according to the number of their years. And if Saturn were in the Ascendant or the tenth, and he had testimony[101] in them, and he were received through the testimony of the planets,[102] he will signify 30 years; and if they were complete, revolve the year.[103] But if the Lord of the Ascendant (or the significator) were combust in the angles, the matter will be destroyed.[104]

But if Saturn were strengthened and the Lord of the Year aided him, he will not cease to be fixed [in power] until the revolution is destroyed, and the testimony and his strength is removed;[105] which[106] if Saturn did not have such testimony, revolve it for him for 30 months, because the time is weak. After this, look at the destruction of the year due to impediment and burning.[107] Which if the one who was in charge of the disposition were retrograde at the end of some angle, the matter will be destroyed suddenly and unexpectedly.

And if Jupiter were in the Ascendant or in the tenth, and he had testimony, it will signify 12 years. And if Mars[108] were in the Ascendant, and the

---

[99] Material in brackets from 1493.
[100] Nowadays this should probably be considered tax revenue.
[101] BN reads, "and he had testimony *more*..." This is ambiguous. If the Latin translator meant that he had "more testimony" than other planets did in those places, he should have written *plus testimonii*. We should probably follow 1493 above.
[102] This notion of testimony sounds like he is being received by aspect or conjunction.
[103] By itself this suggests that if the ruler has already been ruling for thirty years or months (only 1493 says "years"), we should cast another solar revolution chart to see what will happen next.
[104] Reading *destruetur* with BN for *destruent*.
[105] BN reads, "and he will have testimony and his strength."
[106] For the rest of this sentence BN reads, "which if Saturn were not in the angles, such testimony signifies the destruction of the kingdom; and if a malefic were retrograde in the Ascendant, or Lord of the Ascendant were combust, *tale testimonium* ["such testimony"], revolve for 20 months, because the time is weak."
[107] But this could also simply mean the combustion of a significator in real time (and not the prediction of the burning of crops, for instance).
[108] BN does *not* mention Mars here, but speaks as though we are still dealing only with Jupiter. I am not sure which is correct.

Moon in a square or opposition (or vice versa)—unless the benefics would be aspecting—it signifies a mortal impediment.

And if Venus were in the Ascendant or the tenth, and she had testimony, you will note 10 months through her. And if she were combust in an angle, he will withdraw from his kingdom. Indeed if she were received and free from the malefics, it signifies 8 years; and revolve the years. But if she met a malefic in the revolution of the eighth year, and the malefic were retrograde in its own place, it will signify the destruction of the kingdom, and his weakness, and the entrance of impediments upon him.

And if Mercury were in the Ascendant or in the tenth, and he had testimony in that same place, and he were strong and received, it signifies 20 months; and revolve the year. But if he were weak and did not have testimony, count 5 months for him; moreover if he were combust in an angle, and a malefic or the light of a malefic occurred in the angle[109] of the Lord of the tenth, he will withdraw.

And if Mars were in the Ascendant or in the tenth, look to see whether combustion would happen to him in less than 15[110] months: because if he were combust in an angle, the king will withdraw; and revolve the year.

And if the Moon were his Lady, and she were received, and free from the malefics, and she had testimony, it signifies 25 years; and if she did not have testimony, 25 months. Or, look at the planet to whom she is committing disposition: if it were combust in an angle, he will withdraw. But if it were not combust in an angle, and it were received, it signifies the years and months of that same planet.

And look in this topic just as I have indicated to you with the Sun, when his degree arrives to the malefics. If however the Sun were in charge, and he received the testimony of a star, it signifies a year. If the Sun were strong and had great testimony, it signifies 19[111] years, if a malefic who impeded the Lord of the disposition (or the Ascendant or the tenth) did not impede his disposition in the first year; which if he were impeded, he will give months.[112]

And know that if a planet signified the number of some disposition, [and] afterwards were impeded before [this time] in an angle, revolve that year for

---

[109] BN omits "in an angle." But as it reads in 1493, it looks like this means, "if a malefic were in the square or opposition of the Lord of the tenth."
[110] Reading 15 with BN for 20.
[111] BN mistakenly reads 18.
[112] Following BN. 1493 inexplicably says "29 months." But the number should be 19.

him. If it were safe from combustion and from impediment, the matter will be saved until the number is completed: harm and diminution will not[113] enter upon it.

After this, perform, in the revolution of the years of the king, the projection of the rays just as you do in nativities (namely, to each sign).[114] Also, you will look from the Lord of that sign, and see [1] what kind of place it is, and [2] what is his being [or condition], and [3] what is in the signs, in terms of benefics or malefics, and [4] where is the place of the Lord of the sign in terms of the signs and the benefics and malefics,[115] and [5] what kind of being [or condition] he has, and that of his place, and [6] if he is received or not, and [7] if he is impeded or not; even [8] what kind of being [or condition] he has with the Lord of the tenth, toward the Ascendant of the year;[116] and if the revolution of your year [is] by equal hours, so that the Ascendant of the revolution is not destroyed.

After this, look at the Lord of the Ascendant and the Lord of the tenth, to see if they were conjoined:[117] they signify the stability of the king. And if the Moon were free from the malefics and she pushed her own disposition to a planet in an angle, it signifies his stability. Likewise the Sun and the Lord of the Ascendant in the day. And if the Lord of the tenth were combust in the revolution, or there were a retrograde malefic in the tenth, it signifies the withdrawal of the king. Likewise the Lord of the Ascendant. And if the Lord of the tenth of the revolution were oriental, it signifies the restoration of the kingdom and his stability. But if it were occidental, it will signify his destruction and his end.[118] And if the Lord of the tenth of the revolution were joined to the Lord of the fourth, it will signify the withdrawal of the king. But if the Lord of the fourth were joined to him, it will signify the stability of the king. And the withdrawal of the king will be even more so if the Sun had gone out of the angles, and the Moon [were] in the sixth or in the

---

[113] Reading *non* with BN for *sed*.
[114] Omitting *annum* in 1493. Sahl may be talking about annual profections in combination with solar revolutions.
[115] Adding "and the benefics and malefics" from BN.
[116] Reading *ascendens anni* with 1493 for *ascendentis anni*.
[117] BN says only "joined," but both corporal conjunctions and aspects should be considered.
[118] This use of oriental and occidental may refer to pertaining-to-arising and pertaining-to-sinking. See *BOA* pp. lxxxii-lxxxiv.

twelfth from the Ascendant of the year. And it helps in this topic through the application[119] of the year to a sign in which there is a benefic or malefic.

And commingle the luminary of the time of the revolution and the planet which was in the tenth, and the Lord of the Ascendant, and the Lord of the tenth with one another; and seek their testimony according to what I have laid out for you. And then you will discover the time, and you will not go astray, if God wills.

The little book of Sahl on the signification of the time for judgments, is completed

---

[119] Reading *applicationem* with 1493 for *amplificationem*. Again, this sounds like profections.

ON THE KNOWLEDGE OF THE MOTION OF THE ORB

The book in which are the causes of the orb and its motion, and its nature, in the account of Māshā'allāh, begins.

§1: And a discussion on this: that the orb is created [as something] foreknown

I will begin and say that the orb is spherical [and] foreknown, which boundaries grasp, and a diameter inserted in addition to two poles, from which it is not separated nor departs. And in fact the stars of the eighth orb (according to its arrangement) do not depart from nor surpass each other, nor are they inferior to each other; therefore, they are like rivets: its stars are not raised up, nor do they depart, except those of them with which the orb departs, according to the known order and the understood order which the computation of the stars' motion captures, with the orb in its totality and its particularity—whose elevations of arising and setting [are] understood: in all times and moments and days and hours, a star does not arise from them whose arising is not known before it arises, nor does one of them set, whose setting is not known before it sets; whose signs and mansions and degrees [are] understood, all the dispositions of which, know, are neither transformed nor corrupted nor altered.

In this therefore is a recognized signification[1] and true demonstration, whose contradictory is not possible, nor something different than it be said, that the orb is foreknown, created, comprehended, compelled, commanded, ordered, according to its servitude; it does not depart from [its servitude], nor is it transformed into something else: just like a compelled slave for whom it is impossible to give up his servitude; nor does it have a choice to surpass or be postponed or hasten or slow down from that over which it was ordained. And that the arrangement of each one of the stars, planets, and the Sun and Moon is likewise known, and its course understood, from which it[2] is not transformed nor altered into something else, the station of which [planet] is already known in every sign, and up to how much it returns to

---
[1] Throughout this text, "signification" should be understood as "indication, evidence."
[2] That is, the course and disposition of each planet.

itself, and when it departs from it and goes direct, and hastens and is slowed, and arises and sets and is elevated to space and descends to earth, and it begins in length and breadth.[3] Thence the whole is understood by a sound intellect; therefore in it is a clear signification that it is created [as something] foreknown by the Creator unto Whom there is none like, nor is there a God except Him.

And likewise the disposition of the Sun and Moon is known, and the course of each, and without a doubt when they enter a sign, and when they go out of it; there is not a surpassing nor deferral of each, neither choice nor deliberation.

A measure has already been posited for each of the Sun's months from the parts of the orb. Therefore when the Sun dismounts in that part, the known month comes, with its nature, and what pertains in that season concerning the maturation of fruits: that is, the nature of which is in either agriculture, or measuring, or pruning, or germination. It is already known with what the month comes, before his entrance, because it is furnished for him by which its harmfulness from heat or from cold is expelled; it is not transformed nor altered.

Moreover the Moon, in her arising and setting, and her addition and diminution, and her great and small renewal, and her transformation from mansion to mansion, is not transformed nor altered from her disposition. Therefore in this is a fixed signification and a clear demonstration that the orb is foreknown, made, compelled.

And if the orb and the stars were makers, creatures creating things according to what the *Ether*[4] think, and the Indians, who, [being the] first [people] treating of philosophy, said God is the cause of things (just like the Sun is of heat), except for the fact that He knows Himself to be the cause of things—against whom we say:[5] these things (from which God would be for-

---

[3] Or, "longitude and latitude."
[4] Unknown people or thinkers.
[5] Māshā'allāh seems to be saying that some thinkers believed both God and the stars were makers or creators in an automatic and unintentional way, as when the Sun naturally gives off heat—with the difference that at least God knows He is a creator. But then God would be unrelated to things created by the planets, and not having any rational intention in his own creation. Then God would be producing but with no particular concern for the world's intelligibility or consistency. In order to explain its consistency and intelligibility, then, the Indians must be wrong and God is the sole or primary creator, and it is with intellect and rationality.

eign) would become[6] contrary things and of diverse motion, and a day would come whose quantity was an hour, and a second whose quantity would be a year, and years and months and days and hours and the stars would be transformed, and their transformation would not be known, nor would their dispositions be known, and what comes from them before the coming forth of their matters, and their motions would be unknown; and stars would arrive to us which we did not know, and stars which we already knew would depart from us; and diverse figures and shapes would arise from the west—just as if contrary things come from one foreknowing, who does not know that with which it comes, nor does he know what he wants prior to his will, like the operations of a creator of things; like death and life, and poverty and riches, and glory and ignominy, and the hindering of a gift, and health and infirmity, and the masculinity and femininity of creatures, according to different forms and contrary shapes in the earth and sea and air, which, for [their] invention, are not copied from those things, but they are those which walk above its womb; and from those who move upon two feet, and from those who walk upon four. Moreover, plants and trees of different fruits and twigs and leaves and flavors of sweetness and bitterness and sourness and saltiness [are] in one earth and one heaven and one water; and there is not an impression nor sign in a creature except toward the purpose for which its Creator created it. And we do not know how this is, nor do we know its operation, nor how much it does it and until when it does it.[7]

Therefore these are the operations of the Creator of things and of the one having foreknowledge of them, Whose loftiness is to be admired, doing what He wills, and He is the knower of every thing, by means of what is necessary He changes again the four natures (which are fire, air, earth, and water), for there is not a nature from them which is not foreknown, comprehended; it does not depart nor is it transformed; compelled, established in its servitude just its Creator ordained it over it, and He foreknew it in itself.

---

[6] *Venirent* ("they would come"), but my translation makes it run more smoothly.
[7] This is a difficult paragraph, with a seemingly awkward overlap between what the world would be like without God's rational command, and a Platonic conception of what the world *is* like. See Introduction.

§2: A discussion on the four elements, which are fire, air, water and earth, and their places, and how their Creator created them

And I say that the earth is in the middle of the world, round, spherical, which water embraces, and [earth] is covered up in [water], and [water is] above [earth]. Then air is a covering above water; after that, fire is a covering over the air. Then the orb is a covering over the fire which it already comprehends.[8]

Therefore, fire is a hot, dry, light, burning, coursing, mixable body. Then, under it is air, which is a hot and moist, coursing, mixable body, heavy in the presence of fire [but] light in the presence of water. And water is a moist, cold, liquid, mixable body, heavy in the presence of air and light in the presence of earth. Earth is a cold, dry, heavy, fixed, comprehended body, not mixable. And this is its shape:[9]

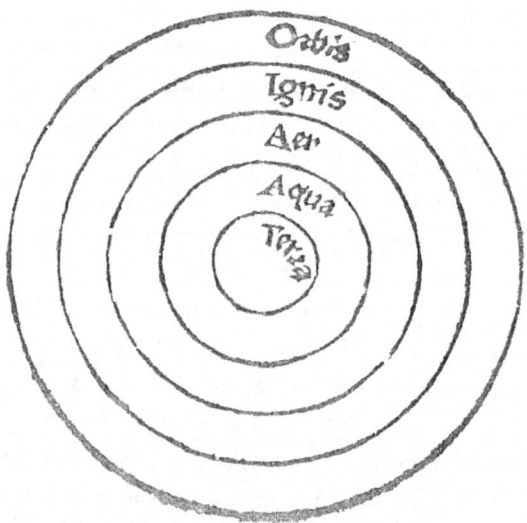

Figure 11: The Four Elements

---

[8] These are idealized conditions based on the "natural place" of the elements, since in the real world the elements are mixed up together.
[9] From the outermost circle to the center the figure reads: "Orb, Fire, Air, Water, Earth."

§3: A discussion on motions

The philosophers said all motions are only three: motion from the middle, and motion toward the middle, and motion around the middle.[10]

"From the middle," namely what is lifted up from the earth toward the heaven; "toward the middle," namely what descends from the heaven toward the earth; and "around the middle," namely what is revolved around the earth. Therefore the aggregate of all motions of the world is of these three, and they are the motions of the four elements,[11] which are fire, air, water, and earth. For certain ones of them are moved from the middle, and certain ones of them toward the middle. Therefore, of those which are moved from the middle, certain ones are more conquering and certain ones toward the lowest [region] of the heights. And of those which are moved toward the middle, certain ones are more conquering and certain ones [are] toward the middle (namely, toward the earth). And the more conquering of the two bodies (of the motions toward the middle) is earth, and following it is water. And the more conquering of the two bodies (of the motions from the middle) is fire, and following it is air. Therefore, that which tends[12] toward the one which is the middle, is heavy, and the one that tends from the middle toward the higher part is light. Therefore, earth is the heavier of these four bodies, and fire is the lightest of these, and the air and water remain behind.[13] And we have found the two dispositions of each to happen likewise through comparison. For water is the heavier when it is compared with air, and the lighter when compared with earth. And air is the lighter in the presence of water, the heavier in the presence of fire.

And let us put it in this shape, so that what is being said might be seen sensibly. Therefore, let us form the Earth, and let us put E in its center; and let me put N in the height. And let us form the orb, and let us put A in its

---

[10] This is based on the Aristotelian doctrine of natural motions, in which fire and air move from the middle of the earth, and elemental earth and water toward it, with the planets moving in circles around the earth.

[11] Or rather, the elements have only two of these motions—the celestial spheres travel according to the third, circular motion.

[12] *Tendit*. Literally this means to "stretch" toward something. We must think of earth and fire as stretching to the extremes, with air and water being in the middle, not so fiercely stretched—hence they are said below to "remain behind" fire and earth.

[13] Reading *remanet* for *remonet*.

east, and B in its Midheaven, and G in its west, and D in the pivot of the earth and in the lower part in which the orb is. And this is its shape:[14]

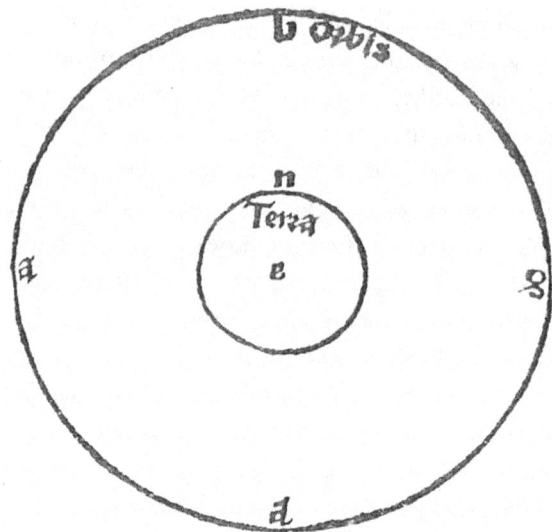

Figure 12: The Four Pivots

§4: A discussion on the motions and natures

And I say that heat and dryness and coldness and moisture are "qualities," that is, things which happen through these four bodies (which are fire, air, water, and earth). And the ancients said that of every body are three dimensions: length, breadth, and depth. And of these qualities—which are heat, coldness, and moisture, and dryness—two are active, and they are hotness and coldness: namely because they impress in us when we touch them. And two are passive, and they are moisture and dryness. Through the "passive" ones it is signaled that what they bring about is not impressed in us with a [sensible] presentation when we touch them. And these four bodies are called simple, and the bodies which are cultivated earth and seed are composite, because they are created from these four bodies: wherefore in every one of the created things these four natures are found.

---

[14] The words at the top and center of the diagram read, "Orb, Earth."

And indeed fire is hot and dry, whose composition is from hotness and dryness—namely its qualities which its body confers. And the composition of air is from heat and moisture. And earth, from coldness and dryness—namely, each one of these bodies confers its quality which is of the two qualities, and in spite of the fact that they are composed of two qualities.[15] But the simples, compared with the composites (namely, plowed earth and seed), are of the four qualities. Therefore, these four elements are simple and composite: simple compared with those four whose composition is from four, composite compared to that in which there is no inward composition from these qualities. Therefore it is true that a simple body has a simple motion, and a composite motion is contained in a composite body.[16]

And again we see greater virtue[17] from the active qualities, namely the heat ruling over fire and air; and lesser virtue from the two passive qualities, namely the coldness ruling over earth and water. Therefore it has already appeared and is clear again that the greater virtue of the two passives (namely dryness) rules over the two bodies quick in motion (namely fire and earth),[18] and that the lesser passive virtue (namely wetness) rules over the two bodies slower in motion (namely water and air).[19]

Therefore, it has already been declared that hotness makes lightness, and coldness heaviness; and dryness makes quickness and victory and advancement in a light body and in a heavy body together in everything, to its own place (namely to the natural [place] belonging to it). And [we say] that moisture rules over water and air, making in each one a slowness in advancement and motion to its own place natural for it. Therefore it already appears through what we have said, that of these four bodies (which are fire, air, water, and earth), the natures are rest and standing still in the places particularly belonging to them, which are, of each one, the standing and end in their mo-

---

[15] *Et ipsa quamvis sint composita ex duabus qualitatibus.* I take this to mean that each element has its own particular quality that is more than merely the sum of the two distinct primary qualities.
[16] For example, the element earth by itself is a "simple body" with its own, internally-consistent and simple motion downward. But actual soil is composed of many elements (earth, water, *etc.*), and so has complex tendencies due to the competing motions of the simple elements in it.
[17] "Virtue" is meant in the sense of power, strength (literally, "manliness").
[18] Normally we do not think of earth as being "quick." But remember that earth is being understood as stretching itself harder and faster toward the middle of the world.
[19] So, this is Māshā'allāh's construction of the notion that heat is the stronger of the hot-cold qualities, and dryness of the dry-wet qualities.

tion and [in] their advancement: when they are elongated from their place just for a moment, they are turned back to it naturally.

§5: A discussion that earth, water, air and fire, and the orb, are spherical

I say that earth is in the middle, namely in the lower part of the heavy bodies. Therefore it is in the middle of the orb just like the center in a circle. And water follows it in place, and [water's] place is above it. For water, as we have said, is moved again toward the middle: therefore it is a coursing, heavy substance which, if it finds a path to advance on, it descends and runs with a motion[20] tending towards the lowest part until it arrives at the last place under which it does not find a path for advancing to the middle (which is the last part of the lower region). Therefore it stands in that place, in the presence of what prohibits it from penetrating to the center of the earth. And if it is extended[21] until it arrives there, it stands still, because there is the last part of the lower region. And on account of this reason, the two shapes of water and earth are spherical, for the very reason that each seeks the middle which is the center, when they are set free[22] or they are coursing; but when they are being restrained they do not seek the center, just as it is in the nature of earth concerning construction (unless an accidental unleashing of earth follows it), for no doubt a certain thing is more distant than a certain other thing.[23] But running water by its nature is not restrained through itself, unless something befalls it and it restrains it, and it falls in a certain part of the water (not all of it).[24] But the restraint of water therefore is of a spherical surface, namely the surface of the water of the sea and the great rivers are of spherical surfaces: and this plain fact is visible. And again, for those of these bodies which are coursing, proceeding from the middle, advancing to the higher regions (namely air and fire), roundness happens [to them] by nature.

---

[20] Reading *motu* for *mota*.
[21] *Elongetur*. That is, if it keeps moving.
[22] *Resolutae*. I take this to mean when they are dropped or set loose from confinement, as when water goes over a waterfall or a support is removed from something heavy.
[23] *Namque quiddam longinquius est quam quiddam aliud*. Significance unclear. This may simply be a comment that if something stands between water or earth and its resting spot, then it is keeping that water or earth away from it.
[24] Maybe Māshā'allāh is imagining something like a tree trunk falling into a river.

But the orb of the Moon is the last one which the motions from the middle reach. For in fact the surface of fire which borders on the orb of the Moon becomes spherical, and is the last path of the motions from the middle. Therefore how much of the fire touching the surface of the Moon's orb (which follows us),[25] is shaped from the part at which the Moon's orb resists it. Therefore fire is spherical. And air is shaped from the portion of the meeting of spherical fire. Its shape is from the portion of the meeting of water and earth, of their spherical shapes to shapes, because there is no absolute void in the world.[26] Therefore air, again, is spherical. And I will tell you this in its own particular place, if God wills.

§6: A discussion on the contrariety of the four elements

And it is plain again that the first four elements, since they are contrary in motion, are contrary by nature. For fire is the more conquering of the motions from the middle; and earth (which is the more conquering of the motions toward the middle) is contrary to fire through the qualities[27] making heaviness and lightness (namely hotness and coldness), because fire is hot and dry, and earth cold and dry—which agree in dryness, which is the passive quality making quickness and victory in advancement. And they are differentiated in heat and cold.

And likewise air is contrary to water through the quality making lightness in the air (and it is heat) and making heaviness in the water (and it is coldness); and they agree in the patient quality (which is moisture), because they are agreeing in slowness, because moisture makes slowness in each (namely in air and water), just as dryness makes quickness in earth and fire. The nature of water is even contrary to fire in two qualities at the same time: through the active one, which is heat, and the passive one, which is moisture. For fire is hot and water cold, and fire dry and water moist. And it is contrary to it through lightness and heaviness and quickness and slowness.

And likewise air is contrary to the earth through two qualities, namely the active and passive. For indeed air is hot and moist, earth is cold and dry; and

---

[25] That is, the Moon's orb is next in order if we start from the Earth and rise up through the spheres.
[26] That is, their curved surfaces touch, with no space in between.
[27] Reading *qualitates* for *qualitatem*.

again it is contrary to it through the two bearings[28] at the same time: through lightness and heaviness, quickness and slowness. Therefore it is already clear and apparent that of the two motions by rectilinear motion, [their] nature is at once rest and standing still in their peculiar and natural places to which they are moved, when they are turned back or elongated from them violently.[29] Then they are divided and an accident prohibiting [their movement] does not befall them. For they are moved through their own nature, returning to their places which belong to them. Therefore when they arrive at them, they stand still in them by nature, remaining still. In such a way their Creator (may Whose names be blessed, and Whose renown be exalted) created them. And it is even apparent that the motion from the middle to the upper parts is hot, and that the motion to the middle is cold, and that the quicker motion by nature, according to comparison, is dry; and that the slower one by nature, according to comparison, is moist.

§7: A discussion on the roundness of the orb, and its motion and its nature

And we should inquire now into the motion of what is round (and it is the orb), concerning its nature—whether it is hot or cold, or moist or dry, whether these qualities are found in it, and which ones of them, whether it is a body not susceptible to one of these qualities altogether, if there are not others.

Therefore I say that a discussion and description has already been set forth, with a clear demonstration: that[30] a light body is that which is moved from the middle, and a heavy body is moved toward the middle, and that these motions are in the four elements of rectilinear motion, concerning whose description we are done.

And indeed the orb is a body not moved toward the middle or out of the middle, therefore the orb is not light nor heavy. Because if it were heavy, its motion would be toward the middle; and if it were light, its motion would be

---

[28] *Habitudines.* That is, through the two pairs of characteristics describing how the qualities make the elements bear themselves.
[29] This is a typical description of non-natural motion in Aristotelian physics. Simply picking up a stone moves it "violently" from its natural resting place toward the center of the earth.
[30] Reading *quod* for *quot*.

out of the middle. Therefore it is already established that this is altogether not a motion to one of these two directions; and it is established that it is not light nor heavy, therefore it is not hot nor cold, because lightness belongs to a hot body (namely fire), and heaviness to a cold body (namely earth). And it is not moist nor dry, because one of the two described is moved toward the middle (and it is water), and the other moved from the middle (and it is air); and of each, the one moved toward the middle is the slower of the two moved toward the middle (namely water); and of each, the one moved from the middle is the slower of the two moved from the middle (and it is air). And in the motion of the orb there is not slowness nor lightness, because the motion of the right orb is one from which its sublime and glorious Creator began it, from which He will end it when He wills—and likewise all the orbs. Therefore it is already apparent that it is not moist nor dry.

Certain people of those who pass through the natural sciences without intellect, and through examinations (though they attained to those having demonstration in the natural sciences),[31] supposed that[32] it is composed of fire and air and water and earth. But it is clearly [a case of] corruption and contradiction compared to those who have gone before in this, and compared to others; and it is because in a composite there is altogether no diversity of impression belonging to the composition out of which it is composed, since it is an individual; something different from that out of which it is composed, is not found in it. And indeed revolving motion is not inwardly in any of the four elements, because it is moved by right motion (which, namely, we have established), nor do they have a durability of their motions by nature in any of them; and that because they are not moved to the places belonging to them except when they recede from them and are elongated violently from them by change.[33]

Therefore if their habit[34] is dismissed from them, then they are moved by returning to their places which belong to them by nature: therefore if they reach them they are fixed [there], at rest. And an example of this is when we project a stone from the earth toward the heavens: it is elevated in the air violently, and when it reaches the furthest point of the projection, it returns, advancing according to nature by seeking the middle (namely, the center).

---

[31] *Et hii quamvis perveniant ad habentes demonstrationem in scientiis naturalibus.*
[32] Reading *quod* for *quot*.
[33] *Per conversionem.*
[34] *Consuetudo.* This seems to refer to artificial conditions that are causing unnatural motion or are blocking their motion.

Therefore when it reaches the earth it is fixed at rest in its own place. And likewise the fire which is among us does not exist except [insofar as it is] bidden by those of the terrestrial bodies in which it stands, like olive trees and wood.[35] Therefore when the fire is extinguished, it is converted into air; and when air is converted to fieriness, fire is converted and it reaches the place belonging to it. And I would state this in its own place, if God wills.

But the motion of the orb is always revolvable in its own place, by the days of its space [by which] its sublime and glorious Creator divided it; it altogether does not stand still, nor does alteration in itself enter into it, nor increase or decrease, or quickness or slowness: therefore, it exists according to one bearing out of which it was created, up until it is ended. But the four elements are those standing fixed in their own places according to how their Creator created them always, until the time He ends them. Which[36] if the orb were composed of these four, then already in the composite of motion, right motion would take place, which is not in their natures.[37] And again, it is not possible that it may be composed of that whose nature is standing still and rest in its own place; but lasting motion is therefore what distinguishes the orb from the four elements—but the durability of its motion in the days of its space; and it is [already] in its own natural place appropriate for it.

And the durability of their rest [is] in the natural places particular to them in the days of its space; that it is joined to them in the taking up of the first qualities (which are hotness and coldness, moisture and dryness, and lightness and heaviness and quickness and slowness). For a composite is by composition from ruling contraries, of which certain ones are corrupted, certain ones are contained—contrary qualities acting until it reaches the consummation of the separation of [the composite's] elements. Or rather, if someone said that these elements are composed from the orbs, [the elements being] of manifest corruption at every time, that will be close [enough] that it would make him who is not perfect in this art go astray by it; but the things subjected to corruption in its particularity, are these elements, and everything which is composed of them is corruptible, dissolvable, [and] flowing in its totality. Therefore the whole of what is plowed and sown [is] what is otherwise similarly corrupted in its totality, and is resolved down to the elements;

---

[35] Māshā'allāh is trying to explain why not all fire automatically rises—it is a component of terrestrial bodies, and is only later released by burning.

[36] Reading *quod* for *quot*.

[37] Translating somewhat freely from *iam accidet in composito ex motibus recti motus quod non erit in naturis suis*.

and it is already apparent and clear that the orb is unresolvable to any particular one of the elements, and it appears to the senses (just as we have set forth before) that the motion of the orb is revolvable, and that its nature is incorruptible and not changeable in part nor in its totality: because it is according to one bearing. And again it is apparent that the motion of the elements are rectilinear, and that they are transformable in their parts and their totality. Therefore we have already explained the nature of the orb and the elements, and the natures composed of them.

§8: A discussion on the knowledge of the magnitude of the Sun

And I say that the Sun appears small, just like the size of the palm,[38] and the earth appears big; and we do not know its size from the size of the Sun. Therefore we should display, in the knowledge of this, natural reason and geometrical cognition, so we may discover the knowledge of it which we want concerning it, without ambiguity and not by [mere] belief. And indeed Theon, in a book on the composition of the orbs, has already discussed this topic. And we do not want this book to be void of [this topic].

And he said that the Sun is not abolished[39] without it being either equal to the earth, or lesser, or greater [than it]. Therefore he said that the Moon's light, and that of all the stars, is from the Sun, and that they do not have light except what is loaned by the Sun, and that they are dark in their own essences. And I will even show [this], in a chapter appropriate to it, if God wills.

But let us now return to that which we have established. I say therefore if the Sun is equal to the earth, then it is necessary that the earth's shadow (which is of the night), be going out from the earth according to the quantity of the earth's diameter, and the Sun's diameter be crossing over to the heaven, going from one to the other, for which there is no end, until it reaches[40] the fixed stars of the eighth orb, and that they be eclipsed on ac-

---

[38] Omitting *in palmo*.

[39] *Evacuatur*. This seems related to the statements that follow, if the point is that the Sun cannot be taken from the heavens with light still remaining; but it does not seem logically related to the question of the Sun's size. Perhaps there is an error in the manuscript tradition.

[40] This also appears below. My sense is that Māshā'allāh is speaking as though he is gesturing to the diagram, showing how the light moves on up to the sphere of fixed stars. Look at this and below.

count of the fact that they are deprived of the Sun's light: because the earth separates in between them and between the Sun's light. And thence it is necessary that the Moon be eclipsed in every month, with her eclipse lasting through the majority of the night, on account of the size of the earth's diameter, because her light is from the Sun and we do not see it. Thus, let me therefore revolve the orb of the Sun's circle, and within that one a small circle about which let it be said that it is the earth, and let me put the shadow which belongs to the night above the earth, above it and the Sun (in his own orb under the earth). And let me make the Moon be eclipsed by him in the shadow, and let me put certain eclipsed stars in the shadow, in their own superior orbs above the Moon. And let me write *A* in the east, *B* in the west, *G* in the Midheaven, and *D* in the pivot of the earth. And this is its form:[41]

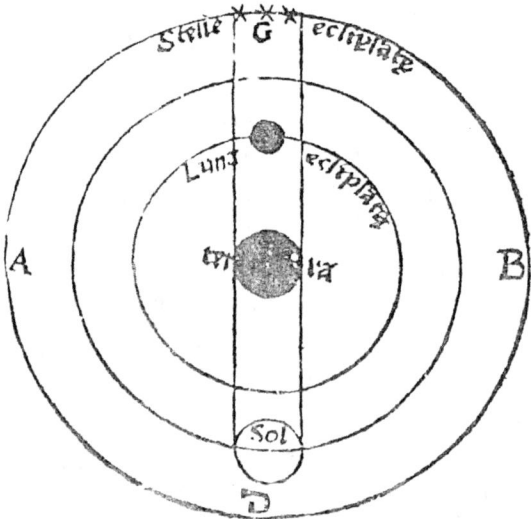

Figure 13: If the Sun were Equal to the Earth

And if the Sun were less than the earth, then it would be necessary that what we have said would happen to the Moon and the stars; and we make it seem to be [thus] in this figure [below].

Therefore now I say again: because if the Sun were less than the earth, then it would have been necessary that by how much more the shadow was

---

[41] From the top to the bottom, the figure reads: "Eclipsed stars, Eclipsed Moon, Earth, Sun."

elevated from the earth to the heaven, it would be enlarged until it would fill up the horizons and would reach the fixed stars of the eighth orb, and all planets would be eclipsed in every month, and the stars with them in every night will be eclipsed when the shadow reaches them, for the whole night, and the Moon will be eclipsed from the beginning of night until morning: and this is unsuitable and impossible. Therefore, by repeating the figure of it, let what we have established be written so that its unsuitableness may be manifest, and that what is not possible be destroyed, and that what is possible be made firm. And this is its form:[42]

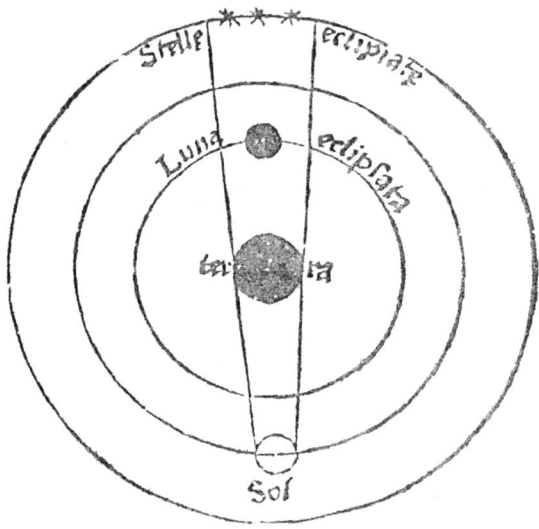

Figure 14: If the Sun were Smaller than the Earth

And it has remained for us to give a discussion making it true according to what we have said, that the Sun is greater than the earth, and that his shadow does not cross through the orb of Mercury, on account of the eclipse of the Moon; and that the shadow of the earth is a cone: by how much more it is elevated to the heaven from the earth it is made fine until it becomes the shape of a cone. Therefore when the Moon meets the cone, she is eclipsed. And her eclipse is according to the quantity of the width of the shadow. And perhaps she crossed through from the right and left shadow, because one-fourth or one-third or half of her is eclipsed, according to the amount of the

---

[42] The words in this diagram reads exactly as the previous one.

shadow she touches. And perhaps she cuts the shadow according to her diameter, wherefore she is wholly eclipsed. And that is what we have seen and known, from which [fact] our discussions reach us.

And I have never seen a star eclipsed, nor a dark star, except for the Moon (who is closer to the earth), because the shadow does not reach the places of the stars, nor those of the five planets, on account of its shortness from them, and since it is already cut off from under them, on account of the fact that the Sun is greater than the earth. And it was already said in the book on bodies that the Sun is greater than the earth by parts,[43] and it circles by reason of the orb, just as is already known and understood. And this is its shape:[44]

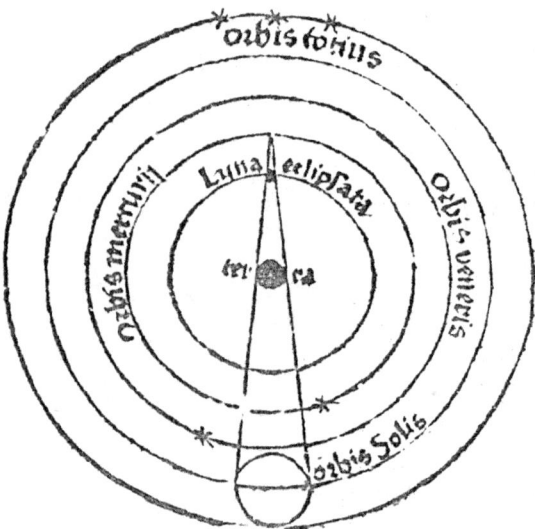

Figure 15: The Sun is Greater than the Earth

---

[43] *Partes.* This must mean that the Sun is many times bigger than the earth, or that it is proportionately bigger.
[44] This diagram reads: at top, "Orb of the whole"; left, "Orb of Mercury; right, "Orb of Venus"; middle top, "Eclipsed Moon"; middle, "Earth"; bottom, "Orb of the Sun."

§9: A discussion of the fact that the Moon gets light from the Sun

And I say that the Moon's light is from the Sun, and that her body is spherical (and likewise the Sun's body)—and their bodies are not surfaces like shields, in the way that certain men supposed. For if what *they* say were true, the magnitudes of the Sun and Moon, when they arise from the direction of the east, we do not see[45] the flat surfaces which would be in their middle: in this therefore [is] the clear signification that they are spherical. Because if someone would look at a sphere, he sees the middle of its roundness from every direction: whence if the Sun were in the east and the Moon were in the west, he will see the middle of the sphere's roundness without a doubt. Therefore I say that the nature of the Sun's body seems to be of his essence; and that the Moon is [like] dark polished iron, and that when she is opposed to the Sun's light, she is illuminated from his light.

And I say that the orb of the Moon is the closer of the orbs to the earth, and that the orb of the Sun is above the orb of the Moon, in the fourth part.[46] Therefore, when the Moon is with the Sun in one degree, then she is under one diameter, and her body [is] below the Sun's body, however much a great space is between them. Therefore, if it were according to this opinion, the middle of a superior[47] body which is opposed to the Sun will be covered by the light of the Sun, and the middle of one which is opposed to the earth [will be] dark.[48] Therefore, on account of this reason we do not see the Moon when she is with the Sun, because we do not see any of her light, since her light is in the upper part of her body, which is opposed to the Sun. Therefore, when the Moon goes out from under the direct line of the Sun, toward the east, the light which is above her body is revolved, and its magnitudes even appear to us from the direction of the west, in a renewed way.

---

[45] Omitting *videremus*.

[46] This must mean that the Sun's orb is fourth in the order of orbs (Moon, Mercury, Venus, Sun).

[47] Reading *superioris* for *superior*.

[48] Māshā'allāh's use of the word "opposed" is ambiguous here. He is simply saying that if a planet superior to the Sun (like Mars) were opposite the Sun, with the earth in between, then it would not be eclipsed and we would see the side facing us as illumined by the Sun. But if a planet below the Sun (like Mercury) were between the earth and the Sun ("opposed to the earth"), then we would not be able to see it, since the side facing us would be dark.

Therefore, by how much she recedes from under his direct line, the light recedes and enters under her body (which is opposed to the earth). Wherefore an addition to her light appears to us, and a signification besides this.[49] And we see at some time the circle of the Moon near its renewal on the first night, and on the second a round circle through the light from him, which flows from his light which is above her. Therefore, by how much more the Moon is revolved in her orb, and recedes from under the direct line of the Sun, by that much more does her light appear derived to us, which is before our eyes, and what is dark is concealed from us, according to the quantity of the Moon's revolution from under the Sun. Therefore, if it were the fourteenth night of the [lunar] month, the Moon will be in her longest distance from the Sun from each of the two sides. Therefore, if the Sun were in the west in that hour, the Moon will be arising from the east: therefore the light of the Sun is entering from under the earth and above it, and from its right and its left, on account of the fact that the Sun is greater than the earth: wherefore his light reaches the Moon and covers her light which is opposite the earth from the body of the Moon.

Therefore her second half is obscured from the other side. Therefore if she is revolved again in her orb, approaching the Sun according to the quantity by which she was elongated from him from the beginning of the month up to its middle, her light is decreased again, and it is revolved from above her, and we see darkness which was above her being added in our eyes, according to what we have seen before: her light is added from her renewal because her light is decreased and her darkness is added, until she returns to her darkness and returns to the degree in which she is assembled with the Sun.

Then her middle comes back luminous in the upper part of it which is opposed to the Sun, and her middle comes back dark, [which is] toward the earth before our eyes, just as it was the first time. Therefore I will form [two] figures [for you] on this.

A figure in which the Moon is seen renewed over 12° from the Sun, and the Sun has already rested; and the Moon has remained so that she may set, and she is renewed—just as it lies under our vision:[50]

---

[49] *Et significatio super illud.* Meaning unclear.
[50] *Subiacet visui nostro.* That is, "just as we see it happening." The diagram reads from left, "Horizon," "Earth," "Moon," "Expressing of a ray to the Moon," "Sun."

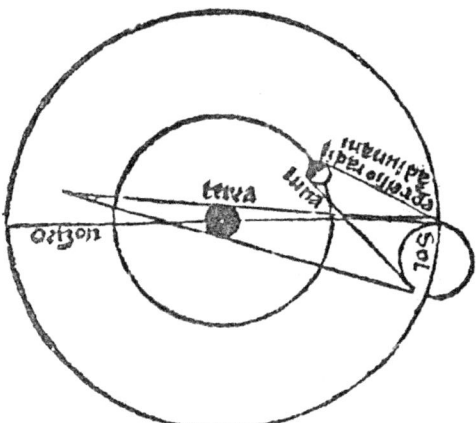

Figure 16: The Moon 12° from the Sun

This is a figure when the Moon is in the orb below the Midheaven, and it is the seventh day of the month, and her half appears bright to men. And | |[51] her middle is dark, and the Sun has already set, according to what is in this figure. And this is its form:[52]

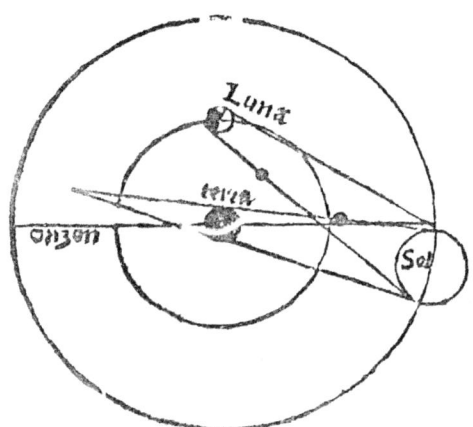

Figure 17: The Moon on the 7th Day

---

[51] Here ends p. 16. The rest of this section has been restored with the material from pp. 29-30.
[52] Reading from the left, "Horizon," "Moon" (top), "Earth" (middle), "Sun."

[This] is a figure in which the Moon is in the fourteenth [day], in the Mid-heaven, whose upper half is dark, which men would not see; and its middle which is opposed to the earth [is] luminous on account of its opposition to the Sun and its derivation of light from him. And this is its form:[53]

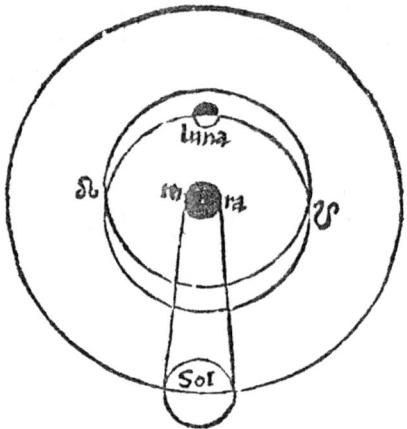

Figure 18: The Moon on the 14th Day

[This] is a figure in which the Moon is arising in the middle of the night, on the twenty-first [day] of the month, half of which is dark; and her half which is opposed to the Sun is luminous, according to what is in the figure. And this is its form:[54]

---

[53] Reading from the top: "Moon," "Earth," "Sun." The symbols for the Nodes are to the right and left.
[54] Reading from the left: "Moon," "Shadow" (top), "Earth" (middle), "Sun" (bottom), "Horizon."

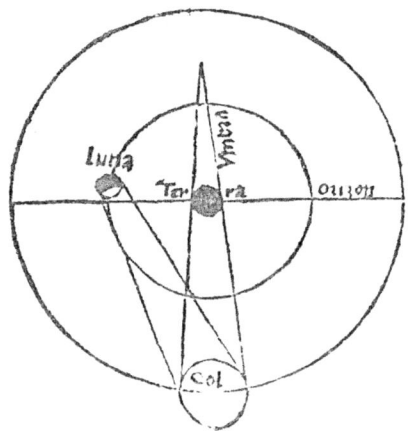

Figure 19: The Moon on the 21st Day

[This] is a figure in which the Moon is with the Sun in one degree, and someone does not see her light in the upper part opposed to the Sun, until she recedes from under the Sun's rays. And this is its form:[55]

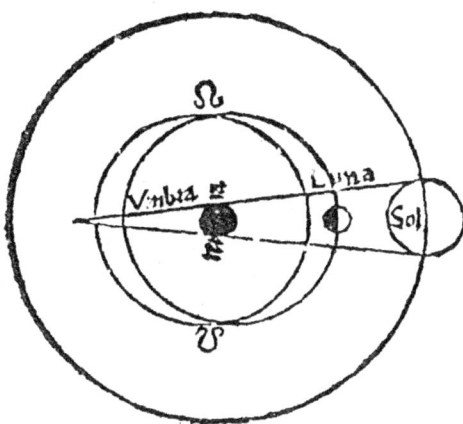

Figure 20: The Moon Joined to the Sun

---

[55] Reading from the left: "Shadow," "Earth," "Moon," "Sun." The symbols for the Nodes are at top and bottom.

[This] is a figure in which the Moon is arising in the morning, and the Sun is not arising, in the shadow which belongs to night, [which] is declined to the west. And such is its form:[56]

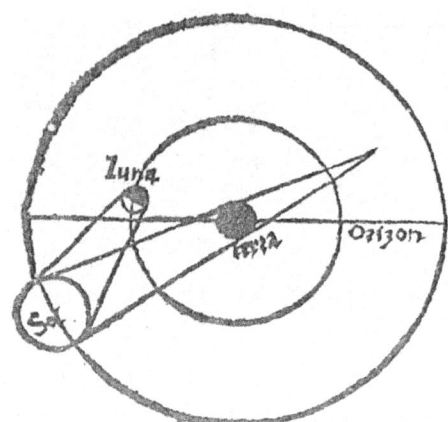

Figure 21: The Moon Arising in the Morning

§10: A discussion on the Moon: why it happens that certain people see her, others do not see her, and why [she appears] big and small

And I say that the New Moon is not seen inwardly[57] until there are 12° between the Sun and her; and what is below this is not seen, because she is under the rays of the Sun, and sight does not reach her there, and because at times it is necessary that her renewal be according to the distance[58] which we have said. Then she is not [apparent to sight] but for a hairline[59] which perhaps is not seen. But he who adds on top of the 12° sees [her as] big according to the quantity of the addition. Perhaps the Sun sets from cities which are in the east, and she herself is beyond a longitude of 11°, because her sight is not necessary among them, and the appearing Sun is extended over cities which are in the west, until the Moon completes the 12° or more in her course; because she is renewed over those who are in the west, and

---

[56] Reading from left: "Sun," "Moon," "Earth," "Horizon."
[57] *Penitus*. That is, while she is still under combustion.
[58] *Longitudinem*, which might also mean "longitude."
[59] In English we would say "a sliver."

toward the second day she is renewed over those of the east. Therefore the month comes one day early among those of the west, before those of the east, and this is manifest and clear—for which a figure is not necessary. But we have already expounded the great and small[60] of her renewal, and her nearness and longitude from the Sun makes this [so]. And God knows [all].

§11: A discussion on the diversity of the Moon's light and that of the other stars, over cities

And I say that the Moon and stars shine over certain people, and they do not shine over others in one [and the same] hour. Therefore, those who see the Moon and the stars shining are in the night, and those who do not see them are in the day: and the reason for this is nothing more than on account of vision, because vision, when the light of the Sun gleams upon it, one does not see any of the luminaries except [the Sun], and it darkens from the vision of the light of the Moon and the stars and fires. Therefore, when the Sun is appearing over certain people, it conceals the light of the Moon and the stars among them, and the Moon and stars glitter over those who do not see the Sun, just as fire is seen in the night over a long space, and it is seen in the day over a near space. And he who wishes to see the stars in the day should go into[61] a well whose depth is dark, then lift up his head toward the sky, for he will see the stars clearly. And it is necessary for us to put down a figure for this, since it would seem that we have spoken sensibly, if God wills.

Therefore I will revolve the circle of the fixed stars and put them in [the circle], and I will revolve the circle of the Sun's orb within it, and I will form it, I will draw the circle of the orb of the Moon, in which I will put her firm on the twenty-first night.

I say that in place *A* is a city for which the Sun is already setting, and they are in the beginning of the night, for whom the east has already begun to be obscured.

And in place *B* is a city for which the night is already in the middle, and they see the stars shining, and the Moon has arisen, shining upon them, the middle of which is luminous in their sight.

---

[60] *Magnas et parvas.* I am not sure what subject these adjectives modify, especially since they are plural. Perhaps this is a misread for "greatness and smallness."
[61] Reading *ingrediatur* for *egrediatur* ("go out").

And in place *G* is a city in which the Sun is already appearing, and the Moon appearing in their Midheaven. The light is already erased from their view, and likewise of the stars of the city.

Therefore, the men who are in place *B* see the stars and the Moon shining upon them in that hour; therefore the sight of these and the sight of others are grouped together. And certain ones of them see the light of [the stars and Moon], and certain ones do not see it, for the reason which we have stated.

And I say that in place *D* is a city, over which [people] the Sun is clear in their Midheaven, and it is their noon, because they do not see a star, and they see the Moon setting in their west, not luminous. And this is its form:[62]

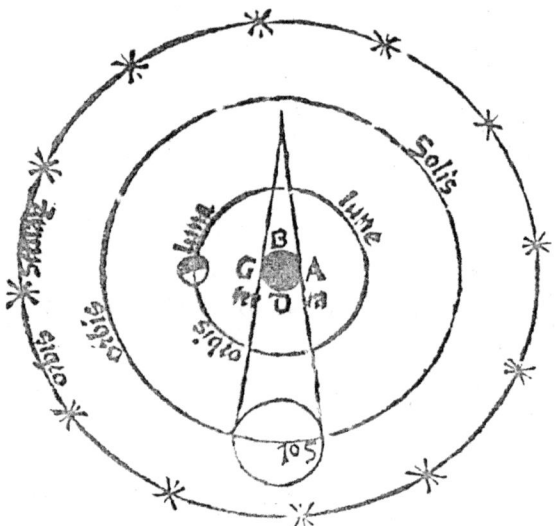

Figure 22: The Moon over Cities

---

[62] The outermost orb is the orb of the stars; the next is the orb of the Sun; the next is the orb of the Moon. The earth is in the center, and the Moon and the Sun each travel on their respective orbs.

§12: A discussion on the number of the Moon's orbs

And I say that the Moon has four orbs:

[1] An orb which is called the "great orb," and it is that which leads her in her course from the east into the west, in every day and night. And if this orb which comes from the east to the west did not exist, the Moon, when she is renewed from the west, running toward the east, [would] be appearing in the middle of the month and would not set from the sky in the night nor day until she reached the east—then she would be hidden and would not appear in the night nor day in the middle of the month. Therefore the great orb guides her toward the west, and she in herself goes toward the east, though you do not see [her] in the first night, just as on the second [night] she is higher in the sky toward the east. Then on the third she is higher than she was, and closer towards the east. Therefore her motion changes her toward the east every night compared to [where she was], and the great orb which she has guides her from the east toward the west every day and night through its motion.

[2] And she has a second orb, which is said to be like the orb of the signs. And it is that in which she appears, entering into the signs and going out from them. Therefore, when the signs are northern, she declines toward them, and when the signs are southern she descends toward them. Therefore it, in its disposition, is not separated from the course of the orb of the signs.

[3] And she has a third orb, which is called the "eccentric orb," because its [center] point does not fall in the middle of the earth, but its middle is separated from the middle of the earth: because its circle approaches the earth from one side, and is elongated from the other. Therefore it is necessary that the Moon descend toward the earth from one side and be lifted up from the other side; and the course of its orb is from the west to the east.

[4] And she has a fourth orb on the border of this [third] orb, which is called the "orb of the revolution," and she is revolved in it toward the east. Therefore when the Moon is in its highest point, she has a faster course; and when she is in its lowest point, she has a slower one, and she is retrograde toward the west, because what happens to the stars in terms of quickness and slowness and retrogradation, happens to her. But in fact it does not appear in her, on account of the quickness of her eccentric orb.

This therefore is the number of the Moon's orbs, and this is its form:[63]

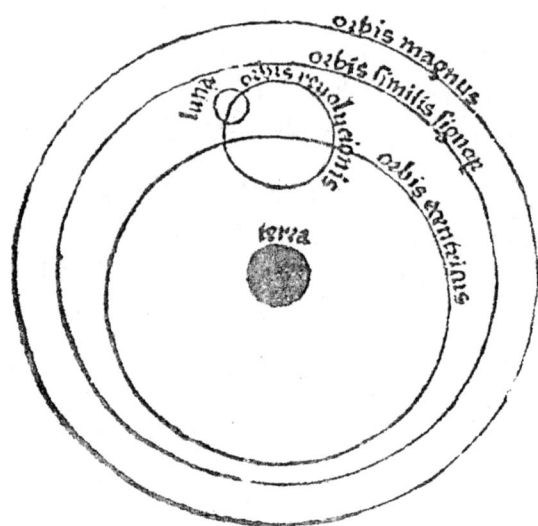

Figure 23: The Orbs of the Moon

[§13: A discussion on the number of the Sun's orbs][64]

And I say that the Sun has two orbs, of which:

[1] One has the motion of the great orb. And it is that which makes him arise from the east and makes him set in the west. And if its motion did not exist, he would run from the west to the east in six months, and would be hidden for six months. But the Sun revolves in his orb in twelve months, until he returns to the place from which he began.

[2] The other orb is called the "eccentric orb," just like the Moon's. And its motion is from the west toward the east. And it is an orb which approaches the earth from one side and is elongated from it from the other side. Therefore if the Sun is in his nearer nearness from the earth, then he runs in the south and scorches what is there. Therefore, on account of this reason it is said that in that place there is no agriculture nor seed. And when

---

[63] Reading from the outside orb: "The Great Orb," "The Like Orb of the Signs," "The Eccentric Orb" (on which travels the Moon on her orb of revolution), "Earth."
[64] I have inserted this heading.

he is in his longer distance from the earth, then he runs in the north, where there is habitation.

This therefore is the number of the Sun's orbs; [and] God knows [best]:[65]

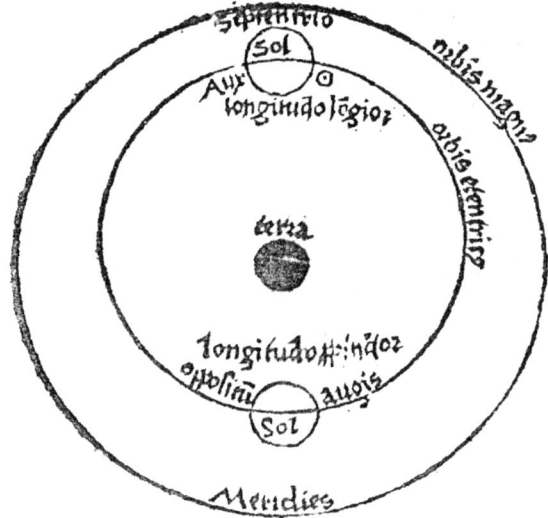

Figure 24: The Orbs of the Sun

§14: A discussion on the number of their orbs and motions

Ptolemy says, I have seen two different motions in the heaven, of which one is from the east to the west, the other from the west to the east. And indeed in the one which is from the east, all motions of the stars and luminaries agree, according to the quantity of the bulk of their orbs. And the motion which is from the east leads all of these stars according to the diversity of their motion which is from the west, and it is the motion of the great orb. And I will show it [to you] by means of a longer discussion (this [will be] in a place appropriate to it), if God wills.

Therefore I say that the motion of all of these stars from the west is one motion, nor is it necessary that of them [there should be] a star quicker or

---

[65] The outermost circle is the "Great Orb," labeled "North" and "South" at its upper and lower extremes. The orb in the middle is the "Eccentric Orb," with two positions of the Sun on it: the upper position of the Sun is the "Farther Distance," where the Sun's *awj* is; the lower position is the "Nearer Distance", the "Opposite of the *Awj*".

slower than another star—or rather, the course of all of them is one course, because [the motion] is one, and not a composition.⁶⁶ Therefore Saturn and the Moon have one, even though in appearance Saturn is slower than the Moon. And this is on account of the reason which I will describe, if God wills.

Therefore I say that the number of the orbs is ten.⁶⁷ And so the motion of the great orb and of the orb of the signs is from the east, and eight of the orbs [go] from the west. Therefore, certain ones of them are within others, and the nearest one of them to the earth is [1] the orb of the Moon; then [2] the orb of the Writer;⁶⁸ after that [3] the orb of Venus; then [4] the orb of the Sun; after that [5] the orb of the Red One;⁶⁹ then [6] the orb of Jupiter; after that [7] the orb of Saturn; then [8] the orb of the fixed stars. And the fixed ones are not named because they do not have breadth,⁷⁰ nor do they run from the north to the south, nor from the south to the north, and they do not run except from the east to the west; and according to quality they do not add nor subtract, nor do they hasten nor slow down as the planets do. Then there are others, and it is [9] the ninth orb, that of the signs, then [10] the great orb (and it is the right orb). And this is its form:⁷¹

---

⁶⁶ Translating somewhat freely from *nec et compositionis unius cursus*, ignoring the *unius cursus* as probably being redundant.
⁶⁷ According to Pingree 1975, this comes from Ptolemy's *Planetary Hypotheses*.
⁶⁸ Mercury.
⁶⁹ Obviously Mars.
⁷⁰ *Latitudo*. In the context of what follows this seems to mean that they do not change latitude (which would give their courses breadth), since they are fixed.
⁷¹ From the outermost circle toward the center, we have the great orb, the orb of the signs, the orb of the stars, the seven planetary orbs, the regions of fire, air, and water, with earth at the center.

Figure 25: The Ten Orbs

If therefore the Moon had been in the place of Saturn, she would walk through that circle in thirty years; and if Saturn had been in the orb of the Moon, he would walk through the Moon's orb in twenty-eight days. And indeed this is so only through the constrictedness of the Moon's orb compared with the greatness of Saturn's orb—but the nature of their course is one in truth. Because if the orb of Saturn were divided into 360°, then 1° of those were made into a circle whose quantity was the quantity of the Moon's orb, and if the Moon's orb were opened to it, [its quantity would be 360 times what was added].[72] And just as the quantity of the orb of Saturn and the

---

[72] This sentence is awkward because, while it is trying to express a simple thought, it is as though the sentence is describing how Māshā'allāh might be motioning with his hands to a diagram. The sentence reads, *quoniam si divideretur orbis Saturni in ccclx partes, deinde poneretur una pars earum circulus cuius quantitas esset quantitas orbis lunae, et si orbis lunae aperiretur ad ipsum adderetur tercentupla et sexagintupla sui esset quantitas eius.* The idea seems to be that each degree of Saturn's orb corresponds to a degree of the Moon's, since every circle has 360°. So if Saturn and the Moon were at the same degree, "attached" as it were by a line, then moving Saturn so many degrees would turn the Moon that many, too, just like different points on the spokes of a wheel all turn the same number of degrees when the circle spins. I think this is the basis of Māshā'allāh's point that the nature of the course of the planets (in this respect) is one. What makes the sentence difficult is that Māshā'allāh is imagining (I think) a degree from Saturn's orb being attached (*adderetur*) to a degree on the smaller circle, and then letting the two circles turn, so that gradually every degree between the two circles matches up.

other[73] orbs are according to this quantity, and they do not slow nor become quick except according to the quantity of their orbs. But their course is one, nor does one star from them cut off something else[74] in its orb, without every star from among them cutting off something like it.[75]

And indeed Ptolemy posited an example regarding these two motions and said, if the other *dārāt*[76] ran from the east in every day and night by one revolution, then even in the *dārah* [there would be] a small circle near its middle, and above a circle equal to twice its size, then another one equal to three times it, after that a circle equal to four times the first, after that a circle equal to five times the first, then a circle equal to six times the first, after that a circle equal to seven times the first, after that a circle equal to eight times the first. And if there were an ant in each of these circles, who was being turned around from the east to the west in the day and night by one complete revolution (and that is the motion of the great orb), then when the first [ant] has walked through its circle once, the [ant] which follows it has walked through half of its own circle; then the third [ant] one-third of its own circle; after that, the fourth [ant] one-fourth of its circle; then the fifth [ant] one-fifth of its own circle; after that the sixth [ant] one-sixth of its own circle; then the seventh [ant] one-seventh; after that the eighth [ant] one-eighth of its own circle. Therefore when the eighth [ant] has walked through the whole eighth circle, then the first [ant] has walked through its own circle eight times. And in the revolution of these eight motions, he has turned around it many times toward the west, and [the ant] runs toward the east, cutting off sign after sign of the *dārah*. Therefore when every ant has completed the revolution of its orb, it will begin with the second revolution—therefore, understand [this].

---

[73] Reading *aliorum* for *alii*.
[74] *Aliud*.
[75] Awkward sentence: *Neque abscidit aliquae stella ab eis Aliud in orbe suo quin abscidat simile illius omnis stella ex eis.*
[76] Lat. *bathara*, a mistransliterated singular form Ar. "orb, circle, orbit" (sing. *dārah*, alt. *dāʾirāt*). The Latin translator probably misread the *hamza*.

§15: A discussion on the motion of the great orb

I say therefore that the great orb is that which is called "right." And it is the more temperate [or moderated][77] of the orbs, and the quicker of them, which turns a revolution of 360° in every day and night with the orb of the signs; and the orb of the fixed stars is revolved away from it by 1° in every one hundred years[78] ([and] after that the other orbs), according to the quantity of its own restraint and greatness. And it comprehends the rest of the orbs, from all of its degrees; and on account of that there are night and day, and the different seasons of spring and summer and autumn and winter, and it changes[79] the planets. And the earth is fixed in its middle. And if the earth were not fixed in its middle, the night and day would always be unequal; and it is not starred; [and] regarding it they have already said it is spherical.

§16: A discussion on the orb of the signs

And the second orb from the great orb is the orb of the signs. And it, again, is not a starred orb, and its motion is from the east just like the motion of the great one. And the authors (that is, the ones making images according to the astronomy of *Altasamec*[80]) said first that it is one of the circles of the great orb, and that all the orbs are nine. But Ptolemy inveighed against this in his book,[81] and said that he has found a difference between them on account of the diversity of the great belt from the belt of the orb of the signs, and the diversity of its poles. Therefore he ordered the number of the orbs at ten—and this is the orb when it is said that a star is in such-and-such degree of a sign, to which this and no other is compared—that is, to this ninth orb. And its northern pole is above the pole of the great orb by 23° toward the Midheaven, and its southern pole is under the southern pole of the great orb by the same amount, when Aries is from the degree of the east, and Libra from the degree of the west.

---

[77] *Temperatior*, probably because its motion is constant and even.
[78] I.e., the precession of the equinoxes. The rate of 1°/100 years is an erroneous figure sometimes cited from antiquity. The true rate is close to 1°/72 years.
[79] *Permutat*. I take this to be a statement about it being partially responsible for the planets' motions.
[80] Unknown person or book title.
[81] Possibly the *Almagest*, if this is an accurate citation.

And this orb is that regarding which something is said to be in such-and-such a degree of Aries and Taurus. And indeed the orb of the signs is not that one at which we nod and say "Aries" and "Taurus" and "Gemini," and so on up to their end. But we do not name these by these names except on account of the fact that they are formed from the figure of their forms; and we cannot name it the orb of the signs, because there is not a form in it, since it is not starred, and all stars are under it, though you do not see [it]; because you say that *Cor Leonis* and [*Cor*] *Scorpionis* and the Vulture and the Fish were in such-and-such a degree of the orb of signs in the times of the Flood, and today they are in more degrees than those degrees would be in it. And the equation of some one of those stars is not completed in the canons, except by the equation of *Cor Leonis*; and that it was cut off from Leo, of the orb of the signs (which is not starred); and indeed these stars which are seen, unless they are the fixed stars; and they cut off from the orb of the signs according to the quantity which they run in their own orb.[82]

And indeed this orb is divided into twelve parts, and every part is called according to what the stars of the eighth orb form beneath it in latitude, according to what we have shown. And every part is called a "sign," and to every sign is posited a month, and it is one-twelfth of the orb of the Sun. Therefore, when the Sun enters into that part, seasons arrive with their own natures concerning which they have been ordered by the elevation of the Sun, and his descending, and his equality. Therefore when the Sun enters Aries, day and night are made equal, and spring comes, and he is in Aries. After that, [he is] in Taurus, then in Gemini, and that is the month of *Nīsān* and *ʾAyār*, [and] *Ḥuzayrān*.[83] Then he enters Cancer and summer comes, and the Sun arrives in the upper part of his orb, and he ignites the earth with his hotness, and by his opposition to the earth—and this is in the beginning of Cancer, then in Leo, after that in Virgo: and they are the months of *Tammūz*, *ʾĀb*, and *ʾAylūl*.[84] Then, the Sun enters the beginning of Libra, and night and day are made equal (and the [beginning] is opposed to the first degree of Aries), and he is in Libra and Scorpio and Sagittarius, and autumn

---

[82] I suspect something might be missing from the text. Here is the Latin (all punctuation being removed), starting from "And the equation": *et non completur aequatio alicuius illarum stellarum in canonibus nisi per aequationem cordis leonis et quod abscisum est ex leone de orbe signorum qui non est stellatus et istae stellae quae videntur nisi sunt stellae fixae et ipse abscindunt de orbe signorum secundum quantitatem quo currunt in orbe suo.*

[83] Lat. *Nizar et Aiar, haziran*. These are the Syriac months for April, May, and June. Māshāʾallāh is not counting the 10 days or so the Sun spends in Aries in March.

[84] Lat. *Zammer, Rab, et Eiul*. July, August, and September.

comes; and that is in *Tishrīn al-ʾawwal* and *Tishrīn al-thānī* and *Kānūn al-ʾawwal*.⁸⁵ Then he enters the first degree of Capricorn, and this is in the winter, in the month of *Kānūn al-thānī* and *Shubāṭ* and *ʾĀdhār*.⁸⁶ Therefore when it is completed, he returns to his working according to what was above him, out of which his glorious and sublime Creator created him.

§17: A discussion on the orb of the fixed stars

However, concerning the stars of the eighth orb: and they are the stars which we see, and we said here it is Aries and Taurus and *al-Ḥout*⁸⁷ and Gemini, and the rest of them, with the exception of the five planets which are under them, and the two [luminaries], the Sun and the Moon—for [the fixed stars] run toward the east, nor does some star of them cut off [anything] except what its comrade cuts off. Nor does any star from among them approach its comrade, nor is it elongated:⁸⁸ because their course is one toward the east, and [the eighth orb] cuts off one degree from the great orb in every 100 years, in accordance with the reminder of it [which] has preceded.

[§18: A discussion on the orb of the revolution]⁸⁹

Then after that is the orb of the revolution. And it is an orb which is revolved from the west toward the east; following it, above it, is the eccentric orb. And its center is above the orb of the eccentric, and [the center] is revolved with it; and it is on it so that if [it is] fixed, it is not removed. Because the stars do not run in the heaven like arrows, but they run with the revolution, and they are, for example, just like if it had been closed up in the belt of a wagon wheel, and the wagon advanced to the east. Therefore if there were a nail up the upper part of the wheel, then the nail would advance to the east; and if the nail were descending, its motion would not be toward the

---

⁸⁵ Lat. *Tisrim primo et tisrim postremo et kemiz primo.* October, November, and December.
⁸⁶ Lat. *Kemiz postremo et Subar et adar.*
⁸⁷ That is, Pisces (Lat. *Alhayot*).
⁸⁸ I believe this strange phrasing is simply meant to say that the fixed stars move at a uniform rate through the zodiac (due to the precession of the equinoxes), and they do not eclipse each other, apply and separate from each other, *etc.*, as do the planets. They are "comrades" (*compares*, lit. "equals, buddies, etc.") because they are all part of the same orb.
⁸⁹ This text begins abruptly on p. 37, but belongs in this place after §17.

east nor toward the west. Therefore if it were descending toward the earth, its motion would be turned from the east to the west, [and] afterwards its motion would be in the upper part of the circle from the west to the east. Then when it would be elevated from the earth, and seeking what is uppermost in the wheel, it would be slowest, and its motion would not be in the upper part of the orb; therefore it would return to its course toward the east. This therefore is the retrogradation of the stars, and their direct motion, and their slowness. And this is its form, and it is a kind of completion of the discussion on the four motions.[90]

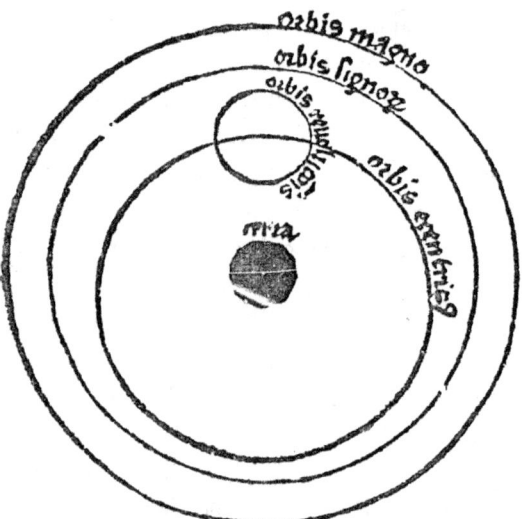

Figure 26: The Four Orbs

---

[90] The outermost circle is the great orb; then the orb of the signs; then the eccentric orb with the small epicycle or orb of the revolution; the earth is in the center.

§19: A discussion on the transformation of the natures of the seasons

And I say that perhaps a winter arrives colder than [the previous?] winter, and dryer and more moist, and likewise the summer. Therefore I say that spring and summer belong to the Sun, and likewise autumn and winter—and we do not see planets likewise. Therefore when the Sun's summer arrives, and it is appropriate that the course of the rest of the planets in the heaven should be in wintry signs,[91] summer will begin, and it will be moist, [with] much rain. And perhaps the Sun's winter arrives, and it happens that the course of the rest of the planets is in summer signs; therefore winter will have little rain and dew, and [will be] dry. And it likewise happens in the two seasons of spring and autumn, by the order of God.

§20: A discussion on the orbs

And I say even that Saturn has four orbs, and that is because he has four motions: the motion of the great orb which is from the east; and his natural motion from the west; and the motion of the orb of the revolution (and it runs from the east to the west), and from that retrogradation and quickness and slowness happens to a star (and I will state it with a plainer discussion here, if God wills); and the motion of the eccentric orb (and it is that which elevates the star in the upper part of space, and makes him descend to the lowest part which is of the nearness to the earth).

These therefore are the four motions of Saturn and of all the planets—with the exception of the Sun, for he has two orbs. And I will describe each of the four orbs in themselves whenever I may repeat [my] statements on them, in order to complete [my] intention. For in the motion of these stars is wonder for him who wonders, and thought for him who thinks, and he knows that it has One foreknowing and ruling it, and that they do not govern anything from themselves nor from their motions, except that with which their orbs run.

Therefore, I will now form the circle of the great orb. And let its motion be from A to B to G to D, and it is from the east to the west. Moreover, let the shaper who formed ones coming before, form this figure—and do not

---

[91] Translated as though the text read *in signis hyemalibus* for *signorum hyemalium* for the sake of clarity and in parallel with the statement below.

let him have disparagement [because of] its crookedness. And this is its form:[92]

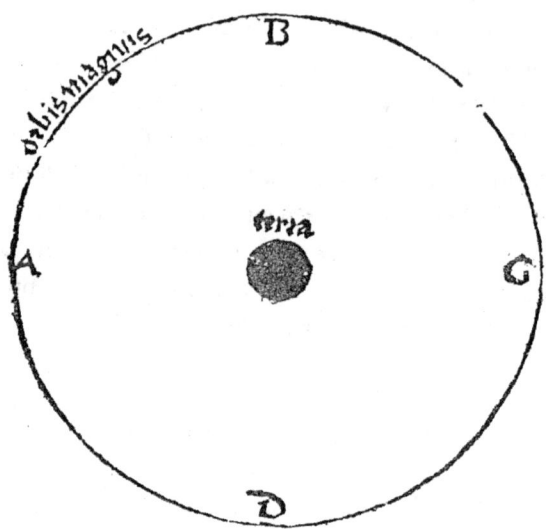

Figure 27: The Great Orb

Then [let him form] the second orb, which is revolved from the west to the east, within this orb, and [let this be] its motion in it, which is opposed to the orb of the signs. Because the orb of the signs is sloping, and the great orb is right: because their poles do not coincide with each other, according to what we have indicated in what has been set forth before. And this is the form of the second one:[93]

---

[92] The circle is the great orb, with the earth in the center.
[93] The outermost circle is the great orb, with the orb of the signs just below it. The earth is at the center.

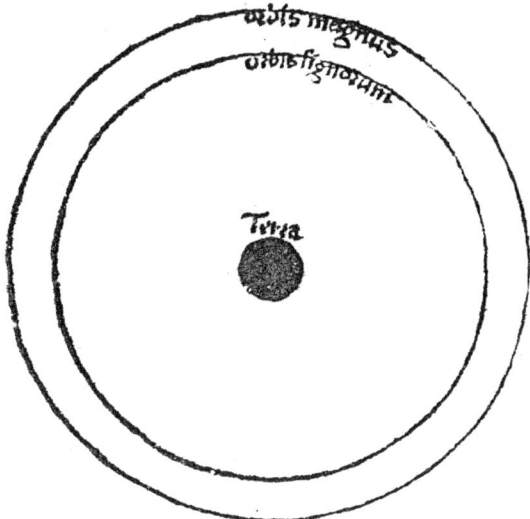

Figure 28: The Orb of the Signs

After this is the motion of the third orb, which is the eccentric orb, because its center does not fall in the middle of the earth, but recedes from its middle by 2°, and the therefore the middle declines toward the earth from one side, and is elongated from it from the other. Therefore when the stars are in the nearby part, they approach [the earth]. And if they are far away, they are elongated from it. And this is its form:[94]

---

[94] The circles in order from the largest to smallest are the great orb, the orb of the signs, the eccentric orb; the earth is at the center.

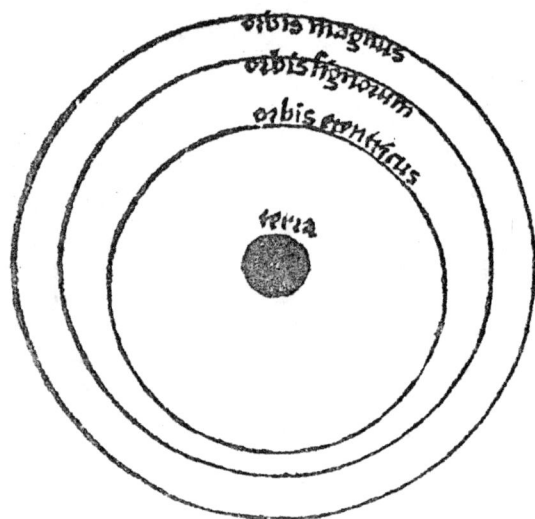

Figure 29: The Eccentric Orb

§21: A discussion on the retrogradation of Saturn, and his turning around toward the sign in which he is[95]

Therefore, after we have already described the orbs of Saturn and his orbs, then we should complete the discussion by expounding the retrogradation which happens to him and to others—and it is when they enter Aries, then he is turned around toward Pisces.[96] Therefore I will project from his orbs in a form in which I want to expound it, and where the orbs (which we have expounded in this our book) are not multiplied—for thus it would become obscure to one looking at it.

Therefore I will form the orb of the signs, which is above the orb of Saturn, in which the stars appear to us, which I will divide into twelve parts according to the number of the signs of heaven. And I will revolve within it the eccentric orb of Saturn. And I will form the earth in its place in it, and I will draw around the circle of the orb of the revolution in its upper part, and I will form Saturn in the orb of the revolution, in the four places: in right-

---

[95] This chapter was originally on pp. 37-39, but I have moved it here after the previous chapter on Saturn's orbs.
[96] Obviously the use of Aries and Pisces is only an illustration.

ness toward the east, and in his first slowness, and in retrogradation, and in his second slowness. And from the earth I will drag four lines toward Saturn, stretching on high to the fixed stars which are in the form of the signs. Therefore I say that they are the lines of sight belonging to men looking toward Saturn. And so I put E in the center of the sights.

Therefore I say that when Saturn is in place A of the orb of his revolution, then he is seen from the orb of the signs [to be] in the beginning of Aries, and he goes toward the east in a straight line.[97] And when he arrives at place B of the orb of his revolution, then he has already walked through many degrees in Aries. And when he arrives from B to G, then he is descending toward the earth, and his course does not appear [to be] either to the east or to the west; and the course of the place is called the "first station." Therefore when he goes out of G to D, then he goes toward the west in the orb of signs, and in the orb of his revolution. Therefore when he arrives at D, those looking from the earth look to him from E in Pisces, after he was in Aries. Therefore when he runs to A from D, then that place D is called the "second station" because he is raised up to the upper part of the orb of his revolution. Therefore his course does not appear [to be] toward the east nor toward the west. Then he returns to his first course, just as it was the first time. And from the significations that the stars approach the earth at the hour of their retrogradation, is [the fact] that they are made bigger to sight in retrogradation—so that their quantities become more (double) than they were. Therefore men look with wonder from that. And this is its form:[98]

---

[97] *In rectitudine.*
[98] The outermost circle is the orb of the signs. In the middle is the earth. The smaller circle about the earth is the orb of Saturn. The two lines A and G from the earth are "lines of vision" to the four stations of Saturn around his epicycle (the small circle on the orb of Saturn), each of which stations is marked by a little cross or star.

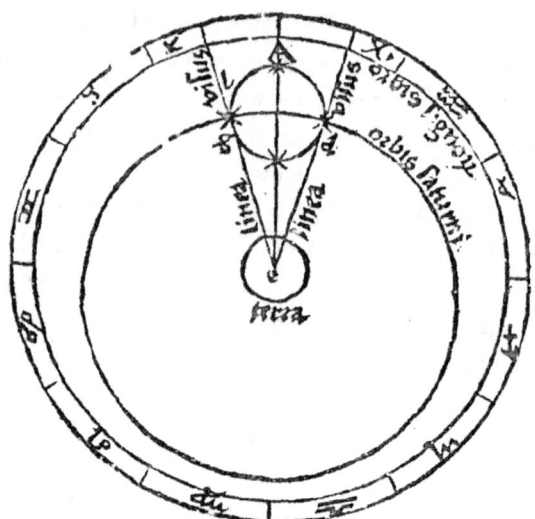

Figure 30: The Orbs of Saturn

We have already gathered [enough] from the description of the orbs of Saturn and his motions, in which there is enough foundation to excuse us from describing the orbs of Jupiter and Mars, because these two and [Saturn] are equal in this. But what happens to those which are above the Sun, in terms of retrogradation and slowness and rightness, happens to Venus and the Writer[99] and the Moon; and a certain reminder of that has preceded [this discussion]. Nevertheless, retrogradation does not appear in the Moon on account of the quickness of the eccentric orb, because she becomes fast toward the east. Therefore if the Moon is being revolved in the orb of the revolution toward the west, the eccentric [orb] becomes quick toward the east; and it carries away[100] the orb of the revolution of the Moon; wherefore retrogradation does not appear for the Moon on account of this reason. But slowness and quickness does appear, wherefore on certain nights we see her walk through one mansion in two nights, and in certain of them she walks through two mansions in one night, on account of these reasons which we stated.

---

[99] Mercury.
[100] Or even, "carries down" (*defert*).

§22: A discussion on circles and chords and points

You should know that he who understands the circles and chords and points by the intellect, understands the quality of the orb. Because by the intellection of these circles and chords and points, the form of the orb stands [firm] in the mind. Therefore when it is erected in the mind, then it already falls in *al-ḥayy*.[101]

Therefore the first circle goes out from the east to the middle of heaven,[102] to the west, to the lowest heaven of the orb of the earth, to the east. Therefore this is named the "circle of the east and west," and it is named the "line of equality."[103] Again, when the Sun is revolved in this circle, night and day is made equal in all climes, and through him is understood that it[104] declines from the stars in latitude to the north or the south.

And the second circle goes out from the point of the north to the middle of heaven and the point of the south, to the interior concavity of the orb below the earth, to the point of the north which is the second pole. Therefore this circle is named the "circle of the south and north," and the "circle of the middle of heaven and the earth."[105]

And the third circle goes out from the point of the east to the point of the south which is the pole of the south to the west, to the north, to the east. And this circle is named the "circle of the horizon." Through it is known what arises from the stars, and what sets in longitude.

And of the three chords there is a chord which goes out from the east to the middle of the earth to the west. And a second chord goes out from the middle of heaven[106] to the middle of the earth, to the lower concavity of the orb below the earth.[107] And a third chord goes out from the point of the north to the middle of the earth, to the point of the south. These, therefore, are the three chords.

---

[101] Lat. *alchy*, "the existent, the living, the Everlasting (esp. God)," again resuming the Platonic tradition of the correlation between eternal reality, the faculty of the intellect, and the world.
[102] I.e., the zenith.
[103] This must be the great circle of the celestial equator.
[104] Or perhaps, "through *it* it is understood that *he* [the Sun]…".
[105] I.e., the meridian circle.
[106] I.e., the zenith.
[107] I.e., the nadir below the zenith.

And the points are the places of the cutting-off of the three circles at the extremities of the chords (and there are six [points]). And the point of the earth which is the middle of the world is the seventh point.

> Therefore the first point is the point of the east, and the point of the section of the circle of the horizon with the circle of the east and west.

> And the second point is in the middle of heaven, and it is the place of the section of the circle of the east and west with the circle of the south and north.

> And the third point is the point of the west, and it is the place of the section of the circle of the east and west with the circle of the horizon.

> And the fourth point is the point of the lower concavity of the orb below the earth, and it is the place of the section of the circle of the south, and it is the point of the north with the circle of the east and the west.

> And the fifth point is in the north, and it is the pole of the north in the place of the section of the circle of the south and north with the circle of the horizon.

> And the sixth point is in the south, and it is the southern pole in the place of the section of the circle of the horizon with the circle of the north and south.

> And the seventh is under the earth,[108] which is in the point of the lower world, which is below every thing—namely, the middle of every thing.

> Therefore he who understands these three circles and three chords and seven points, already understands the quality of the orb. Therefore, I will

---

[108] That is, below our feet in the center of the earth which forms the center of the universe.

revolve the circle and write *A* in the east, and *B* in the south, and *G* in the west, and *D* in the north. I say therefore that this is the circle of the horizon. Therefore I will imagine *V* in the middle of heaven,[109] and *Z* in the middle of heaven belonging to those which are under the earth, because it is not possible to write them in the figure, because the figure is a surface, and what is described is a sphere. Therefore from point *A* which is in the east, to *V* (reckoned in the middle of heaven), to *G* in the west, to *Z* (reckoned in the lower concavity of the orb), is the circle of the east and west. From point *D*, which is in the north, to point *Z* (reckoned in the lower concavity of the orb under the earth), to point *B*, which is in the south, is the circle of the north and south. Therefore these are the three circles and chords.

The [first] chord is that which goes out from point *A* in the east to point *E* in the earth, to point *G* in the west. And the second chord goes out from point *B* in the south to point *E* of the earth, to point *D* in the north. And the third chord goes out from point *V* (reckoned in the highest part of heaven), to *E* in the earth, to *Z* (reckoned in the lower concavity of the orb under the earth). Therefore, these are the chords just as we have shown and expressed them recently.

And the seven points are the place of these letters: and they are point *A* and *G*, *B* and *D*, *V* and *Z*, and point *E*. And for this I will put down a figure so that what we have said may be seen sensibly. And this is its form:[110]

---

[109] Again, the zenith.
[110] The horizontal circle with *A* and *G* at its extremities is the "Circle of the East and West." The vertical circle with *B* and *D* at its extremities is the "Circle of the South and North." The circle *ABGD* is the "Horizon." The chord *AG* from left to right reads "East," "West"; the chord *BD* from top to bottom reads "Midheaven," "Angle of the Earth." The Earth is in the middle.

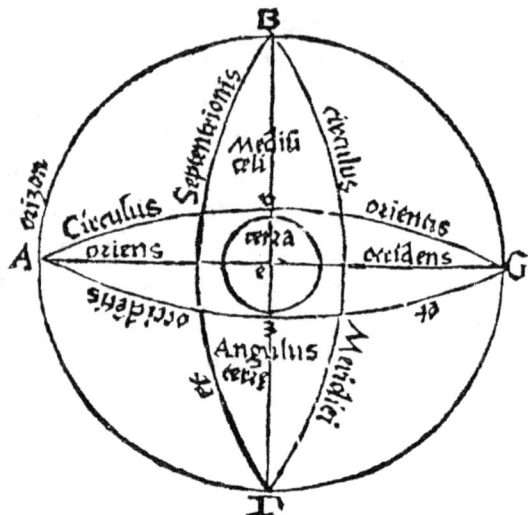

Figure 31: The Circles, Chords, and Points

§23: A discussion on the eclipse of the Moon

And since what we have described regarding the signs (that the light of the Moon and the stars is from the Sun) has been proven true by necessary significations and geometrical demonstrations, in which [mere] belief is not necessary, and ambiguity does not enter in, I say then, that when the Moon is being deprived of the light of the Sun, she is dark; and that is when the earth enters in between him and her, and she meets the earth's shadow: she is eclipsed and she appears dark to men. And perhaps she crosses through from the right of the shadow or from its left, and she is saved, just as happens to her in every month until the time that she meets the Head of the Dragon or its Tail and there is a gathering of orbs: then at this location she runs across the middle of the shadow (wherefore she is wholly eclipsed). And perhaps she touches the shadow from its right or its left, and she is eclipsed by it according to the quantity which enters into the shadow, because she appears to be of diverse colors of red, and off-white and black, according to the quantity of her entrance into the shadow, and her privation of the Sun's light. And a certain view of the eclipse is made different across men on account of the diversity of places and the position of cities. For of them there are those who look at her from the east, and others look at her from the west, and others from the north. And of those, there are those who are in the day at that hour, wherefore they do not see her eclipse; and on account of that reason the wise man lacks her equation and the equation of the regions in the earth (because by that he will know the quantity of her eclipse and its hour).

And if I had not intended to do [anything] in this book except to expound the reason on account of which the Moon is eclipsed, I would have expounded those things which make the eclipse, according to what is in the canons of the *Zij*.[111] And I will state the reason for the eclipse of the Sun in a place appropriate to it, if God wills.

Certain stars eclipse certain others, and this is because when a star enters closer to the earth, between the superior stars and [our] sight, the inferior star covers the superior star, and it does not appear. This, therefore, is the reason for the eclipse of the stars and planets relative to one another. And indeed the Moon eclipses the stars, because when she enters under them she covers them until she recedes from under them. And this is its form (the form of the eclipse of the Moon):[112]

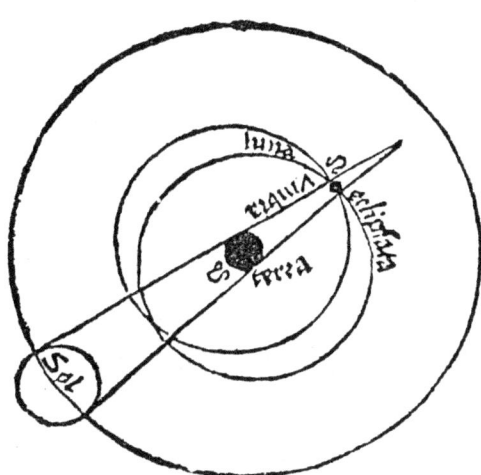

Figure 32: The Eclipse of the Moon

---

[111] Lat. *Zezigii*.
[112] The diagram reads from left to right: "Sun," "Earth" (middle), "Shadow" (on the cone), "Eclipsed Moon." The symbol for the Head of the Dragon is next to the eclipsed Moon.

§24: A discussion on the fact that the stars derive light from the Sun

And I say again that the light of the stars is from the Sun. And they are spheres just like the Moon, though it does not appear in them just as it appears in the Moon, because they are not under the Sun (except for Venus and Mercury). But of the stars which are above the Sun, the middles[113] of [their] bodies to which the Sun is opposed, take up the Sun's light, whether he approaches them or is elongated from them. However, they appear completely [covered] on account of the distance in height from the Sun, wherefore the brightness of sight governs these stars. Therefore the circles always appear; yet when they are in the opposition of the Sun, their light is toward the opposition of the earth, because they appear [to be] of greater quantity than were they in front of it.[114] And that is on account of two reasons—of which one is that the darkness of night in that place is of greater denseness than the middle place of night is, and the light adds clarity in the darkness. And the other [reason] is that when they are in opposition to the Sun in the seventh, retrogradation happens to them in the orb of the revolution, because they approach the earth and their light is filled up until perhaps men wonder at it; and what we have said does not happen except to the planets which are above the Sun. but Venus and Mercury are not elongated from the Sun, nor are they ever in his square nor in his opposition; and they are not [in any configuration] except according to their nearness, sometimes in front of him and sometimes behind him; and then certain ones[115] are lesser if they very much approach the Sun, just as happens to the Moon when she approaches the Sun and she is under him.

Therefore, when they are elongated from the Sun, their quantity is added until they reach their farther longitude; then they return to him, wherefore their light is decreased until they are assembled with the Sun in one degree—therefore their light will be in their loftier [place], just as happens to the Moon when she is with the Sun in one degree. For she does not appear until there are 12° between her and the Sun.

And likewise these two stars then arise from the eastern direction, sometimes when they are in their retrogradation; and sometimes from the direction of the west, when they are direct, from the direction of the east.

---

[113] Reading as *medietates*, to agree with *sumunt*.
[114] *Illud*. I am not sure what subject this pronoun denotes.
[115] This must mean "certain configurations" of Venus and Mercury to the Sun.

And then certain ones are greater when they are in the farther longitude from the Sun, but nevertheless a disclosure of addition and diminution does not appear to the eye in each—as it does appear for the Moon, because the Moon[116] is closer to the earth than these two, [and] because the middle of her circle appears, and it does not appear for the stars on account of their distance from the earth. And their bodies appear small—and likewise for fire, whenever we see [fire's] flame, when it is according to nearness (according to the long or short or stocky size of its body); and when it is according to distance from sight, its flame does not appear except [as something] round, however far away it is. And for us it is necessary that we make a form of the derivation of the light of the stars from the Sun for that which is above the earth, and we should give a form of it; and this is its form:[117]

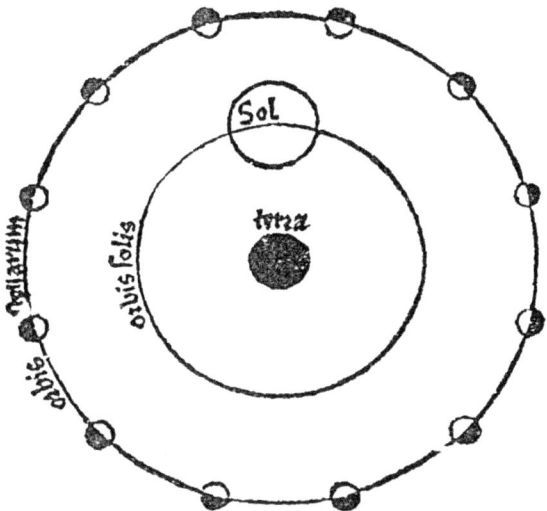

Figure 33: The Stars Receiving the Sun's Light

---

116 Omitting *cum* to make the sentence flow more naturally in English.
117 The outermost circle is the orb of the stars; the next one is the orb of the Sun, with the Sun on it. The Earth is in the middle. The bodies around the orb of the stars are fixed stars receiving the Sun's light from all directions.

§25: A discussion on the eclipse of the Sun

I say therefore that the eclipse of the Sun does not happen except by the Moon. And this is because the Moon is conjoined with the Sun in every [lunar] month, and she crosses below him because the Moon is in an orb closer to earth. And the Sun is in the fourth orb.

Therefore, when the Moon begins to be moved from under him, on the right or left, the Sun is saved from eclipse. Therefore when he meets the Head of the Dragon or its Tail (and that is the place of the assembling of the orbs),[118] the Moon enters between our eyes and the Sun, wherefore he is eclipsed. And the blackness which is seen in the Sun during his eclipse is the body of the Moon. Therefore the Sun is never eclipsed unless the Moon is with him in one degree. And when the eclipse begins with him, it begins from the direction of the west (and likewise the fullness, on account of the fact that the Moon is faster than the Sun, because she reaches him from below him and crossing through to the east). And perhaps [only] something of the Sun is eclipsed, and this is according to the quantity which he covers, regarding the Moon.

And indeed men differ in the sight of an eclipse in the regions, according to the quantity of their readiness and the projection of the rays of sight toward it, from different places. For if he is being totally eclipsed, the stars appear, and day becomes night; and the eclipse of the Sun does not endure as the eclipse of the Moon lasts, because the Moon becomes quick in course under the Sun. And the eclipse of the Moon does not last except on account of the thickness of the shadow of the earth in which she is eclipsed; which if someone were to say that it is necessary that Venus and Mercury eclipse || the Sun[119] because they are under him like the Moon is, it will be said to him that Venus and the Writer,[120] if they were with the Sun in one degree in longitude, they are further than they could ever be in latitude. And sometimes this happens to the Moon, and she would not[121] eclipse the Sun.

Therefore [these two] stars have smaller bodies than the Moon, and they are closer to the Sun. In fact a small body, when it approaches a big one, [the

---

[118] That is, the joining of the ecliptic with the Moon's course.
[119] Here ends p. 36, with the material from p. 17 restored here through the rest of this section.
[120] Mercury.
[121] Reading as *non*.

big one] is not covered by [the small one][122] except according to the quantity of the small body. And when the small one approaches [our] sight, it is covered by the big body by many times greater than one like itself.[123] And at times the Sun is eclipsed at the same time in a region, and the stars appear, and he is not eclipsed in another, and indeed that [would be so] if the Sun had been above our heads and the Moon had been under him: the Moon would mark off between us and between the sight of the Sun, wherefore he would be eclipsed for us; and for those whose region was in the furthest part of the east, with the Sun being among us in the west at that hour, the eclipse would not appear, on account of the fact that their sight enters between the Sun and the Moon, and anything which would have covered him would not be there.

Therefore an eclipse is made different in the regions on account of this reason. I will put down a figure so that one may see how the Sun is eclipsed according to a summary approach, because the first ones[124] form all of the orbs of the Moon and the orbs of the Sun in this figure. And ambiguity enters [the figure], because one will not understand it unless one is perfect in this art. Therefore I have cast it forth, and I have approached and posited the eclipse in two orbs: the orb of the Sun and the orb of the Moon. Therefore someone should not think I have been perfunctory and expressed it ignorantly. In fact I wanted an ease of figure, and its approach to the mind, if God wills.

Therefore, I will revolve the circle of the orb of the Sun, and I will write E in his middle; and I will write C in the earth (I say therefore that the point C is the view of those looking at the Sun); and I will write L in the east of the earth, and M in its west. I say therefore that those who are in place C are not looking at the Sun, because the Moon separates between them and between him. And those who are in L, the place of the east, looking at him, see him not being eclipsed on account of the entrance of their sight between him and between the Moon, since the Sun is a big body and the Moon a

---

[122] Reading *non tegitur ex eo* for *non tegit ex eo*.
[123] *Multiplex sui similis*.
[124] *Primi*. I believe Māshā'allāh is referring to those who drew his source diagram, since he says immediately below that he will fashion one to be less confusing. See below where Māshā'allāh refers to the "first sages" in §26.

small one compared to him, and because there is a great space between them. And this is its shape:125

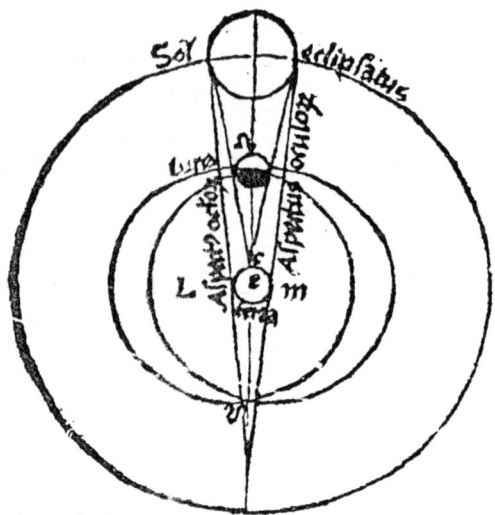

Figure 34: The Eclipse of the Sun

§26: A discussion of winds

And I say that the first sages specified these winds and they differed amongst themselves regarding the different natures in dryness and moisture and hotness and coldness. Therefore they said that the eastern [wind] is hot and dry; and the western one hot and moist; and the northern one cold and dry; and the southern one cold [and] moist. And they differed on the western and southern one, and they said that the western one is cold and moist, and the southern one hot and moist.

And I certainly[126] do not know what regions they wanted by this, whether they signified the whole earth or they signified the natures of the winds of their own regions. And I have found the winds to be different in their regions. For there is a region which brings dew through the eastern one, and another is dried out by the western one, and another brings dew through [the

---

[125] Reading from top: "Eclipsed Sun," "Moon" (next to the symbol of the Head), "The View of the Eyes" (on the rays joining the Sun to the Earth), "Earth" (center).
[126] Reading *quidem* for *quidam*.

western one]. But I will expound these winds by a sufficient discussion according to the quantity of [my] strength.[127]

And in this I will begin from the conclusions of their thoughts, not by rebuking them, nor by making out what they put down to be a lie. Therefore I say that the root of these winds is from the transformation of this air from its course from region to region; and the root of its nature is hotness and moisture. And it takes up all accidents, like hotness and coldness and dryness and moisture, and foul[128] and heavy and aromatic odor, so that perhaps it arrives with the taste of refined things to the mouth, on account of the fact that it takes up these accidents over which it runs. Therefore if it runs above the sea, the nature is made[129] moist; and if it runs over the earth, the nature is made cold; or over hot earth it is hot and dry; likewise it is natured according to the manner which it finds with regard to accidents, transformed from accident to accident, and from heat to cold, from dryness to dewiness, and from dewiness to dryness.

And in its nature it is hot and moist, and the root of its motion is the Sun. For if [the Sun] acts in it, it heats it, and makes it bubble up,[130] because it grows and is increased, and runs, just like waters run toward a city. Therefore if the action of the Sun on it is strong, it runs with strength; and if his action in it is small, weak, it runs with weakness. And on account of the mountains, at times the winds decline from cities according to the quantity of their preparation;[131] and the winds blow stormily[132] over them according to the quantity of the openings in the mountains, and the preparations of the cities because of those openings. For there is a city in which the wind blows stormily, and another in which it does not blow violently, and it blows over them from their eastern and western and southern and northern ends, according to the quantity of the reason which we have said.

And at times the winds are multiplied on the seas by the cold in the air which comes over [the seas]. Therefore if the Sun acts in the air, it grows and

---

[127] Lit., "according to the quantity of virtue" (*secundum quantitatem virtutis*).
[128] *Fetorem*.
[129] *Naturatur* (here and immediately following), lit. "natured," so that its "nature is natured." This means that it takes on the nature of the other quality.
[130] *Ebulire*, the root of the English "boil."
[131] *Praeparationis*. Meaning here unclear—does this refer to how a city is structured to survive strong winds (e.g., through lines of trees to interrupt gusts of wind, or positioning streets to avoid wind tunnels, *etc.*)?
[132] *Procellose*. This word can also mean "gustily," but I will treat it as though it refers to storms (*procellae*).

its blowing and its steaming[133] and dewiness is multiplied, because clouds are lifted up from the steaming of the seas and the moisture of their air. Therefore if they met cold air, their parts would be condensed and thickened, and rain is generated by the virtue of the glorious Wise One. And if that steam and dewiness meets hot air, they are destroyed and evaporate and become air, and it runs to the air of the cold region, because they are hardened and packed, and drag the air of the hot region to themselves. Therefore they run from region to region, just as waters run.

And at times stormy winds blow among the courses of the clouds; but the clouds, when they run in the sky, they lift up the air, and the winds blow through that rolling[134] and their pressure in it. And at times the winds blow at battles and victories, and the arrival of troops, and their motion is on account of the lifting up of the air and its course, which is more subtle than water, and faster in running.[135]

And he who really wants to know what we have expounded on the generation of winds, let him take up a basin and let him put some water in it to the height of two fingers, and let him leave the basin (with the water) standing in the air, and make it stand in the night, a glass vessel with it at its side. Therefore when the day begins to appear, let him take the vessel and turn it upside down onto its orifice in the water which is the basin—therefore the cold, chilled air is caught in it. Therefore when the Sun rises, put the basin with the water and vessel in the Sun. Therefore it will be necessary for the air that entered the vessel that it grow and be increased, and seek a place for going out—therefore it does not find one except for under the water. Therefore you will then see bubbles of water on the circumference of the vessel's orifice. Therefore you will know through this that the air which is in the vessel has already expanded and is going out from what was added regarding the filling of the vessel.[136] Therefore, leave it [there] according to its disposition. When therefore the night will be chilled, and the air which is within the vessel will be chilled and assembled and packed together, and will draw, with this being packed, something of the water, according to the quantity of the air

---

[133] *Vaporatio*, "vapor, steaming, warmth." See also below.

[134] *Involutionem. Involvo* has connotations of being rolled up and turned about, complications, etc.

[135] I am not sure exactly what phenomenon Māshā'allāh is describing. I do not think he is referring to omen-like occurrences. I have heard there are strange acoustic effects during battles, such as "acoustic blindness," in which sounds of battle can be heard from far away but not nearby, due to some phenomenon of the air.

[136] That is, it is going out from the water which was added in the beginning.

which went out of it during its swelling up and increase. This, therefore, is what a small [bit of] air does within a vessel—how much [more], therefore, the air filling up the world, and which fills up the horizons! And we[137] have already stated the reason for the generation of winds and their courses.

§27: A discussion on rains and lightning, thunder, and lightning strikes[138]

I say that when the Sun runs above the seas and rivers and moistening places of the earth, he stirs up and out of them a vapor[139] which one does not see in that hour except the one who applies oneself in seeing it at daybreak, because when the Sun is elevated, it is made finer and thinned by his hotness, wherefore it does not appear. Therefore when that vapor is elevated toward the air, and meets the hot air, it is dispersed and destroyed, and becomes air.

And the nature of its air is one; and if the vapor meets cold air, it is assembled and thickened and packed. Then the hotness and coldness disappear, and clouds come to be from it through the virtue of the glorious Wise One. Then the clouds do not cease to be packed and thickened, and what of them is small, clings to that which is great (since the small is faster), until they become great mountains, and thus their parts are packed together and thickened, and the coldness of the air is contained with them; and the two contraries (hotness and coldness) escape it. Therefore from the sides of the clouds (over which coldness conquers) it is frozen, and snow comes to be, and they go out from the inner part of the clouds, expelling hotness in certain hours, wherefore the frozen clouds are shattered by the power and compression, and thunderings and lightnings happen, and hail comes to be out of them, and it reaches to the earth with a round shape, because it dissolves from its exit from the clouds until it reaches the earth: and at the hour of its exit [from the clouds] it has different shapes. And perhaps the two contraries (hotness and coldness) become violent, and perhaps thunder happens, and a destructive lightning bolt which reaches the earth; and [that portion] of it which does not reach the earth, strikes in the air. And at times

---

[137] Reading *quidem* for *quidam*.
[138] Much of this section bears a close resemblance to Aristotle's *Meteorology* I.9-12, II.9 and III.1, and should be compared with it.
[139] Or "steam" (*vaporem*), here and below.

lightning appears just like twisted lines, according to the quantity of its exit from the place of contrariety; and of the lightning bolts which reach the earth, it splits what meets it, with harshness of motion, and it burns the earth: and it happens in them on account of the strength of the escape of the two contraries of hotness and coldness.

And the sage likened it to green leaves compared with fire,[140] for roaring and ringing are heard, and this contrariety appears when something ignited by fire is taken up and projected into water, for this great voice is heard by [someone even] in something small. How much [more so], therefore, is it in a thing which is like a mountain, and indeed [how much] more is the descent of lightning bolts, and the voice of thunders, and the flashing of lightning in two seasons [in particular]: the season of spring and the season of autumn, which are between heat and cold.

But rains come to be when, with clouds, winds come from the region whose air is cold, fine, [and] humid, without dryness and without hotness (unless it is from the fineness of the hotness of the clouds); there is no contrariety there. And the clouds attract and project from what is heavy that to which it must be raised;[141] in them there is no strength concerning that which is already assembled from parts, which is made larger from the vapor in them; and they sustain what is made fine on account of its fineness, according to the quantity of hotness in them, everywhere they project it; and they meet hot, dry air, and they make it air. But the contrariety in the air between heat and coldness and moisture and dryness, makes great clouds come to be and [make] abundant rain, of which there are great drops assembled; and a cloud of it is thick, and most often this rain comes to be in the spring and autumn, and perhaps it comes to be in the summer. Therefore it will be stronger and more intense on account of the contrariety which we said. Therefore if a wind blows in stormy clouds, it overwhelms them by coiling, and it appears to man as though they are dragons; and when winds happen from the revolving of the wind with dust on the earth, just as that which happens in clouds, and it is an *acubato*[142] (namely, a whirlwind); and I say that thunder and lightning do not come to be except in one [and the same] hour,

---

[140] *Et assimilavit illud sapiens foliis viridibus apud ignem*, treating *apud* as the translator uses it early in this work.
[141] Uncertain whether the clouds are the object or subject of this odd sentence: *Et attrahunt nubes et proiiciunt ex gravi illud ad quod tollerandum [est]*.
[142] Unknown word, but it bears a resemblance to some Arabic words for "tornado" and "whirlwind."

namely at the hour of separation between heat and coldness, however much lightning comes first. Therefore I say that what is sensed by the eye does not have a time—that is, that the eye sees what it is elongated from it, and approaches in one time; and the ear hears it as closely related [in time] according to the quantity of its nearness and farness, according to the quantity of its distance. Therefore on account of this reason, lightning comes before thunder.

§28: A discussion on plants

And I say that the earth brings forth every thing without a sower and without a planter. For in desert mountain peaks we find species of fruits; therefore what is born from them in the desert is not good even though nothing would be born except in a place in which it becomes good, and with which its air (and what is born in it) agrees, and what lives [there] comes to be good and useful.

Therefore I say that the glorious Wise One has measured the seeds so that they would be seed, and he posited them as forms for trees and plants. Therefore when a grain falls, and the Sun rises, [the Sun] heats it up, and acts in it so that it might draw out the moisture which is in it, because the nature of the Sun is to lift up all moistures. Therefore it strains on account of the grain, and what is within it, hidden in it, comes out from the tree, and then the grain swallows[143] what is under the Sun from the moisture of the earth, and it draws it to itself as a support for itself, on account of what the Sun lifts up from out of it. Therefore the soul which the philosophers call "the vegetative [soul]" happens. When the Sun lifts up the moisture which is in the grain, it draws to itself what is under it from the moisture of the earth, and casts veins and twigs under the earth in its search for moisture, in order to swallow the moisture. Therefore whenever it swallows the moisture, it draws to itself, in that moisture, from the fine substance of the earth and its delicateness,[144] and it becomes food for it. Therefore the Sun does not cease to draw the moisture to itself, and grain strains on account of that, until branches and leaves happen, and the tree hidden in the grain goes out, by the virtue of the glorious Wise One, according to the form which God created

---

[143] *Deglutit.*
[144] *Tenui.*

in the grain. For we have already found in the earth a grain of the pine-fruit created from the pine tree, and this is discovered for him who seeks it in the pine tree and in other trees. Therefore the Sun does not cease to draw moistures toward himself, and a tree to swallow the moisture of the earth under it, and with [something] subtle that would be thinned and made refined from it,[145] up to the point at which it becomes a great tree, and those forms which are the seeds of the plant come out in it, just as God created a seed for every thing, Whose majesty is great; [and] there is no God besides the glorious Wise One.

---

[145] An uncertain clause: *et subtili quod attenuatur et subilitatur ex ea*. The idea simply seems to be that the plant converts moisture and other fine nutriments in the earth into what it needs for growth.

ON THE ROOTS OF REVOLUTIONS

Chapter 1: On the system[1] of the circle of the stars, and how they operate in this world

Māshā'allāh said, since the Highest Lord made the earth in the likeness of a sphere, and he made the higher circle spinning in the circumference[2] of the same, and he placed the earth fixed and immobile, and in the middle of the circle, not declining to the right nor to the left; and he placed the four movable elements (that is, he made them to be moved by the motion of the seven planets); but the Head of the Dragon and the signs and all of the stars participate with the seven planets in their works and natures. And therefore the work of the planets in this world is like the magnet stone and iron:[3] because just as iron is withdrawn from this stone by a known distance, so every creature and everything which is upon the earth is effected by the motion of the planets and of all things which are above the earth—both that of seeds and animals, namely fortune or impediment. Also, fitness or destruction comes to be from the motions of the planets in their works, the greatest signification[4] of which matter is the diversity of men in their conditions, and in fortunes and misfortunes. And since we see certain rational beings deprived of goods, but certain stupid men enjoying goods to the fullest, [we must ask] whether[5] this does not have any cause signifying that fortune and misfortunes would come to be apart from the decision and will of those who undergo fortunes or impediments—and all of this, by the will of God, is the work of the planets, and their fortune and misfortune.[6]

---

[1] *Ratione.*
[2] *Circuitu.*
[3] Compare with *On Elect.* §10b.
[4] I.e., "indication."
[5] *Numquid hoc.*
[6] This is a rough attempt at a theodicy, using the planets and God's will as an explanation as to why the wicked flourish and the virtuous suffer. See also Bonatti's slightly more extended take on this in *BOA* pp. 637-38. Here it is awkwardly phrased, but Māshā'allāh is suggesting that God's will and the actions of the planets are responsible, since under normal circumstances one would expect virtuous or rational people to be successful, and wicked or stupid people unsuccessful.

Chapter 2: On the diversity of the traces[7] of the stars in the regions[8] of the earth

Māshā'allāh said, know that the planets have diverse work according to the diversity of the climes. Because in certain climes certain planets come to be benefics, and certain ones malefics in another clime (by different arrangements[9]). And therefore every rational being ought to understand the reasons for the climes and regions: like the land of the Ethiopians, in which there is always heat, and the land of the Slavs, among whom there is always cold. And if the planets signified overflowing cold for the citizens of Ethiopia, their air is tempered;[10] and if the planets signified this for the Slavs, their air will be corrupted, and their habitation will be ruined. And therefore the knowledge of the reason[11] for the climes and regions and airs is necessary.

And know that the knowledge of the stars is very serious, and that the most worthy thing can be known from it, that is, namely, every general thing and what pertains to many,[12] as are the revolutions of years and eclipses—understand the significations of all of these. And this is not known except by the examination of the natures of the signs and whatever each one of them signifies in terms of the regions and provinces, and universal matters. And we have already said this before in our books, but now we would state briefly a part of these matters, and we would begin with the aid of God.

Chapter 3: On the natures of the signs

Māshā'allāh said the signs are twelve. In every sign are 30°, and in every degree 60', and in every minute 60", and thus up to the quantity of a point[13]—that is, up to the infinite. And these are their names: Aries, Taurus, Gemini, Cancer, Leo, Virgo, Libra, Scorpio, Sagittarius, Capricorn, Aquarius, Pisces.

---

[7] The body text of BN reads, "of the work of the stars."
[8] Reading *plagis* in the classical sense.
[9] *Ordinibus*.
[10] *Temperatur*, lit. "combined properly."
[11] *Rationis*.
[12] *Plurales*.
[13] Omitting *primi* in BN.

And they have significations over fire, and air, water and earth.[14] Of them, three are fiery: namely Aries, Leo, and Sagittarius. And three earthy ones: Taurus, Virgo, and Capricorn. And three airy ones: Gemini, Libra, and Aquarius. And three watery ones: Cancer, Scorpio, and Pisces.

For[15] the fiery ones are hot, and the watery ones cold; also, the earthy ones are cold, and the airy ones hot. And know that all of the hot signs are masculine, and the cold ones feminine; and all the masculine ones are diurnal, and the feminine ones nocturnal.

Also, four of the signs are movable (namely in which the weather is moved), which are Aries, Cancer, Libra and Capricorn. And four [are] fixed (in which the weather is fixed): Taurus, Leo, Scorpio and Aquarius. Also, four are bicorporeal or common (in which two bodies[16] are joined): which are Gemini, Virgo, Sagittarius, and Pisces. These are the natures of the signs.

Chapter 4: On the revolution of years

Māshā'allāh said, if you want to know what would happen in the world from winds and from rains, and the rest, set up the Ascendant at the hour of the Sun's entrance into the first point of Aries, and set up the seven planets for that same hour. And, the figure having been made, consider which of them is in charge of it. Which if it were a benefic, the time will be made fit; but if it were a malefic or impeded, the world will be corrupted. And do likewise in the quarters of the year, and its months.

And know that if more planets were conjoined in watery signs in the revolution of the year, they will signify a multitude of rain; and in fiery signs, an overflowing of heat and dryness or the sterility of the land; and in the airy ones, a multitude of winds; and in the earthy ones, frost and snows. And likewise in the quarters of the year, if the planets were in cold signs, they will signify the severity of the cold and the decrease of heat.

Also, know that if Mars and Saturn were in charge of it, and the benefics did not aspect them, they will signify a multitude of war, and the destruction

---

[14] This sentence is in 1533 but not in BN.
[15] Following 1533 for this passage, which in BN reads only: "The fiery and airy ones are masculine, the earthy and watery ones feminine. And all the masculine ones are diurnal, and the feminine ones nocturnal."
[16] Following BN. 1533 reads, "seasons," which was evidently meant to parallel the above statements about weather).

of the world. And even if Mars were the Lord of the summer quarter, and he were in one of the domiciles of Mercury, he will signify a multitude of rains and pestilences. And you should know that the severity of the dryness and the sterility of the earth, or the dearth of the *annona*, does not come to be except from the conjunction of the planets in the fiery signs. Understand this, and test it (according to what he has told you),[17] and you will discover.

Chapter 5: On the eclipse of the Moon, and its signification

Māshā'allāh said, it behooves you to consider the eclipses of the year (both the lunar ones and the solar ones), and to know the Ascendant of the middle of the eclipse, and the one who is in charge of that same Ascendant and its figure.[18] Which if it were a malefic, it will signify impediment and destruction. But if it were a benefic, it will signify fitness.

And know that the eclipse of the Moon, if it were in the cold signs, signifies the severity of the cold, and in watery ones the severity[19] of rains, if the season supported it (that is, if it were winter). But if it were summer, it will signify the temperateness of the air. Understand and test the rest thusly. You should understand this: because if the benefics aspected the Moon and received her, [the eclipse's] signification will be on those things which they signify concerning good and profit.[20]

Chapter 6: On the changing of the seasons through the changing of the planets (namely, of the heavy ones)[21]

Māshā'allāh said, if you wished to know the variety of weather over the diverse things of the corruptible world, know the signs of the heavy planets,

---

[17] This parenthetical remark is in 1533.
[18] That is, the planet ruling the rising sign at the middle of the eclipse. If Māshā'allāh is following *Tet.* II.7, then by "figure" he probably means the type of sign that the eclipse is in, and the sign that the Lord of that Ascendant is in—for instance, human signs show good or bad for humans, *etc.* But Ptolemy's method for determining the ruling star is more complicated. See note to Ch. 7 below.
[19] 1533 reads, "excessiveness" (*nimietatem*).
[20] *Proficuum.* This should be taken broadly, to include whatever is beneficial or profitable (including good weather).
[21] This extra remark is from BN.

namely whether they are hot or cold. Which if they were hot, it will signify heat in the summer, [but] the temperateness of the air in the winter. And if they were in the cold signs, it will signify cold in the winter and temperateness in the summer.

Likewise, if the planets were conjoined in watery signs it will signify overflowing rains (and the corruption of the air by those same rains)[22] in the winter, and[23] the good mixture of the air, and a multitude of dew in the summer. And test according to this, because you will not go astray. But the heavy planets are Saturn, Jupiter and Mars, and you ought to combine the Sun with them, too.[24]

In short, know that the heavy planets, if they were in the direction of some one of the regions, they will signify dryness and the sterility of the earth; but if they were elongated from it, they will signify a multitude of rains. By "nearness" I want it to be understood that they are in northern signs, and by "distance," in southern ones.[25]

Know[26] also that the heavy planets, if they were all[27] oriental, they will signify dryness; and if they were all occidental, they signify a multitude of rains in the winter and the good mixture of the air in the summer. And likewise in arising [out of the beams] they signify the fitness of the air in the winter and excessive dryness in the summer.

---

[22] This parenthetical remark is in 1533.
[23] Following 1533 for the remainder of the sentence.
[24] That is, include the Sun along with them when looking at the signs.
[25] Meaning unclear. What exactly does he mean by a planet being "in the direction" (*in directo*)? This can also mean being in a straight line, and it recalls Abū Ma'shar's descriptions of planets being "parallel" to signs (*OGC* VI), which simply means they are "in" the signs.
[26] This may be a reference to *Tet.* II.8.88, but Ptolemy himself only says "by their phases with reference to the Sun." So it is unclear which form of orientality and occidentality is means. However, my guess is that being "oriental" means being from pertaining-to-arising to the first station, and being "occidental" means being from the second station to pertaining-to-sinking. See the following sentences.
[27] Only 1533 has the comment about being oriental.

Chapter 7: On the eclipse of the Sun and its signification

Māshā'allāh said,[28] know that in the eclipse of the Sun, it cannot come to be but that some great accident[29] is signified, according to the quantity of the eclipse—that is, that it comes to be from the square of the Sun's body, and above that.[30] But the knowledge of those things which happen from the eclipse of the Sun is that you should know the Ascendant of the middle of the eclipse, and the planets conquering over the figures of the eclipse. Which if they were malefics, they will signify evil and detriment, and the death of kings and the wealthy. And if they were malefics, they will signify fortune and the fitness of the condition of matters.

And you should know that the eclipse of the Sun, if it were in Aries, will signify the ruin[31] of kings and the wealthy, and dryness or the sterility of the earth, and famine; and so in the rest of the fiery signs. But in the watery ones, it will signify a multitude of rains, and detriment from them. Understand also that if the benefics aspected, they will subtract evil. But if the malefics aspected, they will amplify [the evil] and will subtract fortune.

Know even that if the Sun or the Moon were the *hīlāj* or the *kadukhudhāh*, and it were obscured, it will signify for him whose *hīlāj* or

---

[28] Source of Māshā'allāh citation unknown, but this chapter and the next should be read along with *On Rev.* Chs. 24, 35, and 40. I follow 1533 through the rest of the paragraph. BN reads: "Know that in the eclipse of the Sun it cannot come to be but that something great is signified, happening according to the quantity of the eclipse and the planets conquering over the figure of the eclipse. Which if they were malefics, it will signify impediment and the corruption of kings and the wealthy; and if they were benefics, they will signify fortune and the fitness of the condition of matters."

[29] Remember that "accident" is simply anything that befalls us.

[30] My sense is that this sentence and the next (which speaks of planets "conquering") derive ultimately from *Tet.* II.4 and II.6-7. In II.4 and II.6, Ptolemy says that we must observe "the movements of the stars at the time" of the eclipse (and during the time of its effect), especially planets that are pertaining-to-arising, pertaining-to-sinking, or in a station, and then especially if they are in some aspect to the sign the eclipse is in. Superior planets in a station and aspecting the sign of the eclipse would either be in a square or trine, hence they would be in a "square of the Sun's body" or "above that," *viz.*, in a whole-sign trine. In II.7, Ptolemy says that the planets that "govern" or "rule" these matters are planets having relationships of rulership over or aspect the sign of the eclipse and of the angle which follows it—and then he gives rules for deciding which planet is the most powerful.

[31] *Interitum*, which can also mean "death," but I take it that the translator would have used *mortem* if he had meant death.

kadukhudhāh it was, a great danger or serious infirmity, unless the benefics aspected.[32]

Chapter 8: On the conjunction of the planets and their effect

Māshā'allāh said the conjunction of the planets signifies the accidents of this world and its matters, which are thus to be considered at the time of the conjunction of the higher and lower planets. Because the benefics signify fortune and a good effect, if they conquered over the figure of the conjunction. But if the malefics conquered, they will signify evil and the effecting of evil. Wherefore, were you even to know if they were conjoined in some one of the signs, they will signify detriment and a multitude of evil according to the substance of that same sign.[33] That is, if the conjunction were in watery signs, it will signify the detriment of the rains; and thusly in the rest of the signs. If however they were conjoined in feminine signs, they will signify pestilences and the death of animals of the feminine sex (and the same is said concerning masculine [signs and sexes]).

And know that the conjunctions and the eclipse of the luminaries, if they were in fixed signs, will signify the lastingness of evil and its detriment; and if they were in movable signs, they will signify the smallness of the lastingness of the evil and its detriment; but if they were in common signs, they will signify mediocre evil. And say thus about the good.

Chapter 9: On the conjunction of the superior planets

Māshā'allāh said, know that the greatest things, and those to be marveled at, happen from the conjunction of the superior planets. And this comes to be on account of the slowness of their motion. And if these three were joined in one bound or face, and the Sun aspected them, they will signify the destruction of sects and kingdoms, and the changing of them, and the great-

---

[32] In other words, see if your *hīlāj* or *kadukhudhāh* is a luminary in your natal chart: when that luminary undergoes eclipse in real time, it indicates difficulties unless the benefics aspect. But Māshā'allāh does not say whether these are the transiting benefics' aspects to the natal luminary, or to the eclipse itself, or they are the natal benefics' aspect to the position of the real-time eclipse, or what.

[33] Obviously this statement refers to the malefics' conjunctions.

est matters, according to the quantity of the stronger of them, and of the one conquering over their signs—and this is their greatest conjunction,[34] which signifies prophecies[35] and the destruction of certain climes, and the greatest matters, and especially of some one of the inferior planets gave aid to them. And you should know that the one stronger than the rest will be the significator—which if it were a benefic, it will signify fortune; and if it were a malefic, it will signify evil and tribulation.

Understand even that these planets, if they were conjoined in their own exaltations, they will signify good and the fitness of the weather, and a multitude of the stirring-up of wars, and the demonstration of miracles. But if they were conjoined in their falls, they will signify the detriment and dryness and sterility of the earth, and famine—unless they are made fortunate. Wherefore, know that if they were conjoined in a fiery sign, they will even signify the sterility of the earth; and in a watery sign, they will signify a multitude of rain; in an airy one, the strength of the winds; and in an earthy one, the overflowing of cold and detriment. And if they were conjoined in masculine signs, they will signify the detriment of masculine animals; and thus with the feminine ones.

Chapter 10: On the greater conjunction

Māshā'allāh said, we have already stated that the principal things happen from the greater [kind of] conjunction, which is of the superior planets.[36] But these superior planets have other conjunctions, even ones signifying greater accidents. For the conjunction of Saturn and Jupiter is a greater conjunction, and it signifies accidents and sects.

But the knowledge of the accidents from this is had by looking at the Ascendant, and at the planets at the hour of their conjunction, and which of them rules in the figure. Which if it were a benefic, it will signify good and the fitness of the weather. And if it were a malefic, [it will signify] detriment and dryness, and moreover the sterility of the earth, and wars.

---

[34] This could refer to the climacteric conjunction in Aries, which happens every 960 years—ideally, it takes place in the first bound of Aries, which in the Aries Ingress would also put the Sun there.

[35] But we should probably also take this to include prophets themselves.

[36] Māshā'allāh has made this sound as though it refers to a conjunction of *all three* superior planets.

And know also that if Jupiter were stronger than Saturn, he will signify good[37] in that same conjunction; but if Saturn were in charge, it will signify detriment and tribulation.

And know that their conjunction in the fiery and airy signs signifies dryness and the sterility of the earth, and moreover the severity of the cold.[38] And in earthy ones, the destruction of seeds, and famine. In watery ones it will signify the excessiveness of rains and of pestilence, under the condition that they are impeded. Finally, if they were made fortunate,[39] they will signify the increase of goods in all things signified by them; and if malefic, decrease.

Moreover, know that the greater conjunction, if it were in some one of the angles, and especially in the angle of the Midheaven, it will signify the appearance of a king or a prophet from the direction of that same sign.[40] But if that sign itself were made fortunate, and its Lord of good condition, this will signify his triumph and domination—but if [the sign] and its Lord were impeded, it will signify his ruin and dejection. And the conjunction will have to be won[41] after the noted years of that conjunction, which we have brought up elsewhere.

Chapter 11: On the middle conjunction

Māshā'allāh said the middle conjunction is namely the conjunction of Mars and Saturn, and it signifies the accidents of wars and the contrarieties of battles. If you wished to know the accidents, know the one ruling in the figure of their conjunction. Which if it were made fortunate, it will signify good and its fitness; and if it were malefic, it will signify evil and its impediment.

Know even that their conjunction in the signs of men signifies the multitude of their infirmities; and their conjunction on some one of the angles of the year signifies the contrariety of the wealthy or the kings, and a multitude

---

[37] Reading *bonum* with BN for *locum*.
[38] Reading *frigoris* with BN for *fori*.
[39] Here and later in the sentence ("malefic") Māshā'allāh might be contrasting either planets made fortunate or made bad (no matter what their intrinsic benefic or malefic natures are), or else benefic *versus* malefic planets.
[40] This probably means from the south for earthy signs, the east for fiery signs, *etc.*
[41] *Meruenda. Mereo* means to win, gain, award, deserve. Its exact meaning here is unclear, but Māshā'allāh could be suggesting techniques like those of Abū Ma'shar in *OGC*, where he applies timing techniques to determin when the promised effects will come to fruition.

of wars, and the matter will last until they are joined another time. And their conjunction in fiery signs signifies the dryness (namely the sterility) of the earth; and in airy ones, winds; in the watery ones, a multitude of rains; in earthy ones, frost and snows, and a multitude of cold spells. Know even that the benefics, if they aspected, subtract evil; and the malefics will increase [evil]. Test[42] this in the way I have described for you, and you will discover it, if God wills.

Chapter 12: On the lesser conjunction

Māshā'allāh said the lesser conjunction is the conjunction of Jupiter and Mars, and this signifies accidents which come to be in rains and clouds, and the corruption of the air and war. But if a benefic conquered in their conjunction, it will signify fortune; and if a malefic, evil. And know that Jupiter and Mars, if they were conjoined in the Ascendant of the year, or in some one of its angles,[43] they will signify the stirring-up and diversity of the kings, unless the benefics aspected.

Know even that however often a benefic were conjoined with a malefic, the nature[44] of the stronger of them will appear. And if a malefic were joined to a malefic, evil will abound, unless the one who is in charge of the conjunction is a benefic—understand.

And this is the last thing of those which we have brought forth in this book, and it is of the secrets of the science of the stars.

And [the book] of Māshā'allāh translated by John of Spain, in Lunia,[45] from Arabic into Latin, is completed.

---

[42] This sentence appears only in 1533.
[43] I believe this means we are to see where the position of their *future* conjunction appears in the *ingress* chart cast for earlier in the year.
[44] Reading *natura* with 1533 for *fortuna*.
[45] See Thorndike 1959 for a lengthy and somewhat torturous exploration of all of John of Spain's appellations. Lunia (or Limia, or Luna) is a region in Galicia.

CHAPTER OF THE RAINS IN THE YEAR

From the sayings of Māshā'allāh

§1

When it is desired to learn the abundance of rain or its scarcity, or if there will be more in the first [part] of the year or in the last [part], then observe when the Sun has entered into Scorpio. Then look to Venus: and if she is appearing in the east in the early mornings, the first [part] of the year will have little rain, and the last [part] of it will have more rain. And if she were in the west in front of[1] the Sun, then the first [part] of the winter will have more rain. Know that when Venus was with the Sun in a sign, there was more rain in the month that they meet. It is like the woman under the man, receiving his water.

Then, when knowledge of the abundance of the rain or its scarcity is desired, observe when the Sun enters the first minute of Aries, and erect the rising at the time of its connecting to the first [part] of the sign. Then observe how many degrees the rising is from it, and then take an owner of the part[2] of the degree of the rising. Then erect the four stakes. And know that if an owner has a part of the rising it is owner of the year in the rains.

Then look to the owner of the year—does it make connection with Venus or Mercury, and is it assembled with either of them in a sign? Then look to the rising to see if it is of the water signs or not. Then when that has been judged, look to the placement of Venus, the Moon, and Mercury, and [see] if these planets are found in water signs. And if the Moon is found connected with them, and [she is] not connected with one of the unfortunate planets, there will be more rain in that year.

And if Mercury is found to be made unfortunate by Mars, [or] is under the rays, and the Moon is found to be connected with Mercury, then know that the rain will be scarce in the first [part] of the year, and in-

---

[1] One would think this should read "following," i.e., setting after the Sun.
[2] I.e., a dignity, here and at the end of the paragraph.

crease in its middle [part]. And the rains will be with thunder and lightning and obstructive weather and much wind.

And if Venus is found connected with Mars or under the rays, then less rain in all of that year.

And when Mercury is found connected with Saturn, and the Moon is connected with Mercury or Saturn, then it is said that the rains will increase in the first [part] of the year, and an increase in moist atmosphere and the obstructive [weather].

And if Jupiter is found in a sign of water, and Venus and the Moon are connecting with it, then judgment is for less rain that year.

Then look to the owner of the bound of the rising, which is the owner of the year,[3] and if there were a connection in the stakes, or [...].[4]

And regarding the indication of the rains in the first and last [parts] of that year: if the owner of the year is found to be made unfortunate by Mars, or Mars was with it in the sign, then less rains in the first [part] of it and last [part] of it, with great difficulty for you. And when the owner of the year is found with Venus and the Moon is connected with Mars, then the clouds and winds will increase and the rain will lessen. And if the sign which gathers within it the owner of the year with Venus is of one of the signs of air, and the Moon is connected with Mars, so then say that the air is spoiled from moisture other than rain. And if Venus is found connected to Saturn, or the Moon was connected with Saturn, then say that the moisture and the fog will increase until it is as a semblance of rain, and it will burden the earth in that year from moisture other than rain.

Then look to the owner of the year, which is owner of the bound of the rising:

And if it were Mercury and were made unfortunate, then the rains will lessen and increase in that year with corruption from the winds and the clouds.

---

[3] Note that he did not say earlier that the lord of the year ought to be the Lord of the bound.
[4] There is a lacuna in the Arabic.

And if the owner of the year was found to be Jupiter and it were made unfortunate by one of the unfortunate planets, then the rains will lessen and there will be no deterioration in the atmosphere or the winds like there was with the corruption of Mercury.

And if Venus were the owner of the year and were made unfortunate by Mars and she were under the rays, then the fog will increase and the moisture on the earth will be from other than rain.

And if the owner of the year were Mars, the moisture, rains and clouds [would be] decreased.

And if it were Saturn, the rains [would be] decreased and there [would be] more fog.

And if it were one of three planets, which are the Moon, Venus, or Mercury, then they are the planets which indicate an abundance of rain and its scarcity, as well as connections of the fortunate and the unfortunate planets, and the planets which prohibit the rains—which are the Sun, Mars, and Saturn, except if Saturn were in a sign of rains.

§2: Chapter of the rains in the quarters of the year

Observe when the Sun has entered the first minute of Libra or Capricorn, then erect the rising and record the stakes (record that which I prescribe to you), and the rising of that sign. And look to where Venus, Mercury and the Moon are in that quarter, and with whom they connect. And look to where Mars is placed in each quarter, and the connections of these planets. Then judge these planets. Then judge each of these in the topic of the moisture: the rains, the clouds, the fog and the winds. So you make judgment on what you desired, when you know the first connections of some of them, then observe them like we have done in [the chapter on] the first [part] of the year, if Allah wills.

So then the Sun, when it has entered Libra, infers what will happen in that quarter to the beginning of Capricorn, and it is the autumn season. And when it has begun to be Capricorn, then erect the rising to the time of the entering of Capricorn or Aries like I have demonstrated for you in [the chapter on] the first [part] of the year, if Allāh wills.

§3: Chapter of the knowledge of the year in gathering and the reception[5]

When it is desired to know the rains in each month, look to the time of the gathering of the Sun and the Moon within one degree, or a time that the Sun receives a degree of the Moon (this is at the time that the Moon moves into a sign which is seven from the Sun, changing to the degree of the Sun).[6] Then erect the rising to that time just as you evaluate a rising of each month, then surely from it you will know what will come to be.[7]

Then look to the Moon. And if it is found connected with Venus or with Mercury, it [would] rain in that month. And if you want correction of that,[8] then if the Moon, when it has reached the stakes and is connected with Venus or Mercury, then in that day it rains. An exception is if the Moon is connected in the first of the [lunar] month with Mars, then as such there will be more thunder, lightening, and winds and less rain until the reception is met, and there won't be a root in that half.[9] And if the Moon is found connecting with the fortunate planets at the time it separates from the Sun, then after that bisection there [would be] much rain.

And the placement of the gathering of the Sun and its reception falls upon you, and it is half of the month to the moment of calculation of the rising in each half-month.[10] Then you will know what will be of the rains in each half. So if the Moon is found at the moment of separation of the gathering or reception to be connected with Saturn, and Venus is connecting with Saturn in a rainy sign, then know that the rains increase in that gathering

---

[5] "Gathering" refers to the conjunction, "reception" to the prevention or Full Moon.
[6] In other words, at the times of the conjunction and prevention.
[7] Māshā'allāh may be distinguishing here between the quarterly (and by implication, monthly) ingresses of the Sun into the signs, and the halves of the lunar months which may take place at any point in the signs. He seems to be saying we should use the same procedures for both.
[8] I.e., if we want to know the exact time.
[9] I'm not sure what Māshā'allāh means by a "root" here. Surely the chart of the prevention acts as a kind of root?
[10] Again, we are simply to cast a chart for the moment of the conjunction or prevention.

and reception, except if Saturn is in a fire sign. And if Mars were found already in a connection with Saturn, then surely the clouds [will] increase and there [will be] an increase in the winds and a decrease of rain, and the atmosphere is spoiled from not having moisture other than what is not already acquired by it—then there [will be] a scarcity of rain during the gathering and reception.

§4: The rains in the days

And when knowledge is desired of what the rain in which day will be in half of that month, make a connection of the Moon with a sign. So when it enters one of the stakes and it is connected with Mercury or Venus or with the planets which were connected with it in the first of the month and it has entered a sign of water and is connected with these planets which I have mentioned to you, rain will come that day, if Allah wills.

§5: Chapter of the rain in each day the Moon is entering the rainy signs

Know that the rainy signs are Scorpio, Cancer, Aquarius, and Pisces. The strongest planets of rain are Venus and the Moon.

And when Venus [would be] in one of these rainy signs and were in the first [part] of the sign or in its middle [part], and when the Moon has passed in these signs and is connected with Venus, it is an indication that there will be rain in that day, and it will continue until the country is swimming from an abundance of rain; and [likewise] if Venus and Mercury were in the rainy signs and the Moon has passed in the rainy signs and connects with one of them, and it[11] is in the last [part] of the sign, this is indicative of much rain, but less [so] than the first [part].[12]

And if the Moon and Venus were found in the rainy signs and Mercury was not in the rainy signs, it also is indicative of rain.

---

[11] The text is unclear which planet is meant, but since by definition the Moon has to be in the same respective degree in order to join with them, it is moot: all of the planets would have to be in the last part of the sign.

[12] That is, there will still be rain if it is in the last part of the sign, but not as much as in the previous case, where Venus was in the first or middle parts.

And if the Moon and Mercury approach the rainy signs and Venus was not in the rainy signs, it is an indication of rain.

And if the Moon were in one of the rainy signs and connecting with Venus and Mercury, or [one of them] were in the sign that the Moon was in, it is indicative of continual rains until it departs the Moon.

And when the Venus, Mercury, and the Moon have not connected with unfortunate planets, and the unfortunate planets were not assembled with them in the signs, it is an indication of rain on that day. And if they were connected with the unfortunate planets or were with them, that indicates a retention of the rains.

And Venus, Mercury, and the Moon, when they have entered into the rainy signs, it is indicative of rain that day. And Venus, [if] she [were] with the Moon and Mercury in a sign, or gathered with Mercury and the Moon, it is indicative of rain that day.

Mercury and Venus, [if] either of them [were] in Capricorn, and the Moon were in Taurus, Cancer, or Pisces, it is indicative of rain in that day.

And [if] the Moon were in Taurus, Virgo, or Capricorn, and connected with Venus or Mercury by reception, it is indicative of rain.

And the strongest is [if] the Moon [would be] with the Tail of the Dragon in a sign. [If] the Moon were in Taurus with the Tail, and the Moon is departing from Saturn, and Venus and Mars are in Aquarius, and Mercury is in Pisces or Capricorn, it is indicative of rain, if Allah wills.

ON RAINS

In the name of Holy and Merciful God, the letter of Māshā'allāh on rains and winds, translated from Arabic into Latin by Amagro Drogone.[1]

Māshā'allāh said, inspect the inferior planets and the parts of their heavens. And you should know that the heaven of the Moon extends up to the heaven of Saturn,[2] and the Moon takes from it and allots much concerning dew and hail, and the Moon receives the vapor of the earth.[3]

When therefore it is connected from the heaven of Saturn up to the heaven of the Moon, and were the Moon descending[4] and Saturn standing still, it will be a sign of rains lasting a short time. And [this] happens if clouds meet each other in the air, part to part, to each other.[5] If however Saturn were descending and the Moon ascending, and the gate of the heavens were open, that of one to the other, it is a signification of rains in that hour—especially if Saturn were in Cancer and the Moon in Capricorn, and the Tail were in agreement (or the Tail were in Aquarius). And [if] one of them is descending and the other is ascending, and the Moon quickened in [her] advancing,[6] the year will be very rainy and watery. But if the Moon were, along with this description concerning Venus, occidental and descending, Venus[7] signifies a multitude of winds and dew and their lastingness. And

---

[1] Or Amager/Amagrus Drogo. The *CCAG* editors believe this is Hugo of Santalla; otherwise, unknown.

[2] Although it seems here that Māshā'allāh is making a statement about their orbs (which are the highest and the lowest orbs), later on he will speak about different planets' "heavens," and it seems he means their signs: so for instance the "heavens" of Mars and Venus are linked, as are those of Mercury and Jupiter. These planets' domiciles are in opposition, as are those of Saturn and the luminaries.

[3] See *Tet.* I.4.

[4] This vocabulary sounds like "slowing down" and "being stationary."

[5] *Obviant sibi, pars parti ad invicem. Obvio* can also mean to oppose or go against, so this sounds like a clashing of clouds; but I am not sure exactly what Māshā'allāh means.

[6] *Addiderit Luna in incessu.*

[7] Reading the sentence so far with *CCAG*, which seems to contain a grammatical error in *descendenti* (*Si autem fuerit Luna cum hac narratione in Venere et occidentalis et descendenti, Venus significat...*). But BN reads differently, though again with ambiguity about what the role of the "description" plays here: "But if the Moon were, along with this description concerning Venus, and Venus occidental from the Sun and descending, it signifies..." (*Si autem fuerit luna cum hac narratione in Venere, et Venus occidentalis a sole et descendens, significat...*). Either way, I'm not sure what it all means.

if Saturn were retrograde, and the Moon advancing less, it will be reduced in its number.

And the Tail in Aquarius signifies a multitude of obscurities[8] and a scarcity of rains, and the condensing[9] of cold, and snows; and they will be multiplied up until where the snows approach,[10] up to a six-day period[11] or more.

And you should know that the Moon is bound up[12] in the heaven of Saturn; therefore, if Saturn were in Cancer, and the Moon in Capricorn or Pisces or Scorpio, it is a signification of waters. And in Libra (which is the exaltation of Saturn), and Aquarius (the domicile of Saturn) are signified the duration of rain and the multitudes of snow.

And if Saturn were in Aquarius, but the Moon in Leo (the opposite to [Aquarius]), and one of them [were] ascending and the other descending, it signifies plenty of waters. And however much the Moon will proceed up to Leo, descending, and the waters of the springs which are in Aquarius come down to the riverbank; and this signifies rain. And if both were ascending, there will be strong and hot winds with obscurity, and rains will come to be until they descend. After[wards] there will be winds, and the rains will be ceased. And when Saturn were in another place from this one (namely that he is in Aries or Taurus or Gemini), nor will he be in signs in which his nature is strengthened, there will not be rains.

And you should know that there are places in which rains are bound together, just as in Armenia, in elevated places, in the third[13] clime, from the entrance of the Sun in nineteen degrees of Taurus—and this because the Sun's heat is not reinforced in the third clime—and that obscurity heats up in the air and becomes still in the air, and it will be reinforced.[14] But if the Sun were in the nineteenth degree of Taurus up to the nineteenth degree of Scorpio, rains will be multiplied in the southern villages; and those[15] which are from the direction of the south, and the villages which are near to the line of the equator of the day (and they belong to the blacks and the *Zingi*

---

[8] I.e., difficulty of vision, shadiness, darkness.
[9] *Constrictionem.*
[10] Reading *accedant* with BN for *accederant.*
[11] Tentative translation of *6 diaetas.*
[12] *Ligatur.*
[13] CCAG reads "seventh," but this is contradicted by the statement below about the third.
[14] Following BN here in word order. *CCAG* also breaks off the sentence in appropriately.
[15] One would expect the translator to say "and *in* those," *etc.*, using the ablative; but the following is in the nominative.

and *Oaden*),¹⁶ and the southern villages; and the villages which are near the equator of the day in the first clime.

And they even look in this [matter] from the first minute of Aries and Libra in the root of the signification, and where the planets of rains are from the entrance of the Sun in the ten degrees after they will be made equal.¹⁷ And if Venus were with the Sun, and she were conjoined with the Moon, and if certain planets [were?] in the hours of the Moon,¹⁸ it is a signification for rain; but the stronger signification belongs to the Moon, because she has moisture. And whichever planet [were] in the nineteenth degree of Taurus, is a signification of rain, but not like the Moon's signification, because she is opposite Saturn's heaven.

Therefore, if you wanted to know this, look at the entrance of the Sun in the first¹⁹ minute of Aries, or nineteen degrees of Scorpio, and if the planetary Lords of their heavens, and they inspected it,²⁰ and the Moon would assist them, it signifies a multitude of rain. But if [she?] did not inspect the Lord of the Midheaven of her fluid,²¹ nor to a planet, and she will be decreasing in her advance, then it signifies rain.²² And likewise the Moon signifies just as Saturn [does] if she were under the rays of the Sun or in his opposite, for then she signifies concerning rain. Because in these two hours she receives and has thrown down²³ in place.

And then inspect²⁴ the place of Saturn and the Moon: and if it were then as I have said, and you want to know the hour of the rain in that year, see

---

16 Unknown.
17 Māshā'allāh seems to be speaking about the first ten days or so after the *days* are made equal in length, after the equinoxes.
18 This sentence seems to have suffered greatly in the manuscript transmissions. I am following *CCAG*, with an addition in brackets based on an alternate reading in the footnotes.
19 Adding from BN.
20 This sentence is difficult to understand. It is unclear to me which domicile Lords are meant (Mars rules both Aries and Scorpio). "It" (*eam*) could mean the domicile, but it could also refer to the Moon, who is spoken of again immediately below in connection with inspecting (aspecting).
21 Following *CCAG*'s *liquamenti* for BN's *ligamenti* (bandage, binding), though I cannot find another record of this word. See the following footnote.
22 *Si vero non inspexerit domino medii caeli sui liquamenti/ligamenti nec planetae, et minuens erit in incessu suo, significat tunc pluviam.* But what is also odd is the translator's use of the dative with *inspicio*, which is a normal transitive verb taking the accusative. Therefore my translation is somewhat tentative, though I do not see how the Latin could be otherwise translated.
23 *Deiecit*.
24 Here the translator uses *inspicio* in its normal transitive sense.

when the Sun is in Aquarius and the Moon turns[25] with him: it signifies a scarcity of rain. Likewise if Venus were to turn with the Sun in that sign, and likewise Mercury. And if they were being conjoined, the rain will not cease in that year, until[26] Venus and Mercury will be removed from the Sun. If therefore the Sun were in Aquarius (namely, the domicile of Saturn), and the Moon in Leo (the domicile of the Sun), it signifies many rains in that hour. And if Venus and Mercury were with the Sun, it signifies many rains. And if the Sun were in Pisces or in Aries, and the Moon in Cancer or in Libra or in Virgo, it signifies rain (and Sagittarius, namely up to the first part, because of the vapor which is in it).[27]

And if Mars aspected the Sun or the Moon or Venus or Mercury, or one of the two luminaries,[28] it signifies many rains, especially if they aspected each other by the conjunction[29] or the opposite aspect: because it signifies great fearful things like lightning flashes,[30] and like things of this kind. And if Mars were retrograde, those fearful things will be many.[31] And if the Moon were in Taurus and Mars in Scorpio, or the Moon in Scorpio and Mars in Taurus (which is the exaltation of the Moon), and the Sun in Aquarius or Pisces or in Aries, it signifies many rains and lightnings and lightning flashes. And if Mars were in Pisces and the Moon in Sagittarius, and the Sun in Pisces, it signifies rain and lightning flashes. And if the Sun were in Scorpio or in Sagittarius, and the Moon in Scorpio or in Sagittarius or Pisces, and Mars in Gemini or Virgo or Taurus, it signifies the movement of lightning flashes, and not much rain; and the connection[32] of lightning-flashes for the Sun in Aries, because it is the domicile of Mars.

But if it[33] aspected the Moon, or it were in Pisces (the which sign is the exaltation of Venus), and the Sun in Scorpio (the domicile of Mars) or in Libra (the domicile of Venus), there will be cold winds, and with the Sun

---

[25] *Vertit.* I am not sure what it means to "turn."
[26] Reading *donec* with *CCAG* for *cum.*
[27] *Et Sagittario quo ad primam partem scilicet, pro vapore qui est in eo.* The Latin *vapor* can also mean steam or the warmth of the Sun—so Māshā'allāh is speaking about heated moisture in the air.
[28] *CCAG* reads, "or one of the two [or a] different one" (*unum duorum vel varium*).
[29] Reading an odd abbreviation as *con.*
[30] *Fulgetrum.* Specifically, this refers to heat-lightning or lightning unaccompanied by thunder.
[31] *CCAG* reads, "the rain will be fearful."
[32] *Continuitas*, following *CCAG*; but it should be in the accusative, not the nominative.
[33] Unclear which planet is meant.

appearing in Capricorn or Aquarius (the domiciles of Saturn).[34] Note even that the heaven of Jupiter and Mercury are gathered together; likewise that of Venus and Mars.[35]

For the superior planets do not have power in themselves and through themselves (nor likewise the inferiors, except from the superiors). Therefore if Mercury aspected Jupiter in the revolution of years (which I have reported),[36] and one of them were falling[37] and [the other one] ascending, and the falling one aspected the ascending one, it signifies a multitude of winds in that year, because the heaven of Jupiter is a multiplier of winds, and Mercury signifies concerning winds.

But if the Moon were in Taurus, and Mercury aspected her from Aquarius or Pisces, and Mercury were received by Jupiter in the root of the revolution, it signifies winds.

And if Mercury were in Aquarius, and the Moon in Leo, or Mercury in Pisces and the Moon in Sagittarius or Virgo, or the Moon with Jupiter or Mercury[38] in this sign, it signifies winds. Or, were[39] Jupiter in exaltation and Mercury in Aries or in Pisces, and he aspected Jupiter, and will be connected with him, then winds are signified.

And if Mercury were in Scorpio and Jupiter in Taurus or Leo, and the Moon will be connected with Mercury from Aquarius or from Pisces or Taurus or Leo, winds are signified.

And if Mercury were in Scorpio and Jupiter in Taurus or in Sagittarius, and the Moon will be connected to him from Gemini or Virgo, winds are signified.

And if the Sun were in Scorpio or Aquarius or Sagittarius or Libra or Pisces or Aries, and Mercury [were] under the rays of the Sun, many winds are signified. And if Venus aspected him, there will be rains. And if Mars aspected him, there will be lightning flashes and lightning.[40] And if the Moon transited by him, there will be rains. And inspect concerning Mercury as I have said. But the heaven of Mars and Venus are gathered to one another.

---

[34] Ending the sentence here with *CCAG*.
[35] Following *CCAG* for this sentence.
[36] Reading as *quam retuli*.
[37] *Cadens*. Normally I would translate this as "cadent," but this passage might refer to falling and ascending in zodiacal latitude. Therefore I have kept its literal meaning.
[38] BN reads as though the Moon could be with Jupiter or Mercury in this sign; *CCAG* reads as though the Moon is with Jupiter there, *or* Mercury is there by himself.
[39] Reading *fuerit* for *erit*.
[40] *Fulgura*, presumably to be distinguished by being accompanied by thunder.

And in a revolution of the year, inspect the Moon and Venus from their opposition or in the hour of an aspect, which signify that it will be (and it will not be completed) in that hour. But if it were from Scorpio, the rain will not last.

But if Venus were[41] in Taurus or in Aquarius, and the Moon aspected her from Scorpio, and Mars[42] [were] with the Moon, there will be rain with lightning-flashes and thunder, and there will be hail; and perhaps if Saturn aspected the Moon, there will be hailstorms harming the harvests and killing birds.[43]

And if the Moon were in Scorpio or Sagittarius or Aquarius or Pisces in the revolution of the year, if Mars were aspecting the Moon from the opposite (and so he was not in Scorpio), it signifies the decrease of the aforesaid. And if it were from Scorpio, it will not make harm on account of the vapor which is in Scorpio.

And when Venus is in Scorpio or Sagittarius or Taurus, it signifies rain. The[44] retrogradation of Venus in Scorpio or Capricorn or Aquarius signifies many rains. And when the Moon recedes in the foundation of the question[45] from a superior planet, and she applied to an inferior or equal planet, it will signify rains.

But if Mars were falling and Venus ascending southern, it signifies rain if the Moon aspected him from Virgo or Leo.

If Venus were under the rays of the Sun, and the Moon aspected her from Pisces (with Venus being in[46] Taurus), or were the Moon to aspect her in Aries from Libra, it signifies much rain in that time.[47] And [if] Mars cut off her aspect, it will subtract from that rain.

If the Moon and Venus and Mercury, in the revolution of the year, were in Pisces, rains are signified. And if the Moon and Venus will be in Aquarius, there will be rains. But if they were in Aries or Taurus, a decrease of rains is signified.

But the Moon opposite the Sun in a revolution, or [opposite] Saturn or Venus, signifies the corruption of the air, and rain from dew. But if the

---

[41] Reading *fuerit* for *erit*.
[42] *CCAG* reads "Mercury."
[43] *Volucres*, a rare word for "bird" (usually *avis*); but it can also mean insects or other flying things.
[44] Adding the rest of this paragraph from *CCAG*. In BN this passage appears at the end.
[45] This sounds like a horary chart, *viz.*, the "root" chart of the question.
[46] Lit., "going along in" (*eunte in*).
[47] Or, "season."

Moon and the Lord of her domicile were adding,[48] there will be corruption from much dew, if God wills.

When the Sun enters the first minute of the twentieth degree of Scorpio,[49] take the Ascendant. If it were a watery sign, and the Moon is in a watery one, and likewise Venus, the beginning of winter will be raining, and the end moistening. And if Venus were occidental-weak, and the Moon and the Ascendant in watery signs,[50] it will be likewise: the beginning and the end moistening. It must be noted that Venus under the rays of the Sun is like a woman under a man, making waters descend.[51] And if Venus were oriental[52] of the Sun, it will be the beginning of dryness.

But if the Ascendant were not of the watery [signs], nor were the Moon in a watery one, the beginning of winter will be rainy, and the last part dry. And if the Ascendant were fiery, and its Lord in a watery [sign], then the season will be temperate, with neither much nor little rain, and it will be inclined a little bit to moisture and lightning flashes. And if the Ascendant were of the fiery [signs] and its Lord in a fiery sign, the decreases[53] of rains are signified in that year. And if the Ascendant were a fiery [sign], and its Lord in a windy sign, there will be few rains and many winds in that year. And if the Lord of the hour were wet and dewy, the year will be good. And if it were dry, it will corrupt the year. And if the Ascendant were an earthy sign, and its Lord in a watery sign, the year will be good, with many rains and dews. And if the Lord of the hour were in a fiery sign, and the Lord[54] in an angle, there will be great dryness in that year. And if the Ascendant were a watery [sign] and its Lord in a windy sign, there will be many dews in that year, and winds and mists. And if the Ascendant were a fiery [sign], and its Lord in a watery sign, that quarter of the year will be very moist with little rain, or the fair weather[55] will be multiplied and the rain decreased. And if the Ascendant were a windy [sign] and its Lord in an earthy sign, it signifies many winds, few dews.

---

[48] *Addentes.* This must mean adding in number.
[49] *CCAG* reads, "the first minute of Scorpio," but adds *minuti vigesimi gradus* two lines later.
[50] Following *CCAG*, in parallel with the previous sentence. BN reads, "and the Moon ascending in watery signs."
[51] Reading as *facens descendere aquas.*
[52] *Orientalis.* This probably means pertaining-to-arising.
[53] Following BN. *CCAG* reads, "the duration of rains."
[54] This could be the Lord of the Lord of the hour (as before), or perhaps the Lord of the Ascendant. It is unclear.
[55] Following *CCAG*. BN reads, "coldness."

Likewise, when the Sun will be conjoined with some one of the three superiors in the Ascendant, and one of them is in the 4th house [domicile?], it signifies rain in the first quarter of the month or year. Likewise if it were in the 7th house [domicile?], it will be in the middle quarter of the year. Likewise if it were in the 10th, the dew will be in three quarters of the month or year. Likewise if it were in the 4th,[56] it will be in the end of the year. Likewise in its opposite and in its square [aspects]. Principally in winter or the spring, the signification hastens.[57] Take its signification rightly, and believe in the rains and the flowings of the waters.

Likewise, if it were in the summer, it will signify great and strong hail—this is if the conjunction or opposition were in earthy or watery signs, for this signifies a multitude of rain and flowing. But if they were in fiery signs, they signify wars, battles, captivities, slaughters, arsons, fires, and the wasting of vegetation. If their conjunction were in a sign of winds, and one of them will square one of the earthy signs, it is a signification of winds and their roaring, and the corruption of the fruits, and a multitude of tempests.

If you want to know the hour, [it will be] namely when the Sun would apply to the place of a planet which was in the square.[58] And this signification will be elongated when the Moon is in the Ascendant or in the opposite. Moreover, if someone said "where will this be," inspect the conjunction of the planets: if they were in the Ascendant, it will be from the direction of the east; if in the Midheaven, from the south; if in the seventh, in the west; if in the fourth, in the north. Secure [the matter] on this basis and you will find [the answer], God willing.

When there is great dryness, if you wished to know when it will rain upon the face of the earth, it will be seen where the Head of the Serpent[59] is, or the star which is called *Azaphora*.[60] When one of these is in a domicile which

---

[56] The only problem is that the 4th will have been used twice here: once to mean the start of the year, then to mean the end. So it could be that the text itself is wrongly attributing the quarters.

[57] Following BN. *CCAG* inexplicably says, "Principally in the winter, it hastens with Sagittarius or Venus."

[58] Following BN. *CCAG* reads, "know when the Sun would apply to the place of rain, which is in the square." But note the similarity between this and the last paragraph of *Chapter of the Rains in the Year* above, where the Arabic Māshā'allāh speaks of the Head of the *Dragon*. So this could simply refer to the North Node.

[59] That is, α Ophiuchus, *Ras alhague*.

[60] I am uncertain about the identity of this star. The name looks Greek, but I have not been able to find it. It may be from an Arabic word *al-z—*.

is called water, calculate the Moon. When she dismounts in a watery domicile, it will rain quickly.

ON THE REVOLUTION OF THE YEARS OF THE WORLD

The book of Māshā'allāh on the revolution of the years of the world, begins

May God watch over you, and increase life for you; may God raise you up and lay open for you the revolution of years, the knowledge and disposition of which is that you should know when the Sun enters the first minute of the sign of Aries. And when you know this, you will set up the Ascendant and the four angles, and the rest of the places of the celestial figure by degrees and minutes, and you should set up the places of the planets in the signs by degrees and minutes, and their condition according to the order of the circle (namely by their direct motion and by retrogradation, slowness and[1] quickness, and their elevation and latitude, and the projection of their rays). And know that a retrograde planet has no strength over good, until it goes direct.

After these things, look at the Ascendant and its Lord, and at the Lord of the exaltation of the Ascendant (if there were an exaltation of some planet in that sign), and the Lord of the bound and of the triplicity, and the place of the Lord of the hour from the Ascendant, and see of what kind are their places relative to each other, and what kind they are in the place of the enmity of the Ascendant, and which in a place of friendship. For if the Lord of the Ascendant appeared in an inimical or hostile place from the Ascendant, it signifies the detriment of that same clime, according to the quantity of the hostility or contrariety of the Lord of the Ascendant with the horoscope. And if it were in the sixth place, it will be infirmity; if it were in the eighth, it will be death; if it were in the twelfth, it will be enmity or discord, according to the nature of the sign in which the Lord of the Ascendant is. Likewise if the Lord of the bound, and the Lord of the exaltation and triplicity were in the said places [that are] inimical to the Ascendant—but this will be below what is signified by the Lord of the Ascendant.

---

[1] Following BN for the rest of this paragraph.

Chapter 1: On the places of the luminaries from the Ascendant

After these things, look at the places of the luminaries from the Ascendant, and from the Lord of the Ascendant. Because if the revolution were in the day, and the Sun aspected the Ascendant or[2] its Lord, and the Sun were free from the malefics, it signifies the strength and attainment or victory of the citizens of that clime—and better than that if the Sun ceded his disposition to the Lord of the Ascendant, and if he were received in the place in which he was. Because if it were just as we have said, the wealthy and powerful of that clime will be humbled by and subjected to the master of that clime, and prosperity and peace will be bestowed upon him, and health, with a good condition, by the will of God. And likewise the Moon, if she bore herself toward the Ascendant and its Lord just as we stated regarding the Sun, if the revolution were in the night.

And if the Lords of the luminaries (or one of them) were aspecting them from a strong place, and received them, there will not be detriment in men, nor any disturbance, but they will be secure and calm, seeking justice, and judging by means of it. But if it were the reverse concerning the Sun, Moon, and the Lords of the Ascendant and the Lords of the luminaries, say everything to the contrary, and turn the good things which we have said, into bad. And look at the reception of the planets toward each other, and their hostilities, and pronounce according to what you saw regarding lands and plagues[3] in the areas which they were in charge of.[4]

Chapter 2: On the triplicities

Know that the signs signify parts of the world through their own natures, not through their places. Wherefore if a part of the world agreed with the nature of its sign,[5] what is signified will be stronger for it.

---

[2] Reading *aut* for *ut*.
[3] *Plagis*, reading it in the medieval sense. In the classical sense, "afflictions, wounds, gashes."
[4] Following primarily BN, and transferring *de partibus* to the end of the sentence.
[5] That is, with the triplicity of the sign on the angle in question. See the following chapters.

Aries and its triplicity (Leo and Sagittarius) are signs of the east; which if they came together with the Ascendant,[6] their signification will be stronger.

Taurus and its triplicity (Virgo and Capricorn) are signs of the south; wherefore if they came together with the sign[7] of the Midheaven, their signification will be greater.

Gemini and its triplicity (Libra and Aquarius) are signs of the west; which if they came together with the sign of the angle of the west, what is signified by them will be stronger.

Cancer and its triplicity (Scorpio and Pisces) are signs of the north; wherefore if they came together with the angle of the earth, what is signified by them will be stronger.

Moreover, these things which we have said are even adapted to the planets appearing in these places.

Chapter 3: On the division of the earth

Know that the earth has two divisions: the east and the south is one, because they agree in heat; and the west and the north is another, because they agree in cold. After these, the earth is divided by the seven divisions of the seven planets in the climes, according to the order of the circles. Therefore, the climes are known from the circle according to the order of the planets, just as in the Lords of the hours.

For the first clime is Saturn's, the second Jupiter's, the third Mars's, the fourth the Sun's, the fifth Venus's, the sixth Mercury's, the seventh the Moon's. But the climes are according to the nature of the circle; then there is a known thing belonging to each sign, in terms of lands and cities; and likewise in the bounds. Because perhaps there will be a city belonging to some

---

[6] *Convenerint.* That is, if one of them *were* the rising sign; and so in what follows.
[7] Reading singular here and in the next paragraph.

sign, and the bound of some planet of that sign conquers in it. Like Iraq,[8] for example, which is said to belong to Cancer, and its planet is Jupiter, since the place of Iraq is in the place of the Jupiterian bound, from the nineteenth degree of Cancer up to its twenty-seventh, which is the bound of Jupiter.[9] And the dismounting of the benefics onto this place signifies fitness around Iraq in particular; and likewise the dismounting of the malefics onto the same place signifies evil around Iraq. Likewise you will know this from the dismounting of the benefics and the malefics in the rest of the bounds, as we have already expounded this to you. Therefore, know them just as I have told you, because if you did this, it will not be concealed to you which sign or which bound belongs to a city.

Chapter 4: When it is necessary to revolve the quarters of the years

After this, look to see whether the ascending sign is fixed, movable or common, and look likewise at the Lord of the Year. Because if the Ascendant of the year were a movable sign, revolutions of the quarters in the year will be necessary, and more so if the Lord of the Year were in a movable sign. And if it were a common sign, there will be exactly two revolutions necessary in the year—that is, at the beginning of Aries and Libra—and more so if the Lord of the Year were in a common sign: therefore do even with the entrance [of the Sun] into the first minute of Libra as with the beginning of the year. And with the movable [signs], do likewise through all the quarters of the year. But if the Ascendant were a fixed sign, the revolution of the year will be conquering all the quarters of the year, and more strongly so if the Lord of the Year were in a fixed sign.

But if the Lord of the Year were in a movable sign, the abundance or want which it signified will be only in the first quarter of the year—unless [such a] distinction is even in the second, third, and fourth [quarters]: then it will be according to what that same quarter signified, in terms of abundance or want.[10]

---

[8] Reading for *Alirac* here and throughout this paragraph. Iraq is traditionally associated with Cancer, perhaps because of its southern marshes and the dominance of the Tigris and Euphrates.

[9] The bound of Jupiter in Cancer runs from 19°—25° 59'.

[10] That is, although the Aries ingress stands generally for the whole year, if the rising sign is movable certain features (like agricultural abundance or want) will only be relevant for

Chapter 5: On discovering the Lord of the Year

Therefore, if you wished to know the Lord of the Year, look in the hour of the revolution at the planet which was stronger than the rest in its own place, and which had more testimonies, and make that one the Lord of the Year in the clime in which you are. After this, give to the seven climes (from out of the clime in which you are),[11] according to what I told you before, in terms of the seven planets.[12] And I will expound to you the portions of the planets and their testimonies, so you may know the Lord of the Year.

Chapter 6: On the portions and testimonies of the planets, from which the Lord of the Year is identified

Know that the stronger of the planets is that one which is in the Ascendant, not removed from the angle, nor cadent, or the one which was thus in the Midheaven; but in the setting [angle] and the angle of the earth it will be lower than what I told you regarding strength, by one-fourth. And the eleventh sign is below the setting [angle] and the angle of the earth; and the ninth [sign] below the eleventh, and the fifth [sign] below the ninth, and the third [sign] below the fifth.

If the Lord of the Ascendant were in the horoscope, namely by 3° in front or behind its cusp, not cadent nor removed from the angle of the Ascendant,[13] it will not be necessary with it to look at another planet. Likewise the Lord of the exaltation of the ascending sign, if it were in the degrees of its exaltation. But the Lord of the triplicity, if it were in the Ascendant, will have one-third of the strength of the Lord of the Ascendant; also the Lord of the bound has one-fifth of the strength, and this according to the quantity of their strength in the signs; and the Lord of the hour has one-seventh.[14]

---

that quarter; we have to look at the other quarters individually to determine what they predict.
[11] *Ex climate in quo fueris*. The function of this is unclear to me.
[12] Māshā'allāh is probably referring to Ch. 3, in which various cities and peoples receive planetary attributions.
[13] I take this to mean that it is still in the same sign as the cusp—so if the cusp were at 2°, he would not accept its Lord at 29° of the previous sign.
[14] This paragraph could be one source for the later idea that the dignities themselves can be assigned numerical values.

And know that this comes to be if they were in the Ascendant or the Midheaven. But if they were in the west or in the angle of the earth, their strength will be decreased; likewise if they were in the eleventh, the ninth, and the fifth, it will be decreased more.

Chapter 7: On the luminaries, if they were in the angles

Know that the luminaries, if they were in one of the angles, will be the Lords of the Year—unless the one which was in an angle was impeded. Which if it were so [that it was impeded], it will signify the impediment and weakness of that same clime which is subjected to that sign. And better than that [is] if the Sun in the day were in an angle, and the Moon in the night in an angle. And likewise the nocturnal stars[15] thrive in the night, and the diurnal ones in the day. Therefore, once you have set up the revolutions of the years, begin afterwards with the consideration of the strengths, according to what I have told you.

Chapter 8: When the Lord of the Year commits dominion[16] to another

And if the Lord of the Year appeared to you, see if perhaps it would be committing its own disposition to another: that is, like if it is in the domicile of another planet, and that planet appeared in an optimal place from the Ascendant, and the Lord of the Year is also conjoined to it. Because if it were so, the one who is the Lord of that sign in which you found the governor of the year, is made the Lord of the Year, because it receives [the original Lord of the Year] from its own domicile; and better than that, if the luminaries aspected it, or [if] the Lords of [the luminaries'] signs (in which they were found) did. But if it did not[17] commit its own disposition to the Lord of its own domicile, look to see whether it has strength in its own place on top of the disposition, and its strength is just as I designated to you in the sixth chapter.

---

[15] Planets.

[16] *Dominium.* This words has a special connotation of "ownership," but it is clearly meant as a synonym for disposition (*dispositio*).

[17] BN lacks this "not" (*non*).

Chapter 9: On the strength of the Lord of the Year

If planets were joined to the Lord of the Year, and committed their own disposition to it, joy will come to that clime from every direction, according to the disposition and strength of the planets.

Chapter 10: When the Lord of the Ascendant is made into the Lord of the Year

If the luminaries (or one of them) committed their own disposition to the Lord of the Ascendant, it will not be necessary to look at another with this, because he himself is the Lord of the Year without a doubt.

Chapter 11: What things must be looked at in judgments about kings and the rustics

You will also look, for the rustics and their condition, from the Lord of the Year and its place, and from the aspect of the planets toward him. But for the king of the clime you will judge from the Lord of the Midheaven and from the Sun (namely from one [of these]), and from the conjunction and the separation of the planets from them. And of the Sun and the Lord of the Midheaven, you will choose the stronger one according to the strength of the places, and you will put down the conquering one as the significator of the king.

And if you knew the significator of the king, his condition with the rustics (in terms of good and evil) and whatever will come out for him in that same year (in terms of difficulty,[18] and abundance and want) will not lie hidden from you, by the command of God—namely, about every matter of his empire: that is, about his rustics, and his substance, about his children too and his women, and about his health and infirmity, about a foreign journey, and his strength and weakness, or about his ruin.

And know that this chapter on the king is clearer than the chapter on the Lord of the Year and the condition of the rustics, because you are looking for the king as an individual, and the rustics as a group.

---

[18] Reading *districtione* with BN for *distractione*.

And if you knew the Lord of the Year and the significator of the king of that same region, look to see who aspects it, and what kind of strength belongs to the one aspecting it, and whether they are in their own light or in the light of another, and whether it is necessary that they aspect their own places. Because perhaps the Lord of the Year will be strong, not in need, or perhaps it will be weak and in need.[19] But how this happens, I will expound to you in the following chapters.

Chapter 12: When the Lord of the Year is cadent

If the Lord of the Year were cadent from the Ascendant, not aspecting the Ascendant (in the eighth, sixth, second, or twelfth sign), then he will be in need, and therefore weakness will befall him, because he fell in a place removed from the Ascendant: and therefore he needs a planet to whom he is being joined, who would render his light to the Midheaven—and [this other planet] would strengthen him. Because if a planet had more testimonies and it were the Lord of the Year, and it were in the eighth place, then it needs a planet who would aspect it from out of the Midheaven. And every planet which does not aspect the Ascendant *does* aspect the Midheaven from a trine or sextile aspect—except for one which was in the third sign, where it is weakened and does not aspect the Midheaven.

And if the planet who was strong out of the Midheaven were the Lord of the sign in which the governor of the year (to whom more testimonies were joined) appeared, and the Lord of the Year himself were joined to him, [the planet in the Midheaven] will receive the disposition of the year and its signification, and it will be the Lord of the Year. But already before I have expounded to you this topic in the beginning of this book, and how the Lord of the Ascendant will be made strong in its own place by the Lord of its domicile, or by another.[20]

---

[19] See the next chapter.
[20] See Ch. 6.

Chapter 13: On the strength and weakness of the Lord of the Year

After this, look at the one who aspects the Lord of the Year, and pronounce what it would signify according to the quality of its place, in terms of good and evil; [and] if it were strong, strongly; and if it were weak, weakly.

Know that the aspect of the opposition signifies discord and contention, and likewise the square; but the trine or sextile aspect [signifies] friendship and concord. If the malefics aspected the significator of the year or the significator of the king from the opposition, the impediment will be from enemies. And if they aspected from a square aspect, it will be from certain people who are thought to be peacemakers, whose enmity was previously concealed. And if it were from the trine or sextile aspect, it will be from friends.

After this, look to see whether the impediment would enter upon the king or over the rustics: which if it entered upon the king, look to see whether the rustics will help him or not. But if it entered over the rustics, see whether the king would help them or not. But whether [they do or not] can be known from the status of their (the king's and the rustics') significators.

Chapter 14: On the adversary of the king

After this, look at the domicile in which there was a malefic, to see whether the significator of the king or the Lord of the Year had some testimony in it: which if it came out [like that], there will be enmity from that clime, according to the quantity of that testimony. Look even to see if perhaps the Lord of the Year were in charge, and the significator of the king were not in charge:[21] because if it were so, the enemy will be from that same clime, but the king will be weakened, and another will be led into his place. But if the significator of the king were in charge, and the Lord of the Year were not in charge, the enemy will not be from his clime, nor from his kingdom: but the king will bring them under his sway, and he will subjugate them.

Indeed once you have completed this, look at the place of the malefic planet, what kind of direction it is [in]: because the destruction will be from that direction, from the city or clime, or from the clime of that same sign.

---

21 I am not sure what situation Māshā'allāh is imagining.

The age of the general and the princes is also known from the place of the malefic from the Sun: which if it were oriental,[22] it will be a young man; and if it were occidental it will be an old man; and pronounce in this what is between them, according to what the place of the planet was, from the conjunction of the Sun up to its combustion.

Also, if a malefic were in the Midheaven, and it impeded the Lord of the Year, this will enter between all men. And if it were in the east, the evil will be from the direction of the east; and if it were in the west, it will be from the direction of the west; and likewise in the north and south, if it were in the angle of the earth or the Midheaven.

And know that nothing is worse for the status of the citizens of the land, and of a city (which belongs to that same sign in which there was a malefic), than if it is retrograde in the revolution of a year; and more strongly than that if the malefic were in an angle.

Chapter 15: On the impediment of the king

After this, look at the malefic who aspects the Lord of the Year or the significator of the king: because if it aspected from the Ascendant, it signifies that the impediment is communal;[23] and if it were in the 2nd, it will be in connection with substance; if it were in the 3rd, it will be in connection with brothers; and if it were in the 4th it will be in connection with fathers and real estate; and if it were in the fifth, it will be in connection with children; and if it were in the sixth it will be in connection with infirmities; and if it were in the seventh, it will be because of war and contention; and if it were in the eighth, it will be in connection with death; and if it were in the ninth, in connection with foreign travel; and if it were in the tenth, it will be in connection with the king and his supremacy; and if it were in the eleventh, in connection with friends; and if it were in the twelfth, in connection with enemies. And speak likewise concerning the good which it signified, by the will of God.

And if there were a malefic in a common sign, it is feared concerning the king, if his significator aspected it just as I told you before. And if the Lord of the Year were not the significator of the king, it is feared concerning the rustics, because there will be mortality in them.

---

[22] I am not sure what sense of *orientalis* and *occidentalis* is meant here.
[23] I.e., it afflicts all people generally.

Say likewise in the revolution of the years of a native, just as you have spoken in the revolution of the years of the world.

Chapter 16: On the place of the Lord of the Year

After this, look at the Lord of the Year to see in whose domicile he receives the year, and in what bound, and in what exaltation or triplicity. Then look to see of what kind his place is, out of those which we have said before. Because if [his Lords] aspected him and received him, he will be stronger.

After this, look at the sign in which the significator of the year is, whose clime it is, or whose city: because the master of that clime will be stronger, and will have happier successes, beyond the rest of the climes.

Then, put down a planet for each clime;[24] nor will it be concealed from you, by the will of God, what will come about for the king of that clime. And know that the stronger of the kings will be he whose city or clime belongs to the Lord of the Year. Then look at him who follows by succession, and everyone who is born under that same sign in that land, or under the sign of the Lord of the Year, will be fit for the good, and there will be trust in him—unless he were impeded. And when you have done this, look to see who is making a peace agreement with or is turned against him, in terms of the places of the planets and their aspects (the opposition, and the square, the trine, and the sextile aspect), and from the domiciles out of which they are aspecting.

And know that a planet which is under the rays is like one suffering, for when it enters the solar rays, its strength recedes; and when it goes out from under the rays, it signifies increase and progress.[25]

Chapter 17: On the signification of Mercury and the Moon

Know that, of the seven planets, there are none for which fortune or misfortune varies more quickly than for the Moon and Mercury; and this comes to be on account of the multitude of their diversity and combustion. Be-

---

[24] I think this means we are supposed to look at each planet in the chart, and its condition will say something about its clime: for instance, a bad Saturn will mean something bad for the clime ruled by Saturn, *etc.*
[25] *Profectum*, which can also mean "profit" or "success."

cause a planet, if its combustion were overflowing, signifies evil, and especially every planet which was under the Sun,[26] if one of them were the Lord of the Year or the significator of the king, and one of the malefics aspected it: then the condition of the year and the king will be worse in this way than it [ever] could be. And if a diurnal planet were in his rays in a revolution of the day (and a nocturnal planet in a revolution of the night), the Sun signifies the king, because then he receives the strength of the planets. And if the Lord of the domicile of the Ascendant were under the rays of the Sun, [he will be][27] more worthy for the annual rulership. And look thoroughly at the place of the luminaries, and at the aspects of the Lords of their domiciles to them, and their own aspects to each other.

Chapter 18: On the strength of the luminaries

Consider even whether their[28] aspect had strength, because a planet will be stronger by aspect if it aspected from out of its own domicile, or its own exaltation or triplicity, or bound, or from out of a place of strength, or were it the Lord of the Lot of Fortune, and it were (in addition to what I have said) oriental or direct: for then it will be stronger than it could [ever] be.

Look also at the Lot of Fortune and its Lord, and at their places in the signs, because these [places] strengthen the Lord of the Year and the significator of the king. Which if [they][29] were impeded, look at them and their places in the signs: because the Lot of Fortune is the strength of the luminaries. But if the said significators were fit in the place of Fortune, they signify good and fitness; and if they were impeded under the rays, they signify detriment and loss according to the substance of the signs in which they are.

---

[26] This must mean the inferior planets.
[27] I take this to refer to the Sun.
[28] This must still refer to the luminaries.
[29] I believe this refers to the Lord of the Year and the significator of the king.

Chapter 19: On the planet to which the Lord of the Year is being joined

After this, look at the Lord of the Year to see to whom he is being joined: because from this direction will be trust and fear. Look also to see if the significator of the king were the Lord of the Year; and I will expound to you by means of what reason this could come about: namely like if the Lord of the Year [were] having testimony in the Midheaven, or if the Lord of the exaltation of the Midheaven committed his own disposition and strength[30] to [the Lord of the Year], or if the Lord of the Midheaven were in his[31] domicile, aspecting him.[32] For if it were so, the Lord of the Year will be the significator of the king. And if you knew this in a revolution of years, know even the significator of the king from the Lord of the Year, and know his condition from the condition of the rustics. Which, if he were the Lord of the Year, look just as I have told you in the first heading.

Look even at the Lord of the Midheaven, to see if he were under the rays, entering combustion: this signifies the death of the king. And if he has already gone out from combustion, and is not yet appearing, the Sun will be more worthy than he in the signification of the king.

After this, look to see to whom the significator of the king is being conjoined. Because if he is being conjoined to the Lord of the Year, he will commit his disposition to the rustics; and if he were separated from the Lord of the Year, and were joined to a malefic planet who is inimical to the Ascendant, he will go on his knees regarding them,[33] and the king will send in detriment upon them.[34] And if the significator of the king were joined to some planet in the eighth or in the seventh, from the opposition or the square aspect, death will be feared for the king in that same year. Likewise were he joined to their Lords outside of these places which I told you, and more strongly so if they were joined to malefics. And infirmity will be feared for him if he were joined to a planet in the third or sixth domicile (just as I told you in the beginning), or to their Lords.

---

30 This probably refers to pushing strength/virtue. See *Introduct.* §5.12.
31 I.e., the Lord of the Year.
32 This is the pushing of nature, *Introduct.* §5.13.
33 *Supplicabitur super eos.*
34 I think this means that the king will be very weak, and through this weakness will be disastrous for the country.

Likewise, you look, on every day of [the revolution] in this way (and I have told you these things), to see if the Lord of the Midheaven committed his disposition to the Lord of the Year. But if the Lord of the Midheaven did not commit it to him, [the Lord of the Midheaven] will be more worthy in this which I have said.

Look even in the twelve places of the region[35] in terms of difficulty and abundance, and in terms of fear and sorrow, and look likewise regarding the general regions of the climes and the directions.

After this, consider who is the Lord of the domicile of the Lord of the Year: which if it aspected him, and received [him], joy and security will find them; and if it did not regard[36] him, fear and trouble will find them. Which if the Lord of the Year committed disposition to the significator of the king, it will send in difficulties upon [the rustics] on account of the acquisition of substance, if their commingling were from the square aspect or the opposition; but if it were from the trine or sextile aspect, it signifies the rendering of the *census* without the coming of difficulty upon the rustics. And if it committed its own disposition without an aspect, this will be without the king's knowledge. And if it aspected the Lord of its domicile, the king will extract substances in that same year; and if it did not aspect, he will extract substance without bad intentions.[37]

After this, look at the substance of the king: and if the significator of the king were the Lord of the Midheaven in the eleventh, and the Lord of the Year in the second sign[38]…and look at the condition of the soldiers toward the king, from the Lord of the sign in which it was, and from the Lord of the bound or face, and assist these through the Lot of Fortune and its Lord: because if the significator of the king aspected [the Part's Lord], or [the significator of the king] were with [the Part], it signifies the good fortune of the king. Judge clearly in the same way for the rustics, from the Lord of the Year. And know the condition of the king from his significator; that of the powerful and the nobles, from the Lord of the Year. Because if you did this, their condition will not be concealed [from you], and what is going to come about for them in the year (of good or of evil), and in what way or for what reason, of God wills.

---

[35] Reading *regionis* for *regioni*.
[36] *Respexerit*, a rare synonym for *aspexerit*, meaning simply an aspect. I take this to be a whole-sign aspect.
[37] Lit., "without his own bad will."
[38] I have inserted this ellipse because something seems to be missing.

Chapter 20: When the Lord of the Year and the significator of the king are retrograde

After this, look at the Lord of the Year and the significator of the king, to see if they were retrograde: they signify the loss and weakness of the king, and of the citizens of that same kingdom. Indeed if they were both (or one of them) retrograde, look to see in whose bound it is retrograde, whether it is in the bound of a benefic or a malefic, and pay attention to it[39] in your work—and likewise the Lords of the domiciles [they are in]: because if a planet were retrograde in the domicile of a benefic, it will be better than in the domicile of a malefic or in the bound of a malefic. The retrogradation of the significator of the king signifies the weakness of the king, and the retrogradation of the Lord of the Year signifies the weakness of his rulership.

Chapter 21: On war

After this, look at war from the direction in which Mars was: which if he were direct, it will be from eager men who do not want to flee; and if he were retrograde, the war will be with robbers who do not rest in one place, and will not advance to war.

Indeed, Saturn signifies the difficulty of the cities of the region in which he was, according to the substance of the sign in which he appeared, and according to the substance of his place in the houses through succession (like the Ascendant and the domicile of substance) until he arrives at the 12th [domicile]. And if he were retrograde, it will be just as I told you about Mars, and this will be more severe from the conjunction. And if he were joined to the Lord of the Year, it will be more severe for the king from the lands in which he was, and the clime.

After this, look at the attainment and victory from the stronger one of the planets, because it signifies the multitude of the soldiers and their strength, just as elsewhere you look at the testimony of the planets and their strength in their own places.

---

[39] *Mitte eum.* Here and below, I take this to be the continued use of medieval meanings of *mitto* to translate the Arabic *wajuha*, "direct, guide, channel, face, confront," as in *On Elect.* §36. Clearly we are supposed to "use" this planet, but it is unclear whether it is allowed to overrule the signification of the retrograde planet.

After this, look at the quickness of the victory (or its slowness) from Jupiter, Saturn, and the testimonies of their conjunction, and the nature of their profection in the root, according to the course of the circle in the greater years (in which the middle conjunction comes to be, which is changed from triplicity into another triplicity); the lesser one, which comes to be from their profection in the root, [signifies] a change[40] of sects and kingdoms.[41] For this signifies what I have told you regarding their conjunction in three ways, which I will reveal to you in the following chapter.

Chapter 22: On the signification of the three superiors

If you sought concerning this, do just as you do in the revolution of the years of a native regarding the root of the nativity, because you will take the signification of sects and kingdoms from the conjunction of Saturn and Jupiter, and their change from triplicity to triplicity. Look even at the presence of the three planets which are above the Sun, and at their places in the fixed and movable signs, and the common ones, and pay attention to it[42] in the hour of the destruction of things, as I will reveal to you concerning the course of Saturn and Mars, and I will expound all of these things.

Know that if the malefics (namely Saturn and Mars) were in a sign [made] in the image of men, and one malefic were joined to the other, and it were direct or retrograde, from the conjunction and the square aspect or the opposition, there will be pestilences in men. But if it were retrograde, it will be more insidious[43] and faster. And it behooves you to see whether the aspect or conjunction is from some angle: which if it were so, it will be more insidious and strong. Look then to see in which angle it is.

But if it was Saturn who is slower, in the fourth or in the Midheaven, and a retrograde planet who is being joined to him in the seventh, this evil will come from the direction of the west, and the king will be made great, and will be extended and strengthened. And if he were slower in the west,[44] or

---

[40] Reading *[significat] mutationem* for *mutatio*.
[41] *Cf. On Roots* Chs. 10-12. There, Māshā'allāh attributes changes of religion to the greater conjunction of Saturn and Jupiter. The middle conjunction, that of Saturn and Mars, signifies wars.
[42] *Mitte eam.* See note above. *Eam* is feminine and so could refer to the "presence" or "signification"; but presumably we should pay attention to everything mentioned.
[43] *Calidius.*
[44] I.e., in the seventh.

the one who is being joined to him [were] retrograde in the fourth, this will begin in the region I will tell you, until it comes to the west.

After this, look at the manner of the inception from the direction of[45] the quicker planet who is being joined to the heavier one; and know that evil will come about when the quick planet proceeds to the place of the heavier and slower one. And know that the retrograde and conjoined one, that is, he who is being joined to the heavier one, if it were in a common sign, there will be death from war or from killing; and in fixed and immobile [signs] it will be according to what the stronger of the malefics signified in its own places. If the stronger one were Mars, it will be from war or an infirmity which is hot; which if Saturn were stronger, the death will be from every infirmity which was of the likeness of Saturn. And commingle the strength of Mars to him. And if what we said before were outside the angles, [the evil] will be small, [and] afterwards it will be dissolved.

Chapter 23: On a year to be feared

If you wished to turn the years[46] in which one should have fear, see[47] whether there is a conjunction of Saturn in that same year:[48] which if there were one, it will be more evil; and if there were not one, it will be easier. Likewise the Lord of the Year or the significator of the king, if they transited past a slow and malefic planet in an angle: then it will be feared because of its signification, just as I told you concerning destruction and death.

Also, look at the malefics, to see if they were in such a condition as we have described above in their place of the night or day. Because Saturn in a diurnal and masculine sign impedes less, and Mars in a feminine sign and place of the night is of lesser impediment.

After this, look to see whether [the malefics] are received in their places or not. Because if they were received, their impediment will be less; and if there were an infirmity in that same year, [people] will not die (except for a few). And if they signified killing, there will not be wounds, and there will not be killing (except for moderately), and men will feel pity with each other.

---

[45] *Parte*. That is, from what he represents—this is not a reference to primary directions.
[46] Does this refer to looking at successive revolutions?
[47] Reading *aspice* for *accipe*.
[48] But a conjunction with whom?

Chapter 24: On the signification of the Head and Tail of the Dragon of the Moon

Know that the Head of the Dragon corresponds to the benefics, and the Tail aids the malefics.[49] And so, look at the conjunction of the Head and Saturn, because it signifies the substance of the sign in which they are conjoined, just as it signifies in an eclipse of the luminaries. For if it were in some way in Aries and his triplicity, it will be in beasts and wolves according to the substance of the sign in which they are being conjoined. And if it were in Taurus and its triplicity, it will be in trees and herbs, and there will be few rains and [little] *annona*. And if they were conjoined in the airy signs, men and birds will find impediment, and the winds will blow. And in watery signs, rains and water will be multiplied, and fish and cold, and locusts and the creeping things of the earth will be multiplied.

And look for the square aspect of a malefic and the Tail, and their conjunction, because they would signify war and famine, and a multitude of fear; and there will be great cold, and a multitude of evil. And if Saturn were joined with the Tail, it signifies famine and a scarcity of good, and the strength of cold, and the destruction of trees, and therefore it will be in the direction[50] in which it is. And if the Sun burned up a planet in that direction, this will be stronger in that direction than in the rest of the directions.

Chapter 25: On the signification of a planet in the signification of wars if it were slow, retrograde, or direct

Know that a slower planet signifies war, and a retrograde one signifies flight. Indeed a direct one signifies peace, and especially if a benefic aspected it from the Midheaven. And if the Lord of its domicile (or the Lord of the triplicity, or the Lord of the bound, or the Lord of its exaltation) aspected that planet, it signifies a multitude of allies from relatives and others, according to its quantity (which I have told you).

---

[49] Normally a medieval text would say that the Head is of the nature of the benefics, and the Tail of the malefics, and that the Head aids both (it aids the benefics in their goodness, and the malefics in their badness), and the Tail harms both. We should not read too much into the word choices here regarding corresponding and aiding.

[50] *Parte*, here and in the rest of the sentence. It could refer to the cardinal directions of the signs (fiery signs the east, *etc.*), but might also refer to lands ruled by the various signs.

Look even at the condition of the master of the war from the planets from which the signification is taken. Because if it were in its own domicile, he will be from the household members of the king, and is known; and if it were in its own exaltation, he will be noble and useful to the kingdom; and if it were in the triplicities, he will be below what I said, but he will be known, and he is below them. But if it were not one of these, he will not be known nor influential, and perhaps it will be said about him that he was born from fornication.

And know that the diurnal planets are the Sun, Saturn, and Jupiter, and [they are] masculine in the day, and feminine in the night. And the nocturnal planets [are] the Moon, Mars, and Venus, and they are feminine in the day, masculine in the night. But Mercury is masculine with the masculine ones, feminine with the feminine ones, also nocturnal with the nocturnal ones, diurnal with the diurnal ones.[51]

Chapter 26: On the condition of the king when his significator is entering combustion

If the significator of the king is entering combustion in the revolution of the year, the king of that region will die in that same year. And if it were in the extremity[52] of the rays, grief and sorrow will enter upon him—but if a benefic aspected it, he will escape. And if what I told you were the case, and he has already transited combustion, anger and contention will enter upon him, [but] afterwards he will be loosened from it, and his condition will be made fortunate—unless a malefic aspects him, because then it signifies the prolongation of those things which I said, and their difficulty; and it will be feared concerning him according to the nature of the sign—whether it was an infirmity or death.

Therefore, look at the hour of that signification from the time of the significator and the malefic. And likewise, if a malefic aspected the significator of the king from the opposition or the square aspect, or from the conjunction, it will be feared concerning him, if what I said were in an angle; and the

---

[51] According to Ptolemy (*Tet.* I.7), Mercury is considered diurnal when he rises before the Sun, and nocturnal when he rises after the Sun. But other Hellenistic authorities give other formulations. Valens's comment on this same topic suggests aspectual relations as well (*Anth.* II.1).
[52] *In summitate*. This probably means the outer edges of combustion.

time of it will be in the combustion of the significator, and in the arrival of that same malefic to the significator or to the Midheaven, or to the Ascendant, unless a benefic would relieve him by aspect, and this malefic would be an ally in nature. And if he who was a malefic will be the significator of the king, destruction will enter upon men from the direction of the king, and more strongly so if it were in an angle: then it signifies that he will not be bothered[53] by their destruction.

And if what I told you with him were in the Midheaven, there will be difficulty from certain strangers, and this will be wholly in the place of the malefic if it were in the east, and likewise if it were in the west; and if it were in the Midheaven, it will be generally in the rest of men, and especially in the area of *Banāt na ͨ sh*[54] (that is, Ursa Major, through which the north is signified); and if you said in the northern direction, and if it were in the direction of the angle of the earth, it will be in the direction of the east and *Accenden*,[55] that is, of the blacks; and the benefics likewise will bear the significations. Therefore, examine the directions in which [the benefics] were, unless the benefics were retrograde and in a bad place (that is, in their descensions, or in the oppositions of their own domiciles): because these places belong to their bad fortune, in which they are weakened. And look at the planet from which the king and his condition is signified, and pronounce according to the being of the planets and their profection through individual days, concerning difficulty and want and abundance, concerning good or evil.

After this, look for the receiving of light and its pushing, because this signifies what is going to come about for the rustics.

Chapter 27: Whether there is going to be war, and who would attain victory

And if you were asked about war, whether there was going to be one, and who would attain victory, look for him (for whom you wished to look) to see what kind of condition he would have in that year, and how the significator of the king and the Lord of the Year aspect him: which if [the significator of

---

[53] *Fatigabitur.*
[54] *Benetnaas.* Lit., "daughters of the bier/coffin," the grouping of stars Ursa Major *α—η*, especially *η* (who is also known as Alkaid). See Kunitsch and Smart 2006, p. 57.
[55] Unknown, but undoubtedly a region in Africa south of the lands conquered by the Arabs.

the querent]⁵⁶ were [in] a strong place, and the significator of the king did not aspect him, and the Lord of the Year *did* aspect him, it will be a grave matter for the master of the question, and the king will not help him, but there will be allies from the household members of the king. And if the significator of the king did aspect him, predict the aid of the king towards him, according to the aspect in terms of strength and weakness. Which if it were of the nature of an enemy,⁵⁷ say he is going to be affected by an injury from him; and if it were of the nature of making peace, judge according to what you found; and therefore I have indicated this to you so that you may imitate it, and you may know how you should look at his concern; because something will not be concealed from you by this method in the description of it. And know his departure rationally, just as I have told you before in the chapter on the revolution, and you should not lose [sight of] the destruction nor fitness without looking at it, and you should see with this the aid of the planets toward him according to the substances of the domiciles, through the longness and shortness⁵⁸ of their Lords.

Chapter 28: On the impediment of the citizens of that clime

Know that a planet which was under the rays impedes the citizens of that clime, and destroys their condition, so they may acknowledge themselves to be subdued and to be subjects; and more strongly than that if it were in an angle with the revolution, or [if] a malefic aspected [the planet].⁵⁹

Because if it were just as I have told you, under the rays, and it were at the end of the sign in which it is, and a malefic planet aspected it from the front part, and another malefic from the back part,⁶⁰ this clime will suffer according to the quantity of the aspect of the malefic. But if it were a conjunction in one sign, the whole of them will suffer; and if it were an opposition, half of them; but if it were from the square aspect, one-fourth of them. But if Saturn went before him, and Mars were after him, they will be taken captive,

---

⁵⁶ It is unclear how to differentiate this from the other significators—or perhaps we are now speaking about a horary chart *in relation to* the revolution of the year of the world?
⁵⁷ E.g., by a square or opposition; the rest of the sentence ("making peace") must refer to sextiles and trines.
⁵⁸ *Per longitudinem ac brevit[at]em.* I am not sure what this means.
⁵⁹ Presumably this refers to a retrograde planet who is the Lord of the Year, or perhaps in the Ascendant.
⁶⁰ This must refer to besieging.

and only a few of them will be killed. But if Mars went before him, and Saturn were after him, they will be killed.

Chapter 29: On the enemies of the king

For these people, look at the malefic who aspects the significator of the king. If it aspected him from out of a sign in which the king had testimony, the enemy will be from his land, by the quantity of the testimony. And if it aspected from out of the domicile of the significator of the king, the enemy will be from his household members. And if it aspected him from his own exaltation, [the enemy] will be of the nobles, from those who are like him, and of his rank. But the triplicity and the bound signify the citizens of his rulership.

And know that the trine and sextile aspects signify relatives. And the opposition [signifies] enemies, and the first square aspect[61] signifies the house of the father, but the second square signifies influential people and those well-born, similar to the king, and of those who are fit for a kingdom. For the conjunction, look to the sign about which we have spoken: because if [the significator of the king] had testimony in it, he will be of those relatives who were nourished with him. And if he did not have testimony, their lineage will be one.[62] Observe this chapter very well.

Chapter 30: On the power of the luminaries

After this, look at the places of the luminaries, and at their strength, and at their separation and conjunction, likewise to whom they are being joined, or by the same token being separated: because the conjunction of the sextile or the aspect of trine is weak, but the opposition, square, and [corporal] conjunction strong. Observe this chapter very well, because it signifies the

---

[61] Again, this aspect is cast forward in the order of signs, into a later degree. The second square aspect is cast backward against the order of signs, into an earlier degree. Here Māshā'allāh is saying that if the malefic falls on the fourth from the significator (i.e., the significator casts a "first" square aspect to the malefic), then it pertains to the father; on the tenth, it pertains to an authority.

[62] *Erit eorum progenies una.*

quantity of their strength; and I will indicate to you generally the work of the seven planets, and their signification:

The Sun signifies the king, the Moon the generality of the vulgar, Jupiter signifies nobles, Mars signifies warriors, Saturn signifies the religious men of faith, Venus signifies women, Mercury signifies businessmen and boys. Therefore look to see, if one of these were a significator, whether it has a portion of rulership in that year. Because if it had a portion in that year, destruction and detriment will enter in beyond that which I said. And its portion is like if it is in the Ascendant or in the Midheaven by its own degree and sign—except for Venus and the Moon, because these, if they were in their own domiciles in the west or in the angle of the earth, signify a strong impediment, because these two are of the same nature;[63] and Mars likewise is nocturnal, but he is below them [in strength]. But Jupiter and Saturn and the Sun will be of their nature; and more strongly than that if the Ascendant and the Midheaven is in their domiciles. Every masculine planet will be stronger in the east, and likewise its domicile. Thus, even if it were eastern, and the feminine planets are stronger in the west; and it will be better than that if they were southern, and likewise their domiciles.[64]

Chapter 31: On the division of the world according to the three superior planets

Know that the world is divided into three divisions according to the natures of the three planets which are above the Sun—namely according to their substances and complexions. Therefore, the upper part of the world belongs to Saturn, and the middle part of the world belongs to Jupiter (and it

---

[63] I.e., by sect. the Ascendant and Midheaven are conceived of as being masculine and diurnal.

[64] Māshā'allāh is drawing together the planets and the angles by the analogy of sect and elemental qualities. In other words, if a given planet is aspecting the luminaries, then that type of person will be affected most during the year; and if they are in angles appropriate to themselves, and especially if their domiciles are on those angles, then the significations will be even more relevant and powerful. So if Venus (a feminine, nocturnal planet) is in the seventh or fourth (both signifying a loss of light, and akin to femininity), and especially if Taurus or Libra is on that (or an) angle, then the people she signifies will even more certainly be affected.

is the temperate[65] part, like the substance of Jupiter); but the lower part belongs to Mars, which is the hot part, and it is according to the substance of Mars.

And the Moon participates with Saturn in his part, because her sign is opposite the sign of Saturn. Therefore, from the quality of the intemperate years of this part of the citizens, there is a scarcity of wisdom and customs, and a cutting-off of piety, and forgetfulness; also, their colors are red and white, but the whiteness is like leadenness.[66] Their complexion is even of the darkness of the earth, and of their air.

And Mercury participates with Jupiter, because his domicile is opposed to his domicile. Also, the quality of the year of the citizens of this part effects wisdom, certitude, religion, variety and the conjoining of piety, and the unique shrewdness of [their] minds;[67] and their colors are of diverse complexion, namely commingled of whiteness and blackness and redness, because their domiciles are commingled from the cold of the earth and the heat of the air. Therefore the division of these is more worthy and more valuable than the rest of the divisions, and their land (the land of the philosophers and the wise) is better than the other lands.

And Venus participates with Mars, because her domicile is opposed to his domicile. Also, just as we have said before in terms of the quality of the year of that same part of the citizens, there is the shamefulness and desire of Venus, and drinking parties and games, according to the places of its planets; and their colors are commingled from the heat of the earth and the air.

And the Sun participates with Jupiter and Mercury in their parts.

Chapter 32: On the division of the climes

Also, the climes are divided according to these ways, in worldly quality and colors of bodies according to the order of the circle in the latitude of its circle. Even after this [the climes] are divided over the twelve signs, which are the parts of the circle; and in these are 360 lesser segments divided by the degrees of the Sun, which make 21,600 minutes. But the lesser minutes are

---

[65] Remember that "temperateness" in traditional thought has to do with proper *mixtures*. So, Māshā'allāh is saying that the part of Jupiter is a harmonious mixture of the extreme qualities of Saturn and Mars, tempering their extremes.
[66] *Livido.* This word can also mean "black-and-blue."
[67] *Singularia ingeniorum acumina.*

not necessary, except in a revolution of the years of the world, and namely in a revolution of the year pertaining to the topic of the Sun,[68] so that the degree of the Ascendant and the quarters may not be concealed from you.

Chapter 33: On the nature of the winds and triplicities

The east and its wind is hot and dry; the west and its wind is cold and moist; the south and its wind is hot and moist; the north and its wind is cold and dry. Thus also Aries and its triplicity is hot and dry. Taurus and its triplicity is cold and dry. Gemini and its triplicity is hot and moist. Cancer and its triplicity is cold and moist.

Chapter 34: On the number of cities in each clime

Also, they described that in the seven climes which is the world, there are cities and castles and villages according to the number of the twelve signs of heaven.

Likewise, the cities [are] just like the twelve signs, which are great cities, out of which there are two in every clime: namely two of Saturn, two of Jupiter, two of Mars, two of Venus, one[69] of the Sun, one of the Moon, two of Mercury. And I will reveal to you how many cities, villages and castles they said there were in the seven climes. For in the first clime they said there were 3,100; and in the second clime, 1,713; in the third, 1,077; in the fourth, 2,944; in the fifth, 3,006; in the sixth, 3,408; in the seventh, 3,300.

Chapter 35: When the Sun commits his own disposition to the Moon

Therefore, look at the revolution in which, if the Sun commits disposition to the Moon—that is, if the revolution were in the night—look at the Moon and her place from the Ascendant, to see if it agreed so that she would be the Lady of the disposition; [then] look at the Lord of her domicile, and the aspect of the planets to him, and speak according to what you saw concern-

---

[68] *In capitulis Solis.* I think this may refer to a revolution of the years of a nativity.
[69] Reading *una* for *duae*.

ing the aspect of the malefics and benefics, and their conjunction. And look at her place from Saturn, what kind it is (namely whether she is being joined to him or being separated from him). Moreover, look for the increase or decrease of her light.

Also, look to see whether an eclipse would happen to her in that year, or not. After this,[70] look at the eclipse of the Moon, and at its place, and at the eclipse of the Sun, and at its place, and at the aspect of the planets to it.

And know that if the Lord of the Ascendant were impeded in that year, the king will send in detriment upon the rustics, and their condition will be made severe according to the substance of that sign, in that same land which belonged to that sign. For example, if the Ascendant of the year were Libra, and Venus were cadent or retrograde, or under the rays, the land of Libra will be destroyed, and infirmities and pestilence will happen to it.

After this, look to every sign according to the nature of its Lord, and its place from it, and their fitness and detriment will be according to the aspect, and speak concerning this according to what you saw. And if you made good concerning these things, look at the second sign, and at its Lord, then at the third and its Lord, just as I have told you, until you complete the twelve signs. And you will look better in the signs of the angles, because they have a strength beyond the rest of the signs.

Chapter 36: On the signification of Mars and of the other planets in the angles, if they were the Lords of the Year

Know that if Mars were in the Midheaven at the hour of the revolution, it will signify this: that the king will put some people in the gibbet; and if he were in the Ascendant or in the angle of the west, he will cut off the hands of some people of his rulership; and in the angle of the earth, he will kill [them].

And if Saturn were in the Ascendant, it signifies famine, death, infirmities, and vehement and harmful winds.

And if Mercury were the Lord of the Year, and he were free from the malefics, and the benefics aspected him, the year will be good and useful for the wise, merchants, and boys. And better than that if he were received by

---

[70] I.e., if indeed an eclipse *would* happen.

the Lord of the domicile in which he was. But if you found contrary things, say the contrary.

And if the Moon were in the Ascendant, and she were free from the malefics, rains will be multiplied, and rivers and cold will overflow, and men will find good and joy—and better than that if she were received.

And if Jupiter were in the Ascendant, it will be a year of security, and the matters of men and the wealthy will be made fit, and will profit. And if he were received, the generality of the vulgar will find good from the king, and will esteem their king.

And if Mars were in the Ascendant, there will be an earthquake in that land, and the rain will be little, and there will be a moderately-sized war.

And if the Sun were in the Ascendant, and he were the Lord of the Year, and free from the malefics, the wealthy will rejoice and good will overflow, and matters will be successful; but if he were impeded, it will be to the contrary of what I have said.

Chapter 37: On the calamities of the year

Know that the year will be made severe if there were malefics in the part of the upper circle, and in the northern part,[71] and especially if Mars committed his own disposition to Saturn: because Saturn signifies grave things, and long-lasting ones, concerning the appearance of detriment in the earth, and the weakness of the king, and the taking away of faith and religion; and robberies will be multiplied, and contentions, and especially if one of the malefics were in the Midheaven.

And in addition, look at the Moon: because if she committed her own disposition to Saturn from the lower part of the subterranean circle, it signifies tribulation and detriment and the changing of the kingdom. And if the Moon pushed her light to Saturn, and were with him [in the same sign] or in the square aspect or in the opposition, it will be that much worse.

And look likewise at the Sun just as you have looked at the Moon: because if he were received, it signifies the fitness[72] of the evil.

---

[71] Perhaps this means in signs of northern declination? But see a further statement in the next paragraph. It could be that this has a technical astronomical meaning that escaped the Latin translator.

[72] *Aptationem*, here and in the next paragraph. Here it might mean something like the "temperateness" or "mitigation" of the evil, since the Sun is being received.

And know that the benefics signify the loosening of evil, and its taking-away, if they were strong in their place, having good testimony. And if they were direct, they signify good and fitness.

Chapter 38: On the signification of a planet when it enters combustion or goes out from it

Know that when a planet goes out from under the rays and combustion, it will be just like a boy who progresses and is increased—so long as the malefics did not aspect it. And likewise when it enters under the rays and combustion, it will be like a worn out old man. Therefore, consider this chapter very well.

Chapter 39: On the signification of Saturn when he is in his own exaltation

Consider the entrance of each planet into its own exaltation—and particularly Saturn, because then he is stronger. And in addition, [see] what he would have in terms of testimony and strength: look even to see if he received disposition, because it will signify great things. And likewise Jupiter and the rest of the planets. And while the year is being revolved, look at the benefics and the malefics to see if they aspected from out of a fixed sign: what they signified in terms of good or evil will be prolonged. And if they aspected from a movable sign, this will be moderately [so]; but if they aspected from a common sign, it will be something in the middle.

Chapter 40: On an eclipse, if there were one that same year

After this, look at the topic of an eclipse, if you knew that there would be an eclipse in that same year. Accordingly, look in that year at the Lord of the sign in which the eclipse will be, at what his condition is, and what kind of place he has with the Lord of the Ascendant of the eclipse, and what kind of condition he has from the Lord of the Year and the significator of the king, and how the benefics or malefics aspect him. Because if he were impeded by the aspect of the malefics, what he signified will be irritated[73] and multiplied, and more strongly so if the Lord of the eclipse were the significator of the king. Because if he were the significator of the king, and there were malefics aspecting him, it will be feared concerning him when the Sun arrives to the Midheaven of the eclipse; and if he were the Lord of the Year, it will be feared concerning the rustics when the Sun arrives at the Ascendant of the eclipse, according to the rationale[74] belonging to the nature of the Ascendant: if it were according the image of a man, there will be impediment in men; and if it were according to the substance of animals, it will be in animals; and if it were regarding the substance of water, it will be in waters, according to the substance of the ascending sign.

And know that, of the hours of the eclipse of the Moon, there is a provision of one month to every hour; and for the eclipse of the Sun, a year through every hour.

After this, look at the malefics: if they were in the Ascendant or closer to the Ascendant, there will be impediment in the middle part of the earth which we said belongs to Jupiter and Mercury; and if the malefics were in the Midheaven, or closer to the Midheaven, it will be in the upper part of the orb, which we have said belongs to Saturn and the Moon. But in the west, or closer to the west, it will be in the lower part of the earth, which belongs to Mars and Venus.

Chapter 41: When the Sun is made the significator of the king

And if the Sun were the Lord of the Ascendant in the revolution (wherefore Venus is then the Lady of the Midheaven),[75] and were Venus under his rays, then the Sun will be the significator of the king. Then, look at the condition of the king through his place from the malefics and benefics, and from his strength in his own place, and from the aspect of the Lords of the domiciles to him, according to what I have expounded to you concerning their testimonies and aspects, until he completes[76] the twelve signs. Therefore, look to see which of the planets is in an optimal place, and which of

---

[73] *Exasperabitur.* Or, "made angry."
[74] *Rationem.*
[75] This assumes Leo rising and Taurus as the 10th domicile. For present purposes Māshā'allāh is ignoring issues of whether the Sun is fit, *etc.*
[76] This sounds like we are to make note of his transits throughout the year.

them is impeded, and which combust, or which is removed from the angle and domicile [house?], and pronounce the strength of evil from the malefics, and the fitness of good from the benefics.

Moreover, if the Sun were northern in his latitude, or he committed his disposition to a northern malefic from the opposition or conjunction or the square aspect, or a trine or sextile, his signification will not be concealed from you. And likewise if a malefic committed its own disposition to a planet in the sixth, it will signify infirmity; and likewise in the eighth it will signify death, and in the twelfth sorrow, distress, captivity and enmities.

But if Venus had gone out from under the Sun's rays in her own light, she will be more worthy for the signification of the king, and better than that if she were in the Midheaven.[77]

Chapter 42: On the condition of the king in that same year

Indeed if you knew [it] through what I said, and it was revealed to you concerning the signification of the king and the nobles and the rustics, look to see what will be concerning the king's condition in that same year, whether he will be made free not, and what kind of being he will have with his rustics, and whether he will have a faraway or nearby foreign travel, or war, or what will be concerning his matters.[78] But look at this from the Lord of the domicile of foreign travel at the hour of the revolution, and from his place in the circle: because if it were direct or received in its place, he will go *exaciatum*,[79] by roaming; and if it were slow and in its station, it signifies slowness on the foreign journey. And if it were retrograde and received, he will go out and turn back quickly; and if it were retrograde without reception, it signifies detriment in the king's foreign journey, and it will not be completed.

---

[77] Suddenly the text takes up the question of Venus again: do the above paragraphs only pertain to when Leo is rising and Venus is under the rays, *etc.*, or did Māshā'allāh stray from the topic and is only now returning to it? I think the latter is the more likely explanation.

[78] Reading *rebus* for *re*.

[79] Unknown word. It could be related to *exactare*, "to collect (taxes)," or *exagito*, "to drive away," or perhaps *exatio* (*exsatio*), "to satisfy one's passions." But while I can see a king collecting taxes or satisfying his passions on a journey, I'm not sure how these are related to roaming (*vagando*). The verb *vago* might be a variant on *vaco*, which means for land "to be ownerless, vacant," but that does not really help.

After this, look at the domicile[80] of foreign travel. If its Lord were retrograde, aspecting its own domicile from the square aspect or the opposition, he will go battle [with] an enemy. And if it aspected from the trine or sextile aspect, he will to go make peace.[81]

After this, look for his being safe[82] on his foreign journey and the condition of his body, and to his significator, to see if it were free from the malefics and from his enemies (of the planets), and [that] the Lord of the domicile of foreign travel is not in the domicile of infirmity or in a place of impediment: the king will be kept safe on his foreign journey.

Which if the significator of the king were free from those things which I said, and the Lord of the domicile of foreign travel were impeded, it signifies difficulty for the king on the journey, and grief and infirmity, according to the quality of the substance of the sign.

And if the Lord of the domicile of foreign travel were free from the malefics, and [the king's] significator were impeded, what he was fearing will happen to him from difficulties or infirmity.

After this, look at the Lord of the domicile of foreign travel. If it were in the second, he will go out to gather substance. And if it were in the third—because it is in the opposition of its domicile—he will go out to the contention of war. And if it were in the fourth, it will signify that the foreign travel will be bad, and death will be feared concerning him in that year.[83] And if a malefic aspected it from the square aspect or the opposition or conjunction, what is signified by the matter will be more severe, and it will be feared concerning him.

And if the significator of the king were in the Ascendant at the hour of the revolution, it signifies tranquility, and he will not go on a foreign journey. But if it were removed from the Ascendant, and in addition another planet

---

[80] Reading *domum* for *dominum*.
[81] This seems to be related to the idea that the type of aspect shows the type of person or purpose; the key here is not that the Lord is aspecting his own domicile, but what kind of aspect it is. And this seems different than speaking of whether the malefics are aspecting: the Lord of the 9th represents not just the foreign travel, but the king's control over it, and his intentions; so if the Lord aspects, it shows actual control and intention, and the type of aspect shows the purpose.
[82] Here and below ("kept safe") the noun/verb pair is *salvatio/salvo*, which has connotations both of being saved (including in the religious sense), safe, and healthy.
[83] The fourth domicile is the eighth (death) from the ninth.

[were] in the Ascendant,[84] not removed, look to see who that planet is: because if it were an enemy of the significator, he will go out regarding him who seeks his kingdom, and he contends with him in it. And if it were a friend, he will hand over his kingdom to the man whose significator that planet is, and he will be put in charge of that kingdom.[85]

And if the significator of the king were in the second from the Ascendant, he will seek substance in that same year. But if a malefic were with it, or aspected it from the square aspect or the opposition or the conjunction, he will squander his substance, and will extract his treasures.

And if it were in the third, he will multiply his cavalry, and he will desire a foreign journey.

And if it were in the fourth, he will not go on a foreign journey but he will desire quiet.

And if it were in the fifth, he will have a son, and he will long for[86] him.

And if it were in the sixth, infirmity will befall him.

And if it were in the seventh, his sexual intercourse will be multiplied.

And if it were in the eighth, death will be feared concerning him.

And if it were in the ninth, he will go on a foreign journey.

And if it were in the tenth, he will be strengthened in his kingdom. And this is so known from its condition in its direction and retrogradation and station: because being direct signifies fitness, and

---

[84] This could also read, "and [there was] another planet with it in the Ascendant…" This would be the case if being "removed" simply meant "far from the degree of the Ascendant." I am not sure which reading is correct.
[85] This must mean that he will set up a friend to rule the kingdom in his absence while he is abroad.
[86] Or, "he will miss him" (*desiderabit*).

retrogradation signifies detriment, and its first station is just like retrogradation, and its second station is just like being direct.

And if [it] were in the eleventh, it signifies fitness, esteem, piety, liberality and expenses: because this domicile is the 2nd from the domicile of the king.

And if it were in the twelfth, it signifies his enemies' acquisition,[87] and his purpose in that. Which if then the significator of the king aspected the Lord of his domicile, he will get them, if God wills.

And say likewise if the significator of the king committed disposition to the Lords of these domiciles which I said. For it will signify the same there as it would signify if it were in their domiciles. And if the significator of the king were joined to a planet appearing in the ninth or the third, it signifies a foreign journey; and likewise a conjunction with the Lord of the domicile of infirmity, or with the Lord of the domicile of death: it signifies the infirmity or death of the king. And if the significator of the king were under the rays or near them by 12°, it will be feared concerning the king in the hour of combustion, and this will be at the hour of its combustion. And likewise the Lord of the ninth: if it were cadent or in a bad place, it will be feared for him on his foreign journey.

Chapter 43: On the impediment of the rustics

And if the Lord of the Ascendant were combust in an angle, impediment will enter in upon the rustics. And if he were combust in the Midheaven, this impediment will be from the direction of the king. And if the Sun were the Lord of the Midheaven, and the Lord of the Ascendant combust, men will find difficulty from the king, because it is under the rays. If the combustion were in the fourth angle, which is the angle of the earth, it signifies that death will fall on men. Which if the Ascendant were a feminine sign, this will be in women; and if it were masculine, this will be in men. And if Mercury were the Lord of the Ascendant, this will be in boys; and if it were Venus or

---

[87] *Acquisitionem inimicorum suorum.* This verb *acquiro* can also mean to obtain, get, or win. I take it to mean that his enemies will have advantages over him.

the Moon, it will be more in women; and if it were Jupiter or Saturn, it will be in the middle class; and if it were the Sun or Mars, they signify young men. And if they were oriental, it will be in boys and youths. And if they were occidental, it will be in old men and poor old ladies.[88]

Chapter 44: On the detriment of the king

Look for the king (at the hour of the revolution) from the Sun: which if Mars aspected him, or were joined to him, killing will be feared concerning him. And if he were joined to Saturn, difficulties and poison will be feared for him. And if the Lord of the Ascendant of the year were combust in the Midheaven, what I said will be feared in the same ways, and it will be in his own region in which he is, and it will not be outside of that land. And if the combustion were in the angle of the earth, or in the opposite from the seventh, what I told you will be from someone who will come outside the land in which he is. And in this topic, the opposition of the malefics and their square aspect is more severe than their conjunction. And if the Sun were the significator of the king, and he aspected Jupiter from the opposition, the king will become angry with his household members, and he will hold them in suspicion, and he will be burdened by them. And likewise if the Lord of the Ascendant were opposed: he will get angry with his rustics, he will mistrust them badly, and will impede them. Finally, know the reception of the planets with one another, and the projection of their lights. And know the concord or discord of the Ascendant and its Lord.

Chapter 45: On the signification of Mars

Know that each malefic (namely Saturn and Mars), if one of them were in an angle in the revolution of the year, and it were direct in earthy signs, it signifies the destruction of trees and the death of animals.

And if Mars aspected the significator of the king, and he were commingled with the light of Saturn, it signifies contention and the shedding of blood.

---

[88] *Cf.* Ch. 14 for a similar statement about ages.

And if he were in an airy sign, it signifies injuries and enmities. But if it were not in an angle, and it aspected the Ascendant, it signifies infirmity from winds and blood,[89] and more severely in every land in whose sign its light was [corporally], or the opposition, or the square aspect.

Which if he were retrograde, it signifies pestilence. And if he were in a sign which does not aspect the Ascendant, and he were direct, it will signify infirmity and the detriment of seeds. But if he were then retrograde, it will signify death and infirmity and blood.

And if Mars were the Lord of the Year, and he were in fiery signs, and he were in an angle, direct, he signifies a hot and dry infirmity, and the powerful will contend with each other. And if he were retrograde this will be more severe, and destruction and robberies will be multiplied.

But if he were in watery signs outside an angle, and he did not aspect the Ascendant, men will afflict each other with injuries, and this will be more severe in the sign in which his square aspect or opposition is.

And the impediment which I told you [about] will be according to the substance of that same sign, and the nature of the planet.

Chapter 46: On the signification of Saturn in the triplicities

If Saturn were the Lord of the Year, and he were in Aries and its triplicity, and he were direct in an angle, it will signify many rains, and the contentions of the wealthy, and more strongly so if he received the disposition of Mars and his strength: because it signifies that the rustics would contend with the king. And if he were retrograde, the condition of men will be burdened. And if he were removed from the angle, aspecting the Ascendant, difficulty will enter in on top of the nobles, if he were direct; but if he were retrograde, he will destroy the houses of substances.

And if he received disposition from Mars and the Moon, it signifies a severe cold and the death of animals, along with what I told you about wars and lawsuits. And if he were cadent and did not aspect the Ascendant, and he were direct, the cold of winter will be made severe; but if he were retrograde, there will be contention and rebellion among the rustics.

---

[89] This must be related to ancient and medieval notions of the passage of air into the blood through the lungs. See *On Sig. Planet.* Ch. 7.

And if Saturn were the Lord of the Year in earthy signs, in an angle, direct, it signifies contention and war, and the death of animals, particularly in that land in whose sign he was. And if he were retrograde, he will destroy harvests and seeds, and youths will die, and more strongly so if he were in the Midheaven. And if he were removed from the angle, aspecting the Ascendant, seeds will be destroyed, and youths will die, and the harvests will be little. But if he did not aspect the Ascendant, the evil will be moderate.

And if Saturn were the Lord of the Year and were in Gemini and its triplicity, and he were in the angle of the Ascendant of the kingdom, northern winds will be stirred up, and they will be strong and harmful, and infirmity will befall the rustics because of the substance of Saturn, and there will be war and contention and the shedding of blood in men. And if he were retrograde, it signifies the contention of the wealthy and the nobles. And if he were removed from the angle and were direct, severe winter cold and winds will arise. And if he were retrograde and removed, it signifies infirmity and winds. And if he were cadent, and did not aspect the Ascendant, and he were direct, the southern winds and infirmities will be multiplied, and this will be collectively in low-class persons.

And if he were in the angle of the earth, and he were the Lord of the Year in this triplicity, it signifies earthquake. And if he were not the Lord of the Year, and he received the disposition of the Lord of the Ascendant, and he[90] were in this place, men will die in an earthquake. And if he received the disposition of the [Lord of the] Midheaven, it signifies contention and lawsuits in the acquisition of the kingdom.

And if Saturn were the Lord of the Year, and he were in watery signs in an angle, the cold will be severe, and locusts will be multiplied. And if he were retrograde, there will be the greatest discord and powerful death. But if he were removed from the angle, rains and waters will be multiplied. And if he were cadent, not aspecting the Ascendant, it signifies the infirmity of the citizens of the sign in which he is. But if he were retrograde, severe cold will come, and locusts will be multiplied. And if a benefic planet is joined to him, it decreases the said hardships.

---

[90] It is unclear whether this refers to Saturn or the Lord of the Ascendant. I suspect it refers to Saturn, as an alternative to his actually being the Lord of the Year. See the following sentence: if Saturn were still in the fourth but receiving the disposition of the Lord of the Midheaven, then he could show disputes over the kingdom by his being in the sign opposite that of the king.

ON THE SIGNIFICATIONS OF THE PLANETS IN A NATIVITY

The book of Māshā'allāh on the significations of the planets in a nativity, of which these are the chapters:

The first chapter, on what is signified by Saturn in his own domicile or others'
The second, on the signification of Jupiter in his own domicile or others'
The third, on the signification of Mars
The fourth, on the signification of the Sun
The fifth, on the signification of Venus
The sixth, on the signification of Mercury
The seventh, on the signification of the Moon
The eighth, on the signification of the Lord of the Ascendant, when he is in the Ascendant and the other eleven domiciles
The ninth, on the signification of the Lord of the second in the twelve places of heaven
The tenth, on the signification of the Lord of the third
The eleventh, on the signification of the Lord of the fourth
The twelfth, on the signification of the Lord of the fifth
The thirteenth, on the signification of the Lord of the sixth
The fourteenth, on the signification of the Lord of the seventh
The fifteenth, on the signification of the Lord of the eighth
The sixteenth, on the signification of the Lord of the ninth
The seventeenth, on the signification of the Lord of the tenth
The eighteenth, on the signification of the Lord of the eleventh
The nineteenth, on the signification of the Lord of the twelfth
The twentieth, on the signification of Saturn when he is in his own or others' bounds
The twenty-first, on the signification of Jupiter in his own or others' bounds
The twenty-second, on the signification of Mars in his own or another's bound
The twenty-third, on the signification of the Sun in his own or a strange bound

The twenty-fourth, on the signification of Venus in her own or a strange bound

The twenty-fifth, on the signification of Mercury in his own or a strange bound

The twenty-sixth, on the signification of the Moon in her own or another's bound

Māshā'allāh on the significations of the planets in a nativity, when they are in their own domiciles or strangers', begins:

Chapter 1: On the signification of Saturn in his own or another's sign

If[1] Saturn were in his own domicile, his works will be strong, and the native will be mixed with those who know sciences; and if the nativity were in the day, it will be stronger; if in the night, it will be with anguish.

If Saturn were in the domicile of Jupiter, it signifies that the native will live long, and will have much substance, and honor before princes—if he were born in the day. But in the night, he will endure poverty and harm to the father's substance.

If Saturn were in the domicile of Mars, the native will be wounded,[2] and will suffer harm in the father's substance, and he will see the death of his successors.

If he were in the domicile of the Sun, the native will have an open face, and he will be like a mischievous person and joker, and irritable; and he will have little expectation[3] or stability. And if it were in the day, he will be subject to goodness and much fortune, and the works of his father will be good; if in the night, he will not have honor, but he will have lawsuits and labor, impeded by his brother.

If he were in the domicile of Venus, his works will be evil with women, and he will take old women [as partners], and he will enjoy the sexual intercourse of poor old women, skinny women, and disgraced women—and from this fact he will hear bad words, and he will see dishonor.

If he were in the domicile of Mercury, his tongue will be heavy, and he will have a gentle heart, and he will esteem philosophers and astronomers and the inventions of events or games,[4] and he will see the depths, and he will seek the sciences, and from this fact he will discover harm, his mind or heart will become heavy, and he will have bad discourse [with others], and he

---

[1] Chapters 1-7 and 20-26 ought to be studied in conjunction with *Carmen* II.18-19 and 28-33, whence they derive.
[2] Reading *laesus* for *laetus* ("happy").
[3] That is, he will not be impatient.
[4] Reading *causarum vel ludorum* for *causarum vel ludum*, but this statement about having fun does not really fit the rest of the paragraph. Bonatti's version omits this.

will have much envy, and he will readily believe whatever gossip [people] say concerning him.

If he were in the domicile of the Moon, he will have a scandal with women and associates, and his infirmity will be from phlegm and spleen, and his infirmity (and likewise that of his mother) will be from his middle below, or from the navel below, and he will do harm with his mother's substance.

Chapter 2: On the signification of Jupiter if he were in his own domicile or those of other planets

If Jupiter were in the domicile of Saturn, he will have moderate honor, and he will serve princes and greater men, and he will have many designs, [be] greedy, and will endure great harm, and will labor so that his poverty will be apparent, and he will have a bad heart, be negligent and very lazy, and dull, and he will do his deeds in private, and from that fact he will find harm.

If he were in his own domicile, he will be subject to goodness, fortune, good works, honor and riches. And if it were in the day, it will be more useful; and if a malefic did not aspect him, he will have much honor before princes. And if it were in the night, the above-said will be small, and he will make his life [going] from this to that.[5] And if he is chosen for something, from that event a position like that of the religious will come to him.

If he were in the domicile of Mars, he will be subject to honor and exaltation, and will esteem those who know laws, and he will serve learned people and greater men, and he will be conjoined to the king or a prince, and he will be a drinker of wine. And the deeds he does will be praised, for the most part, by all; and his place of reclining or recreation and elevation will be with princes. And if the Sun and the Moon were in the angles or the succeedents, he will be like a prince, and his name will be divulged[6] in the world.

If he were in the domicile of the Sun, he will be honest and wise, and will have goodness alike with princes and great men. And if he were in an angle, and were not impeded, he will be very wealthy, and he will be a great man like a prince, or likened to such people, and it will be more useful if the nativity of the boy were in the day.

---

[5] *De parte in partem.*
[6] But *diffamo* can also mean "defamed." I take it to be the positive sense.

If he were in the domicile of Venus, he will *bursabit*[7] much. And were the native masculine, his discourse (namely [his] recreation and residence) will be with princes, and he will have honor and dignity, and he will take some wife who will have great honor. And he will see much happiness, and will have wealth from women. And if [the native] were feminine, she will be religious, and like a nun, and of good faith, and honest, and from this fact she will find goodness.

If he were in the domicile of Mercury, it signifies [he will be] involved in the greatness of instructing a man over great men;[8] and he will have soldiers, and will be a merchant or minter of coins; and he will take much and give much; and he will be a philosopher and wise, and he will be like a prince, and will earn much substance.

If he were in the domicile of the Moon, he will have goodness and greatness, and much substance, and his recreation and residence will be with princes and great men. And if he were in the angles or the succeedents (and if it were in the day), it will be better. Indeed if it were in the night, he will be of those greater of faith, and he will do good deeds, and will be acknowledged or known in his own land or in his own town.[9]

Chapter 3: On the signification of Mars in his own or another's domicile

If Mars were in the domicile of Saturn, he will have an easily-affected[10] heart, and will have much anger. And if he were in Aquarius, he will be made unfortunate. If he were in Capricorn, he will have a bold heart, and will not have carelessness. And whatever deeds he wants will come forth from his hands, and he will diminish the substance of his father, and his brothers will die.

If he were in the domicile of Jupiter, he will be mingled in goodness with soldiers and the masters of arms. And if Jupiter were with him, he will be a

---

[7] Uncertain meaning. But *Carmen* II.29.3 says that the native will be an "overseer" in the houses of kings, and in the medieval period a *bursarius* was a pursekeeper or treasurer, deriving from *bursa*, a purse or pouch.
[8] *In magnitudine praecipiendi hominem super magnos.*
[9] *Castro.*
[10] *Teneri*: tender, soft, delicate, weak, impressionable. *Carmen* II.30.1 says the native will be pleasant. I have chosen "easily-affected" because Māshā'allāh's sentence suggests he will be impressionable, reacting overmuch to influences and impulses.

great soldier, and lovable, he will not be involved in evil deeds; and if [Jupiter] saw him from the domicile of Mars with an aspect of friendship,[11] he will be great, and like a count, and he will have an army, and his hand will be upon all of those turning against him.

If he were in his own domicile, he will be a soldier, and a braggart, and he will be a geometer and fortunate, and he will have much honor, and he will be a husband, [and] will fall from a high place if he were in Aries and a benefic did not aspect it.[12] And if he were in Scorpio he will not have fear, and he will be rich; whatever deeds he wants will go forth from his hand, and [it will be] more useful if he were born in the night; and if he were born in the day, he will be evil and have an evil tongue.

If he were in the domicile of the Sun, he will have an infirmity from much heat, but he will be fortunate, and he will have fear of a wound, and his death will be sudden, and he will be killed (and likewise his father) in his old age.[13]

If he were in the domicile of Venus, he will be a fornicator, and will fornicate with his own relatives,[14] and he will be like a sodomite; he will take a wife from those with whom he will fornicate, and he will find bad things from women. And if he were in Libra, he will have fear from the sword,[15] and from fire, and in hidden places. And if he were in Taurus, he will have many male children, and be evil in fornication.

If he were in the domicile of Mercury, he will be wise and knowing, and will find evil from deeds which he does not want. And he will have much substance, and will walk around much, and he will find harm in journeys. And he will be an astronomer and writer and a philosopher, and he will know how to free others from their own things,[16] and it will be when he will have little substance, and his wealth and life will be from thieving,[17] and they will be evil works, for the most part.

If he were in the domicile of the Moon, he will serve princes, and will suffer many evils, and his infirmity will be diverse, in the belly and in a hid-

---

[11] This would be a case of mutual reception.
[12] *Eum*, which could mean either Mars or Aries. I take it to mean Aries.
[13] The Latin is somewhat ambiguous as to whether the native will die in his own old age, or the *father* in the *father's* old age. But I take it to be the native dying in his own old age.
[14] *Proximis*.
[15] Or, "iron." *Ferrum* generally means any sharp instrument made of iron.
[16] Reading *liberare alios a propriis*, though the meaning is unclear.
[17] Or, from things done in secret (*ex furto*).

den place; and the infirmity of his mother will be prolonged, and he will have or give great harm, and he will have fear of a sudden death.

Chapter 4: On the signification of the Sun in his own domicile and that of others

If the Sun were in the domicile of Saturn, it is his good and that of his father; and if it were in the day, he will have great works, and will have an open face, either stammering and a reviler, or a keeper of the Sabbath day,[18] and all works will go out from his hands. And if it were in the night, it will bad for his father, and he will have little substance, and he will grow angry quickly, and will be unstable in works, and will be changed from one to another.

If he were in the domicile of Jupiter, he will be subject to its goodness and exaltation; he will have good works and wisdom, and he will be mingled with princes, and will stand over fine works and guide them into good, and will be a good man, but mistrusted in his own house with his relatives. And if it were in the day, he will be mingled with princes and will commit malice, and it will be with the wife of his father, and with the wives of his own neighbors.[19]

If he were in the domicile of Mars, it will be as though to the loss of his father and mother; and he will find evils from swords[20] or from iron, and he will have a fear of sudden death, and of death in old age, and he will have a pain in his bowels and in his liver, if it were in Scorpio. And if it were in Aries, he will be subject to exaltation and fortune, and his honor, in all of his life if it were in the day; but if it were in the night, these will be less.

If he were in his own domicile, and he were in an angle or the succeedents, he will be more admired than a count; and he will be rich, and have a long life, and be strong, and will earn great substance from cities and villages. And if it were in the night, it will be to his folly,[21] and that of his

---

[18] Reading *sabbatharius* for *sabatharius*.
[19] *Proximorum*. This could also mean "relatives" (as I translated it in the previous chapter). The idea here seems to be that the combination of the Sun and Jupiter leads to arrogance and the belief that he can do what he wants, taking liberties with others' spouses.
[20] Reading *ferris* for *feris*, because of the Mars connection between iron and fire. But *feris* indicates wild animals, which may be possible due to the meaning of Scorpio.
[21] *Stulticiam* (*stultitiam*) here and below, which can also mean "foolishness, stupidity."

father, [and] to his separation from his father and mother on a foreign journey.

If he were in the domicile of Venus, he will have good things from women, and his fortune will be from women, and he will open his own heart in profound works, and he will be a judger of dreams, and he will be known and recognized for the associates which he knows, and he will be set up in good works and foreign journeys.

If he were in the domicile of Mercury, he will be an astronomer and will have many horses; and he will be knowing and fortunate. And he will be of good mental character, and have a better memory, and will love scandals. And if it were in the day, it will be better;[22] and if it were in the night, he will have impediment or annoyance from phlegm and choler.

If he were in the domicile of the Moon, it will be to the happiness and folly of the native, and to his little substance, and he will be a bad worker.[23] If he were [still] in childhood he will earn more substance,[24] and he will have a pain in the stomach, and in hidden places. And he will be mingled with those making incantations or conjurors, and those who write short things[25] for curing the infirm.[26]

Chapter 5: On the signification of Venus

If Venus were in the domicile of Saturn, it will be his evil from the taking[27] of women, and he will love the sexual intercourse of old women and of despicable women—from that fact bad things will be said about him; and all of his works will be perfected and he will be happy. And if it were in the night, he will engage in the bad takings or marriages of women, and from that fact he will find bad things and impediment, and he will see the death of his wives.

---

[22] Reading *melius* for *vilius* ("more low-class"). Since the Sun is of the diurnal sect, it makes sense that the signification would be better in the day; but perhaps the Latin is right, and there is something about the domicile of Mercury itself that makes it bad.
[23] *Operator.*
[24] *In pueritia cum fuerit magis lucrabitur substantiae.*
[25] *Brevia.* That is, magical spells.
[26] The sense of this paragraph must come from the fact that the Sun in Cancer is in the twelfth from his own domicile.
[27] This refers either to marriage (i.e., taking women as wives), or in sexual conquests in general.

If she were in the domicile of Jupiter, he is subject to goodness and fortune, and his exaltation, and his substance will be greater from women, or from some feminine work, or from work which one does through women: for instance, if he were the guard of a hospital,[28] or an administrator or manager [of one]. And if it were in the night, it will be less.

If she were in the domicile of Mars, he will find evils from enemies, and scandals, and he will be commingled with honest Slavs,[29] and his marriage will come out unpleasantly, and he will kill his wife on account of jealousy.

If she is found in the domicile of the Sun, he will be happy, and will have a good life, and will esteem dishonest women, and he will love joys and games; and men will say bad things about him, and he will see the majority of the things he wills, which he has in his heart.

If she were in her own domicile, it signifies many joys, the love of stupid women whence he will have evil; but he will be made fortunate in his works, and will pursue the good.

If she were in the domicile of Mercury, he will be mingled with the greater people of faith, and women who serve, and in the works which are likened to this which are conjoined to women (like a painter, or gilders, or the like), and he will love sexual intercourse.

If she were in the domicile of the Moon, he will have the love of women in a bad marriage, and [love] in joy and games, because of an error or by means of a desirable love; and he will be engaged in prevarication or improper activity.[30]

Chapter 6: On the signification of Mercury

If Mercury were in the domicile of Saturn, he will be wise in all works, and an inventor of songs or speeches of praise, or he will be an astronomer

---

[28] *Hospitii.* This is ambiguous. A *hospitium* is a place of lodging, of which there are many forms: inns, pilgrimage hostels, monastic housing, *etc.* But I think a "hospital" might be more relevant, especially if women are working and healing there. Another possibility is that it is an inn for travelers, run by women who do the cooking and cleaning.

[29] *Sclavis.* In medieval Latin *Sclavus* is one word for "slave." Slavic people were used as slaves by medieval slavers, whence we get our English word "slave," and the Germans *Sklawe.* I have retained "Slav" here in order to keep the reader connected to its original sense.

[30] *Praevaricationis vel pravae operationis opus habebit.* "Prevarication" in the medieval sense could mean treason, betrayal, a tendency to sin, perversion, *etc.*

or medical doctor, or he will be unfortunate in earning substance; and his tongue will be grave, and he will be mingled with men of good trustfulness,[31] and he will be plainly honest.

If he were in the domicile of Jupiter, he will be mingled with princes and businessmen, and he will have a mandated authority or prefecture[32] in the works of princes, and he will be wise in the prefecture, a judge in good faith or trustfulness.

If he were in the domicile of Mars, he will have good senses and will be knowing, and he will have moderate wealth; or he will be a soldier, and will write false papers under the name of a judge or king; and he will be a liar, and because of this fact he will find evils.

If he were in the domicile of the Sun, he will have a good discourse and good works, and he will be an astronomer, and knowing in all works, and every day his knowledge will increase, and he will have a good intellect and memory, and he will be a discoverer of the profound sciences and hidden things.

If he were in the domicile of Venus, his heart will desire sexual intercourse, and he will be lazy, and he will render his life in good theatrics, and he will have many friends (and they like brothers), and he will love fun things like lyres and the like, and he will imitate some ancient things well, and will love the calculation[33] of number and the *trivium* of the books.[34]

If he were in his own domicile, he will be irritable, and enflamed, and have an obstinate anger, and he will be knowing the good, and will engage in merchant activities, and he will be a discoverer of the profound and hidden sciences, and he will be an astronomer.

If he were in the domicile of the Moon, he will be stupid, and will travel abroad much, and will be unstable, and he will be a builder of houses, and will be quickly angered and quickly placated, and he will be mingled with greater people of faith, and will conduct his works for the most part with knowledge.

---

[31] *Credulitatis.* Or, "credulity" (here and in the next paragraph).
[32] *Praefecturam.* This is a general word for many types of offices, both civil and ecclesiastical.
[33] *Rationem.*
[34] Reading *trivium librorum* for *tertionem librorum*. The *trivium* was the medieval educational grouping of rhetoric, grammar, and logic.

Chapter 7: On the signification of the Moon in her own domicile and that of others

If the Moon were in the domicile of Saturn, it will be the evil of the native, and of his mother, and he will have pain from windiness[35] and his spleen, and bad things will be said about him. And if she were decreased in light, he will find pain from coldness and the kidneys in old age. And if it were in the night, it will be worse.

If she were in the domicile of Jupiter, it signifies the native's greatness, goodness and fortune, and he will be known among men, and he will have intercourse with a female or male person who is not suitable, and with prevarication;[36] and [it will be a] male or female from his own kin or neighbors.[37]

If she were in the domicile of Mars, he will have a light head[38] in works, and his mother will find evil things, and he will be on fire and of obstinate anger (especially in scandals and wars); and he will be mingled with soldiers and robbers, and in the night [with] those walking around with bad [intent].[39]

If she were in the domicile of the Sun, it signifies happiness and the native's good life, and he will be mingled with princes, and will be renowned, and will have a pain in the head and in the stomach; and it will be more likely [so] if she were in the third of the sign.[40] And it will be when he will have little substance and little wealth.

If she were in the domicile of Venus, it signifies love, and his heart will desire sexual intercourse, and his marriage will transpire with joy, and with a good life.

If she were in the domicile of Mercury, he will have a good sense, and he will be cleansed, and will be good in faith, and will desire women, boys, and girls, and he will be knowing in his works.

If she were in her own domicile, he will have great wealth, and it will be with honor; and he will be mingled with princes. And it will be better if the benefics aspected—if the malefics, less so.

---

[35] *Ventositate.* I am not sure what kind of ailment this indicates; but some traditional theories of blood circulation postulated types of air in the veins, and both the Moon and Saturn do signify fluids. See *On Rev.* Ch. 45.
[36] See Ch. 5.
[37] *De proximis suis, vel propinquis.* Both of these words can mean broader kin or neighbors: literally, people who are "nearby."
[38] *Leve caput,* which could range from being fickle to being a simpleton.
[39] *Pro male ambulantibus.* My translation is somewhat speculative.
[40] *Tertia signi.* Meaning unclear. But it could also be read as *tertio signo,* "the third sign."

Chapter 8: On the signification of the Lord of the Ascendant in the twelve domiciles

If the Lord of the Ascendant were in the Ascendant, it will be good; and if a planet aspected from the Midheaven, he will find a great inheritance.[41] And if it[42] were in its own exaltation, [it will be] from a prince.

If the Lord of the Ascendant were in the 2nd, substance will come to his hands, and he will lose it by means of one who is likened to the sign in which it is.

If it were in the third, his brothers will be older[43] than him, and he will make many foreign journeys; and if it aspected a benefic, he will have good faith or belief, and he will be faithful. And if it aspected a malefic, he will be unfaithful.

If it were in the 4th, he will love his own father and mother, and he will find impediment or a lawsuit from greater men. And if the Lord of the Ascendant were in honor, he will see wealth from his parents.

If it were in the 5th, he will nearly generate children in his youth,[44] and he will have virtue from their arrival.

If it were in the sixth, he will be practically likened to slaves in his works, and will be in much infirmity.

If it were in the seventh, he will find many goods from the arrival of women, and from favoritism.[45]

If it were in the eighth, it signifies goods in something of ancient things, and because of inheritance.

If it were in the ninth, he will be good in faith, and in prayers to God, and he will be much on foreign journeys, and will excel in every science.

If it were in the tenth, he will seek a princely position, and he will find victory in greatness and exaltation.

If it were in the eleventh, he will be eminent in the discovery of faith and victory, and with many friends, and he will have good fortune from them, and they from him.

---

[41] Or perhaps, "real estate." In the medieval context this probably means it will be granted by a 10th house personage.

[42] I believe this refers to the planet in the Midheaven.

[43] Or perhaps, "greater."

[44] *In infantia sua*, here and below. This probably means more precisely, "while he is still a minor."

[45] *Acceptione*. This medieval usage may not be exactly what is meant. It does suggest accepting funds from other people, whatever the motive.

If it were in the twelfth, he will have many enemies and rivals, and he will be their master or overcomer or victor if it were strong and fortunate there; without this, were it weak and unfortunate, say the contrary.

Chapter 9: On the signification of the Lord of the second in the twelve domiciles

If the Lord of the second were in the 1st, he will make money from his works, and will be fortunate, and will have substance.

If it were in the second, it signifies a good life, and he will be rich.

If it were in the third, there will be a contention between him and his brothers on the occasion of substance.

If it were in the fourth, he will have substance from his parents.

If it were in the fifth, he will have fortune from children, and his children from him.

If it were in the sixth, he will have fortune from quadrupeds and Slavs, and he will spend on the occasion of infirmities.

If it were in the seventh, his substance will be earned from women and partners, and he will have wealth from women.

If it were in the eighth, he will find much inheritance.

If it were in the ninth, he will earn wealth from a foreign journey, and he will not have wealth in his own place or habitation.

If in the tenth, his life will be sustained by princes, and by their services.[46]

If in the eleventh, he will have fortune from friends, and his friends from him.

If in the twelfth, he will be a pauper, and he will perform heavy or bad works, and he will not do them quickly, and in his works he will speak many lies, and he will be impeded, not perfecting what he wants.

Chapter 10: On the signification of the Lord of the third in the twelve domiciles

If the Lord of the third were in the first, he will see many good things from his brothers, and he will be made fortunate by his brothers and kin, and

---

[46] That is, through *his* services to *them*.

he will be a roaming person because he will always be changed from place to place, from land to land.

If it were in the second, he will earn substance in a change from place to place, and from on the occasion of his brothers and kin.

If in the third, his brothers will be renowned, indeed so that he goes to them.[47]

If it were in the fourth, it signifies the evil of his father,[48] on the occasion of his brothers.

If it were in the fifth, his children will be called by the name of his brother, and his brothers will see good things from his[49] children.

If it were in the sixth, it signifies evil for him and his brothers.

If it were in the seventh, his brothers will take his wife.

If it were in the eighth, it signifies the evil and death of his brothers in his own days.

If it were in the ninth, his wife is not from his own land, and not from his brothers,[50] and on the occasion of women he will fall into a foreign journey.

If it were in the tenth, he will have few brothers and kin, and he will be a person roaming from place to place.

If it were in the eleventh, his brothers will themselves be good, and he will be fortunate on the occasion of them.

If it were in the twelfth, enmity will fall between him and his brothers and kin.

Chapter 11: On the signification of the Lord of the fourth in the twelve domiciles

If the Lord of the fourth were in the Ascendant, he will find evil from princes, and will be weak or bad.

If it were in the second, it signifies the goodness of his father on account of [the native].

---

[47] That is, he goes to them for help due to their greater position.
[48] Reading *patris* for *partis*.
[49] *Suis*. This could refer to the brothers' own children, which is how I would normally translate it.
[50] I believe this means that she is not from any of the lands in which his brothers live—so there is no family connection, whether by knowledge or blood, with the wife.

If it were in the third, it signifies the loss or division of his brothers from the substance of his father.

If it were in the fourth, his father will be renowned and have a good life.

If it were in the fifth, his children will be six,[51] and he will find discord or impediment on the occasion of them.

If it were in the sixth, his children will be like Slavs or slaves, and they will perform the services of slaves.

If it were in the seventh, it signifies the goodness of the marriage.

If it were in the eighth, he will be fortunate in inheritances, and in something of ancient things.

If it were in the ninth, he will die on a foreign journey, and his infirmity will for the most part be in hidden places.

If it were in the tenth, it signifies the glory of his father along with princes, and he will be involved in the works of princes.

If it were in the eleventh, he will have goodness from friends.

If it were in the twelfth, it will be the evil of his father and kin.

Chapter 12: On the signification of the Lord of the fifth in the twelve domiciles

If the Lord of the fifth were in the Ascendant, he will have fortune from children and friends.

If it were in the second, he will have brothers on a foreign journey, and he will have wealth from his children.

If it were in the third, he will have fortune from women.

If it were in the fourth, his father will be rich in substance, and have a long life, and he will see the children of his children.

If it were in the fifth, his children will have goodness and a long life, and they will be renowned.

If it were[52] in the sixth, his children will have much sluggishness, and will have a weak life.

If it were in the seventh, he will take a wife older[53] than himself, and he will have goodness and much substance.

---

[51] The exactness of this number (*sex*) seems suspect to me, and I cannot see the rationale for it.
[52] Reading *fuerit* for *fuerint*.
[53] Or perhaps "greater" (*maiorem*) in status.

If it were in the eighth, his children will die in his days, and he will find something like a princely position and exaltation.

If it were in the ninth, he will not generate children in his own land.

If it were in the tenth, his children will have much sluggishness, and will have evil days, and he will not find evil from princes.

If it were in the eleventh, his children will have fortune from princes.

If it were in the twelfth, it signifies the enmity of his children with him, and they will never rejoice together.

Chapter 13: On the signification of the Lord of the sixth in the twelve places

If the Lord of the sixth were in the Ascendant, he will be unfortunate, and will be likened to Slavs; and for many days after that he will be successful and he will have fortune from Slavs and quadrupeds.

If it were in the second, he will be fortunate in medicine, and from Slavs and quadrupeds.

If it were in the third, his brothers will be turned against him, and one will desire evil and the death of the other.

If it were in the fourth, his father will be obscure.

If it were in the fifth, it signifies the evil of the children and his slaves.

If it were in the sixth, he will be a medical doctor, and knowing, and will get to know herbs.

If it were in the seventh, his father will be made unfortunate by women.

If it were in the eighth, he will not have fortune from Slavs.

If it were in the ninth, he will be made fortunate in buying quadrupeds, and he will have much infirmity on a foreign journey.

If it were in the tenth, he will have moderate wealth and bad love from princes.

If it were in the eleventh, he will be a pauper and have a bad life.

If it were in the twelfth, he will feel pains on the occasion of quadrupeds and Slavs, and he will never be delighted.[54]

---

[54] This must mean he will never be delighted by quadrupeds and Slavs, not that he will never be delighted by anything at all.

Chapter 14: On the signification of the Lord of the seventh in the twelve places

If the Lord of the seventh were in the Ascendant, he will often be contentious, and better in the works of women.

If in the second, it signifies his contending on behalf of the matters of women.

If it were in the third, it signifies the native's enmity with his brothers.

If it were in the fourth, his enmity with the father and brothers.

If in the fifth, his enmity with his children.

If it were in the sixth, it will be his evil on the occasion of women and slaves.

If it were in the seventh, it signifies his goodness because of marriage and the knowledge of his wives.

If it were in the eighth, he will take a wife and she will die; and he will take her substance.

If it were in the ninth, he will take a wife of good descent, or from the stock of princes.

If it were in the tenth, he will take a fortunate wife, and one of long life, and she will be exalted.

If it were in the eleventh, it signifies his goodness due to marriage, and the goodness of his wives.

If it were in the twelfth, he will take a marriage or wife from bad men, and she will never be glad.

Chapter 15: On the signification of the Lord of the eighth [in the twelve domiciles]

If the Lord of the eighth were in the Ascendant, he will be weak in body and heart.

If the Lord of the eighth were in the 2nd, he will find substance because of inheritances.

If it were in the third, he will be happy on the occasion of female relatives.

If it were in the fourth, it signifies loss for his father, and [the father's] low-class status.

If it were in the fifth, his children will die.

If it were in the sixth, he will always be healthy.

If it were in the seventh, he will consume the inheritance[55] of women, and his wives will be harmful to him on a foreign journey.

If it were in the eighth, in his heart he will want to earn substance, and it will happen.

If it were in the ninth, the same.

If it were in the tenth, in youth he will seek to have power over men, and he will not have it in that time.

If it were in the eleventh, he will be knowing, and he will use sordid or bad words.

If it were in the twelfth, he will have few friends; his Slavs will kill him.

Chapter 16: On the signification of the Lord of the ninth in the twelve places

If the Lord [of the ninth] were in the Ascendant, he will make many foreign journeys, and he will be knowing, and exceedingly thrifty.

If it were in the second, he will find happiness from an inheritance,[56] and it will be abundant.

If it were in the third, his brothers will get married while on a foreign journey.

If it were in the fourth, his father will be obscure.

If it were in the fifth, he will have many foreign journeys, and many children.

If it were in the sixth, he will fall ill on a foreign journey.

If it were in the seventh, he will make foreign marriages.

If it were in the eighth, the same.

If it were in the ninth, he will be on a foreign journey, and on the path of his father, and he will be a good workman, and will have a good faith.

If it were in the tenth, he will find something like a princely position on a foreign journey, and he will earn from some such.

If it were in the eleventh, it will be his goodness on a foreign journey, and he will have a long life.

---

[55] Or perhaps, "real estate."
[56] Or perhaps, "real estate."

If it were in the twelfth, he will have bad belief or faith, and on a foreign journey he will see impediment from enemies.

Chapter 17: On the signification of the Lord of the tenth in the twelve places

If the Lord of the tenth were in the Ascendant, it signifies his goodness from princes, and he will be renowned.

If in the second, he will gather substance on the occasion of a prince.

If in the third, it signifies the goodness of his brothers and sisters.

If it were in the fourth, his father will be known because of his goodness.

If it were in the fifth, it denotes the infirmity and evil[57] of his children.[58]

If it were in the [seventh],[59] he will get married to the greater people of princes.

If it were in the eighth, it denotes the goodness of his wives from him.

If it were in the tenth,[60] it signifies the stability of [his] rule.[61]

If it were in the eleventh, it signifies his rule in his youth.

If it were in the twelfth, he will make enmity with princes, and he will always be in the discord of princes.

Chapter 18: On the signification of the Lord of the eleventh in the twelve places

If the Lord of the eleventh were in the Ascendant, he will exhibit good social discourse to men, and will have many friends.

If it were in the second, it signifies his goodness from friends.

If it were in the third, it will be related to the good name of his brothers and sisters.

If it were in the fourth, it signifies the loss of his father, and his evil.

---

[57] Not in the sense that the children *are* evil, but that they will encounter or suffer evil.
[58] The text is missing the statement on the sixth domicile. The following statement begins as though it should be the sixth (*in sexto*), but the interpretation is a traditional one for the Lord of the tenth in the *seventh*, and I have read it as such.
[59] Reading *septimo* for *sexto* (see previous footnote).
[60] The statement on the ninth is missing.
[61] *Principatus*, here and in the next sentence.

If it were in the fifth, it will be good in his residence, and for his children.

If it were in the sixth, he will love bad and sordid women.

If it were in the seventh, it signifies his goodness, and that of his wives and children.

If it were in the eighth, it signifies the loss of his neighbors and friends.

If it were in the ninth, he will have foreign or external[62] marriages.

If it were in the tenth, his friends will find goodness from him.

If it were in the eleventh, he will be honored and rich and exalted.

If it were in the twelfth, he will be unfortunate and have a bad life.

Chapter 19: On the signification of the Lord of the twelfth in the twelve places

If the Lord of the twelfth were in the Ascendant, he will be unfortunate and have a bad life, he will have many enemies, and everyone will be above him.

If it were in the 2nd, he will have little substance, and will be lazy in works.

If it were in the 3rd, he will have enmity with his brothers and neighbors.

If it were in the 4th, it signifies the evil, and the few foreign journeys of, his father.

If it were in the 5th, it signifies the evil of his children.

If it were in the 6th, it signifies the evil of his quadrupeds, Slavs, slaves, and hired labor.[63]

If it were in the 7th, it signifies the evil of his wives, and their mutual enmities.

If it were in the 8th, his enemy will labor to kill him.

If it were in the 9th, he will have a bad faith.

If it were in the 10th he will see harms and impediments from princes.

If it were in the 11th, he will have little inheritance,[64] and few friends, and many enemies.

If it were in the 12th, he will not fear from enemies and rivals.

---

[62] *Extranea.* Normally I would translate this as "foreign," but the Latin translator has already used *peregrina*, "foreign." Māshā'allāh clearly means marriages with people abroad or from distant or "strange" places (*extraneus* can mean a stranger).
[63] Or, "mercenaries."
[64] Or perhaps, "real estate."

Chapter 20: On the signification of Saturn, when he is in his own bounds or those of other planets, in the nativity

If Saturn were in his own bound, it will give greatness and many things to the native, and gain in many things; but he will be infirm. And he will have civil power from greater men, and in their services, and in the services of the religious, and because of faith he will gain by all things.[65] And he will be very rich, and everyone will run to him for counsel regarding diverse matters. And if the benefics aspected him, all of the aforesaid will be increased; and if the malefics, they will decrease.

But if he were in the bound of Jupiter, the native will have many things, but he will lose everything in youth, and spend it, and he will be sad. But he will have a great name, and he and his household, and his services, will be mediocre up to thirty-eight years,[66] and from thence he will be glad in his progeny, and he will see his own will in them, and before it is born;[67] and he will see many good things from the one born. And in that house where he will be born, there will be a man having a defect or infirmity in the eye; and his substances will be many, and after he has passed the twenty-eighth year,[68] the services of the above-said first native will be good. And he will alter many matters, and he will find great services. And if he aspected with a benefic from its[69] exaltation, the aforesaid will be increased.

If he were in the bounds of Mars, the way is demonstrated thus, because the native's parents are foreigners and paupers, and this native will spend and tear away at their substance. And he will kill his relatives in obeisance,[70] or he will pierce some brother with a sword (whom a doctor will heal), and he will find discord from his first wife. And after the years of this planet have passed from his nativity, and he is made an old man, he will pass over to the

---

[65] Or perhaps, all *people*.
[66] This sum could be gotten by using Capricorn's 27 years, added to Jupiter's 12. This would equal 39 years, at the end of the 38-year period of mediocrity.
[67] Reading *nascitur* for *noscatur* ("before it comes to be known").
[68] Again, this could mean that we take the Capricorn years first, and then the minor years of the planet ruling the bound: the twenty-eighth year is at the end of the 27 Capricorn years.
[69] *Sua*. It is unclear whether this means Saturn's or the benefic's exaltation. I suspect the latter.
[70] *In adulatione*, lit. "to be in obeisance, flattery, fawning." This could mean he kills relatives who are obedient to him, or perhaps that he kills them due to his master's command.

services of religious men, and many pains will find him—but if the benefics aspected, he will be freed.

If Saturn were in the bound of Venus, it seems thus: wherefore the native will have much infirmity in his youth, and his father will die with his mother, and he will have children from two wives, and he will devise a lawsuit for his wives; but to the last he will rejoice, and he will gather together the children of his relatives. And pain will appear in his testicles so that he cannot lay down with a woman. And he will see moderate abundance, and poverty until the years of this planet have passed over—and afterwards he will rejoice with his kinsman and his children, and he will be in the first place. And if the benefics aspected, he will take a wife with much substance.

If Saturn were in the bound of Mercury, it seems that the native will devise a lawsuit for women, and he will see the death of his children, and many days will pass by and his wife will not be impregnated—and afterwards she will give birth to a daughter who will live until he will give her a husband, and he will see her nuptials, and she will generate sons and daughters. And he will appear great in the view of men, and they will not approach him, and from them certain ones will have a great name, and men will honor him and will consider him good for the works of his hands. And he will devise a lawsuit from princes or great men, and he will be made needy, nor will he have anything, and he will be captured as booty. But if the benefics aspected, he will be freed.

Chapter 21: On the signification of Jupiter in his own or others' bounds

If Jupiter were in his own bounds, the native will be over great services,[71] and he will see the children of his children. And whenever Jupiter enters into his own bound[72] he will find substance. And great men will confide in him, and above his hand there is no other in that service; and he will find sub-

---

[71] This refers to medieval traditions of personal loyalty and service. The text is saying that other people will owe him their services, and below it says that there will be no one above him in whose service he is. This model should be understood throughout the text below, where it speaks of the native being "over" or "above" other people.

[72] This must mean by transit (here and below), *provided that* he is in his own bound in the nativity.

stance from business matters, and he will take care of the household of his father: he will comfort and support it.

If he were in the bound of Saturn, he will find headache, and he will be captured by hostile armies, and he will be ransomed for money by them. And he will discover diverse things, and usefulness from business matters. And his enemies will not have power [over him], and he will know or discover how to attach [himself] to the secret matters of women.[73] And he will rejoice in his wife and children. And whenever Jupiter entered the bounds of Saturn, he diligently wishes to see his substances. And if the benefics aspected him,[74] he will be freed from the above-stated things. And if the benefic were in its own domicile, his services will be open,[75] and he will find truth from greater men. The usefulness or work of his underofficials will not be of equal importance[76] up to seven years.

If Jupiter were in the bound of Mars, he will find much malice, and will be captured by hostile armies, and will die a bad death; and he will be mustered to do something with iron [or a sword]. And his son will die, and he himself will die before his child will be born. And if the benefics aspected him, the evils will be decreased, and he will generate a son in his old age, and will see [the son's] death.

If Jupiter were in the bounds of Venus, he will be handsome, serious and honest, and he will take an honest wife. And he will be over the service of greater men, and his usefulness and fortune will be greater from business matters. And he will be instructing male and female slaves[77] who will honor him as a master; and men will speak well of him, and after him. And by taking care of manorial products[78] he will be subject to great riches, or he will be over great services by taking care of manorial products. And he will always be happy, and near the end of life he will be a religious man.[79]

---

[73] *Addere secretis mulierum.*
[74] Or perhaps "it," referring to the bound itself. But most of the time these two will coincide.
[75] *Aperta.* This means a combination of being honest and being well-known or unconcealed.
[76] *Aequale.* The significance of this is unclear to me.
[77] *Praecipiens servis et ancillis.* Normally this verb only takes the accusative. Perhaps the Latin translator meant it to work like *praesum*, which means "to be in charge of."
[78] *Supellectiles.* I follow Niermeyer here instead of Latham ("bedding," or "penis" for *supellex*), also following *Carmen* II.29.3, which speaks of being an overseer in the houses of kings.
[79] This must mean that he will enter an Order or take some official religious position.

If he were in the bounds of Mercury, he will desire to know books of diverse religions and beliefs, and men will esteem him and magnify him. And he will find fortune from the success of women, or he will have his usefulness from some adventure[80] or army. And he will not be a pauper, and he will be over the services of a [religious] belief, and he will be over the services of princes just like a prince. And he will be over towns,[81] and he will have great villages. And he will be just, honest and religious, the end of his works will always be useful. And if he[82] were in his own domicile, all of the above-said will be increased.

Chapter 22: On the signification of Mars in his own and others' bounds

If Mars were in his own bound, he will be the associate of soldiers in proportion to the occurrence of [his?] years,[83] and he will become practically a great man; and men will be grateful to him, and they will speak good things about him. And his life will pass over through a middling amount of discord and lawsuits; and the king over him will be angry, but he will be freed from him. And he will find pain from haste and from those wearing arms, since he stands in the middle of battle. And if a benefic aspected him, he will find a princely position, and there will be kings from him and after him, or they will say good words, and he will be over great services, and over great matters. And he will have many enemies, and the end of his works and life will be good and praiseworthy, and he will do malice to his wife.

If he were in the bound of Saturn, he will see the death of his children and his kinsman, and poisons or a toxin will be toasted to him. And if a benefic aspected him he will be freed, but he will destroy the substance of his own father, and he will find[84] a lawsuit in his old age; and he will go into places from which malice will arise. And whenever Mars entered into the bound of Saturn, he will devise a lawsuit, until the powers of his years[85] have

---

[80] *Casu.* Other possibilities are misfortunes, chance events, *etc.*
[81] *Castra.* This could mean a fortress or a walled-in town.
[82] This probably refers to Jupiter.
[83] *Pro eventu annorum.* I take this to mean the time of Mars's own minor years.
[84] This could also mean "devise" (*inveniet*).
[85] Reading *annorum* (pl.) for *anni* (sing.), probably referring to the minor years of either Saturn or Mars. But it is unclear which one it would be. Perhaps this is a case of primary directions of Mars through the bounds of Saturn, and not a transit at all—in which case,

passed by—and then much substance will come into his hands, and he will generate children and will rejoice; and on that account he will be subject to tribulation, and from these things many people will die a sudden death.

If he were in the bound of Jupiter, much substance will come to his hands, and he will find pain and tribulation, and infirmity, and he will be made stupid or out of his mind. And if he had a wife, she will not be impregnated. And he will make many foreign journeys, and he will destroy all of his own substance. And he will find lawsuits and pain on the occasion of slanders in which he has not done wrong, and he will enter into scandal and quarrels. And if the benefics aspected, he will find exaltation; and if the malefics, humiliation.

If he were in the bound of Venus, he will have a bad life on account of women, and he will take a wife because of a sin, and [women] will take him in sexual intercourse in sin or fornication,[86] and he will take prostitutes, and he will have them, and many days will pass and his works will not be good, and he will do nothing good with his wife and with his children, because the children which he will generate will die while tiny. Then he will be turned from the bad path in which he was, and he will spend much money on women, and he will not remain steady in his own faith, and he will be made insane because of women, and he will be taken and given as booty. And he will make many foreign journeys, and he will take a wife unequal to and unlike him. And if Mars were in the domicile of Venus, whatever would happen to him of the good and evil, will be mixed. And whenever Mars enters into the bounds of Venus, he wants to advance or see what belongs to him.[87]

If he were in the bound of Mercury, he will be a commissioner,[88] or will have a similar duty, and many different ones; and nothing good will be spoken about him, and his enemies will accuse him concerning everything which he does; and he will have many good things from the office which he exercises, and in his office it is not he alone;[89] and he will always become angry with his wife and children; and men will seek someone else instead of him,

---

Māshā'allāh is speaking of the years corresponding to the oblique ascensions of the bound of Saturn.
[86] *Capient eum in concubitu peccati vel fornicationis.*
[87] *Sua ipsius.*
[88] *Commissarius.* Or, "executor." He will be specially charged or commissioned to complete some duty.
[89] I think this means his special duty or office will somehow be shared with others.

and they will be turned away from him. And if a benefic aspected Mars, he will be freed from all of these evils.

Chapter 23: On the signification of the Sun in his own[90] and others' bounds

If the Sun were in the bound of Saturn, he will live long, and will be made fortunate. And if he had brothers, they will be likewise, and he will be like a prince in the houses of kings, or a judge, and all of his services will be open, and he will rejoice over his own children.

If the Sun were in the bound of Jupiter, he will be like a prince, and clothed in gold and silver. And he will fear God, and will adore much, or he will be a great businessman, and the end of his services will be good.

If he were in the bounds of Mars, he will have an intense mind,[91] and he will get angry quickly, and he will be made fortunate, and will make a journey by sea; and he will find discord and a bad infirmity from the clashing of iron.[92] And if some malefic aspected the Sun, he will be the gatekeeper of the residence in which he prays,[93] or he will be like a swift merchant. And if a benefic aspected, he will be freed from these things.

If he were in the bounds of Venus, he will always be happy, and will esteem women, and will be involved in many services, and will seek or take a wife from among his relatives, and will be in a place of the greater men of faith, and he will always be in that place, and he will approach it, and he will do good works from which he will find the income of people going on pilgrimage for God. And he will engage in something of the sciences, and wherever he would walk, his works will be good, and his substance will abound.

If he were in the bounds of Mercury, his livelihood[94] will be from writing, and he will be like a medical doctor, and he will be made fortunate, and speaking rightly, or administering justice, and he will be next to kings.

---

[90] This is an error of a later editor, as the Sun does not have any bounds.
[91] Reading *ardentis animi* for *ardenti animo*. Lit., "burning mind."
[92] Especially by sword.
[93] *Portarius erit hospitii in quo oratur.*
[94] *Vita*, lit. "life."

Chapter 24: On the signification of **Venus in her own or others' bounds**

If Venus were in her own bound, he will rejoice because of women and children. He will be like a city councilor,[95] and will be like a master over male and female slaves, and his heart will be good toward them. And he will be in a place of religious men or priests, and he will be like a bishop over priests. And he will become great[96] wherever he might be, and it will be good for his parents. And he will have good children who will be strong. And whenever Venus would enter into her own bound, his services will be good, and the laity will make much of him.

If she were in the bounds of Saturn, he will find a headache due to women, and he will seek or take [as a wife] a talkative woman, one liable to anger, proud and insubordinate. And he will stand many days without a wife, and after that he will take an old woman or one lower than himself, and low-class, and he will see little of old age. And whenever Venus would enter in the bound of Saturn, he will be made clean, and he will not do disgraceful or bad things. And if a benefic and malefic aspected it,[97] whatever of good and evil will find him, will be mixed.

If she were in the bound of Jupiter, he will be wise, and will rejoice in every work which he does, and he will be over an inheritance[98] and a multi-faceted estate, and he will have a brave and firm heart, famous and renowned, and he will be a manager[99] of religious places, known to princes and kings, and his wife will be good and wise, and the end of his works will be good and praiseworthy.

If she were in the bound of Mars, he will have a pain in taking a wife, and he will be a fornicator, and he will be taught in fornication. And he will find pain because of a slave-girl or female Slav, and [will find] a lawsuit from women, and will have a headache because of his own sons,[100] because they will be rustics. But he will have a dispute and pain by iron, and when he will speak many lies; and his fortune will be greater from robberies, and the occasion of a woman will be his death. And whenever Venus would enter into the

---

[95] *Consiliarius.*
[96] *Magnifiet.*
[97] *Eum*, referring to the bound.
[98] Or perhaps, "real estate."
[99] *Praeceptor.*
[100] *Liberorum*, a rare word. If it should be read as *libertorum*, it means "freedmen."

bound of Mars, he will want to be practically cleansed of evils. And if Venus were in her own residence,[101] whatever he would find of good and evil will be mixed.

If she were in the bound of Mercury, he will see joy from his wife and offspring, and he will take a wife from whom he will see many good things, and he will rejoice on the occasion of the works of entertainers; and he will find substance and an office from kings, and he will be over male and female slaves; and he will have a position over the crowd. And he will be a good writer, and he will know something well in all things; and his honor will be high, and like a chancellor and a judge in his own castle, and his works will be open, and they will listen to him in everything which he would instruct; and if someone did something evil to him, they will find harm and evil. And if Venus were in a common sign, he will find a great dignity, and his life will last through many days of joy. And if a malefic aspected it,[102] it will reduce the above-said things.

Chapter 25: On the signification of Mercury in his own and others' bounds

If Mercury were in his own bound, he will be high, and will have an official position in a place where they write compositions, and he will always be spending his time on a foreign journey. He will never be a pauper, he will have a great name, and he will be a member of the court,[103] and will seek the sciences. And he will be light and not severe, and he will teach men lightness,[104] and he will be the scribe of princes or kings, and will gather together substance from substance; and the crowd will rejoice in him, because he will benefit them, and he will always be involved in the good by virtue of his knowledge,[105] and he will have good dreams, but he will become anguished because of women, and afterwards he will rejoice.

If he were in the bound of Saturn, he will be happy on account of his virtue, and enmity will come between him and his brothers, and he will see the death of his brothers, and many days will pass by and his wife will be im-

---

[101] I.e., domicile.
[102] *Eum*, referring to the bound.
[103] *Curialis*.
[104] Reading *docebit hominibus levitatem*, for *docebit homines levitatem*.
[105] *Semper erit in bono pro scientia sua*.

pregnated, and he will be of lesser fortune for women, and he will stand many days on a foreign journey, and he will become wealthy, and afterwards he will find harm; and a relative will have a scandal with him, and they will go bring their suit to a prince, but his hand will be stronger than their hands. And he will be infirm from hidden things, and he will pass the years in joy and goodness. And whenever Mercury would enter into the bound of Saturn, he will want to be made clean.[106]

If Mercury were in the bound of Jupiter, he will be knowing and a city councilor, and a merchant, and he will be exalted, and will have a great name, and he will be like a master in the midst of the laity or idiots, and he will be above many matters, and over the services of princes and priests, and a long life will pass for him in happiness, so long as his father would be alive. And men will want to serve his offspring, and his male and female children will be Mercurial, and his enemies will be weak before him.

If he were in the bound of Mars, he will have much desire, because of which pain and discord will always be born for him; and his works are not good, and he will find harm and headache because of women, and he will lose his temper,[107] and moreover he will go to bed with his own offspring. And if Mercury were in his own domicile, the above-said things will be lesser. And he will always want to be cleansed whenever Mercury would enter into the bounds of Mars.

If he were in the bound of Venus, he will be a master of priests, and he will be happy for his children and his wife, and he will be wealthy and a counselor of those like him, and he will always be happy in his works, having rule over slaves, Slavs, and foreigners; and if he were of the faith of the priests, he will be knowing in every work, and he will be over the services of princes, and over religious houses. And death will be in his house, and he will flee due to his soul's fear. And if Mercury were in his own residence,[108] his days will pass in exaltation and goodness; and if Mercury were in his own fall, his works will be mediocre, and he will know the arts. And if the malefics aspected, he is of those who do not know the arts.

---

[106] *Mundificari.*
[107] *Evanescet cerebrum eius.*
[108] I.e., domicile.

Chapter 26: On the signification of the Moon in her own[109] or others' bounds

If the Moon were in the bound of Saturn, he will find a lawsuit from women and his offspring. And he will not take a wife unless the years of Saturn[110] had already passed. And whatever would come to his hands, he will destroy, until Saturn has run through the zodiac[111]—and afterwards much substance will arrive in his hands, and he will rejoice because of his wife and children, and his wife will pass just as is appropriate.

If she were in the bound of Jupiter, his fortune will be greater from mercantile dealings and a foreign journey. And he will devise a lawsuit, and he will have the honor of his son in his days; and just as his years grow, so will his substance grow, and his life will pass through many days in old age, and his life will always be good.

If she were in the bound of Mars, he will be liable to anger, and burning in anger, and his works will be from fire and iron, and he will find discord and harm from arms or from quadrupeds, or from wild animals. And if a benefic aspected, he will be freed from all of the above-said things.

If she were in the bound of Venus, he will be good, and he will have exaltation, and he will take a wife due to the event of fornication; and he will do it rudely in his own house, and a separation will come in their midst, and it will pass over concerning this.[112] And he will have children by two women, and he will take a wife unlike him, and he will find much substance without a lawsuit, and he will have honor from princes.

If she were in the bound of Mercury, he will be a good writer, and he will have many thoughts and wills[113] in his heart; and he will find usefulness from that; and he will be a member of the court,[114] and above the orders [given by] princes; and writers will consider him great and dear; and he will be in the services of a vulgar person. And he will have good sense and advice, and the end of his works will be good, if God wills.

---

[109] Again, this is a later editor's error. The Moon has no bounds.
[110] Typically 30, but we have seen above the reference to 27 years (which belong to Capricorn in the Hellenistic technique of "releasing").
[111] Again, approximately 30 years.
[112] *Transibit super hoc.* Meaning somewhat uncertain.
[113] *Cogitationes & voluntates.* That is, his mind will be full of things he thinks and wants to do.
[114] *Curialis.*

ON NATIVITIES

Māshā'allāh's book on nativities begins:

§1

And first, whether a boy would be weaned or not. Māshā'allāh said that among all books of astronomy, none is found to be more useful than a book of nativities,[1] nor so good in judgments. He who was skilled in it will find good sense and wisdom in it, and will delight in its knowledge.[2]

In the first place, it must be known if a boy will be weaned or not. And you will know this by:[3]

What is ascending, namely by the Lords of the triplicity;[4]

And by the [triplicity][5] Lords of the domicile of the Sun (if the nativity were diurnal) or the domicile of the Moon (if it were nocturnal);

And from the Lord of the conjunction or the Lord of the fullness,[6] if he were born after the conjunction or the fullness;

And if it were from the conjunction (or[7] the fullness), you will look from the Lords of the triplicity.[8]

---

[1] Holden (*JN* p. 79) suggests that this might be the title of the book whence Māshā'allāh seems to have taken some of his charts (see below). Since Latin does not have a definite article, we cannot be certain whether Holden is right, or this is a reference to books of nativities in general, or a reference to this work itself. At present I take it as a statement about books on nativities generally.
[2] *Peritia*. This is knowledge in the practical sense of expertise, not theoretical knowledge (*scientia*).
[3] This is the first of three lists given by Māshā'allāh. While they agree on certain features, none of the lists are identical, though they are reminiscent of, and probably derive from, passages in Dorotheus like *Carmen* I.4. See my introductory remarks to this work.
[4] I take this to mean the rising sign *and* its triplicity Lords (see below). Normally the rising sign or the Ascendant is referred to as the *ascendens* in the accusative, but here it is uncharacteristically put as *ascendentem*. Therefore I have written "what is ascending," on the off-chance that something else is meant.
[5] Following the order below.
[6] Otherwise known as the "prevention."
[7] Reading *aut* for Pingree's *et*.

On top of this you will look at Jupiter and Venus.

Which if the nativity were diurnal, you will look from the diurnal stars; and if nocturnal, from the nocturnal stars.

And you will begin to look to the Lord of the triplicity of the 1st domicile, that is, of the Ascendant; and to the second Lord and at the third Lord—these are the Lords of the triplicity of the 1st. Which if they were free from the malefics, namely in the Ascendant or in the 10th domicile or in the 11th or in the 5th, the native will live.

Which if they were cadent from the angles and they were bad,[9] you will look to the Lords of the triplicity of the domicile in which the Sun was then, if it were a diurnal nativity; but if the nativity were nocturnal, you will look to the Lords of the triplicity of the domicile in which the Moon was then. Which if they were in a good place and safe from the malefics, the native will live.

Which if they were in bad places, and [they were] malefics, you will look to the Lords of the triplicity of the domicile in which the Lot of Fortune was then.[10] Which if they were in good places and free from the malefics, the native will live.

Which if the nativity were diurnal, you will look to the Lot of Fortune; and if it were nocturnal, you will look to the Moon.

Which if [the Lot or the Moon] were in bad places, you will look to the Lords of the triplicity of the domicile of the conjunction of the Sun and the Moon (if the nativity were around the conjunction), or you will look to the Lords of the triplicity of the domicile of the fullness (if the nativity were around the fullness). Which if they were in angles and free from malefics, the native will live.

Which if they were malefic and impeded, look to Jupiter, who is a partner in nativities. Which if he were in an angle or in a succeedent of an angle, and

---

[8] I take this to mean the triplicity Lords of the sign in which the conjunction or prevention was.

[9] *Mali*, here and below. I normally translate this as "malefics," but I believe Māshā'allāh is only speaking about planets in a bad condition. See below, where the Moon is spoken of as being "bad in an angle."

[10] Note that the Lot of Fortune does not appear on the list above; but it belongs to the standard list places pertaining to life, which are considered when choosing a *hīlāj*.

free from the malefics, [the native] will live; but if he were in a bad place and impeded by a malefic, you will look at Venus. Which if she were in an angle or in a succeedent of an angle, and free from malefics, [the native] will live.

But if [Venus] were in a bad place and impeded by the unfortunate [planets], you will look at the Moon. Which if she were in the Ascendant or in the 10th domicile, and free from malefics, or joined to a diurnal star (if the nativity were diurnal) or joined to a nocturnal star (if the nativity were nocturnal), and free of the malefics, [the native] will live.

Which if [the Moon] were bad, you will look to the *mubtazz*.[11]

And[12] you will know by the Lords of the triplicity of the Ascendant; and if the nativity were diurnal, by the Lords of the triplicity of the Sun; and if the nativity were nocturnal, by the Lords of the triplicity of the Moon; and likewise by the Lords of the triplicity of the Lot of Fortune; and by the Lords of the triplicity of the domicile of the conjunction of the Sun and Moon (if the nativity were around the conjunction) or by the Lords of the triplicity of the domicile of the fullness (if the nativity were before the conjunction). Which if they were in angles or in the succeedents of the angles, and free from the malefics, [the native] will live; which if they were in bad places and impeded, he will die.

Then, look at the planet which was the *mubtazz*, and to whom it communicated its own disposition, and what degrees were in between. Which if it[13] were in a fixed sign, you will give a year to every degree; and if it were in a common sign, you will give a month to every degree; and if it were in a movable sign, you will give a day for every degree. But if the *mubtazz* were in a cadent, and a malefic planet in the Ascendant and the Moon joined to a malefic, he will live as much time as there were degrees—that is, if the one who [is] the receiver of the disposition were impeded, and he were in a fixed sign, it will be years; and if in a common sign, it will be months; and if in a movable sign, it will be days.

---

[11] Here and below it seems as though the *mubtazz* is the best planet from the above list (and not a separately determined planet); but if all of the other planets have failed, then how could any of them succeed as the *mubtazz*? Perhaps it is some other planet, but Māshā'allāh does not explain how to determine it.

[12] This paragraph is a repetition of the previous points. Then we return to the topic of the *mubtazz*, though without an explanation of what exactly that is—but probably it is the *hīlāj*.

[13] I take this to refer to the planet receiving the disposition (see below).

Then look to the degrees of the Sun or Moon. If they aspected each other from the square aspect (if the *mubtazz* [were] one of them),[14] or they had a conjunction in one domicile, or they aspected each other from the opposition, it will be bad unless the degrees of the *tasīrāt*[15] were there. And if some of the degrees of the *tasīr* were there, he will live so many years or months or days, as was said above, as there were degrees.

But if the *mubtazz* were joined to a malefic planet from the square aspect or from the opposition,[16] and some benefic did not aspect it, he will live only a little. Which if the Moon were conjoined between two malefics, and one were in the Ascendant, the other in the seventh, and the Moon bad in an angle, he will die.

But [if] the Lords of the triplicity of the Ascendant or the Lords of the triplicity of the domicile in which the Sun was,[17] and the Lords of the triplicity of the domicile in which the Lot of Fortune was, and the Lords of the triplicity of the domicile of the conjunction or the fullness, were impeded or in the cadents, and some planet were in strength,[18] he will have grave illnesses. And if the Lords of the triplicity of the domicile of the Ascendant were in the cadents, he will die; and it will be worse if one of the aforesaid were Saturn (in a nocturnal nativity) or it were Mars (in a diurnal nativity)—namely, in one of the angles.

Which if the Moon were received, and the Lord of the Ascendant in a good place, he will live and will be honored, and will have many brothers; which if there were not a reception there, it designates poverty.

If the Lot of Fortune were with the Moon, and she[19] aspected Venus in a nocturnal nativity (or Jupiter in a diurnal nativity), it designates height and a life just like if the Lot of Fortune were in a good place.

Every planet which indicates concerning the nativity, and was oriental[20] in a diurnal nativity and in a masculine sign, or occidental in a nocturnal nativity

---

[14] Holden (*JN* p. 87) reads this as though one of the luminaries is aspecting the *mubtazz* itself. But I do not see how he gets this: *Ex quarto aspectu si se aspexerint, cum [fuerit] almuptez aliquis eorum...*

[15] I.e., of primary direction, from the Ar. "to move/march." Holden (*JN* p. 87 n.2) reads this as indicating certain lunar stations based on al-Bīrūnī §254, but in the context of natal theory it indicates primary directions, as described in al-Bīrūnī §521 (and footnotes).

[16] *Septimo*, lit. "from the seventh [sign from it]."

[17] Presumably in a nocturnal nativity we would look at the same for the Moon.

[18] I am not sure what planet counts, but below he seems to define "strength" below in terms of sect, phase relation to the Sun, and zodiacal sign.

[19] I say "she," indicating the Moon, since the Lots do not cast rays.

[20] I am not sure exactly what form or orientality and occidentality is meant here.

and in a feminine sign, the planet will have a good strength, and its testimony [will be] good, and designates the loftiness of the native.

Which if the Lord of the Ascendant or the Moon were in evil, and the Lord of the domicile of the Moon [were] in an angle, it designates death.

And if you knew the native would not live long, you will perform a *tasīr* from the degrees of the Ascendant up to the bad planet who impedes, and you will give a month to every degree; but if the native escaped from these months, he will live as many years as were the aforesaid months.

Then look to the Lord of the 5th domicile: which if it were in a good place, the aforesaid must be judged good; if in a bad one, it will perplex his mind in poverty.

§2: When there is a *hīlāj* in the nativity, or not

A[21] chapter on the *hīlāj* in the knowledge of life, if the nativity of the boy designates life. And if you wished to know this, direct the *hīlāj* in a diurnal nativity from the Sun. Which if he were in an angle or in a succeedent of an angle, and in a masculine sign or in the masculine quarter (that is from the 7th house and previous [to that]),[22] and the Lord of his own domicile, or the Lord of his bound, or the Lord of his exaltation, or the Lord of his triplicity or his face aspected him, he will be the *hīlāj*. And if one of these did not aspect [the Sun], he will not be the *hīlāj*.

Then you will look at the Moon. Which if she were in an angle or in a succeedent of an angle, and in a feminine sign or in a feminine quarter, and [one of her Lords] aspected her just as I said for the Sun, you will take her as the *hīlāj*.

Which if the Sun or the Moon were not the *hīlāj*, you will look to the Lord of the domicile of the conjunction or the fullness; if it were not the *hīlāj*, you will look to the Lord of the domicile of the Lot of Fortune;[23] and if you did not find this [Lord] to be the *hīlāj*, you will put down the degree

---

[21] §§2-4 seem to be a mixture of elements from *Carmen* I.24 and III, possibly with some of *Tet.* III.11.

[22] That is, from the 7th backwards to the 4th. The Latin translator seems to have omitted that the space from the Ascendant to the Midheaven is also a masculine quarter.

[23] It is unclear whether the Lot of Fortune itself would be the *hīlāj*, or its dispositor. Usually in this tradition, the degree of the Lot of Fortune (or the conjunction, *etc.*, below) is being considered as a possible *hīlāj*, not its dispositor.

of the Ascendant as the *hīlāj*, if the Lord of the Ascendant aspected the Ascendant. But if all of the aforesaid failed, there will not be a *hīlāj*.

§3: On the acquaintance of the time from the *kadukhudhāh*

A chapter on the *kadukhudhāh*, through which the computation of life is known. And when the *hīlāj* is found, you will look at the *kadukhudhāh*, and you will look at the *hīlāj* and to the Lord of its bound, and to the Lord of its triplicity, and to the Lord of its domicile, and to the Lord of its exaltation, and to the Lord of its face—and of these, the one who aspected the *hīlāj* will be the *kadukhudhāh*. But if one of the planets, or two or three, looked to the *hīlāj*, that planet who was more in its own strength[24] and closer by degrees will be the *kadukhudhāh*.

You should know that if the Sun were in Aries or Leo, he will be the *kadukhudhāh* [and] he will be the *hīlāj*; and likewise if the Moon were in Taurus or in Cancer, she will be the *hīlāj* and the *kadukhudhāh*, if [the Lords mentioned before] aspected her or not (likewise for the Sun).

And if you found the *kadukhudhāh*, look at it: if it were in an angle by degrees[25] or in its own domicile or in the exaltation or triplicity, safe from impediment (namely from retrogradation or from the combustion of the Sun), you will give it the greater years of the planet; which if it were in a succeedent of the angle and safe from malefics, you will give it the middle years; and if it were in the cadent of an angle, and did not have any dignity there, you will give it the lesser years.

And you should know that the increase of a planet's years, or its decrease, does not exist except from the strength of a planet or its weakness. But if that planet were oriental[26] and in a good condition, you will give the greater ones; and if were not oriental and it had a bad aspect with some [planet], you will give it the lesser years; and if it were occidental and had a bad aspect with some [planet] and were retrograde, you will give it weeks [corresponding to] how many its lesser years were; which if it were in a bad place, in which it

---

[24] For Māshā'allāh's understanding of this "strength," see above. But I imagine also that a planet being in one of its own dignities would also count for its strength.

[25] *Ex gradibus.* Holden believes this is an error, but I am not so sure. It could be a reference to one of the 15° rules in *Carmen.* See Introduction.

[26] Again, it is unclear what sense of *orientalis/occidentalis* is meant here.

could not be worse, if [it were] retrograde, and of the lighter planets,[27] you will give it so many days as there were the lesser years of that planet.

And you should know that the Head of the Dragon, if it were in one sign with the planet who was the *mubtazz*,[28] within 12° or more, in front or behind, it adds one-fourth of the years of the planet which was the *mubtazz*. And if it were closer in degrees, it will be more useful yet. Which if the Tail of the Dragon were there, it subtracts one-fourth of the years. And if it were with the Sun or the Moon in the same degree,[29] it subtracts nothing; but if the Sun were the *kadukhudhāh* and were elongated from [the Tail], it subtracts from the years. Ptolemy says[30] the Head with the benefics adds fortune, and the Tail subtracts from the years. Which if the Head or Tail were with the Sun and the Moon, their strength will appear, whether to the good or the bad (and more strongly for the Moon). But if the *kadukhudhāh* were in a bad place, it will subtract from the years.

Which if Jupiter were with Venus in the Ascendant, each one of these adds [its own] lesser years in the nativity, unless the malefics impeded them—and likewise the Moon in a bad condition.[31] But if the aforesaid benefics (namely Jupiter and Venus), [or] one of them, were the Lord of the domicile of death, and were in the Ascendant, he will die before he lives a little bit.

§4: How many years the planets add to the *kadukhudhāh*

A chapter on knowing what the planets add or subtract.[32] And if you knew how many years you ought to put down through the *kadukhudhāh*, and you wished to know how many are subtracted or added, you will look at the *kadukhudhāh*. If there were a benefic with it, and it aspected with it from a sextile aspect or some good one, and if it were in a good place, it will

---

[27] I do not feel that Holden is justified in his reading of this sentence. He writes: "And if it is in an evil house in which it cannot be worse than retrograde [and is aspected by one] of the lighter planets…".
[28] Here *mubtazz* is being used as a synonym for the *kadukhudhāh*.
[29] *Gradualiter*.
[30] This is perhaps a conjecture based on *Tet.* III.11, p. 37.
[31] I.e., if the Moon were in a bad condition and were in a bad aspect (or perhaps any aspect?) with such a Venus or Jupiter in the Ascendant.
[32] In all of these following cases, it seems that the other planets will add to (or subtract from) the *kadukhudhāh* using *their own* years. The *kadukhudhāh* already gives years based on its own years and its own condition; the others will add or subtract to that number based on *their* years and conditions.

increase the lesser years of that benefic.³³ But if the benefics which aspected the *kadukhudhāh* were weak, you will give it so many months as the lesser years. And if the benefic planet who aspected the *kadukhudhāh* were retrograde, and a malefic impeded it, give it so many weeks as are the lesser years of that retrograde planet. But if the *kadukhudhāh* were with the Lord of the domicile of death, and some bad star impeded [the *kadukhudhāh*], it will be days [according to] how many the lesser years were. Which if there were a malefic star with the *kadukhudhāh*, and that star will be the receiver of the degree of the *kadukhudhāh*,³⁴ and they aspected each other from the square aspect or from the opposition, and they had a conjunction with the Lord of the domicile of death, how many the lesser years of the *kadukhudhāh* were, will be so many hours.

But if Mercury were in a good place and aspected the *kadukhudhāh* by a good aspect, the lesser years will be increased for [the *kadukhudhāh*]; and if it were the converse, how many its lesser years were, so many years will be subtracted. And the stronger of the planets' aspects is the aspect of Mars with the *kadukhudhāh*. But if you wished to know the exactness of death, look to the malefic who impedes the *kadukhudhāh*, and when the *kadukhudhāh* reaches those degrees,³⁵ he will die.

§5: What kind of will the native has

A chapter for knowing the native's will. Look to the Lord of the Ascendant and Mercury (who indicates concerning the native's way of speaking). Which if it³⁶ were strong and in a movable sign, it indicates he has a good way of speaking, and an honored one, and one fearing God. And if it were in a common sign, it indicates he has little wisdom, and is liable to anger, and as a rule he does not believe the advice of another. And if it were in a fixed sign, it indicates he is going to be honored, and by means of truth and goodness and counsel in his life, and his advice will be most truthful in every way, and he will free hindered advice from its hindrances.³⁷

---

³³ I take it that all of these conditions (being in a good place, *etc.*) pertain to the benefic, not to the *kadukhudhāh*.
³⁴ I am not sure what this means—perhaps it simply means that they will perfect their aspect.
³⁵ By primary direction.
³⁶ Māshā'allāh probably means we are to look at both. See below, where he says "they."
³⁷ *Liberabit consilia impedita ab impedimentis.*

Which if they were oriental[38] and in the angles or in the succeedents of the angles, it indicates a good nature and sharp talent,[39] and whatever he wanted to do he will do without impediment. Which if they were occidental and cadent from the angles, it indicates he is malevolent in heart, and [has] the association of low-class persons, and he will be excessively liable to anger.

And everything which was said before[40] is from the Lord of the Ascendant and the Moon: which if they were in a good place, say good; if however the reverse, [say bad].[41]

Every star maintains a rulership in the human body. But if the Lord of the Ascendant were the Sun, and in a good place, safe from the malefics, it indicates height and honor and rulership; which if he were bad and in a cadent place, it indicates he has a bad spirit and little fortitude and has little acquisition of wealth.

But if the Moon were the Lady of the Ascendant, and in a good place, free from the malefics, it indicates he is honest and modest; and if she were in a bad place, it designates him to be shameless and sad, and from his mouth will proceed...[42] through which his body will be beaten and pierced.

If Saturn were the Lord of the Ascendant and he were in a good place, free from the malefics, it designates him to be honored and popular and strict in oration and in aptitude, prudent in counsel. And if he were in a bad place, it designates him to be sad and lamenting, and a deceiver.

---

[38] Again, I am not sure of the sense of *orientalis/occidentalis* here.
[39] *Ingenium*. This could perhaps be translated as "sharp wit," with the understanding that this pertains to character and skill, not the sense of humor.
[40] I believe this only refers to the previous paragraph. But note that this is *not* how Abu 'Ali understands this material (*JN* pp. 7-8). Abu 'Ali says that all of the foregoing material in this chapter pertains to Mercury and the Lord of the Ascendant, and that the Moon and the Ascendant only signify the body.
[41] Pingree does not add anything in brackets to finish this phrase, so I have supplied it.
[42] There is a lacuna indicated in Pingree. But clearly it suggests that the native will say things that will get him into trouble. Abu 'Ali says nothing along these lines, suggesting only a bad mind and ugly body.

If Jupiter were the Lord of the Ascendant and in a good place and free from the malefics, it designates loftiness and honor and a good spirit. And if he were in a bad place, it designates him to be shameless and stingy.

Mars, if he were the Lord of the Ascendant and free from malefics, designates him to be extravagant, and he will have a strong heart. And if he were in a bad place, it designates he will be *alhagem*,[43] and he will be a drainer of blood or a butcher.

If Venus were the Lady of the Ascendant, and in a good place, it designates him to be handsome and humble. And if she were in a bad place, it designates he is hot [in desire][44] (and if were a woman, it designates her to be a prostitute).

Mercury, if he were the Lord of the Ascendant, and safe from the malefics, designates him to be wise and a medical doctor. Which if he were the Lord of the Ascendant and joined to Saturn, it designates him to be a stammerer in speech and a good medical doctor, involved in powerful matters,[45] and luxurious or a sodomite. Which if he were joined to Jupiter, it designates him to be good and wise, and he gets hold of a preferred rulership. But if he were joined to Mars or in his aspect, it designates him to be a king or the writer for a king. Which if he were joined to Venus, it designates he esteems wisdom and judgments, and will be treacherous in the law, enduring in strength or his weakness, whether in the arrogance of the mind or in the detriment of his knowledge.

You will know from the ends[46] of the signs concerning their strength or weakness, just as I have taught in the book on the nine parts of Māshā'allāh, where[47] it is written in Sahl bin Bishr, *al-ʾiqbāl* and *al-ʾidbār*,[48] and so on.[49]

---

[43] Uncertain. Some possibly related words are: *hajjar*, "to break away"; *hajr*, "desertion, abandonment"; *hujūm*, "attack, assault"; *hāja*, "to be agitated, stirred up," which has a related phrase which means to burst with anger; *hājaz*, "divider, partition." All of these boil down to anger and violence, or division and sundering, both Martial themes.

[44] *Calidum*, not *callidum* ("clever").

[45] Reading *in fortibus rebus* for *in forcibus rebus*.

[46] *Finibus*. I believe this should probably understood as *terminis*, the "bounds" of the signs.

Then, for the children of kings you will look to the degree of the Ascendant: if there were some hot star joined to the aforesaid degree, or in the Midheaven, and the degree of the Ascendant were a lucid one, or the Sun were there in a diurnal nativity or the Moon in a nocturnal nativity, and the native were from a lineage of kings, it designates he is going to be under the power of a king, and he will be lofty. Which if the nativity were diurnal, and the Sun [were] in Aries, or the Moon were in her exaltation in a nocturnal nativity, and in the Midheaven or in the degree of the Ascendant, and the Ascendant were of the signs which designate kings,[50] and the Lord of the Ascendant [were] in a good place, it indicates for a kingdom and for loftiness. But if the two luminaries were joined to the Lord of the Ascendant in its exaltation, it designates he will have a strong kingdom.

Which if the Lord of the Ascendant were joined with the Lord of the 10th domicile, and they were oriental and in their own exaltation, he will be a most powerful king. But if many stars were joined with Jupiter in the Midheaven or in his exaltation, it indicates he is an emperor; and every star which was the *mubtazz* and were as was said before, it will be for him concerning loftiness.[51]

Which if the Lord of the triplicity of the Ascendant were joined with the Lord of the Ascendant in the Midheaven, and it were oriental, it designates he is a king.

Operate with the diurnal stars, with the Sun; and with the nocturnal stars, with the Moon. And if the Sun were in his own domicile or in an angle or [his] joy, and the stars aspected each other, it designates he is a king.

---

[47] Reading *ubi* for *uti*.
[48] Lat. *Alichel et Alicherz*, the first two items on Sahl's list of planetary conditions in *Introduct.* §5. The statement about the "nine parts of Māshā'allāh" suggests that this little paragraph was inserted by the Latin translator.
[49] Following is the second half of the sentence, with Pingree's addition in pointed brackets: *sicuti docui in libro <De> ix partibus Mesalla uti scribitur in Zoelbembris, Alichel, et Alicherz, etc.*
[50] The fiery signs.
[51] *Erit ei super sublimitatem.*

§6: On the fortune and misfortune of the native

A[52] chapter for knowing the fortune and misfortune of the native in his nativity. You will look to the Lords of the triplicity of the luminary which it matched: in a diurnal nativity, that of the Sun; in a nocturnal nativity, that of the Moon. Which if they were in angles and free from malefics, it indicates the native's good fortune in all the days of his life. And if the first triplicity Lord were in the Ascendant, from the first degree up to the fifteenth,[53] he will ascend to great riches; and if it were in an angle, closer[54] in degrees, it will be more useful for him. Which if it were in the second sign, from the first degree up the fifteenth, [it will be likewise].[55] But if the first Lord of the triplicity were in a good place, he will have good in the first time; and if [it were] the second Lord of the triplicity, it will be in the second time; and if [it were] the third Lord, it will be in the third time; and if it is the converse, it will be the converse.

But if the Lord of the triplicity of the luminary were cadent and in a bad place, it designates he has poverty, namely in what time it was, in the first period or in the second or in the third. But if the Lords of the triplicity of the luminary were in bad places, and benefics were in the angles, and the Ascendant aspected them, and they were not impeded, it designates he has fortune. And if the luminaries were not impeded, it will be more useful for him.

Which if the Lord of the Ascendant and the Moon were in the angles, and free from the malefics, they indicate he has riches, and more if they were received. But if the Lord of the Ascendant will be joined to some one of the luminaries in its[56] own domicile or in the exaltation, or the luminaries joined themselves to the Lord of the Ascendant, it designates him to be eminent in riches.

And if the Lot of Fortune and its Lord [were] in an angle (namely in the east), and they aspected the Ascendant, it indicates him to be very wealthy; which if they were in the cadents and the bad places, it designates him to have detriment and more, unless the Lords of the triplicity of the Ascendant

---

[52] This section derives largely from *Carmen* I.22-26.
[53] This is a reference to one of the 15° rules in *Carmen*. See my Introduction §6c.
[54] Reading *proprior* for *prior*, also following Abu 'Ali (*JN* p. 11): "And the closer it is to the degree of any angle…".
[55] Following Abu 'Ali (*ibid.*): "likewise if the planet is in a succeedent." See my Introduction for my interpretation of this phrase.
[56] That is, if the luminary is in its own exaltation or domicile (following Abu 'Ali, *ibid.*).

aspected the Ascendant. Which if they were in the cadents of the angles and were joined with benefics in angles, it designates him to have good before the detriment; if the Lord of the Ascendant were cadent and in its own detriment, and were joined with a planet which was in its[57] own exaltation or in its own domicile, it designates he has good after the detriment.[58]

---

[57] That is, if the other planet being applied to is in its own exaltation or domicile.
[58] In the following examples, I will present the charts in the standard square medieval chart form, using whole-sign houses unless otherwise noted. While some charts are based on Dorotheus, others come from other sources (see below). I note that while Abu 'Ali has a chart corresponding to every one of these, his own charts differ in details; thus Holden rightly suggests (*JN* p. 80) that Abu 'Ali was not taking his charts directly from Māshā'allāh, but from their common (and unknown) source. The reader should compare these delineations below with Dorotheus and Abu 'Ali, since they differ in interpretive detail despite reaching generally identical conclusions.

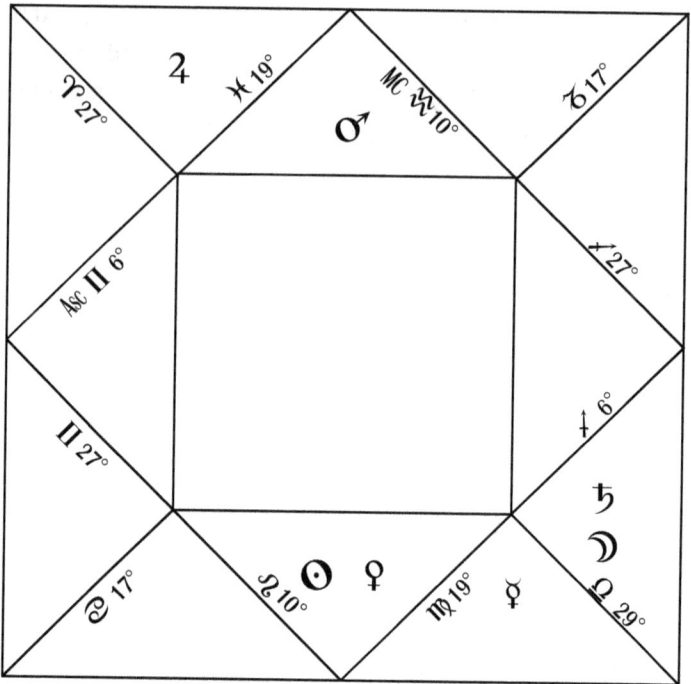

Figure 35: Example 1, A Nocturnal Figure[59]

I looked at the fortune of this native from the Lords of the triplicity of the Moon, because the nativity was nocturnal. And the first Lord of the triplicity was Mars, Venus the second one, and the Moon the third Lord of the triplicity. And they were cadent. I judged him to be in poverty, and at the appointed time I saw he was a beggar. And he died in misery and in poverty. And all of this is laid bare in this figure.

---

[59] This chart is based on *Carmen* I.24.2; *cf. JN* p. 13. But the medieval translator of this work has evidently recalculated the chart with intermediary quadrant cusps at a location around 43° N, so the descriptions do not make sense in terms of the original angular/succeedent/cadent *signs*. In the original, no degrees of the Ascendant or Midheaven are shown; the Sun and Venus are in Leo, a cadent sign; Mercury is in Virgo, an angular sign; the Moon and Saturn are in Scorpio, a cadent sign; Mars in Aquarius, a cadent sign (though he is actually in Scorpio); Jupiter in Taurus, a cadent sign. Holden dates this chart from August 2-3, 43 AD GC. A chart cast for 12:11 AM on August 2, for Marseilles, France, gives us almost exact cusp values with Alchabitius semi-arc houses.

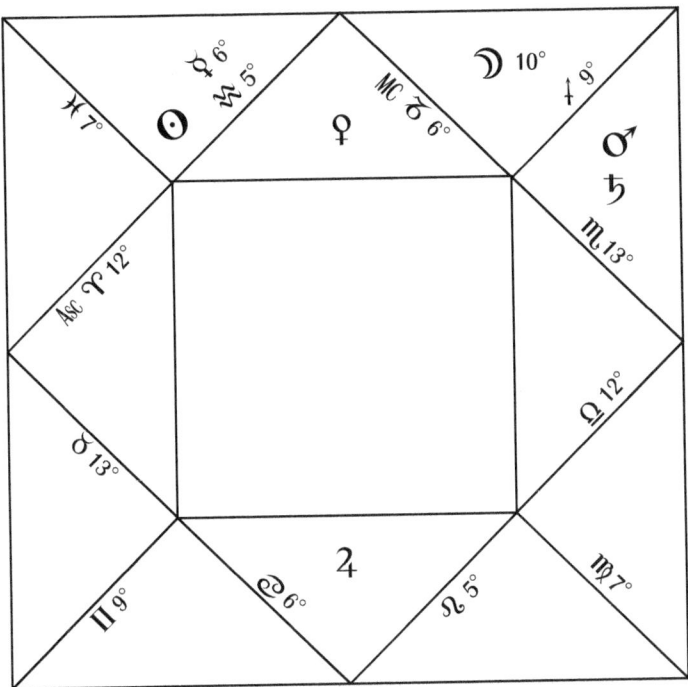

Figure 36: Example 2, A Diurnal Figure[60]

I looked at the fortune of this native from the Lords of the triplicity of the Sun, because the nativity was diurnal. And Saturn was the Lord of the triplicity, and the second one Mercury, and he was nearly[61] in an angle; and one in the descendant, and another in the Midheaven. Then I judged him to have goodness and much forbearance, and so it was always good.

---

[60] This chart is based on *Carmen* I.24.5; *cf. JN* p. 14. Again, the chart was originally whole-sign, with no degrees of the Ascendant, Midheaven, or planets. The medieval translator or editor has recalculated it for quadrant houses. In the original, Jupiter is in Libra and Venus in Pisces. Also, only Māshā'allāh says that Mercury is "nearly" in an angle. Holden dates this chart to January 29-30, 425 AD. The cusp values can be obtained by casting the chart for Marseilles, France, at about 9:45 AM, with Alchabitius semi-arc houses. Note that no value is given for the Sun.
[61] *Fere*.

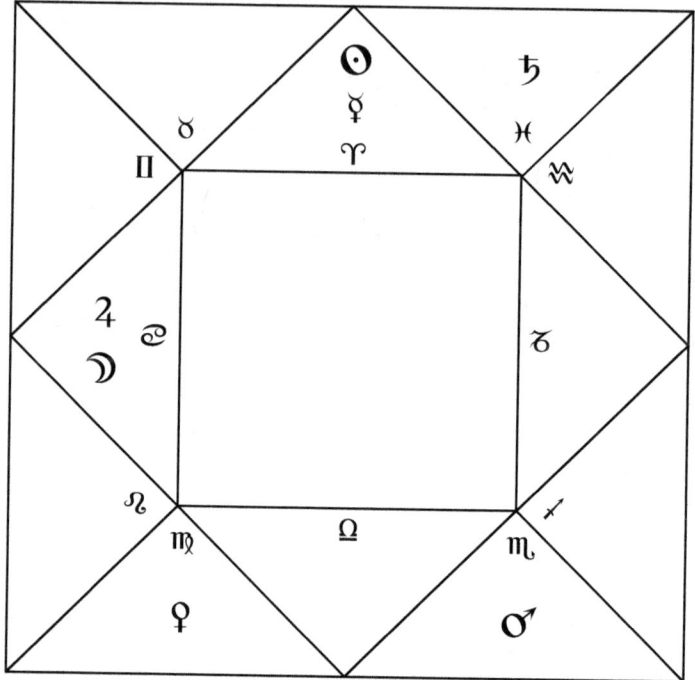

Figure 37: Example 3, A Diurnal Figure[62]

I looked at the fortune of the native from the Lords of the triplicity of the Sun. And the first Lord of the triplicity is the Sun, and the second one Jupiter, and the third Lord is Saturn. And I found these in the angles and in their exaltations; it was designating him to have fortune and loftiness, and therefore Saturn did not kill him because he was in the domicile of Jupiter, and was aspecting him by a good aspect.

---

[62] This chart is based on *Carmen* I.24.7; cf. *JN* p. 16. Pingree and Holden date it to March 29-30, 22 AD. In the original, Mars did not appear (he is in Cancer), and Venus is misplaced in Virgo (she is in Aquarius).

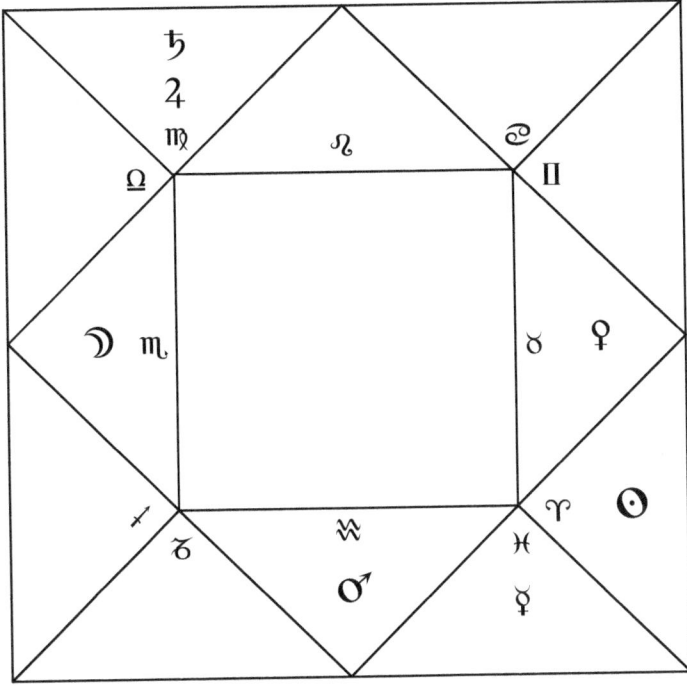

Figure 38: Example 4, A Nocturnal Nativity[63]

I looked at his fortune from the Lords of the triplicity of the Moon. And the first Lord of the triplicity is Mars, and the second Lord is Venus, the third Lord the Moon. And I found these in angles; therefore I judged that he would ascend in exceeding loftiness until he acquired the gold crown; and it was so.

---

[63] This chart is based on *Carmen* 1.24.9; *cf. JN* p. 15. Pingree and Holden date it to April 1-2, 36 AD. Based on that date, Mars should be in Pisces, Mercury in Taurus, and Saturn in Leo.

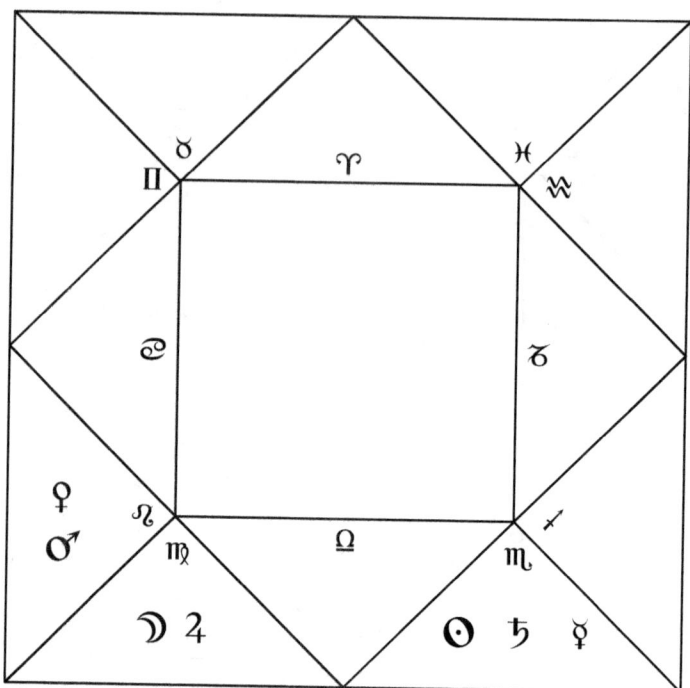

Figure 39: Example 5, A Nocturnal Nativity[64]

I looked at the fortune of this native from the Lords of the triplicity of the Moon, which were Mercury first, Saturn the second, Jupiter the third. And these were cadent.[65] I judged misery and poverty concerning him, and it was so.

---

[64] This chart is based on *Carmen* I.24.12; cf. *JN* p. 17. But there seems to be some dispute over its date, possibly because Abu 'Ali's version puts Jupiter in Gemini rather than in Virgo. In *Carmen* p. 166 (Appendix 1), the date is given as October 31, 12 AD; but Holden discusses several different possibilities from the 5th and 6th Centuries. In the version from *Carmen*, Venus is in Virgo, the Moon and Jupiter in Libra. If we date the chart to 12 AD as above, then Mars is actually in Virgo, and Venus with Jupiter and the Moon in Libra. My sense is that the confusion is due to a copyist's error, since the Mars-Venus and Moon-Jupiter groupings are always together, but they get pivoted into the wrong signs.

[65] But Saturn and Mercury are *not* cadent in this chart. Dorotheus makes the same comment.

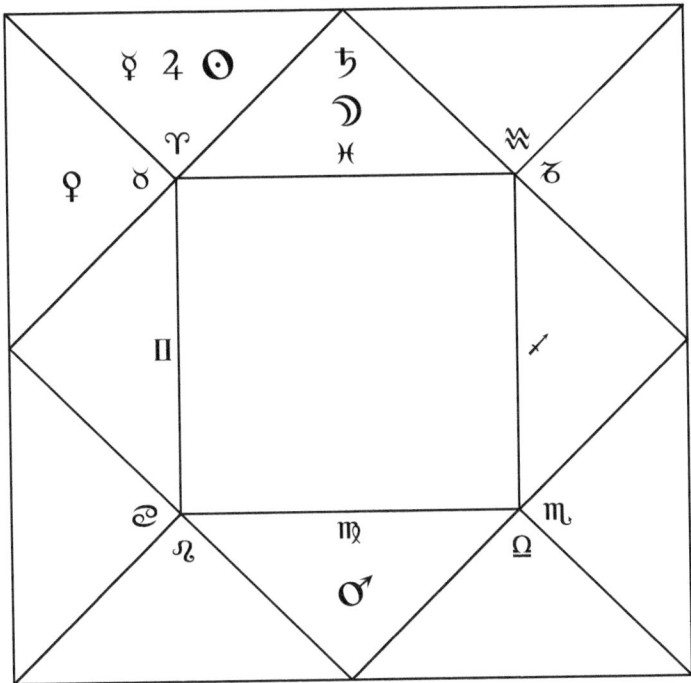

Figure 40: Example 6, A Diurnal Nativity[66]

I looked at the fortune of this native from the Lords of the triplicity of the Sun, of which the first is the Sun, the second Lord Jupiter, the third Saturn. And I found these in angles. I judged him to have loftiness and high rank and honor in all the days of his life; and it was so.

---

[66] This chart appears to be based on *Carmen* I.24.15; *cf. JN* p. 18. In the *Carmen* version, Jupiter is in Pisces. Again there is a dating issue. But Appendix 1 of *Carmen* (p. 166) gives the date of March 29, 7 BC. According to that date, the Moon, Jupiter, Saturn, and Mercury are all in Pisces.

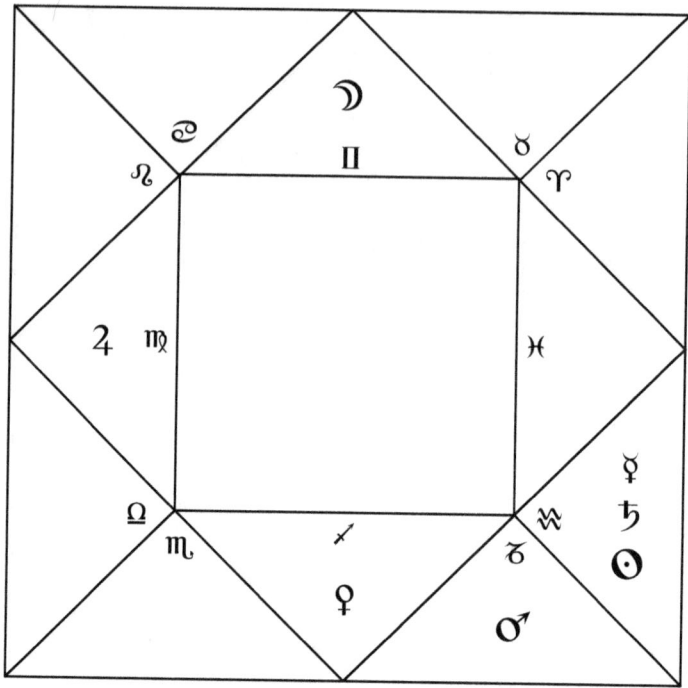

Figure 41: Example 7, A Nocturnal Nativity[67]

I looked to the Lords of the triplicity of the Moon, of which the first one [was] Mercury, the second Lord Saturn, the third Lord of the triplicity Jupiter. And I found these cadent from the angles and in bad places. I judged him to be miserable and a beggar.

---

[67] To me this chart appears to be based on *Carmen* I.24.17; *cf. JN* p. 20. *Carmen* puts Jupiter in Sagittarius, and Saturn and Mercury and the Sun in Scorpio, not Aquarius); *cf. JN* p. 20. Again there is a dating issue. According to *Carmen,* Appendix 1 (p. 167), the date is November 26, 14 AD. In that chart, Saturn is in Sagittarius, Jupiter is in Scorpio, Mars is in Libra, the Sun in Sagittarius, Venus in Sagittarius, Mercury in Scorpio, the Moon in Gemini.

MĀSHĀ'ALLĀH: ON NATIVITIES

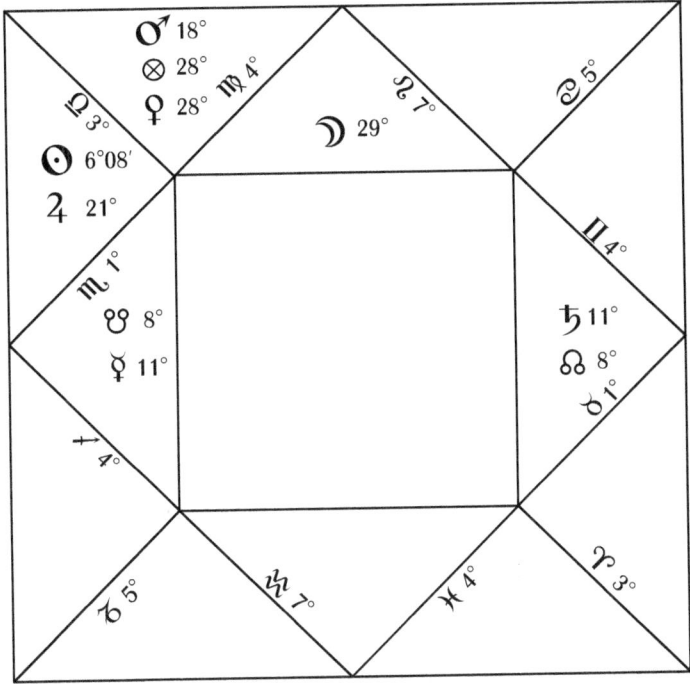

Figure 42: Example 8, A Diurnal Nativity[68]

I looked at the fortune of this native from the Lords of the triplicity of the Sun, of which the first was Saturn, the second Mercury, the third Jupiter. I found these aspecting from the opposition, and Mercury joined with the Tail, and Saturn with the Head, and Jupiter cadent, and the Lot of Fortune with Mars, and the Lord of the Lot of Fortune joined with the Tail, and Saturn was in the fullness.[69] Then we judged [him to be] very stupid[70] and miserable; and all of this is made clear in this figure.

---

[68] This chart is from an unknown source, but appears in *JN* p. 19, with only a few minor differences. Holden dates the chart to October 19, 439 AD. We can get a close match for cusp values if we cast it for Marseilles, France, at 6:53 AM, with Porphyry houses. Note also the Lot of Fortune is off by almost exactly one sign.
[69] I am not sure what this means. It cannot mean that Saturn is in the sign of the prevention, because that took place in Aries, not Taurus.
[70] *Perstultum*.

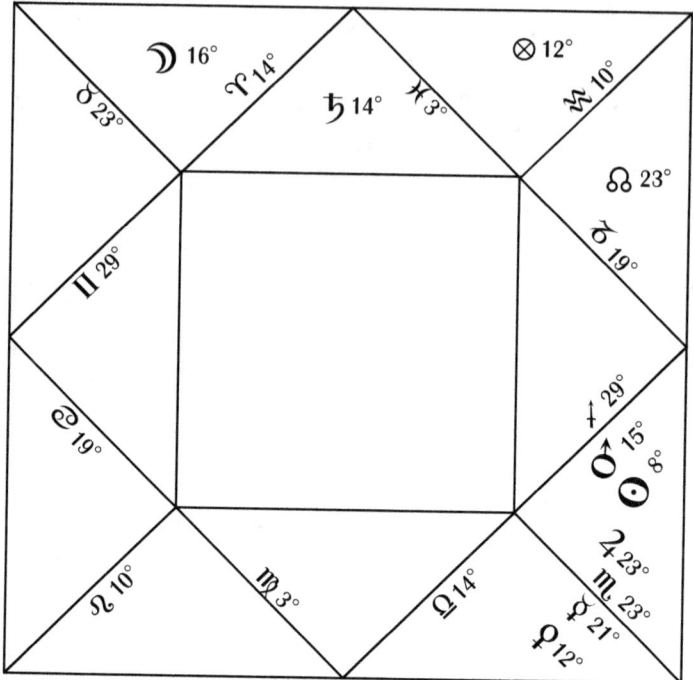

Figure 43: Example 9, A Nocturnal Nativity[71]

I looked at the fortune of this native from the Lords of the triplicity of the Moon, of which the first is the Sun, the second Jupiter, the third Saturn.[72] And I found them cadent in the 6th domicile.[73] Therefore it indicates for evil and insufficient good, [and also] in accordance with the testimony of the Lot of Fortune, which [also] indicates for evil.[74]

---

[71] This chart is from an unknown source; *cf. JN* p. 21. The Midheaven value, which was 8°, has been corrected to match the IC value. According to Holden, Pingree dates this chart to November 25, 464 AD. A chart cast for this date at 6:00 PM in Marseilles, France, matches all the cusp values with Alchabitius semi-arc houses.
[72] Since it is a nocturnal chart, the order should be Jupiter, Sun, Saturn.
[73] But in the chart the Sun is in the 7th domicile and Saturn in the 10th. But by quadrant houses, the Sun and Jupiter are cadent in the 6th house. Since the source of this chart is currently unknown, we cannot be certain of the intention of the original text.
[74] Abu 'Ali (*ibid.*) says this is because the Part is cadent, its Lord not aspecting it.

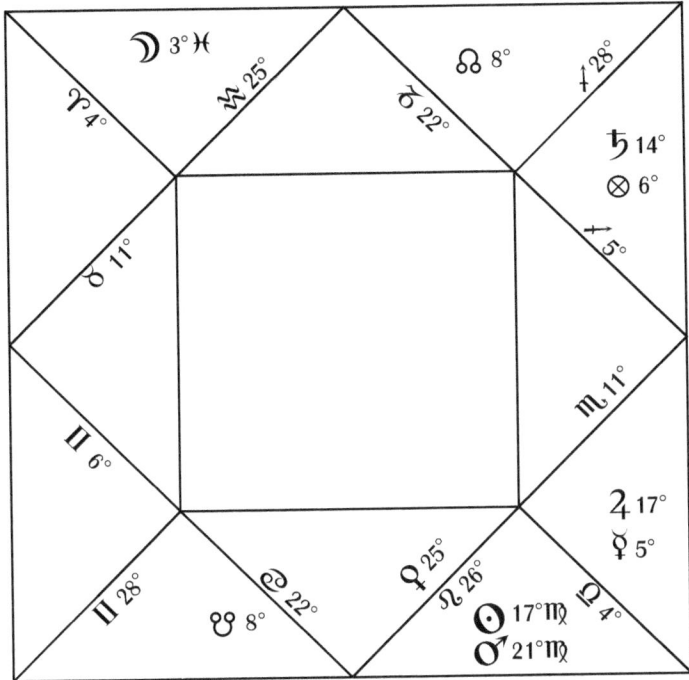

Figure 44: Example 10, A Nocturnal Nativity[75]

I looked at the fortune of this one from the Lords of the triplicity of the Moon, of which the first is Mars, and he was under the rays of the Sun in the square aspect. It indicates for loss and evil in the first time of his life, and in the second part of his life it indicates for good, because Venus was the second Lord, and she was in a good condition. And it designates that in the second time of his life he will have good before much labor. But Jupiter and Aquarius were in the 6th domicile from the Lot of Fortune;[76] it designates him to have honor and advancement.[77] It was so.

---

[75] This chart is based on Rhetorius (Holden locates it in *CCAG* VIII.1); *cf. JN* p. 22. The degree of the Ascendant is given differently by Abu 'Ali. Here I have reproduced Māshā'allāh's version, which is dated by Pingree to September 8, 428 AD. Again, the chart cast for Marseilles, France, gives almost exact cusp values with Alchabitius semi-arc houses. The only change I have made is to the 12th house, which the Māshā'allāh text gives to Pisces (when it should be Aries). Note the other minor errors, such as opposite cusps receiving different values.

[76] Actually they are not. Jupiter is in the 6th domicile from the Ascendant, and Aquarius's position seems irrelevant.

[77] Reading *profectum* for *prospectum*.

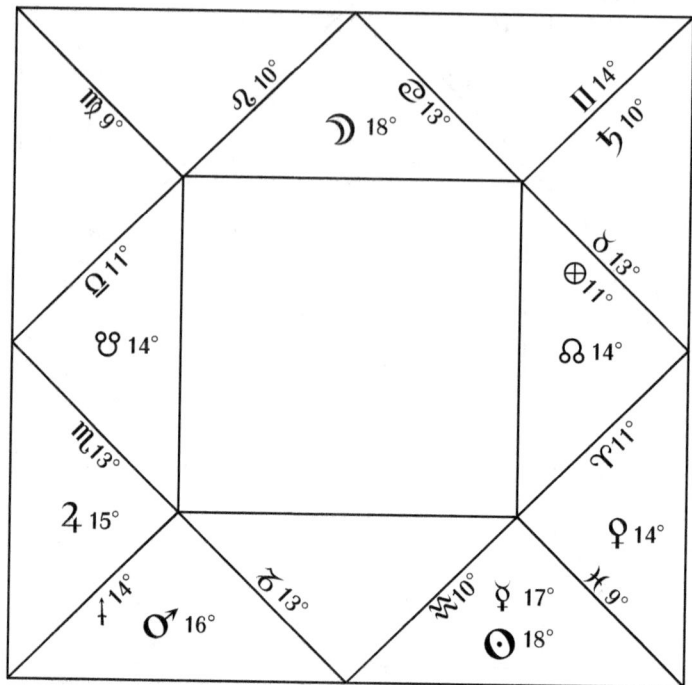

Figure 45: Example 11, A Nocturnal Nativity[78]

I looked in the nativity of this one from the Lords of the triplicity of the Moon, of which the first was Mars, the second Venus. And I found these cadent from the angles. It designates he has a bad life and loss. When we looked at the Moon, and she was in the 10th, and the Lot of Fortune in Taurus, it indicates he will have good for the last period of his age.

---

[78] This chart is based on an unknown source; cf. *JN* p. 23. According to Holden (*JN* p. 84), Pingree dates the chart to February 7, 442 AD. A chart cast at Marseilles, France, at 9:46 PM gives very close cusp values with Alchabitius semi-arc houses.

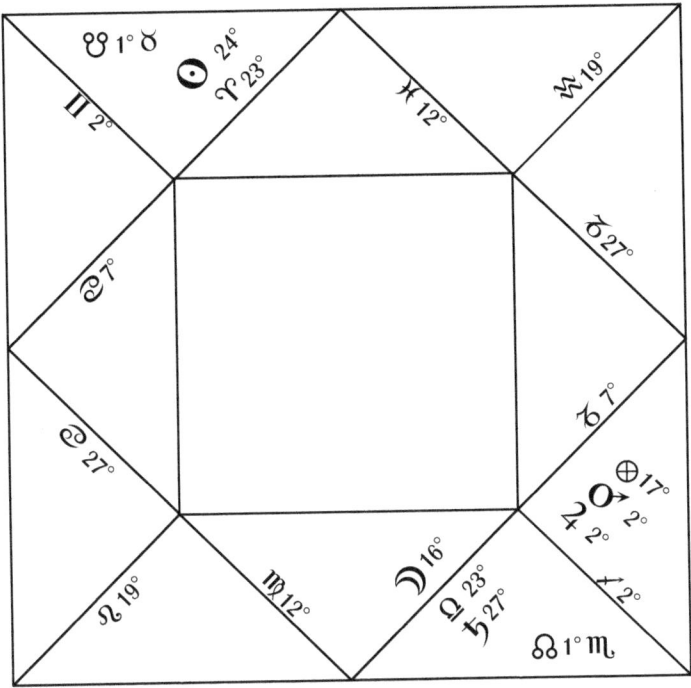

Figure 46: Example 12, A Diurnal Nativity[79]

I looked from the Lords of the triplicity of the domicile in which the Sun was, of which the first one was the Sun, Jupiter the second, Saturn the third; and I looked to the Lot of Fortune. It indicates he has good and honor, and more in the middle of his time. And this appears in the figure.

---

[79] This chart is from an unknown source; cf. *JN* p. 24. Holden (p. 85) disagrees with Pingree on the dating and proposes April 3, 394. The chart cast for 10:10 AM in Marseilles gives us almost exact cusp values using Alchabitius semi-arc houses. Note that Mercury and Venus do not appear in the diagram (nor do they appear in Abu 'Ali's description). I have added in both Nodes after consulting the modern calculation: the diagram originally had "Tail in Scorpio 1" placed up where Taurus is.

ON THE INTERPRETATION OF COGNITION

The Book of Māshā'allāh on the interpretation of cognition begins:

Māshā'allāh instructs that you should set up the Ascendant by its degree and minute, and the houses,[1] most precisely. And he said that questions come to be[2] by three ways:[3]

First, for what reason the questioner has come, so that you might know [it] and about what he is asking.

Second, that you should know what was the cause of the question.

Third, that you should know whether it might be perfected or not, and what end it will have.[4]

Therefore, if you wished to know this, first know the significator according to what I will tell you—the knowledge of which is that you should look at[5] the Ascendant and its Lord, and at the Moon, and the Lord of her domi-

---

[1] If Māshā'allāh were working only with whole signs, then there would be no need to determine the *domos* precisely (apart from the degrees of the Ascendant and the Midheaven). Therefore I have retained "houses." But the open question is still whether these houses are to be used topically, or only for determining a planet's strength.
[2] Reading *fiunt* for *sint*.
[3] The "reason" is shown by the condition and the nature of the significator; the "cause" is shown by the planet the significator separates from; the "end" is shown by the planet to which it is being joined. See below.
[4] Heller reads these differently, but is not much more helpful in making sense of these different causes: "First, that you should know the cause, concerning which he is asking; second, what cause impelled him; third, that you should know whether the matter would be perfected or not, and what end it is going to have."
[5] Note that Māshā'allāh gives two slightly different lists. The first list includes: the Ascendant, the Lord of the Ascendant, the luminary whose authority it is, the Lord of the sign of that luminary, the Lord of the hour, and the Lot of Fortune. The second list given below includes: the Lord of the Ascendant, the luminary (as above), the Lord of the sign of that luminary, the Lord of the Lot of Fortune, and a planet in the angles.

cile; the Sun, too,⁶ and the Lord of his domicile, and the Lord of the hour, and the Lot of Fortune. And operate through that one which had more authorities⁷ and was in a better place. Which if you did not find one from those which I told you, look at the Lord of the Ascendant or the Lord of its exaltation, also the Lord of the bound and the triplicity and the face—and know which one of these is stronger in the Ascendant by the multitude of its dignities. And you would look, and you would set up this one as the significator if it were in a good place. (And the goodness of a place is that it is in one of its own dignities, or in a good place from the Sun, or in the angles, free from malefics). Therefore, operate through him who is stronger and had more dignities and were in a better place.

And know that the Lord of the Ascendant, if he were in the Ascendant, is more worthy,⁸ more so than the rest. Which⁹ if he were [not]¹⁰ in the Ascendant, and the Lord of the exaltation of the Ascendant were in it, he alone will be the significator. Indeed if both were in the Ascendant, they will both be partners. If however one of them had, in addition, another dignity, and it were stronger by place, this one will be the significator and will be more worthy. If some planet who had a dignity in the Ascendant would be joined to one of them, or were the Moon in the domicile of one of them and she were joined to it—which if it were so, that one will be the significator on account of the multitude of dignities. Which [if] it were not in the Ascendant, [seek]¹¹ the significator or the Moon or a planet which was in the Ascendant or in the rest of the angles, and was stronger than the rest in the figure.

And know that each sign has a Lord, and ascends in two hours, and many things can be asked in them. And if the Lord of the Ascendant was the significator of all things, [then] all things asked under the same sign would be all good or all bad according to the signification of the Lord of the Ascendant—but it is not so. Likewise, the Moon is being joined to some planet

---

⁶ Below, Māshā'allāh clarifies that this is in diurnal charts.
⁷ See *On Hidden Things*, §6.
⁸ Omitting *ascendente illo*.
⁹ Heller's text reads rather differently for the rest of this paragraph: "Which if he were not in the Ascendant, and the Lord of the exaltation of the Ascendant were in it, he alone will be the significator and more worthy; and you would look thus at the one who was stronger in the circle by the multitude of dignities, even if he were not in the Ascendant or in the rest of the angles, and he was stronger than the rest in the sign."
¹⁰ Adding *non* with Heller, else these sentences would not make sense.
¹¹ Reading *quaere*.

through the whole day, and through the greatest part of the day, but the significations[12] of matters are diverse in that same day: because certain ones of them are effected, but certain ones not. Wherefore it is necessary for us always to seek the significator.

Therefore, know which one is the significator, and I will tell you out of which ones you should choose—namely, out of the Lord of the Ascendant, and the Moon, and the Lord of her domicile, and from the Sun, too (in the day), and from the Lord of his domicile, and from the Lord[13] of the Lot of Fortune, and from a planet which was in the angles (and especially in the Ascendant or in the Midheaven), the one which was stronger in the figure.

And know that the more truthful intention is the one which the questioner has had in his heart for one day and night,[14] or more.

Therefore, if you found the significator, and you wished to know the cause of the question—that is, whence the question has arisen—look to see from whom the planetary significator of the intention is being separated. And know that the cause of the intention would be according to the nature of the planet from whom the significator is separated. And if you wished to know the end of the intention, know to whom the significator is being joined. And know how the end of the intention will be through the signification of the planet to whom it is being joined.

And now I will erect for you an example, through which you would be able to perceive all questions generally, and the significations of matters, if God wills:

---

[12] Omitting *significatorem*.
[13] Reading *domino* for *domo*. Heller omits this consideration.
[14] That is, for 24 hours.

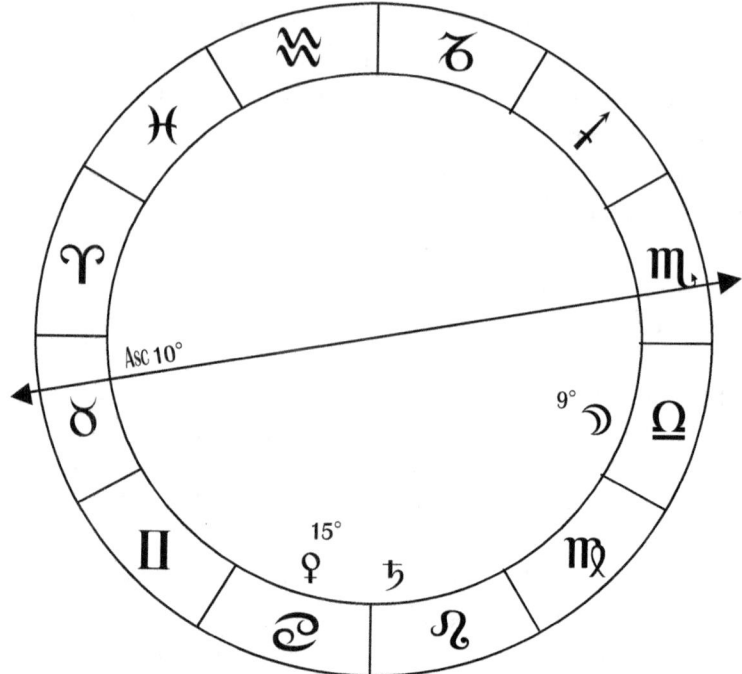

Figure 47: Discovering the Intention

A question, the Ascendant of which was Taurus, 10°. And Venus, its Lady, in Cancer, 15°, namely in the domicile of the Moon. And likewise the Moon in Libra, in the domicile of Venus, in the tenth degree. And the Moon was peregrine, because she was not in her own domicile nor her own exaltation or triplicity.[15] But she was being joined to Venus from the square aspect, and she was received. Also, the Lord of the Lot of Fortune was *Zuhal*[16] (that is, Saturn), who was in Leo, peregrine; nor was he received.[17]

---

[15] Note that Māshā'allāh does not consider bound or face relevant here, at least for purposes of peregrination.

[16] Lat. *Zoal*, a transliteration of the Arabic for Saturn. Here and below the text suddenly begins to use transliterated Arabic, often with little Latin translations written above the word. I have retained (but have corrected) the transliterations and supplied the English words in brackets, to give the reader a sense of what the medieval Latin astrologer would have encountered.

[17] Due to the position of Venus, the chart must be nocturnal. A nocturnally-calculated Lot of Fortune in Capricorn or Aquarius puts the Sun between 29° Taurus and 28° Cancer. But if the Sun were in Cancer, Venus would most likely be under the beams or combust, which is not mentioned. Moreover, I am not an expert on the ephemerides used by astrologers like Māshā'allāh. At any rate, possible dates for the chart include July 14, 799

And I looked at all the planets but I did not find in them one stronger in place than Venus was, because she was the Lady of Taurus, *al-Thawr*,[18] and she was in her own triplicity. Therefore I looked at the Lord of the domicile in which she was,[19] and she was in the domicile of the Moon. Therefore I began to look afterwards to see where *al-Qamar* [the Moon][20] was, so that[21] I might seek the significator from her,[22] because she was the Lady of the domicile of *al-Zuhrah* [Venus][23] (the which Venus was the Lady of *al-Thawr* [Taurus]),[24] whom I found [in] *al-Miyzān* [Libra][25] in the sixth domicile from *al-Thawr* [Taurus],[26] and in the fourth place from the significator, which was *al-Zuhrah* [Venus].[27] And *al-Qamar* [the Moon][28] signifies mothers. Therefore I knew that he was asking about the infirmity of his mother.[29]

And since I wanted to know [the infirmity's] nature, I looked to see from whom *al-Qamar* [the Moon][30] would be separated, [and] she was being separated from *Zuḥal* [Saturn].[31] And I knew she was suffering a cold and dry infirmity. And I wanted to know in what member [of the body] the infirmity was, and I looked at *Zuḥal* [Saturn][32] in the first face of *al-ʾAsad* [Leo][33]—

(during Māshāʾallāh's lifetime), July 17, 446, August 7, 623, or even June 14, 34, all on the Julian Calendar.
[18] Lat. *Athalf*.
[19] Looking at the dispositor of the Lord of the Ascendant was not in either of Māshāʾallāh's lists.
[20] Lat. *Alcamara*.
[21] Reading *ut*.
[22] Reading *ea* for *eo*.
[23] Lat. *Azore*.
[24] Lat. *Athale*.
[25] Lat. *Almizene*.
[26] Lat. *Athala*.
[27] Lat. *Azura*. Here he says Venus was the significator, but below he says the Moon is.
[28] Lat. *Alcama*.
[29] This paragraph is full of information but little exposition to explain it. First, Māshāʾallāh has identified Venus as the significator. But then he looks at the Moon, apparently because she disposes the significator Venus. He identifies two things: first, that she is in the fourth sign from the significator; second, she is in the sixth natural domicile. This means that the Moon's place will say something about the question, through a relationship to Venus and the Moon's own house position. The Moon is in the fourth from the significator, signifying family members; of family members, the Moon signifies the mother, so it is the querent's mother; and since the sixth signifies illnesses, he concludes it is about the mother's illness.
[30] Lat. *Alcamara*. But notice that, contrary to his rules stated above, he is using the separations and applications of the *Moon* here, and not Venus (who is the significator).
[31] Lat. *Azoal*.
[32] Lat. *Zoal*.
[33] Lat. *Alased*.

and *al-ʾAsad* [Leo][34] has, of the members of the body, the stomach. And I said that she was suffering in the stomach. But since I wanted to know what end it would have, I looked to see to whom *al-Qamar* [the Moon][35] (who was signifying the intention) was being joined, [and] she was being joined to *al-Zuhrah* [Venus].[36] And I said that she would be liberated on account of *al-Zuhrah* [Venus],[37] who is a benefic and was receiving her. And since I wanted to know the time of the liberation, I looked at the degrees of the conjunction which were between *al-Zuhrah* [Venus][38] and *al-Qamar* [the Moon].[39] I said that she would be liberated after so many days as there were degrees. And I put down days, because *al-Qamar* [the Moon][40] was in a movable sign. For if she had been in a common sign, I would have put months. And if in a fixed one, years. And if *al-Qamar* [the Moon][41] was being joined to *Zuḥal* [Saturn][42] or *al-Mirraykh* [Mars],[43] I would have said that she would die in so much time.

Look thusly for the intention and for hidden things, and in all general matters about which you are asked—that is, know by this means what end it will have. And likewise, set up the time of the effecting of matters according to this example, and commingle the significations of the planets [with] the significations of the signs, and the matter of every intention and question will be made plain to you according to what I have expounded to you, if God wills.

And know that if it had been Venus instead of the Moon, I would have said that he was asking about a woman; if then she had been in the seventh, I would have said that he was then asking about a marriage; and if then [she had been] in the fifth,[44] about children; and if in the eleventh, about friends. And if it had been the Sun instead of the Moon, I would have said that he was asking about his father; and if [he had been] in the tenth, about the king; and if he had been in the Ascendant, about some princely position; and in

---

[34] Lat. *Alased.*
[35] Lat. *Alcamara.*
[36] Lat. *Azoare.*
[37] Lat. *Azoram.*
[38] Lat. *Azoram.*
[39] Lat. *Alcamaram.*
[40] Lat. *Alcamara.*
[41] Lat. *Alcamara.*
[42] Lat. *Zoal.*
[43] Lat. *Almaret.*
[44] BN seems to read "fourth" (*iv*), but it must mean the "fifth."

the ninth, about faith; and in the third, about a foreign journey. And if it had been Mars instead of the Moon, he would have been asking about a fugitive or about a robber; and if he had been in the Ascendant, it would have signified fear; and in the second, stolen goods and the taking away of substance; and in the third, a brother; and in the seventh, an adversary fighting against him; and if it had been *al-ᶜUṭārid* [Mercury][45] instead of *al-Qamar* [the Moon],[46] he would have been asking about a letter or about wisdom. And if it had been Jupiter in the ninth, I would have said that he was asking about a dream. And I have already expounded to you above how to mingle the significations of the planets with the significations of the signs.

---

[45] Lat. *Arcarit*.
[46] Lat. *Adgoek*. A small superscript reads *Lunae*.

ON HIDDEN THINGS

In the name of the Lord, the little book of interpretations which I reckon to be by Māshā'allāh, begins. For I have found it extracted from his book on questions.

§1: [How the astrologer can go astray]

Know that the one looking (that is, the astrologer) can go astray in four ways:

First, if the astrolabe were false, or he took the shadow in an uneven place, or with a crooked plank.

Second, if the questioner did not know how to ask.

Third, if he did not know whether the Sun had already receded from the Midheaven or not.

Fourth, if the benefics and malefics were equal in assent,[1] then he could go astray—that is, he could be deceived in the strength of the benefics or malefics.

But in every question which is free from these ways, if you came to know the significator well, you could judge rightly, and you will not go astray. Nor should you be operating by estimating (that is, do not judge through your own free choice[2]) without reason: because if you did so, you will rarely find [the truth].

---

[1] *In probatione.* This can also mean "proof." The idea is that the balance of information from the benefics and malefics was roughly equal.
[2] *Arbitrium.* The earlier word translated as "estimating" (*aestimatio*) and *arbitrium* do not primarily have to do with freedom, arbitrariness, and subjective opinion. *Aestimatio* originally meant to assess the financial value of goods, and *arbitrium* originally meant decision, control, authority. But the Latin translator seems to be using them in a later, more subjective sense. The idea is that we are not to use a subjective, "it feels like this to me" attitude, but rather judge the planetary combinations carefully through reason.

§2: On discovering the significator

A chapter on the knowledge of the significators of an intention, from the different sayings of the ancients. Know that the intention will be more accessible if his reflection[3] retained it in his heart for one day and night (or more). For if he did not know how to ask about his intention, you[4] would not be able to find the significator of the question. Because the circle will be according to the intention of the one asking, and according to the reflection of his heart. Therefore, [if] he who asked you [did so] well, you will not go astray—but not every man knows how to ask. And now I will tell you something about the intention, inasmuch as[5] if the questioner were to ask well, you will not go astray, if God wills. This is what I have found to be stronger, concerning the significations.

Now you should set up the Lord of the Ascendant [as] the first significator, and the planet who receives his disposition, because the intention will be concerning the place of the Lord of the Ascendant (out of the circle),[6] or according to the place of the reception of disposition (out of the circle)—that is, the signification of the intention is taken from these places. The intention is also found from that same ascending degree: that is, that you should look to see to what planet the degree of the Ascendant is being joined, because the intention will be according to the place of that planet (out of the circle). Nor should you overlook a planet which is in the Ascendant, if it were not removed from the degree of the Ascendant: because the intention or deliberating will be according to the nature of that same planet. Therefore, look to see of what domicile of the circle [that] planet[7] is Lord, because the intention will be according to that domicile which it aspected.[8]

---

[3] *Cogitatio*, the same word used in *Cognition*. *Cogitatio* (also translated as "reflection" below) has especially to do with the process of judging, reflecting, meditating, resolving on something.

[4] Reading *potueris* for *potuerit*.

[5] Reading *quatenus* for *quatinus*.

[6] I.e., where the planet is actually located. This phrase seems to be used in order to distinguish it from the sign ruled by the planet, which may be somewhere else.

[7] I.e., the one near the degree of the Ascendant.

[8] Clearly we are to see what domicile it rules; the clause about aspecting may mean that the domicile it rules can only contribute its topic if the domicile is in a whole-sign aspect to the rising sign. For instance, if Taurus is rising and Mars is in it, the intention cannot be from 12th-house matters, because Aries (in the 12th) doesn't aspect Taurus. But perhaps 7th-house matters (Scorpio would be on the 7th) would work. Still, that would mean no planet in the rising sign could signify wealth, servants, death, and illness, since these domiciles never aspect the rising sign—and that seems unreasonable.

Also, the second significator is according to Dorotheus and Antiochus and Ptolemy, and Vettius Valens:[9] this is that you should look at the sign in which the Lot of Fortune is, because the intention will be according to the nature[10] of that same domicile from the Ascendant. That is, if it were in the Ascendant, the question will be about himself; and if it were in the second, it will be about substance; and if it were in the third, it will be [about] his brother; and thus concerning the remaining twelve signs.

The third significator is according to the Indians, who said if you were asked about some matter which he was concealing from you, look at the Lord of the dignity of the degree of the Ascendant, and at the Lord of its bound or face (that is, the one which is stronger), and see to whom it is being joined. Because what he was concealing will be by[11] that.

And[12] what is stronger than all of these is that you should look at the twelve-degrees of the degree of the Ascendant—upon which sign they fell.[13] Which if the Lord of that same sign were there, or another planet were there, the intention will be according to the place of that domicile in the circle. If however you did not find a planet in that place, look to see where the Lord of that domicile is: because the intention will be according to the twelfth of the Ascendant[14] from the Ascendant, and according to its Lord. An example of which is this: that the Ascendant was the twelfth degree of Aries, which, when I had projected two-and-a-half degrees for each sign, beginning from Aries (which was the Ascendant), the number was ended in Leo,[15] which, from the Ascendant, is the domicile of children—in which neither the Sun nor another planet was journeying.[16] Therefore I looked at the Sun, whom I found in the seventh from the Ascendant. And I said that

---

[9] *Velium*. I am not sure where Māshā'allāh is getting these alleged cites.
[10] *Substantiam*.
[11] *Apud*. That is, it will pertain to or belong to matters associated with that planet.
[12] I cannot be sure that this paragraph is not connected to that on the Indians, but it does seem to be a fourth, favored option.
[13] *Aspicias xii gradus ascendentis super quod signum ceciderent*. Based on the instructions below, this is a statement about the *duodecimae* or twelfth-parts of a sign. Each sign is divided into twelve sections of 2°30' apiece, allotted to the zodiacal signs. The first twelfth-part of each sign belongs to the sign itself, the next one to the next sign, and so on. Thus the first twelfth-part of Virgo (0°—2°30') belongs to Virgo, the next (2°30'—5°) belongs to Libra, and so on.
[14] That is, the twelfth-part.
[15] The twelfth degree of Aries is from 11°—11°59'. The twelfth-part of Aries corresponding to Leo is from 10°—12°30'. Hence the degree of the Ascendant falls in the twelfth-part of Leo.
[16] *Peregrinus*.

the question was about a child who sought a woman, wanting to take her as his wife. And if the Sun had been in the sixth, I would have said that he was seeking concerning an infirm child; and so on with the rest of the twelve signs.

§3: The division of a place into quarters[17]

A chapter on the hiding of a ring or other thing, according to Dorotheus.[18] If someone were to hide a ring (or any other thing) from you, in some place in the house, and you wanted to find it, set up the Ascendant most precisely, just as well as you can. Then, divide the home into four parts. After this, look to see where the Lord of the Ascendant is: which if he were in an eastern sign, then look at [the home][19] and divide it into four parts, and discard the remaining parts. After this, look at the Lord of the aforesaid eastern sign, from which you found the Lord of the Ascendant. (Which if it were in a northern sign, look at the northern part of this division, and look to see where the Lord of this sign is. Indeed if it were in a western sign, look at the western part, and discard the rest.)

And look to see where the Lord of this sign is:[20] which if it were in a southern sign, look at that southern quarter, and discard the rest. And look to see where the Lord of that southern sign is, and likewise divide that quarter by four, until you come to the place of concealment, and you will find it, if God wills.

§4: The division of the quarter itself[21]

A chapter on the quadrant—that is, the figure of the extraction of hidden things, according to the rule of the *hīlāj*.[22] Hidden things are discovered

---

[17] See my Introduction for a clearer description of this method and the related one described below in §5.
[18] Unknown source.
[19] *Ipsam*.
[20] Now I believe we are talking about the Lord of the Lord of the Ascendant, who was alluded to in the previous paragraph.
[21] Reading the faint title as *Divisio ipsius quartae*.
[22] *Hyles*.

through it,[23] by means of the quadrant, by the will of God, if [the astrologer] knew well the [Ascendant],[24] and he knew how much all the planets had walked through in their own signs. But if he did not know the measure,[25] and he did not know how much every planet had walked through in their signs, in terms of degrees, and he did not know the part of the sign, he will find a part but will not find the place.[26]

And this rule: you will look at the Ascendant and its Lord, and the Lord of the hour, and see which of them better aspects the Ascendant—and set this one up as the significator. And you will look to see where it is. Which if it were in the Ascendant, the hidden thing which is sought will be in the middle of the east: that is, if it were in the degree of the Ascendant, it will be in that very eastern line in the quadrant. And if it were in the tenth, it will be toward the south (and to your right while you are looking at the east). And if it were in the fourth, it will be toward the north (and to your left if you were looking at the east). And if it were in the seventh, it will be in the west, behind your back (namely when you are looking at the east).

But if you found the significator between the Ascendant and the fourth, it will be between the east and the north. Which if it were in the second from the Ascendant, it will be closer to the east than to the north. And if you found the significator between the fourth and the seventh, it will be between the north and the west. And in the decrease of the measurement you should do as we have said above: that is, if it were in the fifth, it will be closer to the north; and if it were in the sixth, it will be closer to the west; and for the south you will do [it as] in the decrease of the measure above. And if you found the significator between the tenth and the Ascendant, it will be between the south and the east. And in the decrease of the measure you should do as above.

---

[23] *Eam.* I believe this refers to the *hīlāj*, which is often treated as a feminine noun in Latin.
[24] The ungrammatical Latin reads: *si bene sciverit aequator aequatae ascendens.* If the case endings were changed, this might read, "if the assayer knew well the equated Ascendant," or "if [the astrologer] knew well the equated equator of the Ascendant," and so on. But the basic point simply seems to be that we should know the Ascendant exactly.
[25] *Signum mensuratae.* Again, this seems ungrammatical. It could mean, "the sign of what was distributed," or "the measured sign," but that would demand case changes. At any rate the phrase seems to refer to knowing the Ascendant.
[26] I am not sure what the distinction between "part" (*pars*) and "place" (*locus*) is here. If place means "quadrant house," then it is possible that one might know (inexactly) the part of a sign the planet is in, but not know the quadrant house.

But before everything you ought to look at the Moon, to see whether she aspects the Ascendant or the significator, and likewise the benefics. Because if she[27] aspected one of them, it signifies the quickness of the discovery; and if she did not aspect the Ascendant, it signifies the slowness of the discovery.

But if the hidden thing were in his house, [know] that the airy signs signify the roof; and the fiery ones the walls; and the watery ones the foundation; and indeed the earthy ones the floor of the house. Therefore, know of what nature the Ascendant is, and seek in a place just like it. So, seek hidden and lost things in this way, [and] you will find it, if God wills.

And know that if the significator[28] is between two signs—that is, between the end of one and the beginning of the next—the thing was neither stolen nor concealed, but fell in a fall.[29]

Again concerning the discovery of a hidden or lost thing. If someone were to ask you about a lost or hidden thing, whether he would find it or not, look at the Ascendant, to its Lord, and the Lord of the hour. If the Lord of the Ascendant and the Lord of the hour were in angles, he will find his thing. But if they were in the dark domiciles—that is, in domiciles which do not aspect the Ascendant—he will not find it. And if the Lord of the hour or the Lord of the Ascendant were in the Ascendant, his thing is already with him, and not lost. But if one or both of them were in the seventh, he will find it after several days. And if the Lord of the hour or the Lord of the Ascendant aspected the Sun, he will find it. And if the Moon aspected him, it will be better; and wherever the Lord of the hour is, there will be the things. Understand.

§5: According to Dorotheus

The treatment of Dorotheus on hidden things.[30] Dorotheus said, if you were asked about a treasure or about some hidden thing, look at the seventh sign from the Ascendant—in which, if you found benefics, know that some hidden thing is in that same place. Likewise look in the angle of the earth

---

[27] I take this to refer to the Moon, here and in the rest of the paragraph.
[28] Reading *significator* for *significatio*.
[29] Reading *sed casu ceciderit*. This verb tense would not usually be used for a straightforward statement of fact, but I take this to mean that the object has fallen in between two places—like between the couch and the wall, or something like that.
[30] Much of this chapter seems to be a mixture of information from *Carmen* V.35.

(that is, in the fourth[31] from the Ascendant)—in which, if there were some benefic, know that there is something buried there.

Which if [the object] were in the house, and you wanted to know where it is, look at the Sun and the Moon. Which if they aspected the Ascendant, it will be above the door of the house. And if the Lord of the hour were in the Midheaven, it will be in the middle of the house. And if it were in the seventh, it will be in the western part of the house. And if it were in the fourth, it will be toward the north. But if the Lord of the hour were eastern,[32] the thing will be buried recently—that is, newly[33] buried. And if it were western,[34] the buried thing will be ancient.

And look at Mercury: which if he were in the Ascendant, it will be buried in the ground. And if Venus were in the Ascendant, it will be under the bed.[35] And if Jupiter were in the Ascendant, it will be under a wall. And if Saturn were in the Ascendant, it will be in a stinking and dark place, or in a deserted and destroyed house, or in the latrine. And if the Sun were in the Ascendant, it will be in a better place of the house.

And if the Moon were in the seventh,[36] it will be in a place of women or wine. And if Mars were in the seventh, it will be in a hallway[37] or in the house oven,[38] or in the kitchen, or where fire is kindled. And if the Head were in the seventh, it will be in a higher place like in the dining room; and if the Tail were in the seventh, it will be in a stinking and dark and moist place.

After this, look at the Sun and the Moon to see if they were[39] in the Ascendant, or both or one of them aspected it: they will signify the quickness of the matter.

Also look to see whether some planet is in the eighth, because it will be the significator of the buried thing—that is, it will indicate what it is.

After this,[40] divide the home or place into four parts: namely the eastern, and the western, the southern and the northern. Then look to see how much

---

[31] This probably means the fourth sign.
[32] *Orientalis*. Precise meaning unclear, as with "western" in the next sentence.
[33] Reading *noviter* (as below) for what looks like *noverit*.
[34] *Occidentalis*.
[35] Or, under the couch (*lecto*).
[36] I am not sure why the author suddenly switches to the seventh.
[37] *In itinere*. Or, "duct, passage."
[38] Reading as *in domo furni*.
[39] Reading plural instead of singular, due to the next clause.
[40] See my Introduction for a clearer description of this method and the related one described above in §3.

the Lord of the hour has traveled through in the sign, and in which one of the degrees it is, and multiply those by 12; and what was collected together, divide by sign, giving to each sign 30°, beginning from the Ascendant until the number is finished. After this, look to see what kind of sign it is in which the number is ended—that is, look [to see if it is] eastern or western, southern or northern—because it will be in that quarter, if God wills. Aries, Leo, [and] Sagittarius [are] eastern. Gemini, Libra, [and] Aquarius [are] western. Therefore, know in what part [it is]. Taurus, Virgo, [and] Capricorn [are] southern. Cancer, Scorpio, [and] Pisces [are] northern. If the finished number which you multiplied were in the twelfth...[41] And know that it will be in that same direction, if God wills.

After this, divide that part again[42] by four parts, and look to see where the Lord of the sign (where your number fell) is, and how much of the sign it walked through, in terms of degrees, and divide [the degrees] through the signs, giving seven-and-a-half degrees to each,[43] beginning from the sign in which the planet is: and where the number is ended, look at that sign to see whether it is eastern or western, and so on. And know that it is in that same direction.

After this, divide that part[44] into four parts, and look at the Lord of the sign in which your number fell, in whose domicile it is, and how much the Lord of that domicile has walked through in terms of degrees [in the sign] in which it is, and divide those degrees through the signs, giving to each sign seven-and-a-half degrees; and you will begin from the sign in which it is. And where the number were ended, see what sign it is—that is, whether it is eastern and so on, and know that it will be in that [direction]. Work in this way as much as you want, until the place is rendered in the measure of one cubit in its breadth and length, and you will discover it, if God wills.

And[45] this [next method] of measuring, according to certain people, is said to belong to Jirjis,[46] who says that we should seek the direction of the hidden thing from the Lot of Fortune and its Lord: that is, if these were in eastern signs, it will be in the east, and so on.[47] But he says that we should

---

[41] The sentence ends here.
[42] Reading *iterum*.
[43] Dividing 30° by four yields 7°30'.
[44] The sign in which the Lord of the other sign is.
[45] The author is now introducing a new method.
[46] Reading as *Et haec mensura secundum quosdam dicitur esse Gergii*.
[47] This is more like the method attributed to Dorotheus, Antiochus, Ptolemy, and Valens above.

seek what the hidden thing is from the fourth domicile and from its Lord. Moreover, he says that if the Lord of the Ascendant and the Moon were in a good place, strong and fortunate, there will be something buried, if God wills.

§6: According to Ptolemy

Ptolemy said[48] if the significator[49] aspected the Ascendant, the kind of the hidden thing will be of the nature of the Ascendant; and if it did not aspect it, it will be of the nature of the significator's place. And the Lord of the hour signifies its color. And the place of the Moon signifies its time: which if she were above the earth, it will be newly buried; and if she were under the earth, it will be old. And from the Lord of the Lot of Fortune is signified the length or shortness of the thing—that is, the length and shortness of the mater whence it was taken up.[50] And from the Lord of the bound of the degree of the fourth,[51] and from the Lord of the Midheaven—that is, from the one of them which was in an angle—and from the Lord of the bound of the Moon, is known its nature. (He wants the bound of Ptolemy to be understood here.)[52]

The significator of which Ptolemy speaks is not the Lord of the Ascendant, nor [the Lord of] the Moon,[53] nor he who was more worthy in the Ascendant[54]—but rather he to whom are joined many strengths, namely, he who was more worthy in the Ascendant *and* in the places of the luminaries. And were it joined to no one,[55] that is, it did not commit its own disposition to another, and it were strong in its own place (or perhaps it were joined to another, and that other were joined to no one, and it were strong in its own place), such a one will be the significator of the intention and the thinking.

---

[48] Source unknown, but definitely a pseudo-Ptolemy.
[49] See the next paragraph for the definition of the significator in this instance.
[50] I am not sure what distinction or clarification is being made here.
[51] That is, the degree of the IC itself.
[52] Lit., "the bound of Ptolemy wants to be understood here." This may be a comment by the Latin translator, or by the original compiler/author. At any rate, we are supposed to use Ptolemy's bound rulerships when using Ptolemy's method.
[53] *Lunae*. But it could be a scribal error for *luna*, meaning simply "the Moon."
[54] This probably means the planet with the most rulerships in the Ascendant, giving a single point to each dignity.
[55] Reading *nulli* for *ulli*.

And the place in which it was, will signify the intention or thinking:[56] and if it were in the tenth sign, the question will be about the king; and if it were in the domicile of foreign travel [it will be about foreign travel], and so on with the rest.

Also, for the increase of the strength of this significator, other authorities[57] for seeking this are namely that it should have a dignity in the degree of the conjunction or the prevention which was before the question, and in the Ascendant of that same conjunction or prevention,[58] because then it will be stronger. Also, one must seek out whether it would have a power or dignity in the Ascendant of the revolution of that same year, and in the Ascendant of the lesser[59] conjunction, and in the present conjunction of Saturn and Jupiter; and in the sign to which the profection of that same year is coming.[60] Such a one, if it were strong in the figure (that is, if it were direct and free from every impediment, and it were in an angle, and had some dignity in that same place, and it were in the rest of its own praiseworthy conditions), it will be made fortunate, stronger than all of the planets, or more worthy than the others in signification. Which [if] you were not able to have all of these (because such a one is rarely found), at least it should have a portion of them—that is, it should have a part in the Ascendant of the question, and in the places of the luminaries, and in the Ascendant or degree of the conjunction or the prevention just finished, and let it be strong in its own place in the figure (that is, let it be direct and strong just as it is said concerning the strength of the planets), and let it lack every weakness, and let it be in an angle, and let it have [something] of those authorities[61] which we stated—that is, let it have a role in the Ascendant and in the places of the luminaries,

---

[56] *Cogitationis.* This description is reminiscent of Māshā'allāh's accounts in *OR* of which planet in a horary will have final disposition over the nature and outcome of a question. But compare this method with Māshā'allāh's other two ways of determining the significator of the intention, as described in *Cognition* and in §2 above.

[57] The author does not mean astrological authorities, but planetary conditions that will give the *planet* more authority (see below).

[58] That is, the Ascendant of the chart cast for the moment of the conjunction or prevention itself.

[59] Reading *minoris*, but the text might also be read as *maioris* ("greater"), especially considering the following clause about the current Saturn-Jupiter conjunction (which is considered to be lesser than the conjunction signaling a change in triplicities).

[60] That is, the profection of the most recent Saturn-Jupiter conjunction. It would be amazing if a planet had to have so many testimonies—asking the astrologer about your missing watch does not seem like it should have import in relation to Saturn-Jupiter conjunctions.

[61] Reading *auctoritatibus* for *auctoribus*.

or in the Ascendant of the revolution of the year, and in the Ascendant of the present conjunction of Saturn and Jupiter, or let it be the Lord of the conjunction of the prevention just finished. The Lord of the conjunction or the prevention is said to be the one who has dignity in the degree of the conjunction or the prevention, and in the sign which is ascending at the hour of the conjunction or the prevention—for this one, as the philosophers say, had authority in all things which come to be in that same conjunction or prevention, and it must participate with the Lord of the Ascendant in all questions which come to be [asked?]⁶² in that conjunction or prevention. And certain experts of the astrologers, if they found this one strong in an angle, they used to give it some⁶³ partnership. But they used to *judge* by him alone and [they used to declare with true vision].⁶⁴ Such a one, therefore, to whom two or more of the aforesaid authorities were joined, and was in a good condition (as we said above) in the hour of the question, will be the significator of the philosophers. And there will be no doubt in all judgments that they are judged by him.

And know that it is of the secrets of astronomy, and the astronomers hid it, and the ancient sages of the astrologers used to hide it from the rest who were less learned in this art.

The book of Māshā'allāh on hidden things, is done

§7: A chapter on the knowledge of places: if something were in them or not

If you wanted this, take the altitude and set up the twelve domiciles. Then look to see if there were a benefic in one of the angles: there will be something there. And [whether it is] much or little is known from the strength which the benefic had in that place in which it was. And if the malefics (or some one of them) aspected that benefic which was in the angle, by an evil aspect, there will not be something there. And if they did not aspect, and the aforesaid benefic in the angle were free from the aspects of the malefics and [from] every impediment, there will be something there.

---

62 BN has an unclear abbreviated word here.
63 *Ullum*.
64 This is my best rendering of *vera fitebant eorum viditia*, assuming the Latin translator meant *fitebant* to be a version of the verb *fateor*.

But if you wanted to know whether he who asked would find it or not, look at the Lord of the Ascendant and at the Moon. Which if they were joined to the aforesaid benefic, or they aspected it by a good aspect or received it, he will find it; without this,[65] not.

And if you knew that he would find it, then [look at] the place (namely the twelve equal parts) from the port[66] of the Lord of the place. Drag out one line from the port to every part.[67] And know how much the benefic (which is in the angle) has walked in its sign, in terms of degrees and [unclear], and take from the port toward the outermost from all the lines, how much the benefic has walked. Which if it has walked a fourth or a fourth, and if a third or a third;[68] and know that the Ascendant will be the east of that place. But if you knew this, know how much elongated the Lord of the benefic was from the Ascendant, because according to its remoteness, that which you seek will be remote from or near to the east. And if you wished to know whether it is toward the point or toward the outermost, know the latitude of the planet, and if it were northern or southern. Then take up from the place of the planet in that part in which the latitude was, but[69] toward the point or toward the outermost, how much its latitude was—because the thing will be there, if God wills. But if it lacked latitude, the thing will be there where the Lord of [the Lot of] Fortune is, if God wills.

And if you wished to know whether it was deep, look at the place of the planet: which if it was in the *awj*, it will not be deep. But if it were in the opposite of the *awj*, it will be deep (and likewise if it [were] in the middle).

And if you wished to elect an hour for extracting it, let this be when the Moon is conjoined to benefics by a good aspect, or corporally. And beware, in taking it out, lest there be malefics in the angles, and lest the Moon be in the signs of evil spirits.[70]

---

[65] The manuscript is damaged or unclear on this word, but this is the meaning.
[66] Reading *porto* here and below. If this translation is right, then it sounds like a Latin translation of an Arabic work that treats the signs as ports of call.
[67] This might also be translated as "direction."
[68] Reading as *quartam vel quartam et si tertiam vel tertiam*. Meaning unclear.
[69] Reading as *tamen*.
[70] *Demonum*. I am not sure what signs these are.

MĀSHĀ'ALLĀH'S BOOK ON RECEPTION

Of which these are the chapters:

The first chapter: what is reception?
The second chapter: on a matter which is hoped for, whether it would come to be or not
The third chapter: whether an infirm person would be liberated or die
The fourth chapter: a question concerning an infirm person
The fifth chapter: on substance
The sixth chapter: on substance lent
The seventh chapter: on things left behind by a certain dead person
The eighth chapter: on a kingdom, whether it would be acquired
The ninth chapter: a question about a kingdom
The tenth chapter: a question about a kingdom
The eleventh chapter: on discovering the *hīlāj* of the native
The twelfth chapter: a question about a kingdom

Māshā'allāh's book on reception begins:

A certain man from among the sages discovered a book from the books of the secrets of the stars, concerning those things which kings treasured. And he expounded it, and laid bare its intention in all things of which men are in need in their own affairs concerning questions. And it was in accordance with that, that he put down and laid bare in the matters of questions, whether the matter would be or not, and when it will be (if it ought to come to be), and when it will be apparent that it is not (if it ought not to come to be), and what would prohibit it so that it is not, and by whom, and whence it is (if it ought to come to be).

And the knowledge of this matter, and the exposition of it, is on the seven planets, and in their twelve domiciles, and in the seven exaltations, and in their descensions,[1] moreover their conjunctions and separations, and in the receptions toward one another, and in the rendering of reception, and the

---

[1] Māshā'allāh omits the detriments.

pushing of their disposition to each other. And the one to whom the disposition arrives, will be the significator (by the command of God):² which if it were in the nature of the effecting of the matter, it will signify its effecting. And if it were in the nature of prohibiting, it will signify its prohibition (by the command of God).

---

² Let us call this the "final dispositor."

Chapter 1: What is reception?

Know that reception comes to be from the exaltations and the domiciles, in the causing of matters, whether they are or not: this is, that some planet of the seven is in the exaltation of another planet, or in its domicile, and it is joined to it from the seven known aspects; or, were both in one sign, and some one of them is in the exaltation [or domicile] of its associate, joined to it. Therefore, then it will be joined to it by its own body, an example of which matter is [this]: if Saturn is in Aries, in the twentieth degree, and Mars in the fifteenth degree of the same.

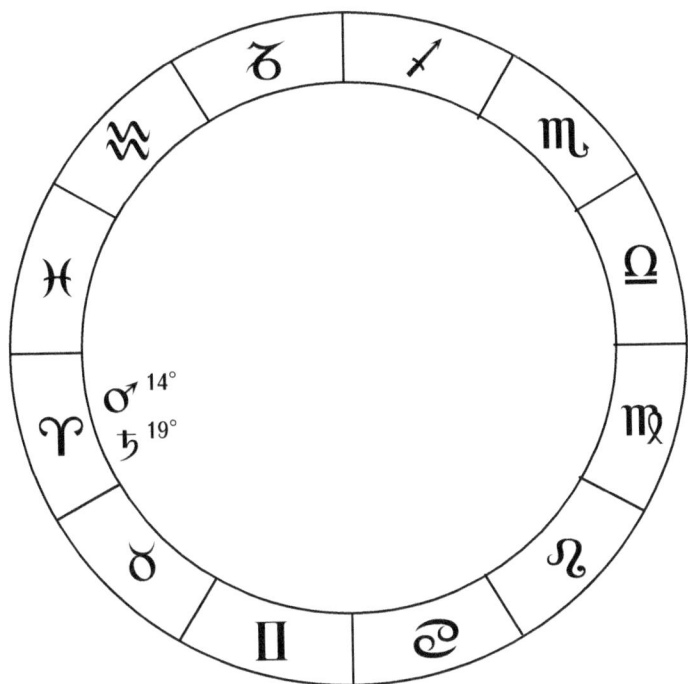

Figure 48: Mars Receiving Saturn by Domicile

Then Mars is being joined to Saturn by his own body, and Mars receives Saturn in his own domicile, but Saturn does not receive Mars. This comes to be if some planet were not in the known aspects, who is closer to the conjunction of Saturn (namely degree by degree), in front of Mars. Which if there were a planet in the known aspects (or in Aries) who is closer to the conjunction of Saturn, that one will be more worthy for the conjunction of Saturn than Mars is, for a true conjunction is degree by degree (both for a [corporal] conjunction and an aspect).

And there is another example of reception: if Saturn were in Aries, the twentieth degree, and Mars in the tenth degree of Capricorn, and none of the planets is closer than Mars to the conjunction of Saturn (namely, degree by degree). And when Mars would be joined to Saturn degree by degree, then they receive each other mutually in their domiciles, for Mars receives Saturn (because [Saturn] is in [Mars's] domicile), and Saturn receives Mars (because [Mars] is in [Saturn's] domicile).

Likewise the exaltations are just like the domiciles, but the exaltations are of greater authority in a kingdom—namely if [something] is done concerning a king, the Lord of the exaltation is stronger than the Lord of the domicile. Therefore, if the Sun were in Aries in the tenth degree, and Mars in Capricorn in the tenth degree, then the Sun is being joined to Mars, and Mars receives the Sun because [the Sun] is in [Mars's] domicile; but the Sun does not receive Mars, because [Mars] is not in the domicile of [the Sun].

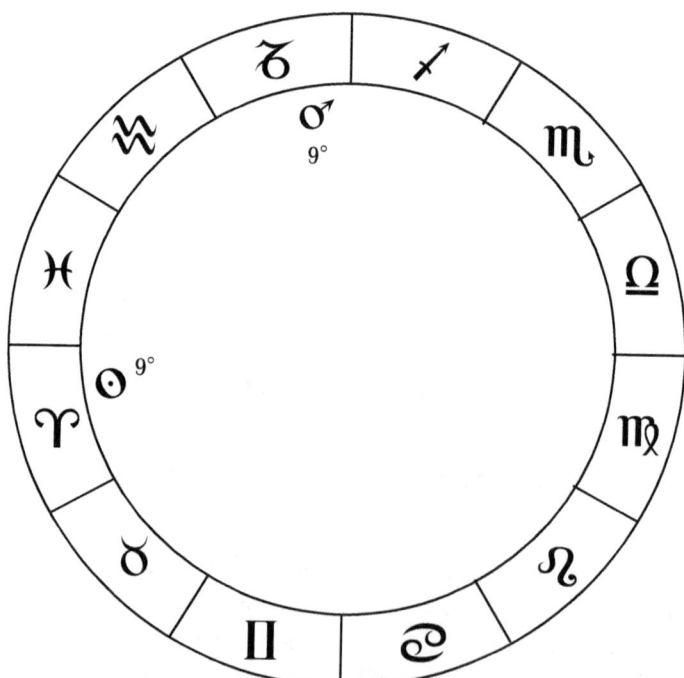

Figure 49: Mars Receiving the Sun by Domicile

Likewise[3] the rest of the seven planets, whichever one of them were joined to its associate from its domicile or exaltation in the known aspects, or in one of the signs, and it projected or committed its disposition, [then] if the one to whom it is committed receives [the disposition],[4] it will perfect the matter, by the command of God. And the Sun in this aspect [above] does not receive Mars, because [Mars] is not in [the Sun's] domicile, nor in [the Sun's] exaltation; and Mars receives the Sun because [the Sun] is in [Mars's] domicile.

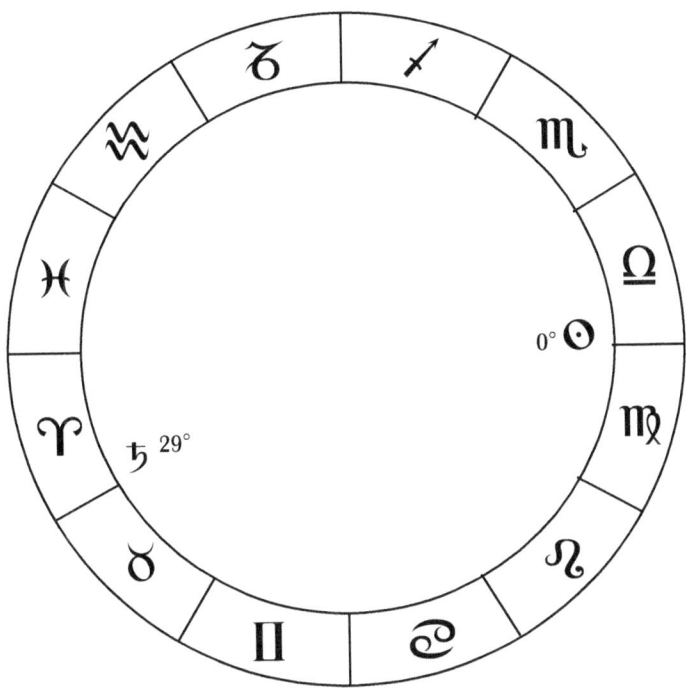

Figure 50: Saturn and the Sun Receiving Each Other by Exaltation

---

[3] This paragraph is ambiguous. First, it seems strange that after these examples Māshā'allāh would feel the need to mention the other planets specifically—could this be a new topic? Besides, this new discussion of committing disposition is also ambiguous because it is unclear to me whose dignities we are in.

[4] Remember that reception proper is not the same as receiving a disposition which is pushed to a planet.

And if the Sun were in Libra in the first degree, and Saturn in Aries in the thirtieth degree, and no planet were in Aries, nor [one] in all of the aspects closer than the Sun to the conjunction of Saturn, nor did Saturn go out from Aries until the Sun is joined to him degree by degree, [then] the Sun receives Saturn, and Saturn the Sun: each one receives his associate in this place by exaltations.[5] And if it were in the square aspect or the opposition, it signifies labor and error, and anxiety, and contrariety; and in the trine and sextile aspect, and in the conjunction, smoothness and piety and loftiness. And if the Sun were joined to Saturn, and [Saturn] received the Sun, with [Saturn] even being received in turn by the Sun, from their own domiciles or exaltations, they will make peace[6] and perfect the matter, by the command of God.

Likewise, all of the benefic planets with benefics increase the good.

And the malefics with malefics come to be good on account of withdrawal—that is, they make good, and their evil and impediment withdraws.[7]

And the benefics with malefics make an agreement, and their evil recedes, and the matter is perfected—unless they were in the square aspect or opposition, because there is a certain labor and error in this.

But if the Sun were in Aries, and Saturn in Libra (just as I told you before about the conjunction), there will be enmities and contrarieties, ignorances,

---

[5] Note the ambiguity here, based on this statement about Saturn leaving the sign before reception. Do they receive each other *already* because the aspect *will* perfect while they are in their own signs (in which case the perfection of the aspect is merely preferable to being in a whole-sign reception), or are they not in reception at all *until* the aspect actually perfects?

[6] Here and elsewhere two related verbs are being used: *pacifico*, "to conclude peace, make peace, pacify," and *pacificor*, "to enter into an agreement." Both of these suggest that reception makes planets discard their differences and come to an agreement (even if certain aspects make this agreement brief and unstable).

[7] Abū Ma'shar discusses this (and attributes the concept to certain "ancients") in *Gr. Intr.* VII.4.483*ff.* According to him, if Saturn and Mars were joined by corporal conjunction, they would help to temper their respective cold and hot qualities (which could be further changed by their sign placement or solar phase, *etc.*). But this seems hard to square with the claim that the Saturn-Mars conjunction in Cancer is a terrible thing—as Māshā'allāh says in *On Roots* Ch. 11 and Abū Ma'shar describes at length in *OGC* II.8.

and refusals, because [neither] of them receives its associate.[8] And all of the planets do likewise.

For a conjunction[9] comes to be from the known aspects (namely from the opposition, trine, square and sextile aspect) and from the [corporal] conjunction. And this comes to be in the noted domiciles. And whatever would be less than two signs, is being separated from conjunction. This comes to be if a planet entered the following sign before a planet who is going toward it, would be joined to it—nor is it [then] joined to it.[10]

And know that the conjunction comes to be in this way, whichever of the seven planets it was: a light one is joined to a heavy one, and a heavy one is not joined to a light one, because a light one overtakes a heavy one, and a heavy one does not overtake a light one. For a conjunction comes to be from degree by degree when they are conjoined (namely the light to the heavy): then they are joined from degree by degree, and [the light one] commits its own disposition to [the heavy one]. After this, [the light one] is separated from [the heavy one], and does not stop aspecting him (from [the aspect by which]) he is being joined to it, until he is separated from it. But a conjunction is an aspect, because however long a planet were going to another planet, it will aspect it with its own light and own nature, until it projects its own light upon it, from degree by degree: than it will be a true conjunction, and [the light one] will commit its own matter to the other.[11] After that, it is being separated from it, and the end of its aspect is in this way.

And a planet, if it were going to the conjunction of another, will indicate what does not yet exist. And the one who is being separated from [the conjunction] will indicate what is past and is already done. Namely, a star will indicate what is past from the star from which it is being separated; but what is going to be will be indicated by the star to which it is being joined.

---

[8] Both planets are in their own exaltations. In fact one might say their opposition is made worse, because each will be proud, powerful, and puffed-up—not a good situation for people seeking agreements.

[9] Here and elsewhere the translator (and probably Māshā'allāh) uses "conjunction" equivocally, sometimes meaning any conjoining of the planets whatsoever, and sometimes only the corporal conjunction.

[10] This situation assumes that the planets are in the same sign, and one planet goes to the next sign. But we still have the same ambiguity as above, due in part to the use of the subjunctive. For while the conjunction cannot be *perfected*, does reception exist at all, or does it not exist because it will *never* be perfected?

[11] This suggests that committing disposition only takes place when the aspect perfects—which raises the further question, whether the disposition can be committed at all if the aspect will not be perfected while they are in their current signs.

Chapter 2: On a matter which is hoped for, whether it would come to be or not

Therefore if you were asked, about some matter, whether it would be perfected or not, or, about some rumor, whether it is[12] or not, you will take the shadow immediately, at that hour when the word goes out of the mouth of the one seeking the matter. And let the man who seeks the matter be asking on his own behalf, or let him write to you in letters of his own hand (which if he did not know how to write, let him send you such a person who is anxious about his matter), and let him not seek another matter besides [this one] with it, until you comprehend [this one]; and let this not be except in a matter about which there is great anxiety, or in a very necessary matter. However, it is not consistent with the wise person that he should ask for himself, but it behooves him to ask another.

And once the ascending sign and its degree were laid out for you, and the sign of the Midheaven and its degree,[13] and you took note of the seven planetary dispositors (by the command of God) in their own degrees, and in the domiciles in which they were, and in their minutes, with a most precise and pure number, from which nothing shorter nor greater fell,[14] then look at the Lord of the Ascendant and the Moon, and the one of them whom you found stronger, operate through that one, and the other will participate with it. That is, you will begin to look at the Lord of the Ascendant: which if he aspected the ascending sign, this will be in accordance with[15] the strength of his testimony—therefore operate through him, and the Moon will participate with him, in whatever place she was. And if the Lord of the Ascendant did not aspect the Ascendant, you should look to see whether he would be joined to a planet who aspects the ascending sign from *its* own place, and renders [the Lord of the Ascendant's] light to the Ascendant itself; or [if the Lord of the Ascendant] would be joined to a planet cadent from the Ascendant,[16] and that cadent planet would be joined to another one aspecting the

---

[12] That is, whether the content of the rumor or news is *true* or not.
[13] Note he does not mention the intermediary cusps.
[14] That is, do not estimate the planetary positions, but calculate the positions exactly.
[15] *Ex*. It could also be translated as "of" or "from," but the idea is that the strength of his testimony (in the search for the querent's significator) goes along with, or is caused by, the aspect to the rising sign.
[16] I.e., not aspecting the rising sign.

ascending sign, who lifts it up[17] and render its light to the ascending sign. Thus if the Lord of the Ascendant is being joined to a planet aspecting the ascending sign, or that planet is being joined to another who renders its light to the ascending sign, it will lift up [the Lord]. And if there were a conjunction from a planet to the seven planets, the work in these will be by means of a system,[18] namely where one renders and lifts up the light of one to another, until it arrives at the last of them. But as I said, if the Lord of the Ascendant pushes his own light to the ascending sign, operate simply through him, and let the Moon participate with him.

And if the Lord of the ascending sign did not aspect the Ascendant, nor were he joined to a planet aspecting the Ascendant, and to one rendering his light to it, and pushing it (because the push is its aspect to the Ascendant), then his fall is there:[19] when he neither aspects the Ascendant, nor renders the light to an aspecting planet.

Which if the Lord of the Ascendant did not aspect the Ascendant, either through himself or through another to whom he renders his light, then he will be impeded[20] and bad. Wherefore then, operate through the Moon in the same way you operated through the Lord of the Ascendant: which if she aspected the Ascendant, or some one of the planets rendered her light to the Ascendant, operate through her, and the Lord of the Ascendant will participate with her.[21] (And know that, according to the quantity of the impediment which has entered in upon him—that is, upon the Lord of the Ascendant—that same amount of impediment will enter in upon the matter about which it is asked.)

Therefore, operate through the Moon if she aspected the ascending sign, and the Lord of the Ascendant will participate with her—namely under the condition that the Lord of the Ascendant did not aspect the Ascendant, nor were he joined to some planet who would render his own light to the Ascen-

---

[17] Remember that if a planet does not aspect the rising sign, then it is cadent or "falling from" (or "falling away from") the Ascendant—therefore if such a planet can somehow get its own light over to the Ascendant through a second planet, it is as though the second planet is "lifting" the first planet up from its falling away.
[18] *Ratione.*
[19] That is, since no planet will lift it up (by rendering its light to the rising sign), the Lord of the Ascendant has fallen completely away from the rising sign and has little or no control over it.
[20] He will not be impeded in himself, but insofar as he wants to have control over the affairs of the Ascendant.
[21] Obviously, though his participation will be weak, since he is now impeded.

dant. Afterwards, see to which of the seven planets the Moon would be joined, and operate through her, even with the Lord of the Ascendant adjoined.[22]

And if [1] the Moon did not aspect the Ascendant, nor were she joined to some planet who would render her own light to the Ascendant—or even if she did aspect the Ascendant and she was not joined to any planet (which happens while she is void in course), and [2] likewise the Lord of the Ascendant did not aspect the Ascendant, and he were void in course in the same way, then look to see which of them ought to go out more quickly from the sign in which it is, and which one would have fewer degrees for going out. After this, you will change the Moon to the following sign from her own place. After this, you will look to see to which of the planets she[23] would first be joined, and judge through that. And all of the planets are changed, but the lighter planet is more worthy in a change than a heavy one. In this way, Saturn, if he were void in course, will be worse than all the rest, because the emptying of the course of the planets (that is, when they are being joined to none) indicates the malice of the matter and its slowness. And every planet, with the emptying of its course, indicates a multitude of slowness. Also, the fewness of the degrees (or the multitude of them) of the planet which it ought to walk through in the sign in which it was, after the question, indicates the slowness or quickness of the effecting of the matter.

Therefore the one who goes out more quickly from the sign in which it is, will be quicker in the matter; but a light one and heavy one, if they were void in course, indicate the slowness of matters, and their worthlessness.[24] Therefore, if you found the Lord of the Ascendant and the Moon void in course, joining themselves to no one, foretell the slowness of the matter, and its prolonging, and that it ought to be postponed[25] according to what you saw.

---

[22] This probably means, "along with the Lord of the Ascendant." Then we have three planets participating.

[23] The Latin could just as easily read "it," i.e., whichever the quicker planet was. But the instruction is ambiguous. In almost every case the Moon would be the one to leave her sign more quickly, which accounts for the instruction to change her specifically. But then the whole point seems moot, since the instruction also implies that one could use the Lord of the Ascendant as well.

[24] So, even if we can change the planets into the next sign and look for perfection there, there will still be slowness and difficulty due to their hindrance in their *current* signs.

[25] This "ought" pertains to the planets, not to the querent. That is, it is not as though the *querent* ought to postpone things, but that the planets *will* postpone the matter because of *their* situation.

And see to whom the Moon is first being joined after her going out from the sign in which she is: judge the effecting of the matter according to [that planet], and the Lord of the Ascendant will participate with it according to his strength or weakness in the place in which he is. Also, a planet who was in the Ascendant will participate with them in the work, [and] moreover a planet which was in the domicile of the quaesited matter—which if it were concordant with the sign[26] in which it is, and it were received, it indicates the goodness of the matter, and its worthiness. And if were not concordant with the sign in which it is, nor were it received, it indicates the impediment of that same matter, and its worthlessness. But the effecting of the matter and its prohibiting does not come about from that one which is in the Ascendant, but it comes about from the role[27] of the Lord of the Ascendant or Moon, and from the stars to which they are being joined, and their conjunction and reception, and the rendering of their reception.

And know that the Moon would always be the partner of the Lord of the Ascendant, in whatever place she was, by the command of God. Therefore, if you found the Lord of the Ascendant impeded, operate through the Moon just as you operate through the Lord of the Ascendant.

---

[26] This probably includes having a dignity there, or it being a sign of the same gender, or having similar elemental qualities, *etc.*

[27] *Parte.*

Chapter 3: On an infirm person, whether he would be liberated or die

Which if you looked for a man who asked you about his life, namely whether he would die in that year or not, you will look for him just as you looked for an infirm person.[28] Namely, look to see to whom the Lord of the Ascendant is being joined: which if the Lord of the Ascendant is being joined to a benefic planet, and that benefic were the dispositor of the disposition (which it undertook),[29] nor did it render his light to another (and unless that benefic were itself the Lord of the domicile of death), say that he will not die in that year, by the command of God.

And if the Lord of the Ascendant were conjoined to a malefic planet, or to the Lord of the domicile of death, whatever kind [of planet] the Lord of the domicile of death was, whether malefic or benefic, and the Lord of the Ascendant were not received, nor did the malefic planet receive him, nor[30] the Lord of the domicile of death (whether it was a malefic or benefic), then look at the Moon: which if even she were bad, he will die in that year, by the will of God.

Then look to see when the Lord of the Ascendant will be joined to that malefic planet or to the Lord of the domicile of death (who does not receive him), degree by degree, and put down the number of their distance, in place of days. Which if [the death] were not then, it will be when he is commingled with it by his own body, and arrived to its degree[31]—*then* he will die.

If however the Lord of the Ascendant is being joined to a planet who receives him, then the infirm person or questioner will escape death in that year, by the command of God, and he will regain strength from his infirmity.

And if the Lord of the Ascendant were impeded,[32] operate through the Moon just as I have told you before about the Lord of the Ascendant, and judge through her just as you have judged through the Lord of the Ascendant. Which if prosperity and health from the infirmity would attend [the querent], look to see when the Lord of the Ascendant is being joined to that

---

[28] As we will see below, this assumes the querent has a reason to suspect his death—from a serious illness, perhaps. Māshā'allāh is not assuming that the querent is a healthy person who is simply worried about his own death in general. This assumption makes the question more of a particular question, rather than a universal question.
[29] *Ad quam accessit.* That is, if it is the final dispositor.
[30] Reading *nec* for *vel.*
[31] This must mean by actual transit, rather than the symbolic progression just described.
[32] This probably means, if the Lord of the Ascendant does not aspect the Ascendant, *etc.*, which was said to define his impediment in Chapter 2.

planet who will signify his health, degree by degree, and put down the distance of the conjunction for days. Which if [the healing] were not then, it will be when he will be joined to it by his own body in the sign in which it is. And if he would be joined to it in some place or in one of the angles from which it[33] is already removed, then he will escape, if God wills. But if the Lord of the Ascendant were joined to the Lord of the domicile of death, or, *vice versa*, the Lord of the domicile of death were joined to him, he will die, by the will of God, and the Moon would not be considered in this.

And if the Lord of the Ascendant were strong, and not impeded, and the Moon were joined to the Lord of the domicile of death, he will be liberated by the command of God. For the Lord of the Ascendant rules more in life and in death than the Moon does, and the Moon participates with him in every matter except for this one.

And behold, I am setting up for you a question on this matter, namely a question about an infirm person, whether he would be liberated from his infirmity or die, by the command of God.[34]

Let [this] be the question, the Ascendant of which was the sign of Virgo, in the fifteenth degree, and the Midheaven in the fifteenth of Gemini. And Mars in Gemini in the seventeenth degree and thirtieth minute; and the Moon in Taurus in the twenty-sixth degree, twenty-fifth minute; and Jupiter in Taurus, in the nineteenth degree and fifteenth minute; and the Sun in the twentieth degree and thirtieth minute of Aries; and Saturn in Aries, in the tenth degree and fifteenth minute; and Mercury in Aries, in the twenty-fourth degree and fiftieth minute; and Venus in Pisces, in the fifth degree and thirty-seventh minute.

---

[33] I take this to refer to the other planet, not the Lord of the Ascendant.
[34] This chart's latitude possibilities are wide: from about 13°—31° N. But it does include Basra, Māshā'allāh's hometown. Cast for Basra, one can get something very close to this chart at about 3:19 PM on April 11, 791 AD JC.

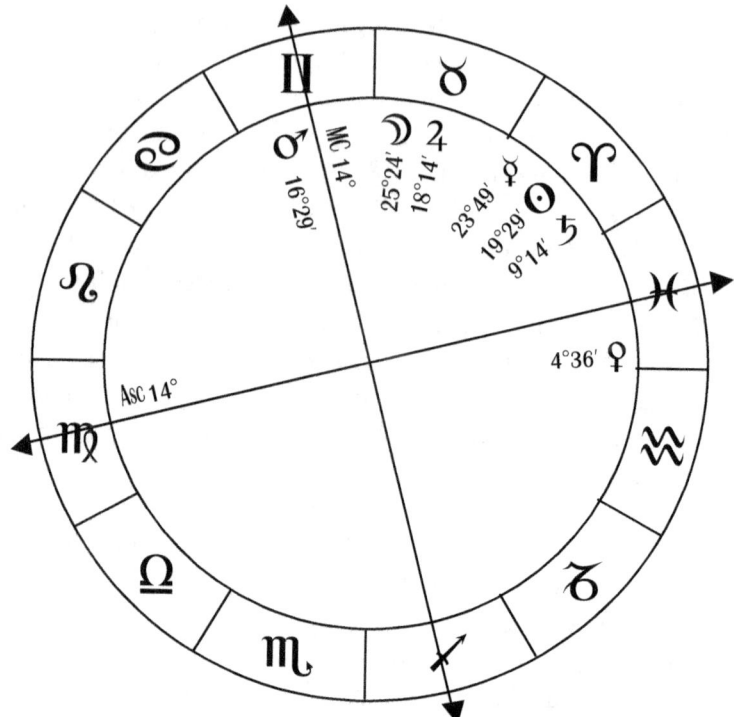

Figure 51: An Infirm Person, Will he be Liberated or Die?

I looked, by the will of God, at the Ascendant of this question, and at its Lord, with the Moon and the rest of the planets, and moreover the angles. And Mercury, the Lord of the Ascendant, was void in course, and in the domicile of Mars he signified the strength of the pain, and the fear of death. And Mars was the Lord of the domicile of death, in the Midheaven, aspecting the domicile of life, he also signifying the strength of [the querent's] pain, and the loss of hope.

After this, I looked at the Moon, whom I even found void in course, but she was aspecting the domicile of life from the 9th domicile; and the Moon was stronger than the Lord of the Ascendant in signification, because she was aspecting the ascending sign and [was] quicker, and was supposed to go out first from the sign in which she was.

Therefore, through the emptying of their course they signified the prolongation of the infirmity, and its weightiness. The Moon went out from the sign in which she was, because she had walked through more degrees in her sign than any of the rest of the planets or Mercury (the Lord of the Ascendant) had. Therefore she went out from her sign more quickly. And she was stronger than Mercury because she aspected the Ascendant. And she was joined to Venus, to her first conjunction,[35] committing her disposition to her; and Venus was being joined to Jupiter,[36] and she was receiving him,[37] and she was received by him, by domicile and from the conjunction; and Jupiter, when the disposition arrived to him, was not committing his disposition to another. Because he was not being joined to Saturn (who is heavier than all the planets), and Jupiter is joined to none of the planets except for him. Therefore, Jupiter signified, when the disposition arrived to him from Venus (who was committing it to him, and was receiving him, and she was being received by him by domicile and from the conjunction), that the infirm person would come to health and prosperity, though the infirmity was going to endure in increase, until Venus would be joined to Jupiter from degree by degree. And when Venus was separated from Jupiter by one minute, the infirmity would begin to be decreased, by the command of God, and health and liberation would come.

And the master of this question[38] was just as we said before, and his pain did not cease to be in increase and the fear of death, until Venus was joined to Jupiter from degree by degree. Therefore, when Venus was separated from Jupiter, health and rest began, and the pain was diminished, by the command of God.

And if the conjunction had come to Mars (that is, if Venus had been joined to Mars instead of Jupiter), who was the Lord of the domicile of death, and he was not receiving her, we would have said that he would die, by the command of God, when Venus was joined to Mars and projected her own rays and light upon him, degree by degree (which is a true conjunction). Because Mars is the Lord of the domicile of death, which is the matter about which the questioner is asking.

---

[35] That is, it is the first aspect she will make in the next sign. Note that she is said to commit disposition without there being any reception between them: the Moon will be in the bound of Mercury with no other dignities for Venus there, nor does the Moon have any dignities where Venus is, except for the secondary triplicity rulership, which Māshā'allāh ignores.
[36] The only way Venus could be joined to him is if we use the wide orbs given by Sahl in *Introduct.* §5. It must also be that Mars will have travelled far enough by the time she reaches Jupiter, that he will not cut off their sextile.
[37] Again, she cannot be receiving him *yet*, unless we use Sahl's wide orbs.
[38] The querent.

And so, always, if the Lord of the Ascendant and the Moon were joined to the Lord of the quaesited matter (of all matters), the matter concerning which the questioner is discussing would come about, by the command of God. But[39] death is not like other matters: but if there were death, one does not look to see what is going to be after it. Just as in other matters to be inquired about, when the Lord of the Ascendant and the Moon are joined to the Lord of the matter, we[40] say that the matter will be. After this, the planetary Lord of the domicile of the matter is looked at, to see to whom it commits its own disposition after its effect: which if it were a benefic, we say the matter is going to follow and come about in a happy way. And if it were a malefic, we say that the matter will be taken away after it existed. But if you looked concerning death, and you found the Lord of the Ascendant and the Moon joined to the Lord of the domicile of death, the infirm person will be dead from the infirmity, by the will of God, unless the Lord of the domicile of death (who is the Lord of the quaesited matter) receives him. And know [that] because, the Lord of the domicile of death, if it would be joined to the Lord of the Ascendant, you will judge him likewise to be dead, by the command of God.

And[41] know [this]: because Venus, to whom the Moon is joined, if she had been joined to the Sun, and the Sun had been the Lord of the domicile of life, and he himself had been joined to Jupiter from the known aspects (which is weaker) or by his own body (which is stronger), if there had not been a strong reception between them, and the Sun was not impeded by Jupiter in this figure (because [Jupiter] would be Lord of the quaesited matter), and Venus was joined to the Sun, and the Sun joined to Jupiter, and Jupiter is a benefic and the Sun a benefic, and the Moon was being joined to Venus, and Venus was being joined to the Sun, and the Sun was being joined to Jupiter—therefore the Sun signified[42] the cause of life, and it is his signification, and conferred his light to Jupiter (who is the *mubtazz*, that is, who has rulership in this figure).[43] And he had life, and did not destroy himself,

---

[39] *Quia*.
[40] Here and below, reading *dicimus* for *dicunt* ("they say").
[41] Now Māshā'allāh is imagining what he would say if the chart were somewhat different.
[42] From here the verbs change tense, as though the hypothetical example were real. It should still be read as a hypothetical.
[43] This seems to be an example of *mubtazz* being used generically, not in a technical sense like through a point system. Jupiter seems to be the *mubtazz* because he has the final disposition—see also below, where the planet with the final disposition is said to be the "Lord of the quaesited matter," and "in charge over it," and its "author."

because the benefics even have the nature of life, unless the benefics themselves are the Lords of the domicile of death. But then the Sun destroys stars by combustion when he does not receive them by a strong reception (namely by domiciles and exaltations).[44] And were the stars already falling into combustion by conjunction, or were the Sun to project his own light upon a star from the known aspects (without strong reception), and he were not the Lord of the Ascendant, and[45] if he impeded some planet who was closer to him than the rest in the conjunction or aspect, and it were not in one degree, he destroys it and every matter it is in charge of, by the will of God, whether it is a malefic or benefic, if in fact the Sun were *not* the Lord of the domicile of life, nor did he receive it with a strong reception.

And know that if there were a planet in the domicile of death, and it were a malefic, and it had the Lord of the Ascendant attached to itself (or were it a benefic and it had dignity in the domicile of death), and there were no reception between itself and the Lord of the Ascendant, it will even signify death. And likewise the conjunction of the Lord of the domicile of death with a planet who is in the domicile of life.

Also, the multitude of the conjunction of the planets, and reception and no reception, signifies the diversity of the condition of this infirm person: namely, first health and soundness, and then a new illness, as well as the diversity of their natures in good and evil. Because when the Lord of the Ascendant (or the Moon) is being joined to a benefic or malefic who receives him, the infirm person will not cease to bear it more easily, until [the Lord of the Ascendant] commits his disposition to it from degree by degree. Then, if the planet to which the Moon or Lord of the Ascendant is committing its disposition is being joined to no one, the infirm person will be liberated, and his soundness will be perfected. And if that planet committed its own disposition to a malefic planet who did not receive it, or to a benefic (who is the Lord of the domicile of death) not receiving it, and the disposition were his and not another's (that is, if it committed disposition to it and not to another), he will die.

And if the Lord[46] of the Ascendant (or the Moon) were separated from that planet who receives him, and that planet itself committed its own dispo-

---

[44] So the Sun will not destroy by combustion if he receives the combust planets by a "strong" reception; and a "strong" reception is by domicile or exaltation.
[45] Reading this as a continuation of the previous sentence. Māshā'allāh seems to be listing several ways in which the Sun will destroy matters.
[46] Omitting an extra *dominus*.

sition to a malefic planet who did not receive *him* (or to a benefic not receiving him, who was the Lord of the domicile of death), the infirm person will be broken: that is, he will become infirm again, or will return to [the first] infirmity. And if that planet were conjoined to the same malefic from degree by degree, he will die, by the command of God. And if it were received, his infirmity will be prolonged until its disposition arrived to that planet: afterwards, he will be liberated, by the command of God. Therefore, look at the planet at which the conjunction arrives, because it is the Lord of the quaesited matter, and it is in charge over it, by the command of God.

And the good fortune of the planets, and their malignity or impediment, also their reception or not-reception, will indicate the lightness of the matter to you, or its weightiness (also, its effecting and prohibiting). But the end of the matter will be where the conjunction and committing of disposition will be ended. Because that planet at which the disposition is perfected, is the Lord of the matter and its author.[47] You will judge thusly in all matters generally—which, when the disposition arrives at the planet who receives the Lord of the quaesited matter, the matter will be made fortunate, and be perfected (by the command of God). And when it even arrives to a benefic, it will be advantageous in the disposition of the same. And if its disposition were perfected, and it committed it to another, the dispositor will operate by the quantity of its nature, and its being, by the will of God.

In the above figure, Mercury was being joined to Venus after his going out from Aries, [and] she was receiving him from Taurus, and Venus herself was being joined to Jupiter, and Jupiter was receiving her, and he himself was being received by her. Therefore this same Mercury signified that the Moon, as a partner (because he was the Lord of the ascending sign), certainly [signified] the liberation of the infirm person.

---

[47] Again, the final dispositor.

Chapter 4: A question about an infirm person

Leo[48] was ascending in the twenty-eighth degree, and the Midheaven the twentieth degree of Taurus. Saturn was in Aries, the fourth degree, fifteen minute; and the Moon in Aries, the twenty-seventh degree, thirty-seven minutes;[49] and Jupiter in Taurus, in the ninth degree, thirteenth minute.

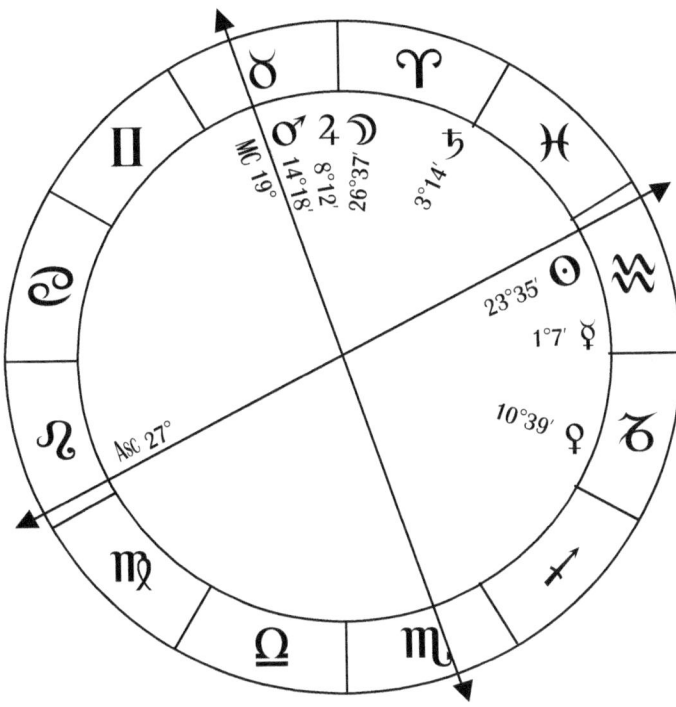

Figure 52: An Infirm Person

And Mars in Taurus, the fifteenth degree, eighteen minutes;[50] and the Sun in Aquarius, the twenty-fourth degree, thirty-five minutes;[51] and Mercury in

---

[48] This chart could only have been cast at latitudes from about 40°-45° N, which again suggests European latitudes. Thus Māshā'allāh could not himself have been responsible for this particular chart, unless perhaps it had been cast for areas like modern Azerbaijan, Uzbekistan, and so on, some parts of which were under the control of the 'Abbāsid Caliphate at the time. However, it is absolutely clear that under no quadrant house system would Venus be in the 6th house, as Māshā'allāh says she is, so he evidently uses whole-sign houses in this chart. Cast for Marseille (as I do for several charts in *On Nativities*), one can get very close to this chart at 5:21:47 PM on February 11, 791 AD JC.
[49] Or perhaps, "by 20° 37'." The Latin reads *28 grad. 37 minutis*.
[50] Or perhaps, "by 15° 18'." The Latin reads *15. grad. 18 minutis*.

Aquarius, the second degree, seven minutes,[52] direct; and Venus in Capricorn, the eleventh degree, thirty-nine minutes.[53]

I looked at this question by the command of God, the Ascendant of which was Leo. And the Sun was in the seventh sign, namely in the domicile of nuptials, void in course or joined to no one. And I looked at the Moon, whom I found void in course. Therefore I looked to see which of them would be stronger in place. And they were both aspecting the Ascendant, but the Sun was in an angle stronger than the rest.[54] I also looked to see which of them had more degrees in the sign in which it was, and which would go out more quickly from its own sign, and it was the Moon, and [so] I worked through her first. But if they had each been each conjoined [to some planet],[55] or the Sun were conjoined to some planet, I would have begun from the Sun, who was in the angle—but he was void in course. But I looked at the Moon, whom I found having more degrees than the Sun, and she was going to go more quickly out of the sign in which she was. Therefore, I began to judge first through the Moon, then through the Sun.

After this I looked to see to which of the seven planets the Moon was being joined to first at the time of her going out from the sign in which she was, into the following sign. But the Moon was being joined to Mercury in the following sign, and she was committing her disposition to that same Mercury. And moreover, Mercury was being joined to Saturn, and committed his own disposition to [Saturn]; and [Mercury] is received by [Saturn] by place, because [Saturn] was the Lord of [Mercury's] place. Therefore, Saturn signified his soundness, by the command of God, because Saturn receives Mercury in his own domicile.[56]

After this, I looked to see to whom the Sun would first be joined when he went out to the following sign,[57] and the Sun was being joined to Jupiter

---

[51] Or perhaps, "by 24° 35'." The Latin reads *24. grad. 35 minutis*.
[52] Or perhaps, "by 2° 7'." The Latin reads *2. grad. 7 minutis*.
[53] Or perhaps, "by 11° 39'." The Latin reads *11 grad. 39 minut*.
[54] Technically the Moon is not in an angle at all; but he seems to be using "angle" or "stake" here as a generic term for any house.
[55] That is, instead of being void in course.
[56] Note that nothing so far has involved the 6th or 8th—we are still only dealing with the succession of disposition and aspects and receptions coming from the Moon. Note also that all of this committing of disposition involves reception.
[57] Māshā'allāh seems to have two reasons for turning to the Sun. First, even though the Moon leaves her sign first (and so has a central authority here), the Sun is still the Lord of the Ascendant, and aspects the Ascendant—so he will still have something key to say about the outcome. Second, Māshā'allāh has stated above that the Lord of the Ascendant

(who is the Lord of the domicile of death).⁵⁸ But [Jupiter] was receiving [the Sun] from his own domicile. Therefore, the Sun also signified his soundness and prosperity (by the command of God) on account of the reception by Jupiter (who received him). And if Jupiter had not received him, this would have been a testimony of death, because Jupiter was the Lord of death. And when the Lord of the domicile of death is being joined to the Lord of the domicile of life, and commits his disposition to him,⁵⁹ it will signify death, by the will of God, unless it is something else which God willed. For, whether a benefic were the Lord of the domicile of death, or a malefic, it signifies death, because it is contrary to the Lord of life, unless reception would intercede between them, which repels death—namely where the Lord of the domicile of death receives the Lord of the domicile of life, or it receives the announcer⁶⁰ of his disposition from the Lord of the domicile of life:⁶¹ because then it will be a strong reception. And were the Lord of the domicile of life to receive the Lord of the domicile of death, this will be a weak reception;⁶² nevertheless the Lord of the domicile of death will not destroy him totally, by the command of God.

After this, look to see if you found the Lord of the domicile of life and the Moon both signifying soundness: then begin from the one who more quickly arrived at the planet signifying soundness for him, and the one which was stronger in its own place, and the other one will participate with it. Which if you found one of them signifying life, and the other signifying death, the signification of the Lord of life will be more worthy and stronger, because life does not suffer detriment except through the detriment of each. And the Lord of life rules this matter, so that it should be considered more than the Moon [should be].⁶³ But they should be partners in every matter, nor does one of them particularly have some matter without its associate: and therefore if one of them were advantageous, and the other suffered im-

---

has more authority than the Moon in cases of life and death. So whatever we might want to say about the Moon's role here, the Lord of the Ascendant is still crucial.
⁵⁸ Note this is the situation Māshā'allāh described in Chapter 3.
⁵⁹ That is, when the Lord of the 8ᵗʰ is applying to the Lord of the 1ˢᵗ.
⁶⁰ *Delatorem*, a planet transferring light between them.
⁶¹ That is, if the Lord of the 8ᵗʰ received the planet who transfers the light from the Lord of the 1ˢᵗ.
⁶² This is something new—here weakness has to do with the ability of the reception to perfect things—in this case, the reception is weak because receiving the Lord of death into your house will invite death. He is not making a particular point about dignities here.
⁶³ See earlier footnote.

pediment, it will enter upon him who was advantageous, and upon the matter, from necessity, according to the quantity of the detriment of his associate.

And know wherefore, if you inspected concerning death and infirmity, that beyond all the planets the worst one turned against the Lord of life [is] the Lord of death. And [this is so for] the Lord of death and the Lord of infirmity, unless it is one in common (namely the Lord of the domicile of life and the Lord of the domicile of death)—then it will not impede itself, even if it is malefic, but the rest of the malefic planets will impede it. And you should know wherefore, [that] every planet of the seven, whichever one you found to be the Lord of the domicile of life, it will not impede itself even if it were malefic, but the rest of the malefics will impede it.[64] And on the contrary, whichever planet of the seven you found, who is Lord of the domicile of death, it is the enemy of the Lord of the domicile of life, even if it is a benefic—but it destroys life if it is the dispositor,[65] or unless it receives or is received by another (then it takes this away,[66] by the command of God). And if the Lord of the domicile of life and the Lord of the domicile of death had been Saturn or Mars,[67] it will not make an agreement with another Lord of life except by reception, because death is the enemy of life, unless the Lord of them[68] is one [and the same].

Then one looks to see to whom the Lord of the domicile of death (and the Lord of the domicile of life) would commit his own disposition, or which one is joined to him, committing to him *its* own disposition, and judge according to this. If the Lord of the domicile of death and the Lord of the domicile of life committed their own disposition to a malefic planet not receiving them, they will signify his death, if God wills. And if one of them committed his own disposition to a malefic planet, and that malefic received him, [the infirm person] will be liberated, by the command of God. And if the Lord of the domicile of life (or the Lord of the domicile of death) committed his own disposition to some [planet], the infirm person will be

---

[64] Omitting a partial repetition of this sentence which follows.
[65] This must be if it is the final dispositor.
[66] I believe this means "reception takes away the signification of death."
[67] Māshā'allāh must mean "or," since only Mars is able to rule both the rising sign and the eighth (when Aries is rising). His point (in partnership with the previous sentences) seems to be that the malefics are natural enemies with life, so ruling either of these signs will look especially bad for life.
[68] I.e., of life and death.

liberated from death, God willing, and a benefic will not impede [the planet], whether [the benefic] received [the planet] or not.

After this, I looked concerning the decrease of the infirmity of this infirm person, and concerning its increase. I looked (I have said) at the Lord of the domicile of infirmity, and it was Saturn, who is not being joined to any of the planets (for none of the planets is being joined to Saturn, nor is being separated from him, because he is heavier than all). Therefore I looked to see which of the seven planets was being joined to him, or which of them was being separated from him (namely from Saturn, who was more worthy in the infirmity)—and I found Venus, separated from Saturn (who was the Lord of the domicile of infirmity) by seven days from the domicile of infirmity (because Venus was in the domicile of infirmity).[69] Therefore Venus signified the decrease of the disease, because she was being separated from Saturn (since he was the Lord of the domicile of infirmity) by 7°, and she was being joined to Mars, who received her—and in turn is being received by her (in fact he is receiving her from his own exaltation, but she receives him from her own domicile). Therefore, both signified the easing of the pain, and the arrival of health, by the command of God. Look in this way concerning pain and concerning death.

---

[69] Māshā'allāh means that Venus, who signifies infirmity already because she is in the sixth sign, had been separated from Saturn (the Lord of the sixth), for seven days. Her signification is therefore doubly relevant, being located in the sixth and separating from its Lord.

Chapter 5: On substance

Which if you wished to know, concerning substance, what kind it was, and someone asked you whether he would discover substance or not, and the question were absolute (namely the place of it is unknown, and it is not to be sought from someone [specific]),[70] look for him from the Ascendant, and the Moon, and from the domicile of substance (which is the 2nd from the Ascendant).

Therefore, when you have erected the Ascendant and its degrees, look at the Lord of the domicile of life: which if you found him aspecting the ascending sign, or if some one of the planets rendered his light to the Ascendant, operate through him. But if it were not so, and the Moon were just as I told you before concerning the Lord of the Ascendant, operate through her. And if they each did not aspect the Ascendant, nor were they joined to a planet which would render their light to the Ascendant, you will change the one who had transited more degrees in its sign, and who was supposed to go out more quickly, to the following sign: then operate through that one.

Which if the stronger of them were joined to the Lord of substance (which is the Lord of the 2nd domicile), he will find substance and get it, whether [the stronger significator] were received by the Lord of the domicile of substance or not, whether [the Lord of the domicile of substance] were a benefic or malefic. Because a conjunction of the Lord of the Ascendant with the Lord of the quaesited matter is attainment through himself, and nothing forbids its effecting, if God wills. Which if the Lord of the domicile of substance commits its own disposition to another planet, then one looks to see if it were a malefic and received the Lord of the domicile of substance: the matter will be perfected (if it did not receive, it will not be perfected). And if it were a benefic, it will be perfected and he will find substance, whether it received him or not, if only the dispositor were in a strong place or in the angles. For reception effects matters, so that it can in no way happen but that it comes to be—whether it were delayed or is going to come about shortly—but the angles hasten the matter, and strengthen it, and the following domiciles or those succeeding [the angles] are useful; but the cadents, which do

---

[70] A universal or general question lacks certain specifications like time: "Will I ever marry?" "Will I (ever) be successful?" A particular or specific question is more focused: "Will I get *this* job?" "Will I get *this* money back?" "Will I have good luck *this year*?"

not aspect the Ascendant,[71] delay the matter, and postpone it. But reception cannot pass over into nothing, even if a period of time came in between, by the command of God.

Which if the Lord of the Ascendant or the Moon (namely some one of them) were joined to the Lord of the domicile of substance, [1] even [if] to a malefic planet who at least had a power or dignity in the domicile of substance, though it is not receiving the Lord of the Ascendant, or [2] if it were joined to a malefic planet in the domicile of substance who even lacked a dignity in that domicile, provided that it received the Lord of the Ascendant—the quaesited matter will come about.[72] And if the Lord of the 2nd domicile (which is the domicile of substance), or a planet which was in that same domicile, is being joined to the Lord of the Ascendant, the matter will come to be without any difficulty, and it will be perfected, by the will of God.

The conjunction of the Lord of the Ascendant with the planets signifies the pursuing of the matter by the master of the question before it is given. And the conjunction of the Lord of the domicile of substance with the Lord of the domicile of life signifies that the matter would come without pursuing [it], and it will be more from that side than was hoped for.[73]

Which if the Lord of the Ascendant (and the Moon) is not being joined to the Lord of the 2nd domicile, nor to any planet in his place[74] (that is, who is dismounting in that same domicile), then look to see to whom the Lord of the Ascendant or the Moon would be joined. Which if they were both (or some one of them) joined to a benefic, and that planet did not commit its own disposition to another, and it were in an angle or in a strong place, the

---

[71] Māshā'allāh is mixing up two kinds of cadence (unless the phrase "which do not aspect the Ascendant" has been added by the Latin translator). Here he begins speaking about the angles and the succeedents, so we would expect the cadents to be the 12th, 9th, 3rd, and 6th. These places are cadent from the angles. However, two of these *do* aspect the Ascendant (3rd, 9th). On the other hand, the places that are cadent from the Ascendant (because they do not aspect it) are the 12th, 2nd, 8th, and 6th—and the 2nd and the 8th are *succeedent* places. My conjecture is that Māshā'allāh only means the places cadent from the angles; but it is reasonable to assume that the places cadent from the Ascendant likewise show sluggishness and delay.
[72] In other words, the matter can be perfected by joining to [1] a malefic who has a dignity but does not receive, or [2] a malefic who lacks a dignity but *does* receive.
[73] This is a standard rule in the horary techniques of Māshā'allāh and Sahl. If the Lord of the Ascendant is doing the joining, the querent must strive to perfect the matter; but if it is the other way around, the quaesited matter seeks the querent out, and the querent has to do little.
[74] Reading *in loco eius* for *in vice eius*.

matter will be perfected, and he will find substance, whether the benefic received it or not. And if the Lord of the Ascendant (or the Moon) were joined to a malefic, if [the malefic] received him the matter will be perfected; and if it did not receive him, it will be destroyed, if the malefic were the dispositor and author.[75] Because a malefic planet makes the detriment of matters,[76] if it will not receive another or be received.[77] But the benefics render matters more useful, by the command of God, even if they did not receive others or were [not] received. For if they receive, it will be a greater good, and if they do not receive they still work good, and do not impede (by the command of God). Which if a benefic committed its own disposition to a malefic planet who did not receive [the benefic], its matter will suffer detriment when the disposition arrives to the malefic; but if [the malefic] did receive [the benefic], the matter will be perfected without detriment.

---

[75] This seems to be a variant on earlier statements, that the planet receiving the disposition last becomes the planet in charge of the matter. In this case, if that planet is a malefic, and there is no reception, then he will destroy the matter.

[76] Here we should remember that Sahl's Latin translator uses *detrimentum* to render the Arabic "corruption." See *Introduct.* §5.0 and my Introduction.

[77] This makes it seem that the reception can go in either direction, generally speaking.

Chapter 6: On substance lent

If however you sought substance from someone, which you lent out, or you were asking if he would give to you from his own substance (or in whatever way you demanded it), the Lord of the Ascendant and the Moon will be the questioner, and the Lord of the seventh will be he from whom the substance is sought. And the querent's domicile of substance will be the 2nd domicile from the Ascendant; also, the domicile of substance of him from whom it is sought, will be the 2nd from the seventh—that is, the 8th from the Ascendant, which is the domicile of death.

Which if the Lord of the Ascendant (or the Moon) were joined to the Lord of the domicile of death (who is the Lord of the domicile of the substance of him from whom it is sought), or to a planet which was in that same domicile, just as I have told you before in the preceding chapter, he will acquire his matter which he sought. And if there were [1] no cause of a conjunction between him[78] and the Lord of the domicile of substance of the aforesaid debtor (that is, between the Lord of the Ascendant and the Lord of the domicile of death), nor [2] were he joined to some planet which is in that same domicile, just as I have said before in the chapter above, nor [3] were the Lord of the domicile of death (which is the Lord of the domicile of the quaesited substance) joined to the Lord of the Ascendant nor [4] to some planet agreeing with it which was in the Ascendant (whether it were a malefic or a benefic)—and its agreement is reception, and if it had some dignity in the Ascendant—then look to see to whom the Lord of the Ascendant or the Moon would be joined. Which if one of them (or both)[79] were joined to a malefic planet who receives them, or to a fortunate one which is in a strong place, the matter will be perfected and he will find it, by the command of God.

And if the questioner asked you about substance which is in the house of the king's substance, whether he would have it or not, look for him according to what you saw: to the domicile of substance of the one asking, and to the Lord of the substance of the aforesaid quaesited—that is, from the eleventh sign, which has the second place from the domicile of the king (which is the tenth sign), and judge according to that, by the will of God.

---

78 The Lord of the Ascendant or the Moon.
79 Again, the Lord of the Ascendant or the Moon.

Which if he asked you when this will be, look at the planet to whom the Lord of the Ascendant is being joined, or at a benefic which had a closer reception from the Lord of the Ascendant or the Moon, or at a malefic who received the Lord of the Ascendant or the Moon, in the domicile of the signified matter—that is, at him who signified the effecting of the matter.

Then, if there were an effecting of the matter by conjunction from the known aspects (and not by body), look to see when the Lord of the Ascendant or the Moon will project its own light upon the significator, degree by degree, and make the time according to the number of degrees which there was between them: that is, how many degrees there were, make that many days.

Which if [the effecting of the matter] were not then, it will be when the Lord of the Ascendant or the Moon arrived at that significator, and were joined to him by its own body in the sign in which it was, degree by degree.

Or, on the other hand, when the significator arrives at the Lord of the Ascendant, and there were a conjunction between them in that same sign, and the Lord of the Ascendant appeared heavier than that significator: then the matter will be, by the command of God. And this will be in a strong place in the angles, or in a place in which the Lord of the matter rejoices.

Which if [the effecting of the matter] were not in that hour, it will be when the author of the matter[80] arrived at the Sun, and it pertained-to-arising (that is, if it began to arise after its going-out from under the Sun's rays): for then [the planet] will be renewed, and it will renew its matter, if God wills. And if it were under the Sun's rays, it will be when it goes out from under the rays. Therefore, look at the day when this will be, by the degrees which were between them. If they were lighter stars (namely Venus or Mercury or the Sun), you will put down days for them according to what there was between them in terms of degrees, until one projects its own light upon the other, degree by degree (which is a true conjunction). Then, one will look at the degree in which the author of the matter is, to see when the one seeking the matter would be joined to it, degree by degree. And when the Lord of the Ascendant (or the Moon) arrived to him, the matter will be perfected, by the command of God, of which matter [this] is an example: if some man promised another man something[81] in some place, [and] after this he said, "I will put it here for you," and he put it [there]. After that he set out

---

[80] Again, this is the final dispositor, as described in a footnote above.
[81] *Causam*.

to go abroad, and he left it in that same place until its owner[82] would come and find it and take it. If however it were not in the named place, [the owner] would seek it until he arrived to [the other man]—that is, to the one promising it. And when he reached him, if he found him in a place of his strength, it will perfect the matter, by the command of God. You will do likewise with the Lord of the Ascendant, if the Lord of the matter is being joined to him. And I will put down a likeness[83] through which you will work, and through which you would go forward, if God wills.

---

[82] *Dominus*. There is a play on words here, since *dominus* means the Lord of a house, and in this context signifies the owner of the thing.
[83] I.e., the chart in the following chapter.

Chapter 7: A question concerning things left behind by a certain dead person

A question about the things left behind by a certain dead person, about which a certain relative of his asked whether he would have something of them or not.

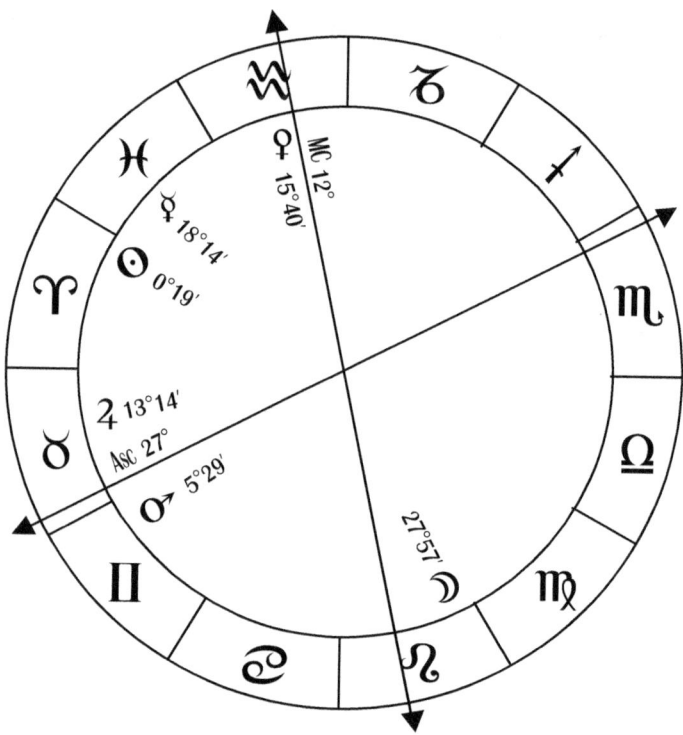

Figure 53: Will the Relative get the Decedent's Goods?

Its stars were posited in this way: the Ascendant was the twenty-eighth degree of Taurus; and the Midheaven the thirteenth degree of Aquarius; and Venus in the sixteenth degree, forty-first minute of Aquarius; and the Moon in Leo, the twenty-eighth degree, fifty-eighth minute; and Mercury in Pisces, the nineteenth degree and fifteenth minute; and the Sun in Aries, the first degree, twentieth minute, and Jupiter in Taurus, in the fourteenth degree, fifteenth minute; and Mars in Gemini, in the sixth degree and thirtieth minute.[84]

And I looked at this question, by the command of God, and its stars were just as I have told you before. Namely, the Lady of the Ascendant, Venus, was void in course, joined to no one, but separated from Jupiter (who was the Lord of the domicile of the substance of the dead person, which is the 8th domicile from the Ascendant).[85] And Jupiter was in Taurus, in the domicile of Venus, and she was separated from him from out of reception, the which separation from out of reception is a certain foulness and a horrible thing.

After this, I looked at the Moon in that same hour, [and] she was void in course, but she was being separated from Venus. Therefore I looked at their places, and I found each in angles, aspecting the Ascendant. But I looked at the one who had more degrees of the sign in which it was, and who ought to go out more quickly from it. And they were both in angles, but the Moon was supposed to go out more quickly,[86] and she had more degrees in her own sign. Wherefore I changed and transferred her to the following sign from her place, and she was joined first to Mars. And Mars is a malefic, and he did not receive her (nor was Mars received by her), nor was Mars the Lord of the domicile of the substance of the aforesaid dead person (which is the place of the querent's purpose): therefore, he signified the prohibition of the purpose. After this I even changed Venus to the following sign, for Venus signified what the Moon had signified, because she is joined first to Mars.

Which if Mars had been the Lord of the domicile of the substance of the dead person, or he had received Venus or the Moon, or he had been a benefic star, or appearing in an angle,[87] or in a place of his own strength, I would have said that the matter would be perfected, and [the querent] would acquire from the substance of that dead person.

And if there had been some benefic in the domicile of the substance of the dead person, and Venus had been joined to him, the matter would come

---

[84] Saturn does not appear in the diagram nor in the text. Hand dates this to March 22, 791 AD. The latitude for the chart must be around 27° N, which passes through the middle of Egypt, Saudi Arabia, and southern Iran and Pakistan.
[85] Note that Māshā'allāh treats the dead person as a 7th house personage, even though the querent is a relative (*propinquus*). Normally we might expect the dead person to be the 3rd because he is a relative, and his substance to be the 4th.
[86] Again, this will happen in almost all such cases involving the Moon.
[87] Note that Māshā'allāh is treating the rising *sign* as the angle or stake, so that Mars, who is only a few degrees from the rising degree, is not yet considered angular.

about; or it if were a malefic, and it had some dignity in that same place, and had received Venus (or, had it not received, if Venus were joined to it), the matter would have come to be.

Or if there had been a malefic planet in that same place, receiving Venus or the Moon, although having no dignity in that place, but still it would affect the matter if Venus had been joined to him, because reception will not perish however it were, by the command of God, if a planet who receives were in charge of the matter, and it were [the matter's] dispositor, and the disposition arrived to it, and if it did not commit it to another. Because if it did commit it to another after its reception, the reception will signify the effecting of the matter, and the committing of its disposition to another signifies the end of the matter, and to what its end would come down to. Because the perfection and effecting of a matter will be understood to be from the planet to which the Lord of the Ascendant and the Moon is first joined, or from the second one who receives what is committed, or from the last one—namely in whatever way the reception was. The end of the matter will even be thus either from the Lord of the quaesited matter, or from the benefic who was in a good place (even without reception).

And so the planets [in this example] signified what they had signified in their own places, and the desperation was from him who sought, [namely] the master of this question. And the hour in which he understood already that it would not come to be, was when [1] Venus went out from Aquarius to the following sign from her own place, which is the sign of Pisces, [2] and when the Moon was joined to Venus by her own body, [3] [and] after she was separated from Venus and was joined to Mars from Pisces, degree by degree. In that hour he lost hope about what he sought. Because the Moon is the significatrix of matters, and she was joined to Mars before Venus was, at the hour of the question, and the Moon knew that she was with Mars before Venus would be joined to him; and when the rumor would have arrived to Venus, the Moon indicated a rumor for Venus. After this, the Moon was joined to Mars by body, and from this came the detriment of the matter, and the matter was then dispersed and dissolved.[88]

And know [that] since the angles strengthen matters and they hasten, and they reinforce matters both good and bad, therefore whatever good there was is fixed by its Lord, and will last (and likewise whatever evil there was, for the one suffering it).

---

[88] Again, linking *detrimentum* with dissolution and corruption.

Chapter 8: About a kingdom, whether it would be acquired

Which if you looked concerning a kingdom, and a man asked whether he would be in charge of a kingdom or not, and his question were absolute (that is, he did not ask you whether he would be in charge in this year, or in this month, or in this week), look to see if you will see that he will not be in charge. In this way, know when there will be a loss of hope concerning it, and what would prohibit him from being in charge.

And if you saw that he would be in charge, and he asked you absolutely, not indicating to you the day nor year, nor a noted month nor week, look for him (if you saw that he will be in charge, and he spoke to you when it seemed to you [that] this could come to be). Set up for him the time just as you saw it in his question: that is, you will foretell for him when this will be in his life, and what part of that life. And general questions will be in this way in all matters.

Which if he asked you about a year or month, or less than this or more, and you saw that it will not come to be, point out to him that it will not come to be in that time about which he asked. And if he asked you when there will be a loss of hope from this matter, point out to him when it will be from the hour in which he asked you. And if you saw that the matter will come to be, indicate to him when it will be, from out of the time concerning which he asked (namely, in the beginning or in the middle, or in its end, or in whatever hour it was of it).

The knowledge of which matter you will observe thusly: namely, you will set up the Ascendant and the Midheaven, and their degrees by the ascensions of your city in which you were then, and by equal hours, and with all of the things generally which are necessary for that about which it is asked. Therefore, adjust the Ascendant by equal hours, [and] after this look at the Lord of the Ascendant and the Moon—which always belong to the one asking, whoever he was of men generally, in general questions, whether the questioner were a man or woman, whether he were small or great. After this, look to see which of them (namely the Lord of the Ascendant or the Moon) is stronger, and see whether the stronger of them would be joined to the Lord of the Midheaven (which is the domicile of the king), not committing its own disposition to another:[89] the querent will attain his matter, that is, he will find the kingdom which he sought, whether the Lord of the Midheaven received

---

[89] That is, if the Lord of the Midheaven does not commit it to another.

the Lord of the Ascendant or not, whether it were a benefic or malefic: then the one seeking the kingdom attained his matter, by the will of God.

If however the Lord of the Midheaven received the Lord of the Ascendant or the Moon, then it is good, by which it could not come to pass better or more strongly, and the matter will be provoked more to this, so that it should come to be, and it will be stable and lasting. But if the Lord of the Midheaven were the one who is being joined [to the Lord of the Ascendant], that is, if he himself seeks the conjunction of the Lord of the Ascendant, then the one asking will acquire the kingdom without his own seeking, for it will come to him of its own accord while he is sitting in his own house, and without labor. For if the Lord of the Ascendant would be joined to the Lord of the Midheaven, it cannot come to be without he himself (or someone on his behalf) seeking the kingdom. Because the conjunction of the Lord of the Ascendant is the acquisition itself, and the reception is its esteem.[90] And if it were a conjunction from the opposition or square aspect, there will be some difficulty in the matter, and delay, and labor. But if it were a conjunction from a trine or sextile aspect, the matter will be without labor, and without duress. It is likewise in the conjunction by body.

Which if the Lord of the Ascendant or the Moon was not joined to the Lord of the Midheaven, nor were the Lord of the Midheaven joined to either of them or both, nor were there some one of the planets between them, committing the disposition until it guides it to them,[91] then look at the Lord of the Ascendant or the Moon:

> If the stronger of them is being joined to another [planet] which is not the Lord of the kingdom or of the Midheaven, and that planet were a benefic, and it were in an angle or in a strong place, the matter will be perfected by the command of God, whether it received him or not.
>
> And if it were a malefic and received him, the matter will be perfected if God wills.
>
> But if it were a malefic and it was not the Lord of the Midheaven, and it did not receive the Lord of the Ascendant,[92] and the malefic did not

---

[90] *Dilectio*, which also denotes non-sexual love and being valued.
[91] In other words, by a transfer of light.
[92] This still seems to assume the above scenario, such that the Lord of the Ascendant is the stronger planet (between it and the Moon), and that it is applying to the malefic.

commit its own disposition to another planet, then the matter will not be perfected—because the malefic destroys it, by the will of God.

And if that malefic committed its own disposition to another malefic who does receive the Lord of the Ascendant, the matter will be perfected, by the command of God.

After this, look at the planet which was in the sign of the Midheaven, and in the sign of the Ascendant:

If there were a malefic in the sign of the Midheaven, who had no dignity in it, and it received the Lord of the Ascendant or the Moon, the matter will be perfected; and if it will not receive one of them, it will not be perfected.

And if it were the exaltation of that same malefic in the sign of the Midheaven, and [the malefic] were in its own exaltation, the matter will be perfected, by the command of God, whether it received the Lord of the Ascendant (or the Moon) or not, if God wills.

And if there were a benefic in the sign of the Midheaven, and the Moon or the Lord of the Ascendant were joined to it, the matter will be perfected, God willing, whether the benefic received it or not, whether it had a dignity in the sign of the Midheaven or not.

Look also at the conjunction of the Lord of the Midheaven with the planets which were in the Ascendant, just as you have looked in the matter of the Lord of the Ascendant, and in his conjunction with the stars which were in the Midheaven.

And know that the planets which are in charge of the matter, if they were in the four angles, dispose matters and hasten, stimulate, and perfect [them]. Which if he asked you about the good or bad in which he was [at the time], or that he expected was going to be afterwards, and you found planets which are in charge of the matter in the angles, it will be lasting, whether it were good or bad. And look at the conjunction of the planets which were in the angles, and at their reception, and [their] assistance through this concerning your matter, if God wills.

And if the one speaking asked you when this kingdom will be, look at the Lord of the Ascendant and the Moon to see which of them were stronger in the signification of the effecting of the matter: operate through that one. But I call the "stronger one" the one who was stronger between the Lord of the Ascendant and the Moon.[93] And see how many degrees there are between the stronger one of them and the planet who perfects its matter, by how far it would be joined to it, degree by degree, and put down those degrees for days; which if it were not [perfected] then, it will be when the Lord of the Ascendant or the Moon arrives to him, and were joined to him by its own body in one degree; or the Lord of the Ascendant or the Moon arrived to the degree in which the Lord of the Midheaven was—and were [the Lord of the Midheaven] strong in place (that is, received in angles), or in an optimal place, and in the middle domiciles (or the succeedents of the angles), and it had some dignity in that same angle, it will be then.

Then know what the strength of the place is—that is, what are the strong places in which the mind of the one perfecting the matter and preparing the matter, delights—because this will indicate to you when the matter will be (concerning which you were asked), by the command of God: that is, you should look to see to whom the Lord of the Ascendant or the Moon is being joined, degree by degree, and you will know in what degree the author of the matter is. Which if [the perfection of the matter] were not when [the Lord of the Ascendant or the Moon] projects its own rays upon him, degree by degree, it will be when it arrives with its body to the degree in which the aforesaid author was—if it were in a strong place, and had some manner of strength in it, in which it rejoices. Which if it were not then, either, [then] the matter will be when the Lord of the Ascendant arrived to him when he aspected him, and the author was in a strong place, by the command of God.

But if it were not this about which you were asked, and you saw that it would not come to be, look then at the planet which signified the impediment of the matter, and its loss of hope. And so, look in it just as you looked regarding that one who perfected the matter, and when it will be (if you saw that it will come to be): his loss of hope will be then, by the command of God.[94]

---

[93] This is a redundant repetition of what was just said.

[94] In other words, the same timing mechanism that predicts when something *will* come to be, can be used to predict when something will be definitively *hindered* and hope lost. The only difference is that in the first case, the delineation of the planets supports perfection, and in the second case it does not.

And if the Lord of the Ascendant or the Moon were joined to the author [of the matter] by its own body in one sign, and the author were in the angles, look to see how many degrees there are between them, and put them down in place of days if the stars were light; and if they were heavy, put months according to the number of degrees. And it will be according to that same number, if God wills. And know that the light stars are the Moon, Mercury, Venus and the Sun; but the heavy ones Saturn, Jupiter and Mars. And now I will set up for you an example through which you should judge and know the things we have already said.[95]

---

[95] I.e., the chart in the following chapter.

Chapter 9: A question concerning a kingdom

A[96] certain man asked whether a kingdom for which he strove (which had even been promised to him, and [specifically] named) would be perfected for him or not. The Ascendant of his question was the sign of Gemini in the fifth degree; the Midheaven Aquarius in the twentieth degree; and Mercury in Gemini, the thirteenth degree, sixteenth minute,[97] retrograde; and the Moon in Sagittarius, the eighth degree, eighteenth minute;[98] and the Sun in Gemini by 51'; and Jupiter in Taurus by 28° 13'; and Saturn in Aries by 16°; and Venus in Aries by 24° 13'; and Mars in Cancer, the eleventh degree, fifty-eighth minute.[99]

I looked at this question by the will of God, and Mercury was the Lord of the Ascendant, retrograde, for he was turning back towards the Sun and was being joined to him; and the Sun was seeking the conjunction of Saturn from the sextile aspect. And Mars was going toward Saturn so he might be joined to him from the square aspect—and all were in aspect, and therefore they had testimonies.[100] But Mars conquered,[101] because he came first to Saturn, and was joined to him degree by degree (which is a true conjunction), and he cut off the conjunction of the Sun from Saturn and destroyed the matter (because he separated the Sun from Saturn). And the Sun was the one to whom the Lord of the Ascendant and the Moon were committing disposition, and he was in the middle between the Lord of the Midheaven (which is the Lord of the matter for which [the querent] was striving) and the Lord of the Ascendant. And if Mars had not cut off the conjunction between the Sun and Saturn, and the Sun had been joined to Saturn before Mars had been joined to him, the matter would have been successful, by the command of God. But since Mars was in a place in which he was being joined to Saturn before the Sun was joined to [Saturn], Mars destroyed the matter when he separated the Sun from Saturn and cut off their conjunction. Therefore,

---

[96] This chart was cast at a latitude of approximately 25°-28° N, which cuts a swath across Egypt, Saudi Arabia, southern Iran, and Pakistan. Hand dates this chart to May 23, 791 AD JC.
[97] Or perhaps, "13° 16'." The Latin reads, *13 grad. 16 minut.*
[98] Or perhaps, "8° 18'." The Latin reads, *8. grad. 18 minut.*
[99] Or perhaps, "11° 58'." The Latin reads, *11. grad. 58. minut.*
[100] Here we see an association between testimony and aspects, similar to the Hellenistic tradition.
[101] The idea seems to be that Mars "conquers" or overrules the Sun's aspect, because his square with Saturn perfects before the Sun's sextile does.

Mars is joined to Saturn, and the Sun is joined to none, since the light of Mars segregated each—the Sun and Saturn (who is the Lord of the purpose of the one asking).

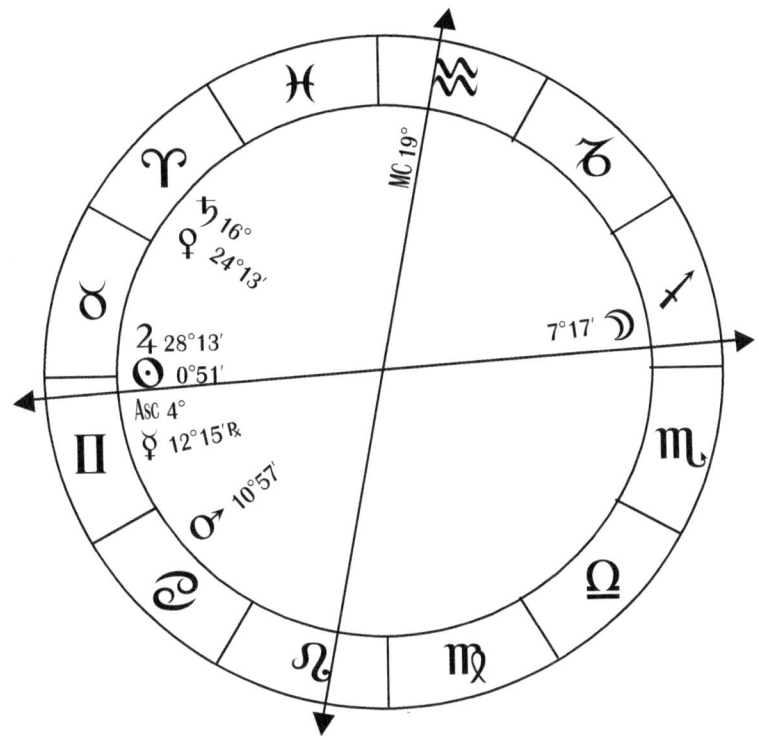

Figure 54: Will he Acquire the Kingdom?

I also wanted to know when the loss of hope was going to be, or when it would be made clear to him that what he demanded would not come to be. And this was when Mars was joined to Saturn, and projected his light upon that Saturn from degree by degree: on that same day there was a loss of hope concerning the purpose.

And know that the Moon, if she were in the sign of the Midheaven, joined to the Lord of the Ascendant, the purpose is even perfected, by the command of God. Since she would be[102] in the place of the purpose, and is a significator of matters, and she is a benefic, therefore she perfects pur-

---

102 Reading *sit* for *est*.

poses, by the command of God, whether reception would be added[103] or not, even if the Lord of the Ascendant had been Saturn or Mars.

And know that the effecting of matters might be in the beginning of the conjunction, in its middle, or in its end, namely in whatever way the concord and reception was. And the perfection of the matter is due to the *mubtazz* or author, to whom the latest [committing] of disposition and conjunction arrived. And if the *mubtazz* or that author received him who commits disposition to him, and he were harmonious with the purpose, then the matter will be perfected and will not suffer detriment, whether it were prolonged or happened quickly, by the command of God.

---

[103] *Accedat.*

Chapter 10: A question concerning a kingdom

A certain man asked whether he would acquire a kingdom in that year or not, at which time the Ascendant was the fourteenth degree of Cancer, and the Midheaven the third degree of Aries. And the Moon was in Libra in the fourth degree, twenty-second minute; and Saturn in Aries, the eleventh degree. And the Sun in Aries, the twenty-ninth degree, tenth minute.[104] And Venus in Pisces, the seventeenth degree and ninth minute.[105] And Jupiter in Taurus by 21° 10'. And Mercury in Taurus, 10° 15'.[106] And Mars in Gemini, by 22° 26'.[107]

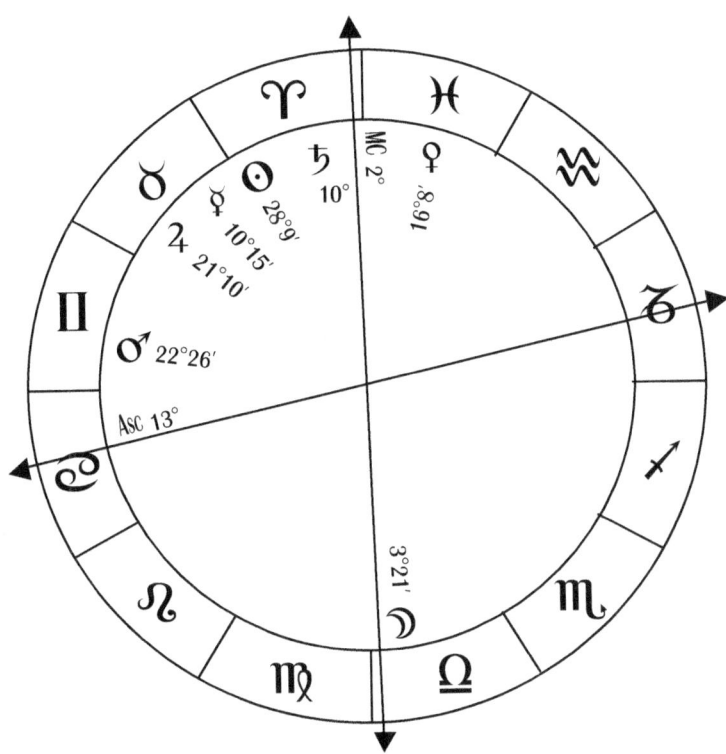

Figure 55: Will he Acquire a Kingdom this Year?

---

[104] Or perhaps, "29° 10'." The Latin reads, *29. grad. 10. minut.*
[105] Or perhaps, "17° and 9'." The Latin reads, *17. grad. & 9. minut.*
[106] Or perhaps, "10° 15'." The Latin reads, *10. grad. 15. minut.*
[107] Hand dates this chart to April 21, 791 AD. It was cast at a latitude of about 28° N.

Therefore I looked in this question (by the will of God) at the Lord of the Ascendant, which was the Moon, whom I found joined to Saturn from his exaltation in Libra. And Saturn received the Moon from his exaltation, and signified the effecting of the matter (by the command of God), since Saturn was receiving the Moon (who was the Lady of the Ascendant), and he was in the royal domicile,[108] which is the place of the matter, and [the querent's] principate was from the reception of Saturn, who was receiving the Moon. But this will not be until it is striven for by the master of the question, and there will be some difficulty or labor there, because Saturn receives the Moon from opposition or contrariety; and the mind of the one striving for the matter will be made anxious on account of his place, because Saturn, who receives the Moon, is in his descension (or in fall), and in [a place of] worthlessness: so Saturn is restricted in his own place. For that reason, we saw that this man will be restricted in his work, and will hate it on account of Saturn's hatred which he has toward his own place. Because Saturn is the one who bestows the kingdom to him (by the command of God), and [the querent's] nature and condition is just like the nature of Saturn and the condition of Saturn.

And the master of the question will find (at the home[109] of him who sets him up) a place of reception and honor and esteem, because Saturn is the Lord of the seventh from the Ascendant, and he received the Lord of the Ascendant, and the Lord of the Ascendant belongs to the one asking—but the Lord of the seventh belongs to him who appointed the one asking. Since therefore it is joined and received by him, we said that there will be esteem and reception between them, and he will be in a good place in his home, if God wills.

And if you wished to know when the kingdom of this man will be, look to see how many degrees there are between the Moon and Saturn, until she is joined to him by her light, degree by degree—and there were 6° between them, so we said that there are six days. Which if it was not going to be then, it will be when the Moon arrives to that degree itself in which Saturn was when he received the Moon degree by degree, in his light. And if it were not then, it will be when Venus arrives at the degree of the Ascendant, since Ve-

---

[108] Aries is also one of the royal signs (along with Leo and Sagittarius).
[109] *Apud.* This means "among, with, in the house of." Māshā'allāh is drawing a parallel between the Moon being in Saturn's exaltation, and the querent (signified by the Moon) being welcomed or received into the good graces and "home" of the man who appointed him to the post (signified by Saturn in his role as the Lord of the seventh).

nus is the Lady of the domicile of the Moon (the which sign is Libra), in which the Moon, the Lady of the Ascendant, was.

And know that if the Lord of the Ascendant and the Moon were cadent, or they perfected their work and disposition [and] yet the matter which you foresaw still did not exist, you must operate through the Lord of the sign in which the Lord of the Ascendant is. And so the principate of the man was toward sixty days from the day in which the question was—that is, when Venus first arrived in the degree of the horoscope (from the ascending sign).[110] For she came into a strong place, and she strengthened the matter, and the works of the stars were then perfected,[111] and the matter was done, by the command of God.

For [a planet effects] both good and bad if it were in a strong place, in higher and fixed places (since these are those that signify and reinforce matters, both good and bad, by the will of God); also, they move [good and bad] at the time of their effecting. Therefore, put your heart into knowing the falling of the planets from the angles, and their loftiness or height in the angles, both for their motion and their receding, both for decrease and for their reinforcement.

And if the man's principate did not exist when Venus arrived at the ascending degree in the east, we would have said that it would be when Venus came to the degree of the fourth sign or the degree of the seventh, or to the degree in which Saturn was at the hour of the question, or when the Sun left Saturn behind and [Saturn] became pertaining-to-arising and went out from under the rays of the Sun and was renewed—and he renewed his matter of which he was in charge. And the transit of Venus to the degree in which the Moon was is a strong place [as well]. But this man for whom she perfects [the matter] went out to his work when Venus arrived at the degree of the ascending sign.

And know that the slowness of this matter happened for the reason that the Moon was in the fourth angle, and was being joined to Saturn from the opposition (from which you knew the effecting of the matter), and Saturn was in the tenth angle, namely in the place of the matter or the kingdom. And if the Moon had been in the seventh angle, at least the matter would

---

[110] By my calculation it would have taken about 83 days for Venus to enter Cancer (not 60), and more than that to reach the ascending degree. Perhaps Māshā'allāh is estimating based on the fact that the Sun is a little over 60 days (actually closer to 70) from the rising degree, so Venus will enter it thereabouts, too. But 23 days off is a significant error.

[111] Reading *stellarum...perfecta sunt* for *stellae...perficiuntur*.

have come to be more quickly; and if she had been with Saturn in the tenth sign, it would have been more quickly yet. And in the ascending sign it would have been faster than the rest of the places. And know that the strength of the Lord of the Ascendant, and the strength of the Moon (or their weakness, if they were weak), makes matters slow down and accelerates them. For if they were in the angles, it will hasten matters, by the command of God. And if one of them were cadent, and the other in a strong place (that is, the planet which is being joined or that to whom the other planet is joining itself), likewise it will impede this matter, and make it slow down according to the quantity of its falling,[112] and according to the impediment which enters in upon him, in the place in which it is. And know that planets falling from the angles make every matter which does not yet exist (and is expected to come to be), slow down. And planets falling from the angles are good, or rather the best, for every good matter whose going-away[113] is expected, like for a pilgrim or traveler having set out, or for a king for whom one looks to see when he will fall and withdraw from his kingdom, and an official[114] when he will withdraw from his rank, and for every good or bad man, when he will withdraw from his master and be removed from him. Therefore, look at this from the receding of the strong planets from the strength of the angle.

The [planets] are elevated in the four angles, of which the more worthy and quicker is the Ascendant, in the good angles, and in the effecting of the purpose; and the second is the angle of the Midheaven or tenth sign.[115] The third is the seventh, namely the domicile of wedlock or nuptials. And the fourth is the angle of the domicile of fathers.

But the more worthy of the middle domiciles[116] is the domicile of hope, and it is faster than the domicile of nuptials and fathers for doing things, and it is the 11th domicile. And the second among them is the domicile of foreign travel or the 9th.[117] The third is the domicile of children, or the 5th. The

---

[112] I.e., its cadence (*casus*).

[113] Here and below *recedo* is used both for a planet receding or falling (i.e., cadent) from an angle, and for someone withdrawing or going away from his current position. In Hellenistic astrology, cadent places are linked with travel.

[114] *Praefectio*.

[115] An unambiguous identification of the Midheaven with the tenth sign.

[116] Earlier Māshā'allāh identified this term with the succeedents, but in this list he includes all domiciles in between the angles. Here he is only concerned with (a) those which are good domiciles, and (b) those which aspect the ascending sign. See next note.

[117] Of course this is a cadent domicile, but probably Māshā'allāh is including it here (along with the 3rd) because it aspects the Ascendant.

fourth is the domicile of brothers, which is the 3rd. These are good and praiseworthy.

But the domiciles cadent from the angles[118] are worse than all the domiciles: namely the domicile of death (which is the 8th) and the domicile of infirmity (which is the 6th), and the domicile of enemies (which is the 12th), and the domicile of substance (which is the 2nd from the Ascendant). These domiciles are inimical to the Ascendant, because they do not aspect the Ascendant.

And the outcome of the man about whom I spoke before, was of little advantage, [and] he did not find in it what he was striving for, except for a middling thing. But he received his authority, and his time [in it] until he turned back to his own house, was fifteen days.[119] And the stability of his authority therefore happened, and the strength of his office,[120] because of his planets in the angles; and the smallness of its usefulness came about because of the fact that Saturn, who decreed a kingdom to him, by the command of God, was in the sign of his own descension, and of his evil and worthlessness, and [his] well,[121] and in a place in which he had no dignity. Even what of [the position] was given to him was hateful, on account of the hatred which Saturn had toward his own place. But the firmness of his stars in the angles fixed[122] all of his matters.

---

[118] Technically, Māshā'allāh should have said the "cadent *from the Ascendant*," since the following domiciles do not aspect the Ascendant.

[119] Or technically, *within* fifteen days, due to the use of the ablative; but the Arabic might read fifteen days exactly.

[120] *Operis*.

[121] I.e., like falling into a well.

[122] *Fixit*. Not in the sense of "correcting them" or "making them better," but in the sense of effecting them and making them happen.

Chapter 11: On discovering the *hīlāj* of the native

If you wished to know the life of the native, by the command of God, if he were born in the day, begin from the Sun. If he were in the Ascendant or in the Midheaven, the root of which (that is, the opposite) is in the seventh from the Ascendant or in the fourth,[123] and he was not receding from the degree of the house[124] in which he was by more than 5°,[125] and he were received by the Lord of the domicile or the exaltation of the sign in which he was, by conjunction,[126] then he will be able to be used as the *hīlāj*. And the planet who received will be the *kadukhudhāh*, and that is the one who is in charge of the nativity (namely, the significator or giver of years or months or days).[127] And the division of the months, years or days is directed from the degree in which it (and that is the degree of the *hīlāj*) is.[128] Which if the Sun were not in one of the places which I told you before, or he were in them and appeared removed by more than 5° from the degree of the place in which he is, or if he were in them and there will not be a conjunction between him and the Lord of the domicile or exaltation of the sign in which he was[129]—if it were so, he will not be able to be used as the *hīlāj*.

Therefore dismiss him and look at the Moon: which if she were in the four angles and in the succeedents of the angles (which are the 11th, 5th, 8th,

---

[123] I am not sure what we are supposed to do with this notion of the seventh and the fourth being the "roots" of the Ascendant and Midheaven. Māshā'allāh is not necessarily saying that the Sun is eligible to be the *hīlāj* if he is in these "roots."

[124] *Domus*. Here and below I will uses "house" and "domicile" as seems fit, but the reader should keep in mind that the same Latin word underlies both. Probably Māshā'allāh has equal houses from the Ascendant in mind, as Ptolemy seems to use in his famous longevity treatment in *Tet*. III.11.

[125] That is, that he is not more than 5° earlier than the cusp.

[126] This should be taken as including aspects.

[127] Throughout this chapter, the planet "in charge of" (*praesse*) the nativity is the *kadukhudhāh*, the planet or point giving the expected years of life. Then we direct the *hīlāj* by primary directions to fine-tune the timing of various illnesses and death. Māshā'allāh is not always clear whether the *hīlāj* is to be directed simply by ascensional times (as when we direct planets or points through the bounds), or whether we are supposed to use the more complicated system of primaries which distinguishes between directions of the ascending degree, the MC degree, and intermediate points.

[128] Māshā'allāh gives ideas throughout on how to judge this directing, but only in the last paragraphs of the chapter does he summarize the procedure.

[129] Note: "there *will* not be." Perhaps this means that the planets do not actually have to be in orbs at the time, but they need only be positioned so that they *will* conjoin or be in aspect while they are still in their respective signs. If so, then this statement by Māshā'allāh is very much in line with Hellenistic practice.

and 2nd), these are eight places in which, if the Moon were not removed by more than 5° from the degree of the house in which she is, and she were conjoined to the Lord of the domicile or exaltation of the sign in which she is, she will be able to be used as the *hīlāj*. Then direct the division of years or months or days, by the command of God. Which if then the Moon were not in these eight places which I have named for you, and she were removed by more than 5° from the degree of the house in which she appears, or she were in them, not removed, [but][130] she was not joined to the Lord of her domicile or exaltation—if it were so, she will not be suitable for becoming the *hīlāj*.

Then look at the degree of the Lot of Fortune to see if it fell in one of these eight places, and was not removed by more than 5° from the degree of the house in which it is; and were the Lord of the bound of the degree of the Lot of Fortune, or the Lord of its domicile, joined to it, it will be able to be used as the *hīlāj*. And the Lord of its bound or the Lord of its domicile which is joined to it, will be in charge—that is, it will be the giver of years or months or days.[131] And direct the division of the years or months and days from the degree of the Lot of Fortune.[132] Which if it were not the Lord of the bound of the degree of the Lot of Fortune, and[133] the Lord of its domicile were joined to it, [the Lord of the domicile] will be in charge: [the Lot] will be the *hīlāj*, and from its Lord is known the granting of years, months, or days. And you will direct for him the division of years, months, and days from the Lot of Fortune, by the will of God. But if the Lot of Fortune were not in these eight places, or it were in them and it were removed by more than 5° from the degree of the place in which it is, it will not be able to be used as the *hīlāj*—therefore dismiss it.

Which if it were in a conjunctional nativity (that is, one which a meeting[134] of the luminaries just recently preceded), then look at the degree of the conjunction of the Sun and the Moon before the nativity of the one born. Which if the degree of the Sun's and Moon's conjunction before his nativity were in these eight places, not removed by more than 5° from the place in which it is, and the Lord of its bound or the Lord of the domicile in

---

[130] Reading *sed* for *aut*.
[131] I.e., the *kadukhudhāh*.
[132] Again, we direct the *hīlāj* through the bounds.
[133] Reading *et* for *aut*, with Hand.
[134] *Synodus* (Gr. *sunodos*), i.e., a conjunction.

which it is were joined to it, it[135] will be in charge over the signification of the giving of years, months, and days. And you will direct the division of the months, years, or days from the degree of the conjunction, since it was made the *hīlāj*, by the command of God.

If however the boy were born in the conjunction, and the Lord of its bound or the Lord of the domicile in which it is, was[136] joined to the degree of the conjunction, and the conjunction were in the aforesaid eight places, not removed by more than 5° from the house in which it is, the degree of its conjunction will be the *hīlāj*, and its Lord will be in charge, as well as the conjunction itself (that is, both at once), and from them will be known the granting of years, months, and days. And from them is directed the division of the years, months, or days. But if the degree of the conjunction of the Sun and the Moon were not in the aforesaid eight places, and it were removed by more than 5° from the degree of the house in which it is, it will not be able to be used to become the *hīlāj*—therefore dismiss it.

Look likewise concerning the degree of the prevention or opposition of the luminaries (which is elsewhere called the degree of the filling-up[137] of the Moon) which was most recently before the nativity: if the nativity were in the aforesaid prevention, the which degree, if it were in the eight places stated earlier, not removed by more than 5° from the degree of the house in which it is, it will be able to be used as the *hīlāj*, and direct the division of the years, months, and days from it. Which if the Lord of its bound or domicile were joined to it, the one of them which was then joined will be in charge of the nativity, and the one who will signify the granting of years, months, or days—only if the degree of the prevention were in the aforesaid eight places, not removed by more than 5° from the degree of the place in which it is. But if the Lord of its bound, or the Lord of the domicile, is not being conjoined to it, nevertheless still the degree of the prevention will be the *hīlāj*, and [its Lord] will be in charge, and from its place is known the granting of years, months or days, by the will of God. And if the degree of the prevention were in the eight places, but it were removed by more than 5° from the degree of the house in which it is, it will not be able to be used as the *hīlāj* — therefore dismiss it.

---

[135] This must mean the Lord of the bound or the Lord of the domicile, whichever it is.

[136] Omitting *non*.

[137] Māshā'allāh recommends that we use the degree of the Moon for the prevention (as opposed to the degree that is above the horizon, or other ways of determining the proper degree of the prevention).

And [then] look at the degree of the Ascendant, because it will be the *hīlāj*, and the Lord of its bound, or the Lord of domicile (the one which was joined to it) will be in charge of the nativity, and it will be the significator and giver of years, months, or days. And from the degree of the Ascendant would be directed the division of the years, months, or days. Which if the Lord of its bound, or the Lord of the domicile, was not joined to it, that is, if neither of these were joined to the degree of the ascending sign,[138] still the degree of the Ascendant will be the *hīlāj*, and it will be in charge of the nativity, and from it will be directed the division of the years, months, or days.[139]

And you will operate in the night just as you operate in the day, equally in all hours, but you will begin in the day from the Sun, after that from the Moon, thence from the Lot of Fortune, [then] in order from the conjunction or prevention (in which the nativity happened), [and] finally from the degree of the ascending sign.

And when you have run through the aforenamed headings from those places, and were your work from the degree of the Ascendant,[140] the life of the boy will not be prolonged, unless the degree of the Ascendant is free from the projection of the malefics' light (namely that of Saturn and Mars) upon it. And you should not give up on this, if you found the Lord of the nativity, so that you might look at the extension of the [malefic] planets' rays to the *hīlāj*, because the [malefic] planets' rays is a certain strong matter, unless the Sun or Venus or Jupiter or the Moon should aspect with them. Because the aspect of these [latter planets] breaks the virtue of the malefics. Indeed if the malefics were in more degrees than the benefics were, you should not even dismiss with this the hurling[141] of the malefics to the *hīlāj* through their own rays. And thus if the one who is in charge of the nativity is strong, the master of the nativity[142] will not perish, by the command of God, but difficulties and labors will find him, by the command of God, and he will be liberated from them.

---

[138] This must refer to the degree of the Ascendant.
[139] In this case it seems we have no *kadukḥudhāh*.
[140] That is, if all of the other candidate *hīlāj*es failed.
[141] *Iaculationem*. This is related to the word used below for the Greek-based "hurling of rays" (*iactus*), and Māshā'allāh or his source is undoubtedly drawing on the discussion of primary directions and the hurling of rays in *Tet.* III.11, pp. 36*ff.* My sense is that *in this paragraph* Māshā'allāh is only referring to aspects in general.
[142] I take this simply to be the native, just as the "master of the question" is the querent.

And if you found the one who is in charge of the nativity in the Ascendant or the Midheaven, or in the seventh angle, gone out from under the Sun's rays, and direct, nor were it in its own descension, it will give its own greater years. And if it were in the fourth angle (which is below the earth), or it were in its own bound, or in its own domicile, or the exaltation, triplicity, or face, and it were oriental,[143] it will give its own greater years.

And if it were in the eleventh or in the fifth, and it were not oriental, nor were it in its own bound, nor in domicile, or in the exaltation, or in the triplicity or in the face, it will give its middle years.

And if it were in the second from the Ascendant, or in the eighth, and it were in its own bound, or in domicile or exaltation, or in its own triplicity or face, it will give its own middle years.

And if it were in none of these, neither in the bound, nor in domicile, nor the exaltation,[144] nor the triplicity, nor in its own face, or[145] were it in its own descension, or in a well,[146] or in a place in which it is made sad, it will likewise give its own middle years.

And if it were in the ninth from the Ascendant, or the third, it will give its lesser years; and if it were in the 9th from the Ascendant, and it appeared oriental in its own bound or in domicile, exaltation, triplicity, or its own face, it will give its own middle years, if it were a diurnal nativity, and the Lord who was in charge of it were diurnal (or if the nativity were nocturnal, and the one who is in charge, appeared nocturnal in the same way).[147]

And if it were in the sixth from the Ascendant, or in the twelfth, and it were not in its own descension, it will give its own lesser years. But if it

---

[143] Here and throughout the paragraphs below, it is impossible to say exactly which meaning of *orientalis* (or *occidentalis*) is meant.
[144] Omitting a redundant *nec domo*.
[145] Reading *aut* for *nec* ("nor") throughout the rest of this sentence.
[146] This is probably not a reference to a welled degree (as Hand suggests), but a synonym for the planet's descension, as Māshā'allāh wrote at the end of Ch. 10.
[147] I am not sure what to make of one planet "being" diurnal, and the other "appearing" (*extiterit*) nocturnal. Probably it simply means belonging to the sect in favor.

were in its own descension in the twelfth or the sixth, and it were retrograde, it will give months according to the number of the lesser years—that is, by counting individual months for individual years. And if it were under the rays of the Sun, retrograde in its own descension, and it were in the twelfth place or the sixth from the Ascendant, it will give days according to the number of its own lesser years: that is, by counting individual days for individual years.

And if you found the one who is in charge of the nativity in an angle, retrograde or under the rays of the Sun, it will give the middle years. And if it were in the followers of the angles, retrograde or under the rays of the Sun, it will give the lesser years. And if it were cadent from the angles, and it were under the rays of the Sun, or retrograde, it would not be able to give the lesser years, but it will give a month instead of one year.[148]

And if the one who is in charge[149] decrees years, and the benefics aspected it from the square aspect or from the opposition, or from the sextile aspect, or they were with it in the same sign, they will increase for it according to the quantity of the degrees which there are in the time of the hours of that degree in which it was, a year for one degree—if the [benefic] who increases were not retrograde or under the rays of the Sun. And if the planets which signify increase were in the sixth from the Ascendant, or in the twelfth, they will increase nothing. And if one of the malefic planets aspected the one who is in charge, from any aspects, from the square, from the opposition, from the trine, sextile, or, finally, however it were with it, [the malefic] subtracts from it according to the number of the degrees which are in the time of the hours of that degree in which it is in the clime in which the nativity was, one year for every degree of the degrees of the times of the hours.[150]

And I have discovered in a certain book—but I have not tested it—that if you found the Tail of the Dragon with the one who is in charge of the nativity, not far from it, within 8°, it will subtract from it one-fourth of the years

---

148 That is, it will give months according to the number of the lesser years.
149 The *kadukhudhāh*.
150 This is an explicit reference to the use of "hourly times" in *Tet.* III.11, pp. 37*ff*.

belonging to the one who is in charge. And if it were the Head of the Dragon, it will likewise subtract one-fourth of the years.[151]

And know that the extension of the rays of the planets comes to be by equal degrees, but it gives years to the *hīlāj* by the degrees of the ascension; and you should not leave out the granting of years from the Ascendant by the degrees of ascension.

And know that if you directed[152] the division of the years, months, or days from the degree of the *hīlāj* (or from the degree of the Ascendant), [giving] one year, month, or one day to every degree, in whatever way you might find a malefic being aspected, with which the degree (which you directed from the *hīlāj* or from the Ascendant) came out.[153] And know that the degree to which the division comes (which you have led down from the *hīlāj* or from the Ascendant), if some one of these four benefics aspected [the *hīlāj*], he will escape and be liberated from death, unless the degrees of the malefic[154] which aspect the place where the division arrived at, are greater in degrees—that is, unless the degrees of the malefic in its sign were more than that of the benefics: for this signifies [that] the native will endure until the degrees which you have directed from the *hīlāj*, transit the degrees of the benefic. And once it had crossed these, and it arrived at the bad degrees, then they will signify death.

And know that if it were a nativity in which[155] the one who is in charge[156] were in a strong place, and a malefic projected its own rays upon the degree of the sign of life,[157] or upon the degree of the Sun or the Moon, or [upon] the degree of the *hīlāj* (in whatever kind of degree it touched it), the native will not be subjected[158] to death until the one who is in charge of the nativity would perfect the number of years which it signified, according to the quality of that place in which it were, in terms of greater, middle, or lesser years, in terms of months, days, or hours, if God wills.

---

[151] Normally (and in *On Nativities* §3), the Head is said to add years, not subtract them.
[152] *Duxeris*, lit. "led."
[153] This sentence is incomplete or garbled. Māshā'allāh is simply envisioning that the direction of the *hīlāj* or the Ascendant might come to the aspect (or body) of a malefic. The next sentence tells us what to do about it.
[154] This could also read, "the bad degrees," since Māshā'allāh uses that formulation below.
[155] Reading *qua* for *cui*.
[156] The *kadukhudhāh*.
[157] That is, the degree of the Ascendant. Reading *signi* for *ligni*, with Hand.
[158] Reading *subiecibitur* for *subiacebitur*, with Hand.

And[159] I will expound for you the hurling[160] of rays, understand it: certain people consider the hurling of rays to be thus—namely a planet which is in the tenth receives rays from the one who looks back from the fourth from him, and the one who is in the fourth from him projects[161] its own rays to him who is in the tenth from him. And therefore it is called a hurling of rays with respect to these four ways[162] which I said before: because he who is in front of it in the fourth, projects rays to the one who is set over him in the tenth; or, with respect to that one which is in the fourth, since he who goes in front of him, projects its own rays likewise to the area put behind him. Because he who is in Aries aspects him who is in Cancer, and he who is in Cancer projects its own rays to him who is in Aries.

And the majority of the wise agree that they should make the 5° which are before the degree of the Ascendant[163] [to be] of the strength of the Ascendant: which if the Sun were in them, they say he is able to be the *hīlāj*, if he were received (and likewise the Moon)—from which [degrees], and in the other places, the *hīlāj* is likewise found. But they said the one who is in charge, or who signifies the granting of years, if it were removed from the degree of the Ascendant, and it were in the 5° which are before the angle, they said it could *not* give the greater years, but [it could] grant the middle years. In fact it seems to us to adapt this book thusly in order that the one who is in charge, and the *hīlāj*, will be known.

After this it will be known what it would signify concerning years, months, days, or hours. But if we came to know what it had concerning these, we

---

[159] This paragraph is pure Hellenistic doctrine, called the "hurling of rays" (see Rhetorius Ch. 21). It is purely a whole-sign dynamic, though I have not added "sign" in brackets. Suppose we have two planets, one of which is in Aries, and the other in the tenth sign from it, namely in Capricorn, forming a "superior square" to it by whole signs. Then the planet in Capricorn will "look ahead" or aspect the planet in Aries, but the planet in Aries will "hurl its rays" back at the planet in Capricorn. This whole-sign situation is also called "overcoming," where the planet in the tenth sign (Capricorn) "overcomes" and has an overwhelming influence on the other planet (Aries). "Overcoming" is the source of the later use of the word *elevatio*, which many medievals took to mean being "elevated" or high up in the chart. That said, Māshā'allāh does not tell us what to make of this doctrine or its relevance to longevity calculations.
[160] *Iactum*, from *iacio*, "throw, cast, hurl."
[161] *Proiicit*, from *proicio*, lit. "to throw away, fling away, extend."
[162] In an earlier paragraph Māshā'allāh speaks of the four benefics, but it is hard to see how this is relevant. Another possibility is that *hos...modos* is a misread for *has...domos* ("these four houses")—this would make some sense if we were talking about planets in angular relations to another, but still its application is unclear.
[163] That is, those that rise just above it in earlier degrees.

would direct from the degree of the *hīlāj* to the square aspect of the malefics, and their opposition, for the purpose of investigating the death of the native. Afterwards, we look to see some benefic projects its own light upon the place of a bad degree,[164] or not. Which if there were some benefic planet projecting its own light upon the place of the light of a malefic, [the native] will be freed after the pain. After this, you will direct it even to the square aspect of another malefic, and to the opposition. Moreover the malefics even give testimony for a disease or infirmity if they were in a trine or sextile aspect. But what they signified concerning degrees from the *hīlāj* up to the light (that is, to the rays of a malefic), we say that they will be years or months or days or hours, according to what the one who is in charge signified. And if you knew the division which the one who is in charge signifies, namely whether they are years, months, days or hours, you will direct that division from the degree of the *hīlāj* up to the square aspect of the malefics and their opposition, for investigating the death of the native.

---

[164] *Locum gradus mali*. This could also be, "the place of the degree of a malefic."

Chapter 12: A question about a kingdom

A question of a certain general whom the King of Africa put [into position]. And he who was then in charge of Africa was rebellious against them,[165] and worthy of deposing.

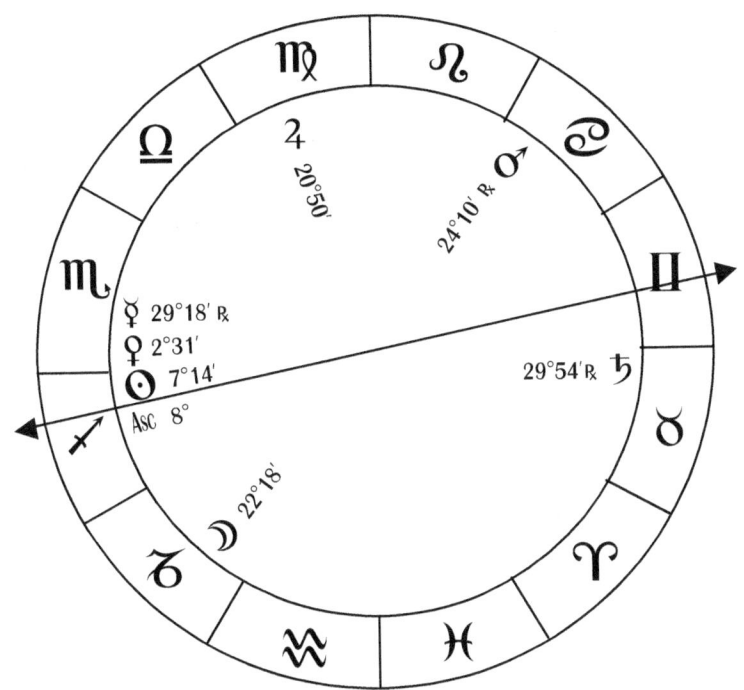

Figure 56: The Condition of a New General and a Rebel

And the general asked whether or not what the King had ordained earlier (concerning the command of Africa) would be given to him, and what was going to be concerning his condition, and concerning the condition of the one who was in charge of it [at that time],[166] by the command of God.[167]

---

[165] *In contrariete eorum eis rebellis.* Throughout the rest of this chapter, Māshā'allāh keeps saying the man is *suspected* of being a rebel, is *considered to be, reputed to be,* and so on. Is this tentativeness a function of the querent's own beliefs (so that he wanted Māshā'allāh to confirm whether the man was rebellious)? Or does it reflect Māshā'allāh's own doubt?

[166] That is, the man who was in rebellion, whom the querent was supposed to fight and replace.

[167] Hand dates this chart to December 1, 794 AD, at 4:00 UT. Note that no degree of the Midheaven is given.

And its planets were of such a figure. I looked at this question by the will of God, and its planets were just as I will describe to you. The ninth degree of Sagittarius was ascending, and the Sun in Sagittarius, the eighth degree, fifteenth minute.[168] And Venus in Sagittarius by 2° 31', the Moon in Capricorn by 22° 18'. And Saturn in Taurus by 29° 54', retrograde. And Jupiter in Virgo by 20° and 50'. And Mars in Cancer, in the twenty-fifth degree, ten minutes, retrograde. And Mercury in Scorpio by 29° 18', [retrograde].[169]

And so I looked at the Ascendant in this question, and at its Lord, and at the planet from which the Moon is being separated. And the Ascendant was Sagittarius, and the Sun and Venus in it. And Jupiter in the angle of the Midheaven, direct, and he is of the higher planets, and he himself was aspecting both of his own domiciles, and all four angles in the higher and lower place. And of the angles generally the master of the question stood out more worthily, namely in the place of the exaltation of the master of the question and his kingdom.[170] And the Sun and Venus were being joined to Jupiter from his own domicile, and he was receiving them from his own domicile by a strong reception. And the Sun was receiving him by his light,[171] and the testimonies were joined concerning fortune,[172] by the will of God. And this signified the strength of the master of the question over his enemy, and the firmness of his honor,[173] and that he would attain his kingdom which extended to that which had been committed to him by his emperor, and it was in his hand, and there was nothing he would not attain, by the will of God.

After this I looked for him who was [currently] in charge of Africa (who was reputed to be rebellious, and contrary, disobedient, and was to be deposed), from the nadir (that is from the opposite of the Ascendant), and from its Lord, and from the planet to which the Moon was being joined. But the nadir was the sign of Gemini, and none of the seven planets were in it, and its Lord was Mercury, of the inferior planets; and he was retrograde and

---

[168] Or perhaps, "by 8° 15'." The Latin reads, *8. grad. 15. minut.*
[169] Below, Māshā'allāh says that Mercury is retrograde, which is confirmed by modern calculation.
[170] In other words, the Lord of the Ascendant, who *signifies* the querent or master of the question, was in the best angle for this purpose: in the tenth, which signifies exaltation and kingship.
[171] I am not sure what this means. Could it relate to sect?
[172] *Super fortunam.*
[173] Not his own personal sense of honor, but the political position of honor he had been given.

falling toward the twelfth sign from the Ascendant,[174] and he was being joined to Saturn by his [direct line][175] from the opposition; but Saturn was cadent in the sixth sign from the Ascendant, and he was retrograde. Therefore, Mercury had signified, by his retrogradation and descension,[176] and through his conjunction with a cadent and retrograde planet, the loss of those things which the enemy and contrary person had undertaken—that is, the loss of his counsel,[177] and the dissolving of his right to command. And his falling[178] in the twelfth from the Ascendant, and Saturn's falling[179] in the sixth sign, [falling] from the nadir, signified weakness falling on the enemy and the adversary, namely a powerful weakness, and the dispersion of his social relationships,[180] and the fall of his name and memory, and the loss of those things which he had fitted for himself and had gathered together, and their destruction, by the will of God.

After this I looked, for the master of the question, even from the planet from which the Moon was being separated. And she was being separated from Jupiter, who is the Lord of the Ascendant; and Jupiter was in the angle of the Midheaven, and he is of the higher planets, having the higher place [in the planetary spheres] after Saturn. Also, Jupiter signified, by the will [of God], by the height and goodness of his place, the strength of the master of the question, and the firmness of his honor, and the attaining of his principate, and of those things about which he had asked—namely, about honor and the position of command which his emperor had committed and ordained for him, by the command of God.[181]

Then I looked, for him who was considered rebellious and was to be deposed, and who had been disobedient, from the planet to which the Moon

---

[174] Actually, Mercury is *in* the twelfth sign, but he is "falling" because he has fallen away from the horizon or the Ascendant.

[175] *Per directionem suam.* Since both Mercury and Saturn are retrograde, Hand (p. 61 n.5) thinks that *directionem* definitely must refer to primary direction. This does not seem plausible to me. I think the answer is much simpler: since Mercury and Saturn are in corresponding degrees, their exact opposition is a "straight line." *Dirigo* and *directus* have being "straight" and "lining up" as their primary meaning.

[176] Usually the Latin translator (or Māshā'allāh) uses "descension" in the way we use "fall" (i.e., being in the sign opposite one's exaltation). But here he is using the term as a synonym for cadence.

[177] That is, his position of providing counsel and aid to the king.

[178] I.e., being cadent.

[179] I.e., being cadent.

[180] *Congregationis*, which means a grouping, assembly, association, a flock. It must refer to the social network which was destroyed when he turned against the king.

[181] Note that Jupiter's being in detriment does not seem to concern Māshā'allāh.

was being joined, and I found that she was being joined to Mars. And Mars was falling[182] in his own descension, and retrograde in the eighth domicile from the Ascendant, which is the 2nd from the Nadir [of the Ascendant], and is the place of the allies or soldiers of him who was suspected of being rebellious, and his substance. The conjunction of the Moon with Mars, and the retrogradation of Mars, and his falling in his own descension, signified the dissolution of the work of the enemy and adversary, and his turning back from the counsel which he had gone out of, and his repentance[183] concerning that which he had moved,[184] and his subjection and loss of honor, by the command of God.

And the place of the Moon in the second from the ascending sign (which is the beginning of the one asking),[185] signified [the condition] of his allies and his substance.[186] And the Moon was the Lady of the significator of the enemy and the adversary, and the significatrix of his soldiers and allies.[187] And the Moon was joined to Mars from the opposition, and each of them was receiving its partner by a strong reception. Therefore, by the will of God, the entrance of the Moon (who is the significatrix of the enemy and the adversary) into Capricorn (which is the place of the allies of the master of the question and the place of substance) signified the seeking[188] of the soldiers of the enemy turning against [the querent] for substance, namely seeking the fulfillment of their hope concerning the acquisition of substance, and that they would accept part of those things which they reckoned [they were owed], by the will of God, and that they would enter into the obedience

---

[182] Here *cadens* simply means "to be in," although it could also reinforce the notion of the descension or fall as falling from a height. At any rate, it does not mean "cadent."

[183] *Poenitentiam*. Technically this word in medieval Latin means "penance," but Māshā'allāh seems to be referring to his mental state, not any punishment he will incur.

[184] I.e., set in motion.

[185] Hand reads, "of the question," but my text reads *interrogantis*.

[186] Adding *esse*.

[187] This is stated imprecisely. The Moon is not the dispositor of Mercury (who is the Lord of the seventh), but as a general significatrix she can indicate what will happen with the enemy (as seen in the previous paragraph). Perhaps Māshā'allāh takes her application to signify the upcoming engagement with the rebel. She is however definitely the Lady of the eighth, the enemy's allies.

[188] *Petitionem*. In classical Latin this work has heavy legal connotations, as when someone is pursuing a legal claim or making a legal petition. But the medieval astrological texts very rarely use this term in a legal context. So we should not assume that the enemy's allies and soldiers had a legal foundation for wanting to be bought off, or that there was something judicial about the process. They were probably making threats in order to be bribed into obedience.

and assistance of the master of the question after accepting those things in which they had hope—that is, after the gifts[189] [were] given, which they were hoping they would accept for themselves, by the will of God.

Also, the place of the Moon in Capricorn, and the place of Mars in Cancer, signified that they would not get everything which they hoped to take (or such as they were reckoning). And the conjunction of the Moon with Mars from the opposition signified that the soldiers of the adversary would be troublesome in the seeking of substance, for this was in their boundary,[190] and they were seeking this, by the will of God.

After this I looked for the enemy turning against [the querent] to see what was going to be concerning his condition, and concerning the condition of him who was succeeding him.[191] Therefore I looked at Mercury, who was the significator of the enemy—namely I looked to see to whom he was being joined, and who was being joined to him. And I found him to be joined to Saturn by his [direct line][192] from the opposition, which is an aspect of contrariety and enmity. And Saturn was the Lord of the 2nd domicile of the one asking, and the Lord of the 3rd of the same, which are the places of his soldiers and allies,[193] and there was no reception between them. Therefore this signified that the enemy will find certain people of these brothers and soldiers opposed to him, who would render unto him in turn, and would renounce his word (that is, obedience to him),[194] by the will of God.

After this I looked to see which one of them would have the victory and the attainment of the kingdom, from the Lords of their domiciles, because the significators[195] were cadent from the angles. I also looked for those who were fighting against the enemy Mercury [who was] turning against Saturn,[196]

---

[189] *Dona*, "gifts, sacrifices, presents." So the rebel enemy's allies were offering to betray him if the querent gave them at least a portion of some kind of payment or booty which they thought they deserved.

[190] *Terminus*, the same word used for the astrological bounds, and meaning "boundary, limit." The passage suggests that the enemy's allies were using their presence in the region as a bargaining chip to get more money, since it would be difficult to expel them if financial negotiations broke down.

[191] I.e., the querent, since the querent was sent in to replace the rebellious man.

[192] See earlier footnote for this phrase.

[193] Perhaps if we assume that relatives and tribesmen of the querent are his natural allies.

[194] Lit., "his obedience."

[195] That is, of Mercury (the enemy) and Saturn (the brothers and soldiers of the querent, who are turning against the enemy).

[196] The sentence is awkward because Māshā'allāh is trying to pack too many relationships into the sentence. He is now going to look at Saturn, who represents those who are fighting Mercury, who is turning against Saturn.

and from the Lord of [Saturn's] domicile. And Saturn was cadent, retrograde, and the Lady of his domicile was Venus, and Venus was in the ascending angle,[197] combust under the rays of the Sun. And her place in an angle, in Sagittarius (which is a common sign) signified the repetition of the battle by those who are turned against the enemy—that is, that those who were turned against the enemy will repeat the battle twice or more, and that they would be enflamed with the zeal of battle; and the combustion of Venus signified their being consumed, and their flight, and their destruction, by the will of God.

After this I looked for the same enemy turned against [the querent] to see what his strength and victory would be against those who were turned against him. And so I looked for him from his significator, and from the Lord of its domicile. And the significator was Mercury, and the Lord of his domicile was Mars, and Mars [was] in Cancer, in his own descension, retrograde: and this signified weakness in the beginning of his work, by the command of God. I also looked to see whether Mars would be joined to someone who would strengthen him, or if some planet would be joined to him who would assist him, and I found the Moon joined to him from the exaltation of Mars, and each of them was receiving its partner by a strong reception. Therefore, this signified the victory of the enemy turning against [the querent] over his own enemies, and that he would subject them to himself, and he would take whatever they had in their hands concerning the kingdom, by the command of God.[198]

Then I looked to see what there was concerning the master of the question and the enemy turning against [him], and in what way the master of the question would attain the kingdom,[199] and whether he was going to have it by means of battle or by means of peace. Therefore I looked at Jupiter, who was the significator of the master of the question, and at Mercury, who was the significator of the enemy turning against [him], who was reputed to be rebellious, [to see] from which part of the circle they were aspecting each other. And I found each one of them projecting his light upon his partner from the sextile aspect, which is an aspect of peace and concord. And this

---

[197] I.e., the rising sign, which is defined here as the entire angle. She is 7° from the ascending degree, so this can only be a whole-sign reference.
[198] So far, then, we have seen that the querent's allies and brothers will not prevail over the rebellious enemy, though they fight him more than once. The rebellious enemy will conquer them all and take what they have. All of this is after some of his own soldiers have been arranging to be paid to betray the rebellious enemy. Now we turn to the querent himself in the next paragraph.
[199] Remember, the chart has already shown that he *will* attain the position.

signified that the attainment of the master of the question, in those things of which he was in charge, and his exaltation over [the enemy], would come about by means of peace and clemency, and that the enemy who was thought to be rebellious would seek security and peace, because Mercury was returning back to Jupiter, and he was the lighter of these two stars: and therefore he was being joined to this Jupiter, by the will of God.

The end of Māshā'allāh's book on reception

WHAT THE PLANETS SIGNIFY IN THE TWELVE DOMICILES OF THE CIRCLE

The significations of the planets in the domiciles, begin.

The Sun, if he were in the Ascendant, signifies sovereignty and loftiness, and the greatness of matters.

And in the second, the beauty of being, and the appearance of esteem, and the happiness of the eyes.

And in the third, the effecting of matters and in connection with the king, and change from region to region.

And in the fourth, treasure and the appearance of a stolen thing, and praise and loftiness between men.

And in the fifth, a description[1] in connection with a child, and a multitude of reverence by the vulgar, and joy, and a bestowal.

And in the sixth, infirmity and tribulation in connection with slaves, and griefs, and reproaches from ignoble people.

And in the seventh, contrariety from the wealthy and nobles, or from kings and powerful people.

And in the eighth, loss and death and the taking away [of things by] princes and nobles and the all-powerful.

And in the ninth, divine culture,[2] faith, and the fear of God the Highest, and the remembrance of angels.

---

[1] *Narrationem.* This probably means that the *astrologer* should declare something about a child (for instance, that the querent will have a child). Latin medieval texts tend to use *narro* to describe something the astrologer should say.

And in the tenth, a great kingdom, and glory, and honor, and benefit.[3]

And in the eleventh, joy in connection with friends and the wealthy, and underofficials too, or allies, and skill[4] in every matter in which there is trust.

And in the twelfth, the killing of the wealthy, and the taking away of a kingdom and honor, and tribulation from slaves and enemies, and from all ignoble people.

Venus, if she were in the Ascendant, signifies joy and the appearance of doing what one pleases,[5] also eating and drinking, and clothing, and golden and silver ornaments, and fragrant things; also the honesty of morals, and greatness of blessings, and the enjoyment of the body.

And in the second, substance and benefit in connection with women, and the nobility of benefit, and the honesty of help in connection with benefits.[6]

And in the third, a lack of self control, and grief in connection with bad works and injustices, and a multitude of friends against[7] God.

And in the fourth, grief and sorrow in the beginning of matters in connection with mothers (and their end will be useful and praiseworthy).

And in the fifth, at first tribulation from a child, after that joy and happiness.

---

[2] *Divinum cultum*. This generally refers to ways in which God is worshipped and people apply themselves to divine things.
[3] *Proficuum*. Although this word can mean "profit," I will tend to translate it as "benefit" or "advantage" generally, which could include monetary profit.
[4] *Ingenium*.
[5] *Voluntatum*.
[6] Treating as a plural.
[7] Reading tentatively as *contra*; also cf. *BOA* p. 97.

And in the sixth, infirmity and tribulation in connection with male and female slaves, and mothers; and it signifies widows.[8] But still, the master of the question will attain everything of the matters which he sought. And if the question were about an infirm person, he will be freed from his infirmity, and the time of his liberation will be according to what I expounded to you at the beginning of the book. And know that if a benefic were in the domicile of infirmity, the infirmity of the one suffering will be lightened. But if there were a malefic there, it will be made worse, by the will of God.

And in the seventh, marriage and joy in connection with women, and from every matter sought in terms of partnership, and every matter which he wanted is effected easily for him.

And in the eighth, the death of mothers and maternal relatives,[9] and the older ones of them.

And in the ninth, foreign travel and change in the houses of religion, and divine culture, and religion and true dreams.

And in the tenth, joy in connection with the king.

And in the eleventh, friendship and joy, and the use of good things, and happiness and trust in connection with friends, and [good] fortune with them.

And in the twelfth, the greatest tribulation and enmity from women, and especially from ignoble people.

Mercury, if he were in the Ascendant, signifies teaching[10] and wisdom and writings, and good eloquence and disputations, and geometry and arithmetic.

And in the second, the benefit of substance, and honor with the king, and a good condition.

---

[8] Or, "spinsters."
[9] Word unclear, but it has to do with people connected to the mother.
[10] *Disciplinam.* This can also mean a science or a discipline.

And in the third, brothers and sisters and a multitude of them; also a multitude of friends and noted people.

And in the fourth, grief and deliberation, also contention and speech.

And in the fifth, the arrival of letters and rumors; and joy about a preceding grief, and [good] fortune in connection with a child.

And in the sixth, contention and destruction, and the confusion of the mind, and deception from slaves and ignoble people, and contentions.

And in the seventh, contention in connection with women, and a multitude of luxury.

And in the eighth, the greatest enmity from neighbors, and contempt because of a lie which is said about him because of the dead, on account of substances left over by the dead, or on account of an old, settled matter.

And in the ninth, teaching and wisdom, also the knowledge of the stars, and honest praise by those who know him.

And in the tenth, great power from writing and arithmetic and geometry, and from princes.

And in the eleventh, a multitude of friends, and joy, and the association of sages.

And in the twelfth, stupidity and perversity[11] and a scarcity of sense, and lightness in going and returning, and in asking about these things which lack a basis.[12] But if he had knowledge, it will be concerning quadrupeds.

---

[11] This should not necessarily be taken in the sexual sense (and probably not at all that way). It rather means something that is distorted.
[12] *Radice*, lit. "root." In other words, the querent will ask pointlessly and aimlessly.

The Moon, if she were in the Ascendant, signifies sovereignty and the effecting of matters, and change from place to place, and joy in connection with mothers and of great women.

And in the second, the taking away of substance, grief, and sorrow.

And in the third, joy and happiness from the wealthy, and loftiness from kings, and the effecting of matters, and their purposes;[13] also foreign travel, and the getting of friends, and trust,[14] and being with nobles, and an increase of love.

And in the fourth, grief and sorrow in the beginning of the question if it were in the day, and its end will be praiseworthy. If it were in the night, she signifies ruin,[15] both in the beginning of the matter and in its end, unless the question is about a hidden treasure or a buried thing: because in this it is the best, for the thing will appear and be uncovered; and God knows best.

And in the fifth, a multitude of children, and that the children will be masculine, if the question were nocturnal; if it were diurnal, it signifies a multitude of daughters; and the repulsing of horrible things, and powerful rumors from a distant place, with joy regarding a child. And if you wanted to know what the rumors are, look to see from whom the Moon is being separated, because the rumors which come will be according to the nature of the planet from which the Moon is being separated. And if you wished to know whether the rumors which come are in a written document, or a legate will make them known by his mouth, look at the Moon and Mercury, to see if she is being joined to him or is being separated from him. Which if she were separated from the Lord of the seventh and were joined to the degree of the Ascendant, the legate will relate the rumors by his own mouth.

And in the sixth, quarrels and contention in connection with fathers, and wealth from quadrupeds, and the health of the body.

---

[13] *Causas eorum.* I take this to refer to the wealthy and kings just mentioned.
[14] Reading as *fiduciam*.
[15] Reading as *interitum*.

And in the seventh, a good condition in connection with women and marriage, and benefit because of them.

And in the eighth, ruin and destruction and the deposing of the king,[16] or his death, and disorder in works, and false testimony, and quarrels, and flight and tribulation, and the anxiety of the mind (as lunatics suffer), and fear and incantation, and instability of the mind, and bad thoughts.

And in the ninth, partnership and bad thoughts, and changes of the kingdom from region to region, and the command[17] of women, and knowledge of the arrangement of the kingdom, and the knowledge of things. And if the 9th domicile were of the domiciles of Mercury, it signifies the knowledge of the stars. And if it were of the domiciles of Venus, it signifies the knowledge of fine things[18] and of old songs and happiness. And if it were of the domiciles of Mars, the mastery of instruments, and the work of arms. And if it were of the domiciles of Jupiter, it signifies divine culture and knowledge in the law, and the position of judges.[19] And if it were of the domiciles of Saturn, it signifies the knowledge of alchemy and all masteries of it. And if were the domicile of the Sun, it signifies knowledge and foresight in all quadrupeds. And if she were in Cancer, it signifies the knowledge and foresight of all substances which go out of the water. And know that this is the peculiar property of the Moon among the planets.

And in the tenth, the effecting of matters and of questions, but there will be a command from the king concerning this, if it were in the day; but if it were in the night it signifies the effecting of matters in connection with the king and women, and this will be quickly; but matters in each of the times (namely in the day and night) will not be lasting; and if a woman undertook to reign in it, the king will be deposed

---

[16] I am taking ruin and destruction to be distinct from the statements about the king, but it is possible that they are meant to be connected to them.
[17] Reading as *nutus*. I believe this means women having command, not that there is command *over* women.
[18] *Subtilitatum*. This has connotations of simplicity and precision.
[19] Reading as *iudicum*.

quickly, because this place is powerful in the signification of the Sun; but the Moon is not sufficient except for something middling in this signification.

And in the eleventh, joy in connection with friends, and the attainment of every matter in which he was hoping, and in which he had trust. And in the twelfth, impediment and duress, and the instability of the kingdom, and quarrels; and prisons[20] in connection with enemies.

And if you were asked when it will be concerning some matter, and the Moon were your significatrix, and she were in the twelfth, it will be at the hour of the Moon's exit from that same place; for through this will the matter be perfected, and [the absent person will come],[21] and especially if this were in the end of the lunar month, and the Moon were impeded by Saturn; for then judge it to be horrible and bad; and you should not doubt in this, if God wills.

Saturn, if he were in the Ascendant, signifies grief because of a debt and lands.[22]

And in the second, the taking away of substance, and the disorder of friends.

And in the third, the destruction of the brothers by the thrusting of a quarrel between them.[23]

And in the fourth, the destruction of a building and lands and seeds and treasures; and danger or ruin because of them.

And in the fifth, the destruction of children, and contention with a legate.

And in the sixth, the infirmity and disobedience of slaves.

---

[20] The phrase suggests that the querent is in danger of imprisonment by enemies, not that the enemies are in prison.
[21] Reading with Bonatti, *BOA* p. 978.
[22] Reading as *terrarum*.
[23] The last part of this sentence comes from BN 7316.

And in the seventh, the destruction of the wife and lands, and the effecting of a malign matter in the end.

And in the eighth, the pursuit of things left behind by the dead, and of an old and ancient thing, and grief and sorrow because of death; and a long lamentation.

And in the ninth, the destruction of faith, and going out to [accomplish] a bad plan, like lunatics and those who dig up tombs in order to plunder the dead; and grief and anxiety on foreign travel, and a long duration in grief.

And in the tenth, grief and sorrow and severe unpleasantness, and danger in connection with the king; and a prolonged imprisonment. Which if the Sun were the Lord of that same domicile, the king will kill him in his prison. And if the Moon were the Lady of the 10th domicile, it will signify what the Sun signified, unless the Moon is joined to Saturn. And if Jupiter were the Lord of the 10th, the king will kill him without blame, and will do injury to him. And if Mars were the Lord of the 10th, he will perish by his own fault. And if Venus were the Lady of the 10th, he will pursue loftiness after this tribulation, and benefit and joy. And if Mercury were the Lord of the 10th, he will be killed with injury, for a lie will be told about him. And if Mercury aspected Mars, he will be beaten with whips. And if Mercury were with the Sun, the king will do injury to him, and will take substance from him, and will make injuries to him in computation,[24] and will examine him. And know that this particular quality belongs to Saturn in the tenth, among the rest of the planets.

And if he were in the eleventh, [it signifies] a multitude of grief and sorrow in connection with friends, and a scarcity of benefit in those things which he was hoping for, and in which he had trust for the

---

[24] I believe this means the king will cheat him on things that are counted, like taxes or other assessments.

good; and complication in matters, and their hardness, and a multitude of trust in false matters which profit nothing.[25]

And in the twelfth, impediments which happen in connection with the king, and he will be strong and bold in this, and he will be captured by enemies, and he will be afraid in all of his matters.

Jupiter, if he were in the Ascendant, signifies reverence and beauty and the honesty of faith and religion, of teaching also, and reason, and the end[26] of those things in which he is involved, will be toward salvation, and sovereignty will be handed to him in this.

And in the second, the collection of many substances with skill and a good disposition,[27] with the attaining of all things which come to be because of substance.

And in the third, fortune in connection with brothers and greater associates, and a multitude of joy in connection with relatives.

And in the fourth, benefit from things left behind by the dead, and from lands and their inheritances and treasures from every ancient thing; and the taking away of griefs and bad thoughts, of quarrels too, and sorrow; and security from every horrible thing.

And in the fifth, a multitude of children and the goodness of their condition; and a multitude of benefit through them; and honest praise; the conjoining of the wealthy and the nobles, and the benefit of all things in which they have trust.

And in the sixth, a scarcity of infirmity, and the health of the body, and loftiness in connection with slaves, and benefit from quadrupeds.

And in the seventh, joy in connection with women and marriage, and the getting of every enemy.

---

[25] Reading with BN 7316.
[26] Reading *finis* with BN 7316.
[27] Reading *dispositione* for *disponsione*.

And in the eighth, the taking away of the substance[28] of the master of the question, and that they[29] will fall in the hands of their enemies; and it will happen to him because of this difficulty; but it will have a praiseworthy end.

And in the ninth, joy from a foreign journey, and the honesty of faith, and the expounding of dreams, and the truth of dreams, if God wills. And if he asked you what he saw in the dreams,[30] look at the planet from which Jupiter is being separated, or who is being separated from him, and speak according to the nature of that planet from which Jupiter is separated or who is separated from him. And if he wanted to know the interpretation of the dream, look to see from which of the planets Jupiter is separated, or which is separated from him: because the interpretation of his dream [will be] according to the nature of the planet: know this.

And in the tenth, enrichment[31] and the collection of substances, and the honesty of praise; also loftiness and honor in all things.

In the eleventh, praise in connection with friends, and benefit in those things which he hopes for, concerning every matter or those in which he has trust.

And in the twelfth, servitude and poverty and need; also sorrow in connection with quadrupeds, and grief from slaves.

Mars, if he were in the Ascendant, signifies sorrow and fear and contention, and a horrible thing; also craftiness and contrariety, and the taking away of substance without praise; and entering into a matter which does not pertain to him.

---

[28] Reading with BN 7316.
[29] His substances.
[30] This sounds like a reference to a consultation chart (like Sahl's material on dream interpretation), since presumably the client already knows at least roughly what he dreamt—else there would be little point in consulting the astrologer.
[31] Reading as *ditationem*, presumably an invented noun form of *dito*, "to enrich, get rich."

And in the second, the taking away of substance, and poverty and need, and the disarray of [the querent's] underofficials.

And in the third, the enmity of the brothers, and the thrusting of hate between them, and their killing one another. And if the 3rd domicile were of the domiciles of Venus, it signifies joy from brothers and sisters. And if it were of the domiciles of Jupiter, it signifies a multitude of substances from business dealings. And if it were of the domiciles of Saturn, it signifies the digging up of graves and walls, [and] the seeking of stolen goods.[32] And if it were of the domiciles of Mercury, it signifies his loftiness through divination and writings, and false testimony because he would speak outside of the sayings of the wise; and he will suffer dangers or tribulation. And if it were the domicile of the Moon, it signifies the breaking of walls, the seeking of stolen goods, and the harmfulness of robbery in business.[33] And if it were the domicile of the Sun, it signifies the cutting of roads and the plundering of villages.[34] And know that this peculiar quality belongs to Mars among the rest of the planets.

And in the fourth, ruin and killing and the shedding of blood, and the suspicion[35] of blood, and the end of this matter will be into grief and lengthy tribulation.

And in the fifth, a multitude of daughters from fornication, and defects from the same,[36] and a scarcity of benefit and joy because of them; and his livelihood [or sustenance] will be wholly good.[37]

And in the sixth, a multitude of infirmity and hot and dry fevers, and the rousing of the blood; also grief and sorrow in connection with slaves.

---

[32] *Latrocinii*, here and below.
[33] *Detrimentum latrocinii in foro.*
[34] Reading as *villarum*.
[35] *Suspicionem sanguinis*. I am not sure what this is supposed to mean—perhaps family suspicion generally, or suspicion about the paternity of a child?
[36] This might mean sexually transmitted diseases, but it could also mean some physical defect in the daughters.
[37] Reading with BN 7316.

And in the seventh, business dealing and contention and sexual intercourse with injustice, and harm on account of this; and disarray in every matter, and contention, and horribly [so], and grief because of them.

And in the eighth, killing and the cutting off of hands and feet, and the most disgraceful censure, but he will acquire from the substances of the dead (and the greatest substance), and he will suffer excessively on account of them. And they will have [it][38] from his own hand, and he will fall into the greatest poverty.

And in the ninth, the pursuit of horses and wars and armies; also the drinking of wine, and lack of self-control, and infidelity,[39] and multitude of divisions and the lying of dreams.

And in the tenth, tribulation in connection with the king, and the beating of whips, and distress, and prison, and need[40] in his lifestyle; and a multitude of war and contention in those things which do not pertain to him.

And in the eleventh, a scarcity of benefit, and the enmity of friends, and the loss of substance, and the taking away of trust in those things which he has in his heart.

And in the twelfth, the skills of a robber in all ways, and delay in all things which he can do, and the taking away of substance, and a multitude of enemies, and committing something horrible,[41] and grief because of beasts, if God wills.

The Head in the Ascendant signifies increase and loftiness and strength according to its conjunction with the planets.

And in the second, the increase of substances and the greatest good fortune.

---

[38] Reading *habebunt* with BN 7316, for *habebit*.
[39] I believe this is meant in the religious sense, not in the sense of disloyalty.
[40] That is, he is in a state of need and dearth.
[41] *Perpetrationem ad audiendum horribile.*

And in the third, the acquisition of success, and the fitness of faith, and the truth of dreams.

And in the fourth, the increase of benefits if it were in the fiery and airy signs. But if it were in the earthy or watery signs, the statement would turn—that is, say the contrary.

And in the fifth, the increase of children and freedom from men turning against him.

In the sixth, the strength of an infirmity, and the increase of slaves, and the enlarging of beasts.

And in the seventh, the increase and association of women.

And in the eighth, the strength of life and the scarcity of death.

And in the ninth, faith and the increase of religion[42] according to what is conjoined with it (of the benefic or malefic planets).

And in the tenth, a question about the Highest God or about a good matter not able to be seen; and it signifies loftiness and strength, and veneration and reverence, and the strength of fortune in professions.

And in the eleventh, it has no work in it (and likewise the Tail).[43]

And in the twelfth, it signifies the increase of evils and a scarcity of fortunes.

The Tail in the Ascendant signifies separation and detriment, and uprooting; also dangers and tribulations and the decreasing of matters.

And in the second, poverty and preoccupation,[44] and a fall from places from which it is not suspected.

---

[42] Following BN 7316 for the rest of the sentence.
[43] That is, neither Node is effective in the eleventh. I have not heard of this before.

And in the third, the destruction of the brothers, and the severity of friends' quarrels, or perhaps one of his brothers or sisters will perish.

And in the fourth, want or need; and searching into matters, and benefit.

And in the fifth, it signifies the expulsion of fortunes, the descending of horrible things onto the children, and the great age of [one's] clothing, and the need of the children.

And in the sixth, the infirmity and laziness[45] of the male and female slaves, and the weakness of beasts—understand.

And in the seventh, the destruction of [unclear],[46] and the strength of enemies, and scorn.

And in the eighth, death and things left behind by the dead, and the presence of death and ruin.

And in the ninth, the strength of change and moving, and the scarcity of faith.

And in the tenth, deposing and dangers and a foreign journey or a fall.

And in the eleventh, they have no work in it, just as we stated above.

And in the twelfth, it signifies the scarcity of evils, if God wills.

These are the significations of the planets and the Head and the Tail. And in the twelve domiciles, if it were in a better condition, say better; but if it were in a bad condition, turn the statement—that is say the opposite, bad for

---

[44] *Occupationem.* Normally this word means a job or employment, but it would seem strange to pair poverty with a job. Still, "preoccupation" does not seem that intuitive either.
[45] Reading with *BOA* p. 989. I cannot determine the exact word in BN.
[46] *BOA* p. 989 describes difficulties in marriages and between men and women generally.

good, and speak boldly. And do not doubt nor dismiss what I say to you, and you would discover something else and you will find,[47] if God wills.

---

[47] *Proferas aliud et invenies.* This seems somewhat unclear. *BOA* p. 990 reads: "nor should you dismiss what I have told you; nor should you say otherwise, and you will discover [it], if God does not oppose you."

BIBLIOGRAPHY

Abū Ma'shar al-Balhi, *The Abbreviation of the Introduction to Astrology*, ed. and trans. Charles Burnett, K. Yamamoto, and Michio Yano (Leiden: E.J. Brill, 1994)

Abū Ma'shar al-Balhi, *Liber Introductorii Maioris ad Scientiam Iudiciorum Astrorum*, vols. IV, V, VI, IX, ed. Richard Lemay (Naples: Istituto Universitario Orientale, 1995)

Abū Ma'shar al-Balhi, *The Abbreviation of the Introduction to Astrology*, ed. and trans. Charles Burnett, annotated by Charles Burnett, G. Tobyn, G. Cornelius and V. Wells (ARHAT Publications, 1997)

Abū Ma'shar al-Balhi, *On Historical Astrology: The Book of Religions and Dynasties (On the Great Conjunctions)*, vols. I-II, eds. and trans. Keiji Yamamoto and Charles Burnett (Leiden: Brill, 2000)

Abū Ma'shar al-Balhi, *The Flowers of Abū Ma'shar*, trans. Benjamin Dykes (2nd ed., 2007)

Al-Bīrūnī, Muhammad ibn Ahmad, *The Chronology of Ancient Nations*, trans. and ed. C. Edward Sachau (London: William H. Allen and Co., 1879)

Al-Bīrūnī, Muhammad ibn Ahmad, *The Book of Instruction in the Elements of the Art of Astrology*, trans. R. Ramsay Wright (London: Luzac & Co., 1934)

Al-Khayyat, Abu 'Ali, *The Judgments of Nativities*, trans. James H. Holden (Tempe, AZ: American Federation of Astrologers, Inc., 1988)

Al-Qabīsī, *The Introduction to Astrology*, eds. Charles Burnett, Keiji Yamamoto, Michio Yano (London and Turin: The Warburg Institute, 2004)

Al-Rijāl, 'Ali, *Libri de Iudiciis Astrorum* (Basel: Henrichus Petrus, 1551)

Bonatti, Guido, *Book of Astronomy*, trans. and ed. Benjamin N. Dykes (Golden Valley, MN: The Cazimi Press, 2007)

Bonatti, Guido, *De Astronomia Tractatus X* (Basel, 1550)

Brennan, Chris, "The *Katarche* of Horary," *Geocosmic Journal* (New York: NCGR, Summer Solstice 2007), pp. 23-34.

Burnett, Charles, Jill Kraye and W.F. Ryan eds., *The Liber Aristotilis of Hugo of Santalla* (London: The Warburg Institute, 1997)

Burnett, Charles and Gerrit Bos, *Scientific Weather Forecasting in the Middle Ages* (London and New York: Kegan Paul International, 2000)

Burnett, Charles, "Late Antique and medieval Latin Translations of Greek Texts on Astrology and Magic," in Magdalino, Paul and Maria Mavroudi eds., *The Occult Sciences in Byzantium* (Geneva: La Pomme d'or, 2006), pp. 336-37.

Carmody, Francis, *Arabic Astronomical and Astrological Sciences in Latin Translation: A Critical Bibliography* (Berkeley and Los Angeles: University of California Press, 1956)

Crofts, Carole Mary, "*Kitāb al-Iktiyārāt 'alā l-buyūt al-itnai 'asar*, by Sahl ibn Bišr al-Isra'ili, with its Latin Translation *De Electionibus*" (Ph.D. diss., Glasgow University, 1985)

Della Vida, G. Levi, "Appunti e Quesiti di Storia Letteraria Araba," in *Rivista degli Studi Orientali* 14/1934, pp. 249-83.

Dorotheus of Sidon, *Carmen Astrologicum*, trans. David Pingree (Abingdon, MD: The Astrology Center of America, 2005)

Grant, Edward, *Planets, Stars, and Orbs: The Medieval Cosmos, 1200–1687* (New York, NY: Cambridge University Press, 1994)

Hertz, J.H., *Pentateuch and Haftorahs: Hebrew Text, English Translation, & Commentary* (London: Soncino Press, 1988)

Holden, James H., *A History of Horoscopic Astrology* (Tempe, AZ: American Federation of Astrologers, Inc., 1996)

Ibn Ezra, Abraham, *The Beginning of Wisdom*, trans. Meira Epstein, ed. Robert Hand (Arhat Publications, 1998)

Kunitzsch, Paul and Tim Smart, *A Dictionary of Modern Star Names* (Cambridge, MA: New Track Media, 2006)

Latham, R.E., *Revised Medieval Latin Word-List from British and Irish Sources* (Oxford: Oxford University Press, 2004)

Lemay, Richard, *Abū Ma'shar and Latin Aristotelianism in the Twelfth Century* (Beirut: American University of Beirut, 1962)

Leopold of Austria, *Compilatio Leupoldi ducatus Austrie filii de astrorum scientia* (Augsburg: Erhard Ratdolt, 1489)

Manilius, Marcus, *Astronomica*, ed. G.P. Goold (Cambridge & London: Harvard University Press, 1977)

Māshā'allāh, *On Reception*, ed. and trans. Robert Hand (ARHAT Publications, 1998)

Māshā'allāh, *De Scientia Motus Orbis*, ed. Joannes Stabius (Nuremberg: Johann Weyssenburger, 1504)

Māshā'allāh, *De Receptione*, in *Messahalae Antiquissimi ac Laudatissimi Inter Arabes Astrologi, Libri Tres*, ed. Joachim Heller (Nuremberg: Joannes Montanus and Ulrich Neuber, 1549)

Māshā'allāh, *De Revolutione Annorum Mundi*, in *Messahalae Antiquissimi ac Laudatissimi Inter Arabes Astrologi, Libri Tres*, ed. Joachim Heller (Nuremberg: Joannes Montanus and Ulrich Neuber, 1549)

Māshā'allāh, *De Interpraetationibus*, in *Messahalae Antiquissimi ac Laudatissimi Inter Arabes Astrologi, Libri Tres*, ed. Joachim Heller (Nuremberg: Joannes Montanus and Ulrich Neuber, 1549)

Māshā'allāh, *De Cogitationibus*, in *Messahalae Antiquissimi ac Laudatissimi Inter Arabes Astrologi, Libri Tres*, ed. Joachim Heller (Nuremberg: Joannes Montanus and Ulrich Neuber, 1549)

Māshā'allāh, *De significationibus planetarum in nativitate*, in *Messahalae Antiquissimi ac Laudatissimi Inter Arabes Astrologi, Libri Tres*, ed. Joachim Heller (Nuremberg: Joannes Montanus and Ulrich Neuber, 1549)

Māshā'allāh, *Epistola in rebus eclipsis* (Basel: Iohannes Hervagius, 1533)

Māshā'allāh, *Epistola Messahalae de rebus eclipsium et de coniunctionibus planetarum in revolutionibus annorum mundi*, in *Messahalae Antiquissimi ac Laudatissimi Inter Arabes Astrologi, Libri Tres*, ed. Joachim Heller (Nuremberg: Joannes Montanus and Ulrich Neuber, 1549)

Māshā'allāh, *In radicibus revolucionum* (Paris: BN 16204, pp. 387-391)

Māshā'allāh, *Liber revolucionis annorum mundi* (Paris: BN 16204, pp. 391-404)

Māshā'allāh, *De interpretatione cogitationis* (Paris: BN 16204, pp. 422-24)

Māshā'allāh, *Liber de occultis* (Paris: BN 16204, pp. 424-28)

Māshā'allāh, *In pluviis et ventis epistola* (Paris: BN 7316a, pp. 69v-71v).

Māshā'allāh, *Epistola Mašallah in pluviis et ventis*, in *Catalogus Codicum Astrologorum Graecorum (CCAG)* XII, pp. 210-16.

Māshā'allāh, *De Nativitatibus* (Paris: BN 7324 15c, pp. 73r-75v).

Māshā'allāh/Jirjis, *Quid significent planete in 12. domibus circuli* (Paris: BN 16204, pp. 428-32.)

Māshā'allāh, *De septem planetis* (Paris: BN 7316, pp. 80v-82v).

Mannan, Abdul Omar, *Dictionary of the Holy Qur'ān* (Noor Foundation International, 2005)

McEverdy, Colin, *The New Penguin Atlas of Medieval History* (London: Penguin Books, 1992)

Michelsen, Neil F., *The Koch Book of Tables* (San Diego: ACS Publications, Inc., 1985)

Morin, Jean-Baptiste, *Astrologia Gallica Book Eighteen: The Strengths of the Planets*, trans. Anthony Louis LaBruzza (Tempe, AZ: American Federation of Astrologers, 2004)

Niermeyer, J.F. ed., *Mediae Latinitatis Lexicon Minus* (Leiden: E.J. Brill, 1993)

Paulus Alexandrinus, *Late Classical Astrology: Paulus Alexandrinus and Olympiodorus*, trans. Dorian Gieseler Greenbaum, ed. Robert Hand (Reston, VA: ARHAT, 2001)

Pingree, David, "Astronomy and Astrology in India and Iran," *Isis* v. 54/2 (1963), pp. 229-46.

Pingree, David and E.S. Kennedy eds., *The Astrological History of Māshā'allāh* (Cambridge, MA: Harvard University Press, 1971).

Pingree, David, "Māshā'allāh," in *Dictionary of Scientific Biography* vol. IX, pp. 159-62 (New York, 1974)

Pingree, David, "Māshā'allāh: Some Sasanian and Syriac Sources," in George F. Hourani ed., *Essays on Islamic Philosophy and Science* (Albany, NY: SUNY Press, 1975), pp. 5-14.

Pingree, David, "Classical and Byzantine Astrology in Sassanian Persia," *Dumbarton Oaks Papers*, v. 43 (1989), pp. 227-239.

Pingree, David, *From Astral Omens to Astrology: From Babylon to Bīkāner* (Rome: Istituto italiano per L'Africa e L'Oriente, 1997)

Pseudo-Ptolemy, *Centiloquium*, ed. Georgius Trapezuntius, in Bonatti (1550)

Ptolemy, Claudius, *Tetrabiblos* vols. 1, 2, 4, trans. Robert Schmidt, ed. Robert Hand (Berkeley Springs, WV: The Golden Hind Press, 1994-98)

Ptolemy, Claudius, *Tetrabiblos*, trans. F.E. Robbins (Cambridge and London: Harvard University Press, 1940)

Rhetorius of Egypt, *Astrological Compendium*, trans. and ed. James H. Holden (Tempe, AZ: American Federation of Astrologers, Inc., 2009)

Sahl bin Bishr, *Introductorium, Praecipua Iudicia, De Questionibus, De Electionibus*, and *De Significatione Temporis* in *Tetrabiblos*, ed. Girolamo Salio (Venice: Bonetus Locatellus, 1493)

Sahl bin Bishr, *Liber Introductorius, De L. Preceptis, De Interrogationibus, Liber Electionum*, and *De Significationibus Temporum* (Paris: BN lat. 16204, pp. 433-500).

Sahl bin Bishr, *De Electionibus* (Venice: Peter of Liechtenstein, 1509)

Schmidt, Robert E., *Kepler College Sourcebook of Hellenistic Astrological Texts* (Cumberland, MA: The Phaser Foundation, 2005)

Stegemann, Viktor, *Die Fragmente des Dorotheus von Sidon* (Heidelberg: Self-published with F. Bilabel, 1939)

Stegemann, Viktor, *Dorotheos von Sidon und das Sogenannte* Introductorium *des Sahl ibn Bišr* (Prague: Orientalisches Institut in Prag, 1942)

Thorndike, Lynn, "John of Seville," *Speculum*, v. 34/1 (1959), pp. 20-38.

Thorndike, Lynn, "The Latin Translations of Astrological Works by Messahala," *Osiris* vol. 12 (1956), pp. 49-72.

Valens, Vettius, *The Anthology*, vols. I-VII, ed. Robert Hand, trans. Robert Schmidt (Berkeley Springs, WV: The Golden Hind Press, 1993-2001)

INDEX

'Abbasids, 455
Abimelech, xxvi
Abraham, xxvi
Abu Bakr, ix
Abū Maʿshar, viii, lx, lxxx, 9, 57, 147, 160, 303, 307, 442
aḍ-ḍaʿf (weakness), 12
Africa, Africans, xii, 344, 491, 492
aḥwālu-l-qamar (condition of the Moon), 13
al-ʾidbār (falling-back), 11, 13, 400
al-ʾinṣarāf (departure), 11, 14
al-ʾiqbāl (approach), 10, 13, 400
al-ʾittiṣāl (connection), 11, 13
al-Bīrūnī, lx, 210, 394
al-Hasan, Vizier, viii, x
al-jamʿ (collection), 11
al-kadukhudhāh. See Nativities: kadukhudhāh
al-Khayyāt, Abu ʿAli, lii, 225, 399, 402-03, 408, 412-13, 415
al-Ma'mun, Caliph, viii, x
al-manʿ (prohibition), 12, 20
al-mubtazz. See mubtazz
al-Qabīsī, xli
al-Qasrani, ix
al-qubūl (reception), 12
al-quwwah (strength), 12
al-Rijāl, ʿAli ibn (Haly Abenragel), ix, xxxv, lix, lxv, lxvi, 210
al-Tabarī, ʿUmar, vii, ix, lxiii
Angle of the earth, xlii, xlvi-xlviii, 5, 8, 50, 73-74, 76, 106, 112, 120, 138, 140, 142-43, 225, 256, 327, 329-30, 334, 344, 347, 350, 357-58, 360, 430
an-naql (transmission), 11
annona 113, 302, 342
an-nūrah (depilatory creme), 206
Arabs, Arabia, 344
Aristotle, xxviii, lxxv, lxxx, 295
Armenia, 316

ar-radd (return), 12
Aspects
 first/leading, 346
 first/leading aspect, 10
 second/following, 346
 second/following aspect, 10
 their natures, 9
 whole-sign, (general description), 9
Astronomy
 awj, 200, 269, 436
 eccentric orb, 267-68, 275-77, 279-80, 282
 great circles, 283
 great orb, 267-70, 272-73, 275-79
 orb of the fixed stars, 275
 orb of the revolution, 267, 275-77, 280-82, 288
 orb of the signs, 267, 270, 273-74, 276, 278-81
 precession, 273
Azerbaijan, 455
Baghdad, vii, xi, xii
Besieging, 43, 45, 48, 128
Bonatti, Guido, viii, xxxv-xxxvi, xxxviii, lx, lxvi-lxvii, lxviii, lxxx, 7, 68, 75-77, 88, 100, 116-20, 133, 136, 138-39, 141, 147, 160, 180, 299, 363, 505
Brennan, Chris, v, xxxiv, xxxv
Burnett, Charles, xli, lxxiv, lxxxi
Burnt path (*via combusta*), 2, 46, 194, 197, 216
Byzantium, Byzantines, xi
census, 147, 338
Christians, Christianity, xxiv
Consultation charts, vii, xxxv-xxxviii, xxxiv-xxxviii, lxxvi, 67-68, 185, 188, 277, 355, 412, 419, 422, 417–23, 426-27, 433-34, 437, 508

Cutting-off of light, 78, 95, 474
dafᶜ at-tadbīr wa-aṭ-ṭabīᶜah (pushing of arrangement and nature), 12
dafᶜu-l-quwwah (pushing of strength), 12
Descension, xxvii, xxix-xxx, xxxii–xxxiv, lxxix, lxxxi, 32-34, 40, 43, 45, 53, 70, 72-74, 90, 122, 125-26, 132, 138-39, 158, 160, 161, 164-65, 167, 193, 203, 224, 236, 478, 481, 486-87, 493-94, 496
Detriment
  as corruption, xxvii–xxix
  as seventh sign, xxix–xxxii, 44, 66, 125, 150, 344
Disposition,
  pushing/committing/receiving, xvii, xix, xxvii, lxvi, lxvii, lxxviii, 12, 27, 35-39, 44, 51, 53, 56, 62-63, 68-69, 71, 73, 76-77, 79-80, 83, 85, 88-89, 95-96, 124, 141, 143-44, 147-50, 153, 158-61, 163, 173, 202, 222, 225-27, 229, 238-40, 243-44, 267, 294, 325-26, 330-32, 337-38, 344, 349, 351-52, 354, 357, 359-60, 393, 426, 433, 438, 441, 443, 448, 451-54, 456-58, 460-62, 468-71, 474, 476, 479, 507
Dorotheus of Sidon, vii, ix-xiii, xxxv, xxxviii, xli, xlviii, li-lvii, lix, lxii-lxv, lxxv, lxxix-lxxx, lxxxii, 35, 83, 97, 105, 111-12, 114, 116-18, 121, 189, 192-93, 196-97, 207, 209, 216-17, 391, 403, 408, 427-28, 430, 432
Drogo, Amager/Amagrus, 315
Eclipses, 194, 255-59, 275, 286-87, 290-91, 302, 304-05, 342, 350, 352-53

Egypt, Egyptians, xi, xii, 467, 474, 520
Elections
  alchemy, 199
  building, 199
  business partnerships, 197
  buying animals, 220
  buying lands, 200
  buying slaves, 206
  buying/selling, 198
  digging, 201
  education, 203
  exorcism, 203
  fishing, 221
  fleeing, 221
  for groups, 188
  freeing slaves, 207
  fugitives, 222
  general instructions, 192, 195, 196
  generating children, 202
  hidden objects, 436
  hopes, 219
  hunting, 220
  investing, 198
  kingdoms, 218
  letters, 222
  making a will, 212
  making enemies, 219
  making friends, 219
  marriage, 208
  miscarriage, 202
  planting, 201
  planting/sowing, 82
  roots, 155, 187, 188, 233
  shaving, 206
  sowing, 202
  taking medicine, 203-06
  taking/lending money, 196
  taxes, 218
  travel, 213-16
  travel with kings, 217
  war, 209, 211, 218, 231

Elements, xxxi, lxxiv, 189, 246, 247, 249-55, 299, 347, 447
Ethiopia, Ethiopians, 300
fasād (decay), xxviii, xxxi-xxxii
Fate, determinism, xxxvii
Firmicus Maternus, xxii, lxxxi
Fixed stars, 255, 257, 265, 270, 273-75, 281, 344
Freedom, free will, xxxvii
ghayr al-qubūl (not-reception), 12
God, xxiv, xxvi, xxxvi, lxxiii-lxxiv, lxxix, 1, 3, 8, 17, 80, 83, 86, 92, 130, 151, 170, 189, 199, 210, 212, 223, 228, 230, 235, 241, 244, 245, 251-55, 265, 269-70, 277, 283, 287, 291, 297, 299-300, 308, 315, 321-22, 325-26, 331, 334-35, 338, 357, 372, 386, 390, 398, 419, 422, 426, 428-30, 432-33, 436, 438, 441-42, 444, 447-54, 456-64, 467-68, 470-76, 478-85, 488, 491-96, 497, 499-501, 503, 505, 508, 510-13
Hand, Robert, lxxix, lxxxii, 467, 474, 477, 483, 486, 488, 491, 493-94
ḥayyiz, 210
Head/Tail of the Dragon, 44, 46, 77, 125, 127, 145, 146, 155-56, 182, 194, 197, 199-200, 208, 217, 286, 290, 299, 314-16, 342, 397, 411, 431, 487, 488, 510-12
Hellenistic astrology, vii, x, xx-xxiii, xxvi-xxvii, xxxiv, l, lv, lix, lxi, lxiii, lxiv, lxvi, lxix, 4, 6, 18, 127, 128, 130, 155, 209, 343, 390, 474, 480, 482, 489
Hephaestio of Thebes, ix, lx
Hermann of Carinthia/Dalmatia, xii-xiii
Hermes, xxxv, lxxvi, 232
Hermetica, xi

Holden, James, vii, lxxv, 391, 394, 396-97, 403-08, 411-15, 520
Houses
 basic meanings, 4–7
 optimal places, lxviii-lxxi, 84, 97, 123, 154-55, 157-58, 166, 219, 221, 330, 353, 472
 quadrants/quarters, xlii, xliv, xlviii, xlix-li, lv, lvii-lviii, lxxxi, 42, 63, 73, 88, 105, 203, 228, 234, 349, 395, 404-05, 412, 428, 429, 455
Hugo of Santalla, xl, 315
ibn Ezra, Abraham, viii-ix, xxx
India, Indians, vii, xxxiv-xxxv, xxxviii, lxxiii, 244
Iraq, vii, 328
Jews, Judaism, vii-viii, x, xxiv, xxvi
Jirjis, lxxx, 432
John of Spain, xii-xiii, xl-xli, lxxii-lxxiii, lxxv, 308
kasmīmī, 41, 62
kawn (being), xxviii
khalā as-sayr (void of movement), 12
Krakow, xii
Leopold of Austria, ix, xxxv, lxxvii
Lilly, William, xxi-xxii, 15
Lord of the hour, lxxvii, 164-65, 177-79, 182, 202, 234, 321, 325, 329, 417-18, 429-33
Lots, lvii, lx-lxi, lxxxi, 225
 of Faith (?), 232
 of Fortune, lxi, 108, 111, 133, 151, 195, 198-99, 211, 221, 231-32, 336, 338, 392-95, 402, 411-15, 417-20, 427, 432-33, 436, 483, 485
 of Necessity, lxi
 of Spirit, lxi
Manilius, Marcus, lix-lxi, lxiii

Marseilles, lxxvii, lxxix, 404, 405, 411, 412, 413, 414, 415

Māshā'allāh, vii-ix, xiii, xiv, xvii-xx, xxvi, xxx, xxxiv-xlii, xliv, xlvi-xlvii, xlix, l-liii, lvii, lxii, lxvi-lxix, lxxii-lxxx, 17, 30, 39, 69, 77, 106, 113-14, 177, 195, 204, 224-25, 229, 234, 236, 243-44, 249-50, 254-55, 259, 271, 274, 291, 294, 299-309, 312, 315, 317-18, 322, 325, 329, 333, 340, 346-48, 353-54, 360-61, 363, 365, 380, 385, 391-93, 396, 398, 400-01, 403, 405, 413, 417-18, 420-21, 425, 427, 434-35, 437, 441-43, 448-49, 451-53, 455-59, 461, 467, 478-82, 484-86, 488-89, 491-95, 497

Moon
  as general significatrix, 51, 53-54, 65
  conjunction/prevention, 97, 312, 392-93, 483
  critical days, 90
  impediments, 45, 193
  phases, 47, 97
  quarters and ages, 112

Morin, Jean-Baptiste, xxxi

mubtazz, lxxviii, 229, 393-94, 397, 401, 452, 476

Mundane astrology
  annual revolutions, 301, 325-59
  climes, xv, 232, 283, 300, 306, 316-17, 325-27, 329-31, 333, 335, 338-39, 345, 348-49, 487
  divisions of the earth, 347
  earthquakes, 351, 360
  Lord of the Year, 309-11, 328-29, 330-33, 328-60
  monthly ingresses, 301, 312
  pestilence, 302, 305, 307, 340, 350, 359
  planets in the Ascendant, 350
  quarterly ingresses, 301, 328
  significations of the planets, 347, 357
  significator of the king, lxxi, 102, 109, 331-34, 336-39, 341, 343-46, 352-53, 355-58
  types of conjunctions, 305-08, 340, 434
  war, 301, 308, 334, 339, 341-44, 351, 354-55, 359-60
  weather, 301-02, 304, 306–23, 359

Muslims, Islam, xxiv

Nativities
  hīlāj, li, lxxv, 188, 229, 230, 304-05, 392-93, 395-96, 428-29, 437, 482-85, 488-90
  kadukhudhāh, li-lii, 304-05, 396-98, 482-83, 485, 487-88
  longevity, 395-96, 482
  quality of life, 394-95, 398, 402
  quality of mind, 398
  siblings, 394
  weaning/longevity, 391

Nature, pushing/committing/receiving, lxvi, lxvii, 38

Nawbakht the Persian, vii

Nechepso-Petosiris, xi

Niermeyer, J.F., 4, 383

Not-reception, xxiii, xxxiii, 12, 32, 453-54

Olympiodorus, lix-lx, lxiii

Paulus Alexandrinus, lix-lxiii, lxvi, lxxvi

Perfection, 74
  collection of light, viii, 11, 19, 70-72, 78-79, 83, 108, 134, 150
  joining, 68-69, 72, 133
  location, 70, 95

INDEX 527

transfer of light, xvii, xxiii, xxvii, lxxviii, 11, 17-18, 70-72, 78-79, 81, 83, 88, 93-96, 101, 107-08, 134, 147, 153, 235, 326, 457, 470

Persia, Persians, vii-ix, xx, xxv-xxvi, xxxi-xxxii, xxxiv-xxxv, xxxviii-xxxix, lv-lvi

Pingree, David, vii-ix, xli, lii, lx, lxiii-lxxv, lxxvii, 236, 270, 391, 399, 401, 406-07, 412-15

Planets

"overcoming", 128, 155, 209, 489

16 conditions (Sahl), 10

above/below the earth, 88-89, 97, 109, 121, 133, 139, 144, 158, 205, 216, 433, 486

angles of the malefics, 52, 56, 60, 73, 95, 98, 129, 132, 148, 153, 239

benefic/malefic, 51-52, 54, 56-60, 63, 65, 132, 442, 470-71

bounds, lxiv-lxv, lxvii, lxxv, 8, 29, 30, 40, 46, 49, 52, 58, 61, 63, 104, 110, 114-16, 125-26, 142, 149, 152-56, 165, 167, 171, 174, 194, 201, 208, 215, 229, 305-06, 310, 316, 325, 327-29, 335-36, 338-39, 342, 346, 361-62, 381-90, 395-96, 400, 418, 420, 427, 433, 451, 482-86, 495

changing signs, lxxviii, 55, 76, 123, 142, 446-47, 451, 456, 460, 467

combustion/under the rays, li, lxviii, 2, 35, 41, 43, 45, 58, 60-62, 70-71, 74, 78, 80, 83-84, 88-91, 97, 103-04, 106-07, 112, 116, 122-23, 128, 132-33, 135, 142, 158-59, 193, 197, 202, 204, 210, 212, 214-17, 221-23, 229, 231, 236-40, 264, 309-11, 317, 319-21, 334-37, 343-45, 350, 352, 354, 357-58, 396, 413, 420, 453, 464, 479, 487, 496

complexions, 56

dismounting, lxxxi, 244, 323, 328, 461

diurnal/nocturnal, 49, 330, 336, 343, 392-94, 401, 486

domiciles, xiii-xxi, xxiv, xxix-xxxiv, xlviii, li, lxii, lxiv-lxvii, lxviii, lxx-lxxi, lxxv-lxxvii, lxxix-lxxxi, 4-8, 10, 18, 22, 28, 30-31, 34, 36-38, 40, 44, 46, 49-51, 54, 56-59, 61-63, 65-67, 70, 73-74, 76-77, 79-80, 83-84, 86-92, 94-96, 99, 101, 104, 106, 109-11, 114, 121, 123, 125-27, 132-37, 140-43, 145, 147-51, 154-155, 158-61, 164-67, 174-75, 176, 181, 183-84, 192, 194-95, 198-203, 208-09, 211, 213, 215-16, 218-19, 221, 230-35, 237, 302, 315-19, 321-23, 330, 332-33, 335-39, 342-49, 351, 353-55, 357, 361, 363-75, 377, 379, 383-85, 388-89, 391-98, 401-03, 406, 412-13, 415, 418-21, 426, 427, 430, 432-35, 437, 439-44, 447-54, 456-61, 463-64, 467, 469, 472, 478-86, 492, 494-96, 499, 501, 504, 506, 509, 512

exaltations, xiv, xvii-xviii, xxix, xxxii, li, lxvii, lxxi, 6, 8, 28, 30-31, 34, 36-38, 40, 44, 49, 51, 56-59, 61-62, 70, 73, 91-92, 110, 114, 125, 126, 149, 154-55, 159, 165, 167, 199-

201, 209, 211, 237, 316, 318-19, 325, 329, 335-37, 342-43, 346, 352, 364, 367, 369, 372, 376, 381, 385, 389-90, 395-96, 401-03, 418, 420, 439-41, 453, 459, 471, 478, 482-83, 486, 492-93, 496-97
faces, lxvii, 8, 29, 40, 49, 62, 110, 118-20, 125-26, 165, 167, 216-17, 305, 338, 395-96, 418, 420-21, 427, 486
feral/wild, 46
hurling of rays, 485, 489
in their own light (by body), 332, 354
in their own light (by sect/gender), 41, 49, 59-60
joys, 8-9, 40, 49-50, 61, 209, 401
masculine/feminine, 41-42, 50, 86, 202, 343, 347
orbs, 14-15
oriental/occidental, x-xi, 41, 56, 61-62, 82, 84, 86, 89, 97, 112, 127-128, 154, 156, 165, 200-01, 203, 207, 220, 223, 227, 229, 232, 240, 303, 315, 321, 334, 336, 358, 394, 396, 399, 401, 486
peregrine, peregrination, xiv, xviii, 44, 57, 58, 60-62, 102, 111, 134, 154, 159, 161, 183, 420
pertaining-to-arising/sinking, lxii, 63, 135, 231, 240, 303-04, 321, 479
planetary hours, 185
retrogradation, li, 35, 43, 53, 56, 57, 61, 65, 71, 74-78, 81-83, 85, 88-89, 97, 101, 104, 116, 122, 124-28, 132-33, 137-38, 143-44, 160-62, 172-73, 177, 198, 203-04,

214, 220, 222, 224, 234, 236-40, 267, 276-77, 280-82, 288, 316, 318, 320, 325, 334, 339, 340-42, 344-45, 350, 354-57, 359-60, 396-98, 474, 487, 492-94, 496
slow in course, 54
solar phases, 61–62
stations, lxix, 54, 65, 75, 76, 104, 137, 203, 224, 281, 303, 354, 357
strengths, 39
triplicities, xiv, li-liii, lxvii, lxxvii, 3, 8, 29-30, 36, 40, 44, 49, 57-59, 61, 70, 92, 98, 110, 114-15, 125-6, 136, 149, 154, 165-67, 189, 199-200, 204, 209, 211, 231, 325-26, 329, 335-36, 342-43, 346, 391-96, 401-02, 404-15, 418, 420-21, 434, 451, 486
void in course, 12, 31, 35, 46, 53, 79, 136, 152, 160, 172, 195, 221, 251, 255, 446, 450, 456, 467
weaknesses, 42
Plants (their growth), 297
Plato, lxxiii-lxxiv, 245, 283
Plato of Tivoli, xii-xiii
Prediction
changing figure, lxviii, 91, 123, 223-24, 464, 479
fast/slow modification, 54, 89, 141, 191, 225, 227, 230, 232, 237, 396, 397, 422, 468, 473, 479-80
hourly times, 487
planetary years, 227, 229, 237-39, 381-84, 390, 396-97, 402, 486, 489
primary directions, lxviii, lxxv, 188-89, 224, 229-30, 234,

384, 394-95, 482-85, 488, 490
profections, lxviii, 161, 189, 213, 238, 340, 344, 434
solar revolutions, lxviii, 92, 161, 189, 213, 236-41, 341, 434
symbolic times, lxviii, 226, 228, 229-30, 234-35, 237, 393, 422, 448-49, 464, 472-73, 478
transits, lxviii, lxxv, 88, 90, 123, 155, 226, 230, 234-37, 239, 339, 341, 353, 383, 384-85, 387, 389-90, 448, 451, 454, 457, 464, 468, 472, 475, 478-79, 505
uncertain method, 343
Prohibition, 20-22, 24-26, 27-28, 55-56, 95, 134, 179, 437-38, 447, 454, 467
Ptolemy, Claudius, vii, ix, xi, xlvii, li, liv, lvi, lx, lxxix-lxxx, 7, 63-64, 269-70, 272-73, 302-04, 343, 397, 427, 432-33, 482
qisma (division), 188
Quantity, lxx-lxxii, 52-53, 67, 122-23, 134, 162, 170-71, 177, 202, 226-27, 230-31, 236, 245, 255, 257, 260, 264, 269, 271-74, 286-88, 290-91, 293-94, 296-97, 300, 304, 306, 325, 329, 333, 342, 345-47, 445, 454, 458, 480, 487
Questions
24-hour waiting period, xxxv-vii, lxxvi
about many matters, 177
absent persons, 132, 143, 233, 234
absolute, 460, 469
affairs, 99
attainment, 148
banquets and parties, 180

buying/selling, 82, 102
choosing between options, 176
death, 132
dreams, 144, 508
enemies, 166
fears, 173
final dispositor, xvii, lxxix, 39, 438, 448, 452, 454, 458, 464, 468, 472, 476
fishing, 179
friends, 163
fugitives, 103, 105-06, 108-09, 111, 114, 118
general instructions, 67, 444-47
genuine/fake things, 176
hidden/lost objects, lxxvii-lxxviii, 428, 430, 435
high offices, 138, 148
hopes, 162, 163
hunting, 177, 179
infirmity and death, 86, 90, 230, 420, 448, 455, 501
inheritance, 94, 466
kingdoms, 147, 151, 153-54, 158, 160, 162, 236, 469, 474, 477, 491
lawsuits, 100
letters, 235
letters and legates, 166, 168, 170-71, 503
loans, 463
lost objects, 103, 105
marriage, 94-97
moving, 92
particular, 460, 474, 477
partnerships, 120
pregnancy, 83-86, 98, 99, 230
prisoners, 140
races, 164-65
real estate, 81
revenge, 175
root chart, 155, 320

rumors, 168, 171, 173, 235, 503
siblings, 80
slavery, 91, 93-94
stolen/missing objects, 106, 108, 112-14
travel, 121, 133, 137, 139, 233, 234
virginity, 98
war, 121, 130, 231
wealth, 79, 230, 460
Reception, xvi-xx, lxxviii, 28-31, 40, 43, 51, 57, 62, 72-74, 77-78, 85, 88-89, 91-92, 96, 101, 122-24, 135, 138, 148-50, 152-53, 158-59, 161, 163, 167, 171-73, 176-77, 190, 197, 201, 210, 218, 220, 229, 237-40, 302, 314, 319, 326, 330, 335, 338, 341, 350-51, 354, 358, 394, 402, 420, 436-37, 439-43, 447-48, 451-54, 456-64, 467-72, 476, 478, 482, 489, 492, 494-96
Rendering of light, xxvii, lxxviii, 88-89, 102, 108, 147, 332, 437, 444-48, 460
Returning of light, 12, 24, 35-36
Rhetorius of Egypt, ix, x, xxxi-xxxii, lx-lxi, 413, 489, 520
Sahl bin Bishr, vii-xiv, xvi-xvii, xix-xx, xxiii, xxv-xxviii, xxxi, xxxiii-xxxv, xxxviii, xli-xliv, xlvi-lii, liv-lv, lvii, lix, lxii-lxix, lxxii-lxxiii, 1, 4, 7, 9-10, 14, 16, 18, 29, 35, 39, 42, 44, 55, 62-63, 69, 73, 75-79, 83-84, 90-93, 111-14, 116, 118, 122, 128, 132-33, 135, 140-41, 143-45, 149, 154, 158, 164-65, 168, 172, 177, 179, 185-89, 191, 195-98, 211, 222, 228, 234, 240-41, 400-01, 451, 461-62, 508

Schmidt, Robert, v, xxi-xxii, xxvii, xxxix, 154
Sect of chart—considerations, 3, 41, 47, 49, 60, 154, 240, 326, 330, 336, 343, 363-68, 392, 394, 401, 419, 482, 485-86, 503-04
Sicily, xii
Signs
  bestial, 206
  common, xlvii, 2, 64, 73, 82, 86, 89, 98-99, 102, 110, 120, 125-28, 141, 161-63, 180-81, 183, 191, 197, 199, 201-02, 206-09, 219-21, 225, 229, 233, 237, 301, 305, 328, 334, 340-41, 352, 388, 393, 398, 422, 458, 496
  dark, 2
  diurnal/nocturnal, 192, 301, 341
  fixed, xlvii, 1, 41, 64, 73, 89, 98, 120, 124-26, 135, 141, 154, 161, 163, 175, 180, 191, 201, 207-08, 215, 218-20, 225, 229, 232-33, 237, 255, 270, 275, 289, 301, 305, 328, 340-41, 352, 393, 398, 422
  four-footed, 2
  half-voiced, 2
  masculine/feminine, 1, 42, 47, 49, 79, 86, 146, 202, 214, 301, 305-06, 341, 357, 394-395
  movable, 1, 64, 85, 89, 98-99, 120, 125-27, 155, 159-61, 163, 172, 175, 180, 190-91, 202, 206-08, 212, 220-21, 225, 229, 237, 301, 305, 328, 340, 352, 393, 398, 422
  straight/crooked ascension, 1, 190, 196, 198, 203, 210

Index

triplicities, lxxvii, 1-3, 5, 82, 98, 112-16, 136, 146, 178-79, 182, 192, 201, 205, 209, 215-16, 221, 301-08, 321-23, 326-27, 340, 342, 349, 358, 359-60, 428, 430, 432, 511
   voiced, 2
Slavs, 300, 369, 373, 375-76, 378, 380, 387, 389
Spain, xii, lxxvi
St. Petersburg, xii
Stakes/angles, xxi, xxv, xxxix–lix, lxxiii, lxxxii, 13, 40, 43, 46, 188, 194-95, 197, 201, 203-06, 210, 213-15, 217, 219-20, 224, 309-13, 456, 467
   15° rule, li-lvi, 64
   5° rule, xlix, l-li, liv, lviii-lix, 63, 482-84, 489
Stegemann, Viktor, viii-xiii, lxiv, lxxii, 10-12, 14-15, 18-19, 22, 27, 32, 35, 40-41, 44, 46-47
Strength/virtue, pushing/committing/receiving, lxvi, lxvii, 12, 36-37, 39, 148-50, 153
tasīr, -394-395
Testimony/witnessing, xx-xxvii, xlv, 7, 32, 42, 44, 58, 70, 74, 114, 125, 128, 138, 142, 149-50, 172-74, 176, 183, 202, 217, 229, 234, 236, 238-39, 241, 333, 337, 339, 346, 352, 395, 412, 444, 457, 474, 490, 504, 509
Theodicy, 299
Theophilus of Edessa, xi, xxii, lxii, 121, 231
Thorndike, Lynn, 308
Tiberius, Emperor, xi
Toledo, xii
Trivium, 370
Tunisia, xii
Twelfth-parts, lix-lxvi, lxxvi, 194, 211, 231, 427
Uzbekistan, 455
Valens, Vettius, ix, lvi, 166, 427, 432
watad (stake), see also Stakes/angles
Weather
   rains, 295
   storms, 295
   winds, 292
Whole signs, xiii-xiv, xvi-xvii, xxi, xxxix, xli-liii, lv-lvii, lxiv, lxix, lxxxi, 47, 61, 70, 88, 98, 100, 111, 128, 134, 142, 144, 150-51, 174, 183, 194-95, 199, 201, 209, 214, 304, 338, 403, 405, 417, 426, 442, 455, 489, 496
Zij, 194, 287

www.ingramcontent.com/pod-product-compliance
Lightning Source LLC
Chambersburg PA
CBHW060400230426
43663CB00008B/1340